ACCLAIM FOR *Gitta Sereny's*

ALBERT SPEER

The Invisible Children
Child Prostitution in America, Germany and Britain

Into That Darkness
An Examination of Conscience

The Case of Mary Bell
A Portrait of a Child Who Murdered

The Medallion
(fiction)

Gitta Sereny

ALBERT SPEER

Gitta Sereny is one of Europe's foremost journalists with a special interest and expertise in the Third Reich. She has written extensively for London's *Daily Telegraph* magazine, *Sunday Times,* and *The Independent,* as well as for *Die Zeit* and *Le Nouvel Observateur.* In America she has written for *The New York Times Magazine, The New York Review of Books,* and *Vanity Fair.* Her previous four books include *Into That Darkness: An Examination of Conscience,* on Franz Stangl, Commandant of the Treblinka death camp, which has been adapted for the stage. She has two children and two grandchildren and lives with her husband, the photographer Don Honeyman, in London.

Albert Speer in 1978, in typically reflective mood

ALBERT SPEER: HIS BATTLE WITH TRUTH

Gitta Sereny

INTO THAT DARKNESS

VINTAGE BOOKS
A Division of Random House, Inc.
New York

FIRST VINTAGE BOOKS EDITION, NOVEMBER 1996

The Library of Congress has cataloged the Knopf edition as follows:
Sereny, Gitta.
Albert Speer: his battle with truth / by Gitta Sereny.
p.   cm.
Includes bibliographical references and index.
ISBN 0-394-52915-4
1. Speer, Albert. 2. National socialists—Biography. 3. War
criminals—Germany—Biography. 4.
Germany—Politics and government—1933–1945. I. Title.
DD247.S63S47 1995
943.086'092—dc20
[B] 94-19764 CIP

Vintage ISBN: 0-679-76812-2

Book design by Anthea Lingemen

Random House Web address: http://www.randomhouse.com/

Printed in the United States of America
10 9 8 7 6 5 4 3 2 1

To my children, and theirs;

to your children, and theirs

People could find no place in their consciousness for such ... unimaginable horror ... they did not have the imagination, together with the courage, to face it. It is possible to live in a twilight between knowing and not knowing.

—W. A. Visser 't Hooft

Acknowledgements

Acknowledgements in books always sound much the same. Not, I think, because writers all feel the same degree of gratitude for each of those who stood by them but rather because, only too often, there are no words to describe adequately our indebtedness.

So I too will have to content myself first to thank those whom you will meet in this book who shared with me their knowledge and their lives, and then just to briefly name the historians and archivists who guided me, and the friends who gave so generously of their time and affection. There are, however, a few whose help went beyond bounds of either professional assistance, or friendship.

There are, first of all, three people who appear in the pages you will read, without whom—I say it without hesitation—this book, as it is now, could not have been written.

For Hilde Schramm, Albert Speer's daughter, and Annemarie Kempf, his private secretary and friend, it was not an easy decision to join my quest. If they did, it was not out of friendship for me, for we were strangers prior to this work. They, and Fritz Wolters, the son of Speer's oldest friend, felt, I think, that "a" book was needed. Annemarie died before she could see it. I hope Hilde and Fritz will feel the book is what they hoped for, and I thank them with all my heart for their trust.

Maria Schwabb and Waltraud and Ulrich Lassek spent many weeks working through the 1,200 pages of Speer's first draft for *Inside the Third Reich*, written in Spandau prison, in order to systematize them sufficiently for me to work with them. It was an incredibly difficult undertaking; for although Speer wrote every day, the entries followed no sequential pattern. The subjects on each page had to be related to the eventual printed version, or separately described. It was a Herculean task, performed with grace.

Two dear friends, Joanna Anstey and Enrique Arias, waded through my first rough 1,500-page draft. Their kind praise, where surely praise could not yet have been due, was badly needed to spur me on.

Elaine Markson is my American agent who read not one but three drafts. I sometimes think she carries a banner "Markson Author: to be handled with care." And that, available to us day and night, is what she does. I thank her for that care.

Frances Gorden, my childhood friend "Franzi," luckily for me lives in London. It is she who, when I started to write, organized many of Speer's indecipherable handwritten letters for my use. At a later stage, when the book was completed, she, with my husband, Don, prepared reams of the letters and documentary material I hold, which had to be made available for verbatim use in the German edition.

I thank my old friend Max Dietlin who found essential material for me in Paris archives; my British agents Tessa Sayle and Rachel Calder and my German agent Ursula Bender, who so generously listened to my troubles even though they had no financial stake in the Speer book; Gwen Edelman in New York who has that rare gift of enthusiasm for the work of others; the eminent historian Saul Friedlander for his warnings, for which I was grateful though I could not always heed them; Elke Fröhlich, the world's leading historian on Goebbels, has added immeasurably to my knowledge; Eberhard Jäckel, the most passionate of Third Reich historians, never once failed to respond to a call for help.

We have a number of rare friends, some of whom have helped for years to keep up my courage:

Aggie and Stephen Barlay never tired of helping me dissect problems as they arose and Marina Henderson never failed to be "there" when needed.

Liz Jobey, editor of the *Independent on Sunday Review,* was never too busy to help me untangle my prose; Phillip Knightley was always ready with tactical advice; with Angela and Mel Marvin, our dearest friends, we share all our troubles, and all our joys; "Hannerl" and Fritz Molden are the best of Austrians, and in their beautiful village, Alpbach in the Tyrol, my favorite retreat, the wonderful "Alpbacher Hof," repeatedly provided warmth and peace.

We will not forget how Rudolf Petzenhauser and Monika made us feel at home during our three years of work in Munich; nor that Isabelle de Reyher, the most gifted of healing osteopaths, and Tim Ladbrooke, our caring doctor, again and again returned me to health. Priscilla and Nat Roe's farm in New Hampshire provided the quiet I needed to begin this book; Virginia and Leo Wilking were unstinting in the gift of their affection and their understanding of the human mind; and Joanna and Dan Rose's generous hospitality in New York and East Hampton, by now legend among their writer and artist friends, has been extended to us over many years.

Tzvetan Todorov is, I think, one of Europe's finest intellectual minds. I am profoundly grateful for his book *Face à l'Extrême,* for his encouragement these last years and for his and Nancy Huston-Todorov's friendship.

One thank-you I have never expressed but must, now, is to Lee Hindley Chadwick, who at Stonar House School in Sandwich, Kent, taught an eleven-year-old child to love the English language and make it her own. Nothing I have done would have been possible without that start from this inspired teacher.

Eight archives have assisted my husband and me in the preparations for this book: the National Archives (and Robert Wolfe) in Washington, Britain's Public Records Office at Kew, the Imperial War Museum, the Wiener Library in London, the Berlin Document Center (and Dr. David Marwell). For photographs, the Bayrische Staatsbibliothek (and Dr. Reinhard Horn) in Munich (and the archive of *Der Spiegel* in Hamburg). For the bulk of my research I owe thanks to the Institute for Contemporary History in Munich and to the German Federal Archives in Koblenz.

I have had nothing but kindness from the Institute for Contemporary History, surely one of the finest archives in the world. Dr. Fröhlich, Hermann Weiss and Martin Broszat, the Institute's director until his death, gave me all the help I asked for and more.

The historical riches of the German Federal Archives are almost indescribable, and here again everything was done to assist me. An archivist who prefers not to be named lent me his house for a whole summer, and two others, Marianne Loenartz and Hedwig Singer, particularly knowledgeable about Speer, spared no effort to solve my many problems.

Let me repeat what I have said elsewhere: that for any researcher into the Third Reich, the Wiener Library is irreplaceable and I, yet again, owe many thanks to its excellent staff.

In 1990, when, after eight years of research, I could see no way of turning this huge mass of information into a book, Knopf's publisher, Sonny Mehta, found a way to "unblock" my mind, and for this I shall always be grateful.

The subject of Speer is not one all editors could have faced with equanimity. Jonathan Segal did, and through months of work never lost his objectivity. I owe him gratitude for that, and for retaining throughout many trying times his belief in what I was trying to do and his enthusiasm for what it became.

I have now spoken of all those who had some association with the work on this book, but not yet of the person who was most important to its creation from the beginning, in the autumn of 1977, to the end, in the spring of 1995. This is Don Honeyman, my husband, who shared my thinking, my concerns and an enormous amount of the work—not only, of course, his own photographs of Speer and his wife, and all picture research and photo preparation, but much of the English-language documentation, the initial pruning and the referencing of the text and finally the technical preparation of the manuscript.

It is my book, but it became a joint effort. Writers, whether men or women, need strong and selfless partners. My Don is the rock upon which my life rests.

G. S., London, April 1995

Contents

ALBERT SPEER: HIS BATTLE WITH TRUTH

Introduction

ALBERT SPEER, whom I knew well and grew to like, might easily have been hanged the night of October 16–17, 1946, when, in the gymnasium of Nuremberg prison, ten other of Hitler's men were executed, some perhaps less guilty than he. The fatalistic part of Speer—for he was always a man not only of many parts but divided in himself—certainly expected that he would be sentenced to death, and many people afterwards thought he should have been.

The condemned men did not know the date of their execution, but Dr. Ludwig Pflücker, the prison doctor, had been told and was very busy that night. On the first floor, the one above both the gymnasium and the cells containing the men sentenced to die, the seven men who had been given prison sentences had been issued the mild sleeping pills they were offered each night at Nuremberg. (Speer always accepted his.) And then, in a compassionate gesture by the Allied prison authorities about which Dr. Pflücker had told Speer a few days earlier, the doctor had been allowed to give a stronger sedative to the condemned men. Not all of them, it appears, had taken it: when at 1 a.m. Colonel Burton C. Andrus, the American commandant of the prison, accompanied by selected German witnesses, had gone from cell to cell and, standing in the open doors, had read the death sentence ending with the words "death by hanging," the condemned men had all been dressed—the two generals, Keitel and Jodl, in their uniforms devoid of decorations, the others in civilian suits devoid of ties—only four of them, three almost somnolent, one nearly demented, had failed to stand up straight for the words.

Despite the sedative, it would appear that Speer slept lightly, for in the depth of that night he shot up in his bunk hearing the calling out of names: "Ribbentrop" (Hitler's Minister for Foreign Affairs); then "Keitel" (Field Marshal and Army Chief of Staff at Hitler's HQ); "Kaltenbrunner" (Head of Reich Main Security Office); "Rosenberg" (Minister for Occupied Eastern Territories); "Frank" (Governor-General of Poland); "Frick" (Minister of the Interior); "Streicher" (Gauleiter and anti-Semitic propagandist); "Sauckel" (Gauleiter and Reich Commissioner for Foreign Labor); "Jodl"

(General of the Army at Hitler's HQ); and last—it had taken two and a half hours from beginning to end—"Seyss-Inquart" (Reich Commissioner for the Netherlands).

He had known all these men very well; two of them, Jodl and Seyss-Inquart, he had liked. With Sauckel, his "unattractive working-class lieutenant in the slave labor program," as Airey Neave described him in his remarkable book *Nuremberg*, he had, by necessity, worked closely. Göring, who was in a position to pay well to learn of the executions in time, had managed to commit suicide a few hours before he was to be hanged. He had sometimes been almost a friend of Speer's, but became a venomous enemy at Nuremberg, where they fought a last bitter leadership battle.

Göring, insisting the trial was a travesty conducted by victors against losers, wanted all the accused to reject the validity of the court and claim innocence before the German law under which they had lived and which, he held, had legitimized their actions.

Speer, on the contrary, asked them all to join him in a recognition of a universal law under which they, as part of Hitler's leadership, had to accept responsibility for acts—crimes in the eyes of all of the civilized world—for which they, but not the German people, could and should be called to account. Whether they had individually collaborated in the crimes or not, in their capacity as leaders, he said, they had to accept a common culpability just as, had Hitler been victorious, they would have accepted the homage of the people for the common triumph.

The morning after the hangings, the seven men who were given prison sentences—Admirals Erich Raeder and Karl Dönitz (life and ten years, respectively); Hitler's old comrade and deputy, Rudolf Hess (life); Minister of Economics Walther Funk (life); former Foreign Minister and Reich Protector of Bohemia and Moravia Konstantin von Neurath (fifteen years); Reich Youth Leader and Gauleiter of Vienna Baldur von Schirach and Speer, first Hitler's architect then his Minister of Armaments and War Production (both twenty years)—were moved down into empty cells on the ground floor and were then assigned to clean out those just vacated by the hanged men. Eight of the cells bore the signs of desperate men: papers strewn all over the floor, remnants of food on the tables, blankets balled up on the bunks. Only General Jodl's cell was spotless, his tin bowl and spoon washed, the floor swept, his blanket militarily folded. And on one wall of Seyss-Inquart's cell was a calendar with the last day of his life, October 16, marked with a cross.

That afternoon Hess, Schirach and Speer were handed brooms and mops and taken to the empty gymnasium. One can't quite think why, for the gallows had been dismantled and the floor had been washed. Nonetheless, they were told to clean and mop it again, watched closely by a GI and a lieutenant.

Speer wrote about this in his book *Spandau: The Secret Diaries,* but when he recounted this story to me years later he had still not got over that particular trauma. His face went red, then pale, and when he almost furtively wiped it, his clean, folded handkerchief came away wet. The gymnasium floor, he said, had been quite clean, except for one enormous dark spot that wouldn't budge. Hess, he said, finally stood at attention and saluted it with a raised arm.

I SAW SPEER in the dock at Nuremberg on three occasions when, by invitation of a friend, the simultaneous interpreter George Vassiltchikov,* I was able to attend the trial. But I was very young, knew nothing about Speer and only noticed him among the twenty-one accused because, then forty years old, he looked young and, with his smooth face and strangely shaped, bushy black eyebrows, startlingly handsome. Contrary to many of the other defendants, who pretended to be bored or asleep, read or fidgeted endlessly with their hands or in their seats, he invariably sat very still, listening intently, with nothing moving in his face except those dark intelligent eyes.

But I never heard his voice until about thirty years later. By then he had served twenty years in Spandau prison and, released in 1966, then sixty-one years old, had written two extraordinary books. I, in the meantime, one generation younger than he, had also become a writer, with two main interests both no doubt originating in my experiences in the war—troubled children and the phenomenon of the Third Reich.

By the time Speer's first book was published—*Erinnerungen* (Reminiscences) in German, retitled in English *Inside the Third Reich*—my family and I were living in England, but I had spent a good deal of time working in Germany. Over the subsequent few years, while Speer's first book became a huge best-seller and he was writing the second one, *Spandau: The Secret Diaries,* I was preparing my book *Into That Darkness,* which, seeking to examine through the personality of Franz Stangl, Commandant of Treblinka, the capability of men to commit the worst of Hitler's crimes, brought me in touch with many of the perpetrators as well as many victims of the Nazi horrors. To finance the years of research for it, however, I simultaneously continued with journalism on related subjects, in the process meeting a number of survivors of Hitler's inner circle, almost all of whom brought up the subject of Speer. Most of them spoke of him with contempt for the "disloyalty" he had displayed at Nuremberg and in his writings and interviews since Spandau.

*This historic family name is spelled differently in various languages. I am using that given in the *Almanach de Gotha.*

By then, of course, I had read his first book and found it fascinating: fascinating how, now both proud and ashamed of it, he had so entirely belonged to Hitler; fascinating how this man had been caught up in the life at Hitler's court and in the power games played there. But by comparison with the suffering and horror I had to confront both in personal encounters and in the literature for the work on my own book, *Inside the Third Reich* was very cool, very controlled, recalling to my mind's eye, on the fringes of my memory, that still, attentive figure I had observed in the Nuremberg dock in 1946.

I felt very differently about *The Secret Diaries,* which I had read in German as soon as it was published. Here he manifested not only a real literary talent but, between the lines, the sadness and loneliness I would find in him later. His handling of his long prison life—the reading, writing, gardening, his "Walk around the World"*—seemed to me astonishing, and his account of it deeply moving, certainly the most striking prison memoirs I had read. By this time, however, I had repeatedly seen Speer on television, being interviewed in German and in English. Despite the remarkable intelligence of his books and the apparent sincerity there of his moral self-examination (unique among former high-ranking Nazis, as I by then knew from my own experience), he seemed to me unconvincing in person.

While his writing was persuasive, in the filmed interviews I saw his mea culpas appeared to flow too readily from his lips; his smile was condescending, his voice too smooth; he was too charming. I had admired the books but, after watching him, felt uncomfortable about the man. In *The Secret Diaries* he had seemed to question himself, but on screen, almost another person, he communicated no vestige of doubt, or of humanity: in his apparent cocoon of success, he seemed too sure. Within two years, I was to find out how wrong I had been.

On July 10, 1977, the *Sunday Times* in London had published an analysis by my colleague Lewis Chester and myself of the British writer David Irving's thesis in his book, *Hitler's War,* that Hitler had not known about the extermination of the Jews, at least until October 1943. Some of Irving's points were cleverly produced, and at first view his theory looked—barely—possible and intriguing, but weeks of research in German archives and interviews with many of his own witnesses showed up the falseness of his premise, and our feature totally discredited his claim.

A few days later, out of the blue, I received a letter from Speer. He felt he

---

*Speer created over several years a large formal garden from the wilderness around the prison, with a circle of paths around it. In 1954, his seventh year in Spandau, he decided to systematize his daily walks into a forty-thousand kilometer "Walk around the World"; coupling physical effort with imagination, fueled by maps and descriptions of the world's cities, rivers and mountains sent by his friend Rudolf Wolters, he had covered nearly thirty-two-thousand kilometers by the end of his imprisonment.

had to write, he said, to express his appreciation of the manner in which we had approached the subject. It was "ludicrous," he wrote, for anyone to claim that this could have been anyone's idea but Hitler's. "It shows a profound ignorance of the nature of Hitler's Germany, in which nothing of any magnitude could conceivably happen, not only without his knowledge, but without his orders." The fact that there was no documentary evidence of such a Führer command meant nothing, he said. He knew from ample personal experience that many of Hitler's most critical orders were issued only verbally.

"From the historical point of view," he wrote, "the matter has now, thanks to your exposé, been dealt with. Nonetheless, unfortunately, Irving has provided fodder for the abominable efforts of those whose one aim is to create a new 'war-guilt-lie,' as it was called after 1918, in order yet again to deceive the German people. It appalls me."

The next day there was another letter from Speer, to say he had forgotten to tell me that a year or two before, the psychoanalyst Erich Fromm had sent him a copy of my book *Into That Darkness,* which had caused him sleepless nights. If I ever found myself in the vicinity of Heidelberg, would I perhaps care to drop in on him and talk?

It was his voice that surprised me when I telephoned him that night to thank him for his letters. When I had heard him speak on television, he had sounded arbitrary and arrogant. Now, on the phone, he seemed very different: hesitant, shy, perhaps a little too warm but with an odd question mark in his voice at the end of a statement. I had not imagined him to be curious or personal, nor had I suspected him of having a self-deprecating sense of humor. And although his books were certainly sad, somehow I had not thought that this sadness could be an essential part of him. I now sensed that it was, and it intrigued me.

From then on we talked on the phone frequently, usually on his initiative. He would tell me about books I might want to read, and often sent them to me, as well as writings from the German press. In return, I sent him articles I thought might interest him. And I read through vast files of clippings about him, many of them fawning but many others vehemently hostile, driven by emotion rather than rationality.

Although there were of course exceptions, most commentators seemed to be giving vent to their anger at what he had been, without adding anything to our knowledge of what he had—perhaps—become. I was not convinced of Speer's integrity, but I was, I admit, taken aback by this apparently huge reservoir of unrelieved pain which found expression, or relief, in verbally assaulting this man—certainly primarily for his sins and omissions but almost as much, it seemed to me, for his conditional acceptance of guilt.

It reminded me of a painful occasion in my own life when I was young. In France in 1940, I was a voluntary nurse with a French charity, the Auxiliaire Sociale, which looked after children found lost or abandoned after the defeat. Just before the Germans arrived, our group left Paris for the Château de Villandry, one of the great castles in the Loire whose chatelaine, Isabelle de la Bouillerie, the daughter of the American owner, was the president of our charity. I was passionately Franco- and Anglophile and, like many young people in France—far more than is perhaps now remembered—prepared to do almost anything to harm the invaders. But in that first year of occupation, except for hiding the occasional British flier stranded in France, the possibilities for active resistance were limited. We had to content ourselves with pointedly ignoring the Germans to demonstrate our loathing of their presence.

This was difficult in my case, for as a theoretically neutral young Hungarian fluent in German, from the kind of background the Germans were likely to respect, I had been asked to act as the charity's interpreter and mediator in the necessary hunt for documents and extra rations.

Most of the German officers who came to visit the famous Villandry were polite enough, considering the coolness with which they were received, but at the time I could only see them as arrogant and threatening. There were two exceptions, however, who refused to be cold-shouldered: one an army doctor, the other a former schoolmaster.

Both took an immediate interest in our children and helped with badly needed food, medicines and, when the district was struck by an epidemic, devoted medical care. They were quite simply—I now know—good men, a fact which at the time, as a more-French-than-the-French teenager, was impossible for me to accept.

The two men—I say it with sorrow and shame—became sitting targets for my fury. For months they accepted my railings and Isabelle's more elegantly phrased criticism of their country without demur. And then, without warning, they disappeared. The doctor, I discovered later, was sent to the Russian front, where he died within weeks. The former teacher, older and not very fit, was sent to a concentration camp.

They had both been devout Christians and opponents of the regime. We had never known. They didn't tell us, only tried to express it by showing affection to the children and helping us to care for them, which was strictly against Nazi rules. Indulging our own emotions, we had abused their kindness. We had never sensed their pain and their dilemma, and that they despairingly wanted to be—and indeed were—our friends.

I don't know how much of a part this buried memory played in my reaction to the pain and fury I sensed in the writings against Speer, and in my suggestion to him, months after his first letter and hours of telephone conversations, that we collaborate on a profile of him for the London *Sunday Times Magazine*. When we finally met face to face for the first time, in the spring of 1978 at his home in Heidelberg, my feelings were very mixed, ranging from curiosity and fascination to a troubling malaise.

Over dinner that first night, I told Speer and his wife, Margarete, about the ambivalence of my feelings toward him. (Her name was Margarete, but he called her Gretel and referred to her as Margret.) I told him I had read everything I could find that had been written about him in three languages, and that I was as surprised by the similarity of the questions he was invariably asked as I was by his own almost monotonously uniform answers, ever since Nuremberg. I warned him that I would attempt, in my own way, to break through this pattern and through the defenses he had manifestly set up over so many years.

Oh, yes, he shrugged, everybody came with that intention. All of them wanted to trap him into admitting the same thing. "Always the same thing," he said with weary resignation, and added meaningfully, "you will too."

I knew what he meant of course; the subject that was always uppermost in his mind and in the minds of all those who questioned him was the murder of the Jews, the knowledge of which during the Third Reich he had always denied.

Conversations such as I intended having with him, though certainly a dialogue rather than questions and answers, needed to be structured. It was most important, though difficult with a man such as this, that the formulating and direction of this structure, avoiding rather than inviting the obvious, remained invariably mine. His denial of knowledge of the murder of the Jews was of course central to the problem, but to my mind it needed to be left in abeyance, in a way refusing him the relief of denial until everything else had been said.

There were two essential matters I wanted our conversations eventually to focus on: one, the origin of Hitler's evil (which to my mind went even beyond his obsession about the Jews and his worst crime, the gas chambers in occupied Poland); the other, Speer's realization of—and participation in—it.

Hitler's genius in part was to corrupt others, but the evidence I have collected suggests that with extraordinary skill he deliberately protected those closest to him—who from 1933 on included Speer—from any awareness which could have disturbed them or the harmony of their relationship with him. But corruption is insidious. Speer, in the course of his growing relationship with Hitler, inevitably became—though for a long time unwittingly—a part of it.

Speer, I was already convinced, had never killed, stolen, personally bene-

fited from the misery of others or betrayed a friend. And yet, what I felt neither the Nuremberg trial nor his books had really told us was how a man of
such quality could become not immoral, not amoral but, somehow infinitely
worse, morally extinguished.

Eventually he had gained knowledge of the abominations and recognized
that they originated with Hitler. What then kept this man in place? What had
prevented him, whose possibilities for escape were unlimited, from taking
himself and his family out of it?

The reasons for this and for his later denial of knowledge, I felt sure,
needed to be uncovered slowly by exploring, with his help, all of his life. So
on that early spring evening, sitting around the old refectory table in the
kitchen of his patrician Heidelberg family home, I told him that I needed to
learn about all of the things he hadn't written or talked about: his childhood,
his parents, "this house where you lived as a boy," I said.

"I hate it," he interrupted, with surprising vehemence. "I hate being here."
His wife winced. "But Albert," she said, helplessly, "my friends . . . the children. . . ." And to me: "He doesn't mean it."

He did. He hated this house of his childhood misery; she, on the contrary,
loved what had been her and the children's refuge during his twenty years'
imprisonment. Yes, I told him, that was what I meant; it was precisely this I
would want to learn about: whom he had loved or disliked, perhaps even
hated and feared from as far back as he remembered.

Showing his feelings had been a momentary slip quickly corrected. He
could see, he said lightly, that I intended to tax his endurance. If it got too
difficult, if I got too near the knuckle—he smiled, "then Don here will come
to my aid." My husband, Don Honeyman, a tall blond Iowan who had been a
Vogue photographer for years, was to photograph him for the article. Speer
had quickly formed an easy relationship with him and called him Don at
once, while he and I—for many weeks and until long after Margret and I
were, at her suggestion, on a first-name basis—rather awkwardly avoided
calling each other by name in order to be neither too formal nor too
informal.

Don, I explained, would be going back to London after taking the photographs he needed in Heidelberg. At the end of the following week, during
which I would stay, as arranged, with the Speers at their isolated farm high
up in the Bavarian Alps, Don would come back briefly for more photographs
there. After that, we would play it by ear.

"Oh, what a pity," he said. "I was counting on him to protect me."

This flippancy and Speer's very real charm were integral parts of his whole
persona and, I would discover later, always had been. I knew well that if anything of value was to come of our conversations, I would have to get him to

divest himself of the glibness which he had cultivated over a dozen years of continuous publicity and behind which I believed there could be another—perhaps a worse, possibly a better—man.

But Margret's life was also part of the story: the origin of their courtship; the distance between them, and yet his very real feeling for her and her iron loyalty to her husband; and Hitler's affection for "my beautiful Frau Speer," as he called her, and her attachment to him.

By the time I completed my original conversations with Speer for the projected profile, we had talked for just under three weeks, about twelve hours every day. But this, as it turned out, was only the beginning of a quite special relationship (I can find no word for it: common interests? curiosity about each other?) that would continue until he died.

During the original weeks of our work together, he often consulted material from his archive, above all his "black" (illegal) correspondence from Spandau prison with his children, his wife and with his friend Rudolf Wolters: thousands of pages of transcripts typed from tens of thousands of flimsy pages and hundreds of thousands if not millions of words in close, hard-to-decipher handwriting. Much of it had originally been written on toilet paper, tobacco or cigarette wrappers, or little bits of notepaper torn off the drawing pads he was in later years allowed to have for architectural sketching.

During those weeks and later, he gave me letters he wrote to his wife when they were both still at school, which clearly showed the fluency, the depth of thought and the morality he evidenced fifty years later in *The Secret Diaries*. He also gave me a manuscript of twenty-eight profiles of Hitler and the men closest to him, which he had written—with helpful questions from a British intelligence officer—in an Allied VIP detention center in the autumn of 1945. As our relationship developed, we planned to work together later to transform these—the most perceptive characterizations of Hitler's circle I have read—into a book comparing his views of these men at war's end with the way he saw them thirty-five years later.

Additionally, Speer gave me two manuscripts he wrote in Nuremberg before being sentenced: one—almost prophetic—on the future of Russia; the other—completed a few days before the sentences, which in his case he expected to be death—a first short draft of what would eventually become *Inside the Third Reich*.

All these documents from Nuremberg and Spandau (plus many others from earlier years) had been cared for and organized by Wolters, whose loyal help to Speer extended to the care of his family during the twenty years of his imprisonment. Smuggled out with the help first of a Dutch medic and then friendly Allied guards, the thousands of letters, some of them thirty or forty pages long, and, over subsequent years, thousands more to his children and to Wolters, were transcribed in Wolters's architectural office in the north German town of Coesfeld. Over fifteen years, this work was done mostly by Marion Riesser, a graphic designer who, half Jewish, had, like a number of others at risk, found employment and protection at Speer's ministry during the war, and became Wolters's personal assistant afterwards.

Speer died in September 1981, and Wolters a year later. When I decided a year after that to undertake this book, Wolters's son, Fritz, gave me full access to the vast documentary collection, including copies of most of the Speer material, which his father had left to the Bundesarchiv, the Federal Archives in Koblenz. This included the remarkable 1,200-page draft for his memoirs which Speer wrote in Spandau between January 1953 and January 1954. (By a majority decision of Speer's children, his own archive, also now at Koblenz, will be closed until the third generation of Speer children are grown.)

Speer's daughter Hilde, perhaps the most moral person I have ever met, who devoted ten years or so of her young life to sustaining Speer's morale while he was at Spandau, entrusted me with some four hundred other letters Speer wrote to her (and, toward the end of his imprisonment, to her young husband), which added uniquely to my understanding of this deeply ambivalent man. Here, written with warmth and love, is the man he wanted to be but could only be on paper: the father, the friend, the thinker—a moral man.

Here, too, is the other man he was, as he displays the qualities that caused him to become the second most powerful man in the Third Reich and afterwards helped him to survive its disintegration: the inveterate schemer and brilliant planner; the ruthless user of others, even those closest to him; and the compromiser, always toward his own good.

Speer also wrote many letters to Annemarie Wittenberg Kempf, a woman of impeccable integrity who became his private secretary when she was eighteen, and who remained his friend until and beyond his death. She married Hans Kempf, a devout Catholic, in 1942. He was reported missing in action in Russia on March 9, 1944. (Speer often referred to her as Wittenberg—for years afterwards.) Annemarie and I too became friends—aside from many other things, she helped me with material from Speer's archive before it was moved to Koblenz. But because of the strength of her feeling for Speer, I decided (and she agreed) that it was necessary, both for my objectivity and for her peace of mind, that we should not meet or even communicate during the actual writing of this book. (I had come to the same arrangement with Hilde.) To my sorrow Annemarie died in 1992 without knowing how much I owe her.

The man who had the greatest influence on Speer's life, aside from Hitler, was Georges Casalis, an exceptionally wise man who, as well as his wife, Dorothée, became my counselors. Sadly, he too has died, as have so many who have helped me. A French pastor, he was the Spandau prison chaplain for the first three years. "When I met Speer," he told me, "he was the most tortured man I had ever met. By the time I left Spandau, I saw him as the most repentant."

It was Speer's profound malaise with his own conscience, his "battle with his soul," as Casalis, who understood him like no other, called it, that essentially brought me to write this book. The ambivalence between his moral necessity to confront the long-repressed guilt of his terrible knowledge, and his desperate need to deny—or "block"—it, was the great dilemma of his life, and dominated it from the Nuremberg trials until shortly before his death.

Although I found that many others today remain weighed down by the memory of their intense feelings of faith, trust and, yes, love for Hitler, Speer was, I believe, unique among Hitler's men in the intensity of this inner battle of conscience. Psychologically the most interesting and morally an extraordinarily positive aspect of his personality, it largely determined the direction of my work with him and inevitably became the focus of this book.

When I started I did not know how many voices would have to be heard, how much he and others would divulge to me nor how much would emerge through the comparisons between Speer's different writings and other peoples' diaries and memoirs and relating these to incidents he described—or passed over in silence. It demonstrated that as it is human beings with a human wish to be remembered who enact and record history, little of it can be kept secret forever. What I was absolutely certain of, from the start, was that Speer's life during the Third Reich could only be understood in the context of his strange relationship with Hitler. Working on this book for more than a decade showed me that there were singular parallels between Hitler and Speer. Not parallels, of course, in historical significance, but parallels in psychological traits which so decisively influence historical events.

What is to be learned about these two men should make us ponder the nature of love, the perils of emotion. Both Hitler and Speer were bedeviled from childhood by thwarted, imagined and withheld love, a deficiency which rendered them both virtually incapable of expressing private emotions. Both of them, though surrounded by people, remained alone. Both of them, capable of great charm and courted by women, could barely respond, though neither of them was homosexual. Both not only shied away from but despised manifestations of feelings, and yet, for each of them in his different way, it was emotion that ruled their decisions and dictated many if not most of their acts. It is doubtful—Speer confirmed this—that, excepting one strange message from Hitler to Speer, they ever consciously thought of each other with affection. And yet, it was a kind of unspoken love, needed, demanded and received, that bound them to each other.

Toward the end of my first week with Speer, he suggested that the theme of my next book should be charisma. "It is the most dangerous quality there is," he said. He meant, of course, people through the ages whose charisma, like Hitler's, had affected human lives and altered the course of history. Speer would never have applied this description to himself. But one after another of his former staff, who shared his almost Spartan way of life and worked for him to the point of exhaustion, pointed out that he too "had an aura."

Many of the people I spoke with in the course of preparing this book—Speer family members, key colleagues on his team during his twelve years with Hitler, prison staff at Spandau and friends, observers and enemies of his later years—liked and admired Speer for the consistent modesty he displayed even at the zenith of his power, for his achievements and for the courageous actions he took on behalf of the German people in the last months of Hitler's rule. But none of those who had worked with him under Hitler had questioned the morality of Hitler and his creed, any more than Speer himself had done until the end approached, and some of their statements now, as they appear in this book, will undoubtedly jar. When you read quotes from Goebbels adoring Hitler, and statements from others defending his ideas, I invite you to remember that any person, man or woman, may speak his own "truth," either as a tactical move or a "truth" he needs to explain, or even live, his own life. But truth or lies, however uncomfortable or, seen in retrospect, even offensive they may be, can serve our purpose of gaining understanding.

The principal aim of this book, throughout, was to learn to understand Speer. It would have been impossible to achieve this if I had only viewed him in isolation, out of context with the environment in which he lived. It was thus necessary to find out how and why some other essentially decent and often talented men and women could become so subject to Hitler and his ideas that no doubt of him could be allowed to intervene. And here, while in such encounters it is essential never to pretend agreement with the unacceptable, moral indignation for its own sake is an unaffordable luxury. As this search turned into the written word, it seemed important to me, even while of course aware of the outrageousness of some statements, not to interrupt the flow too often with critical comments, but rather to trust the reader to see each claim, each admission and each denial as one more necessary detail in a mosaic which in the end might provide a comprehensive whole.

A few of those who had been on Speer's architectural or ministerial teams expressed admiration for his stand at Nuremberg and afterwards, but many more felt uncomfortable, some profoundly angry about it: angry above all, I think, because his publicly expressed derogation of Hitler cast a reflection on their own moral impotence.

I have spent much of my life studying this moral impotence in Hitler's Germany. Hitler was obsessed by the Jews, and among his murders of millions—Orthodox, Catholic and Lutheran Christians, Gypsies and Jews—it was the killing of the Jews in the gas chambers of occupied Poland which struck deepest into the conscience and remained in the consciousness of the world. It is the one action which those who admired Hitler fifty years ago, and those whose nationalist and racist aims today resemble and indeed are modeled on his, are desperate to deny.

The fate of Europe's Jews, so central to Speer's life after Nuremberg, inevitably plays a great part in this book, but it is not its subject. Hitler's evil, I believe, went far beyond even this madness, and my aim here is to put into context all of the crimes against humanity which Hitler initiated, which continue to threaten us today, and of which Speer, who was in many ways a man of excellence, sadly enough made himself a part.

Prologue

THE MORNING OF my first visit to Heidelberg in 1978, Speer had received a letter:

You pig of a traitor:
  We have looked for you for a long time. You who as our Führer's architect profited when he went from victory to victory. You, who planned to gas him and his staff when he defended our Berlin.
  You pig played the penitent, and barricaded in a villa guarded by dogs, betrayed us. Your lying scribbles show your true character . . . with speechifying, toadying to the victors and sending money to Jewish organizations . . . you are trying to get yourself readmitted to society . . . you money-grabbing pig. . . .
  When we put an end to you, no one will care. No one will shed a single tear. And we *will* put an end to you. Rely on it.

The letter was signed with the initials L. P. Hauptsturmführer (the SS rank of Captain) and was stamped with an eagle carrying the swastika and the letters NSDAP AO (National Socialist Party, Auslands Organisation [Foreign Section]). The letter came from Lincoln, Nebraska, and the back of the envelope identified the senders as "The victims of October 16 1946," the day the major war criminals were hanged in Nuremberg.

Speer's "barricaded villa" had "A. Speer" prominently displayed on a post next to the permanently open gates. "Just think what a bore it would be to get out of the car every time to open them, and anyway, it wouldn't do for the children," he said. The grandchildren were "guarded" by one ridiculously soppy Saint Bernard, their play companion, who loved nothing more than slobbering over visitors.

Speer and Margret, both seventy-three when I met them, occupied two floors of the beautiful patrician house on the hill above Heidelberg Castle; the top floor was rented to students, and a guest cottage in the garden was used by their youngest son, Ernst, and his family, who a little later would take over most of the big house. "It's nice to have young people around,"

Margret said. "And then, too, it doesn't stand empty when we are up in the mountains."

There was an intense aura of loneliness about the Speers. Five of their six children, most of them married, lived scattered all over Germany. The parents saw them rarely. Speer's relationship with Ernst, who was a year and a half when Speer was convicted and twenty-two when he was released, was never good. "He is the one who could never say a word when he came to visit me in Spandau," Speer told me. "I too had nothing to say and—it's sad—I still don't."

Ernst, his pretty red-haired medical student wife, and the Speers' second daughter, Margret, and her husband were coming to dinner the fourth day I was there, and Margret, unusually merry, was bustling around the kitchen much of the day. "Would you forgive us if we don't ask you to stay?" Speer asked. "It's the first time in three years we have several of the children here together."

The children wanted nothing to do with his past, or with his life after Spandau. They were close to their mother. "Do you see how she lights up when they come?" he asked after they had come in to say a quick hello. "How she changes when I'm not around, becomes girlish and gay?"

His relationship with the children was formal to a degree. He stood up when they arrived or left; they shook hands without otherwise touching. "Well, hello" or "Well then, goodbye," he said. "Good evening; goodbye," they replied—it seemed impossible for them to say even the word "Father."

Couldn't he be more relaxed with them, I asked the next morning; the tension one felt was awful.

"I can't," he said. "It's all right with some of the grandchildren," he said, and then laughed—it was to be the only time I would hear him laugh happily in connection with his family. "A few of the little girls call me 'Granddaddy' [instead of the more formal Grandfather] and treat me like an old fogey who has to be taken care of. It's rather nice." The laughter stopped. "Just lately there have been indications that something might be salvaged with one or two of the others, but on the whole it's too late. My fault, of course. I have just never known what to do."

It was impossible to talk it out with them, he said. "Last night, after you left, we sat down and had supper. Margret had made it quite festive." He pointed to a charming rustic dining area. "It was pleasant enough. We chatted, about nothing you know, until about 11:30 when I went up to bed. As soon as I got upstairs—my bedroom is above this room—I could hear peals of laughter. There had been no laughter while I was there; there never is. I weigh upon them." He was stating a fact, not expressing self-pity.

I talked with Speer quite regularly over the last four years of his life. He never realized that his distant relationship with his children was a curious echo of his difficulties with his own father.

ON A SUNDAY in 1912 in Mannheim, a smallish but rich industrial city on the Rhine, lunch with ten guests was coming to a close in the French dining room of the imposing Speer town house.

The family lived in fourteen rooms on three floors, with seven servants living in the basement. An annex across the courtyard housed the father's large architectural offices. The parents had separate bedrooms and dressing rooms on the second floor. The three boys—Hermann, nine; Albert, seven; and Ernst, five—shared with their French governess, Mlle Blum, a rear wing which connected through the kitchen with the formal reception rooms, all meticulously arranged with French furniture and fabrics for which Frau Speer, sixteen years younger than her husband and even richer than he, had an abiding passion.

The two footmen in their purple livery and the maids in black and white, all wearing white gloves, were serving the dessert when the boys, dressed in striped French shirts and dark grey shorts in fine gabardine, filed in.

Little Ernst, a charming scamp with piercing black eyes, ran to his father, a tall dignified man with a small, tidy beard and sparse hair who immediately pulled him onto his lap and stroked his fine blond hair. Hermann, dark as his mother and sturdy, was ordered to her side. She was wide-hipped but had a small waist and bust; a tight but pretty face; intensely black, beautifully shaped eyebrows; and thin lips. Extremely elegant, she wore copies of French clothes, for the making of which she kept a French dressmaker occupied almost exclusively. Lightly clapping her hands, she announced to her guests that Hermann would recite a poem he had written for the occasion.

Albert, dark too, with his mother's eyebrows though even thicker, was thin, pale and tense as he stood, his hands straight down his side, almost at attention just inside the door. Nobody looked at him. Ten minutes later, the poem recited, Hermann and Ernst—but not Albert—each received a chocolate. Ernst gave his indulgently smiling father a sticky kiss, and the boys bowed formally first to their mother, then to the guests. Then they walked through the hall with apparent decorum, until at the kitchen door Hermann tripped Albert, who fell noisily, then slammed the door against him as he lay on the floor. His mother didn't ask who had fallen. "Really, Albert," she called from the dining room, "can't you look where you are going?"

This is one of many similar stories about his childhood Speer was to tell me sixty-six years later. He still remembered in minute detail his apprehension going into the lavish room; the overpowering smell of the many flowers and the ladies' scents; his little brother's automatic run to, and welcome from, his father; his older brother being shown off as always by his mother; his own isolation; and even his skinned knee and bruises when Hermann, so predictably, succeeded in hurting and embarrassing him. "It never failed," he said. "Every day I hoped it would be better, but it never was."

He met Margarete Weber when he was sixteen (she was fifteen), and it was her family more than her he fell head over heels in love with. Her father, a solid Heidelberg *Bürger*, was a master carpenter, like his father and grandfather before him. "You are not to see that girl," his mother said. "It is inappropriate."

But the large warm Weber family—they laughed a great deal, ate profusely and welcomed the boy with open arms into their simple house—drew him like a magnet. At home they spoke in a thick Heidelberg accent which, although Albert later discovered that his father sometimes used it when speaking to employees in his office, he had never known. It was taboo in the Speer house, even for the servants. Many years later, just before his release from Spandau, he started to dream in that dialect. "I had completely forgotten it over the years," he told me, "and here I dreamed speaking in it to Margret, more . . ."—he hesitated, and then went on—"more warmly than was our usual way."

These particular dreams, which he was later to describe in detail to Erich Fromm, were to occur almost nightly throughout his last year in Spandau. "They are the expression of your longings for your most innocent times,"* Fromm wrote to him, advising him to give way to this need, even to think and muse in that dialect when awake. "That may bring out the best in you."

One night in 1978, when I stayed with the Speers in their mountain retreat, I heard them speak to each other in that—to me—incomprehensible dialect. They spoke it sometimes, he said in the morning, "when we feel good."

IN MAY 1953, when Speer was forty-eight years old and serving his seventh year in Spandau prison, his then seventeen-year-old daughter, Hilde, a brilliant high school student spending a year with a Quaker family in America, wrote to her father asking him to explain to her about his guilt. He replied,

> You ask . . . about the Nazis. . . . You say how could an intelligent person go along with such a thing. I want to show you by specifically using

*All quotes from the Speer-Fromm correspondence are from the Fromm Collection of Dr. Rainer Funk, Tübingen.

myself as an example, how this might happen. Let me say the hardest bit first: unless one wants, cowardly, to avoid confronting the truth, one has to say that there can be no excuse; there is no justification. It is in that sense that I am convinced of my own guilt. There are things, you see, for which one has to carry the blame, even if purely factually one might find excuses: the immensity of the crime precludes any attempt at self-justification. . . .

By this time, Speer had lived through the two most significant stages of his twenty years in Spandau: three years under the influence of Georges Casalis, who helped him discover in himself the potential of a moral regeneration, and then—unhappily—after Casalis's departure, the next three years during which he had to acknowledge to himself that without help from such a catalyst he was not capable of the required intellectual and spiritual discipline.

His young daughter's grave letter in which, stating very gently her long-pondered and long-hesitated-over question of conscience, she had demonstrated so clearly her willingness as well as her need to understand, had—briefly—shaken his resolve to tread a less difficult path: to remember and recount publicly his years with Hitler, rather than to seek self-knowledge and redemption privately.

As he would admit to me twenty-five years later when, unasked, he brought up the subject of Hilde's preoccupation with his morality, this letter was exceptionally disturbing to him. Before that, it had simply not occurred to him that any child of his—any young person—could ask him such a question, bringing him back so sharply to the state of mind Casalis had provoked in him years before.

This fine-boned, slight girl with silky blond hair, who was only ten when her father was sentenced and who would remain determinedly loyal to him throughout his imprisonment, had already by then established a very special relationship with him. The letters he was to write to her over the following years were the warmest, deepest and most personal he was ever to write.

When their correspondence had started two years earlier, in 1951, when Hilde was not quite fifteen, she, with Annemarie Kempf and Rudolf Wolters, had begun to form what was to become for Speer an exceptionally efficacious triangulate of love and psychological support. Nonetheless, almost from the start, while their concern was almost entirely for Speer, he seemed to be essentially incapable of considering them and their efforts in any context other than his own life, past, present and future. "They kept me sane," he was to tell me years later.

He barely knew his six children—he had hardly spent any time with them

before he went to prison for twenty years—but there is no doubt that he grew
to admire and deeply love Hilde, to whom he wrote from the start as he
could never have spoken to her had life been normal: about the universe of
man, about nature, about philosophy, art and music and, above all, about
religion and faith.

In her earlier letters Hilde had spared him, accepting "in comparative silence," as she said later, his instructions and advice. In July 1952, two weeks
before she left for America, he wrote,

> You will of course be interviewed by the press and, unless your hosts
> suggest it, you should not avoid it. If you are asked political questions, just
> tell them you feel too young to express an opinion. You should not say
> that you knew Hitler, or that you lived on the Obersalzberg [Hitler's
> mountain compound]. . . . You should absolutely read two books in
> which there is a lot about me and with which you can then counter any-
> thing anybody might throw at you about me.*

"It probably did him good to tell me all that stuff," Hilde said later. "I
didn't pay much attention to it."

She conversed with him in her letters about ideas and impressions she had
gained, music she had heard, paintings and buildings she had seen, and to
some extent about the people she had met. All of this, however, was carefully
framed and phrased in the context of what might interest *him*, affect *his* feelings and alleviate the burdens of *his* life.

That grave letter in May 1953 was a new departure for her. On the one
hand, it demonstrated her growing maturity and courage after months in the
unaccustomed and very special moral environment of an educated Quaker
family on the American eastern seaboard. She was now not only ready but
needed to challenge him. On the other hand, it was perhaps an unconscious
attempt to deepen their relationship.

In the final analysis, the most intense relationship he would ever have was
with Casalis. As Protestant chaplain of Berlin's French community since the
four-power occupation in 1945, Casalis was put in charge of the spiritual care
of the seven prisoners at Spandau soon after they arrived in Berlin in July
1947, traumatized by the Nuremberg trial and the death sentences several of
them only narrowly escaped. With this thirty-year-old French intellectual, a
man of impeccable morality and exceptional humanity, Speer had slowly
gone further in his search of self and, had Casalis felt able to stay longer than
the three years they knew each other there, might have got to the point of
articulating his enormous guilt feelings.

*Hugh Trevor-Roper's *The Last Days of Hitler* and G. M. Gilbert's *Nuremberg Diary*.

"He could never say it," Casalis said. "And yet, when I first knew him, he was, under the extraordinary cool he affected, the most guilt-ridden, the most tortured man I had ever known. This gave him a very special value."

Casalis had joined the Resistance straight out of university at twenty-three, and was active in it throughout the occupation of France. He was told that Spandau would be added to his duties as chaplain after a long May weekend which he had spent with a team sent to identify, and bring back for burial, French dead from the Buchenwald concentration camp. He had photographs of the team: the two Soviet guards who traveled with them, the German POWs who dug up the corpses—and himself, with a clipboard, recording what they found. Next to him on the ground in one photo is a large bottle. "Brandy—it was the only way one could manage," he said when I first visited him in 1985 in Noyon, a village near Paris where Calvin was born, and where he and his wife, Dorothée, were looking after the Calvin Museum.

"I was very, very worried when I was told about Spandau," he went on, "full of doubts whether I was the right man for the job. Just imagine me, after four years as an active *résistant*, having to find detachment in myself toward these seven men. What could I say to them? What could I preach?"

He asked these questions of Karl Barth, the great Swiss theologian, just then on a visit to Berlin; he had been Casalis's teacher and had become his friend. "He thought it was a huge challenge. 'It's quite simple, *mon vieux,*' he said. 'Give them the same sermon on Saturday as to your congregation on Sunday—and tell both you are doing it. For the prisoners it will be reassuring; for your parishioners it'll be very sanguine to learn they are getting the same words on the "outside" which these prisoners heard the day before on the "inside": an interesting experiment in Christian charity.' And that's what I did, for three years."

At the end of Casalis's first service at Spandau, Speer asked to speak to him.

"And I was glad he did," Casalis said. "I needed to speak with him too." He told Speer that he was the only one of the group to whom he had wanted to say something, right away. "I told him that I considered him more blameworthy than any of the others. First of all, because he was the most intelligent. But secondly, he was, to my mind, not only more responsible than the other six prisoners but perhaps more than anyone in Germany except for Hitler himself, for extending the war. Thanks to his efforts, I told him, this terrible war had lasted at least a year longer than it might have, and as a result killed many of my friends."

Speer thanked him for his honesty. "And then he said, 'I'll be as honest in return. I would have said this to you anyway, having listened to your sermon and watched you as you delivered it—it was because I wanted to do this that I asked to speak to you just now: I've been sentenced to twenty years,' he said, 'and I consider it just. I want to use this time that has, in a manner of speaking, been given to me. What I want to ask you is: Would you help me become a different man?' "

Casalis left Spandau in 1950. "I could have stayed on for another term—a further five years," he said. "I was very tempted—it was of course very interesting. Seen in retrospect, if only from the point of view of my relationship with Speer, perhaps I should have stayed. But the fact is that neither I nor Dorothée could accept any longer to lead the really quite extraordinarily privileged life as 'occupiers' we had in Berlin. It was wrong. So we went to Strasbourg, where I took my Ph.D. in theology."

As Casalis realized much later, for Speer, in his very real effort to become "a different man," the departure after only three years of the man he would later describe as "the most important person in my life" was almost catastrophic. It had not only been his first experience of that very special thing, a French intellectual mind, but, rare for anyone, of a pure spirit and a total man. "Casalis is in my eyes entirely unique," he had written to Hilde a few months earlier. "So much so that I would like him one day to officiate at my funeral." (Casalis didn't. "I wasn't even asked to attend it," he said sadly, years later.)

With Casalis gone, Speer was virtually alone, for his relationship with the other six prisoners, although it would, necessarily, improve with time, was difficult, and that with the five subsequent chaplains merely courteous. With Casalis, for the first time in his life, he had learned to use spoken language to search for inner meanings and thereby let go of some of the iron self-control imposed upon him, by himself as well as others, since early childhood. Casalis's departure didn't stop Speer's process of change, but—as he would say many years later—it altered it. Whereas for those three years he had been helped to look inwards, beyond himself, thereby beginning to discover hitherto unsuspected imaginative freedoms, this introduction to abstract thinking had been too brief.

"He was a man with quite exceptional facilities," Casalis said. "They were indeed so exceptional that his thinking—as well as, I fear, his actions—had become facile. What he needed to do, you see, to become the 'different man' he wanted to be, was to give up everything that was easy. A determined human being of quality can achieve this if the circumstances are right. For Speer, who I suspect was the most determined of men at whatever he undertook, the quasi-monastic life of Spandau was ideally suited for such an endeavor."

It was, but, as he realized very quickly after Casalis left, not on his own, without support. He had begun to think—or dream—of writing quite some time before the end of the Third Reich. A number of his former associates recalled quips about turning himself into a biographer, and early in April 1945 he had worked out with his pilot friend, Werner Baumbach, Nazi Germany's ace dive bomber, a crazy and soon abandoned escape plan to Greenland. There he and a few selected friends could sit out the first few critical months after defeat in a sophisticated weather station the Germans had put up there in an isolated bay, where he could "start on [his] memoirs." Instead, he actually began to write them during a recess of his trial in Nuremberg, when, in a kind of euphoria of *Das Ende*, he had become increasingly convinced that, like most of the other accused, he would be sentenced to death. It was then he produced the 103-page précis which, seven years later in Spandau, he would develop into the 1,200-page draft that after his release in 1966 eventually became *Inside the Third Reich*.

"I was intensely affected by Nuremberg," he said later, "especially by the final speech by Britain's Chief Prosecutor—it devastated me." On July 27, 1946, Sir Hartley (now Lord) Shawcross, ending his summation with the most difficult and emotional subject of the trial, the horrors of the extermination of the Jews, read from a description by a German eyewitness of a mass execution of Jews by one of Himmler's Action Groups (Einsatzkommandos) in the Baltics.

> Without screaming or weeping, these people undressed, stood around in family groups, kissed each other, said farewells, and waited for a sign from another SS man, who stood near the pit . . . with a whip in his hand. During the fifteen minutes I stood nearby, I heard no . . . plea for mercy. I watched a family of about eight people, a man and a woman of about fifty with two daughters of about twenty to twenty-four and boys of about one, eight, and ten. An old woman with snow-white hair was holding the one-year-old in her arms and singing to it and tickling it. The child was cooing with delight. The couple were looking on with tears in their eyes. The father was holding the hand of a boy about ten years old and speaking to him softly; the boy was fighting his tears. The father pointed to the sky, stroked his head and seemed to explain something to him. At that moment the SS man at the pit shouted something to his comrade who then counted off about twenty persons and instructed them to get down behind a mound of earth. Among them was the family I have mentioned. . . .
>
> An SS man . . . sat on the edge of the narrow end of the pit, his feet dangling . . . a tommy gun on his knees. He was smoking a cigarette. The people, completely naked, went down some steps which were cut in the clay wall of the pit and clambered over the heads of the dead lying there, to the place to which the SS man directed them. They lay down in front of the dead or injured; some caressed those who were still alive and spoke to

them in a low voice. Then I heard a series of shots. I looked into the pit and saw that the bodies were twitching or . . . lying motionless on top of . . . those before them. Blood was running from their necks. . . .

"What special dispensation of Providence kept these men ignorant of these things?" Sir Hartley asked, pointing at the two rows of accused in the dock. ". . . Mankind itself, struggling now to re-establish in all the countries of the world the common simple things, liberty, love, understanding, comes to this court and cries, 'These are our laws, let them prevail.' . . . You will remember [this description] when you come to give your decision . . . not in vengeance [but] in a determination that these things shall not occur again."

"This account," Speer said thirty years later, "haunts me to this day. You know, when one hears of a thousand or a million people murdered it is out of scale, it's unimaginable. But this . . . it was the first time I could visualize what happened, what was done. And yes, it made me feel personal guilt. The others largely discounted the most terrible parts of the testimonies. They said the so-called eyewitnesses lied; the Germans, such as Ohlendorf, Höss* and others, were accusing each other or even confessing to monstrosities because this was what the court wanted to hear and they were bargaining for their lives; and that the films which were shown were fakes. I didn't think so. Oh, there were emotional exaggerations, how could there not be? But on the whole it was manifestly all true. I knew that the Russians would demand the death sentence for me, and after Shawcross's speech I thought they were right. How could we—just we—be allowed to remain alive after that?"

IT IS REMARKABLE that the man and the relationship most significant to Speer's life throughout his years at Spandau has remained entirely unknown. And yet, without understanding Rudolf Wolters and what he did, it is impossible to understand Speer at Spandau, which he himself considered the most important period of his life.

Wolters and Speer had known each other since student days in Munich in 1924. Over the years, with Wolters's feelings for Speer curiously similar to those Speer felt for Hitler, they developed a relationship that was to become decisive for Speer's survival at Spandau and his subsequent career.

Wolters was two years older than Speer, and their social world was different. But both their fathers were architects, and their education and early career ran almost parallel, though with Speer always a few steps ahead. Thus, if

*Gruppenführer Otto Ohlendorf interrupted his bureaucratic career in the Main Security Office in Berlin to head (for exactly one year after the invasion of Russia) Einsatzgruppe D, which operated in southern Russia. He testified that he and his unit had killed ninety thousand people, and justified his actions with ten pages of historical precedents. Standartenführer Rudolf Höss was Commandant of Auschwitz.

Wolters just managed to get his *Abitur* (qualification for higher education) in 1923 when he was twenty, Speer graduated the same year at the top of his class, both in German and mathematics, at eighteen. When they first met, Wolters was beginning his fourth term in architecture at the Munich Technical College, while Speer was transferring there after three terms at the rather second-rate technical school at Karlsruhe. Wolters preceded Speer on to Berlin, to study under the distinguished architect Heinrich Tessenow, but Speer, following him a year later, managed to get his architect's license at the same time as Wolters, in the summer of 1927. He even got an appointment as Tessenow's assistant—a plum Wolters had coveted from the start.

Nonetheless, the two students had become friends, or almost friends. "We had amicable relations," Wolters would write fifty years later in his superb reminiscences, *Lebensabrisse* (Segments of a Life). Speer from his side did indeed have "amicable relations" with Wolters, about the same as he had with most of his fellow students: friendly but distant. But Wolters had very soon come under the spell of Speer's personality, where he would remain for more than forty years.

They both had talent, a high degree of intelligence and ambition and a pronounced gift for writing. Wolters had kept a diary since his father gave him his first one on the day World War I began, when he was eleven, and in 1973 privately published his reminiscences. Speer, at sixteen, wrote long, rather earnest but brilliant essays in school, and over the next year and a half almost daily letters to Margret. They shared another quality not then frequently found among educated Germans—a sense of humor. Wolters's was almost ribald and somewhat studied, but rarely unkind; Speer's was either impersonal and sharp or, very much like a clever child, mischievous sometimes to the point of malice.

One thing that set Speer apart from his peers was that in the 1920s, at a time of economic catastrophe in Germany and dire penury for students, he had money. As he has written, the sale of his maternal grandfather's firm and factory for "dollar treasury bills" provided him with a monthly allowance of $16, a princely sum in inflation-ridden Germany. And in 1928, when he was promoted to being a senior rather than junior university assistant, while others, including Wolters, got their Ph.D.s on soup, bread and water, he earned the equivalent of $200 a month, secured by the state against inflation. "Gretel [by then his wife] and I," he would say almost fifty years later, "gave huge spaghetti dinners every week for our student friends."

Wolters, writing later in *Segments of a Life*, credited him with great generosity. "He would help any student in need, including quite often myself." For two years Wolters worked for the German Railways without pay, except for food, then in early 1932 accepted a two-year contract to build railways in the

Soviet Union. He was therefore away when Speer's career first took off. When he returned to Germany, he briefly worked for Speer in his still tiny Berlin office but then married and returned to work for the railway, this time with pay.

In 1937, however, when Hitler named the thirty-two-year-old Speer Inspector General for the Construction of Berlin (GBI), Wolters accepted a job offered by his old friend. "I had viewed Hitler and his movement with some skepticism," he would write later in *Segments of a Life*, "but when the abolition of the multi-party mess removed the obscenity of unemployment, and the first 1,000 kilometers of *Autobahnen* (motorways) opened up a new era of mobility, I too saw the light: this was the time when Churchill said he hoped Great Britain would have a man like Hitler in times of peril, and when high church dignitaries and distinguished academics paid the Führer homage."

From that moment on, Wolters, always in Speer's shadow, entirely trusted but always taken for granted, worked for Speer. While Speer was Hitler's architect, Wolters was part of Speer's design team, but as Speer's role changed upwards, so did Wolters's, sideways. He traveled with and for Speer, and had ready access to him, but as an old friend rather than advisor. He became his press representative and his chronicler,* rather than an executive in his own right in Speer's huge and powerful ministerial hierarchy. Holding Speer in awe for much of his life, it was a role Wolters appeared to accept readily.

The tribute Wolters paid Speer in his reminiscences, written well after Speer had been released from Spandau, by which time Wolters had become bitterly disillusioned with him, clearly showed the admiration he had had for him:

> The task [Speer] had been given—the rebuilding of Berlin—exceeded anything until then imaginable in city-planning. His concept was brilliantly simple. . . . If I were to characterize briefly the man who received this incredible assignment I would put it as follows: despite his academic training [he was] a self-made man, artistically inclined toward purity and nature. With an absolutely unfailing instinct for management and organization, Speer had the gift of transmuting complications into simplicity. What was especially to Hitler's liking was that he could function with minute backup, demonstrating with great elegance an almost casual nonchalance in the tensest moments.
>
> Despite the resolute determination he needed to achieve his enormous projects, he remained sensitive: he was never loud or uncontrolled. . . . Although he was incredibly hardworking and recognized no conventional office hours—his closest staff had to be available at all hours of the day

---

*Wolters kept the *Chronik*, the official record of Speer's activities—travel, speeches, memos, meetings—from January 1940 until September 1944. A fuller discussion of the *Chronik* is in Chapter IX.

and night—he himself, oddly enough, always had time. At least, so it seemed to all who worked close to him. . . .

At Nuremberg, when to Speer all seemed lost, it was to Wolters he turned. On August 10, 1946, he wrote him a letter which was to all appearances his Last Will:

My dear friend Rudolf Wolters,
    You have been among those closest to me and we have known each other since our early youth. I therefore want to ask you to get together a collection of my work and to set down, for the future, some of what you know of my life. I think that one day it will be appreciated.
    I visualize this as follows: Part I. The architectural work, which you know better than anyone. I hope the photographs still exist and it should be possible to get hold of the designs which we deposited in Hamburg. This should be presented quite matter-of-factly.
    Part II. The work as Minister: "the Wittenberg'sche" [Annemarie Kempf] should be consulted on this part. She knows best who of the old crowd is still around and one of them should be put in charge. It should be, again, a purely factual account of the organization and its achievements.
    Part III. The essential points of my life: I think I'm entitled to be seen by posterity in a different light than all these repulsive bourgeois "revolutionaries." My idealistic attitude toward Hitler—for that is what it was—should here be described. The contributors—aside from those you know such as Wittenberg'sche, [Manfred] von Poser [his Wehrmacht liaison officer], [Walter] Rohland [head of the German steel industry], [Hermann] Röchling [an armaments manufacturer]—should also include my parents, parents-in-law, and many old friends such as [Robert] Frank [an industrialist friend], Wilhelm Kempff [the pianist], Josef Thorak [a sculptor] . . . also [Werner] Baumbach [his pilot] . . . and [Adolf] Galland [Luftwaffe General, Commander of the Fighter Force]. . . .

Here Speer's always-hard-to-decipher handwriting begins to go all over the page, becoming almost illegible as he appeared to reach out desperately for others who might contribute to a positive record of his life.

    . . . the barber Witkamp from Werne an der Lippe, Westphalia, the barber Dinand from Konstanz, the peasant Mayr from Michelhausen/Moosbier, near Tulln in Austria—these three were here in the prison and are good people; and of course Dr. [Hans] Flächsner [his counsel], Berlin.
    Then, my wife has letters from our youth which she won't like to hand over. But she must, as well as the letters I wrote her from here. You will also be able to get things from testimonies at the trial. And you will be

interested in some sketches I produced on impulse for my children—my wife has them, and you have "a nose" for all this.

Part IV. I'm going to try in my last weeks here to put down some of the things I remember: perhaps in the decades to come, this could be published as a little book: it is intended as an open and honest account.

That is all: I know you will do it well. Perhaps it will even give you some satisfaction to thus complete your task as my official chronicler. In any case, I shall be grateful to you.

In memory of many wonderful times together, I send you my warmest wishes.

> Always your friend,
> Albert Speer

On August 31, 1946, Speer made his final statement to the court, in which he made no attempt to support his defense but, with the entire proceedings being broadcast to the country, addressed himself directly to the German people.

After explicitly condemning Hitler and his dictatorship, he ended by trying to boost the morale of the Germans who, he said, had for centuries contributed much toward the creation of a civilized human society. They would now, recognizing Hitler as the proven author of their present misfortune, not only forevermore hate and fear dictatorship as a form of government but out of this misery come to create new and lasting values. "A nation that believes in its future," he concluded, "will never perish. May God protect Germany and Western culture."

The characteristic recklessness of this last sentence, with its open contempt for the Russians, was deliberate. He intended to acknowledge openly his realization of the dissension between East and West during the trial, and to reinforce the sympathy for him he believed he sensed among the Western members of the court. One month later, on October 1, 1946, when Speer was sentenced to a long term of imprisonment, many people attributed the court's leniency toward Speer to a kind of "old school tie" sympathy, particularly on the part of the British and American judges.

Historian Bradley Smith in his book *Reaching Judgment at Nuremberg* refutes these claims of prejudice and demonstrates that, on the contrary, the principal American judge, Francis Biddle, voted for the death sentence, as did the Soviet Union's General I. T. Nikitchenko. The twenty-year prison sentence was only agreed to after two days' discussion and some rather bitter horse trading. According to Smith, only the American and British alternate judges, John Parker and Norman Birkett, were possibly influenced in Speer's favor by his upper-class demeanor.

The chief American prosecutor, Justice Robert Jackson, whose cross-examination of Speer was considered by some critics to be unduly gentle, demonstrated his true feelings very clearly in his guideline to the U.S. War Department two weeks before the verdicts. He stated bluntly that, as concerned appeals, he saw no reason for clemency to anyone. ". . . Clemency," he wrote, "is a matter of grace, not of right." As none of the defendants had "rendered any service whatever to the prosecution," there were no grounds for clemency.

Lord Shawcross told me many years later that in his opinion Speer was "quite lucky to have avoided a death sentence. . . . My own view," he said, "was one of great surprise that Speer was so leniently dealt with, and I still think it quite wrong that his subordinate, Sauckel, who worked under his instructions, was sentenced to death while Speer escaped."

Six weeks after the end of the trial, on November 13, 1946, Wolters wrote to Annemarie Kempf, setting in motion the process which would dominate much of their lives for the next twenty years and provide the foundation for Speer's future. She was still living in the VIP detention complex in Kransberg Castle, near Frankfurt, called Dustbin, which housed almost the entire technical and scientific leadership of the Third Reich. She had gone there in late July 1945, when Eisenhower moved his HQ to Frankfurt and the castle became the VIP interrogation center, to assist Speer during his questioning by U.S. and British intelligence.

Speer had suggested in 1978 that Annemarie Kempf and I get to know each other, and from 1982, when I began the research for this book until late 1990, when I began to write it, we met frequently. Her hair was white, but she was still slender and quite beautiful. We talked sometimes for days and even weeks, in Hamburg where she lived, in the Tyrol where she joined us for working holidays, and in London where she came to stay with us.

"He sent word that he needed me, so of course I went," she said during one of our earliest talks. "It was called an exploitation camp, and both American and British experts, officers and civilians, came to ask Speer questions. They had shipped an enormous amount of documentation there, from all over the place. Almost the whole ministry staff was there. Edith Maguira, who had been [Fritz] Todt's secretary and whom Speer kept on when he became Minister after Todt's death, came along to help me.* They gave us a room in the castle tower."

---

*Fritz Todt was the great construction engineer who had conceived and built the *Autobahnen*, which became the model for motorways throughout the rest of Europe. His Organization Todt (OT), so named by Hitler in 1938, built the West Wall fortifications and the U-boat pens and eventually was in charge of all road construction in occupied Europe.

He became Minister of Armaments and Munitions in 1940, and after his death in a mysterious plane crash in February 1942, Speer was appointed Minister in his place and took over the OT and all his other functions.

While Speer was in Kransberg, the two young women—who knew more about the documents than virtually anyone else—helped with research, and Annemarie took down and then typed all the interrogations. When Speer, four months later, was moved to Nuremberg, she was able to keep her Kransberg room and mess privileges by assisting other ministry staff being questioned there, but went as often as possible to Nuremberg to help Speer's counsel.

For twelve years Annemarie had lived at the center of power. "It is impossible to describe adequately the excitement of the first years, or the strain and then the pain of the last ones," she said. Being at the center of events that last year had meant early awareness of the impending defeat and Hitler's disintegration, as Speer saw it, and, once Speer had begun to act deliberately and openly against Hitler in order to save what he could of the country's living potential, it meant continuous anxiety not just for his safety but also, she said, for his life: first from Hitler, then, after the war, from the Nuremberg court. "By the time the day of the verdict and the sentencing came," she said, "I was worn to a nub, just so tired. . . . You know, one just wanted it all to end: I would never have committed suicide, but I wouldn't have minded dying."

On November 7, 1946, Annemarie had written to Wolters suggesting that perhaps they should meet to discuss what could be done for Speer in the future. Wolters replied a week later, carefully avoiding throughout his letter any mention of Speer's name (he refers to him as "Father"), as he suspected, probably quite rightly, that letters to Kransberg would be subject to censorship:

Dear Annemarie,
  Many thanks for yours of 7 November. I have since then, via Dr. F. [Flächsner, Speer's defense counsel], received Father's letter in which he charges me to get together whatever I can about his life and work and eventually to write something appropriate about it. It goes without saying that I will very willingly take on this commission. . . .
  I will try first of all to collect the material and I still hope that I can just hand it over to him one day so that he can write his reminiscences himself for this would be of much greater significance. . . . In his letter he says among other things that important material is in your care. . . .
  I have of course written to Heidelberg [where Speer's wife and children were living in a cottage on the family property, the big house having been requisitioned by the Americans] and am now awaiting the reply. . . . Your information that one can write to Father was quite new to me, and I will most assuredly hasten to do so. Again, I would be grateful to hear from you how this will work in the future, i.e., whether one will be able to write

[once Speer was transferred to a permanent prison] and how the letters should be. If he were cut off there from all correspondence, it would be very hard on him. . . .

It was Speer's devastating letter of August 10 that gave birth to Wolters's feeling of guilt about the fate which he felt Speer was carrying for all of them, and his eventual determination to alleviate it somehow. "His Last Will," he wrote in his *Segments*, "was a goodbye which shook me to the core."

Within two years, only just professionally re-established in his hometown, Coesfeld, which he was commissioned to rebuild after bomb damage, Wolters began to take charge of the Speer family's precarious finances. By 1951, he had succeeded in setting up a fund which some two dozen of Speer's former architects and industrialist friends, under Wolters's steady pressure, continued to support, contributing enough money to allow some security for Margret and the six children and indeed some small luxuries for Speer in prison. But besides the money, he provided—at some cost to his own children—affection and care for the family. Over the years, he organized most of the worldwide but unsuccessful efforts to obtain early release for Speer. Toward the end of the twenty years, Wolters tried to prepare the ground for Speer's professional life after his release by getting a few of Speer's successful former friends to arrange consultancies.

First and foremost, however, Wolters provided an outlet throughout these years for Speer's thinking and writing from the isolation of Spandau. The organization of the smuggling and transcribing of this vast correspondence, scribbled almost illegibly in minute writing, often in old German script, on any scrap of paper Speer could find, was incredibly demanding, given Wolters's increasingly busy architectural practice. The commitment to Speer's cause, both from Wolters and Marion Riesser, was staggering.

The most important part of Speer's writing from Spandau was the thousands of letters from 1953 which, transcribed by Marion Riesser, became the 1,200-page "Spandau draft" of *Inside the Third Reich*.

All the original letters and the transcription of the draft remained in Speer's archive, and when we worked together, he often brought out letters or pages to show to me or prove a point. But it was only after his and Wolters's death, when Wolters's son, Fritz, gave me access to his father's archive containing duplicates of all the material, that I was able to obtain a copy of the entire "Spandau draft."

After Spandau, Speer would write three further drafts, and the book that resulted showed some significant changes from the original. There is no doubt that this first, most immediate feat of memory represents the true, unvarnished record of his own actions and motivations, as well as those of others. When he came out of Spandau and had to confront "real life," as he called it, he became very vulnerable. In Spandau he had been the only one of the seven prisoners to assert continuously his recognition of the Nazis' wrongs. The isolation he suffered over those twenty years as a result of this stand was basically the price he paid—it was a kind of triumph, an immense moral victory.

The shock on coming out was to find that others—indeed most of the world—had gone much further than he in condemnation of the wrong. This is what he meant when he said (see Chapter VII) that "what I said and the way I said it somehow had to take into account these gradations of understanding of which . . . I was entirely ignorant. . . ."

When Speer was in Spandau, his blunt criticisms of Hitler in the draft had already provoked Wolters into carefully voiced complaints. Speer's way after Spandau to "bridge the void, not in others but in myself" (as he would tell me), was to accentuate the negative about Hitler wherever he could. This was to have the result of alienating him from most of his former friends, above all, most painfully, from Wolters.

"What Rudi Wolters wanted," said Marion Riesser, "was for Speer, as far as Hitler was concerned, to recount history as it happened. What he came to deeply resent, as time went on, was Speer's demonization of Hitler, his continuous negative interpretation of virtually every side and every act of his, as he saw or interpreted it in retrospect."

Wolters could never have managed the transcription of Speer's nearly twenty-five thousand letters from Spandau without Marion's work on them over fifteen years. She had never met Speer personally, and her family suffered under the tyrant he served with such passion. What drove her to help him so generously? This too is a mystery.

"It's hard to explain," she said. "I can say that what he wrote fascinated me and that, after a while, yes, I came to like him very much. He tried to be honest, tried even when he failed, and that seemed to me admirable under the circumstances."

Marion had been reluctant to talk with me; she too is a very private person, and was particularly concerned how Rudolf Wolters's children would feel if her story and her complicated private relationship with their father became public. After changing her mind several times, she finally agreed to my visit only after Fritz Wolters, who like his wife, Lore (also a fine architect), is an open and articulate person, invited me to stay with them in the beautiful annex they built to the old Wolters home in Coesfeld. When we talked, it turned out that Marion had never known how much Fritz had suffered under his father's twenty-year concentration on Speer and his family, and his father's indifference toward his own children. Fritz, on the other hand, had known virtually nothing of Marion's life history.

Once she overcame her reservations, Marion and I quickly became friends. Still very attractive at seventy-three when we met in 1985, she must have been stunning when she was young. We talked in her flat, beautifully converted from Wolters's former office; over late dinners in a *Gasthaus* where I stayed on later visits; and during long walks along the river that runs through Coesfeld.

Wolters's unique twenty-year-long act of friendship for Speer was astonishing, but one could understand it, given their many years together, the reflected glory of Speer's relationship with Hitler which Wolters had enjoyed, the admiration he felt for Speer during those twelve years and his compassion for him afterwards.

Marion Riesser's huge part in Wolters's psychological rescue of Speer is more difficult to comprehend. Marion is half Jewish; her grandfather, the eminent Frankfurt banker Jakob Riesser, was vice-president of the Weimar Reichstag. His son Otto, Marion's father, was a professor in pharmacology and physiology at the University of Breslau until he was pensioned off under the Nazis' racial laws and eventually fled to Holland.

Marion's mother had died in 1914, when Marion was one-and-a-half, and six years later, in 1920, her father fell in love and married the beautiful young war widow of a north German aristocrat who had two children, a girl two years older and a boy one year older than Marion. "We immediately became inseparable," Marion said. "I was blissful: a ready-made brother and sister of a sensible age." And she also adored her lovely new mother. "A girl at school said pityingly, 'Oh, you have a stepmother now,' and I said, 'No, I have a second mother.' My parents were wonderful. They treated us all the same— we were all their children, their family, we and then the two they very quickly had together, my brother Julian and my sister Birgit."

But things were not to remain quite so wonderful. After the advent of the Nazis, the two oldest left, the then twenty-one-year-old stepbrother to study farming on an estate, the twenty-three-year-old stepsister to enter a nursing school run by the BDM (Bund Deutscher Mädel; Association of German Girls). "Two years later," Marion said, "she killed herself. Both she and my stepbrother had loved my father very much. The BDM had forbidden her to communicate with him, so she never saw him again after she left home. They had expelled her a few days before she did it. Was it because she had always been mildly manic depressive, or was it because of my father? We never knew.

"By then we were living in Frankfurt, and my mother and we children traveled to Breslau to attend the funeral, which was organized by the BDM." When they got there, they were refused entry. "It was dreadful," Marion said, "dreadful for my mother, but dreadful for us too. And less than a year later, our stepbrother also killed himself. He apparently just picked up a shotgun one day and shot himself—again, we never knew why. But I have always thought that for both of them it had to have been the impossible conflict between their love for my father and for us, and the loyalty imposed upon them by the party."

And only days after they returned to Frankfurt, fifteen-year-old Birgit was to feel the power of the party too. "Until then, she had been all right at school," Marion said, "but now the party's attention had manifestly been drawn to us. Birgit's class was told that they were not to associate with her, in breaks or outside school. Her life, and that of my parents who suffered with her, became very difficult."

In 1940 (by which time her father had long escaped to Holland) Marion moved to Berlin to live with her Jewish grandmother, whom she adored. Half-Jews were forbidden to study science or humanities, but her choice of graphics was allowed. Had she and her grandmother been frightened? I asked her. She shook her head. "No, we weren't. It's so hard to explain now. Perhaps we lived in a fool's paradise. But the fact is that until catastrophe struck three years later, our life was more or less normal. Nobody bothered us. My grandmother's friends remained her friends; we shopped, went for walks, to theaters, concerts, films. After the Nuremberg Laws [against the Jews], I was barred from getting a degree, which meant that one did necessarily live to some degree in a state of heightened awareness. But in the context of the country as a whole, Berlin had always been different, freer, more democratic than other cities, and I managed to study and work. Also, my grandmother was, of course, very well connected—it did help. We knew [through her connections] that my father was getting by in Holland." Her grandmother was under the protection of a high-ranking army officer on the general staff who had known her husband. "But late one night in 1943," Marion said, "he came and said he was being transferred to Russia; he wouldn't be able to help her anymore. Not long after he had gone, they came one night to fetch her for deportation."

The old lady was sent to Theresienstadt, the Nazis' "model camp" which they exhibited repeatedly and successfully to the International Red Cross. "She died there," said Marion, "just before the end of the war."

Marion owed her own comparative safety during the last years of Nazi rule to Wolters—and to Speer—in whose Town Planning Directorate, the GBI, she as well as several other half-Jews were able to find refuge. "It's quite common in our place," she was told by a university friend who got her in. "Nobody cares, and the old man [Speer] backs us up."

As of the summer of 1944, when Speer's various organizations—the GBI, the ministry and the Organization Todt—worked increasingly in conjunction, a number of people, Wolters above all, went from one to another or at times worked for all three.

Late that year there was a rumor that all people of mixed ancestry would be called up "as cannon fodder," Marion said. She had come to be very much under Wolters's protection. "But not only I," she said. "There were four half-Jews hiding under the umbrella of Speer's organizations, and Wolters told all four of us that if it looked as if this was about to happen, he had arranged that we would be moved quickly into one of the factories producing essential war supplies, where we would be safe. 'With Albert Speer's help one can do anything,' he told us, and we believed him and stopped being afraid.

"Wolters was not that much of a Nazi, as you can see," she said, and smiled. "But it is true that the more explicitly and aggressively Speer in his writings in Spandau and afterwards turned against Hitler, the more Wolters defended him. This was of course partly involved with Wolters's very complicated feelings about Speer. But partly too, it was because of his real feelings about Hitler. He could never believe that Hitler was—or wanted—evil. He remembered the good things, and he felt that Speer, who had so vastly profited from them, should have remembered them too."

Speer was determined to show Hitler in his writings as the criminal he finally realized him to be. To Wolters, this was the rankest kind of disloyalty and ingratitude to the man they had both served and admired.

"I kept hoping they would somehow find a way to remain friends," Marion said. But it was not to be. The conflict between them would deepen swiftly after Speer left Spandau, and the complete rupture came after the publication of *Inside the Third Reich*. For in this book, which could not have been written without Wolters's support during his time in Spandau, Speer never publicly acknowledged what this most loyal and devoted friend had done for him.

He said it was for Wolters's own protection. He believed, he told me, that it would have been risky for Wolters—and his architectural work, much of it governmental—to be identified as having for twenty years contravened the law by assisting a convicted war criminal. But the fact is, that in the face of Wolters's growing disapproval of the moral stand he had taken, it was not in Speer's interest to publicize this old friend who knew so much about him. His decision not to acknowledge Wolters's extraordinary merit in print, and his publishing advisors' failure to change his mind on this matter, remains unforgivable.

For Wolters it was a profound disappointment which blighted the last fourteen years of his life. Remarkably, despite everything, it would appear that his love for Speer, just as Speer's for Hitler, survived. When Wolters died, his last uttered word, Fritz told me, was "Albert."

I

An Infusion of Stable Stock

Nuremberg, June 19, 1946

DR. HANS FLÄCHSNER [defense counsel]: With the permission of the High Tribunal, I should like to call the defendant Speer to the witness box.

THE PRESIDENT [Lord Justice Lawrence]: Will you repeat this oath after me: I swear by God—the Almighty and Omniscient—that I will speak the pure truth and will withhold and add nothing. . . .

FLÄCHSNER: Herr Speer, will you please tell the tribunal about your life up until the time you were appointed Minister?

"THE COURT WAS not really interested in my youth," Albert Speer said decades after the Nuremberg trials. "Why should they have been? What does it have to do with what happened?"

This was true enough for the judicial matters before the Nuremberg court. But it can never be true if one wishes to evaluate a human being, his development, motivations, conflicts and emotions. If there is one thing all psychologists now agree on, it is that the denial of love in childhood almost invariably leads to a damaged adult. And in that sense, Speer certainly had more than scars—he bore the wounds of an emotionally deprived childhood.

By February 1978, when I began my talks with Speer for the London *Sunday Times Magazine* profile, both *Inside the Third Reich* and *The Secret Diaries* had become huge best-sellers throughout the Western world, and he was beginning to plan his next literary project—a book about Himmler's planned SS state. Speer's private world, however, had shrunk. It consisted of Margret and himself, living partly in that old family house in Heidelberg he hated and partly in the old farmhouse he had bought and renovated high in the Allgäu—the Bavarian Alps.

And yet, the large Heidelberg house with its lovely gardens and adjoining fields was beautiful. It had been used only for holidays until life in industrial Mannheim during World War I became dangerous, and the Heidelberg house was vastly enlarged to become the family home. Speer had virtually never lived in it as an adult until after his release from Spandau. Until his parents died, while he was imprisoned, it was their home; then, once the Americans who had requisitioned it released it, Margret and the children moved into it and let the top floor and a cottage in the garden to students to provide extra money.

By the time I met the Speers, five of their children lived elsewhere in West Germany and rarely came to Heidelberg. "I go and see them," Margret said. "I don't," Speer quipped, his flippancy sounding false. "They come here sometimes when I'm not here. That's all right; I can understand that: after all, it was their home—and Margret's—during my twenty years in Spandau. As long as I don't have to live in it more than absolutely necessary," he said, looking with distaste around the big living room, with its many picture windows looking out into the snow-covered garden. "Everything here," he said, "reminds me of the miseries of my childhood."

His face, surprisingly smooth for his seventy-three years, looked drawn, the sudden weariness I would see time and again in the next few weeks somehow emphasized by those thick eyebrows, as black as ever. Usually adding to the strength of his face, they somehow underlined the momentary yielding when he was tired, discouraged or depressed by a particularly distressing memory. It was quite strange how ready this very private man was to speak of his childhood, which he said he had never spoken of before, and how bitter he still felt about it.

"I only begin to breathe," he added, "when I leave here on our way to the mountains. There I feel on neutral ground."

In Heidelberg we usually talked in the living room, sitting in deep armchairs in a window alcove. At first Margret, small, slender and shy with strangers, was only with us during meals—they had a daily cleaner, but she did all the cooking and shopping herself, going down into the city on foot or on the bus since she didn't drive and their house was up on the hill. True to form for a German male of his generation—except for a few days when Margret came down with the flu and Speer turned out to have a deft hand at making tea—I never saw him move a finger, domestically.

As our talks proceeded, Margret's restraint slowly diminished and she began coming in while we talked, rather shyly sidling through the door and, for quite a long time, refusing to come any closer, sitting on a straight chair across the room. Her face, with those light blue eyes and blond eyebrows, had a curious look of innocence and seemed perpetually alight with curiosity and oddly hungry for communication.

As the weeks went on and I lived with them on the mountain, sometimes helping with the cooking or washing up, a kind of closeness developed between us. "He only comes alive when he talks about the past," she said once, "like with you, you see: however unhappy the things are he talks about, he is happy that he can talk." The children, she said, didn't want to be part of his single-minded concentration on this history. "It isn't that they don't like him," she said. "Only the other day," she said, not realizing how sad it sounded, "Margret [their younger daughter] actually said, 'I do like him.' It's just that whenever they tried to talk to him about anything but the past, his face glazed over or he'd just go away, so finally they gave up."

I too saw that "glazed over" look several times during meals when I tried to talk about other things. Margret said she hadn't given up, like the children. "I don't want to talk about those things, but I do now sometimes come to listen. Otherwise," she said, "one is so alone."

Speer was born in Mannheim on March 19, 1905. "I did
nal grandparents," he said. "They died while my father
were rumors my grandfather had committed suicide, but it
about. Suicide, mental illness or diseases such as cancer we
ceptable. My father and his four siblings were brought up
grandmother." His father, he said, instead of going to univer
planned, became an apprentice to a firm of architects because
ther hadn't left any money.

This was no doubt true, but he had written precisely the cont
first page of *Inside the Third Reich*. "My grandfather, Berthold Spee
there, "became a prosperous architect. . . . Though he died youn
enough to provide for the education of his four sons." When I as
about this, he shrugged. "I didn't think it mattered," he said. "Why
these private matters, in print?"

It was his maternal grandfather, Louis Christian August Herrmann
mel, whom young Albert had liked best. "He was a real self-made man
son of a forester who worked himself up to become one of the leading ind
trialists in Mainz—he owned a large machine-tool company. But he alwa
remained a very modest man. I remember his office: a hard chair—a stoo
really—and a standing desk; I liked that." He liked his grandfather's simplic
ity, but more than that, he was, and would remain until his death in 1921
when Albert was sixteen, the only warm person in his family. "My grandmother—his wife—was pretentious, and stingy." "She counted the sugar
cubes in the kitchen," Margret said. "Would you believe it? She had a lock-
able sugar tin."

"She was a cold woman," Speer said. "My grandfather wasn't cold, but he
was a very silent man. I used to go shooting with him, and we would walk
and stalk for hours never saying a word—I loved that. At the same time, he
was a great organizer—I think that's where I got my organizing talent from.
It isn't that technocrats can't be romantics—" he added suddenly. "I think
he was very romantic: nature, music. . . ." Did that include women? "I don't
know." His tone at what he considered a flippant question was dismissive.
"Too much is made of that aspect of a man's personality." Mainz, where the
Hommels lived, was a lively garrison city in his mother's youth. "They belonged to the social elite, of course," he said. "There were many balls, young
officers galore; she led a very social life, quite glamorous, I think."

Dr. Lili Fehrle-Bürger's mother became a close friend of Speer's mother
after the family moved to Heidelberg. "Frau Speer had been desperately in
love with a brilliant and very temperamental young officer," she wrote in a
1979 letter, offering her help after reading my profile of Speer in the German
weekly *Die Zeit*. "He coldly deceived her, which drove her, brokenhearted,

husband. I heard her describe this
and classically humanitarian
pensate her for the loss of her

n heard my mother complain that
er exciting life in Mainz before her
rriage contract," he said drily.

is life, they lived in the fourteen-room
s Speer's father owned in Mannheim. "My
he married my even richer mother," he said.
ospect, I now think that because of my mother
eir means but—above their station. If my mother
horrible provincial nest,' as she used to call Mann-
n sit up and take notice. French and Italian furniture,
broidered curtains and of course a staff of servants: cook
black and white, butler and footmen in purple liveries
ons with a coat of arms—to which, incidentally, we were not

(folded corner, partial text:) n't know my pater- / was young. There / e socially unac- / by my paternal / sity as he had / the grandfa- / rary on the / r," he said / g, he left / ked him / go into / dom- / the / us- / ys / l,

iption of his home life, given in his customary deceptively non-
manner and tone, conveyed an overwhelming impression of cold:
tween the parents, cold between parents and children, cold between
mistress of the house and the staff.

Now that I think of it," he said, "it's true: the only warmth I ever felt at
ome was from our French governess, Mlle Blum. She was Jewish, you know.
My mother was keen on my older brother, Hermann, and he became very
conceited.

"I did love my father," he said, suddenly sounding sad and almost ab-
surdly young. "Well, he loved my brother Ernst, who later died at Stalingrad.
He was the youngest, impetuous and funny, and very what the Americans
call 'cute.' I wasn't cute at all," he said, "I was all angles and sharp corners
and—as I know now—nerves. The only people who liked me were my father's office staff. The office was next door and I used to run over there often.
Mlle Blum understood that that was my way of trying to get close to my father, and also that I needed to get away from my brothers, who were beastly
to me. From when I was about eight until I was thirteen, I became the office
staff's favorite. They arranged a small table just for me. I remember working
for weeks on a sketch there when I was twelve, for my father's birthday—it
was a clock, a very special clock. What I felt for him was more than respect;
even more than love, I think. I revered him, but I honestly don't think he
noticed I was there."

This too was said in a curiously young voice. A group of photographs of the three boys together, in twos or threes, shows clearly the tension of the two boys against him, and in young Albert himself. "They used to beat me up," said Speer. "I fainted quite a bit. I remember it quite well, especially as I had similar episodes again later when I was under pressure. I'd suddenly feel terribly hot then very cold, and then, boom, I'd be out. When I was a child—and on those later occasions too—the doctors attributed it to circulation problems, but today one would probably say it was psychosomatic. Later it was stress, but when I was little it was my reaction to my brothers, who were in cahoots against me, I was always trying to get them to love me—" he pointed at a snapshot in which he, at the age of six or seven, leans toward his elder brother, Hermann. "Look how I'm trying," he said, mocking himself.

As a small boy, his only real playmate was a girl, the daughter of their porter. "Already then," he said, "I sought the simplicity of such lives, and their warmth." At his Mannheim secondary school, his only friend was a boy named Quenser. "He came from a poor family, so I wasn't allowed to invite him home. But he was cheeky and so was I, so at school he was my friend." Speer laughed. "That's where I first demonstrated my passion for statistics: I had a little pocket diary and I used to keep a record of classbook entries for misdemeanors, in which Quenser and I competed. It was a matter of pride for me, I remember, that I led the field time and again. Now I know why: I wanted to be different from the way I was expected to be."

As an industrial center, Mannheim was particularly exposed to the increasing rigors of World War I and, when it was over, to the consequences of defeat. In the summer of 1918, when Speer was thirteen, the family moved to the house above the ancient castle in lovely old Heidelberg. Now they had a big garden where vegetables could be grown to supplement their diet, and they were within a stone's throw of hills for skiing and the woods of the Odenwald for hiking.

His passion became rowing. When he was fourteen, he made a new friend, an older boy named Ehret, the top rower in the school. With Ehret's help he got into a rowing club and not long afterwards was made cox. "It was my first real achievement. It was the first time"—Speer grinned impishly and watched for my reaction—"the first time I could impose my will on others. I had eight people under me. The cox is the king, the others are mere slaves."

It was a part of that oddly childlike side of him that he frequently said provocative things in the way a child uses bad language to try his elders and to assert his independence. "I had certainly never been able to do that before, either with my two brothers, who, being two to one against me and invariably supported by one or both of my parents, were bound to win any argument—or at my Mannheim school where, aside from misbehaving, I had never found any way to stand out."

For those first two years in Heidelberg he went quite crazy about rowing, at the expense of all other sports. His mother was furious. Ordinary people rowed; the upper classes, she told him—as he could see by his brothers' example—played tennis.

"But as time went on I became rather interested in schoolwork—especially mathematics and German, so there wasn't really anything to threaten me with, and she let me be."

His parents did not, however, "let him be" when he met Margarete Weber, who would later become his wife. He described how it happened in one of his "Spanish-Illustrated" letters. (In his humorous Spandau letters to the children, he called Spandau "Spain" and the letters the "Spanish-Illustrated.") On October 26, 1953, he wrote:

My dear children,
   I was not yet seventeen . . . when I became aware of two girls who, self-confident and unapproachable, were like me on their way to school. Every time I came down [a certain street] we appeared to bump into each other at the . . . crossing. They could of course have been going to school that way for years, but that's when I noticed them. One of them was very dark-haired, the other—the one I liked—light with exactly the same coloring and hairstyle and eyes like Hilde's when she came to see me the other day, only a bit younger.
   Soon we covered the short distance together, and that little daily stroll—as you will have guessed by now—turned into what is by now a lifetime of thirty-two years. If only I hadn't been so shy with the opposite sex. It's easier for you boys, growing up as you do with two sisters.

For many years, in his letters to the children, Speer created for them an image of lightness and fun, both as concerned his life as a child, and as that of a prisoner. He told me that these letters, contrary to those he addressed to Rudolf Wolters, were solely to and for the children, "to maintain communication with them; to show that one could keep up one's spirits, even under conditions such as I was living through; and to forestall pain they might suffer if they allowed their imaginations—about punishments, dungeons and all that—to roam."

In fact he did achieve this goal. At the end of the war, his six children ranged from two to eleven, and while they were small they did appreciate his Spanish-Illustrated. "It made us laugh," Hilde told me. "I thought it was wonderful that he could be so funny about it: about the prison staff, about his co-prisoners and about himself."

In the course of time, even while continuing to write his Spanish-Illustrated, Speer also wrote quite regularly to each child, discussing their problems which he learned about from his wife, Wolters or Annemarie Kempf. Because he had so carefully created a lighthearted basis of communication, they were able to accept his comments and advice. Had he not laid this groundwork or, more than that, if he had been with them all the time as the conventional German paterfamilias, they would probably have resented and resisted his opinions and suggestions.

These individual letters to the children were private. But the Spanish-Illustrated letters were not, although the children and Margret were not yet aware of his literary plans. He made this quite clear to Wolters, in whose office all the Speer letters were transcribed before being sent on to the addressees. Throughout the Spanish-Illustrated there are instructions in brackets to Wolters, or possibly reminders to himself for later editing. When he tells the children that their maternal grandfather's ancestors were longtime residents of Heidelberg and solid artisans, he puts, "(add later which professions)." When he uses a literary quote, as he often did, he adds, "(check this)," and when he quoted from memory his own letters to Margret as a boy, he suggested, "(here possibly rectify quotes from my letters)."

One wonders whether, when sometimes he manifestly tailored the content of his letters, he embellished his descriptions for the children's peace of mind to support their illusions about the family, or if he did it in the isolation and introspection of his imprisonment to comfort himself. Both certainly apply to his romantic—or romanticized—description of his courtship and later relationship with his wife, but even more so to the impression he seeks to convey to his children about his childhood and his parents, who had only recently died. He, who loathed his mother's pretensions, the unending parties, the formalities of their life, and whose only friend as a small boy was the porter's little daughter, and who later turned to the simple wholesomeness of Margarete Weber's home for solace, provided his children in 1953 with a false, emotionally laundered impression of his boyhood life:

> . . . Just about the time [I met your mother] a considerable event occurred in my parents' life. My mother's father had died and her three brothers urged the sale of his business. My father felt that this immediate postwar period of economic pressures and inflation was not the proper moment for such a transaction, and would have preferred to tighten his belt for a while.
>
> But when a reasonable offer came, in dollars, he was unable to ward off your grandmother's mother's family's pressure and the factory was sold for a million marks. We therefore ended up with $250,000, plus 10 percent annual interest payable in gold. Although this was far less than the busi-

ness was worth—and my father never forgave himself for having given in—this gold "pension" did in fact provide us, in the last two years of inflation, with literally "golden times."

Aside from everything else, it easily allowed the building of the extensions to the [Heidelberg] house. . . . There was the car—a 28/95 Mercedes . . . and above all there were the far larger parties. . . . I'm sure they were nice parties, though they were not to my taste: I rejected all that sort of hollow nonsense. . . .

What I did like about the parties were the lovely table settings, with blue Limoges china, long-stemmed glasses and heavy silver. Tall silver candleholders illuminated the occasions, and flowers from our gardens and greenhouse decorated the table. I think my mother enjoyed the preparations more than the parties. . . .

In the warm Heidelberg spring nights, many of the parties took place on the terrace. . . . When the punch bowl happened to be put on the table close to the hedge, we boys would creep up under cover of the leaves and swipe and empty the bowl. . . . These were doubtlessly happy days, but I must admit that in some ways I preferred the years of restriction which, money not then being a divisive element, somehow brought the family together. . . .

This one letter was the only indication he ever gave to the children that there was anything but harmony between their grandparents, and it is entirely overshadowed by his tale of glamorous parties and boyish mischief on the terrace. His idealized version here was part of the image making he was indulging in in these letters, as he continues, now attempting to extend this idealized past to the children's own early childhood:

You probably can't understand all this, as no doubt you have not experienced such carefree times in these last eight years, and as we, your parents, already showed you during our time of plenty that [material wealth] could not affect our family life. . . .

"I found his letters to the children absolutely astounding," Margret Speer was to say. "In some ways, of course, his determination to be humorous and funny, so as to relieve them of fear that he was suffering, was quite admirable."

Margret, though not an intellectual, was considerably more intelligent than she was allowed to show in the presence of her husband, but long inexperience in articulating her thoughts had made her exceptionally guarded. To speak about herself was torture; to voice an opinion about others appeared to feel presumptuous to her. And yet when—in Heidelberg and later, during my long stay with them in the mountains and during subsequent years—she did become sufficiently reassured to speak her thoughts, she showed spirit and perception.

"When I read some of the things he wrote to them about our life before, and his life as a child . . . I did sometimes wonder whether he had lost his mind. Later, of course, I understood that it was all part of his plan for his survival—his survival as part of the family. . . . It was very odd, you know, because in truth he had never been a father. . . ."

Continuing his account of getting to know Margret, Speer wrote to the children:

> Your mother was very reserved. . . . Even after months of regular visits . . . I could count myself lucky if I could exchange a few friendly words with Gretel . . . until I discovered that she shared my and her cousin Fritz's passion for the theater.
>
> From that moment on the three of us journeyed regularly to Mannheim . . . seeing Wagner operas, *Egmont, Fidelio* and many other plays and operas. Imagine my pleasure when I was able to give her a box of chocolates in the interval, and the thrill on the rare occasions when, overcome by the excitement of the unfolding drama, she clutched my hand. Strange how one can relive such moments thirty years later. . . .

His description to me, another twenty-five years later, in his wife's presence, was more sparing. "We met when she was fifteen and I was sixteen," he said, "and fell in love."

"*He* fell in love—" Margret said, with rare spirit. "I was mainly curious, to begin with. Later," she added, "I came to love him . . . gradually."

"I fell in love as much with her family as with her, I think," he said, ignoring her remark. "They were very warm, very close—and much simpler people than mine. They lived down in the town. Gretel's father was a joiner. He employed fifty people, so he was a man of substance. He was also a city councillor; they were of old Heidelberg stock."

His letter had continued:

> I felt very comfortable at their home. . . . And my parents must have been surprised by my sudden enthusiasm for the Mannheim theater. . . . But in fact, a blind man could see what I was really about. . . .

Speer didn't tell his children that in fact his parents obviously did see and were furious about this growing relationship. "Now he is down there again," his father would say. To the children—growing up in a very different time and, as he had obviously realized, surrounded by very different social ideas—Speer carefully minimized their grandparents' snobbery, while at the same

time lauding the simple solidity of their mother's background, to which he
had so happily responded. He wrote,

At least half of you is true Heidelberg, and I think this part of your genetic inheritance compensates for the influence of the conflicting elements in my own restless blood. All of your mother's maternal ancestors
were well-to-do peasants, who farmed and grew wine in the immediate
vicinity of the formerly much smaller Heidelberg. Neither they nor your
grandfather's artisan forebears were in any way conspicuous; they just led
a diligent, quiet life.

This meant that, contrary to my parents' forebears who, highfliers on
both sides, always alternated between climbing way up and slipping way
down, they—although perhaps never experiencing the indubitable thrill
of great material success or achievement—also never exposed themselves
to the stress of real want.

I think one can summarize your maternal grandparents' life as one
bound to the tranquillity of the soil. And thus, in spite of the disturbing
events the last forty years brought to Germany, their joyful and modestly
prosperous life has continued basically in a straight line, without interruption. They were faithful to the church when most people turned their
backs on it . . . and in good and bad times, they always stuck to their moral
standards. . . . They don't go in for socializing, but their friends are their
friends for life.

You only know your grandfather as an old man, plagued by ill health,
but when I knew him first he worked from dawn to dusk, was proud of his
. . . [joinery] and wouldn't, I think, have exchanged it against any easier
living. . . .

What a wonderful partner he always was for your grandmother who I
always admired so much. . . . [I] thought quietly to myself, "This is what
your future wife will be like one day when we are older; you'll be in good
hands with her. . . ."

I already told you that at that time I was inclined to resist my parents'
social doings. But actually, even then, hardly seventeen years old, I saw
further and realized that our family had bred children who were endangered by their own instincts; who lived—and would always choose to
live—on an edge, in constant danger of slipping; without the biological
strength—what Schopenhauer called the will to live—which once having
slipped, would allow them to climb back. And so you see, I felt in my
bones that an infusion of quiet, stable stock was needed if one was thinking of founding a new family. . . .

"Incredible," said Margret Speer twenty-five years after that letter was
written, when he had showed it to me. "If you think that this is the man who
virtually never said a word to me. . . ."

Perhaps even more extraordinary is the care Speer took in Spandau to "re-habilitate" his mother, even at the cost of rather unfairly laying blame on his father.

> My father obviously eventually realized that I was "going with" a Weber girl, but as he told me later, he comforted himself at first that it was only a passing fancy. When he had to admit to himself that it was much more than that, he wasn't at all pleased. I can tell you this now, because with time he came to appreciate his daughter-in-law very much; but then he tried every which way to change my mind. . . .
>
> My mother, on the other hand, in her kindness, although no happier than he at the thought of this impending connection, was forbearing.

In fact, it was to be seven years after their wedding—which his parents did not attend—before Margret was asked to stay at the house.

> They meant well for me, but I knew better. Or do you think the sort of rich spoiled girl they wanted for me would have stood up to these last eight years as your mother has?
>
> I was so full of happiness those years, I can't even describe it. It wasn't only the proximity of . . . my Gretel, or the ambition she woke in me which suddenly resulted in surprisingly high marks at school. No, it was quite simply a glow, a tingling in me, such as I felt sometimes later when, wrestling with the concept of a design, I suddenly hit upon the solution. Sometimes . . . I stood still in the street and felt an inner music which had nothing to do with sound. . . .

They didn't talk much, but they laughed a lot then. "That first year was a very happy time," said Speer. "I went climbing and canoeing, first with her family, and after a while with her alone. Our best times were up on the mountains, in alpine huts. We would walk for days, in silent comfortable companionship: it was happiness for both of us. But even when we hiked for long hours we never talked."

"Actually he did tell me about his doings, what happened at school, and later at university," said Margret. "And we discussed books he read, po-etry. . . ." But he had never told her about his unhappy childhood, his home life, about his hate-love for his mother, his need for his father's affection. "He never talked about himself in this way, ever. I never heard about his un-happiness," she said, "until today."

As they continued their hikes, Speer began a photo album which covered the years 1922–27, as much a statistical as a pictorial record: "Year's sum-mary: 9 touring days; total height climbed, 6,223 meters; daily average, 691.4 meters; longest climb in one day, 1,458 meters; longest descent, 1,689 meters."

It became clear, from what Speer told me, that it was above all his mother who had rejected Margret and her socially unacceptable family. "My father would actually have fitted in well with them," Speer said. "I remember, when I was a boy, we boys were brought in one day to meet a lady—who he told me much later was his first love. I don't know why she came, but I really liked her—she was my kind of person. But I remember my mother telling my father that she was never to come to the house again. . . ."

Speer had "A Schoolboy's Letters"—his letters to Margret—bound in two volumes and copyrighted. Not because he wanted to publish them, he said, "Just a precaution in case they are stolen or something. Just to protect them."

I had my doubts about this: in both his houses—the "patrician" one in Heidelberg and the old farmhouse in the mountains—there were rooms full of meticulously organized files, no document, no record he could not put his hand on in a minute: all of it, I was quite sure, in preparation for continuous publications. I don't think there was finally anything—old and more recent private letters included—he was not prepared to make use of.

If one wanted to gain real understanding of Speer, one had to realize first that almost everything he did—though, as shown by some of our talks, not quite everything—had a purpose, generally directed toward his own benefit. This, I believe, applies to his giving me these particular letters, a gesture which virtually ensured their existence becoming known.

A year and a half after Margret and he met, her parents, concerned over this rapidly maturing friendship, sent Margret away to boarding school in Freiburg, today a car trip of perhaps two and a half hours, but then—evidently considered a necessary safeguard by Margret's parents—seven or eight hours away by train. "You'll see when you read the letters," Speer said. "There too I never speak about feelings, never the sort of thing you might expect to find in such letters."

Though there is no sentimentality and certainly not even a smidgin of sensuality in these always respectful and romantically tinged letters, the very schoolboy wordiness of them reveals the young Speer's losing battle with his own need for expressing feelings: the "wall between myself and others," which he would later describe in our conversations, was evidently already fully established and is clearly demonstrated in the letters.

Everything he says about himself, much of it with strained humor, is about his external life: "I sleep . . . ," "I went to the opera . . . the theater. . . ." There follow, often in intolerable detail, descriptions of the opera, critiques of the play and the actors. There is hardly a question about Margret, her life at school, her academic progress, her thoughts: the cascade of essentially impersonal words gives the impression of talking in order not to speak. Even when he does talk about her, it is not in the form of questions but telling her what she is doing: "You are in sewing class," "You are wondering what I mean. . . ." "You want to know how to travel when you come on holiday."

It is almost as if, fearing rejection, he anticipates her answers or the possible lack of them. In one letter, he offers to go to Freiburg and travel back with her to Heidelberg. And when she replies, "No, thank you; I want to travel with my girlfriends," he is clearly amazed: not that she doesn't want him to come, but that she says so. "Of course, of course," he answers quickly. Exactly as he would do all his life, he preempts any feeling of rejection or hurt. "Of course you want to travel with your girlfriends; I perfectly understand. If I had known that this possibility existed for you I probably wouldn't have made my suggestion. After all, it doesn't matter whether we see each other one day sooner or later and . . . I'm glad you told me honestly."

Friendship, more often than not, brings about a revelation of one's inner life, one's thoughts and dreams, but not between young Albert and Margret. She was far too modest to think that her little dreams could be of any interest to this brilliant boy from up on the hill. And as for Albert, one must conclude that he had by then already hidden his inner life—much of which revolved around his love-hate for his mother—even from himself, taking a classic refuge in sleep. Thus, the only revealing information he gives her again and again about himself in these letters—if she had known how to look for it—is a daily record of the time he spends sleeping. "I slept fourteen hours." "Yesterday slept eighteen hours: I never did manage to get to school." " . . . I sat down at my desk at one o'clock and promptly fell asleep, woke up just in time to write these few lines, before having to run down to supper when the gong sounded, came back up afterwards, wrote these last four lines and will now go to bed where I know I'll be asleep in seconds."

"I must begin to work tomorrow," he writes three days before his final school examinations (the *Abitur*), saying that he is bound to fail, but clearly implying that he won't because he has a star over him which won't allow him to fail. Indeed, he passed top of his class in composition and mathematics. On January 8, 1923, just after Margret had gone back to school after the Christmas holidays, he wrote:

Dear Gretel,

Of course you mustn't think that this "effusion of my heart and of my soul" [a quotation from Goethe] is meant to proffer you great literary enjoyment; on the contrary, I expect I'm acting entirely along your ideas if I spend as little time as possible on these letters, only telling you the most necessary to lay to rest your apprehensions about my coming *Abitur*.

After this promising beginning, let me get right away to the actual theme: my experiences, my thoughts and feelings, my diligence, my sleep, my appetite, my weight and changes therein, my school successes, my enjoyments of art . . . in short, everything that has happened since you left. I won't be able to avoid putting funny and ironic accounts next to serious matters and descriptions, but am certain you won't object.

But I think it's high time that I come to grips with the first day of school after the holidays. . . . That first afternoon—thanks to your departure I was incapable of anything else—I had nothing more urgent to do than to close my shutters, lie down on my bed and sleep.

Cont. Tuesday, January 9: . . . nearly late for school; slept again after lunch; nearly missed the Mannheim train for the concert.

Cont. Wednesday, January 10: . . . night in Mannheim . . . early train back to school. After lunch I slept again—from half past three to half past six. . . .

Cont. Thursday, January 11: Exceptionally I didn't sleep this afternoon. I went to pick up your photographs. What do you think of them? On the first one, your face looks flat and devoid of expression; the shadowless lighting emphasizes this impression. The best feature, decidedly, is your eyes, even though our late night at the Harmonium Ball the previous evening is reflected in the shadows underneath them. . . .

Cont. Friday, January 12: Nothing of importance has happened so far today. . . . I hope you agree that I now close this letter. The moment I post it, I'll probably remember all the things I've forgotten to put in. Well, be good, don't lose your umbrella, sit up straight, don't forget your hankie if you go dancing or to the theater, study hard, don't feel you have to answer me this week, be good, pious and diligent, sleep well, wake and get up early in the morning, next week I'll write you again, and receive my warm and affectionate regards.

> from your friend,
> Albert

It seems extraordinary that on January 12 he should have written that "nothing of importance has happened," for the day before the French and Belgians, using the pretext of unpaid reparations, had occupied the Ruhr, two hundred kilometers north of Heidelberg. Every newspaper was full of it, and the German government tottered even as he wrote. But the seventeen-year-old Speer, by all accounts a brilliantly clever boy, seemed oblivious to these events and indeed—perhaps a significant indicator for the future—to politics altogether.

But what these boyish outpourings show, despite their self-conscious literary demonstration of recent obligatory reading of great literature, is his preoccupation with morality. What emerges clearly is the kind of boy one would have imagined would grow up to loathe and passionately oppose Hitler's rule, finding it contrary to everything he traditionally, intellectually and ethically believed in. So what astounds is that this is the same person who only ten short years later was to abandon almost every vestige of morality.

This is borne out by several essays, one of which was written on January 16, discussing Kleist's *Prince of Homburg*:

> According to the Duke's battle plan, the Prince, at the head of his cavalry, was to wait some distance off for the order to join the battle. The moment comes, quite soon, when the Prince, waiting at the appointed place, sees the rows of enemy soldiers falter and believes the Duke will win without his help. But he wants a share in the glory of victory and therefore, although there is no order from the Duke, he orders the trumpets blown for the attack, storms the enemy with his cavalry and thus wins the battle.
>
> The Duke is very angry and, without knowing who it was, orders the guilty man court-martialed. And even when he finds out it was the Prince, he will not exempt his relative from justice. The court sentences the Prince to death and the Duke signs the order for the execution. Natalie, who loves him, throws herself at the Duke's feet and begs for mercy for him. For a moment the Duke hesitates, but then he says that the Prince himself must make the decision about his guilt. . . .
>
> And the plan succeeds: the Prince admits he has done wrong and says he merits death, which enables the Duke to feel that justice has been done: the Prince, by his honesty and courage, has shown himself to be the ideal citizen who will from now on be an example for the army.

At the end of the typescript of the essay, Speer had added a remark after his release from Spandau. "This shows my ideas about the ideal citizen," he wrote, "who himself judges his guilt and who, submitting himself to justice, can consider himself reborn."

Was this stating his own position at Nuremberg and after Spandau? "Up to a point I suppose I do feel that," he told me. "Still—" he added, quickly changing the subject, "the essay itself is interesting; I mean that I felt this instinctively while I was still a boy."

The relevance of Speer's moral attitude in 1923, both to his recognition of his deficiencies as of 1933 and his acknowledgement of them as of Spandau, was of course quite obvious. I suggested that the essays did indeed show how he "really felt" at seventeen, and now again at seventy-odd. What they didn't explain was how he could have totally abandoned this moral stand between the ages of twenty-seven and forty.

"It is a mystery," he said, sounding tired. It was another indication of Speer's ambivalence that while readily provoking challenge and criticism, it visibly drained him. Time and again I saw the sudden stress in his face, the

sudden aging, and then, always surprising, there was an almost physical effort of will and a return to vitality. He often joked then, mocking his momentary weakness, always declining if I suggested a break or a rest.

His parents appear to have been entirely unaware of the seriousness of his
affection for Margret and her parents. Margret's parents were evidently entirely aware and were careful but approving. "They liked Albert," Margret
said, simply. Certainly they went out of their way to help this—for that
time—unusual relationship, even to the point of assisting them to circum-
vent the rules of Margret's school and of course those of Albert's parents. The
envelopes of young Albert's letters to her at school were always addressed by
Margret's aunt, with her name as the return addressee, and Margret's much
less frequent and much briefer replies were sent care of her parents. Speer
continued to go to the Webers' house every day, on the way to or from
school. It would have been impossible for him to have received the letters at
home, he said. "Besides, it gave me a good reason for going there. I felt happy
there."

But the complicated postal route had its difficulties. On January 22 he
wrote,

> After school I went by your house and picked up your letter, which
> much improved my mood. . . . [Her aunt, he said, was so entertained by
> their correspondence, she wanted him to read his letters to her before he
> sent them off.] I don't dare just to say no—they might begin to wonder
> what I'm writing.
> [On January 31 he adds] Your mother, in fact, who has shown so much
> tact about our friendship, would never have asked me to read the letters
> aloud. . . . But your aunt would only consider the obvious aspect of the
> letters' contents, while the truth lies within myself, or better said, in my
> feeling that reading the letters aloud desecrates them both for you and for
> me, and necessarily diminishes their value to us. . . .

But he found a solution to the problem:

> You gave me great joy with your long letter, and what you say about
> reading my letters to others agrees entirely with my own feelings. So I've
> an idea: from now on I'll write two letters every time; the one on white
> paper I'll read to your family, let your aunt write out the envelope and
> then I'll put my "real" letter in with the "official" one. In that one I'll only
> write about things your aunt is bound to get bored with in the end,
> like theaters, concerts, etc. Sooner or later she'll give up asking to hear
> them. . . .

This foreshadowed the two kinds of letters he wrote three decades later
from Spandau: the "formal and boring" ones, which had to pass through the

Allied censorship, and the thousands of "black" ones, which didn't. His letter of January 22 continued, on an unusually personal note,

> My dream last night . . . played in the period just before Easter, just before your return from Freiburg: the French had occupied all of the *Badische Land*—there were no more trains and thus no more postal service either. All connection with you was broken off. As my *Abitur* was over, I got onto my bike, took yours too, and after many problems got to Freiburg. . . . You changed, with fantastic rapidity, sat on your bike as I did again on mine, and we happily biked toward home. When you tired, I towed you with a rope I had carefully brought along. I don't know how we made it home, but we did. . . . For me the explanation is simple: my imagination is mixing up the occupation of the Ruhr with my longing for you. You are laughing, I know, and thinking, "How sentimental!"

Margret said that she—and her school friends to whom she read all the letters from Albert—did in fact have that reaction, but at the same time his literary expertise so intrigued her and the other girls that, to their teachers' amazement, they began, voluntarily, to read the classics. "Of course, I would never have written to him about that; I would have been afraid of making a fool of myself. I wrote him once or twice a month about what was important to *me*: my friends and schoolwork, and skiing and hiking. That's all we really had in common," she said with a touching kind of artlessness. "I never did know what he saw in me."

She was too young for falling in love, she said firmly. "I didn't know what love was, except in mushy books, and we didn't get to read many of those. I suppose I was flattered," she added thoughtfully. "He was so handsome, and so clever; nobody else knew a boy like that."

GERMANY CONTINUED to suffer the consequences of the lost war, but the shortages of food and materials barely affected either the wealthy Speers or the solid, *bürgerliche* Webers, and there is virtually nothing in the letters of either material want or politics. Speer had been barely aware of World War I, he told me. He was nine in 1914, thirteen when that war ended. There was no talk about it at home, even during meals. His father never explained to his sons what was happening.

"I thought about this when I started to write my reminiscences in Spandau," he told me once, "and I realized then, for the first time I think, that no one in my childhood talked with us about politics. We rarely ate with our parents, but when we did—I realized later—politics was taboo. Of course, our French governess left, and that was a loss for me personally. But I don't know how much I associated that with the war. Not much, I would think—I just wasn't conditioned to think about it. And of course, I wasn't a militaristic sort of boy. The boys at school often played soldiers—it could become quite violent. I didn't."

He didn't remember if other boys talked about the war. "But I did fantasize a lot about it—you know, the suffering of the soldiers and their heroism, so I must have heard somebody talk about it, but it wasn't my father."

In *Inside the Third Reich* he wrote that he would "often sleep for several nights running on the hard floor beside [his] soft bed, in order to be sharing the privations of the soldiers at the front." He did do that a few times when he was quite small, he told me, just after he and his brothers had been taken to see a Zeppelin that was stationed in Mannheim. The commander of this airship and several of his officers had become part of his mother's social coterie, no doubt the reason the boys were so honored. "Seeing this incredible airship from the inside, so to speak, and actually having met the man who flew it on air raids to London fed my imagination," he said. "I think that was the most powerful impression I had of the war: it gave me many nightmares."

RUDOLF WOLTERS'S unique significance in Speer's life during his imprisonment in Spandau has already been described, but in order to understand how this perhaps peculiarly German hero-worshiping relationship came about, it is necessary to parallel Wolters's development with Speer's.

Born two years before Speer, Wolters, as he described in *Segments*, had happier, gentler memories of his childhood than did Speer. All of Wolters's ancestors, on both sides of the family, were master carpenters and master builders—on his mother's side shipbuilders on the Rhine, on his father's side architects, as his father and he would also become. His parents, he writes, were very different: his father was "a serious, conscientious and diligent man, always worried about the future, deeply interested in the natural sciences and art; his mother was "a highly practical woman, full of zest for life, who in hard times thought nothing of serving a delicious roast without letting on that it was horsemeat." The simple household where Wolters and his younger sister grew up was often given a helping hand by his mother's brother, who had built up a successful industrial concern.

Cushioned by this rich uncle's generosity, the boy Rudolf had a life of comparative ease until the outbreak of war in 1914, with the smell of his father's cheap pipe, he writes, sometimes replaced by the smooth scent of imported tobacco, and their frequent one-dish pea soup by Beluga caviar. He continued,

A thin freckled boy with short reddish hair, I grew up in the best of all worlds, with life reassuringly organized like clockwork. School from eight to one, Silentium nightly from five to seven [they were Catholics], Vespers Wednesday and Saturday. . . . My father's [passion] was astronomy; he would frequently wake me up, carry me out to the balcony and point out to me the wonders of the night sky. . . .

On my eleventh birthday, my father put a thick book in front of me on the table. On the cover was my name and a title: "War Diary, Begun on August 3, 1914." It is thus my father I must thank for initiating me into a habit which I never abandoned from that day: weekly entries, for the first years of my own observations, and as of ten years later, collections—which I had bound every year—of important correspondence, reports, documents and notations.

I was fifteen when the war ended. The defeat and liquidation of the empire was incomprehensible to me, but it made me aware for the first time that my world was not as firmly anchored as I had thought.

A long, gangling boy when World War I ended, Wolters was taken out of school for a year when he became ill with malnutrition. During that year, taught at home by two "exceptional priests," he became fascinated with music, religion and the life of the monks in the nearby Benedictine monastery. He was tempted to enter the religious community, he wrote, until a thirteen-year-old girl, kissing him, one dark evening, with visible enjoyment, dissuaded him from this path. Except for Wolters's love for music—which Speer developed around the same time—it was up to then, as one sees, a life very different from the young Albert Speer's.

In the autumn of 1923, Wolters entered the Munich Institute of Technology to begin his architectural studies. "My academic freedom began, one might say, to the sound of drums: the Hitler Putsch and its consequences to us students, most of whom were in agreement with it. . . ."

Speer never understood until much later that it was the postwar suffering in Germany, of which Hitler made so much, that got Hitler on the road to power. "I must admit," Speer said to me, "that it was only when I met up with much more politicized students that I began to become aware of what was going on."

By 1923, Hitler had headed the new National Socialist German Workers' Party (NSDAP—*Nationalsozialistische Deutsche Arbeiterpartei*, soon shortened to Nazi Party) for one and a half years and was giving endless fiery speeches in Munich and elsewhere. He asked for a classless Germany, with a strong nationalistic youth under a strong Führer; the Jews, he cried in speech after speech, had to be deprived of their power. The very days during which Speer wrote the letters quoted earlier, Hitler gave three major speeches at the meetings preceding the first NSDAP Party Day in Munich. Since 1921, he had been *Der Führer* and had adopted and was soon using with enormous effect the phrase "Germany Awake!" which—often with the outrageous addition of "Juda Verrecke!": "Jewry Perish!" (literally, "Croak")—would within months become the battle cry of the masses.

But as far as young Speer was concerned, this might never have happened. In his letter to Margret of January 31, he does mention the lack of coal, but only in the context of the forced cancellation of half of Germany's express trains—the D-trains.

> In forty days there will be no more coal. If by that time the Ruhr remains occupied we will have nothing but slow trains . . . which I would not recommend to you, because even without changing you would need ten and a half hours to get to Heidelberg. . . .

Two days before this letter was written, speaking in Munich on January 29, 1923, Hitler described his vision for Germany:

> There are three things central to the future Germany: 1) The social concept: This presupposes the awareness of duty. The German civil service [the *Beamtentum,* whose support he then needed but of which, only eight years later and until the end of his life, he would speak only with contempt] and the German Army were models of social organization, and although these two groups could not offer bountiful remuneration in money or property, they turned out individuals who were prepared to offer up their lives for their people and the state. . . . 2) The national concept: identical for us Germans with social awareness. The more fanatically national we are, the more we must be concerned with the welfare of our society. . . . 3) The anti-Semitic concept: It confirms the racial rejection of what is essentially hostile to all that is German. Nationalism is above all inoculation against a bacillus, and the anti-Semitic concept is the necessary defense, the antibody if you like against a pestilence which today has a grip on the whole world. . . . If one goes even further, then two fundamentally opposed forces are engaged in a battle to the death. One force defends the validity of the creative personality, the other the power of money. . . . The first one at present is silent, the other is dominated and guided by stock market shares . . . whose victory would result in the destruction of our culture and [our] people. We live in a time when the external and internal enemy is ready for the final strike in order to destroy the German people.
>
> What is happening now is the consequence of the Versailles Treaty, which was signed by the same people who today shout out their lying protests. . . . Any possibility of an effective German foreign policy presupposes a radical change in policy within. No state can make agree-

ments with governments one . . . can only despise. . . . We say we make
no more concessions. We expect others to adapt themselves to our demands and needs or else be eliminated from the scene. . . . There is only
one differentiation: one is either German or anti-German. The National
Socialists spearhead the march of Germany, and we declare that we
will not sit down at a table with criminals who already once stabbed us
in the back. . . .

Speer wrote to Margret almost every day throughout that February, the
month of his *Abitur*. Most letters continued to report outings: to theaters,
concerts, hikes, rowing, plus meticulously worked-out plans for the holidays,
when she would be home.

The Saturday before his exam week, he told her that that morning his professor of German had advised the class not to work anymore that weekend,
but to spend a good Sunday, perhaps going for a long walk with a friend—
" 'or even better, a girlfriend,' he said. Good man, that. But how can I follow
his advice—you are not here, so I can't walk with you. Or could I . . . ?" What
he wrote to her then not only shows a lively imagination but inevitably brings
to mind his extraordinary "Walk around the World" in Spandau forty years
later.

> You know what I will do? I will make up for your absence by going for a
> walk with you in my thoughts. (One could say that all my letters are such
> thoughts.) I will describe my thoughts to you as I picture it [them]: I come
> to see you and ask whether you'd like to come with me to see Ibsen's *Wild
> Duck* on Sunday.
>
> Do you think your father will permit you to come? Do you want to? I
> will telephone at once to Mannheim and order the tickets. *Auf Wiedersehn*
> [*sic*] then until tomorrow when I'll let you know about the tickets. . . .
>
> Next day, 24 January: we have the tickets, so I'll come to your house
> tomorrow around three to pick you up for our walk. The train is at 4:25.
> But so that you will understand what Ibsen is trying to tell us in his *Wild
> Duck,* let me briefly take you away from your domestic chores (for I imag-
> ine you in the sewing room) and tell you what I know. [He then gives a
> summary of the play.] And on our trip home in the train we'll discuss it.

A few days later he wrote the most explicit paragraph about his feelings:

> One more bit about our friendship. I think we are much too careful
> about each other: this has got to change. Of course it's good that we both
> try not to hurt the other. But surely you, as I, are eager not to have our
> friendship be one of those one-day wonders, but rather something that
> will continue for a long time, perhaps for always. But we will never
> achieve this goal if we don't sometimes tell each other off, if we don't from

time to time have a real good fight. Even the deepest friendship cannot last with this kind of unnatural harmony—we'd be sick of each other in one or two years.

Perhaps you have realized that it is I who will have to do the most to change. And of course you mustn't imagine anything drastic: outsiders would hardly notice it. Only then you must also change. Like for instance when I give you a present—when I do something to give you pleasure— you mustn't think I am doing it to win your friendship. If I give you a present, it is because you are my friend and I value you—not to dispose you kindly toward me.

In his next letter, dated March 15, he reports rather briefly on his very good exam results: "first" in math and German composition, "good" in everything else, except only "pass" in religion, French and English. In *Inside the Third Reich* he described his results:

To my amazement, my *Abitur* essay was judged the best in my class. Nevertheless, when the head of the school in his farewell address told the graduates that now "the way to highest deeds and honors" was open to us, I thought, "That's hardly likely for you."

Since I was the best mathematician in the school, I had intended to study that subject. But my father presented sound reasons against this choice, and I would not have been a mathematician familiar with the laws of logic if I had not yielded to his arguments. . . .

That is how Speer, in his usual manner, played down the most fatal decision of his life which he took only to please his father—from whom he had tried vainly throughout his childhood to obtain some manifestation of love.

II

"I Felt He Was a Human Being"

Nuremberg, June 19, 1946

SPEER: I attended the universities at Munich and Berlin and in 1929, at the age of twenty-four, I was First Assistant at the Technical University in Berlin. At the age of twenty-seven[*sic*], in 1931, I went into business for myself until 1942. . . .

ONE MIGHT THINK that his statement in court was a curious way for Speer to describe his first eight years of working for Hitler, or the Nazis. "That's how I saw myself," he said, "as an architect, first with a number of clients and then just one, Hitler. To my way of thinking, my work as an architect did not concern the court, only that as one of Hitler's ministers."

Nonetheless, it is easy to see how his interpretation of his life could, at the very least, sound like an attempt to be "clever." But the Nuremberg record shows no one—neither the very skeptical President of the Tribunal, Lord Justice Lawrence, or the tough chief prosecutors, Sir Hartley Shawcross (for Britain), Justice Robert Jackson (for the United States), M. Auguste Champetier de Ribes (for France) and General R. A. Rudenko (for the USSR)—questioning it.

Of course, when he began his architectural studies in 1923, he was years away from Hitler, indeed years away from committing himself to the Nazis. Here again, as in his happy description of his childhood in *Inside the Third Reich* and from Spandau in his letters to the children, he makes light of his huge disappointment at not being allowed—for that is what it came to—to study mathematics. He wrote to the children about it from Spandau in October 1953:

> Exams over, the pressure of school behind me, I looked ahead to the free and easygoing university life. I knew exactly what I wanted: to study mathematics, for which I had a passion. . . . But my father presented me with cogent reasons against my intended studies. . . . After that architecture, of which I had absorbed so much since early childhood, seemed the next best choice and I thus decided, to my father's delight, to become an architect as he was, and as his father had been before him.

Again, for his children's benefit, he was "laundering" what had really happened between him and his father that fateful day. "I loved mathematics," he told me dreamily. "I can't describe to you how much or why I loved it. But becoming a mathematician was all I had ever thought of. It did everything for me that was . . . well . . . joy. It was my way of playing games, of experiencing triumph. . . . Well—" he said quickly, "a kind of triumph, anyway." He laughed. "Do you know what I did when I took the *Abitur* exam in math" He laughed again—a happy laugh. "Well, I finished the algebra very quickly— you know, I mean *very* quickly, and looking around the classroom I saw that everybody was still hard at it, so of course I didn't want to make a point of having finished so fast, by handing it in. So I just did the whole thing again— twice—attacking the problem from two different perspectives. It was fun: I came out with exactly the same result three times. I don't suppose it hurt me when they evaluated the tests but that wasn't why I did it. It was just for fun." Many parents would have been highly amused by such a story—his son Fritz did that sort of thing later; Wolters had written to him about it in Spandau, he told me—but Speer would never have dreamed of telling his father.

His voice hardened now when he told me of his father's reaction to his wish to study mathematics. "He was totally dismissive. 'Can you imagine yourself spending your life teaching in some backwater university?' my father asked me. 'You'd never make any money. You'd probably end up cramming snotty-nosed little morons. Is that the life you want?' "

The young Speer had not really considered those aspects. "But when he brought it up, I remember quite distinctly thinking to myself, 'Yes, that is what I want.' Frankly, teaching at a university had never occurred to me. I mean, *professors* taught at universities; I was a schoolboy." He remembered very clearly that day before the math *Abitur*. He had loved spending hours teaching his school friend who was weak in math. "But that's what my father probably meant by 'snotty-nosed little morons.' I wonder—" he suddenly said, "what my life would have been like if . . ."

Margret probably wouldn't have minded in the least, I suggested. He showed real surprise. "Do you know, I've never thought of that. I must tell her . . . well . . . maybe." He didn't: except for generalities, they found it as impossible to communicate in 1978 as they had in 1923.

Speer began his undergraduate studies that autumn of 1923 in the nearby city of Karlsruhe. "I hate it," he wrote to Margret, who was now back in Heidelberg. "The professors are boring, the curriculum inane, this town a ghastly provincial nest."

He had little faith in his own talents as an architect, above all since the Karlsruhe college provided no one able to teach him to draw—his greatest weakness. In the spring of 1924, however, he moved to the much more reputable Institute of Technology in Munich. From Spandau, he described it to the children:

This was very different. Not only that there were good teachers but, above all perhaps, I found other students to make friends with, which—as all of you will understand—lent a different quality to life, and to studying. And among these new university comrades there was one, like me taller and thinner than anyone else, who was conspicuous by his merry blue eyes and his—then still full—head of blond hair.

Athough both the slim figure and rich chevelure are things of the past, you will have recognized from this description our R. W. In the difficult last eight years he has become your mother's and my—and your—best friend and the guardian angel of our family.

But it embarrasses me to have to admit that I have little of note to tell you about the year and a half I spent in Munich. It seems to me we worked as little as possible, just enough to pass exams; for the rest, we communed with art and nature. Frankly, I had little hope ever to get anywhere in architecture: as could be expected, I could do well enough in figures—statistics etc., but I couldn't draw, so how could I be an architect? To tell the truth, I lived for the holidays—hiking, boating and skiing with Gretel; by now we were well versed in tricks which allowed us to avoid being chaperoned and we managed to spend many days, even weeks, in the mountains on our own. . . .

Seen from the perspective of our time, I said to Speer, their relationship in the mid-1920s seemed incomprehensible.

Anything to do with the physical part of relationships could only be approached with great care when talking to Speer. Though he would talk readily enough about the many peccadillos in Hitler's immediate surroundings, if always with an air of contempt, any personal discussion of sex was inadmissible. Even so, he was quick to pick up even unspoken questions.

"I doubt that anyone can understand this today," he said. "We were different; respect for convention was inbred in us as, I suppose one might say, was shyness. Margret's parents, I am sure, knew perfectly well we were on our own, even though they pretended to be fooled. But they knew, too, that there was no risk in letting us appear to fool them."

This iron respect for convention certainly applied to Speer's social class in those years: the German *haute bourgeoisie* were far stricter, far more buttoned up than either the aristocracy, who were socially above them, or the respectable *Bürger* and laboring classes, below them.

In trying to understand how Speer became what he was, it is necessary to consider those who would share the pinnacle with him in the gothic tragedy of the Third Reich. Joseph Goebbels, for instance, whose respectable middle-class background was some degrees lower than Speer's, had very different early interests, and very different sexual morals.

In 1926 Hitler, as head of the rapidly growing NSDAP, would name him as his Chief Administrator—Gauleiter—for Berlin, and two years later made him the party's propaganda chief. Two months after Hitler was named Chancellor on January 30, 1933, Goebbels, while retaining his title of Gauleiter for Berlin, became Minister of Propaganda. Aside from Speer himself, he would no doubt always be the most intelligent man in Hitler's circle: he was also the most loyal and devoted. On May 1, 1945, only hours after Hitler and his wife of a day, Eva Braun, killed themselves in the Berlin Bunker, Goebbels and his wife, Magda, after killing their six young children with poison, followed them into death. Goebbels left a remarkable record of his personal and political life in his diaries, which are now becoming available in their entirety.*

In 1920, when Goebbels at twenty-three was preparing his Ph.D. in Heidelberg, where Speer, then fifteen, was still at school, his sexual conduct was not too unlike that of students in the turbulent 1960s and 1970s. Clearly, neither his life nor that of his fellow students was subject to the restraints we sense in Speer's letters.

Goebbels's love interest then and for the two previous years had been Anka Stalherm, the daughter of a wealthy Freiburg family. In Goebbels's 1920 diary notes he describes journeying there to see her at the beginning of the summer:

> I look for Anka everywhere . . . then bump into her at the university; a happy encounter. I take a room at the [Hotel] Post; we pass three wonderful days. Anka wants to come back to Heidelberg with me. Idiot that I am, I discourage that idea because I want to work. So we agree on Whitsun for our next encounter. . . .
>
> During Whit-holidays meet with Anka in Neckargemüd—a sweet night . . . commute there every day [from Heidelberg]; we row and swim . . . Erna is jealous [he loved to provoke jealousy in other girls]. . . . Wonderful days with Anka, no wish remains unfulfilled . . . a hard goodbye when she leaves. . . . Alone again . . . work, library, seminars . . . swim in the Neckar . . . lonely. . . . Then Anka's letter . . . she meets me for two days in Karlsruhe . . . once more happiness consummated to the last dregs . . . in the Christian Hospice!! [a very proper student's hostel]. . . .
>
> She takes her revenge [when he teases her with fictitious tales of involvements with other girls]: she tells me of [her affair with] Mumme. I return her bracelet—a hard goodbye. . . . I write to her, offer to become

*Fragments of the diaries were found and published as long ago as 1948. The most complete version has been edited by Elke Fröhlich, at the Institute of Contemporary History in Munich, in nine volumes, published by K. G. Saur, Munich. Her discovery, in Russian archives in 1992, of glass microfilms of the entire original diaries, made for Goebbels near the end of the war, will now fill in gaps left in all previous versions. Eventually there will be sixteen volumes.

engaged . . . she withdraws . . . Hard days; I become lonely. Write and ask
her for a last meeting and offer to come to Freiburg. Within days, she appears in Heidelberg as if nothing amiss . . . stays with me in my room, with
me first on the chaise-longue and then, at 6 a.m., into her bed.

Like Speer and Wolters, young Goebbels did only a minimum of work
while a student, but a maximum of dreaming and loafing. Unlike Speer and
Wolters, however, he was, almost from childhood, a political animal. By
1924—when Wolters and Speer were pursuing leisurely studies in Munich—
the diary notes of the now twenty-seven-year-old Joseph Goebbels, a mish-
mash of sexual sagas, romantic yearnings and half-baked political ideas (the
most developed of which was a frantic kind of anti-Semitism), show him
moving, in the curiously haphazardly way of those times, toward his political
future.

On June 28, 1924, he romanticizes about his summer idyll with another
girlfriend, Else Janke: "I would like to go on a honeymoon with her." He had
of course no real intention of formalizing the relationship, which was already
doomed—ironically enough—by her confession a year before that she was
half Jewish.

The first magic is gone. I feel skeptical about her. . . . I'd like to travel
with her down to Italy and Greece, with lots of money, lots of loving, and
no worries. [Then a quick change of thought:] This morning I read Richard Wagner's *The Art of Conducting*—what a treasure trove for musicians.

The battle in him continues, half of him devotedly loving Else, "this lovely
bud of a girl," the other half a fanatic anti-Semite.

Read Maximilian Harden's (alias Isidor Witkowski) *Trials.* . . . What a
lying hypocrite *Schweinehund,* this damned Jew. These pigs, traitors,
gangsters, suck the blood from our veins; vampires. . . . I sit in the newly
installed arbor in the garden and revel in the beauty of this wonderful
summer day: sunshine; soft air; the fragrance of flowers; how lovely the
world is. . . .
June 30: Yesterday a meeting in Elberfeld [a town in the Rhineland
which, eight months later, was to become the seat of a new *Gau,* North
Rhine, to whose board Goebbels, having established his residence, was ap-
pointed]. So these are the leaders of the People's Movement in the occupied territory. Well, you Jews and you, Messrs. Belgians and French, you
need have no fear; they will not be any threat to you. I have rarely attended a meeting where so much nonsense was spoken, and mostly
against their own comrades. In the unoccupied areas, the battle between
the People's Freedom Party and the National Socialist Workers' Party I
have been expecting for so long, is now in full flower. And quite rightly,

for they certainly don't belong together. The former want Prussian Prot-
estantism—they call it the German Church—the others an all-German
unity bringing in the Catholics. It's a confrontation of Munich and Berlin,
or one can also say of Hitler and Ludendorff. There can be no doubt
whom I will join: the young, who really seek to create a new human being.

The political activities Goebbels describes here occurred in Hitler's absence during his imprisonment that had started in April 1924. Following the
failed Nazi Putsch of November 8, 1923, Hitler had written a proclamation
for national distribution:

> Comrades! We stood in the field, shoulder to shoulder, of one mind.
> Nonetheless, upon orders of [traitors] the state police of Augsburg drew
> their guns on Germany's leaders, Ludendorff and Hitler, and shot at the
> people's liberators. The tank *Hindenburg* fired from a distance of thirty
> meters spilling the best of German blood. I, Hitler, was wounded; Luden-
> dorff, as if protected by God, remained unhurt. But twenty of our best
> men were dead, and about a hundred men, women and children injured.
> The opponents suffered no losses. Comrades! Do you wish to be part of
> the murderers or will you help to liberate Germany? You will not fight for
> treacherous Jews. Your German loyalty brings you to our side. . . .
> Tutzing, November 11, 1923, Adolf Hitler

Shortly after this, Hitler was arrested and three months later, on February
26, 1924, put on trial before the People's Court in Munich. After twenty-four
days of trial and 2,912 pages of transcript—most of it Hitler speaking in his
own defense, probably the most extensive spoken explanation of his political
position on record—he was sentenced on April 1 to four and a half years'
probation and six months' detention in specially arranged, comfortable
quarters at Landsberg prison. He used this time to dictate his statement of
political philosophy and his intentions for the future which became *Mein
Kampf* to Rudolf Hess. After he came to power nine years later, millions of
Germans bought the book, and every young couple at the end of the (civil)
marriage ceremony received a copy as a gift.

On December 20 Hitler was ceremoniously released from custody. Even
while he was in prison, however, the party's battle for power went on. Joseph
Goebbels, more and more obsessed about the Jews, although continuing his
love affair with Else, continues in his diary on June 30:

> If only Hitler was free. . . . Will it be possible to beat the Jews with any-
> thing but their own weapons of shrewdness, wit and satire? I am appre-
> hensive about the people's future. The idea of a people's Greater Germany
> is good. But we lack capable, diligent, intelligent and noble leaders. Good-
> will and fine intentions are not enough. We must all work; it will take

endless work, otherwise we are lost. . . . We need to find a Führer who will
give [us] new courage and self-confidence. . . .

July 4th: We must stop spouting phrases and experimenting. We must
seriously begin the work . . . and throw out the Jewish rabble who will not
submit to the concept of a responsible people's community. . . . As the
earth cries for rain in the heat of the summer, so Germany longs for the
One Man . . . God, bring about a miracle for the German people! A miracle! A man! Bismarck, come back! I am desperate for my fatherland. . . .
Help me, God, I'm at the end of my strength. . . .

Goebbels in his diary was of course both highly emotional and already
politically extreme, but on the whole, this was the feeling among young—
and many older—Germans: Hitler was by no means a sudden phenomenon,
arriving on the scene unannounced, unknown or, as has often been claimed,
ridiculed. His picture, on the contrary, was on every front page for months
and years, and his name on all lips.

Except, it would appear, at least consciously, on young Albert Speer's and
Rudolf Wolters's. Wolters had at least noticed—and noted—Hitler's November 1923 Putsch, two months after arriving in Munich. Speer, then still
studying in the comparative quiet of the "provincial nest," Karlsruhe, had
simply ignored it.

"I must have known about it," he said, fifty-five years later. "Now, thinking back, I have this vague memory of reading about it in the papers. But it
simply didn't mean anything to me; above all, Hitler meant nothing to me."

Wolters transferred from Munich to Berlin in the autumn of 1924, preceding Speer by one year. In his reminiscences, however, Wolters seemed little
more concerned the next few years with the political situation of that time
than was Speer: his writings are as full of theater and concert experiences as
are Speer's, and equally deficient in social insight. They both sound as if, perhaps because their chosen subject bordered closely on art, they lived a
charmed existence outside what had become the average German's norm:
unemployment, poverty, even hunger. Much more meaningful to Speer—
and incidentally to Wolters—was the arrival in Berlin from Dresden, at the
beginning of 1926, of Heinrich Tessenow.

Speer had originally wanted to study under Hans Pölzig who, together
with Gropius, Mies van der Rohe and one or two others, was among Germany's great architects. But Speer's ability for drafting was insufficient, and
Pölzig—who only accepted ten new students that year—rejected his, as well
as Wolters's, application.

Speer wasn't surprised, since he had thought so little of his chances in the
profession. "I have wondered, though," he said, "how differently my life

would have turned out if Pölzig, who was very much on the political left and surrounded by students of the same persuasion, had accepted me."

Tessenow was a somewhat pedestrian architect but an idealist, a champion of simplicity and evidently a teacher of genius. "Also," said Speer, now speaking as the pragmatist and realist he certainly became, "he was much more generous than Pölzig: he accepted fifty new students. He was exactly right for me." Wolters also greatly admired Tessenow:

> He was the philosopher-architect, passionately admired by a whole generation of students. He guided us away from everything formally fashionable and false toward the real, uncomplicated and human. I was never to forget, to the end of my life as an architect his introductory sentence in one of his books
> "The simple concept is not always the best, but the best is always simple."

"He didn't believe in competitiveness," said Speer, "only in competition as a means of encouragement." Every month he and Wolters would compete for first place in tests—"One month he won; the next one I would," Speer said. "Tessenow didn't set boring themes. It was always imaginative, even adventurous, exciting. 'A bridge in a park' or 'a houseboat'—that sort of thing which, you see, forced us to imagine people's lives and made us see architecture in a human context."

Tessenow must have sensed Speer's penchant toward simple things and simple people, for over the next few years—during which he became what Speer later described as his first "catalyst"—he expressed his favor in many ways.

"He was a very shy man," said Speer. "He spoke in a whisper. Instead of addressing us from the lecture-room platform as all the other professors did—from up above, so to speak—he would come down to us, sit at one of our long tables, and people from other tables would crowd around, standing on stools to see over the heads of those who had managed to grab a seat. It was very informal, relaxed—it made for an atmosphere different from any other lecture room." He laughed happily when he recounted this. "Looking at it in retrospect, one might say that it affected, not our inner respect for him, which was enormous, but the more extreme manifestations of what now is often caricatured as German attitudes—you know, standing at attention, clicking heels and all that. When I visualize it now, I realize how much we changed—how very much we grew, and grew up, under his liberating influence. He used to talk to us, not just about architecture, but about life, about love for nature, for the land and also for one's country."

To many of his young students, Tessenow's ideas seemed to parallel the rising Nazi doctrines, and paradoxically enough—for he was a declared anti-Nazi who would later be in considerable danger—his course became a center for Nazi agitation. It is of course baffling that Speer remained unaware of these currents.

"How can I explain it to you when I cannot explain it to myself?" he said. "Politics to me was noise and vulgarity. If I thought of it at all, it was only as an interruption to the quiet and the concentration I sought. My ideal, you see, was my teacher, who whispered; his concept of life and of art, which was pure and simple: fanaticism of any kind simply had no place in it."

In 1928, while Speer continued postgraduate studies in Berlin, Baldur von Schirach, later the Hitler Youth Leader who after Nuremberg would share Speer's twenty years' imprisonment in Spandau, was also a graduate student in Berlin and became head of the National Socialist German Student Alliance. A year later he called for the "storming of the universities." In Berlin there were so many street battles between Nazi and Communist students that the university repeatedly had to shut down. In the student elections in 1929 and 1930, the National Socialists won 38 percent of the votes, receiving the highest percentage at the Institute of Technology, where Speer worked. In 1931, this rose to 66 percent.

Wolters's reminiscences, all the more significant as they were written post-Spandau, when he had become very disillusioned about his old friend, appear to confirm Speer's picture of himself at that time as a fundamentally unpolitical man. Wolters remembers Speer in Munich and Berlin as an easygoing sort of person:

> [Speer's] background was the Protestant *haute bourgeoisie,* and he impressed me as totally unconventional, religiously as well as politically uncommitted . . . with an entirely rational way of thinking. He was the typical loner: except for his wife, who was his only friend, he had no attachments, no liking for—or therefore comprehension of, I felt—social mores.

Wolters had recorded more of his impressions of Speer's background in his diary on June 2, 1943, when he met Speer's parents in Heidelberg for the first time:

> Their house, set in a huge garden, almost a park with a large orchard, is built on the side of a mountain. . . . His father . . . 80 years old, shows an almost unbelievable vitality. He eats and drinks prodigiously, smokes fat cigars and walks for hours every day. . . . He has designed many buildings in his life, he told me, but only for money. "I often had to sue to get paid,

but the money was all I cared about," he told me. He is totally different from his son, both in looks, language and personality.

It is his mother whom Speer physically resembles; even their handwriting is similar. She is 65, but still very attractive. During the first twenty years of her marriage, she said, she lived—as women did then—very much under the dominance of her husband and master. She was very quiet then, she said [not the way Speer remembered his mother!], had worked a great deal on herself and only discovered her social talents much later. [Not the way the daughter of her good Heidelberg friend, Frau Dr. Lili Fehrle-Bürger, remembered her, either!]

She told me about her three sons; the youngest, Ernst, had died in the battle for Stalingrad; it emerged quite clearly that he had been the parents' favorite. She said she didn't really have much contact in earlier years with Albert; he passed all his exams without any trouble and went his own way. He had been difficult when young. She didn't say it in so many words, but I already knew that one of the reasons for this difficulty was that the parents, particularly Speer's mother, had considered his wife socially unacceptable. "Albert was very stubborn," she said, "and avoided his home and his parents for years." The whole family, she admitted, had been surprised by his sudden career.

It is part of Speer's ambivalence that while on the one hand he is proud of his upper-class background, he manifested [in college] his indifference and indeed contempt for the parental "style" by an almost aggressive sloppiness. What I mainly remember about him when we first met was that he was disheveled from head to foot: shirt of indefinable color; tie, if any, knotted any old way; trousers unpressed, presenting horizontal rather than vertical pleats. . . .

His friend's unconventional exterior at the time inspired Wolters to produce a caricature of him which he hung up one day in Tessenow's studio. "Speer had an excellent sense of humor," wrote Wolters, "he laughed and kept the drawing." According to Wolters, he was equally casual about his work. "He seemed to me a genius but a loafer," he wrote. "He hired poor students more diligent than he to do his drafting." But Wolters also commented on Speer's generosity. "If any of his students were in financial difficulties, he was always ready to help. . . ."

After Speer graduated, in the summer of 1927, Tessenow appointed him as his graduate assistant. "This was a job everybody wanted," Speer said, "not only because it provided a degree of security and enabled one to continue with postgraduate work, but also because it allowed one to be a comparatively intimate part of Tessenow's world. I admired—no, I worshiped him, but it never became a personal relationship in any way. He was much too closed up, really quite a bit like me. My feelings for him were very different from those I would later have for Hitler: Tessenow could give me nothing tangible—no 'task,' no goal in life, if you see what I mean. My admiration for him, therefore, was much more detached, much freer really, than eventually for Hitler; it was . . . purer. He only held seminars once or twice a week. For the rest of the time," Speer laughed, "can you imagine—I taught for him. But if I say 'teaching,' you mustn't misunderstand. I really 'taught' nothing that came from me; I copied him. But it was good, in the way rote teaching used to be quite good. His was a sublimely pure, or, better said, puritan, architecture. As I transmitted it to others, I could feel it affect me as a person; it made me feel like a good person, as he was a good person. Of course, I didn't know this then; it is now that I understand this and am able to put it into words."

Speer was now on a respectable salary of RM 800 a month—about the equivalent of $200. From Spandau, he described this period in his life for the children:

I had just turned 23—the youngest assistant ever appointed at this college. The best thing about it—aside from working for Tessenow and being with him much of the time—was that the job, being an academic appointment, offered five months paid holiday a year. Thus if I could obtain commissions, there was no reason why I couldn't begin to work independently. . . .

Gretel and I decided to get married. My parents would of course have tried to persuade me to wait, so we went ahead without telling them: we invited your mother's parents—and our loyal chaperon, Cousin Fritz, to come to Berlin, and on August 28, 1928, we had a simple wedding ceremony, the way we liked things. . . .

Afterwards a street photographer took a picture of us—very nice; I must show it to you one day. And we sent my parents a telegram: "We have got married, Albert and Gretel." And the next day, we stacked our luggage into our canoes (a single for your mother, a double for me) and launched them into the Spandauer Kanal—just 500 meters from where I am writing now—and went off on our honeymoon into the lovely solitude of the Havel and the blue lakes of Mecklenburg. For three wonderful weeks we were at last—legitimately—alone. Except on your mother's birthday, which we celebrated festively on dry land, we canoed every day, and slept in our tent at night. It was a wonderful time. . . .

Following a quick visit to Heidelberg, where Speer's parents (who had never yet met Margret) "received their new daughter-in-law very kindly," as he put it in his letter to the children twenty-five years later, they returned to Berlin.

Although times were dreadfully hard for most people then, life was good. We had a small house in a suburb. Most students didn't have a bean, and as we had a little, our house became a meeting place for all kinds of people. But all of us believed fervently in the simple life which Tessenow preached.

"I cooked noodles and rice for dozens every day," Margret recalled happily fifty years later. "It was the purest, the happiest time we ever had," Speer added. And this happiness is reflected by the memories of someone else who met Speer at that time and who was later invited first to become his partner and then, when Speer's fortunes improved, to join his team of architects.

Willie Schelkes was born in Freiburg in 1904. His father was a wealthy industrialist who headed a hemp factory in Austria until 1917, when the family moved to Munich. Their son passed his *Abitur* in 1925, did a two-year course in landscape gardening and then switched to the Institute of Technology—where Speer and Wolters had studied—to study landscape architecture. In 1929, when his father took over a hemp factory in Hungary, twenty-five-year-old Willie moved to Berlin.

"When I went to sign up [for Tessenow's course] I was told that it was full—no hope whatsoever for transfer students," he said. "I was miserable: everything I had learned about Tessenow convinced me that he was the man I wanted to study under. And then, as I stood there in that office, a young man came in—my age—and asked why I looked so unhappy. I told him. He said, 'Where are you from?' and I said 'Freiburg.' So he said, 'Well, I'm from Heidelberg and I'm Tessenow's assistant and one *Badener* has to help another. You hold on, I'll get you in.' I thought it was wonderful. And he did."

We met in 1986 in his charming villa in Freiburg, a beautiful old university town in Baden. Schelkes had recently handed his practice and the house over to his son. He and his wife, who had become too fragile for housekeeping, were about to move into a flat in a sophisticated retirement development on the other side of town. He was depressed about the move because, as he no longer drove, it would become difficult to go to his beloved studio, which he was keeping on top of the family house. Schelkes is, and probably always was, a quiet and civilized man—landscape architecture suits his personality.

Speer, he said, had been very helpful and friendly in those early years in Berlin. "He seemed to take life very easy," he said. "He and his wife had people over for supper all the time—that was quite exceptional. I mean, it wasn't part of the culture then. He wasn't showing off with this; he just wanted to share.

"Speer was central to our lives," he continued. "He had this charisma already then. Of course, I didn't agree with him about the political aspect of the Tessenow seminar: he thought that it was a focal point for the National Socialists. I didn't feel that then and I don't now either. There were of course some Nazis—they tried to get me to join up, but I said no, I didn't want to. I *was* politically interested—one couldn't not be—but I was looking for political purpose in a different direction." He had for years belonged to the vaguely Protestant but also nationalist-oriented youth movement, the Bündische Jugend, which went in for mountain tours and canoeing. "I didn't like the fanaticism, not to speak of the violence, of the Nazis—they were too much for me."

Another of Speer's contemporaries, who much later in his life was to become enormously, indeed uniquely, important to him, lived in Berlin at this time. Robert Raphael Geis, nineteen years old, was the only son of a wealthy assimilated Jewish family in Frankfurt, and arrived in Berlin in the autumn of 1925 to begin rabbinical studies.

Raphael Geis—as he would sign the many letters he wrote to Speer between November 1969, when their relationship began, until May 1972, when he died—was born on July 4, 1906, and, though for very different reasons, was to suffer childhood frictions not dissimilar to Speer's. But the origin of his conflicts with his father—cultural rather than psychological—was not untypical of a considerable number of Germany's assimilated Jews, and thus significant for what was to happen among them under Hitler.

Geis's father was above all else a German, loyal to his Kaiser. Although, somewhat like "Easter Christians," he attended the synagogue at Yom Kippur, he was, if anything, embarrassed to think of himself as a Jew. Fourteen years older than his wife, he had made his fortune and retired early. He was a strict, disciplinarian father who had planned his son's future almost at birth. Raphael would be brought up as an upper-middle-class German, attend the best schools, after his *Abitur* be offered a trip around the world (the customary reward for the sons of Germany's wealthy elite) and prepare afterwards for a career in banking.

Speer's father, no doubt, had similarly planned his sons' lives, with similar unconcern for their individual personalities and preferences. In Speer's case, tragically enough, the father, passionately loved and admired by the most talented and least understood of his three sons, succeeded, and Albert Speer did as he was told—for his father.

Geis, who neither admired nor, one suspects, loved his didactic father, was made of different stuff. He started to say "no" when he could barely speak, and, at considerable cost to himself and those close to him, continued to stand up for his moral decisions until the end of his life.

Very much like Speer's letters to Margret—and later to his children— nothing can illustrate better Geis's development and feelings than *A True*

Childhood Tale, an autobiographical parable he wrote in 1934 to use when he briefly taught in Mannheim:

> Once upon a time the Jews fared well. They weren't thrown out of their homes, their children could play in peace, they could study what they wanted and if they were good and diligent, they could choose to work at a profession they loved. As life was so good for the Jews, many thought they really didn't have to be Jews any longer, and many a Jewish child grew up without knowing what a Jew is. . . .

He described such a boy—himself at about seven years of age—on a first visit to his grandparents, and his fascination with these relatives, so different from his parents.

> "Grandfather, may I touch your beard?" he asked, as they walked home from the station. And the old man leaned down at once, and the little boy very gently stroked the beard, and thus they became good friends. . . . One day the grandfather asked, "Would you like to go to the synagogue with me, child?" "Oh, yes," said the boy. But he had no idea what a synagogue was because his father had never taken him. . . .
>
> It was a big beautiful building with many big lamps which brightly lit the room. In the front was a curtain, bright red and full of shimmering embroideries in many colors, stretching across a whole wall. . . . And suddenly there was total silence and then, from way above, came singing, first very soft and then strong and sure. . . . He kept hearing the word "Jew." . . . God had to love the Jews very much and the people in the synagogue had to be Jews, he thought. . . . The little boy got very scared. . . . Perhaps his grandfather didn't realize that he wasn't a Jew, and the little boy began to cry.
>
> "What is it, sweetheart?" whispered the grandfather, and the little boy whispered back through his sobs, "This is so lovely, but it's only for Jews, isn't it? And I'm not a Jew."
>
> His grandfather laughed and said, "Don't worry, you too are a Jew all right, I know it well, and I hope to God that one day you'll be a good Jew." And the little boy stopped crying. He was so glad that he too was a Jew.
>
> When he returned home he put on his mother's dressing-gown and draped a white cloth around his shoulders, just as his grandfather had done, and began to chant the songs he had heard. His father was appalled at the sounds from the nursery. "What are you doing?" he asked. "I'm in the synagogue," the child answered. "You mustn't disturb me because I'm a Jew—grandfather himself told me."
>
> That summer for the first time, the little boy was allowed to spend a summer holiday in a [Swiss] mountain hotel with his parents. One evening there was a big party and the little boy was allowed to stay up for it. When it was quite dark, the guests assembled on the hotel terrace to ad-

mire the fires which had been lit on top of all the mountains around. And one man called out "Long live Switzerland—" and another "Long live England—" and so on, until all the countries represented there had been called upon to live long. And at the end, when everything had gone quiet, a child's voice rang out—"Long live us Jews."

Everybody smiled, but not the parents of the little boy, for they weren't at all pleased that now everyone knew that they were Jews. The next day the three of them left, because the parents were so ashamed that they were Jews.

In September 1925, when twenty-year-old Speer, after his climbing holiday with Margret in the Austrian Alps, transferred from Munich to the Institute of Technology in Berlin and found Tessenow, nineteen-year-old Raphael Geis began his studies of Jewish theology at the Faculty for Philosophy, under the last of the great German-Jewish academics to teach there: the religious philosopher and rabbi Leo Baeck,* the theological historian Ismar Elbogen, the philosopher and historian Julius Guttmann and the famous philosophers and pedagogues Martin Buber and Franz Rosenzweig. (All of them were to survive the Nazis, though Elbogen died in New York in 1943.)

Protestant theologian Dietrich Goldschmidt, one of Geis's later friends, has written that Geis gained his identity not only by the determined acceptance of his Jewish inheritance and rabbinical mission but also by the full adoption of the German spirit with which the universities at that time inculcated the sons of Germany's elite. Aside from his theological training, he also studied modern German history, in which—transferring in 1930 to Cologne to study under the Breslau historian Johannes Ziekursch—he obtained his Ph.D. with a dissertation on the downfall of Reich Chancellor Caprivi, the successor of Bismarck. Deliberately rejecting his parents' way of life, he elected modestly paid academia and theology as his future.

A year and a half later, twenty-six-year-old Dr. Robert Geis, a "high-spirited, beautifully dressed, passionate young man of slender build," as one of his Munich congregation would describe him, was named "youth-rabbi" of Munich and, outraging the highly conventional Jewish Community Executive (a council in charge of religious-cultural aspects of Jewish life in each German city), immediately proceeded to get on a first-name and *"Du"* basis with his young charges.

Munich had by then for almost ten years been the center of political strife and the headquarters of Hitler's growing nationalist power. Geis, beginning his teaching career, immediately joined the battle—which he would continue

---

*Baeck was sent to the Nazis' "model" camp Theresienstadt in 1943 and, surviving that camp, emigrated to Britain in 1945; his name has since been given to one of Berlin's outstanding scientific institutes.

to the end of his life—against the hubris of nationalism, zealots and, above all, man's inhumanity to man.

"He was a born outsider, anti-establishment, a free spirit, who knew from the start that he would have to walk alone until the end," wrote Harry Maor, who knew Geis as an eighteen-year-old in Munich. "He, who even when young, seemed to me often in dire need of consolation when he found himself rejected and pillorized by narrow minds, was the most gifted of consolers, an artist in pastoral care: we loved him."

By 1932, the young hothead Geis, already then a thorn in the flesh of Germany's traditionalist Jewish Community Executive, had come to the attention of the Christian hierarchy, and when Cardinal Faulhaber, wishing to challenge the National Socialists and their increasingly vicious propaganda, decided to deliver a sermon against anti-Semitism during the 1933 Advent season, he invited the young rabbi to walk next to him in the procession to the altar. It was a remarkable and dramatic first step, from both sides, in Christian-Jewish ecumenicalism with which Geis—fifteen years later, when after vain attempts to sink roots abroad, he returned to Germany—would be closely and controversially involved.

By the end of the 1920s, the generation of Germans born in the first decade of the century (which included Speer, Wolters, Geis, Schelkes and their future wives) had grown to adulthood, with their moral and intellectual potentials presumably fully established. In the economic climate of the time few, it is true, were given the opportunity to prove themselves. Some, like Wolters, who worked in the Soviet Union, went abroad. Some, like Goebbels, and up to a point Speer and even Geis, accepted parental support well into adulthood, while they tried to realize their ambitions or dreams.

By contrast, while Speer was teaching Tessenow's classes in 1929 and he and Margret, supported both by his salary and his father's continued princely contribution, were enjoying their first years of marriage, some young people such as Annemarie Wittenberg became both politically conscious and financially responsible while they were still almost children. She had very early on faced the harsh realities of life. Her father, a newspaper editor, had been blinded by then inoperable cataracts when she was five, and her mother had gone to work in a bank. Money was short; their greatest luxury, she said, was "oat-cocoa—it was hot and filling, and with a little sugar, as my mother made it, we thought it was good." Her father did as much as he could to run the household; the mother worked long hours; the four children knew they had to go to work as quickly as possible.

"Berlin was very political," she said. "By the time I was fourteen, we were profoundly aware of the gaps between rich and poor, between classes and castes. At the end of the school year during which we had studied the Versailles Treaty, we commemorated it with a mourning procession in the schoolyard. At the end of it, we solemnly tore up a copy of the treaty, threw it in a prepared garbage pail and set fire to it." (One got a distinct feeling that young Annemarie was the ringleader in this ceremony.) At the end of the first part of her secondary education, when normally a clever girl such as she would have continued another three or four years to *Abitur* and gone on to university, she entered a business school and learned shorthand, languages and typing. After three or four months—she was then barely sixteen and, as one can see in photographs from that period, a tall, slim, beautiful girl with darkish-blond hair—she decided she knew enough.

"I went to an employment office, told them I had some foreign languages, shorthand and typewriting and almost immediately landed a job in an agency for variety artists imaginatively called Perlen Flitter und Tante [Pearls, Spangles and Aunts]." The salary was RM 120 a month and luncheon vouchers. Helped by her "nonexistent foreign languages," she said, she soon became their secretary-cashier. "I wrote letters with dictionaries—they never knew the difference." She gave her mother almost all her money, keeping only enough for fares.

This paradise—"and believe me," she said, "in a country of seven million unemployed, it was paradise"—lasted about six months. One day she found a box of chocolates on her desk, then an unthinkable luxury. When that same day she went down to the cellar to get some files, the boss followed her, his efforts gaining him nothing except a slap in the face. That afternoon, the boss's wife took Annemarie out to the zoo in a horse-drawn carriage and told her she had been surprised he had waited so long to try something. "And then I joined the millions of unemployed, but you should have seen the reference they gave me—glowing."

She signed up at the labor exchange. "The next job I was offered, they proposed to pay me RM 40 a month. I said certainly not, it's beneath my dignity, and my parents agreed."

Waiting, as it turned out, paid off, though not in money. "I was passionately interested in politics by then," she said, "and passionately concerned with the ills of our society which, with its terrifying class system, had produced this disastrous unemployment. In a modern welfare state, with unemployment, sickness benefits and family allowances, the suffering this caused is virtually unimaginable."

Through a friend of her brother's she heard that the Berlin NSDAP district administration (*Gauleitung*), which had no funds, needed volunteers who would work just for the fare. "My oldest brother worked as an insurance salesman, my sister had a job at the telegraph office, my mother still worked at the bank—they said to go ahead; if I was offered something they'd help me. I didn't care what I was offered in money, as long as I could work there, for our future."

She got into the department that subsequently became the German Work-ers' Front (Arbeitsfront), working as a typist. "I took along a sandwich for lunch; sometimes an apple; I had no money at all aside from my fare, but I was over the moon: I had become part of the struggle—it was all I wanted."

IN THE ALREADY MENTIONED (but only partially quoted) letter which Speer wrote to his daughter Hilde from Spandau in May 1953 in reply to her question about his "guilt," he tried to confront the two main issues of his life: Hitler and the Jews. In her letter, Hilde, partly out of shyness, partly perhaps to protect him even from herself, had almost pointedly avoided the word "Jews." In his reply, however, he brought the subject up of his own vo-lition. He judged this issue quite rightly to be uppermost in the minds of vir-tually the entire Western world, including, perhaps more than most, his profoundly moral young daughter. But that was not the only reason. There was an immense need, a stubborn drive in Speer, to confront it. But while in his "deep" talks with Georges Casalis at Spandau (and, much later, with me) every such mention was tinged with pain, here in what might be called the historical part of his letter to Hilde, he appears only to wish to rationalize it:

> To start out with, when I first—I suppose one can say—encountered National Socialism about 1931, the party, probably in order not to discour-age new applicants, was fairly reticent with regard to anti-Semitic propa-ganda, even though it certainly was part of their platform. In the economic climate of those years, communism—which has always bene-fited from bad times—had grown enormously and many people, includ-ing myself, came to wonder whether National Socialism, with its vitality and energy, wasn't the only valid alternative.
>
> What was decisive for me was a speech Hitler made to students, and which my students finally persuaded me to attend. From what I had read in the opposition press, I expected to find a screaming, gesticulating fa-natic in uniform, instead of which we were confronted with a quiet man in a dark suit who addressed us in the measured tones of an academic. I'm determined one day to look up newspapers of that time to see just what it was he said that so impressed me. But I don't think he attacked the Jews. . . .

In *Inside the Third Reich*, written twelve years later, Speer, apparently loath to admit that he had agreed to attend a major rather than a minor speech, underplayed the importance of that occasion, merely saying,

The site of the meeting was a beer hall called the Hasenheide. Dirty walls, narrow stairs, and an ill-kept interior created a poverty-stricken atmosphere. This was a place where workmen ordinarily held beer parties....

He made it sound, wrongly, like just one more of the thousands of speeches Hitler gave in those years in *Bierstuben,* basically pubs, up and down the land. Even in his "Spandau draft"—the 1953 original which, without the afterthoughts and editorial corrections of the later book, is often more direct and thus more convincing—he says mistakenly that this was not meant to be the kind of mass meeting Hitler was at that point addressing almost daily, but a speech just for students in a "small hall."

In fact this "small hall," though described as a *Bierhalle,* was a huge auditorium and *Der Angriff,* the party daily founded and edited by Goebbels, announced the December 4 speech for two days beforehand and reported it in detail on December 5. Not only did five thousand students come to listen— with many more turned away—but a large number of professors also attended and were seated on the platform, as in fact were Speer and his—one must thus assume politically significant—group of Tessenow students.

Speer knew perfectly well when he wrote his "Spandau draft" why Hitler would not have engaged in his usual hysterical attacks on the Jews before such an audience. In *Inside the Third Reich,* in fact, he specifically remarked on Hitler's "great gift" for adapting himself—consciously or intuitively—to his audience. There is therefore perhaps a degree of sophistry in his remark to Hilde that Hitler had not attacked the Jews in that speech. But Hitler's no doubt carefully calculated respectable appearance that night had the desired effect on his young listeners. The letter continued,

[Hitler appeared]—greeted with incredible enthusiasm. Receptive as I am to atmosphere, already this had its effect on me: I felt gooseskin going down my spine. And then—I had only seen pictures of him in uniform, his hair sort of wild, but here he was, in a good blue suit, looking civil and well-cared for....

(The fact is that Speer not only was "receptive to atmosphere" but, despite the indifference he had shown during his college days for his own dress— surely nothing but a mild gesture of young rebellion—was always enormously affected by appearances. A striking example of this is in a letter he wrote to his two oldest children, Albert and Hilde, after their first visit to him in Spandau prison on September 2, 1953, shortly after Hilde's return from America. To Albert, then nineteen years old, whom he had not seen since this oldest son was eleven, he wrote, "What I noticed particularly about you, Albert, were your beautiful hands and your splendidly well-assorted clothes. And your way of dressing, Hilde, is also full of style...."）

What had made the biggest impression on him on the occasion of that first speech of Hitler's he attended, he wrote in Spandau,

> . . . was first his unexpected shyness and then the restraint he displayed, both in what he said and how he said it. Later I often noticed this tendency of shyness in Hitler when he found himself in the company of highly educated people who were superior to him in knowledge. In the second half of the speech, the shyness disappeared and he spoke with urgency and conviction . . . of the need for young Germans to find pride.

Among the essential elements in searching for the internal motivations of any human being are the external circumstances of his (or her) life, most important of course the people closest to him. Throughout the years I knew Speer, and despite being familiar with his generation's general attitude toward women, I was continually surprised by his intellectual blindness toward Margret. It was not indifference—he cared about her; it was an inbred conviction, emotional rather than intellectually founded, which many men of his generation—not only in Germany—shared, that *their* women did not or could not have the capacity, or even the right, to think for themselves. Such an attitude allowed them, of course, considerable scope. A chosen woman friend could be given leeway—in Speer's case, for example, he certainly admired and enjoyed Leni Riefenstahl's filmmaking talents, and without a doubt respected Annemarie's superior capabilities as his secretary. But even in later years, though far more enlightened by then in his reactions, he could not really allow or maintain his faith in the capacity of women for intellectual originality or depth for any length of time. This emerged very strongly with Hilde, whose remarkable gifts and depth of thinking he certainly recognized and for many years enjoyed in his correspondence with her from prison. But there was a tangible feeling of relief when, a brilliant young husband having come into her life in the early 1960s, Speer could write to *him* about serious thoughts, and to *her* about purely practical matters.

But these were developments after the end of Hitler. What I needed to understand first were the influences which affected him at the beginning.

I asked Speer if Margret had gone with him to hear Hitler's speech. "No," he said, sounding puzzled at my question, "of course not. One didn't take one's wife to a political demonstration." But were there female students in the audience? "Yes, of course," he said, immediately catching the drift. "You are right, of course," he smiled, "there were girl students, but not wives."

I later asked Margret in Speer's presence if she would have liked to go. "I don't know," she said in her soft, hesitant voice. Then she added, unexpectedly, "Well, yes, I think I might have wanted to go."

"You would?" he said, looking at her manifestly surprised, and then immediately turned back to me. "Actually," he said, "it wouldn't have been a good idea. Afterwards—I remember this well—I really needed to be alone. I had left our small car not too far away; I walked there, with crowds of people in the street. . . . My head was ringing. I sat down in the car and drove out of the city, into the woods. And there I went for a long walk."

"It must have been a long walk," Margret interrupted, again unexpectedly. It was always surprising if she spoke up. "I was worried."

"You were?" he said, sounding amazed.

"Well, yes, I was. Don't you remember, just the day before, two SA men had been killed in a demonstration?" The SA was Hitler's first paramilitary organization, set up in August 1921 as "Schutz und Sport Abteilung." Shortly afterwards renamed "Sturmabteilung," known as the "Brownshirts," it became the Nazis' first fighting force.

He shook his head. He didn't remember this and—as he later told me— was astonished that she did. "Isn't it amazing," he said, in a way sounding proud of her, "her coming out with that after fifty years?" He shook his head again and added that he was sure it would never have occurred to him that she could have worried about him. But the meeting, and the lonely walk, changed Speer's attitude to Hitler, and helped change his life.

"Above all else," he said quietly, "—and it was obviously the greatest mistake of my life—I felt he was a human being; I mean with that, I felt he cared: not only about Germany, which in his own terrible way of course he did, but that he cared about people. If you like, though it would never have occurred to me to put it like that at the time, that he cared about me . . . I mean . . . ," he corrected himself, "about us, the young, individually. I am still convinced now that this was his greatest gift: to convey, not in words but by a kind of mass—and individual—hypnosis, that he cared about each of us, even, if you forgive the term, that he loved us. I didn't expect to feel that, you see; I abhor, yes, I abhor vulgarity and loudness, and that's what I had associated with him before that night. So you see, I made a double mistake in judgment, one before that night—for certainly he was not vulgar—and one afterwards, for certainly, at least in the accepted sense of the word, he could not love. But it took me years—a kind of lifetime—to realize that. Then of course, that night, what he said appealed to me. Believe me, in the context of the world then—the enormous growth of communism, and of its danger to Germany—it made sense."

And in a way I saw what he meant: for Germany then, and for that student audience in particular, it made sense. I had a photocopy of the report of this speech, as printed in *Der Angriff* on December 5, 1930, and offered it to him to read. "I know it," he said. "I looked it up some time ago." Hitler, as quoted, had said that the [first] World War had

... eliminated those who were the best and preserved the *Minderwerti-gen* [inferiors; he used here the word *ausmerzen* for "eliminate." Both this and the much stronger *ausrotten,* for "eradicate" or "exterminate," are words Hitler readily applied, throughout his career]. Finally the war and its corollaries left Germany to a preponderance of these inferiors. For the past twelve years the policies of this country—policies of rank egotism—have been those of these inferior spirits.

When nations abandon the old and traditional concepts of honor and heroism in the mistaken belief that they are old-fashioned and outdated, it leads to a slow weakening of the people's fiber. . . . Heroic ideas attract heroic elements. Cowardly ideas rally cowards. . . . Examine our times, examine what you feel gives life and verve to our time. Then make up your minds and make your choice. You need to find a way that allows you to become part of—to absorb you into—the life and future of this nation.

I asked Speer if he had not found the word "inferiors" in Hitler's speech just as grating as he had found it when Hitler said virtually the same thing fifteen years later. (This was on March 19, 1945, as it happened, Speer's forti-eth birthday, when he handed Hitler the last of several memoranda he wrote, explaining that the war was lost and that the only important thing now was to preserve Germany's infrastructure for the sake of the people. "If the war is lost," he quoted Hitler as responding icily, "the people will be lost too; it is not necessary to worry about what they will need for . . . survival. On the contrary, it is best . . . to destroy even these things. For the nation has shown itself to be the weaker, and the future belongs solely to the stronger Eastern nation. The garbage left over after this struggle will anyway be only the inferi-ors, because the good ones will be dead.")

"You are succumbing to the temptation of making facile comparisons out of context," Speer said, "a mistake many people make"—he smiled, to take the sting out of the rebuke—"usually in order to catch me out. I don't think that is your purpose. . . ." (I couldn't tell if he meant this or was flat-tering me. One could never be quite sure.) "I think you really do want to know how I could not react in 1930 to the vulgarity of the word *Minderwer-tigen.* And oddly enough, now that you ask this: Yes, when, during my re-search for my first book, I read the speech in *Der Angriff,* I did feel repelled by the word and, yes, I also immediately made the association you just made. But now visualize that December evening in 1930; imagine the atmo-sphere in that hall, and what Hitler said as a whole. Do you really think one word—even if I had noticed it, and I obviously didn't—would have made a difference?

"Now of course I know—just as you do—that it wasn't a question of one word. It was a question of attitude of mind, or spirit, and even of intelligence. Of course it is grotesque to claim that 'the best' or 'the good' die in a war and 'the inferior' survive—this is paying lip service to some Wagnerian idyll of heroism. Additionally, it is outrageous even to feel this. And in 1945, of course, I knew this. When he said this then, I think I wasn't even surprised— by then I knew him, at least knew him, I think, as well as anybody could know him. But in 1930, I didn't know him and certainly didn't think I ever would."

A few weeks later, the same students who had persuaded Speer to listen to Hitler, evidently in their messianic ardor thinking he needed more persuasion, took him along to a mass meeting at the Palace of Sports which was to be addressed by Goebbels. The description of this occasion in *Inside the Third Reich* (virtually identical to that in the "Spandau draft") seems to indicate that Speer was sufficiently put off by Goebbels's hyperbole and the frenetic and indiscriminate reaction of the huge crowd—"a witches' cauldron of excitement such as I had hitherto witnessed only at six-day bicycle races," he wrote—to begin to question his reaction to Hitler. "I was disgusted," he writes briefly and concisely in the draft, "and it diminished the effect Hitler had had on me. But when after the speech the people, of course excited but quiet enough, left the arena, suddenly mounted police galloped into the peaceful crowd swinging their rubber truncheons. This unwarranted brutality outweighed any doubts I might have had. . . ."

Writing the book thirty-eight years after the incident, he evidently decided the few words in the draft were insufficient explanation for his readers and added, " . . . Until that moment," he wrote, "I had never witnessed such use of force. . . ."

As we sat in the peaceful Heidelberg living room, Margret's beautifully laid tea tray on the round table between us, I asked how he could *not* have been aware previously of the "use of force." Street battles between demonstrators and police had by then been the order of the day for years. How could the police brutality that day have been sufficiently shocking to him to "outweigh any doubts he might have had" about the Nazis?

"I don't know," he said, "and I don't want to make too much of these doubts. That, you see, is the advantage of thinking—really thinking—later, which so many of my critics reproach me for when they discover a difference between something I said or felt years ago, and what I say or feel now. I think now that although my reaction to Hitler was indeed more to him—his magnetism, if you like—than to his speech, what he said did of course fall on fertile soil. Despite my very real disinterest in politics, I doubtlessly knew that Germany had become virtually ungovernable. My father, an old-time liberal, thought as little of the right as he did of the left and, valiantly I now think, continued to subscribe to Coudenhove-Kalergi's Pan-Europe.* But that was manifestly just a dream. In reality, there were only two alternatives to anarchy: socialism/communism or National Socialism. Both by background and inclination, I had to be predisposed toward the latter. Perhaps—and this is what I just don't know anymore—perhaps there was somewhere in me a forlorn glimmer of hope for what was after all still Germany's legitimate government. And here I come back to your question. Yes, of course I knew there were street battles, even riots; I read and heard about them—even saw students demonstrate from my window at the college. It's just . . . I had never been involved before; I had never had to run away from mounted police myself, I suppose. Perhaps it's as simple as that." He was really seeking an answer.

"The other people that night after the Goebbels speech were walking in the street as peaceably as I was. The police just hit out at anybody; this was not rule by law, but mob rule by violence, and it was the police who were the mob—the police, you see, who were after all the representatives of this 'legitimate government.' Hitler's speech a few weeks before had given me a feeling of quiet, of hope for order and stability. Confronted so personally now by these louts on horseback, this feeling came back in me, like a wave. I had no wish whatever to mix in politics even then, only to establish somehow, above all I think to myself, where I stood."

A few days afterwards, on March 1, 1931, he applied for membership in the Nazi Party. His membership number was 474,481.

*Heinrich von Coudenhove-Kalergi (1859–1906) and his son Richard (1894–1972) were, unusual among Central European aristocrats, pioneers in the battle against anti-Semitism. After World War I Richard founded the Pan-European Movement which, not unlike today's European Community, was based on free-market economics, reduction in trade and movement barriers, and a rejection of racialism. He believed that a nation must be defined by its culture, not by its race.

III

Dizzy with Excitement

Nuremberg, July 29, 1946

CHARLES DUBOST [Deputy Chief French Prosecutor]: Speer joined the Party in 1933 [*sic*]. He was appointed personal architect to Hitler, and in this capacity was a close confidant of the Führer. . . .

THE MERE FACT of Speer's joining the party was never a matter for contention: in Nuremberg prosecutors repeatedly got the date wrong—he actually joined, as I have said, in 1931. It was he himself who set up the scenario which led to the attacks against him, by claiming at Nuremberg and afterwards that he was always "unpolitical," including at the time he joined the party. Equally provocative was his claim of ignorance of all specific crimes, first at Nuremberg and then in his two principal books, *Inside the Third Reich* and *The Secret Diaries*.

Given the Nazi horrors of the 1940s, Speer's critics do not admit that the man who, according to his own statements, came as near as anyone to being "Hitler's close friend" could have been unaware in the 1930s of the seeds of the horrors. To them, there are no degrees in assent, and when Speer claims that he was "unpolitical" at the time he joined the party in 1931, they say this simply has to be a lie.

Wasn't joining the party a statement of assent? I asked him.

"Yes, I joined the party," he said, "and of course, given what I became later, this is already against me on the balance sheet. People say, 'Explain yourself; tell us how it could all happen.' But how can one explain, when in order to understand any one thing—any one circumstance, one impulse, one act—you need to understand so many others which, unless one lived them, cannot be understood?"

Very early in *Inside the Third Reich*, he does in fact appear to suggest that there were circumstances in 1931 under which he might have been able to predict the future. Calling his decision to enter the party "frivolous," he poses, hypothetically, many of the questions his critics asked later. Why was he prepared to yield so quickly to the almost hypnotic impression Hitler's speech made on him? As the intellectual he was, why, before committing himself, didn't he collect information about Hitler and his party with the same thoroughness and lack of bias that he had learned to apply to his architectural studies? Why didn't he read the various party programs, at least *Mein Kampf* and Rosenberg's *Myth of the Twentieth Century*? And replying to his own questions, he tells his readers that his "failure was rooted in [his] inadequate political schooling."

But would reading *Mein Kampf* have told him enough about Hitler to persuade him against entering the party? I asked him. Did he really feel—as he says in his book—that "not to have tried to see through the whole apparatus of mystification was already criminal?" There were thousands of other well-educated and decent Germans, many of whom had read *Mein Kampf* and Rosenberg's book, who still came out for Hitler. In a historical context, how immoral—not to say criminal—was it then to join the Nazi Party? Did he really feel it is "political schooling" that makes people ask moral questions?

"It isn't," he said. "That capacity is determined by something deeper," and before I could ask what that "something deeper" was, he said, in that special half-mocking tone he used when he disparaged himself, "I certainly didn't have it." He felt that when he wrote *Inside the Third Reich* (in 1967–68) he was trying to do too much too soon. "I applied then," he said, "not a false but a jumbled perspective; now I wouldn't have put it like that. After 1945 we knew that National Socialism was an immoral concept and Hitler was an amoral man. In 1930 we not only did not know that, but I would doubt that more than a very few—older and wiser heads at that—ever considered it overall in 'moral' rather than immediate sociopolitical terms, even if they had read *Mein Kampf*. While the reading of the party literature would have indicated Hitler's willingness to risk war, or even the inevitability of it if he wanted to carry out his plans, nothing he says in *Mein Kampf*, despite his obvious anti-Semitism, reveals either the intention of murdering the Jews or that of creating an absolute tyranny in Germany and in Europe. I don't know whether these intentions existed concretely when he wrote his book in 1924, but certainly, had he said or even indicated it, he couldn't have been elected."

In March 1931, when the twenty-five-year-old budding architect Albert Speer joined the Nazi Party, the only "faith" on his mind—and on Margret's too—was in the man Hitler and the prospect he held out of a Germany reestablished on the basis of old and proven values and, rid of the shame of the Versailles Treaty, regenerated as a power to be reckoned with on the world stage.

Speer's decision, and that of hundreds of thousands of other Germans at that time, considered in the context of the period, was comparatively undramatic. But while we can believe his statement that, with politics playing "a subsidiary part in [his] thinking," he was then "above all an architect," his much more unequivocal statements—first in a memorandum to Hitler in March 1945, then in Nuremberg, twenty-three years later in *Inside the Third Reich* and countless times afterwards in interviews and broadcasts—that he had always been an "unpolitical" man played havoc with his credibility.

Surely no intelligent young person in Germany in the 1930s could be "un-political," I said. It was already hard to believe his claims of disinterest in the momentous events shaping up during the first period of his university stud-ies, in Karlsruhe. But afterwards? After hearing Hitler address the students and after his long nighttime walk in the forest, the tumultuous weeks which followed, and finally his decision to join the party—could he really expect anyone to believe that he did not know then what he was doing?

"Of course I cannot and do not claim that I was not—or at least did not become—politically committed," he said, quite clearly wishing to clarify the issue. "If you were committed to Hitler, you were politically committed. Yes, if that is what is meant, I became committed when I first heard him speak. I said before: I was enthusiastic, elated; I felt that he could save Germany, give us back faith in ourselves. If that was political, then I was political. When I said, and wrote, that I wasn't political when I joined the party, what I meant was that I wasn't looking for a political career. If I had wanted that, of course I could have had it. They were dying to have people of my background and education; they were desperately short of university graduates. But I wasn't interested. I have not the slightest doubt that if I had not met Hitler, I would have become a provincial architect, as befitted what I considered my modest gifts. But certainly later I played politics, in another sense of the word. I have never for a minute denied that I became intoxicated with power, a power which, as of early 1943, had to be continually fought for. It would have been impossible to do one's job as a Minister, to function effectively, or even—arguably quite literally—to survive, without 'politicking.' "

Both in his trial, in his *Inside the Third Reich* and in talks such as those he had with me over several years, Speer made many both specific and general admissions. In themselves they were both honest and, during his trial, coura-geous acts. At the same time, many seemed deliberately calculated to deflect attention from matters he didn't want to—or couldn't—talk about. Strangely enough, his early feelings about politics, which almost anyone with some understanding of the period could sympathize with, were among these deflections.

A comparison between the "Spandau draft" and the finished version of *In-side the Third Reich* remains the best measure of Speer's real feelings. In the draft he wrote,

I don't intend to go into long political reflections, which would do nothing except show what an amateur I was. But perhaps I should say that the National Socialists at that time, linking up with the respectably con-servative National Party and the Confederation of German Soldiers, made considerable efforts to appear presentable.

In our circles we assumed that, as had happened in other radical movements, rough spots would be smoothed over with time. . . .

When, in early 1931, he and his students had attended a political meeting
during which the speaker attacked their revered teacher Tessenow, they had
written a furious letter of protest to Hitler. Speer, in Spandau, described the
consequences:

> What was important to us political infants was that the polite reply
> we received indicated that the people around Hitler seemed to respect
> our great teacher. Most important of all, we discovered, in the course
> of a seminar . . . that our master himself appeared to view the new Führer
> positively.
>
> "Perhaps what is needed," he [Tessenow] told us, "is someone who
> thinks simply. Thinking has become too complicated. An uneducated
> man, something like a peasant, would find it much easier to solve our
> problems, just because he would not be corrupt. Someone like that, too,
> would have the strength to pursue simple ideas to their fruition."
>
> As anything he said carried for us the authority of ultimate wisdom
> . . . we . . . assumed that what he meant with this rather vague (as I later
> realized) statement was the simple, uneducated, strong man, Hitler. . . .

In this part of the "Spandau draft," Speer avoids mentioning Hitler's anti-
Semitism, or his own feelings about Jews, perhaps because he is addressing it
to his old friend Rudolf Wolters, who knew both him and the situation well.
But in his letter to Hilde in May 1953 (as later in *Inside the Third Reich*), he
feels as always driven to explain and defend himself on this subject:

> . . . I can't remember Hitler berating the Jews in that speech to the stu-
> dents. After I became a member of the party, some very bright Jews I knew
> in Mannheim knew that I had joined and one day not long afterwards one
> of them said, to my astonishment, "If it weren't for their anti-Semitism,
> I'd be joining them myself." You see, it didn't look all that danger-
> ous. . . . But anyway, as far as practicing anti-Semitism or even uttering
> anti-Semitic remarks, my conscience is entirely clear. I really had no aver-
> sion to them, or rather, *no more than the slight discomfort all of us some-
> times feel when in contact with them* [author's italics]. . . .

In 1968, when after three further drafts he wrote the final version of his
reminiscences, he had of course forgotten that passing remark in his letter to
his daughter fifteen years before, and made one of many dangerously unequivocal statements:

> Even after joining the party, I continued to associate with Jewish ac-
> quaintances, who for their part did not break off relations with me, al-

though they knew or suspected that I belonged to this anti-Semitic organization. I was no more an anti-Semite then than I became in the following years. In none of my speeches, or letters, is there any trace of
anti-Semitic feelings or phraseology. . . .

Whatever Speer knew or didn't know about what eventually happened to
the Jews—and I will be examining this subject in detail later—he knew in
1930 that Hitler was an anti-Semite; like millions of other Germans and Austrians, none of whom would have dreamed of advocating or indeed desiring
the murder of the Jews, Speer was at the very least (as he tells Hilde in this
letter, so unperceptively assuming his passionately moral daughter's concur-
rence with his feeling) an instinctive anti-Semite.

CONSIDERING HIS later need to reassure himself as well as others about his motives for becoming actively involved with the party, it is perhaps not too surprising that, recalling those earliest days, Speer emphasized,
to himself as much as to others, a different part of his life between 1931
and 1933: his attempt to set himself up as an independent architect. At least
from early 1932, when the deepening depression caused a cut in university
assistants' salaries, establishing himself professionally became his primary
concern.

Wolters, less taken by Hitler than his old student friend, would later remember asking him why he had joined the party. "That man is no fool,"
Speer allegedly answered. "You'll see; he's going to be someone one day."

In early 1931 (he got this date, like many others, slightly wrong in *Inside the
Third Reich*), Speer very nearly went to work abroad, as Wolters had done.
He was invited to Afghanistan, to teach at the University of Kabul and to
head a German team of young architects and city planners that would rebuild the country. He wrote in Spandau:

> My father was very concerned that a stay abroad for several years could
> alienate me from the fundamental changes which were bound to take
> place in my own country. But what significance did that have by compari-
> son to the fulfillment of our longing for adventures in foreign lands, a trip
> through India and working in a country where we could realize our ideals
> of a simple life? But no sooner had I more or less signed on the dotted line,
> and the great King of Afghanistan, under whose auspices all these idealis-
> tic improvements were to be carried out, had paid a state visit to the Reich
> President, Hindenburg, than the Afghans staged a coup d'état to rid
> themselves of their progressive head of state, who promptly travelled into
> exile in Italy. It was a monumental disappointment, but as fate would
> have it, the same year brought me the first building commission for the

party and soon afterwards a first meeting with the man who would so decisively determine my future. . . .

In all his descriptions of these first two years of the significant 1930s, Speer pointedly skims over his decision, taken almost immediately after joining the party, to accept a—however subordinate—party function when he became a member of the newly founded Motorists Association of the party and, being the only car owner in Wannsee, where he lived, was appointed head of section. He wrote in the "Spandau draft":

> My assignments sometimes required me to call at the district HQ which was headed by a young man whose name I mention here because he would repeatedly have a decisive effect on my life. [Karl] Hanke, a miller by trade [Speer's memory had failed him here—Hanke had a degree in vocational teaching], was an uncomplicated but intelligent man, brimful of energy. In order to live up to the party's new respectable image, he had established the offices of the district HQ in an elegant villa in the select suburb of Grünewald. And discovering that I was an architect, he offered me the job of redecorating the villa.

Hanke in fact did not know Speer or his work. "How could he have? I hadn't done any," Speer told me. "No, I think it was quite simply that I happened on the scene, and I think we liked each other. Explanations are often simple, aren't they?"

Days were spent selecting wallpaper, curtains and paint. "I went quite crazy there in my choice of colors," said Speer. "I still don't know why: it was diametrically opposite to what Tessenow had taught us and I so loved."

"It was fantastic," said Annemarie Kempf. Though Speer didn't meet her until many months later, she was already doing odd jobs around the party offices as a volunteer. "Everybody was talking about him: he'd painted the outer office bright red and all the others canary yellow with red curtains. Some people thought it was crazy—I thought it was wonderful: it was so alive."

However, it was to be the last exciting thing Speer did for almost a year. With his salary cut to the bone, he needed to earn money despite his father's help, and he and Margret decided to move back to Mannheim, where his father (who to his later regret had just retired, at sixty-five) had offered to introduce him to prospective clients and meanwhile—for eating money—to let him manage the buildings the family owned there.

Willie Schelkes had graduated with honors in 1931 and was immediately invited by Speer to join him in the small architectural office he opened in Mannheim—the only one of the thirty-five graduates to be offered employment. "The salary was RM 150 a month," Schelkes said. "But believe me, I was glad to have it. Unemployment had reached its peak, and chances for jobs were as good as nil."

"It was a very discouraging time," said Speer. "Looking back on it—the countless letters I wrote to people my father knew, the polite 'no thank you' replies, the awareness too that I was living on my father's money—I must have been pretty depressed."

"I didn't feel that in him," Schelkes said. "His father owned a lot of property in Mannheim—they were really very wealthy—and managing these was quite a job. And we did do *some* architectural work: reconstructing one of the houses old Herr Speer owned—I think it was a shop on the ground floor—and some other small things too, though admittedly all piddling little commissions. But Speer didn't seem bothered—he always was extraordinarily easygoing, or at least it seemed so. Later, in 1932, he began getting commissions from the *Gauleitung* in Berlin—in fact I went to help him there for two months, but otherwise I stayed in Mannheim"—he laughed—"as his head of office; of course, there wasn't anybody there except he and I, so he was the *Chef* and I the *Bürochef.*"

Speer had converted a dressing room and bath in the back of the Mannheim house where he was born into a tiny flat for himself and Margret. "It was all we needed," he said. "We always went away weekends, and even during the week, if we felt too cramped, we could always use my parents' house in Heidelberg."

Schelkes, in fact, during the unbearably hot summer of 1932, also stayed much of the time at the Heidelberg house—the only one of Speer's friends ever to be so honored. "I received an open invitation from Speer's parents to come there whenever I liked—I still don't know why," he said. He was taken aback—possibly more in retrospect than at the time—at the derogatory manner in which Speer's father discussed his son. "He really thought very little of him or of his talent," he said. Speer's mother on the contrary, he said, was positive and optimistic.

That Speer's mother was suddenly well disposed toward her middle son, whose childhood she had made so miserable, is attributable to the fact that Frau Speer had joined the party early in 1931 and now felt a kind of fellowship with Albert. She didn't in fact know that he too had joined—each hid this from Speer's father and from each other—but she knew of his first working contacts with the party. "I think my father would have been very angry that she joined the party," said Speer. "He despised the Nazis and always said they would be a catastrophe for the country. I don't know how he would have felt about my joining, probably resigned. He wouldn't have expected any better of me."

It was only in 1938 that his mother told him about having seen a parade of

SA men in Heidelberg in the spring of 1931. "She said it was the first time in years that she had sensed energy and joy in the people," Speer said. "She immediately joined, without ever having known anything about the party, because in the sea of pessimism that was Germany at the time, they made her feel optimistic."

Speer's activity for the party in Mannheim was evidently minimal—in the "Spandau draft" he doesn't mention it. In *Inside the Third Reich,* which he wrote when he had no doubt become aware that all the party membership archives had survived and were in American hands,* he briefly explained that "there was no Motorists Association [in Mannheim] so Berlin assigned me to the Motorized SS. At the time I thought that meant I was a member [of the SS], but apparently I was only a guest; for in 1942 when I wanted to renew my membership, it turned out that I had not belonged to the Motorized SS at all."

This—as we will see more fully later—was not a candid account for, as surviving SS records show, Speer joined on March 1, 1931, not just the party but the SA—the Brownshirts, then its active branch—and in the autumn of 1932 he specifically left the SA in order to join the SS Motorized Division. It should be said that many decisions at that time were purely bureaucratic ones. But while this can and probably does apply to the switch from SA to Motorized SS in the autumn of 1932, it is hard to see how it can apply to his originally joining not only the party but also the SA. Unimportant in itself, it points to a stronger commitment than he chose to remember later.

With the forthcoming elections looming in July 1932, the political battle became increasingly critical. En route to a long-planned faltboat holiday on the East Prussian lakes, Speer and Margret drove to Berlin, he said, to feel part "of the exciting election atmosphere and—if possible—to help. . . ."

He put himself and his car at the disposal of the NSKK Berlin West (the Nazi Party car pool) and was assigned to courier duty by its chief Will Nagel, whom six years later Speer would appoint his chief of staff. When he was sent to pick up a party official at the airport where the leadership group was to arrive, it provided him with his second opportunity to see Hitler up close. He described it in both the draft and *Inside the Third Reich*:

> I saw a rather different Hitler there than the quiet, civilized man who addressed the students a year and a half before. He was nervous, obviously annoyed because the cars which were to pick him up had not arrived and he was kept waiting. He spoke angrily to one of his staff and, furiously pacing up and down, hitting his high leather boots with a dogwhip, gener-

---

*The handing over by the United States of the Berlin Document Center, with its millions of files on the Nazi Party, the SS and SA, to the German authorities was effected in July 1994.

ally gave the impression of an ill-mannered and uncontrolled man. . . . [In his draft, but not in the book, he added] but I was already too involved in party doings to allow this unfavorable impression to affect my thinking.

The day after he wrote this, having thought it over, he added, to Wolters:

Re-reading this has made me wonder whether I'm losing myself in details which will interest neither you nor anyone else. I am of course moved, retrospectively, by a lot of probably immaterial matters. Well, later you and I can apply a determined red pencil to all this. I am trying not to conceal, whitewash or gloss over my development in any way, but rather, by putting myself back into that time while writing, to describe it exactly as it was. Thus, just as in the last part [of this draft] I am describing the negative aspects, by the same token I don't want here to diminish the positive ones, as they affected me at the time. . . .

What affected him most, erasing the momentary disappointment at seeing a different, not so pleasant Hitler, was the wild enthusiasm of the masses throughout that day and Hitler's insistence on confronting the equally wild, demonstrating Social Democrats and communists head-on, standing erect in his car. "I wouldn't have liked to be in his place," Speer writes. "I admired his courage then and I do now." Goebbels commented in his diary,

July 27, 1932: The Führer, late at night addresses 120,000 people at the Grünewalder Stadium. The largest open-air rally the movement has ever organized. His words are greeted with indescribable ovations. . . .

The next day was a decisive one for Speer's fate, as he wrote in Spandau:

Our faltboats were packed and we were to take the train to East Prussia that same night, but when I went to take my leave from [Nagel] he told me that Hanke—who had by now become organizational chief [under Goebbels as Gauleiter] of the Gau Berlin—wanted to see me. And when I hurried over there he immediately said, "I've been looking for you everywhere. Wouldn't you like to build our new district HQ?" I said, "Yes, certainly, if you want to entrust it to me."

"I'll propose it to 'the Doctor' [Goebbels] today," Hanke said. A few hours more and I would have been out of reach in the isolation of the Prussian lakes. For years after that, I considered it the luckiest coincidence of my life. And now? Well, anyway, it shows us how dizzyingly one's whole life can be affected by a few hours more or less.

The building in Berlin's elegant Vossstrasse which the party had selected for their *Gau* HQ was in the government district, almost adjacent to the presidential offices. From a back window, Speer could watch the ancient President Hindenburg stroll in the garden accompanied by politicians and Wehrmacht officers. "Moving there," wrote Speer, "was also part of their 'respectability' campaign."

Again the commission was a conversion rather than new construction. "As I was always to do from then on," he wrote in Spandau,

> I worked day and night, easy enough for a 27-year-old with good nerves. A valuable support for me then was a young secretary of Goebbels's, who took on working overtime to type my tenders at night—just as she now works nights on my "case."

This, of course, was Annemarie Kempf, who by the time Speer wrote his "Spandau draft" in 1953, had been working for several years in Bonn, where she had accepted a job for the sole purpose of being close to the government people who might be helpful to Speer in the campaign she, Wolters and Hilde had begun to get him out of Spandau.

"Karl Hanke introduced me to him in the summer of 1932," she told me. "Speer had just been given his first architectural commission and a desk in a kind of reception area in his office. Hanke asked me whether I could help him [Speer] a bit in whatever time I had left over after working—yes, unpaid—at the *Gau* office. I had of course already heard about him when he painted Hanke's office red. So I said, yes sure, and I started giving him a hand. That's also when they began to give me a bit of money.

"If I had to say what my first memory is of Speer," she said, "it would be of a big table, topsy-turvy full of drawings, designs and color patterns and him reaching out and always finding whatever he wanted, without even looking. The order of his mind even then simply cut through—simply ignored—chaos." With her analytical memory, she thus, as Speer himself might have done, pointed me toward Speer's greatest secret weapon: his sharp, orderly mind. "He seemed very poised for someone so young," she said. "But frankly, I didn't pay that much attention to him—I was doing a million things; he was not the center of my life. I was not committed to any man, but to the purpose of a politically and socially changed world."

That's how the long relationship started for young Annemarie, idealistic daughter of idealistic parents. "I had an enormous capacity for enthusiasm," she said. "But not for Speer. He didn't—how shall I put it?—he didn't provoke a personal, an emotional reaction; even later, I think he never wanted it from anybody—indeed, to go further, he probably did everything to avoid it. If there was anything conspicuous about him," she said, "it was his stillness, his calm. In fourteen years, I hardly ever saw him lose it."

"I didn't see much of Goebbels," Speer wrote in Spandau. "They were preparing for the November election and he only came around a few times, hoarse and worn out, and didn't pretend much interest when we showed him around."

On October 1, exactly on time as Speer would always be, the conversion was completed. "Today we moved from our old, by now much-loved HQ to Vosstrasse, smack in the middle of the government district," Goebbels noted. "How long will it be," he wonders, "before we move again—to the Wilhelm-strasse [the Chancellery]?"

But they would have to wait. On November 6, 1932, after Goebbels joined in a wildcat transport strike in Berlin, the Nazis unexpectedly suffered a bad defeat at the polls, losing by more than two million votes. Speer and Margret had returned to Mannheim. "There wasn't anything else we could do," he told me. "The party didn't even have enough money to pay the few builders and painters I had working in the Vosstrasse. It was very embarrassing, both for me and Hanke." A week or so later, when Hitler came to see the recondi-tioned *Gau* headquarters and declared himself satisfied, Speer was already facing the fact that in Mannheim nothing had changed. There was still no work. By the end of that year, Willie Schelkes left.

"I opened my own office here in Freiburg," Schelkes said, when we talked there in 1985. "Actually it took off quite well, and when Speer, back in Berlin after the March elections had put the Nazis into power, asked me to join him there, I said, 'No, thanks.' I was doing all right in Freiburg, and also I wasn't that keen on the political scene that had emerged. You see, I had come out of the Bündische Jugend. We were also nationalists, but different from the Na-tional Socialists—certainly not anti-Semitic."

He was of course aware of the Nazis' anti-Semitism. "How could one not be?" he said. "Of course, one had no idea—I mean just no idea at all that they might actually kill, murder people. . . . That would have been incon-ceivable. Were they really thinking of that then? You know, I really doubt it. But anti-Semitism as a central issue of the campaign—yes, that one *couldn't not see*."

Nineteen thirty-two was Hitler's year of decision: Goebbels in his diary en-tries—and in *Der Angriff*—reported on the Führer's almost daily speeches from one end of Germany to the other.

Watching Hitler on old newsreels, and listening to his orations, it is almost impossible today to understand his phenomenal appeal to the masses. Con-ditioned as we are now to continuous visual confrontation with public per-sonalities, most of whom have been so streamlined as to lose virtually all real personality, the rawness of Hitler's delivery seems ludicrously amateurish now. But as Joachim Fest, writing one of the best analyses of Hitler the speaker, says,

... Those who think [his] success was entirely due to the unbridled, almost sensual extravagance of his delivery are mistaken; what it really was, was the calculated intermingling of frenzy and rationality. Standing always deadly pale and gesticulating in the light of projectors (after a few early failures he only spoke at night, with artificial lighting), hoarsely hurling his accusations and tirades, or almost whispering his declarations of faith and love for his listeners, he was always unfailingly in control. . . .

As possibly no other politician in our time, Hitler understood the art of public speaking, of pauses, of silence, of inducing, inciting and enflaming passion. "I am ashamed of it now," said Speer, "but at the time, I found him deeply exciting."

The political situation was so unsettled that in January 1933 Hindenburg reluctantly had to name Hitler Chancellor in a coalition government. Hitler accepted, on condition that there must be one more election—but promised that would be the last. That was one promise he kept.

Speer and Margret felt desperate about being stuck in Mannheim. Of course, they had no idea they could ever become part of Hitler's circle—the thought never entered their minds. But having had a brief taste of the excitement and energy of that world, Mannheim seemed almost unbearably stale. "A country cannot be governed by such people," Speer thought after attending a membership meeting of the intellectually abysmal local party group. Goebbels wrote in his diary,

> January 30/31, 1933: It is almost like a dream. Wilhelmstrasse is ours. The Führer is already working in the Chancellery. We are standing at the windows up there and watch as hundreds of thousands upon hundreds of thousands stream by their ancient President and young Chancellor and, by the light of thousands of torches, cheer and sing their gratitude. . . . The new Reich is born . . . victory after a struggle of fourteen years . . . we have reached our goal. The German revolution begins. . . .

Four weeks later, on March 5, following the controversial Reichstag fire and a number of acts of terror by the Nazis against the opposition, the Nazis, with the aid of a small right-wing party, were narrowly voted into power. And a week after this electoral triumph, Hanke telephoned Speer in Mannheim and asked how soon he could come to Berlin—there was work for him.

He had the oil changed in their small BMW sports car, they packed "a little suitcase" and he and Margret drove through the night to Berlin, where he reported to Hanke immediately on arrival. "Dr. Goebbels has just been named Propaganda Minister; you are to drive with him to see his new ministry," Hanke told him.

On March 11, 1933, Speer shared Goebbels's ceremonial arrival at the beautiful nineteenth-century building on Wilhelmsplatz, built by the famous architect Karl Friedrich Schinkel. Goebbels in his diary:

> March 11: The sun high in the sky shines warmly upon this wonderful Germany. The joy in work has returned. But an inspection of the working conditions in my new house . . . shows them to be very unsatisfactory. Workmen will have to be brought in to clean up these rooms. They'll have to get rid of all this stucco, and throw away the musty plush curtains: I can't function in these dark rooms; I need sunlight, clean, clear lines—I hate twilight. . . .

According to Speer, Goebbels then and there commissioned him, of whom he knew nothing except for the little conversion of the Gauhaus, to undertake the necessary alterations. Speer wrote,

> Again it was to be done in a great hurry, and again we worked day and night. Aside from designing some new furniture for the Minister's rooms—my first opportunity to apply what I had learned from Tessenow—I tried to respect Schinkel's interior designs.

Speer mentions in neither the draft nor *Inside the Third Reich* the difficulties he obviously had carrying out alterations in an architecturally protected building in a way which would both satisfy his own taste and meet Goebbels's requirements. The latter noted in his diary (his first mention of Speer was not until December 19, 1935):

> March 13: As I have encountered nothing but problems for the reconstruction of the building and even the furnishing of my own rooms, I brought in without further ado some experienced old building hands I knew from the SA and the same night they tore out plaster and wood lining and threw it all down the ceremonial staircase. The next morning, when the worthy old bureaucrats arrived (who will be the next I'll throw down those stairs) they murmured their warning that I could end up in prison for what I had done. They haven't caught on that our revolution will not be stopped either by old men, old files, or old stucco. . . . [After less than two weeks the work was completed.]
> March 23: Today my definitive move to my new ministry. The new rooms suit my taste; sunny, airy, full of light—here one can work. In the evening I celebrate the completion with my construction workers, all old comrades from the SA. . . .

Karl Hanke, who had been promoted to Minister's Secretary, continued his role as Speer's patron when, within days of finishing Goebbels's ministry, Speer saw on his desk the designs of the decor for the May 1 rally at Tempelhof Field. When he remarked that they looked like decorations for a shooting match, Hanke said that if he thought he could do better, to go to it. That same night, Speer designed a platform and behind it three "huge, marvelous flags," as he described them in Spandau, "two of them black-white-red and the one between them the swastika banner, all of them fifteen meters high."

This was to be the first time Speer gave his theatrical talent free rein. "I got the best lighting technicians and together we set up beautiful effects with huge searchlights." Hitler apparently loved it—so much so that Goebbels claimed the idea as his own. (Tessenow's comment to Speer—"They are big, that's all"—stung slightly, but Speer consoled himself with the thought that Tessenow "didn't understand the country's new spirit.") As far as Speer knew, Hitler was still unaware of his existence. His next commission was to redesign the interior of Goebbels's new residence and to add a large reception hall. Speer lightheartedly promised to have it ready in eight weeks. In Spandau he described what happened:

> When Goebbels told Hitler, he said it couldn't be done and Goebbels, no doubt to spur me on, told me of the Führer's doubts. . . . This started a wild 24-hour-a-day construction program in three shifts, with me snatching an hour's sleep here and there. Hitler, with his passion for construction, came over every few evenings to observe our progress and apparently continued to express his doubts—never to me, because Goebbels kept me in the background. . . .

It was during the preparation for the first party rally in Nuremberg after the Nazis came to power that Speer had his first encounter with Hitler, very soon after he completed Goebbels's residence. The rally organizers were having problems with the stadium decor and somebody remembered the architect who had designed the Tempelhof platform for the May 1 celebrations. Speer was flown to Nuremberg and, not unimpressed by this signal honor, rapidly drew some sketches—"not very brilliant," by his own admission. "For a background there I just replaced those huge flags I had invented for May 1 with a huge eagle, about twenty meters across, nailed to a truss like a butterfly."

The organizers didn't dare make a decision when shown the drawing, and sent the unknown young architect to see Rudolf Hess in Munich. "Only the Führer can decide this," said Hess, and he picked up the telephone. "He is here, you are going to his apartment."

"In Spandau I once teased Hess about his indecisiveness on that occasion," Speer said. "He immediately said he would never have dared make decisions such as this on his own; that Hitler reserved all important decisions for himself."

In the Führer's second-floor apartment near Munich's elegant Prinzregentenstrasse, he was immediately taken in to Hitler. "And there I stood," wrote Speer in Spandau, "before Hitler, the Chancellor, who, it would seem, had just taken a pistol apart that was lying in pieces on the table in front of him. 'Put your drawings down here,' he said without looking up, pushing the pistol parts aside. He looked at the sketches with interest, but never looked at me. 'Agreed,' he said then and, ignoring my presence, turned back to cleaning his gun. I left."

He didn't remember if he had said anything to Hitler. "I don't know," he said. "Probably '*Guten Tag*.'" No "*Heil Hitler*" and "*Deutscher Gruss*"? Isn't that what everybody was supposed to do? I asked.

"Well, I was never much one for raising my arm, not later either. I mean, it was so silly. Still, I should remember this," he said. But he didn't enlarge upon these details in either *Inside the Third Reich* or the draft. "I really think I just stood there," he said. "I was pretty confused, and that gun gave me a strange feeling." He laughed it away, as he often laughed away embarrassing topics. "It's probably all nonsense: all in my head, retrospective panic. I was probably just overcome with reverence," he said, mocking himself.

Although Hitler still knew nothing about him, as he would confirm to Speer a few months later, he was now on his way. That autumn, Hitler commissioned Professor Paul Ludwig Troost, one of Germany's grand old architects, to rebuild the Reich Chancellor's apartment in Berlin. "And here," said Speer, "I benefited from the fact that Troost and his wife, who was equally famous as an interior designer, lived in Munich and didn't know much about the Berlin building scene. Hitler remembered that some young architect in Berlin had finished Goebbels's flat in record time. And he gave orders that I was to join Troost's team to assist the building supervisor with local matters: the selection of building and decorating firms, and whatever else I could do to speed up the work."

This began with an inspection of the Chancellor's residence by Hitler, accompanied only, as would become the custom over the next months, by the building supervisor and Speer. "But you know, I had the feeling he didn't even see me; he never looked at me. During the many inspections he made of our progress—although he asked many questions, some of which were up to me to answer—he never addressed me directly. I came to feel that was just his way; I accepted it as, well, normal. Why should the great man talk to me? It was enough for me just to be there."

He hadn't thought it would lead to other commissions from Hitler. "This wasn't a commission for me; it was Troost's. And that seemed quite right to me—he was a famous man; I was nothing. I honestly think I didn't even dream of anything extraordinary then, because even though I was there, in his presence, and certainly always very aware of it, I was aware too that he seemed oblivious of my existence."

During these noontime visits to the site, on which Hitler, accompanied only by an adjutant with two SS men in civvies unobtrusively in the background, would ask the supervisor—and, incidentally, Speer—"terse questions" about progress of the various assignments, his manner apparently changed entirely when talking, as he always did, to the construction crew. "I must say," Speer said, "the way Germany's most powerful man walked about there, unguarded and apparently not a care in the world, did seem quite extraordinary, quite wonderful to me. It was—I can't call it anything else—an ideal picture of modesty, and the workers felt and reacted to this, soon just calling 'Hello' when he arrived.

"There again, you see, no standing at attention or '*Deutscher Gruss*'—they felt at ease with him. It was very evident that he felt at home on site, and this, you know, was likeable—he seemed intent on avoiding any kind of playing to the gallery.

"How to explain this," he said, "so that someone today can understand, can imagine what it was like? Here was this man, who, it seemed as if by magic, had already in a few months changed our country beyond recognition. Everything in Germany was flourishing. The unemployed were back at work; there were work projects everywhere—we lived and breathed optimism.

"I think it's true to say that his lack of affectation captivated me, and, yes, I enjoyed living in this aura of reflected glory. A lot of people—my students and friends at the university, and Hanke and that crowd—they all knew I was working on that site, and questions rained down on me, not about the work, of course, but about him. Was it true, they asked, that he came every day? Virtually alone? Unguarded? 'That's pretty reckless of him,' the party people said, but actually, everybody was delighted, just as I was."

And then one day, at the end of the usual noon visit, Hitler, who had never seemed to notice him, suddenly turned to him as he was leaving and said, "Come along to lunch."

"Can you imagine this?" said Speer. "Here I was, young, unknown and totally unimportant, and this great man, for whose attention—just for one glance—our whole world competed, said to me, 'Come and have lunch.' I thought I'd faint. Just that morning, climbing about on the site, I'd got some plaster on my suit and Hitler noticed me looking doubtfully at my dirty sleeve. 'Don't worry about that,' he said. 'We'll fix it upstairs.' And upstairs he took me into his private quarters and told his valet to get his dark blue jacket. And before I knew it, there I was, walking back into the drawing room behind Hitler, wearing his own jacket.

"The party elite were assembled for lunch—soon afterwards I would discover that he always had large groups for lunch—and Goebbels's eyes popped. He immediately noticed what I hadn't seen, Hitler's golden party badge, the only one of its kind. 'What are you doing?' he said sharply. 'What are you wearing there?'

" 'He is wearing my jacket,' Hitler said, and pointed to the seat next to him. 'Sit down here,' he said.

"Can you conceive what I felt?" Speer said again. "Here I was, twenty-eight years old, totally insignificant in my own eyes, sitting next to him at lunch, wearing his clothes and elected—at least that day—as virtually his sole conversational partner. I was dizzy with excitement."

IV

A Kind of Love

Nuremberg, June 19, 1946

SPEER [in his own defense]: In 1934 [*sic:* 1933] Hitler noticed me for the first time. It was then I got to know him [and] from that moment on I was able to practice my profession as an architect with undiluted fervor, for Hitler was fanatically involved in his patronage of architecture and confided immense commissions to me. Aside from building the new Reich Chancellery in Berlin and the venue for the party rallies here in Nuremberg, he confided to me the reconstruction of the cities of Berlin and Nuremberg.

Because of Hitler's passion for building, I was in [constant] close personal contact with him.... If he had been capable of [friendship], I would indubitably have been one of his closest friends....

GERMANY IN 1933 was in a ferment of excitement, of new measures and of new enthusiasms. The ideals of National Socialism were attractive, even though there were rough spots in their execution. But it was obvious that the new regime was effective in dealing with many of the most worrisome problems: unemployment, housing, the national self-image savagely dented by the defeat in World War I and the Versailles Treaty. Every positive element in the national life was the creation of and personified by one man, the Führer, the leader of his people.

Speer's first lunch with this demigod was to remain in his mind forever. He reported on it several times in varying ways: in the "Spandau draft," in *Inside the Third Reich*, and in additional recollections during our conversations. Here first is the "Spandau draft," marginally fuller than the book:

During and after this lunch was the first time that Hitler asked me some personal questions. Only then did he discover that it was I who had been the designer for the May 1 celebration.

"Is that so?" he said. "And Nuremberg, was that also your design? There was an architect then who came to see me with the plans; but of course, that was you, wasn't it? Well, I would never have believed that you could have finished the Goebbels project by the deadline."

He asked nothing about my affiliation or activities in the party. Later, when I had occasion to observe him with others from whom he commissioned works of art, I realized that with artists he simply didn't care [about their politics]. Aside from my career as an architect, what he did ask a lot about, as I remember, were the buildings designed by my father and grandfather.

It was quite obvious that this luncheon would be of decisive significance for my future. A few years later, Hitler came back to it: "I noticed you during my visits to the site," he said. "I was searching for a young architect to whom I would be able to entrust my building plans one day. He had to be young because, as you know, these plans extend far into the future. I needed someone who, with the authority I conferred upon him now, would be capable of carrying on after my death. And that man I found in you."

"By the time he said this to me—I think it was about two years later—" said Speer, "a great deal had happened; I had become part of his circle and even though my first assignments from him were comparatively minor, I realized that there was now virtually no limit to what I might achieve."

In *Inside the Third Reich,* he said that for a commission to create a great building he would have sold his soul like Faust and that here he had found his Mephistopheles. But did he actually feel this at the time?

"No, of course not," he said. "That's the whole point—I unreservedly admired him, could see no fault in him and honestly could hardly believe my luck."

He could hardly believe his luck because even this extraordinary patronage did not yet convince him of his talent as an architect?

"Yes and no," he said, after some hesitation. "People who have never experienced the effect this kind of man has on those around him can hardly ever understand this. Although my life very quickly was almost exclusively focused on Hitler, and indeed, Hitler became my life, there were of course other people around. And the extraordinary thing was that his liking for me having become so obvious, so quickly, almost everybody around him reacted to it. I mean, architecturally I was still a nobody. All I had proved so far was that I could be quick. But all of them began to treat me, who at twenty-eight was younger than any of them, like 'somebody.' I never analyzed any of this then, but at that time I never analyzed anything; I just accepted—gratefully, I think, rather than as my due—that I was going to have a wonderful life, wonderful beyond any dreams."

Very soon after that fateful lunch, Speer had become part of Hitler's small personal circle. He was expected to drop in at the beginning of Hitler's day in mid-morning for a brief chat or a bracing walk; was called in repeatedly at odd moments during the day to discuss architectural projects, or, more often, some of Hitler's sudden ideas and sketches; and had dinner with him and his intimates every night.

During that period, Hitler's close circle included his adjutants Wilhelm Brückner and Julius Schaub, both SS officers; Sepp Dietrich, the Commander of the SS Leibstandarte (Hitler's own SS regiment, entrusted with, among other things, his personal security); his two secretaries, Johanna Wolf and Christa Schröder; his personal photographer, Heinrich Hoffmann; and his longtime chauffeur, Julius Schreck, whose "peasant sanity" sometimes made Hitler face reality. "Hitler would sit in front with Schreck," Speer once told me, "and I would hear Schreck make caustic remarks about the fawning courtiers who surrounded him. He was the only person who was allowed such liberties."

Speer soon also regularly attended the daily luncheons which Hitler used to keep in touch with—and keep in check—his old political comrades; in those early years Goebbels and Göring also lunched with him almost every day.

Although wives (and Hitler's private secretaries) were frequently asked to the supper gatherings, and the entire household staff was invited in for the nightly film shows both in Berlin and Berchtesgaden, Margret for a long time was not part of this social scene. There were two reasons why this didn't strike her as strange: first of all (as she would tell me after we knew each other much better), she didn't dream that Speer's professional life with Hitler could ever include her in any way—Speer didn't tell her that a number of women were regular guests at his table. Secondly, however, something quite as momentous as Speer's own great experience had happened to her. She had long hoped to have children; in her concept of life that was the main purpose of marriage. And around the time in late 1933, when Hitler had entrusted Speer with his first personal commission—converting a large hall in the Chancellery overlooking the garden into a new office for him and adding a balcony in the front of the building from which he could accept the homage of the masses—Margret became pregnant. (Albert was to be born on July 29, 1934.)

During this pregnancy Speer was hardly ever home. During the last few months of 1933 and the first half of 1934 one commission followed another: all conversions, but all requiring completion in record time.

With Hitler's favor so manifest, approaches came from others too. At one of Hitler's luncheons that exhilarating winter, Göring asked Hitler whether it was Speer who was doing his residence. "Is he your architect [now], my Führer?" he asked. And although it was Troost—greatly admired by Speer—who was then still Hitler's official architect, Hitler blithely answered in the affirmative, whereupon Göring asked permission to have Speer remodel his own—only recently sumptuously refurbished—residence along the simple uncluttered lines of Hitler's new official home.

In order to be available to his patron at all times, Speer had rented a painter's studio a few hundred yards from the Chancellery to use as his office. For the first few months, his only full-time assistant would be Rudolf Wolters, just back from the Soviet Union.

Annemarie, now seventeen and still working for no pay in Goebbels's *Gauleitung*, came over sometimes to lend a helping hand. At the end of that year, however, she came down with TB and had to stay home for six months. After her recovery, she was at last given a paid job as editorial secretary at *Der Angriff*.

This was very different, she said, from the early exhilarating, easygoing days in the *Gauleitung* when there were no bosses or employees. As she put it in one of our early talks in Hamburg, they had all been "young people fired by their passion for a common purpose." It was not, she said, that at *Der Angriff* there were class differences—the party had been very successful in abolishing those. "No, the difference was that now it was no longer a *Kampf-zeit*, a time of struggle. The party was in government now, and there was more pressure on everybody."

I suggested that working among journalists must have given her some indication of the restrictive way the party handled news, but she disagreed. She hadn't known enough to be a judge of that, she said. But as individuals, she said, "one felt no restrictions on how one was supposed to feel, act, or for that matter, talk. I have thought about it a great deal," she said. "As far as our awareness of personal freedom was concerned, I can assure you, we felt if anything freer than before." Nobody, she said, cared whether or not they took part in demonstrations. "I don't like crowds," she said, "so I never did. It was the same later when I was in Speer's office; whether it was during the years of his architectural work, or afterwards as a Minister, there was no question of anyone being required to attend political functions. If they wanted to, they did; if they didn't, well, then they didn't."

Early in 1934 Speer, just put in charge of a section of the Workers' Front named "Beauty of Labor," was told to design a new kind of barracks camp for the workforce constructing Fritz Todt's *Autobahnen*. Speer was delighted. By asking him to develop a model installation with proper infrastructure—kitchens, showers, laundry rooms, comfortable recreation rooms and sleeping cabins with only two beds rather than the depersonalized dormitories which had been the norm until then—Hitler, Speer felt, was showing the social attitude he had always expected to find in the National Socialist Führer.

"Very soon afterwards, though," said Speer, "he only seemed to want big constructions, representational buildings. It was, oddly enough, Goebbels and Hess—he perhaps more than anyone else—who would later keep asking me when I would start designing houses for people to live in. But this was much later; eventually I promised Hess that for every representational structure I built, I would put up a housing estate. In the end, of course, it didn't happen. It would have had to wait until after the war."

The successful design of the barracks camp—which in itself was but a drop in Speer's overflowing architectural bucket at the time—had the interesting sequel of Margret's first meeting with Hitler. Not writing about it in the "Spandau draft," he mentions it in passing in *Inside the Third Reich* but enlarged upon it considerably during our conversations.

At the beginning of 1934, having completed the design for the barracks camp, Speer received his first official appointment—as department chief on Rudolf Hess's staff. (Later, Goebbels, not to be outdone by Hess in this curious wooing of Speer, would confer the same rank on him on *his* staff.) Speer told me that it was because of this new appointment that, in the early spring of that year, he was for the first time invited to one of Hitler's official receptions to which Karl Hanke, as a matter of course, also invited Margret. "And that was going to be a bit of a surprise for Hitler," he said, smiling.

We were walking in the woods above his Heidelberg house when he made that remark. What did he mean, I asked, and he replied, a little impatiently, that as he had never yet mentioned Margret to Hitler, she was bound to be a surprise.

I stopped dead on the path: I could see that in an ordinary patron-artist (or employer-employee) relationship, I said, the artist's private life could be immaterial. But this surely was different: here he had been talking for hours about the joy of Hitler's "total" interest in him, his many questions about his life for what was now almost nine months after that first lunch. How was it possible that his marriage of six years had never come up?

He looked puzzled. "I don't know," he said. Perhaps, he added, he hadn't mentioned Margret because he had been put off by Hitler's behavior toward Eva Braun, his mistress. "He hid her from everybody except his most intimate circle but at that point, even there, denied her any social standing and constantly humiliated her. It was a painful thing to see. She was really a very nice girl," he said, "young, shy and modest. I liked her right away and later we became good friends; she could use a friend."

He sounded sad about Eva Braun, and warm remembering her. Even so, his concern about Hitler's conduct toward his mistress didn't seem an adequate reason for his having virtually concealed from him Margret's existence. Without realizing it, Speer allowed me a glimpse of his complicated feelings for Hitler.

Clearly, Hitler's ill-mannered conduct toward Eva Braun, however disturbing to Speer, wasn't what had stopped him from mentioning his marriage. The real reason was that he had been in an emotional uproar ever since that first lunch. Speer was not—I repeat—a homosexual, but he was a deeply repressed romantic; Hitler created a strength of feeling in him he hadn't known he was capable of. He did not know what these feelings were, would not understand their "erotic" (rather than sexual) component until fourteen years later, when he read and, he told me, agreed with psychologist Alexander Mitscherlich's explanation (of which more later).

His not mentioning his marriage to Hitler was part of this complex storm of emotions into which, without ever making a conscious decision, he avoided injecting anything extraneous which might affect it, such as the fact of his marriage.

There had been a receiving line at the reception, Speer said, just Hitler,

Göring, Goebbels and Hess, with an adjutant to make the presentations. "When we came up to him and I said, 'My Führer, may I present my wife, Margret?' he looked taken aback, but then he just kissed her hand, as he did with all the ladies, and made one of his heavily gallant remarks to the effect that I had no doubt good reason for hiding my wife. But a little later—we were standing around having drinks before dinner—he came up to me and told the person I was talking with that he wanted a word with me. Then he said in what I thought was a curiously serious tone of voice, 'Speer, why didn't you tell me you were married?' I remember blushing, and I stammered something like I didn't know, and then he asked, 'How long have you been married?' I said, 'Six years, my Führer.' And then he asked how many children we had, and I said none. [He was obviously unwilling to say that Margret was then five months pregnant.] 'Six years married, and no children?' he said. 'Why?'

"All I could think was that I'd like the floor to open so that I could disappear. . . . Anyway, as you know, after that we had five children in fairly quick succession, and Ernst, our sixth, in 1943—or 1944, I'm not quite sure." (It was September 1943.)

It almost sounded as though he had the children for Hitler, I said. He looked up sharply but then deflected my impulsive remark with a shrug. "One might say so," he said. "Ah, well. . . ."

As Speer and Margret were standing together after dinner, Hitler joined them. "Your husband," he said to her, cupping her elbow, "is going . . . to put up buildings for me such as haven't been built perhaps for four thousand years."

"With pretty women," Speer told me, "he was, oddly enough, quite physical. He was always linking arms with them or, as he did that night with Margret, cupping their elbows."

According to several survivors of Hitler's circle I have spoken with, Hitler from that evening on took a special liking to Margret, often referring to her as "*Meine schöne* Frau Speer"—"My beautiful Frau Speer."

("Hitler liked Margret Speer very much," said Leni Riefenstahl, who was herself much appreciated by Hitler. "He presented her to me as '*My* Frau Speer.' She was very pretty, and he really liked pretty women. He didn't want to do anything about them, as a man: I think basically he just liked to be— and to be seen to be—surrounded by them.")

But aside from that, Hitler had as little of moment to say to Margret as he did to any of the other wives. With very few exceptions, light banter was virtually his only way of social intercourse with women. Unfailingly courteous to them, warmly concerned for their health, he was very ready to chat about

Above: Albert Speer's mother, Luise Mathilde, and his sixteen-years-older father, Albert Friedrich Speer, when they married in 1900, with her parents, Luise and Hermann Hommel. He was a self-made, immensely rich industrialist; she "counted the cubes in the sugar box." Speer's mother, a social butterfly as a girl, remained enamored of society life after her marriage. *Right:* Speer's parents forty years later, in 1940, in the garden of the Heidelberg house

Above: Albert Speer as a six-year-old *Left:* Bullied by his brothers Hermann and Ernst, Albert (right), as he commented, was "always trying" to get closer. *Below:* Even playing in the snow, exceptionally in the care of his mother, Albert (center) looks as if he wants to hide his face.

Above: Albert (left) and Ernst with Mlle. Blum, the Jewish governess who provided the first warmth in Albert's life. *Right:* Speer, in later life, never liked this photograph from the 1920s: he thought his forelock looked too much like Hitler's.

Above: Margret and Albert as an engaged couple, lunching near Oberammergau in 1925
Right: Snapshot taken in Berlin on their wedding day in 1928. Speer mentioned this photo nostalgically when writing to his children from Spandau. His parents were not at the wedding, and it would be seven years before Margret was invited to stay at the family home.

After Hitler noticed Speer at a construction site in 1934 and invited
him to lunch, the Führer and the young architect soon became ardent
collaborators on Hitler's megalomaniac plans for rebuilding Berlin
and other cities. "After spending time with Speer," said one observer,
"Hitler was always happy and relaxed."

Left: In Berchtesgaden, Hitler's mountain retreat, Speer rented this family house, deliberately some distance from Hitler's lair, the Berghof.
Below: One hundred yards below it, he built his architect's studio, later used as a U.S. Army VIP guest house.

Right: Speer leads an inspection trip of a trial section of the great Nuremberg Stadium, for which Hitler laid the cornerstone in 1937. *Below:* Hitler (right) plans new construction for Munich, accompanied by (from left) Martin Bormann, Speer, his adjutant Julius Schaub and F. X. Schwarz, a Nazi official.

The Cathedral of Light Speer designed for the 1934 Party Congress in Nuremberg, using every available antiaircraft searchlight around the arena. Speer said his lighting aimed to conceal the paunches of the marching Nazis. "This 'theatre'," he told the author, "will one day be the only design I'll be remembered for."

music, theater, actors and, with someone like Riefenstahl, to talk knowledge-
ably about the lighter type of films which, with Wagner operas and the Wild
West novels by Karl May, were his main distraction.

But he could show sharp irritation if, as a few did over the years, women
showed any sign of stepping outside or beyond their role. Both his second
senior secretary, Christa Schröder, a woman of some character and intelligence, and Henrietta von Schirach, the daughter of Hitler's photographer
and constant companion, Heinrich Hoffmann, and wife of Baldur von Schirach (head of Hitler Youth), were said to have run afoul of Hitler when they
attempted to argue with him. Christa Schröder dared to disagree with him
when he objected to young soldiers smoking. He pointedly ignored her afterwards for weeks. "It was a long time before he forgave my *faux pas*," she says
in her book *Er war mein Chef (He Was My Chief)*.

Henrietta von Schirach allegedly asked Hitler if he knew how the Jews in
Holland were being treated, after she had witnessed arrests in Amsterdam in
the spring of 1943. She said in her memoirs, *The Price of Glory*, that she was
forbidden access to the Berghof, where she had more or less grown up, from
that day on.

Speer told me he hadn't been there when she confronted Hitler. "But I
came soon afterwards and found the atmosphere very oppressed. Everybody
was going around with dark faces, because all of us felt very protective of Hitler. On the *Berg* one made it a rule not to bring up anything disagreeable, in
order to protect his short periods of rest." (Hitler's intimates often referred
to his mountain retreat as "on the *Berg*"—the mountain.)

I suggested that unless they were aware of what was happening to the Jews,
their concern about upsetting Hitler was difficult to understand. After all, he
talked a great deal about the Jews himself. But Speer was not to be drawn out.
"Of course, I myself wasn't present," he said again.

Interestingly, Nicolaus von Below, Hitler's longtime adjutant, wrote in his
memoirs that both of the Schirachs were banished, not because of her courage but because of her husband's. Baldur von Schirach and his wife had come
to visit Hitler at the Berghof on June 24, 1943. Hitler angrily recounted to
Below later that Schirach had insisted that a way had to be found to end the
war. "How does he imagine that can be done?" Hitler said to Below. "He
knows just as well as I that there is no way out anymore, other of course than
my shooting myself."

"Hitler was very put out over this conversation with Schirach," wrote
Below, "and made very plain that he wanted nothing more to do with him.
And indeed it was their last encounter."

Below, one of Hitler's relatively long-serving adjutants, was by all accounts an attractive and decent man. Loyal to Hitler virtually to the end, he was without doubt one of those whom, as I wrote earlier, Hitler would have sought to protect as far as possible from gaining knowledge which would have disturbed the harmony of their relationship. This was made relatively easy in his case, as virtually all Below's travels were in Hitler's company, thus never into areas where crimes were committed.

He was the man in Hitler's HQ closest to Speer; this is borne out by the fact that at a critical period in Speer's relationship with Hitler—when he returned to duty in the late spring of 1944, following a four-month illness and convalescence—he obtained the appointment of Colonel von Below as his liaison man to Hitler. The two men were as near friends as Speer could be with anyone; remarkably, Below and his wife, Maria, determinedly remained Speer's friends after Nuremberg, when almost the entire former Hitler circle turned against him as a traitor.

Below's book is probably a unique document in that it represents a serious attempt, by a comparatively uncomplicated but unfailingly sincere man, to come to terms with matters he would ordinarily have considered totally beyond him. Maria, as despairingly loyal to the memory of the Hitler she knew as her husband had been, told me that both of them were absolutely devastated when they learned from the Nuremberg trial what had been done in their names.

I spoke with Below many times on the telephone, but, sadly, he died not long after his book was published, before we could meet. In 1985, however, I spent several days talking with his wife in Detmold, a beautiful small city southwest of Hanover, where they lived in a charming small house (which they rented from Maria von Below's sisters), full of lovely objects and bright colors. Some years later, when she was staying with friends in a Bavarian castle, we spent another fruitful day together.

Maria was nineteen when she married Nicolaus von Below—she shortened his name to Klaus—in 1937. Still beautiful when I met her when she was nearly seventy, she must have been spectacular when her twenty-nine-year-old new husband brought her to the Berghof and introduced her to Hitler. She had not been nervous meeting him, she said.

"I came from a very different world, country rather than city, boarding-school education, a stable Protestant family life, a wonderful home, friends, parties—great security. I had no interest in politics whatsoever. I fell in love with my wonderful Klaus and I became interested in his flying world, but I was not all that pleased to come into that political world. Klaus, too, was entirely unpolitical—he was 'Luftwaffe.' No, I wasn't at all shy. You know, I was used to hunting and shooting, riding in tournaments; I had been out and about in my own world for years—within the safe boundaries of that world, I was left quite free. I was quite sure of my place in the universe. So meeting Hitler was fun rather than anything else—it was exciting, but I wasn't dazzled by the prospect.

"When everything came to an end," she said, "people fell over each other to represent life at the Berghof as horribly boring, with Hitler spouting endless nothings. Speer was guilty of that too—I say this despite our very real friendship with him. We were staying with the Speers at one point before his reminiscences were published, and I remember saying to him, after he gave us his manuscript to read, 'Now look, the Berghof chapter really isn't true. We all lived through this together, and Hitler's knowledge of history and art was phenomenal. Of course, the repetitions became tedious, but those first years particularly—how can you forget how excited we all were?' I asked him, 'And how many moments there were when we were happy?' "

(Speer had apparently given the von Belows his manuscript to read one evening, and then visited them—twice—in the middle of the night to find out what they thought of it. I was struck by this, as he had done a similar thing when I stayed with the Speers in 1978. As always, we had talked until after midnight. Margret had gone to bed hours before, and I finally suggested we should stop until the next morning. Half an hour later I was lying in bed, trying to read myself to sleep, when there was a soft knock at the door.

I got up, put on my dressing gown and found Speer, still fully dressed and clutching a thick sheaf of pages in both hands. "I suddenly remembered this tonight," he said. "I thought perhaps you could have a look at it and tell me what I could do with it." I took the manuscript from him and looked at it rather helplessly; it was well over two hundred pages, and I was already drowning in documentation from his archive. "I thought you might just leaf through it quickly now," he said. "It's profiles of all the men around Hitler," he said with his usual deceptive nonchalance. "I wrote them, with the help of questions from a British Intelligence officer, while I was held at Eisenhower's HQ in 1945."

I did read the manuscript through most of that night—it was impossible to put it down. And just as happened to the von Belows, around 4:30 a.m. I heard him come up the stairs and stop in front of my door. I confess I quickly—and pointedly—turned off my light. He tiptoed away then, but at 7:30 was waiting for me when I came down to breakfast. "What do you think?" he said, forgetting any "Good morning.")

"You know," Maria von Below continued, "I have never understood how diminishing the gifts Hitler so clearly did have made it any easier for people to live with having become bewitched by him. After all, he didn't gain the loyalty of decent and intelligent men by telling them his plan was murder and allowing them to see that he was a moral monster. He persuaded them because he was fascinating. But to say that today is almost blasphemy. I don't know why so many people want to deny that extraordinary . . . spark in him. I often noticed later on how aware he was if one was not awed. I mean, if one seemed at ease with him, I think he liked that. He was immediately very nice to me."

Wasn't it that he was nice to all women? I asked.

"He was very polite to women," she said in that soft upper-class voice, "but he was 'nice' to people in different ways."

Did she *like* Hitler? I asked.

She wouldn't or couldn't answer that. "You know, it's easy to sneer, to criticize now," she said sadly, after a pause. "My children keep asking me how I—how we—could bear it. But my God, it was a different world then. For me, married for two months then to the most wonderful man I could imagine, the world was Klaus; in a way, Hitler was immaterial to me. I suppose you would have thought me rather lightweight, flippant. Klaus was a serious man, and with him seriousness entered my life. Of course, the more involved he became with Hitler, the more difficult it all became. As what Hitler did, thought and also his moods became increasingly important to Klaus, he of course became increasingly important to me too."

But she was flabbergasted when I interpreted this as her having begun to think critically of Hitler. "Oh, no," she said quickly, "I was in no position to judge him. . . ." She stopped and then tried to go on. "Only much later— quite late, and afterwards, when we, when we found out. . . ." The sentence trailed off. It is a reaction I have found time and again among Germans of that generation, especially those who had been close to Hitler. His terrible crimes were always on their minds, particularly when they came into contact with foreigners. Few of them had the courage to talk about their feelings even as much as Maria von Below did.

Margret Speer, however much she came to be at ease with me, could never bring herself to broach this subject.

From the day of that first reception she had attended, Margret came to belong to the Berghof circle Speer had already been part of for months. "Yes, she was always there," Maria said. "In Berchtesgaden always in the evening, but also very often for lunch."

But Margret never joined the party, Speer said. "Why should she have? They were philistines. One of us was quite enough. Hitler didn't care."

I once asked Margret herself in her husband's presence why she hadn't joined. She shrugged. Did she disagree with the Nazis' aims (as one fanciful American TV film about Speer later claimed)? "She was not political," Speer said, conclusively, and Margret was silent.

"She wasn't ever political, that's certainly true," her daughter Hilde said a few years later, after Speer had died. "But I think she immensely enjoyed her very privileged position. I am quite certain that she remained entirely unaware of the horrors. Equally, however, though she never speaks of it, she fully believed what we learned afterwards, and I think she now feels terribly guilty for having lived so close to this man, Hitler, for having so benefited from this proximity. Perhaps too," she paused for a moment, "for having expended so much emotion—a kind of love you know—on such a . . ." Words failed her. "I think she cannot understand, or talk or perhaps even bear to think about it. I just wish she could—it might give her peace."

THERE CAN BE no doubt that the extraordinary relationship between Hitler and Speer, paralleling Hitler's growing passion for huge architectural creations across the land to perpetuate his reign, grew with great speed and intensity in the four and a half years between the day of Speer's first lunch with Hitler and the beginning of 1938, which saw the preparations for the annexation of Austria, followed within five months by the occupation of Czechoslovakia. But when reading the approximately one hundred pages Speer devotes to this period in his "Spandau draft," one is flabbergasted by the virtual blindness he displays to real events which were both indications of Hitler's character and clear portents of the future.

By the autumn of 1934, several things had happened which would be of decisive importance to Hitler and to Speer.

On January 21, Hitler's architect, Professor Troost, whom Speer had begun to consider his second teacher, died after a short illness. ("Congratulations," said Walther Funk, with his customary tact, when he met Speer that day in the ministry; he was then State Secretary in Goebbels's Ministry of Propaganda, later a fellow prisoner at Spandau. "Now you are number one.")

On June 30, the Nazis, led by Hitler himself, "executed" the leaders of the SA, including their Chief of Staff, Ernst Röhm, one of only four men with whom Hitler was on a first-name and "*Du*" basis. And on August 2, Hitler's most illustrious supporter, the Reich President Paul von Hindenburg, died.

In the "Spandau draft" Speer writes of the deaths of Troost and Hindenburg, but except for one sentence describing a "pool of blood" he came across on July 1 in a building he was converting for Hitler next to the Reich Chancellery, he does not mention the Röhm Putsch. (That was the official Nazi name by which they tried to justify the blood purge of June 30 as a "preventive measure" to stop a planned revolt against Hitler by Röhm and his radical cronies.)

In *Inside the Third Reich,* Speer—on his editors' advice—devoted three pages to the political background. "I didn't know about it ahead of time," he told me when I asked if he had been aware of the crisis. "People will never believe me or understand when I say this, but my mind was on other things. When it was actually happening, of course, one could hardly avoid being 'aware,' as you put it, as the streets were full of soldiers and there was a crisis atmosphere. And as I saw Hitler every day, I knew of course that he was very perturbed. But certainly I did not see it as it was considered historically and politically later. At the time, in my rather special, inside-but-not-inside position, one got a pretty one-sided view, you know.

"I think even now, after untold numbers of books," he said, then smiled, "including mine, it hasn't been possible to convey the very special—the peculiar, I now realize—atmosphere of Hitler's world. You see—and I only learned to understand this later, when I had so much time to read in Spandau—when you think of government and those who govern, say, in England or in France, these men are professionals, whether as intellectuals or as civil servants. There were of course such people in Germany, but they were not around Hitler. With intellectuals he felt inferior and therefore distrusted them. And the civil servants he loathed. Furthermore, except for his 'Old Comrades,' he both instinctively and deliberately avoided the professional politicians. Except for the army people who were basically not chosen by him but assigned to him and then—yes, approved by him, if he liked their faces— the people he chose as his men were amateurs. That, after all, included me. When I became his architect, I was perhaps not an amateur, for I had studied, but I was certainly a novice. Later, when he appointed me to what was then probably the most difficult job in the land, Minister of Armaments and subsequently also of Production, for heaven's sake, in that I was a rank amateur. But what I wanted to point to—what I feel has never been quite understood—is the emotional atmosphere which reigned around Hitler and which, believe me, was extremely difficult to avoid. In fact, one was drawn by it and indeed drawn into it—even someone who by nature," he smiled again, "is as unemotional as I am."

But he would surely not claim to have been unemotional about Hitler? "No, I wouldn't," he said. "Anything but. . . . Anyway, to return to the Röhm Putsch: Hitler was very emotional when he arrived back from Bavaria where, most exceptionally, he had actually taken part in the attack on the SA. As a rule, you see, he not only avoided physical but indeed visual contact with violence. During the later stages of the war this meant that, however important it was for morale, it was virtually impossible to get him either to visit the front or the bombed cities.

"But after the Putsch he was full of outraged descriptions of what they had found in the lakeside hotel where the SA leadership meeting had taken place.

He described much of it as a homosexual orgy. Nowadays people—I mean even people in society and the young—talk about these things as if they were nothing. But believe me, for most of us these were very strange and very unpalatable matters.

"And then, a few hours later, he returned, elated, from having called on Hindenburg, from whom he received very specific approval for the action. And that, you see, meant something, to me too: Hindenburg, after all, was 'The Old Man,' a proven man of honor."

Speer has written that Hitler's feeling of guilt (about ordering the murder of Röhm) was noticeable in his address to the Reichstag that night. But in our conversations he said he had not been aware of that until much later. "We weren't allowed [at Spandau] to read anything that had to do with the Third Reich, but when I came out I read up on it all, and then I recalled Hitler's mien and speech that night. You see, when it happened, just like when other things happened later—Austria, Czechoslovakia and so on—I suspect all I would have thought, if I thought at all, was that as Hitler was doing it, it had to be right."

During all those months Speer was rarely far from Hitler. "As I think about it now," he said, "I don't know how I managed to work as I did, because despite my frenetic work rhythm I had to be at his disposal whenever he called. Sometimes this was during the day, a call from an adjutant summoning me to lunch or for a chat about building—and this could be from Hitler in Munich to me in Berlin, and I'd have to drop whatever I was doing to get on a plane and join him. Or it was in Berchtesgaden, where he liked having those close to him around for lunch, for walks, for tea and then for his late suppers, the film shows and then long talks around the fire—these went on until late in the night, two o'clock or even later. Hitler himself never went to sleep until around 3 or 4 a.m. He was a night person; before the war he rarely started his day before 11 a.m. or even noon. It forced his staff into a kind of double life because the working day in Germany has always started at the latest at 8 a.m. But of course, at the time, one would never have thought of regretting—or complaining about—these crazy hours. Even though the long evening sessions were exhausting and, as time went on, increasingly boring, we were young and strong and always intensely aware of the honor of being one of the elect."

The Speers had rented a small hunting lodge in a village near Berchtesgaden. Speer thought it was ideal: close enough to be on call, but far enough away to retain some independence. But even this bit of privacy was soon to end. By mid-1935 Hitler had put at Speer's disposal a large house only minutes away from his own Berchtesgaden residence—the Bechstein Villa, where two other families, including that of Hitler's personal physician Dr. Karl Brandt, were already billeted. Anni Brandt, the doctor's wife, became Margret's closest friend, and Karl Brandt became friendly with Albert.

(Eleven years later, at Nuremberg, Speer discovered for the first time to what extent Karl Brandt, "an excellent man in every way," as he described him, had been involved, first in the Euthanasia Program—the killing of German and Austrian mentally and physically handicapped children and adults—and later with dreadful medical experiments.)

"Two years later," Speer said, "we moved a few hundred meters away: I had designed a studio building where my colleagues could work and live, and we had rented a large comfortable old house only steps away, which I converted into our residence. Basically that's where our children spent their early childhood."

Little is left now of Hitler's legendary Berghof. It is difficult to visualize Berchtesgaden as the lovely virgin territory it was in the 1920s, as Hitler's comparatively modest mountain retreat when he first came to power, or as the virtual fortress it became in the later years of his rule. Today, although still ringed by lovely mountains, the village of Berchtesgaden is spoiled by stylistically uncontrolled building. And on the neighboring Obersalzberg—Hitler's "berg"—almost nothing has been allowed to remain which would remind anyone of that time.

Hitler's Berghof (for which he was his own architect: Speer felt "it wasn't good, but it wasn't bad either") and all the adjacent buildings, including Martin Bormann's and Hermann Göring's rambling domains, were bombed or have been razed to the ground. All that is left is Bormann's folly, the Eagle's Nest, which, accessible only by a lift, he had built on top of the Kehlstein mountain as a surprise for Hitler's fiftieth birthday. It is now run as a public tearoom during the summer months. Down in the valley, the former playground of the Nazi elite—the dreary Hotel Platterhof, renamed Hotel General Walker—was used after 1945 as a U.S. Army R.-and-R. facility.

Ironically, the only two buildings to remain entirely intact, probably because, although only a fifteen-minute walk away, they were just outside the Berghof security complex, are Speer's two houses: his former studio, for years a VIP guesthouse for the U.S. Army, and the large family villa he rented in 1937 from the actor Gustav Fröhlich. Now belonging to a retired couple from the Rhineland, it appears unchanged from fifty-five years ago. The four rooms downstairs, they told me when we went to Berchtesgaden in 1991, are used exactly as in the Speers' time. At the front of the house, which overlooks the studio below, is a simple kitchen adjoining a sewing-*cum*-play room next door to a sitting room furnished in peasant style, with a beautiful white-tiled cylindrical stove which Speer designed. The other side of the house, overlooking the mountains, has a living room and a library with square-paneled ceilings, like the one Speer installed thirty-five years later in his studio in the Allgäu.

"I had no wish whatsoever to have us live too close to anyone else, including the Berghof," Speer told me, and he certainly succeeded. Because even when the mountain was densely populated and policed, his property was kept determinedly private. "Even now," the owner said, "in the winter it's quite a trick to drive up the 30-percent incline of the drive. When the Speers lived here, there was no drive. I always wondered why."

I said that Speer no doubt kept the house deliberately isolated. "I never like to live in places where I look out on houses or where people can, heaven forbid, drop in," he had told me. "I like waking up to the smell of grass and the sight of mountains, and I like to choose who I see, in my own house or elsewhere."

Rosa and Irmgard Irlinger are sisters, and natives of Berchtesgaden. In 1991, when we walked around the "berg" together, they were both good-looking women in their late sixties, Rosa unmarried ("Most of the boys died, didn't they?" she said), Irmgard a widow with two grown children. They were toddlers in the 1920s when Berchtesgaden was a small farming village with only one big villa on the mountain, owned by the immensely rich piano manufacturer Bechstein, who came on rare visits only, in the winter for skiing, in the summer for hiking. But the Irlingers, the Bechsteins' housekeepers, lived in the big house all year round.

Just above the villa was a small house belonging to the Bechstein estate. "It was quite primitive," Rosa said, "but like everything here, strongly built against the snow." And this little house, through the Bechsteins' generosity, was home for long stretches during those years "to a man called Herr Wolf. He almost always had one or two other men staying there with him," Irmgard recalled, "and he had many visitors; we saw them all because they had to climb up past our house."

One day shortly after Herr Wolf had first come there, their mother, as had happened repeatedly, ran up the path to fetch him to the telephone; the Bechsteins had the only phone on the mountain.

"That day, after he finished his conversation," said Rosa, "he asked our mother whether there was a shop anywhere nearby, and she said, yes, the little general store at the foot of the mountain. He thanked her, and we watched him walk down. And about an hour later—it was quite a climb—he came back, knocked on the door and gave our mother a box of chocolates and us each a candy stick."

They realized their mother knew this stranger well because she said—uncannily, they recalled the exact words and her tone of voice now, sixty-odd years later—" 'But why? What is it for?' and he said, 'To thank you for your kindness,' and she said, 'But that isn't necessary, Herr Wolf; we know you have no money.' And that was Hitler," Irmgard said.

As the years went on, the little house—vastly expanded by Hitler with a huge sitting room, one wall an outsize window looking out to the stupendous mountains and Salzburg in the distance—became his Berghof, and the name came to be used for the whole compound. The Bechstein Villa—presented to him by the owners—became the guest house for VIPs, and luxurious establishments were built by Göring, Bormann and others in Hitler's entourage. The buildings on the mountain farms—bought by Bormann, who set up a foundation which raised funds by "voluntary" contributions from industry and a levy on the post office for the use of Hitler's picture on stamps—were torn down to provide the space for these.

The Irlingers, now in Hitler's domestic service, were to live in a flat in the newly built SS security quarters nearby. Before they moved in, Hitler would walk over almost every day to see how the building progressed. To the Irlingers, Hitler always was and, in a way, remained the "Herr Wolf" they knew as small girls. "Of course, life changed on the mountain," Rosa said. "It was very quiet when we were little. And then, after 1933, it became one vast construction site. Everybody our parents knew left; all the peasants, having sold their land to Bormann's foundation, went to live either on the other side of the mountain or in other parts of Bavaria altogether."

They looked puzzled when I asked if the people were angry about having to leave. "Why should they be?" Irmgard asked. "Bormann paid fairly, and people loved Hitler." Like their own parents, they said, most of them voted for him.

The change on the mountain was not only the additional security and the construction. "Above all," said Rosa, "it was people." Very suddenly, they said, "swarms of people started coming, by train, buses, cars, to tramp up the mountain and stand as close to Hitler's house as they could get, chanting rhythmically, 'We want to see our Führer!' until he came out. And then they would scream, applaud, sob, laugh hysterically, even fall to their knees." Rosa shook her head. "We could never understand it. To us he seemed no different; he was friendly, smiled—he was just Herr Wolf."

When Speer and Margret first came to live on the mountain in 1935, their first son, Albert, was one. Hilde was born in 1936, then Fritz in 1937; Margret, like her mother's shortened name, in 1938; Arnold in 1940; and Ernst in 1943. They lived there most of the time until almost the end of the war.

Margret talked to me about all her children, but the two she appeared to feel most at ease with were Arnold and Hilde. Speer spoke almost only about Hilde. Both of the parents—for different reasons—were eager for me to meet her, which I finally did in Berlin in 1982, after many telephone conversations.

Speer was right about her resemblance to her mother. She is blond, blue-eyed, with a delicate face and a slim build. I suspect that Margret must have had a backbone of steel to achieve what she did—bringing up six children on her own—and she certainly passed that on to her eldest daughter. They are both intensely private women, though for different reasons: Margret was essentially inarticulate, perhaps because no one ever asked her to express herself. Hilde can talk to anyone and about every subject under the sun—but only by her own choice, and preferably not about herself.

She and I have talked in many places over the years: in Berlin, either in the apartment-hotel where I often stayed for weeks or in her large house which she shares with several friends and her husband, Ulf (they all live independently, but in a kind of community on separate floors—Hilde shared hers with their two children, Ruth and Moritz, both of whom are now grown); in Munich, where my husband and I had an apartment for the first years of my work on this book; and in London where she came to stay with us. I found in her some of her father's best qualities: curiosity, discipline, humor and of course that exceptional brain. In her, however, all this was very much married to humanity. She is a highly independent modern woman and an exceptional mother—contrary to her father, she knows how to love.

Hilde's memories of Berchtesgaden are in some respects almost idyllic, in others they have become traumatic. "My father, as I remember, only came rarely," she said. "Not more than once a month. I suppose it was only when Hitler was there, though I think he came less often than Hitler. Hitler spent a lot of time there in the years before—and the first years of—the war, much less later. I went up to see our house again in the 1950s and the people who owned it then showed it to me. It made our life up there come back to me with extraordinary vividness."

She had described it to me as "a small farmhouse," and the Speers' life there as "simple" in comparison with the massive Berghof, the Bechstein Villa and the Bormann and Göring properties. The Speer house is in fact fairly imposing but, given their life-style, one can imagine the family being cramped for space; the Speers and their children had a live-in staff of five: a housekeeper, a nurse-governess, two maids and a cook.

"My mother, and my father too, you know, no matter what he designed for Hitler, were anything but ostentatious," said Hilde. "Later I thought how right our parents had been to have us live a 'natural' life, as much like the village children as possible. Maybe it was my mother—she certainly seemed to make all the decisions about us children." She remembered those early years as a happy time. "Looking back, I think it's amazing how little we were aware of security or restrictions of any kind. Particularly when we were small, I remember Hitler going on those walks—no guards; he'd always walk past our house. I don't remember any fuss. If I compare it to the circus now around official people, then the simplicity of life there seems quite astounding."

During all those childhood years on the mountain, she doesn't remember ever being bothered by her mother, the household staff or for that matter her father "with Nazi-ideology nonsense." "My father, of course, we hardly ever saw. I got to know him later, really from the letters when he was in Spandau, but I think the boys and my sister feel they never got to know him at all."

She remembered vividly one day when she was walking through the village with her governess, Paula. "I greeted a passerby with '*Heil Hitler.*' I don't know why I did; normally we always said '*Grüss Gott.*' I think something made me want to try it out, to conform. And I remember very clearly Paulchen saying, quite sharply, 'Don't do that! Don't say that!' And I remember feeling that I had done something wrong, but not daring to ask what and why."

She is certain that her mother chose the staff very carefully, deliberately selecting "unpolitical" people. "I don't think my father had anything to do with that—my mother was in charge of the household and the children. She would never have consulted him about such matters; he wouldn't have required it or had the time for it.

"I don't think she acted out of ideological opposition—I wish it had been, but I don't think so. Just as my father never needed or wanted my mother to involve herself in politics in the sense of joining any of the women's organizations, even in an honorary capacity, by the same token I think my mother didn't want political people around the children." She stopped, and thought for a long moment. "You know, I can't recall a single occasion when—except for Hitler on his walks—any of the bigwigs came to our house on the Berghof. I've never thought about it before, but given the extent to which my father was part of it all and lived in their midst, perhaps that was rather odd."

She had known the Bormann children in Berchtesgaden, and was particularly fond of Irmgard, the third oldest of nine children. "Irmgard was seven when I was six, and she was extraordinarily kind to me at school; I adored her."

But she hadn't known the parents. Hitler's abolition of class differences notwithstanding, there were of course huge cultural gaps between various members of his circle, such as the Speers and the Bormanns, quite apart from the political differences which made Martin Bormann eventually become the bane of Speer's life.

Hilde didn't remember ever talking to Bormann's eldest son (and Hitler's godson), Martin, who, during many conversations I had with him and his wife, Cordula, after meeting them in 1991, also told me about life on the Berghof. He was six years older than Hilde. "I had been lazy at school so my father sent me to boarding school," he said. "I was only home during holidays, but I don't remember any social life involving my mother," he said. "She was totally wrapped up in her family—her husband and us, that was her life."

I usually talked to Martin and Cordula in their charming small flat in a hill village in the Ruhr. They are people of enormous warmth and sincerity, and also became friends of mine. Cordula had been a nun, and a missionary in Africa. Martin is a former priest, a deep and thoughtful man who turned to teaching after leaving the priesthood. I asked him once whether, when the war was finished and he discovered the terrible things the Nazis had done, he continued to love his father.

He pondered the question for a long time. "Yes," he finally said. "Love from a son for a father is not something one bargains about. I think it has nothing to do with the father's qualities or acts—it simply *is*. I deplore and despise what they did—what *he* did—but yes, and it is a puzzle, the love remains."

Martin, deliberately choosing, when still very young, a vocation that offered him time, help and the means for contemplation, has spent a lifetime working through his conflicts about his father, about Hitler and about the terrible Nazi crimes. It has made it possible for him to achieve a degree of liberation.

Hilde on the other hand, though a spiritually free human being, has enormous difficulty in talking about Hitler and the life near him in her childhood. She does not, or cannot bear to, remember the occasions Clara Samuels, the housekeeper, had told me about, when Hitler dropped in, drank cocoa and played with the small Speers. She cannot accept that there were times when he acted like a kind and normal man, and when—perhaps—she even liked him. She insists that, however often their mother might have attended Hitler at the Berghof—daily, when he was in residence—the children hardly ever went there, except on formal occasions "in Sunday dresses, bow in hair," reminded to hold out the right hand properly to shake hands. "I hated it," she said. "Well, perhaps that's putting it too strongly, but I certainly disliked it—I hated the fuss."

As Hilde's letters to her father in Spandau show, she took a strong moral position very early and she has been true to it to this day. Nevertheless, she feels extraordinarily sensitive about her childhood. Despite my understanding and my enormous liking for her, I felt that the quality of her mind and her capacity for remembering were so remarkable and so significant that I persisted with questions when I might otherwise have stopped.

But she simply rejected a question concerning her feelings about Hitler, said she didn't feel like going into that and kept coming back to the formality and rarity of these occasions. She obviously didn't know of the photographs on record in which the Speer children, dressed in the usual Lederhosen and Dirndl, surround Hitler, and other photos of Hitler walking with little Hilde—bow in her hair—hand in hand. "I had to hand him a bouquet for his birthday—I hated it," she said, her voice tense.

I tried once more, implying that surely she couldn't have hated him, the revered Führer, that all children loved him. But she simply cannot bring herself to separate her contempt and loathing for Hitler now from whatever she might or might not have felt then. A retroactive, objective consideration of herself and others about Hitler is impossible for Hilde—her feelings are too raw and run too deep.

"What did small children know?" she finally said, but she said it with despair.

V

A Shared Devotion

THE MID-1930S were years of recovery and expansion in Germany. The Nazi regime laid particular emphasis on image building in every way, whether with press and film propaganda or in grand construction projects. The latter were particularly important to Hitler, who originated all of them, added to the architectural concept of most of them and prided himself on his understanding of every detail in the designs.

By the autumn of 1934, Speer was working on a number of fair-sized projects and—always linked to his architectural work—had also been given several party titles. His first mammoth commission from Hitler, which he received in 1935 following a host of smaller ones, was the construction of a huge complex for the annual Nuremberg party rally. The cornerstone was solemnly laid by Hitler in September 1937, and completion was scheduled for the party rally of 1945. It was to cover an area of 6.5 square miles with a stadium 1,815 feet long and 1,518 feet wide; the stands, more than 300 feet high, were to hold four hundred thousand spectators—the largest structure of its kind in the world. Two years after Hitler had approved the designs, Speer had begun to build the Marchfield, the processional avenue which would lead up to the stadium; it was to be the only part of the plan that would be completed before the war. Speer's design, exhibited as a model at the 1937 Paris World's Fair, received the Grand Prix. Architecturally, that last prewar World's Fair was Speer's triumph, for he was also awarded a gold medal for his German pavilion.

I asked him whether this success made him feel more confident about his talent, but he did not answer directly. "You know, what I find myself incapable of doing," he said after a long moment of thought, "is to separate, to classify in retrospect, if you like, my reactions and feelings. I tried to do that in Spandau, and up to a point I succeeded with respect to my years as a Minister. But now I think that both there and later, when I was writing, or rewriting my reminiscences, I didn't succeed so well with the years before.

"I think I now know why." He paused once more. "In my years of architecture I think it was my heart that ruled me rather than my brain," he said, thoughtfully. "Paris, you see, I loved, so just being there was wonderful. But simply being given the chance by Hitler to do the work—for him and for Germany—that was . . . happiness. It was all emotion, you know," he continued, "very deep and pleasurable emotion. I mean, I couldn't categorize these emotions, either then or later. Were my feelings mostly for the man, Hitler? For the country, Germany? For the work? I didn't know nor, I suppose, did I need or seek to know. It was enough to *feel* something; above all, it was enough to *do* something.

"The prizes, well, I'm sure it must have pleased me, pleased all of us. Because, don't forget—I certainly never did—that I didn't work on my own. By the time of the Nuremberg project, and Paris, I had assembled a staff of brilliant young people. Later, while I was at Spandau, many of them made huge architectural careers." (He pointed this out without bitterness, though later in our talks his tone would change.) "But it was the work that gave me joy, its purpose that gave me fulfillment. Now I quite like the idea of having won the prizes, because I suppose it does prove something about me as an architect, whatever I myself have come to think."

Most of Speer's architects, a number of whom contributed to the fund Rudolf Wolters set up when Speer was sent to Spandau, readily acknowledged the help they had had from him in their early career. Two who became very famous in the twenty years of his imprisonment would in fact suggest his joining their firms after his release. But not everyone agreed that Speer had always remembered the contributions made by his "staff of brilliant young people."

In 1986, Leni Riefenstahl suggested I should go and see a former cameraman of hers, Walter Frentz, who had known Speer since their student days in Berlin and who, thanks to his help, had early in the war become the official Luftwaffe cameraman at Hitler's HQ—a safe and fascinating job.

Frentz was a tall, slim man with a rugged face; he and his pretty wife, a painter, lived what looked like an idyllic life in a rather splendid house on Lake Constance, surrounded by paintings, books and picture-book scenery. What was strangely absent was almost any photographic evidence of his years of activity around Hitler. He claimed that most of it was destroyed or lost after the war (later I saw some of his photographs reprinted in a radical-right book).

Although charmingly talkative—one could see that he had excellent cocktail-party manners—he was exceptionally uninformative. Full of agreeable small talk, he claimed to have forgotten about almost everything connected with Hitler's HQ, couldn't recall a single person or event he photographed or any of many dozens of Hitler's midnight tea gatherings he attended.

The exception to this amnesia (from which a lot of people suffered after having lived close to Hitler during his lifetime) were his memories—and lovely romantic photographs he dug up—of his friend Hans Peter Klinke. "He was a Tessenow student, like Speer," he said. "We shared a flat in Berlin at the time."

Annemarie Kempf, as well as Riefenstahl, for whom Frentz certainly felt great admiration and gratitude, had told me that Frentz had been a friend of Speer's, but they were both mistaken. He felt exceptional bitterness toward him. Klinke, he said, had been Tessenow's most brilliant student, though it was Speer whom, "incomprehensibly," Tessenow appointed as his assistant. Frentz said it was Klinke's work on the designs for the Tempelhof Field—the Maifeld—that launched Speer's career.

His recollection of the sequence of events that led to that assignment for Speer was muddled by his curiously acute anger—he entirely ignored the fact that this was not the first but the third commission Karl Hanke, then Goeb-bels's press and public-relations assistant, had entrusted to Speer. Frentz, to all appearances, is not an emotional man, but the moment he speaks of Klinke, he has tears in his eyes.

"The way this commission came to Speer," he said, "was purely coinci-dental. Hanke lived on the ground floor of the same house in Grünewald where Speer and his wife lived, and Hanke asked his landlady whether she didn't know an architect." According to Frentz's unlikely story, she replied that Hanke didn't have to look far; there was an architect living on the third floor; he might do. So, said Frentz—an interesting example of how myths develop in astonishing detail—"Hanke went upstairs, rang the bell, asked Speer whether he'd like the job, and that was that. Speer got the commission to design a model, and he asked Klinke to help him. Hans Peter never came home for two nights—they spent three days and two nights designing it be-tween the two of them. Speer took it to Goebbels, who was delighted, and it was as a result of that, that Goebbels later commissioned Speer to design his ministry."

In reality, as we have seen, the sequence of events, extending over a period of several years, was the other way round and not nearly as accidental. In *Inside the Third Reich*, Speer wrote that the design was produced in one night, and did not mention that he had help. But when we talked about his archi-tecture, he repeatedly emphasized the team aspect of most of his work. Frentz (talking to me after Speer's death) disagreed bitterly. "For Tempelhof and later jobs," said Frentz, "Klinke really did all his designs, but Speer never gave him credit for it."

He himself met Speer at the end of 1929. "He had unusually close relation-ships with 'his'—that is, with Tessenow's—students," Frentz said. He didn't think, as Speer—and Wolters—had implied, that it was because the students were poor and the Speers, having some money, provided a social focus for them. "The students weren't that poor," he said. "Klinke, after all, lived with me; he did all right. I did too."

Manifestly unwilling to attribute it simply to Speer's being a pleasant man, he said it was probably because of a shared passion for sport: sailing, mountain climbing, kayaking. "Speer's wife was pretty sporty too," Frentz said. "She was usually along; she was a merry sort of girl, with a nice open way with people, lots of laughter. And if he made one of his stiff remarks, she'd try to kid him out of it. I can hear her now, it happened so often: 'Albert, come on. Relax.'

"Speer never showed his feelings," Frentz said—and, as happened time and again the day I spent with him, immediately came back to Klinke—" . . . never once to Hans Peter when he was alive."

Hitler, it was true, had taken a shine to Speer, he said, and Speer made use of this. "We all used whatever connections we could—who could blame him? It was Speer who started me on my career and I didn't say, 'No, thank you,' just because I knew him privately. Leni Riefenstahl, getting ready for her Olympics film, asked him whether he knew any cameramen, and he pointed her my way. She invited me to come and see her in her flat. I didn't like her as an actress, but I had loved her *Blue Light*, which was also the film that brought her to Hitler's attention—he loved it too. Well, when we met, I showed her two films I had made, one on Eskimos, the other on kayaking, and she then made me her cameraman for the Olympics film. We found we had very much the same attitude toward film: I hated wastefulness and so did she; I would shoot eight hundred meters of film and all of it could be used; others shot two thousand and hardly any of it was usable.

"Speer never became a 'friend,' " he said, "but after this, we ran across each other quite a lot in the course of working." He said that when Speer worked on his famous "Cathedral of Light," he had designed the poles carrying the searchlights vertically. "I said, why not curve them, like a tent? And he did." He laughed. "He didn't tell anybody it was my idea, but that was all right."

Oddly enough, Leni Riefenstahl, a few weeks before that day, had told me that the Cathedral of Light had been *her* idea, and she too had smiled and said it didn't matter that Speer had not publicly acknowledged this. If Speer had not been dead by then I might have gotten the three of them together to test these claims—I'm sure with his delighted cooperation. We probably would have found when tracing it back, that this idea—like so many others—rather than being one person's creation, was quite probably the result of shared reflections and shared skills.

"Anyway, I didn't mind," said Frentz. "I was doing all right, and that was, after all, thanks to him. It was very different for Klinke, who gave him not just one idea but did so many of his designs.

"Hans Peter was an extraordinarily unassuming man," he said, showing me a photography book he had done on kayaks—a sport for which he and Klinke (and Speer too) had a passion. The photograph he pointed out to me was of an extraordinarily good-looking young man, almost nude, deeply bronzed and muscular—the ideal Nordic male of Hitler's dreams. "He was a great man, a great spirit," Frentz said, his eyes brimming. "Architecture was the passion of his life—until the advent of Hitler, when he became as passionate a National Socialist as he was an architect. It was totally incomprehensible and reprehensible how Speer failed to grant him recognition, especially from Hitler, whom he worshiped. As I told you, I know I have Speer to thank for my first big chance—and others; nonetheless, I can never forgive him for Klinke."

Frentz is convinced that it was out of despair over this lack of recognition that Klinke finally volunteered in 1943 for active service with Sepp Dietrich's Waffen SS. "After three weeks on the Russian front," said Frentz, "he suffered a bad head wound. Speer sent his personal plane to fly him to Berlin."

It is curious that Frentz believes his friend to have been so neglected, for the record suggests otherwise. While Klinke was lying in Berlin's West End Clinic, in and out of a coma, Speer got Hitler to award him the title of Professor. The Führer conference of April 14 reports the text of Speer's request:*

> Peter Klinke has been my collaborator on all plans since 1933, thus has played a part in all [architectural] designs for ten years. Such [team] operations require of a man of outstanding artistic excellence an exceptional degree of self-effacement, for he must always forgo recognition of his personal achievements. This title will go a little way to acknowledge the great significance of his contributions to many of our designs since 1933.

And the notes record Speer's additional comment that presentation of this title had been planned for after the war, when Klinke intended to take up private practice, but was being conferred now because he had been severely wounded in action in the East. When Klinke died a few weeks later, Speer delivered a eulogy before his assembled family and friends which Wolters recorded in his ministerial *Chronik*:

> We met in 1929 when you were 21 and a student [of Tessenow's] in Berlin. . . . It was your personality that caused you to become the leading student respected by all, with a rare relationship of trust between [us]. . . .

---

*Speer himself jotted down the main points discussed after every conference with Hitler. This collection has been preserved under the title *Führerbesprechungen* and is in both the Speer and Wolters Collections in the Koblenz Federal Archives.

You collected around you the most active of the student body and this eventually grew into our small team of collaborators that has not changed in these past ten years. Those who helped me then to begin my life's work as an architect remain at my side now and will pick up where we left off when the war is over. . . .

For ten years, you shared your artistic knowledge and were my closest collaborator . . . who contributed to every design. . . . Your reward for this selfless work was to be the buildings you would build yourself for the Führer after the war. It was what was intended for you, and all of us are desolated that this is not to be. German art has suffered a terrible loss with your death. . . .

The landscape architect Willie Schelkes, who rejoined Speer's team in 1935, felt no resentment about the comparative anonymity of its members. "It was always quite amazing to most of us," he said, "how often Speer took us along to his meetings with Hitler, encouraging us there to take part very freely in the discussions."

Speer did not formally present his associates to Hitler on these occasions or when Hitler—as he often did—visited Speer's studio. "It wasn't the way we worked," Schelkes said. "One didn't expect that; I mean, just think who Hitler was. But when we spoke up in those discussions, Speer always said, 'This is so-and-so,' or 'You remember Herr So-and-So, my Führer.' But anyway, I certainly always thought that Hitler was very aware that we were a team. People said at the time that the ability of creating and leading a team was one of the talents Hitler most appreciated in Speer."

It was Speer's reconstruction of the Zeppelin Field in Nuremberg early in 1934 that won him his first popular acclaim. An assembly was held there every year for the political functionaries of the party. It was for this he created the Cathedral of Light that Frentz and Riefenstahl had talked about—130 antiaircraft searchlights placed around the field at intervals of forty feet, sending soaring into the sky individual beams which merged finally into a general glow. "It had the advantage of dramatizing the spectacle," Speer said, "while effectively drawing a veil over the not-so-attractive marching figures of paunchy party bureaucrats. As you see, my critics who call me a pragmatist are quite right: I was pragmatic even in dramatic designs. Funny, isn't it," he added, "that if anything it will finally be only these, well, yes, dramatics I will be remembered for."

Certainly, as far as his architecture is concerned, probably more films and photographs of these "dramatics," as he called them, survive than of anything else he did or planned to do. One person who enormously admired this side of his talents and whom he in turn greatly admired and liked was Leni Riefenstahl.

"Speer," she told me in 1986, "was an extraordinarily attractive and impressive man, and I felt this from the moment I met him in 1933, when, after all, he was only twenty-eight. To me, he became the most important—and certainly the most interesting—man in Germany after Hitler."

We were talking in her enchanting modern house set amidst a garden full of blooms and flowering bushes in Pöcking on the Starnbergersee, just under an hour from Munich. Her life, she said, had been very hard since the end of the war; she was being continuously accused of things she had never done during the Nazi time, and had to sue numerous people for libel. "It has taken all the money I had or could earn, even though I usually won." When I remarked on the beauty of her house—the timber-framed glass walls of the ground floor and the flower-filled wide terraces above—she said quickly that it was a very inexpensive prefab. (Many of those who had been close to Hitler felt defensive afterwards about evidence of success and material well-being.) "I saw it in a catalogue, ordered it, and within days—well, a few weeks—there it was, all ready."

When talking to the more controversial personalities from this period, it is always necessary to detach oneself. One can be aware of their evasions and untruths and yet learn from their lives and indeed admire their achievements. This was very much the case with Leni Riefenstahl. There is no doubt whatever that she was a monumental filmmaker; there is no doubt either that, having made some wonderful movies, she put her immense talents to appalling use, in Hitler's service. It was for him and only for him that she made her two most famous films: in 1934, *Triumph of the Will,* her paean to the Nuremberg Party Congress and to Hitler, and in 1936 her hymn to physical perfection, considered by most a glorification of Hitler's esthetic—her two-part film *Olympia* of that year's Olympics. Whatever she now admits or denies, she remains, as I write, one of the last surviving mammoth personalities of that era, which had brought both her and Speer such great triumphs.

Still remarkably good-looking when we met, she lived with her talented young assistant, Horst Kettner, who is ferociously protective of her and almost angrier than she herself—and less restrained in his frankly anti-Semitic comments—about the continuing attacks against her, and their alleged originators. He is not only in charge of the astounding photographic archive he has created for her, and of her darkroom, but worked with her on her assignments in Africa, notably her extraordinary photographs of the Nuba tribe. Since 1970 they have worked together on underwater photography in the Red Sea and the Indian Ocean, where she has done what is perhaps her most spectacular work since the war. At the time I met her, he was looking after her welfare—he also cooks and cleans when necessary—while she was completing her immensely long autobiography, published in Germany in 1987 and in English in the early 1990s.

Like many others in Germany who were profoundly involved with Hitler, she tries almost obsessively to defend herself against the one accusation that seems to matter. She said time and again to me (and in her book) that she had never been anti-Semitic. "I told Hitler once that he shouldn't attack the Jews, that I could never dislike anyone because they were Jews or Negroes, and he said, 'You are young. You will learn to understand.' " Her book is full of such quotes—things many of us may have wished in our daydreams we had said to Hitler, but of course would never have dared say, even if we had had the opportunity. She is a complicated woman with formidable talents, and may well have come to believe her fantasies. Like practically every other contemporary witness I have talked to, she has no memory for dates, and many of her claims and quotes are contradicted by the Goebbels diaries, in which he meticulously noted each night everything he did, everyone he saw and a résumé of what had been said that day.

Goebbels, too, in his last nine years, wrote for posterity. On October 21, 1936, he concluded a very advantageous publishing contract for his diaries, with a huge advance of RM 250,000 and a guarantee after publication of RM 100,000 a year. One must never forget when reading his remarks that they represent *his* attitudes and *his* information at the time, which in our time may well be seen as disingenuous and often outrageous. Certainly his notes from 1936 on were addressed to future readers in a victorious Reich. It was essentially for them, for their appreciation of this glorious part of their history, that he recorded it. This point of view, however—and he stands almost unique in this respect—virtually guarantees the accuracy of his reports at least as far as they involved dates, policies and meetings with Hitler and his cohorts: the war won and the diaries published, these officials would no doubt have been the first to read them. What are less reliable are his reports and analyses of events abroad and, understandably enough, the personal aspects of the diaries. If one has some knowledge of the period and Goebbels's life after the Nazis came to power, one notes with interest his careful avoidance—after his contract was signed—of any mention of his almost compulsive sexual activity, about which he had previously written so frankly. He became remarkably discreet about his wife, Magda; his great love, the Czech film star Lida Baarova; and his longtime favorite assistant and State Secretary, Karl Hanke, with whom the ten-years-older Magda Goebbels, in despair over her husband's endless infidelities, in 1938–39 conducted a mutually passionate love affair until Hitler, using Speer as a messenger and mediator, ordered it ended.

Goebbels's recordings are thus, historically, if for no other reason than the immediacy of the notations, of the most unique significance. As a historical record, Riefenstahl's memoirs, written forty-plus years later, are irrelevant. But then, her book is not intended to teach history; it is meant to tell her own personal story as she needs to—and as she perhaps now does—remember it. If she chooses to underplay her former allegiance to the Third Reich, that is perhaps *her* way of "blocking" the unbearable.

It is obvious that she greatly liked Speer, though in some unimportant details (for example, Speer's first coming to her notice) Speer's 1969 book differs slightly from what she told me in 1986, when she was no doubt marginally adapting the story to fit in with the impression she wished to convey.

"I saw a photograph of him in *Der Angriff* in 1932," she said. "That was just after I had met Hitler for the first time. At that time I was decidedly against the Nazis, not least because, living in the theater and film world, I had many Jewish friends [a fact a number of these friends later confirmed]. And when I saw that photograph, I thought how extraordinary it was that a man with a face like this should be for Hitler—if he was, I thought, then there had to be something to it all." Speer described this differently and perhaps more believably; he quoted her as telling him in 1935 of having clipped that photograph when she saw it in 1932, thinking that "with that head" he might well play a part in one of her future films.

She finally met Speer in Nuremberg in 1934 during the rehearsals for *Triumph of the Will*, which was commissioned and actively supported by Goebbels. Throughout our conversations, and her subsequent book, she described Goebbels as her archenemy. One can only guess at the complications of a relationship between these two people, the desperately ambitious young Riefenstahl and the sexually rampant Goebbels. He was normally incapable of keeping his hands off beautiful women, particularly actresses who, as he was entirely in charge of theater and film, largely depended on his favor. But Hitler's undoubted admiration for Riefenstahl may well have acted as a brake on Goebbels.

Her book, in which, gratingly, she constantly refers to Goebbels as "that cripple" (he was handicapped from childhood with a clubfoot), unfortunately does not reveal the more complicated psychological reason for her enduring fury against him, which, one suspects, is more likely her shame at what she accepted from him, rather than anger at what he refused her. In fact, nothing Goebbels says in his diaries remotely suggests anything but a fairly close working relationship. Nor, aside from occasional impatience with her excitable nature and her tendency for intrigues, does anything he says point to animosity on either side. Remembering that there was no reason whatever for him in 1933 to prevaricate, his entries, particularly in 1933 and 1934, make it clear that he immensely admired her, counseled her and financially supported the films which made her famous. On June 12, 1933, his entry is enthusiastic:

> Riefenstahl at last night's party . . . talked about her new film. She is the only one of the stars who really understands us.

All through that summer there are drives and parties with her and Hitler. Two years later, on October 5, 1935, he still expresses admiration for her:

> Went with Leni Riefenstahl through her Olympic film concept. A woman who knows what she wants. . . .

By late 1936, now in the middle of work on her Olympic film, he begins to show his exasperation with her continual demands. On November 6:

> Miss Riefenstahl [a sign of great annoyance: it was the first time he refers to her as "Miss"!] tries her hysterics on me. One really can't work with these wild women. Now she wants half a million more and wants to make two films instead of one. . . . She cries, the ultimate weapon of women. But her tears leave me cold. Let her do her work and keep her affairs in order. . . .

Even so, a year later it was Goebbels who, overcome with enthusiasm for her Olympic film, suggested to Hitler that "she who has been personally so modest and never sought personal fame or public recognition" should be awarded an "official honor"; Goebbels also made her a member of the government film board.

One of the reasons why her career is relevant to Speer's life is because he had by then become a friend. However contradictory and puzzling her autobiography is on the subject of Goebbels, and however much she may be magnifying in retrospect her relationship with Hitler, her recollections of Speer and his of her entirely coincide. They liked and admired each other, and as he had told me and she later confirmed, they worked together on several occasions. "Much later, during the war," she said, "we became friends." And, to Riefenstahl's credit, one feels, this friendship was to endure.

Speer wrote to Annemarie Kempf from Spandau in early 1952, responding to the information that she was beginning to lobby people in Bonn and elsewhere toward achieving an early release for him.

My dear Annemarie Kempf,
 I really am so touched to read how energetically and loyally you are extending yourself for me. Just don't be disappointed if it doesn't work; I don't have great hopes. . . . There is no reason not to speak openly with

Leni, of course not mentioning [our way of communicating]. She is grateful to me for many things and I think will gladly help. . . .

He was right. On June 29, 1952, Riefenstahl wrote to Annemarie from
Rome:

> As I've been traveling, I only received your letter from June 6 today but
> want to reply at once. Above all to say that I will do anything to help Herr
> Speer. Already before getting your letter, I asked a friend in Berlin to con-
> tact Mr. Lewinsohn [sic: Levinsohn, head of the Berlin Denazification
> Board for the U.S. occupation authorities], to inform him that I am at his
> disposal as a witness for Speer. . . . I suggest that, when you are next in
> Berlin, you pay a visit to my friend, who knows Mr. Lewinsohn and was
> himself present at my own hearing . . . and get him to advise you . . . also
> my own very good lawyer. At all my hearings—and as you know there
> have been many—I have testified about Herr Speer, of course in his favor,
> describing him as I know him. . . . Please keep me informed about him,
> but also about Frau Speer . . . perhaps the day will come when I will be in a
> position to help in one way or another. . . . Is there anything I can send
> him? Can one? Anyway, I'm so relieved that, thanks to you, I can now
> communicate with him. . . .

She didn't think he was a great architect. "As an architect he was run of the
mill," she told me, "but he was extraordinarily intelligent, burningly ambitious, and he had much more than a gift—a genius—for organization. People don't like to hear this now, but you know, there were quite a few men of
stature around Hitler, including, as time went on, some of the generals, such
as [Alfred] Jodl. But among the civilians, the government people, what one
might call the real Hitler circle," she said, "Speer stood out. He was different.
He had distinction; he was quiet; there was a kind of shyness too, not timid-
ity—modesty. He was—how shall I put it?—he was clean. It would have been
unimaginable that he could do anything shifty." Among the Hitler group,
she said, he was her best friend. "My only friend," she qualified. "I never, for
a moment, doubted his total integrity or his total devotion to Hitler."

There can be no doubt—whatever Leni Riefenstahl says now—that they
fully shared that total devotion to Hitler, indeed that it probably was their
primary bond. But while Riefenstahl has tried to minimize Hitler's hold on
her—representing it rather as her hold on him—Speer, far more honest,
tried again and again when talking to me and others, to understand the fascination Hitler had for him and many others of the Führer's top men.

"I ask myself time and again how much of it was a kind of auto-sugges-
tion," he said on one occasion. "One thing is certain: everyone who worked
closely with him for a long time was exceptionally dependent on him. How-

ever powerful they were in their own domain, close to him they became small and timid." ("I try so hard," Göring has been quoted as saying to Finance Minister Hjalmar Schacht, "but every time I stand before the Führer, my heart drops into the seat of my pants.")

Speer used the German word *hörig*, descriptive of a gamut of emotions, from willing submission to servility to helpless passivity. It has no precise equivalent in English, and whenever Speer tried to convey in English this effect Hitler had on his environment, he met with complete incomprehension. This emerged clearly in a long interview (never broadcast) for *Panorama*, a British television program, not long after *Inside the Third Reich* was published. The BBC set up a brilliant panel with historian Hugh Trevor-Roper, American lawyer George Ball and one of their best commentators, Michael Charlton, as moderator. The first two knew Speer well, having questioned him in 1945–46 for British Intelligence and the U.S. Strategic Bombing Survey, respectively.

"From the point of view of most of us . . . ," George Ball said to Speer during the discussion, "[what is] most baffling of all . . . is the constant references to the charisma or mystique or particular charm of Hitler. . . . From the point of view of anyone in my country, or I think in Great Britain, who had the experience of seeing motion pictures of Hitler or of hearing him on the radio, and seeing the things . . . he wrote . . . it was totally incomprehensible. How could anyone find a particular charm in this man? How do you explain it? This is the ultimate mystery I think, as far as we are concerned."

"It is only explicable," Speer replied (I am here slightly correcting his English), "if you agree . . . that there are human beings who have a kind of . . . magnetism or hypnotic quality. You try to evade this influence . . . get away from its effect . . . but you are in their . . . you are . . . [here he cannot do without the term *hörig*, which he realizes he can't explain, and so limits himself to a much weaker and less telling description] you depend on them."

Ball suggested that perhaps just the effect of power could explain charisma and Speer agreed that power exerted its own mystique. But he said that what had always puzzled him was how Hitler's effect on his environment had functioned just as effectively before 1933, when there was defeat upon defeat and crisis upon crisis and yet he succeeded, almost entirely by force of personality. "It remains a mystery," Speer said. "But the fact is that it is impossible to explain Germany before 1933, and from 1933 to 1945, without Hitler. He was the center of it all and always remained the center."

"You paint a picture in the book," said Charlton, "of these excruciatingly boring tea parties on the Obersalzberg. . . . You make it sound almost intolerable. So where did you have your private moments with Hitler which were of such value to you?"

"It was when [we discussed] plans, drawings," said Speer. "It was remark-able how quickly he could grasp the meaning of a plan, how—as very few people can—he was able to think in three dimensions, and how his phenom-enal memory enabled him to recall corrections he made months before. . . . It was amazing to me, because he was the head of the state and had many other concerns and still he could deal with such small details in this, his private field. . . . At these times, when he was acting as an architect, he was really very relaxed, at his ease. You could contradict him, argue. . . ."

Charlton suggested that this may have been because Hitler, in the context of that relationship where Speer was the "professional" in charge, felt himself to be in a sense the weaker partner. Speer was clearly uncomfortable with that interpretation. "I would say," he said, "we . . . we were equals, we were on one level. . . ."

But actually the relationship was more significant than that, and was also entirely different from the one Hitler had with other architects to whom he entrusted large projects, such as Hermann Giesler, the most devout of Na-tional Socialists, who received the plum assignments of Munich and Linz and who, not without good reason, would become one of Speer's bitterest enemies.

One of Germany's most eminent psychologists, Alexander Mitscherlich, would later cause raised eyebrows when he suggested that there was "an erotic component in the Hitler-Speer relationship." But Speer told me, "He was not entirely wrong." Of course, neither Mitscherlich—nor Speer—meant by this active or even conscious homosexuality; that idea would have been absurd.

The truth, as it often is, was both more simple and more subtle. In looks and language, the tall, handsome young Speer probably came close to being a German ideal for the Austrian Hitler; as a member of a patrician family, with a distinctly upper-class but also unfailingly modest and restrained bearing ("He was always quiet, composed and soft-spoken," said Annemarie Kempf), Speer represented a class the lower-middle-class Hitler, when young, had only admired from afar; and the drive Hitler no doubt sensed in him very early responded in many ways to his own. And then, of course, the fact that architecture was his discipline powerfully provided, as Mitscherlich wrote, "the medium through which they [both emotionally uncommunica-tive] could communicate."

Many observers have remarked how the meetings with Speer in those pre-war years elated and relaxed Hitler and how he seemed happily, indeed gaily, to defer to him. Speer to me too vigorously dismissed the suggestion that in a sense he dominated Hitler in these discussions.

"He just loved arguing with me as colleagues do," he said. "It was both

stimulating and restful for him. He was very modest, you know, in a way."
He did add, however, that in the years when their relationship related only to
architecture, Hitler indeed did almost provoke argument, and seemed to
enjoy it for its own sake, almost irrespective of whether he ended up right or
wrong.

"I suppose," Speer said, "that one curious occasion on the Berghof in 1936
has some bearing. I was sitting across the table from him, with a lot of other
people, and suddenly he fixed me with his eyes, quite obviously to 'give in or
hold out'—you know that game, don't you, that children play?" Speer said
he quite deliberately accepted the challenge. "I realize now," he said, "that
the relationship must already have developed a great deal to have this happen. Well, I accepted his stare, returned it and made myself hold on." He
laughed as he told me this, a sudden echo of the excitement of that day. "I
don't know how long it lasted—it felt like a long time, many minutes. I could
hear the buzz of voices around us while I felt this charged silence between
him and me. It was he who looked away first. I had won." He laughed happily, recalling it.

But Speer's victories at that time, in architecture, over himself and
over Hitler, however composed and relaxed he appeared, were not easily
sustained.

"I remember," Margret Speer said at one point in our talks, "that during
those first big years, 1934–36–38, Anni Brandt and I often talked about those
strange attacks Albert had; I was very worried about them."

The "strange attacks" she spoke of started in mid-1934. He had completed
two smaller commissions and had begun on the design of the Zeppelin Field
in Nuremberg; with all this, he was continually on the *qui vive* for Hitler's
frequent visits and summonses, hardly saw his family, hardly had any rest.
"The attacks came often, almost regularly, so regularly that I always lived in
fear of them," he told me. "It was a kind of claustrophobia: I would suddenly
go pale, my heart would beat wildly, I'd have pins and needles in my hands
and feet; I would feel ice cold and panic-stricken and be forced to lie down so
as not to fall. It was particularly bad if I happened to be in an enclosed space,
such as a train. I remember once they nearly stopped a train to get me to a
hospital, until at the last minute, I managed to control it. I just thought it was
fatigue. I was overworking like mad. I was, of course, examined—everybody
was so worried about it. But nothing was found; it wasn't anything physical.
Why otherwise would it have stopped miraculously in 1940 [when his life
began to veer away from architecture], and never happened again even
though, certainly after 1942 when I was Minister, I worked, if anything,
harder, under even greater pressure?"

He knew that it was not his body but his nerves which were in panic. "It was my unconscious realization," he said, "that I wasn't up to what was demanded of me; it was my fear of architecture, and of course my terror of losing the favor of the man I considered the greatest in the world."

Surprisingly, Margret Speer had never heard of the fainting fits he had had when he was six and horribly afraid of his brothers. "Is that true?" she asked him as we sat together that night. "When you were *six*?" He shrugged and suggested we pass on to another topic.

In the spring of 1936, inspecting a newly completed part of Fritz Todt's *Autobahn*, Hitler dropped a hint to Speer: "I have one more building commission to assign—the biggest of them all." Although it would be several months before Speer could see it "in black and white," as he put it to me, he had a pretty good idea that day on the *Autobahn* what it was, and that Hitler was letting him know that it would come his way.

Three months later, in June, Hitler showed him a plan approved by the Berlin City Council and the Mayor, Dr. Julius Lippert, for the reconstruction of Berlin. Lippert, Hitler said, was "an incompetent, an idiot, a flop, a nonentity." He had explained to him time and again the measurements he wanted for the grand processional avenue (in his "Spandau draft," Speer called it the Prachtstrasse—the Street of Pomp, or Magnificence), and time and again the same drawings, with the width of the avenue reduced by 30 meters (from Hitler's 120 meters to 90), were served up to him. In early summer he finally ordered Goebbels, as Gauleiter of Berlin, to replace the Mayor and sent for Speer.*

"I could have imagined the handing over of his 'biggest commission' to be slightly more solemn," Speer wrote in Spandau. "As it was, he just handed me the City Council's designs without further ado, told me what he wanted, and told me to get on with it."

In Spandau, the memory of this, his most triumphant moment, was very important to him; it covers thirty pages of the draft, with many sketches, toward the end of which—in its honesty a particularly poignant revelation—he confesses how much pleasure, and regret, he had found in recalling to his mind this great project. (It seemed to me highly significant, in the context of showing the honesty of the draft, that he did *not* include this "confession" in the eventual book.) In Spandau he wrote,

> [The Berlin project] became my life and I realize that I cannot tear myself loose from it even now. *If I look deep into myself for the reasons now for my rejection of Hitler, then I think that aside from the horror in him that*

---

*Interestingly enough Goebbels didn't; he only informed Lippert that the reconstruction of Berlin was no longer his responsibility.

now stands revealed, my personal disappointment plays a small part—my
disappointment also that his political power game drove us into war and
thereby destroyed what would have been my life [author's italics].

In the "Spandau draft," toward the end of this recollection in the draft of
the planning for the near-total redesign of Hitler's Berlin, to be renamed
"Germania," Speer names the architects to whom he confided the principal
designs—among them, prominently, "my old university friend, Dr. Rudolf
Wolters, to whom was assigned the most essential task, the Prachtstrasse."

When *Inside the Third Reich* appeared in Germany in 1969 (significantly
without this list), there is little doubt that it would not have been in the architects' interest (all doing extremely well by then) to be publicized as co-
creators of Speer's—that is, Hitler's—new Berlin. I only realized after
working through the "Spandau draft" in the late 1980s that this was what
Speer meant when he told Wolters that he didn't mention him in the book
"in order to protect him."

By the time *Inside the Third Reich* appeared, Wolters might well have forgotten these few lines in the 1,200-page draft. But then, he no doubt had not
expected or desired any acknowledgement of his collaboration with Speer
under Hitler. What devastated him was that his help *after* the war, without
which Speer could not have written the draft and therefore his books, was
totally unacknowledged in the published version. Not only was his name un-
mentioned, but even his hometown, Coesfeld, was given a false name.

This would be a bitter blow to anyone, and how much more to Wolters
after all he had done for Speer. His son, Fritz, wise and now very successful,
watched his father's anger and despair for years. Fritz has had to overcome
many bitter memories of his own, of his father, interminably busy with the
Speers, almost entirely ignoring him during his entire life. "Toward the end
of his life," Fritz Wolters told me, "he gave me some of his writings to read.
'It'll interest you,' he said. It was all about 1945 and afterwards; all about
Speer, the Speer children, all that. I read them and I thought, 'Well, hell,
where am I? I was around then—don't I exist?' Not one word about us, about
his own family . . . and he gives me that to read, proudly."

Nonetheless, Fritz had always been intrigued by Speer and admired him;
he knew from his mother, who for years was Margret Speer's best friend, that
losing Wolters's friendship had been the worst blow of Speer's post-Spandau
life.

"If only he had found a way just to mention my father by name, even without going into details," Fritz said, "it would have made all the difference."
Not because it would have made up for Wolters's always having lived in

Speer's shadow, not because it would acknowledge Wolters's immense contribution to Speer's life in Spandau, but because it would have shown Speer's own recognition of his debt to his friend.

Speer, said Fritz Wolters, "had to battle against the demon of his damned love for Hitler; but my father, who loved *Speer,* had to deny and give up this love in order to defend an indefensible devotion to Hitler."

VI

"You've All Gone Completely Insane"

Nuremberg, November 20, 1945

[From the Indictment:] The Defendant Speer between 1932 and 1945 was: a member of the Nazi Party, Reichsleiter, member of the Reichstag, Reich Minister for Armaments and Munitions, Chief of the Organization Todt. . . . The Defendant Speer used [his] positions and his personal influence in such a manner that: . . . he authorized, directed and participated in the War Crimes set forth in Count Three . . . and the Crimes against Humanity set forth in Count Four . . . particularly the abuse and exploitation of human beings for forced labor in the conduct of aggressive war.

On January 30, 1937, Hitler named Speer Generalbauinspektor (Inspector General) for the Construction of Berlin, almost precisely the position held in 1830 by Speer's hero, Karl Friedrich Schinkel as Oberbaudirektor of Prussia. Thirty-two years old, Speer now held the rank of a State Secretary, was entitled to a seat (next to Fritz Todt) on the government benches in the Reichstag, to a place at state dinners and, automatically, to a decoration from foreign state visitors. Suddenly the holder of an enormous, historically established position as Inspector General (GBI, as everyone called it almost at once), Speer became within a very short time a man of power.

Paradoxically, one of the things which so clearly emerges in the Hitler-Speer relationship in the years of his architecture—so different from years later, when Speer became Hitler's Minister—is their mutual shyness. Only Speer commented on it, long after the fact. Other observers' attention had always been on Hitler, and what they invariably noticed and remembered later was his "gaiety," his "happiness," when he was with Speer. It was Speer's precise memory of Hitler's words, and his own reactions to them, which showed that restraint between them which both found not only entirely satisfying but deeply exhilarating.

"Hitler made no more fuss about that official appointment than he had about the commission [to rebuild Berlin] in the first place," Speer wrote in Spandau. "Not uncharacteristic of him, one could almost have thought him shy when, at the end of lunch, he handed me the nomination document. 'Make a good job of it,' he said, and that was that."

Not quite: uniquely, Hitler agreed to Speer's request to carry out the Berlin assignment as an independent architect, under the authority of no one except Hitler as his patron. Speer's office, for which Hitler within weeks ordered the Minister of Education to clear out the fine Academy of Arts building on the Pariser Platz, was separated from the Chancellery only by the Ministry's private gardens. Hitler agreed that although Speer would be supplied with all necessary funds by both the city and state government, his organization would be considered an independent research institute rather than a government department. And he granted Speer's request to continue to retain his private office where he could theoretically accept private commissions.

In practice this was to work out slightly differently. Speer maintained his Lindenstrasse office and team, but there too worked only for Hitler. He also accepted as GBI a salary of RM 1,500 a month, about the same as the Mayor of Berlin, and (although Hitler may not have been informed of this) suggested in a letter to State Secretary Hans Lammers his inclusion in the state pension system, "for the sake of [his] family's security." This request was turned down.

For his Nuremberg buildings he had refused any fee except RM 1,000 a month. Spurred on by Göring, who told him that his restraint was not only ridiculous but unworthy of his new eminence, he would now accept usual architects' fees but, throughout his career, refused any of the perks considered normal by almost everyone else.

"Money was never an issue for him," said Annemarie Kempf. "Perhaps because he was born to money, he wasn't interested in it except as a means to an end. And he wasn't interested in having people work for him whose main incentive appeared to be money. He was always a very easygoing boss— except if he sensed dishonesty or corruption; then he was very hard, merciless." But for a long time, years perhaps, such a problem never arose.

Even before his title became official, he had offered a job to Annemarie, then still working at Goebbels's *Der Angriff*. "He sounded very happy when he phoned," she said. " 'I'm about to become a big shot—a real boss,' he said. 'Would you like to come back to work for me in spite of it?' I didn't have to think twice."

The next person Speer called was Wolters, whose enthusiasm can still be felt in his reminiscences, thirty-five years later:

> The task entrusted to him exceeded anything one could imagine. Berlin was to be rebuilt and expanded to serve a potential estimated population of eight million people. . . . Central to the concept would be a cross of four main thoroughfares of unprecedented generosity [each of them wider and greener than Hitler's favorite avenue, the Champs Elysées in Paris] and, with money no object, an entirely new railway system. . . . My part of the project [aside from the railway network, his specialty]—the most important—was the North-South Axis, the great representational avenue for which I could freely commission our finest architects, painters and sculptors.

With the addition, for the time being, of two further talented young architects long familiar to Speer, he had immediately assembled for the GBI another "brilliant young team."

"I had joined him at the Lindenstrasse already in 1935," said Willie Schelkes. "I had been doing perfectly well in Freiburg, but his position became increasingly extraordinary, and when his star with Hitler kept rising and his invitations kept coming, I finally felt I had to make a choice—basically, because everything in Germany had become political, a political choice: quite simply between left and right. There was no longer any question of splinter parties—they had become irrelevant. And between left and right, of course, I chose right, which was the National Socialists. For me it was a decision I took a long time over because, although it would be within my profession, it was more than a question of architecture. It was an admission to myself that as a German of my generation I could no longer stand aside. I had an obligation—the obligation to be politically active."

In 1935, therefore, he accepted Speer's proposal to represent his "Beauty of Labor" organization in Baden. "Speer appointed representatives for each *Land* [province]," Schelkes said. "We spent three days a week traveling around looking at existing facilities for factory workers—space, canteens, sports grounds, hygiene. Then we made proposals, submitted drawings and estimates, and it was up to the employers whether to accept or not. Some did, others said 'No, thank you.' They were free to refuse, but most of them eventually came around after they saw how better facilities improved output in other factories. In the end the province of Baden spent RM 3 million to RM 6 million a year for these improvements."

When Speer was named GBI, Schelkes very quickly transferred to that bureau. "There were just three of us to start out with: Wolters; Hans Stephan, who became responsible for housing, traffic, the East-West Axis and the planning of the Ring [the ring road]; and myself. I got Berlin-West, which was to become the University City: we were going to combine the university and the Technische Hochschule [Institute of Technology], which had up to then been separate institutions. It was an exciting innovation, and this huge academic area would also contain and link all the main city hospitals, to provide a new system of health and social care. Additionally of course—my pride and joy—I was put in charge of landscape design for Berlin and its surroundings. Speer's concept, believe me, was incredibly innovative and socially conscious. I know, now people can only think of and condemn the outsize representational buildings, as does Speer himself. But there was so much more, so much to give us hope."

He showed me a book he published in 1942 which shows the designs as they were added to and altered from the start of the project. "We had many problems with the Mayor of Berlin, Lippert, who had his own staff of architects whose designs had been rejected and who, understandably enough, deeply resented this mammoth intrusion—particularly as much of the money would have to come from his budget, and our ideas were very expensive. In some areas we did have to compromise—the book shows where."

Professionally, Schelkes has much more reason than Speer to feel vindicated, because two main points of his concept, to keep all lakes and rivers around Berlin *baufrei* (clear of construction) and to change the planting and seeding of all forests from monoculture to mixed forestry, were later put into practice by the postwar administration of West (though not East) Berlin. "I don't know whether it was from my plans they adopted it," said Schelkes, a modest man, "but at least I originated the concept and I'm glad about that."

In this trio of Speer's first collaborators at the GBI, Schelkes had one great advantage. "Speer knew little about landscape architecture and he never claimed knowledge he didn't have—not to Hitler either," Schelkes added. "It meant that I had a great deal of independence. The others too had a good deal of 'space,' but even so, in their areas he eventually took charge."

The task of this team was not actually the design of buildings but planning: "The designs were farmed out to a huge number of people—all the best architects in Germany received commissions. We created the framework—they filled it."

The only outstanding German architect who refused to take part, he said, was Tessenow. "He was of course basically a socialist—he belonged to the 'Ring,' an association of architects of the political left. As such he lost his chair at the Technische Hochschule, although, entirely due to Speer's intervention, he was able to keep his second chair at the Academy of Arts."

Schelkes had not kept up with Tessenow over the years, he said sadly. "I'm afraid I didn't: I did recently find one thank-you letter he wrote me, probably only a reply to a Christmas card."

Although a reticent man, Schelkes doesn't hide his discomfort about his own lack of civic courage during those years. He tries, though not very hard, to justify his inaction by the fact that he joined the army as soon as war broke out, and remained an officer to the end, even though—as he had freely admitted—he was given considerable flexibility in order to continue his work for the Baustab Speer (Construction Authority), as the GBI was renamed when the requirements of war in 1941 interrupted the rebuilding of Berlin. "We then became responsible for all construction work in Germany and the annexed areas, eventually including war construction such as the huge airplane hangars for the Ju [Junkers] 88."

Between 1937 and 1939, he said, the work pace at the GBI was feverish, often keeping everyone there through much of the night. "Of course," he joked, "the days Speer went to the Berghof the place was deserted by 5 p.m.—we'd be off to make merry, Annemarie in the lead."

She was lovely, he said. "People sometimes jokingly said that she was in

love with Speer, but whatever she might have felt in her innermost being—
and I was no more privy to that than anyone else—a liaison with Speer
was . . . it was. . . ." He laughed out loud, and so did his wife. "It is so unthinkable," he said. "Annemarie was his private secretary; true, it's about as
close as he ever got to anybody, but anything else would never have entered
his mind. Not only was he entirely uninterested in anything emotive, but
quite aside from that, both he and Annemarie were incapable of dalliance.
For himself it was unthinkable. In others—and of course like anywhere else,
it went on all around him—he viewed it with distaste."

Annemarie had smiled when she talked with me about "ladies smitten
with Speer—of course there were," she said. "How could it be otherwise?
They'd phone and we'd make fun of them—and of him too, squirming. I
don't mean it literally," she said. "Anybody gushing just made him be terribly polite. Later, in the ministerial offices, there were some long-standing relationships everybody knew about. But not Speer—he couldn't have taken
knowing about such things, so he just didn't."

Wasn't that rather revealing, I asked, refusing to know about things he
couldn't accept? She knew exactly what I meant. "That's right," she said. "In
a way, I think he felt that what he didn't know didn't exist.

"He liked Riefenstahl," she said. "She amused him. He of course attracted
her, and she certainly set her cap for him. Still, in the final analysis I think she
was wise enough to realize it was a no-go situation. But they had a lot in
common, so in a way they did become friends. Sometimes, especially in the
later phases of the war, maybe he could briefly relax with her—you know,
talk about things he loved, music, art. . . .

"It's hard to describe now, though, how much fun we had," she said, "especially in those first years before the war. It was all so very exciting, you
know. And also the extent to which we teased him, and he accepted it.

"We used to go skiing, *en groupe.*" Sometimes Margret went along, sometimes not. "He was very hard to get to be, oh, just relaxed, to have fun. After
all we were all very young, he too. We loved to laugh, to play jokes. Until the
war, you know, it wasn't all so earnest. But it's true, *he* was rather earnest,
even about his fun. We'd want to stay up and dance and drink wine after
skiing—and he'd sit with us after dinner, sort of tolerantly, but then at ten or
whatever—some ridiculously early hour—he'd say, 'Right, up to bed,' as if
we were all in his charge, even on holiday. He always wanted us to be
proper. . . . Nothing to do with sex—that would never enter into his head.
And it wasn't either that he wanted to run our lives. He just didn't want anyone in his circle to be in any way immoderate, conspicuous, excessive. Not
because he cared what other people said; no, simply because of how he felt.
Any kind of conspicuousness or excess was anathema to him. Well, we'd fi-

nally pretend to go to bed when he did, but of course we didn't—we'd go on dancing and drinking wine, or go out for a night walk in the snow, or a snowball fight. . . . I think he knew, but he never said anything."

It sounded as if already then he was consciously lonely, even with his team, I said. "Yes, I think he did feel this, and he retreated. There was that wall between him and others that he talked to you about, and he accepted it. He made do, I think, because he didn't know how to do anything else."

Interestingly, it had been the young Annemarie who, when the first three architects joined, had fixed their salaries. "She asked me what I had earned over the past years, so I told her the maximum," said Schelkes, laughing. "She didn't argue—that's what I got in my contract.

"When Speer was with us," he continued, "we stayed at work at least until 10 p.m. and often later. When we went to work with him on the Obersalzberg, as we often did, he would go and dine with Hitler, and we others would drive into Salzburg and eat at the Peterskeller . . . and then we'd go back to work. Speer would come back from the Berghof around 11—he'd see what we'd done and then, much later, we'd get to go to bed. It was strange, you know, that he became such a workaholic. As a young man he was really quite lazy; even as Tessenow's student he never seemed to work—he just managed, as if by magic."

Schelkes didn't think it was ambition that drove him. "A lot of people are ambitious. But can ambition alone create this kind of total absorption? I don't believe it: I've never seen it happen to anyone else," he said. "I think he was totally fascinated by the challenge. But I don't think one can separate this fascination with the work from his feelings for the man, from the desire or the need to justify Hitler's faith in him. Was that ambition? Was it that simple? I never thought so.

"I never heard anyone say that he 'made up' to Hitler, flattered him or fawned on him, or that he showed off to others in any way; that wasn't his personality. He did of course become very aware of his position, but that is not the same as being convinced of one's own talent. I don't think he thought highly of his own talent at all. And the buildings, the Chancellery and so on—one can't say how much or even whether they were his sole creation. They came out of the *Büro* Speer [Speer's architectural office], and I never heard him claim anything else."

Schelkes thought Hitler's own architectural ideas very amateur. "He was heavily influenced by the Vienna Ring [the wide street lined with representational buildings—opera, theaters, museums, ministries, the city hall—which surrounds Vienna's First District]. This is classicist rather than baroque, and he adapted all his later ideas to it. Even so, all of us were glad to have such a patron. His fascination with architecture assured us almost unlimited support. On the other hand, one was confronted with these bombastic ideas of his which, although some people—Wolters, for instance—didn't mind or even shared them, others didn't like at all. I was quite positively inclined at first, but as they became more and more monumental, I began to distance myself, though in practice that merely meant that I avoided going to the Modellhallen [where the models were displayed] any more than I had to.

"I remember Hitler's first visit there. I recently found a card from my wife to a relative telling her what I'd said about it. He came that night with a large group of people who had dined with him. He walked around the Berlin model. . . . He wore a simple uniform jacket without decorations, and I remember he didn't wear his glasses. He spent quite a long time looking around, and then he straightened up and said, in his heavy Austrian accent which he never used for formal occasions, speeches and all that, 'Das g'fallt mir' ['I like it'], and then he shook hands with us.

"One couldn't separate the man from the position—one was under the spell of that personality. I saw him quite a few times after that when he came to see things. Sometimes he came alone, just with one aide, sometimes with a group like the first time. He'd talk with Speer, and as one of us three—Wolters, Stephan or I—was always on duty at night, he'd greet us. He was always punctiliously courteous, even charming, but I never knew him. . . ."

Hitler and Speer talked in a perfectly ordinary way, said Schelkes. "There was never a feeling of a subordinate talking to the chief. Speer had this very special gift—he really talked the same way to everybody. I suppose one would call it person to person, and he talked like that with Hitler too. It's strange if one thinks about it now—but then one didn't, because that was simply how and what Speer was."

Wolters, in his reminiscences, reports four meetings with Hitler:

> The first time was at Speer's studio on the Obersalzberg. Three or four of us were there that night. Hitler came up to us, joking because all of us, including Speer, were well over six feet tall. He shook hands with each of us and looked quietly in our eyes for rather longer than one usually does [an expression Germans invariably seem to use when describing first encounters with Hitler]. He was smaller than I had imagined. His walk and his movements were slow and relaxed, his manner of speaking unstrained; rather unexpectedly, he spoke in a strong Austrian accent. Oddly, none of us felt in the least shy.
>
> The second time was when Speer took me to one of his lunches at the Reich Chancellery. . . . There were about twenty other guests, among them Goebbels and four other ministers. The conversation at table was mostly [about] how one could best deal with British radio propaganda. Here I noticed how Hitler's factual questions embarrassed [Wilhelm] Oh-

nesorge, the minister of communications, when Hitler showed himself to be better informed than he on broadcast capacity. . . .

The third and fourth meetings were in Speer's Modellhallen at the GBI when Hitler came to view the Berlin plans. . . . He arrived through a back door which had been put in specially for his convenience, dressed in a grey suit. As it was forbidden to make notes in his presence, I always wrote detailed minutes immediately afterwards.

Of course from these few experiences I cannot judge Hitler's personality, but having shared with Speer his virtually daily contacts with him, and being familiar with Hitler's ideas, for example, on town planning, I think that commentators are making it easy for themselves now when, as they frequently do, they resort in their descriptions to simplistic epitaphs such as "buck private," "wall painter," "petit-bourgeois philistine," or "history's greatest criminal."

Annemarie's feelings about Hitler have undergone a profound and profoundly painful change over the years. But she too, in the early years with Speer and well into the war, idolized Hitler. Our talks, of course, went on for years, and like all the others who knew Speer well, on countless occasions when she spoke of Speer, she almost inevitably spoke of Hitler, as if the two were indivisible in her mind.

"For me, from the time I was very young," she said, "it was my country I loved, not any man. However, it is, I think, true to say that as time went on, the cause I supported with such passion and the person of Hitler did in a sense become merged."

She had seen him, watched him talking with Speer many times before she actually met him. "The first time was the evening of the day [in the summer of 1939] Speer completed the new Chancellery. A huge celebration was planned for the opening, but Hitler came to meet us the night before. We all went around the building with him and Speer, us walking behind them. I thought it was beautiful, I don't care what people say now. I was very proud that night. One has to imagine—well, it's almost impossible to imagine—the lights, the flowers everywhere, the excitement of it. I'd like to be critical in retrospect, but I can't be. To meet him on such an occasion . . . it's different from an ordinary meeting. This was still in peacetime, you know. Every day something happened which changed our future for us, and it happened through this man. I'm trying to tell you not what I feel now, but what I felt then. I can't say whether I found him 'likeable' or not; the term has no relevance. It was just joy; he belonged to the joy of it."

And this applied too, she said, to the planning of the new Berlin. "The model Speer had built downstairs took up almost a whole huge room. It was so beautiful, so complete, you know, with all the streets and trees and flowers and fountains, and all the buildings finished and lit to perfection: Speer was an artist at lighting. There was a special entrance to this room from the Chancellery gardens, and that is how Hitler would come. They would phone and say that he was on his way. . . . Sometimes very late at night, sometimes after lunch. But whenever he came—and this went on long into the war too—he would stay for a long time, and however tense he seemed when he arrived, he would visibly change as he looked at this vision of the future. We wouldn't necessarily meet him, of course, but—the hall was enormous—we were allowed in when he came, and we could watch them. Oh, I know what everybody says now about the designs: megalomania, brutality, ostentation. But tell me, just what is wrong with 'large' for ceremonial construction such as palaces, ministries, forums and theaters? Hasn't almost every historical period, in many countries, produced representational buildings?"

Annemarie had an almost faultless memory, not only for words but for feelings. "When Speer was named GBI," she said "and Wolters came over from the Reichsbahn [railways], our office very quickly became a kind of refuge for a number of people who were considered 'uncomfortable' to have around elsewhere. 'Uncomfortable' either because they were suspected of not following the party line or because they had 'problems.' Later we found out that it had very swiftly become known that Speer—and don't forget, Wolters too, with a very important position on Speer's team—simply didn't care about people's politics and even less about their racial 'flaws,' as long as those who applied were professionally capable. I have to say that while that general attitude certainly originated at the top, thus with Speer, he had in fact little to do with the specifics of personnel, except for top people. But one of his great talents always was delegating.

"At the same time one of his less endearing traits was his personal detachment. If he was made aware of somebody having personal or professional troubles, he'd order action taken to assist them. But he never initiated help off his own bat, quite simply because he didn't see when people were troubled. I suppose one could say," she said again, "he didn't see anything he didn't want to see, but really I don't think it was that simple. In fact, I think he would have been glad to have the capacity to see—certainly he was glad whenever we could help people. But he didn't have that capacity; though, in that respect too, there was a change in him after Spandau.

"What he always had," she said, "and I think it was the essence of his success, was a total rejection of anything bureaucratic. He wanted nothing bureaucratic in his organization, and he fought actively against that type of spirit whenever it came up. All the people he surrounded himself with were individualists whom, somehow, through the force of his own personality, he drew together into a tightly knit working organism."

Annemarie, despite her deep affection for Speer, was not blind or insensitive to his deficiencies. When her much-loved father died in 1937, "Wolters immediately reacted," she said. "Speer—oh, he knew about it, but he ignored it. That did disappoint me. I was hurt."

Was it perhaps that it embarrassed him to show feelings, I asked, or did he simply not have them?

"He was the world's most inhibited man, and in time one came to accept it, shrug it off, you know—even laugh it off," she said. "He said to me once how amazingly personal Hitler could be. I asked him what he meant, because of course I never knew Hitler that way—socially, you know. And he went on to describe how often people, sitting next to Hitler at table, would come away feeling he had really wanted to know about them—cared about them. 'I'm really not good at that, am I?' he said, and I said, 'No, you aren't.'

"Although I feel very differently about Hitler now," she said, "I think that the subsequent rejection by so many people of the buildings and the building plans was really the rejection of the system Hitler represented, and of his person. If a benevolent German ruler had decided to build such edifices, representing the stability and grandeur of his country, perhaps the world would not have objected as they did to the Hitler-Speer creations. I remember very vividly one occasion when Hitler came to see us, just after the war had broken out, and I heard him say to Speer, 'We must end this war quickly. We don't want war; we want to build.' Are we to think that that was a lie too? That everything was lies?"

What Annemarie saw in those years was a man who wanted to rule a Greater Germany, and she could understand this, she said, from her own experience. "My mother had been born a German in Lithuania," she said, "which was predominantly German. When I was a child we would travel through Danzig; that was German. Journeying up the Memel, again half of that was German. So to me at that time, you see, the fact that Hitler wanted to unite all these German-speaking areas seemed geographically and morally right. The people there wanted to be German and had never been given a choice."

As for the countries of the East and Russia that Hitler coveted, said Annemarie, "I suppose we thought as we were now at war, one would have to finish the war and then there would be peace talks, treaties, and it would all be reorganized as Europe had often been reorganized in history, and often to the benefit of the people. And you mustn't forget what the vast majority of people in the world have not been able to believe—we knew nothing then of the horrors which emerged later. War in itself, when it broke out, was horrible enough; I knew many people, but I knew no one who wanted war. . . ."

At the time she didn't think that Hitler wanted war. "But afterwards, yes, of course," said Annemarie. "Afterwards, when we learned what had been done in our name, I had to ask myself whether finally there were forces at work in Hitler which were incompatible with what is human. I know such an idea is unacceptable on a rational level. Speer, for instance, would try to avoid such a train of thought. But if one opens oneself to the whole abyss of what was done, and if one is prepared to confront one's own mourning, then one is almost inevitably led to this thought, for how can a man who brought about and allowed such horror have been human?"

On one of the many occasions when Speer talked about how at the outset he could not see Hitler for what he was, he described his own process of reassessment. "In the spring of 1937," he said, "Hitler said something to me that should have made me realize the extent of his megalomania. He came to my Berlin showrooms to look at the seven-foot-high model of the stadium. Talking about the Olympic Games, I pointed out to him that the athletic field did not conform to the proportions prescribed by the Olympic Committee. 'That's immaterial,' said Hitler. 'In 1940 the Games will be held in Tokyo, but after that, for all time to come, they will take place in Germany, in this stadium. And then it is we who will prescribe the necessary dimensions.'

"Thinking of this later, it was almost incredible to me that this didn't open my eyes. I was after all a sportsman, passionately interested in the Olympic Games since childhood, and I knew perfectly well that the whole universal concept of the event presupposed a change of venue every four years. How could he have thought he could bend the powerful world of sports to his will? How could he have wanted it? How could I not have realized that day that he was mad? Well, I didn't; I can almost still see myself smiling in admiration at his prophetic words. He had drawn me into his madness."

On May 14, 1953, Speer wrote to Hilde from Spandau:

> . . . There is such a thing as mass hypnosis which—we have seen it before in the life of nations—can have incredible consequences. Let me remind you only of the witch-hunts of the Middle Ages, the horrors of the French Revolution, or the genocide of the American Indians. . . . In such periods there are always only a very few who do not succumb. But when it is all over everyone, horrified, asks, "For heaven's sake, how could I?"

A few months later, on November 18, 1953, at the end of a paragraph on this theme in his "Spandau draft," he says, "In those first years close to Hitler . . . I was ready to follow him wherever he led. . . ."

In 1937, Speer said, he had no idea where he was being led. He did not even realize that almost imperceptibly his role was changing when he received "the greatest commission" and then the signal honor of being named Generalbauinspektor.

Despite countless Hitler biographies and psycho-profiles, we still do not know to what extent Hitler acted intuitively or tactically. Around the time he appointed Speer GBI, Hitler suggested to Goebbels that it was time Speer got some uniforms. Speer joked about this to me, but this decision of Hitler's might have had some significance. The architect would not be expected to wear a uniform, but an officeholder would be. And if we look carefully at Speer's life with Hitler between March 1937 and February 1942, when it changed radically with his appointment as Minister of Armaments, we can see how he was being slowly brought into the political involvement he was later so fervently to deny. We can see a man who was being groomed either intuitively or by conscious design by Hitler for higher office.

"Of course, having to set up, and being part of, an administration did change things," said Annemarie Kempf. "Everything had to be done just so; we had to learn to account for every penny on printed forms. And although we started out with a small, almost intimate team, within a few weeks or months we were a big organization."

There were about eighty-five on the staff of the GBI, besides many contract free-lancers. One of Speer's early appointments was Karl Hettlage, originally a professor of administrative and financial law, who from 1934 had been in charge of Berlin's financial affairs, and who would after the war be State Secretary for Finance in German Chancellor Konrad Adenauer's government.

Professor Hettlage was in fact one of those Annemarie was talking about when she spoke of Speer's organization becoming something of a refuge for people who were under a cloud. Having been an active member of the Catholic *Zentrum Partei* since his early youth, he might well have been considered politically unreliable.

Perhaps it was this, or the fact of his eminence in postwar Germany, but there was a subtle difference between him and many of the other "Speer men" I met, although many of them also had distinguished careers after the war. With Dr. Hettlage, an elegant, gently humorous and perceptive man, one had the distinct impression of someone who had nothing to regret, unlike so many Germans of that period.

"Speer asked to see me very soon after he was named GBI," Hettlage told me when we met in his house in Bad Godesberg (near the federal capital Bonn). "He wanted to find out how the rebuilding of Berlin could be financed. I told him Berlin alone couldn't manage it; the state, business or industrialists would have to come into it. My first impression was that he would merely be carrying out Hitler's concepts. He seemed very young and much too inexperienced for such a mammoth task. But I could see almost at once that he was most exceptional, highly intelligent and extraordinarily adaptable.

"He told me at that first meeting that he knew nothing about finances and wanted to learn from me. But in fact he had quite a good grasp of it, as he had a good feel about so many things. There was nothing naive about Speer," he said. "I saw him from the start as a very complicated, many-sided personality.

"I was appalled at the idea of rebuilding a whole metropolis; government and representational buildings, roads and even the railway system was one thing, but a whole city? It seemed mad to me. This extravagant concept manifestly came from Hitler. I was sure, and Speer confirmed this later, that many of the actual ideas for buildings also originated with him. But I have to admit that later I was astonished at the care, the quality of the plans Speer produced."

I wondered about the relative input of Hitler, Speer and Speer's team. "Well, the refining of the designs and the building of the models was team-work, of course, as one would expect," he said. "But although you can see from the sketches Hitler gave to Speer that many of the ideas were his, it was Speer who expanded and developed them, perhaps giving them more reality as they talked, and before the war they conferred almost daily, and endlessly."

In those days Hitler clearly considered Speer his architectural alter ego, Hettlage said. "I don't think this was because of Speer's talent as an architect; there were other architects he admired and gave big commissions to. Hitler's whole being was political—in the sense of being primarily or entirely orientated toward political manipulation. He applied this to politics and politicians; to architecture, which was on the one hand his passion and with which, on the other hand, he intended to change the face of German cities; and eventually to the military too. Somehow something grew between him and Speer that enabled Speer to understand and respond to that inner core. It was this capacity—this empathy—that brought about Speer's immense power."

Wasn't that contrary to Speer's claim, both at Nuremberg and in his books, that he was not a political man?

Dr. Hettlage shrugged. "Speer's relationship with Hitler in those first years was not primarily cerebral—it was very special, spontaneous in a way, for both of them. These are very subtle matters," he said. "They can't be categorized into Speer's having been or not having been 'a political man.' He could respond to Hitler, who *was* a political man, in the way Hitler needed because—not a conscious, self-serving decision—he needed to respond to him. That's about all one can say. Nothing is ever just black and white, is it?"

Six months after the initial encounter, Speer invited Hettlage to join his administration and from then on he would be one of Speer's closest advisors, first at the GBI and subsequently as head of the Department of Administration and Finance at Speer's ministry.

"I must say that he interested me very much," Hettlage said. "In the final analysis, there was no one in Germany of his caliber; he was what I would call a 'psychic' [intuitive] organizer, a very special gift which went far beyond architecture or any specialty. And I suppose one must say that it was very perceptive of Hitler to recognize this talent so early.

"It was quite extraordinary how Speer didn't . . . " he paused, "how shall I put it? You know how some people exude strength and power? Well, here was this very young, quite extraordinarily powerful man, and there was nothing about him that showed awareness of that power. What one saw was someone exceptionally courteous, calm, friendly, humorous and modest. For years he never showed anger, even when he was angry, no fatigue even when he was seriously overworked, no tension when one knew of the problems which beset him."

(Oddly, despite his perceptiveness, Hettlage seemed unaware both of Speer's exhaustion and of what Margret described as his "strange attacks," of which Speer himself said, "Everyone was so worried about them.")

"It took a long time before I understood that there was a screen between him and others—a defensive mechanism of quite extraordinary proportions." Dr. Hettlage had seen the profile I had done of Speer, before we met. He smiled at me. "He raised that screen for you, didn't he? You got on together, didn't you? With Speer, that was what always counted," he said. "Strange, isn't it? What really determines the course of human affairs is finally never talent and intelligence. It's feelings, isn't it? Good and bad. For Speer, his father, Tessenow, Hitler—" He shook his head. "And we saw him as the rational man par excellence."

It was Hettlage who put his finger on a strange truth as early as the summer of 1938, as Speer had told me: "He had watched Hitler with me in front of the model of Berlin, and after Hitler had gone, Hettlage suddenly said, 'You know what you are? You are Hitler's unhappy love.' And you know what I felt? Happy. Dear God, I felt happy." When I asked if he had felt flattered, he looked startled. "Flattered?" he repeated and pondered the word. "No," he said. "Joyful."

Speer's first architectural designs—and even the interior decorating he did of places such as Goebbels's ministry—were still strongly influenced by Tessenow. Goebbels, originally delighted with the "quiet simple craftsmanship" of Speer's work, apparently soon tired of its esthetic purity and had his offices redecorated by someone working more to his taste for Germanic *Gemütlichkeit*.

But as Speer came increasingly under Hitler's influence, he changed.

Tessenow, when shown the first Nuremberg designs in 1933, delivered the devastating comment that they were only "big." He was no less dismissive five years later, when Speer showed him the plans for the new Chancellery and pointed out that he had completed them exactly to schedule. "Perhaps you should have taken a little more time," said Tessenow, drily.

And Speer's architect father, by then seventy-five years old and retired, was even more disapproving when Speer took him to see the model of Berlin. "By this time," Speer told me, sounding rather bitter as he recalled the event, "he had suddenly become proud of my success. He carried around a little note-book, and would read from it when he met his friends. 'Now he's been given the German pavilion to design for the World's Fair,' or 'Now he's going to rebuild Berlin,' or 'Now the Reich Chancellery.' But he didn't feel like that about the new Berlin when he actually saw it. He stood and looked at the model for a long moment. Then he said, 'You've all gone completely insane,' and walked out."

Paradoxically, Speer sounded almost pleased about his father's negative reaction as he told the story. But that wasn't what he had felt then. "At that time I was so blinded, I just attributed his reaction to the generation gap. As far as I was concerned, I was following my brief, which was to interpret the political spirit of the time, Hitler's spirit, and this meant gigantic dimensions. Of course I knew about my father's liberal credo, and I just thought he couldn't understand. Because he couldn't understand Hitler, he couldn't understand our time.

"But it didn't end there. The next evening he came to the theater with me. Hitler sat in a box across from ours and sent his aide to say that if the old gentleman was my father, he would like to meet him. As soon as my father stood facing Hitler, I saw him pale and tremble—his whole body shuddered as if he had the ague. He didn't appear even to hear Hitler's hymn of praise about me; he just bowed without having said a word and left the box. Outside, he stood for a long moment breathing deeply, then the trembling stopped.

"Stupidly, I thought he was just unbearably moved, and I was surprised by his unusual display of feeling. Although we had never touched each other in my life except on formal occasions, I remember I touched or perhaps even tried to take his arm. He pulled away quite sharply.

"Now of course I understand: emotionally, politically and, yes, morally on a different plane from the Nazis, he had somehow felt that night that other 'id' in Hitler—whatever it was—which I never sensed until years later."

When asked what he meant by "that other id" (which sounded so surprisingly and unexpectedly like the "not human" Annemarie had spoken of), he shook his head. "I don't know," he said. "I'm not much good at that kind of thinking. Casalis was, of course; we talked about it many times. You know, about the origin and nature of evil. . . . I still don't know how to handle it. Casalis had a great gift, not for rationalizing the perhaps irrational, but for simplifying it. 'Just accept that Hitler was mad,' he said once. 'Leave it at that.' "

("Of course, that wasn't the whole of it," said Georges Casalis when, years later, he heard of this remark. "But Speer's mind—however he tried, and believe me he did try—simply did not lend itself to the metaphysical. One could only deal with him—help him—if one understood and accepted that.")

"I think that is what my father sensed that day," said Speer, "and I suppose from then on he identified me with that madness too. No, he never talked to me about it. I suppose he knew that it would have been pointless."

VII

A Slight Discomfort

Nuremberg, June 20, 1946

FLÄCHSNER: In your documents, as far as you remember, did you ever make statements regarding ideology, anti-Semitism, etc.?

SPEER: No; I never made any statements of the kind, either in speeches or memoranda. I assume that otherwise the Prosecution would be in a position to produce something like that.

SPEER HAD, of course, known that the issue of his feelings about the Jews would come up at Nuremberg, and he gave the only answer one could expect him to give. It would be fair to say, I think, that every one of the accused was anti-Semitic, though of course in varying degrees.

Speer had long managed to convince himself that there was a difference between "social" and "real" anti-Semitism; in truth there is no such difference, except that one makes the other possible. Racialism of any kind begins with a feeling of physical or intellectual rejection of a human being who is seen as different from oneself, and here degrees of feelings or in the expression of such feelings are immaterial.

Just as the moral implications of the Röhm Putsch, followed by the Nazis' murder of the Austrian Chancellor Engelbert Dollfuss, had eluded Speer, virtually all the ominous things which happened between 1934 and 1939 bypassed his awareness. Hitler's "spell" and Speer's incredible rhythm of work do in fact explain a great deal, at least for those early years. But as for the Jews, the crime that preoccupied him most after Nuremberg, the explanation is less simple. An innate anti-Semitism—not confined to Speer or the Germans—may have contributed to his instinctive or deliberate blindness. His conscious mind, however, denied this, as he wrote to Hilde on May 14, 1953:

> My conscience is really entirely clear in that I never took any part in anti-Semitic activities or made any anti-Semitic remarks. . . .

There are not many recorded instances of Germans of Speer's generation accusing each other of anti-Semitism—it would have been unwise. However, the most specific accusation against Speer comes in a letter to him from his brother Hermann, dated July 25, 1973, and this was certainly written, and intended to be used, with malice.

The brothers had not got on since childhood, and Hermann was beset by emotional and financial problems throughout his life which Speer, during his years in power, frequently helped him solve. During the Spandau years, and after their parents' death, Hermann had borrowed against and finally used up his inheritance. By the time he wrote this letter to Speer, he had been financially dependent on him for five years. He was hoping to write a book of his own, and, trying to find a publisher, he sought the help of a German historian he knew to be critically inclined toward Speer. He sent him copies of this and other letters he had written to his brother. Hermann wrote,

> . . . But all of you happily went along with that stupid hatred of the Jews. I remember your telling me in 1938 that you had suggested to Himmler to set up brickworks in [the concentration camp] Oranienburg for the reconstruction of Berlin. And jokingly, you pointed out a precedent: "After all," you said with that total cynicism you habitually manifested toward moral problems, "the Jews already made bricks under the Pharaohs. . . ."

Whatever Hermann Speer's motivation, this story rings true enough and shows Speer's indifference about the Jews and his early cooperation with Himmler. But it is of course irrelevant to any knowledge of the eventual fate of the Jews.

In what I might call our primary three weeks of conversations (very different from many other talks over the subsequent three years), Speer readily agreed to a plan I suggested: to begin with his childhood and youth and move through his architectural work with Hitler, the war and his increasing power leading to Nuremberg, to Spandau and his writings. But in talking about all these facets of his life—in the end, not surprisingly, not as methodically as planned—there were a few subjects he always came back to: his feelings for Hitler, the trial, his years of solitude in prison and the Jews. To a degree, even if these matters when he brought them up were outside the main subject then under discussion, they might be either a link to it, a needed escape from it or simply something he was trying to approach in his own way. (The exception was his feeling of guilt about the murder of the Jews, which I refused to discuss until the time was right.)

Thus one day, when we were talking about Hitler in 1938, he veered away from it to talk about Spandau. "I learned a great deal there," he said thoughtfully, "above all from Casalis, but also from the many books I read. My first book was written partly under the influence of that prison life but also, inevitably, of what I experienced in the immediate post-Spandau years. Many people—above all Rudi Wolters and my children—have reproached me for what they consider self-serving interpretations of people and events which, so says Rudi, I had seen very differently at the time. This is true: I continued to wear blinkers, long after anyone who wanted to see the truth could see it, because they enabled me to hold on to the two things which had become my life: my power and my feelings for Hitler.

"As of the beginning of 1945, however, I passed through what modern psychologists call five stages of trauma, each of which was bound to affect my subsequent reactions."

The first stage, he said, was the months preceding the end of the war. "It was a period of disillusionment and despair." The second and briefest stage, which he did not want to discuss at that point, though we would get to it later, was the days just before and after Hitler's death.

"Then of course came Nuremberg—stage three. With the trial itself, plus six months before and nine months afterwards, there was a period of more than two years when I alternated between euphoria and depression. Oddly enough, mainly euphoria for the ten months before the sentencing, when I was fairly certain I would get the death penalty, but a mind-numbing kind of depression for a long time afterwards, well into the first months at Spandau. We were transferred there at the end of July 1947; my mood only changed when Casalis came, in September."

The nineteen years spent at Spandau was stage four. (His sentence of twenty years began when it was announced, on October 1, 1946.) Despite periods of acute loneliness and the realization of accruing age, "it was an enormous, powerful experience," he said, "but actually, despite some terrible moments, it was peace. And I feel that today when I relive the time in my mind, as I did when I was living it."

The fifth stage was after Spandau. "Leaving there was pure joy, but living again in the world was—yes, traumatic. It was then I realized how sensitive they had been—Rudi, Hilde, Annemarie Kempf—who had done so much to keep my spirit and my mind alive for twenty years. How much they had carefully *not* said in their letters, to avoid my being faced with too much reality; shades and variations of doubts and understanding of our recent history which, in the isolation of my life at Spandau, I simply couldn't have dealt with."

This was the reality—"twenty years of *life* from which they protected me"—which he had to confront after Spandau. "And given that—contrary to me—every single person who would read my book would have fully experienced those twenty years, which would inevitably affect the way they would read and react to it, I felt that what I said and the way I said it somehow had to take into account these gradations of understanding of which I was entirely ignorant. So I talked to friends and the children and [his publisher Wolf Jobst] Siedler and [his editorial collaborator Joachim] Fest about all this: I was trying to bridge a void, you see, not in others but in me. . . ."

This conclusion to his thoughts about the five stages of trauma is what this digression had been all about. It is certainly significant that there was no mention in the "Spandau draft" of the developing campaign against the

Jews, the infamous Nuremberg Laws (the first dated September 15, 1935), or of the so-called Kristallnacht (Night of Broken Glass), the pogrom Goebbels organized on November 9, 1938. But in *Inside the Third Reich* (to which both of us, naturally, often referred) Speer devotes three paragraphs to the latter event, followed by a two-page summary of his feelings about his own reaction—or lack of reaction—to Hitler's words and measures against the Jews.

This passage was included, Siedler told me later, on his and Fest's advice. "He had nothing about the Kristallnacht in his original typescript," Siedler said. "I asked him about it. I said, 'It happened right in front of you, all around you; you cannot simply not have seen it?' And he answered what he then put in his book, that he was mainly disturbed by the disorder in the streets: broken windows, smoldering buildings. He claimed no indignation."

I fear that Speer's lack of indignation, and the similar reaction from countless other Germans, may be due less to insensitivity or cruelty than to Goebbels's brilliance in the comparatively new techniques of propaganda. The insidious preparation of the population first for action against hereditary illnesses—sterilization and eventually euthanasia—then for always stronger measures against the Jews was handled with considerable skill. It was not in *Der Angriff* or Julius Streicher's disgusting anti-Semitic tabloid *Der Stürmer* that the ground was prepared, but in small, slanted items in the quality dailies; long, learned articles in specialist papers; fictionalized stories in popular magazines; and finally—Goebbels's principal weapons—radio and films. All these served his purpose, and his Ministry of Propaganda quickly achieved a sophisticated effectiveness that the Allies were hard put to match.

Even so, Speer seemed exceptionally unaware of what was going on, perhaps because he was unreceptive to the propaganda. Among hundreds of Germans of that generation I have talked with, Speer for a long time was the only one who claimed not to have noticed the Kristallnacht. The truth was of course that he *had* noticed the more obvious results but did not seek to know the reasons. But Annemarie Kempf told me later that she, too, hadn't noticed it at all. "I just never knew about it," she said. "I remember that someone was shot in an embassy abroad, and Goebbels gave speeches, and there was a lot of anger. But that's all."

While this might have been acceptable from someone living an ordinary life in rural Germany, it seemed totally impossible for a young politically minded person living and working in the charged atmosphere of Berlin. Had she known any Jews personally?

"When I was a child, we had a doctor who was a Jew. But he retired before any of this happened. He was the only Jew I knew. In the three schools I attended, I can't remember any Jewish children; certainly, if there were any, it wasn't known."

But what about all the shops in Jewish hands one always heard about later, I asked, rather helplessly trying to get her to admit something. "Yes, that I did know," she said. "Department stores and all that were mostly in the hands of Jews."

Did she not remember even what Speer recalled in his book about that November day? The broken glass on the pavement? "No," she said.

As Professor Hettlage had said, "Nothing is ever all black or all white." I have no hesitation in saying that Annemarie, as I knew her, was a woman of total integrity. But in her, just as in Speer, just as in countless other Germans of the older generations, just as in innumerable other benighted people all over the world, there was and perhaps lingered a moral blind spot about "the Jews." Ignoring and then professing ignorance about this modern pogrom, unprecedented in Western Europe, was part of it, but it shows up in other, almost grotesquely small ways. On March 27, 1952, Annemarie wrote to Wolters about the new Denazification Commission soon to be set up in Berlin. "The people who may be heading it are a Dr. Lippe and a Dr. Levinsohn(!!). . . ."

Liking Annemarie very much, I often wished away those exclamation marks, and I know that if her attention had been drawn to them she would have felt ashamed. But the innate anti-Semitism I found in Speer's letter to Hilde, quoted in Chapter III (page 90), was present in some degree in Annemarie too, though both he and she—as we will see later—battled against those impulses in themselves as perhaps few did.

Willie Schelkes, a man also tortured by self-reproaches, brought up the subject of the Kristallnacht when we talked. He showed me a beautiful book, *Das Herz unserer Städte* (The Heart of Our Cities), by Hans Simon. "He was one of Speer's men," he said, "but then—" He paused. "Well, when [the Kristallnacht] happened, Simon said, 'For people like that, I don't work.' And he resigned from the GBI." Schelkes shook his head. "I thought that that was really something; to give up that chance, that career, for his principles. Since then I have often thought I should have had that strength of character. And I have asked myself why I didn't."

He hadn't been a witness of the Kristallnacht, because he was on a sleeper train during that night. "But I arrived back in Berlin the morning after, very early, and as the train pulled in I saw the smoking synagogues. It made me feel—" He paused again. "I thought this can't be right: this cannot be the right way. But—" He shrugged resignedly, saying, "That's as far as I went. I did not, like Simon, take the consequences." He smiled again, sadly. "He was the better man."

This kind of candid admission was very rare indeed, even by the 1980s. Even for Schelkes, who was so marginally involved politically, it might have been difficult earlier on, and perhaps inadvisable during the years of so-called de-Nazification after the end of the Third Reich. As the guilt of Hitler's men—not only Speer—would necessarily increase with whatever knowledge they gained over the last Nazi years, almost all of them were driven to maintain their declarations of ignorance, not only to others but often even to themselves. Both before their own consciences, and faced later with Allied de-Nazification proceedings which, particularly in the early period, could be very tough, knowledge itself seemed as great a threat as any acts they might have committed.

Every one of the people who had been politically involved, perhaps even every German who had been a party member, had a story prepared that would present him or her in the least damaging light. Knowledge was like a tower built of dominos—the smallest admission and the story tower collapsed, for no admission was likely to be accepted in isolation.

As a matter of survival in postwar Germany these people had every reason to act as they did. As the devastating truth about the Final Solution gradually emerged during the months after the war, an appalled world hardly knew and certainly forgot about the whole process which preceded it. Everyone learned about the concentration and labor camps the advancing Allied troops found in Germany, many of them on the edges or right in the middle of towns. The names of Buchenwald, Mauthausen, Dachau, Ravensbrück, Sachsenhausen, Flossenbürg and Belsen, among many others, within a few short months became part of every Western language. The pictures of pits full of nude corpses and disoriented skeletal inmates in concentration camps overrode all other impressions. But little was known that first year of the four *extermination* camps the Russians had found in Poland.

Even so, the suffering of Jews dominated reports both in the Western media and later—generally if not in specific terms—in the Nuremberg trials. As far as the Western world knew, all concentration camps were death camps, and most of their inmates were Jews. After the Nuremberg indictments in November 1945 cited the figure of 5,700,000 Jewish victims of the Nazis, the specter of nearly six million gassed Jews outweighed the information about the suffering of millions of other prisoners and slave laborers. It invaded all minds and soon became synonymous with Hitler and his rule. To a considerable degree, this partial view of the Third Reich has become history, and endures to this day.

The concentration camps, awful as they were, served first for anti-Nazi Germans and then for many categories of prisoners from many countries, as well as Jews. There were virtually no gas chambers in Greater Germany, other than those where German and Austrian "patients" (a Nazi euphemism) were killed during the Euthanasia Program. While close to six million Jews did perish under the Nazis, about half that horrific number died in various ways other than in the gas chambers of the four death camps of the Aktion Reinhard, and at Majdanek and Auschwitz in occupied Poland.* All these facts became blurred—a confusion which unhappily has played into the hands of the so-called revisionists who hope to whitewash Hitler for their own political aims.

The efforts of a number of historians to set the record straight have almost always been outweighed by the emotional impact of hundreds of books and films based on personal tragedies, most of them—because they were the worst and the most dramatic—suffered by Jews.

Speer was not, as is sometimes claimed, the only one of the accused at Nuremberg to feel and admit to guilt, but his admission, even though much too generalized, was remarkable because he was the only one who, by making it, risked fatally influencing the court's sentence, which for the others who accepted guilt—Hans Frank, Alfred Rosenberg, Otto Ohlendorf—was inevitable.

Speer's aim—to direct guilt toward those in power and away from ordinary Germans—had been quite legitimate, but his admission did not change the world's view. Much of the world to this day blames all Germans—individually and collectively—for Hitler's savagery.

It was the fear of this coming blame that made the citizens of towns and villages whose windows virtually overlooked the roll-call squares of the camps swear they had never known they were concentration camps. Even though in some instances they could see the punishments, beatings and executions being carried out almost daily, and regularly encountered the inmates on their terrible trudges to and from hard labor, on their way back at night often carrying their dead, they claimed not to know that anyone had been ill used or maltreated there.

More often than not, these people had been indifferent to the horrors in their midst. Sometimes, however, theirs were only lies of despair. But the Allied soldiers who had been confronted with the misery of the camps and the hideous task of burying the dead, and who tried to aid the survivors—many of whom were beyond help—were in no mood to give any Germans the benefit of the doubt. They, and with them the world's media, became convinced that all Germans lied, that all Germans knew about the concentration camps and, for that matter—the jump from one to the other was automatic—that all of them also knew about the emerging horror all newspapers and radio stations were talking about, the agony and the murder of the Jews. The world

*The Aktion Reinhard, commanded by the notorious Austrian SS General Odilo Globocnik, with headquarters in Lublin, administered the four camps—Chelmno, Belsec, Sobibor and Treblinka—which existed exclusively for the murder by gas of European Jews.

thus came to believe that all Germans—especially, of course, those who were
close to Hitler—were grievously guilty, if not for anything they personally
did, then for what they all must have known about from the beginning.

Few men could have been closer to Hitler than Speer. What then could he
have known in those early years, and what could he have known in the first
years of the war? What should he have known? And what should or could his
reactions have been?

These questions, although here focused on Speer and on the political and
ethical immorality of Hitler and his regime, cannot be—and are not meant
to be—so limited. For Hitler and his time they apply to all those in his immediate surroundings and to many more, as we shall see, who in the course of
time became exposed to dreadful knowledge.

But personal and national immorality is not reserved to any one crime,
any one place, any one ideology, any one people, any one group or any one
person. The immorality of Hitler is thus equaled by the immorality of Stalin;
the immorality of the Nazi torture camps in the 1930s and 1940s by the South
Africa that murdered Stephen Biko and untold others in their prisons during
the 1960s, 1970s and 1980s, and indeed by the increasingly emerging horrors
of the past twenty-five years in various South American countries. The immorality of the Lidice massacre was duplicated by Americans in Vietnam; the
murder of the Jews, however uniquely awful the technique, was numerically
even exceeded (though the mind recoils at such comparisons) by the Nazi
slaughters of non-Jewish Russians and Poles, and all of it was more than paralleled by the even now not fully known number of Russians whom Stalin,
Yagoda and Yeshov murdered no less determinedly than the Nazis murdered
the Jews. Finally, with the same cynicism the West demonstrated toward
those earlier crimes, nothing was done about the genocide of the Biafrans by
the Nigerians, of the Kurds by Saddam Hussein (whom the West could have
helped, but didn't, remove from power), and of all educated Cambodians by
the Khmer Rouge, whose political ambitions the West today, to our collective shame, continues to support.

I point out these comparisons not to escape from the subject at hand, or to
minimize the Nazi crimes. I do so in order to remind us all that writing,
thinking and judging, if it is to be of any value, must always be—and remain—comparative, open and in context with time, historical events and social developments. When considering individuals, it must be within the
context of the fallibilities and frailties of their lives. Recognizing that human
beings and their actions cannot exist or be judged in isolation from the environment which nurtures them is our first and only safeguard.

Hitler's plans, which he outlined candidly enough in 1924 in *Mein Kampf,*
had as their goal German domination of Europe.

"The nightmare of his overall plans," said Bormann's son Martin, who was born in 1930, "has somehow been, not perhaps forgotten, but certainly overshadowed by the murder of the Jews, which was of course the most appalling of his crimes. But as a result of the fifty-year-long concentration on this horror, millions of people, above all the young, don't even know what might so easily have happened—the changes in the face of Europe which so nearly came about, and which would have affected and fundamentally changed every one of our lives and bred immorality into all human beings."

Rightly or wrongly it is the genocide of the Jews which has dominated not only the world's thinking about the Nazis since the end of the Third Reich, but also the conscience of most Germans.

Again, then, what could Speer—what could anyone in Germany—have known in the 1930s about the eventual fate of the Jews? The answer is that, at least in the early 1930s, aside from Hitler's and Goebbels's polemics, which few people—including Jews—took very seriously, very little. Mass murder was not yet thought of, although persecution of the Jews developed slowly and steadily, an eventually fatal infection of the body politic.

The first *Aktion* the Nazis organized, a one-day boycott of all stores in Germany belonging to Jews, was decided on within days of Hitler's coming to power. Goebbels in his diary describes the week leading up to it. Before the Nazis came to power he had already sold several extracts from his diaries to German newspapers for ready money, and may well already have planned eventual publication for all of them. Even so, his writing is not yet as cautious as it would become later, after he had signed his contract, and he expresses freely his conviction that the Nazis were being wronged by the Jews, and therefore any action was justified:

> March 24 [1933]: We are very concerned about the atrocity propaganda against us abroad. The many German Jews who have emigrated incite everybody against us. . . . I am preparing a very cool and objective article for a large British newspaper to counteract it. . . .
>
> March 26: My article for the *Sunday Express* against the horror propaganda has been well received and will assist us in England. The Führer, after pondering the problem in the quiet of his mountain retreat, called me to join him in Berchtesgaden. His decision is that we will only stop this kind of agitation against us abroad by dealing with the Jews in Germany who so far have lived in peace. We are going to organize a radical boycott of all Jewish-owned shops in Germany. This may make foreign Jews think again. . . .
>
> March 28, 29, 30, 31: Today we announced the boycott: panic among the Jews . . . approval from all members of the government. . . . The boycott is fully organized. We press a button and it starts. . . . It will initially last one

day; if the propaganda abroad ceases, we stop it; if not, there will be no
mercy. . . .

April 1: Boycott fully effective in Berlin and the whole Reich. I drove
. . . [through the business district] to see for myself how it was working.
All Jewish shops are closed, each guarded by the SA. The people support
us with exemplary discipline. An imposing spectacle . . . a huge moral victory for Germany: we have shown to everyone abroad that we can call on
the whole nation for action without the least excesses. Once again the
Führer found the right solution. . . .

Goebbels naturally did not emphasize the objections from Hjalmar
Schacht, Hitler's financial genius (later acquitted at Nuremberg), who
warned him that attacks against the Jewish business community would be
viewed unfavorably abroad and cause Germany economic damage. Whether
it was these warnings or the "success" of the boycott claimed by Goebbels
which led to it being stopped after one day remains a moot point.

As the boycott announcement was made both in the newspapers and on
the radio and, affecting thousands of shops nationwide, brought the business
life of whole streets in many towns to a standstill, it is unlikely that any adult
in Germany could remain unaware that it was happening. But as Goebbels
said, there was no violence, and this may well have led to the reaction Speer
mentioned to his daughter in a letter from Spandau about earlier speeches
and demonstrations, when he said that they didn't "take all this too seriously," ascribing the verbal abuse to "birth-pangs."

It is not without significance that this first consolidated act against the Jewish community is not mentioned in many postwar histories of the period. It
would seem that neither all German nor other historians considered it any
more worthy of attention than did the German population at the time—
including Germany's 561,000 Jews. And indeed the passivity of the population
encouraged the Nazi government to pass a few days later the first of many
ordinances barring Jews from holding office or entering the professions.

Emigration accelerated throughout the 1930s, especially after the first of
the Nuremberg Laws in September 1935, but most people in and outside Germany, including many Jews, still could not accept their significance and danger. Increasingly restrictive decrees were passed during the next three years,
but the Nazis' approach to the introduction of these laws and regulations was
cautious at first. The party leadership was very concerned about potential reactions abroad and wary of possible disapproval in Germany itself.

On August 25, 1933, Goebbels wrote that on Hitler's order the first party
rally, at Nuremberg on September 2, would focus largely on the racial question:

He wants Rosenberg to speak; I warn him against [his fanaticism].

September 1: I rewrite my speech yet again, for reasons of our foreign policy moderating what I will say about the Jews. . . .

The feared reaction from inside Germany was not slow in coming. Time and again Goebbels's diary shows how many people in the arts—actors, composers, writers and conductors (many of them roundly condemned after the war as dedicated Nazis)—made considerable efforts in those first years on behalf of their Jewish colleagues. On June 27, 1933, Goebbels remarks on difficulties he is encountering at—of all places—Bayreuth. This was Richard Wagner's town and the site of the annual Wagner Festival, which Hitler always attended as the guest of Wagner's British-born daughter-in-law, Winifred.

Visit from Frau Thede [identity unknown] about Bayreuth. Another RM 300,000 are needed. [They are] insufferable in their procrastination about the Jewish question. But that's how it is with all the finance people. If [only] Wagner were [still] here. . . . [Wagner was an outspoken anti-Semite.]

July 7, 1933: Yet again arguments with [the great conductor Wilhelm] Furtwängler about the Philharmonic and the Jews.

Furtwängler fought for two more years for the Jewish members of his orchestra, only to give in at the end. Goebbels notes that Hitler agreed that Furtwängler's request to travel abroad was to be denied. And on March 2, 1935, Goebbels mentions what sounds like the final confrontation which caused the conductor to abandon his protests:

Furtwängler still tries to argue but then gives in, and consents to make our [agreement] public. What strange folk they are, these artists. Politically babies, all of them.

And a few months later, in 1936, he mentions that "Furtwängler [is] now good and obedient."

After the war the conductor, bitterly attacked in the British and American press, was asked why he had not taken a stand against the Nazis, and if this was impossible, why he hadn't left. Few of us believed him when he said, "I tried. They wouldn't let me."

Speer, a passionate music lover, had counted many famous musicians among his friends during the Third Reich. I asked him why, if these people had really not been devout Nazis, they—to whom the whole world lay open without language difficulties in practicing their art—had not made the obvious gesture and left?

He shook his head. "I really don't think people understand what it was like. People like Furtwängler, Wilhelm Kempff, Richard Strauss and others were considered to be, well, like national treasures. If they expressed disapproval or doubts, they would be argued with; if they remained unconvinced, they would be warned and put under open supervision. What would never have been allowed under any circumstances would be for them to leave— nothing so damaging to Germany's reputation abroad could have been permitted."

Goebbels's diary presents a whole parade of well-known names, all trying to maintain their friendships with—and protect—Jewish colleagues. In July 1935 he reports that the "*Stapo*" had intercepted a letter Richard Strauss had written to the writer Stefan Zweig, by then safely abroad:

> It is not only impudent but pig-stupid. . . . Now we'll have to get rid of him too. These artists are all politically immoral. Here is Strauss . . . President of the [state] Music Association writing a letter to a Jew. Disgusting. . . .

Two days later Richard Strauss resigned his position and from then on devoted himself to composing. In May 1936 Austria's leading actress, Paula Wessely, tried to get a friend, the screenwriter Walter Reisch, exempted from the increasing restrictions of the Nuremberg Laws.

> May 11: Have rejected Paula Wessely's request. She must learn to obey. . . .
> [Four days later Wessely's husband, Attila Hörbiger, also a mega-star of theater and film, travels to Berlin.]
> May 15: Attila Hörbiger tries to save the Jew Reisch for his wife Paula Wessely. I refuse. We have to be strong about this. He leaves, tail between legs. . . .*

Between March 1933 and September 1935 the "Jewish question" figures prominently in Goebbels's notations, again and again with the admonition (to himself, one must suppose) "Slowly, slowly." In July 1935 Hitler ordered Julius Streicher's *Der Stürmer* to be shut down for three months after it violently attacked Emmy Sonnemann, the actress Göring had married just two months before: she was known to have frequently interceded for Jewish friends and continued to do so after her marriage. Goebbels, who liked to think of himself as a "gentleman," had written repeatedly how much he deplored *Der Stürmer*'s gross style and its constant "idiotic" calls to violence. "At last!" was his comment on Hitler's order, though he noted two days later that *Der Stürmer* had apologized to Sonnemann, whereupon the order was rescinded.

*Walter Reisch went to Hollywood where, among many other films, he wrote (with Billy Wilder and Charles Brackett) the Greta Garbo film *Ninotchka* for Ernst Lubitsch.

A few days later, on July 15, on holiday in Heiligendamm on the Baltic, Goebbels received a telegram from Berlin informing him of "Jewish demonstrations against an anti-Semitic film." Berlin's Jews had evidently not yet been cowed by the Nazi ravings. Hitler had joined him two days before. "This has pushed the Führer to the limit, and it really is hair-raising," he writes. "I expect this will make the balloon go up." He was referring to the announcement of the Nuremberg Laws, which Hitler had had people at the Ministry of Justice working on for months.

The 1935 Nuremberg Rally, which Speer of course attended, opened on Wednesday, September 11; throughout the first three days and well into the night on Friday, September 13, Hitler, Goebbels, Hess and Wilhelm Frick (an "Old Comrade" who became Interior Minister) continued to adjust the speaking schedule. Despite the late date they canceled one speaker as being "too indelicate," and until the last moment "honed" the text of the laws Hitler was to announce and Göring was detailed to explain on Saturday night. "The great day!" Goebbels enthuses in his diary: the balloon was "taking off."

Gerald Reitlinger, in his classic *The Final Solution,* described the Nuremberg Laws as "the most murderous legislative instrument known to European history.... Though for the first time since feudalism the law recognized two degrees of humanity, it was probably not at all evident to the Jews of Germany that pogroms initiated by the police on Tsarist-Russian lines were implicit in the new decree."

This unawareness of what these laws would eventually mean extended far beyond Germany's Jews, to virtually everyone in and outside Germany—in part owing to the extreme care exercised by Hitler and Goebbels in their preparations, even to the detail of entrusting the actual "intolerably lengthy explanation of the decrees," as Goebbels put it, to Göring, who was a particularly tedious speaker on whom people were unlikely to focus attention for long. Speer would confirm this later: "He put one to sleep," he said, and added that he had not been "remotely aware of what Göring was talking about."

Of course, it was not yet genocide they were planning. We cannot know what was in the recesses of Hitler's mind, or even exactly when Reinhard Heydrich, the chief innovator of the "assembly line" extermination methods, first made his suggestions to Himmler. But from everything we have learned, it seems likely that the gas chamber murder of the Jews appeared feasible only when, first, the gassing of handicapped Germans and Austrians in Euthanasia "Institutes" provided a technical precedent, and second, when the shootings in the East brought no effective protest from the public or the armed forces.

But there was a distinct method to the gradual exclusion of Jews from German public life, and a deliberate linking of the Nuremberg Laws to the general ideology of "racial purity." The Nazi drive to "cleanse" Germany of genetic and racial taints had already begun before the first Nuremberg Law, initially not involving the Jews. On July 14, 1933, only weeks after coming to power, the law "for the prevention of the propagation of hereditary illness" was announced, with sterilization measures to take effect on January 1, 1934. From that moment on, a whole series of laws "for the protection of German blood and honor" was passed back to back, on one hand affecting those who were considered genetically imperfect Germans, on the other hand Jews.

The first of the Nuremberg Laws announced by Göring in September 1935, still sufficiently generalized not to appear specifically directed at the Jews, established a new Law of Citizenship with two categories: the *Reichsbürger*, the citizen who had to be of "pure German blood," and the impure *Staatsangehöriger*, who was a subject of the state but not a citizen. The next stage, the Law for the Protection of German Blood and Honor, linking the Nuremberg Laws to the general ideology of "racial purity," decreed that the two categories were forbidden to cohabit, "in wedlock or outside it."

This was quickly followed by another statute on October 6, 1935, the Law to Safeguard the Hereditary Health of the German People, which ordered abortion where either partner suffered from a hereditary disease. Over the following three years, step by step, further clauses (now published without fanfare only in the *Reichsgesetzblatt,* the official gazette) were added. All Jews had to provide information on their financial holdings; all professions became closed to Jews, except that Jewish physicians could treat Jewish patients; Jews were excluded from German schools and institutions of higher learning; Jews were no longer allowed to own factories, publishing firms, places of entertainment or large stores. ("Trustees" took over all these for minute token payments, leaving small shops which could, for a time, sell to Jews only.) Jewish musicians had to leave their orchestras, actors their theaters, dancers their ballet companies, singers their opera houses: Jewish artists could perform only for Jews, and nothing a Jew wrote, drew or painted could be printed or exhibited.

As of October 5, 1936, all Jews' passports had to be stamped with the letter J. Appallingly, this was the joint idea of the Swedes, eager to avoid the threatened invasion of Jewish refugees, and a Swiss, Heinrich Rothmund, the federal Chief of Police, who, wishing to protect the Swiss tourist industry, which would suffer if visas for Germans were reintroduced, thought of this simple device to check Jewish immigrants into Switzerland. As of January 1, 1939, Jews had to add the name *Israel* to their signature (and women *Sara*) unless their first names were already suitably Hebraic. Finally they were forbidden to attend theaters or cinemas, and at the beginning of the war an 8 p.m. curfew was imposed "to prevent Jews from using the blackout to molest Aryan women."

How much of all this should Speer—and of course many others—have known?

Because the publicizing and enforcing of these regulations and events (aside from the Kristallnacht) continued to be kept low-key, the answer is probably that they *could* have known but didn't need to, unless there was a practical need or a psychological or intellectual determination to confront rather than ignore the issue.

As recounted earlier, Marion Riesser, who transcribed most of Speer's letters from Spandau, told me how her father, a Jewish academic of distinction, although pensioned off at the advent of the Nazis from his professorship in pharmacology and physiology at the University of Breslau, managed despite the Nuremberg Laws to find employment, albeit at a less illustrious institution, until he finally fled to Holland in 1939. There were other instances where employers courageously ignored the law.

Equally significant, given their profound involvement with the Jewish community and their commitment in those early 1930s to Zionism, was the reluctance of Jews such as Raphael Geis to leave their beloved Germany.

On November 25, 1934, Geis (at twenty-eight, almost the same age as Speer) wrote from Mannheim, where he had been appointed deputy rabbi, to his professor Ismar Elbogen, an eminent theological historian who continued teaching in Berlin until 1938. Geis had written happily three weeks earlier that it looked as if he was about to be offered a position in a kibbutz in Palestine, but his concern in the second letter—the job had not yet materialized—was not the danger of the Nazis to Germany's Jews, but that of inner conflicts between Jews of different persuasions within the Mannheim community—he feared it would "come to a bitter battle between the liberals and the rest of us, Zionists, Center-party, and Orthodoxy."

At the end of 1936, more than a year after the first Nuremberg Laws, Elbogen, writing from Berlin, advised Geis against emigrating to Palestine. "You are needed here," he said. "Here the demand for rabbis is urgent; in Palestine they are superfluous. . . . You lose nothing by putting it off and gain a great deal . . . quite aside from saving your mother's tears by staying. . . ."

On June 15, 1937, Geis became rabbi for the province of Hessen, Niederhessen and the Jewish community of Kassel. In 1938 he was offered the opportunity (and a visa) to go to the United States but declined in favor of remaining in Kassel, seat of one of the oldest and most distinguished Jewish communities in Germany. There, on November 10, the morning after the Kristallnacht, he was arrested along with thousands of others across Germany, and sent to the Buchenwald concentration camp. Even though his imprisonment was relatively brief, the experience left indelible scars. He rarely talked about it, except thirty years later to Speer. Released after four weeks upon proof of a visa to Palestine, he finally left Germany in February 1939, to return as soon as it was practicable, in 1952.

Whatever explanations countless Germans, including those around Hitler, have given about their reactions to this first pogrom in modern German history, it was a watershed. Not because anyone knew or could know that three years later the Nazis would begin their systematic annihilation of European Jewry. But what it did—in contrast to the one-day boycott in March 1933 and the careful legal moves of the Nuremberg Laws—was to make violence by the state seem almost normal, and as we see from the reactions, acceptable. This is in marked contrast to Speer's reaction in 1931 to the police striking out at innocent people.

The necessity for this indoctrination was, as can be seen in Goebbels's diaries, appreciated very early. It was this achievement, accomplished with what was then unprecedented conditioning techniques, that laid the groundwork for as yet unspecified things to come, and went far beyond the intensification of anti-Semitism which made violence against Jews appear justifiable. It achieved the total personality change of a largely Christian-ethic-oriented and culturally sophisticated people which made possible the sweeping violence Hitler had always intended and which he now unleashed.

None of this happened without the knowledge and, to an appalling degree, the active cooperation of the rest of the Western world. The exodus of Jews, originally seen by the Nazis as a solution, declined as more and more countries—with the United States and Switzerland in the lead—closed their borders. When the war in the East brought additional millions of Jews into German hands, along with huge areas where dark undertakings could be quietly carried out, the decision was not long in coming. It had no doubt already been taken when Germany forbade any further emigration from occupied France and Belgium in May 1941; the Jews had to be kept where they could be caught, for the purpose now was no longer just to rid Germany of its Jews, but to eradicate Jewry in Europe.

Coupled with the improvements the regime had accomplished with employment, a stable currency and a huge wave of optimism among the young, and major coups in foreign policy in the Rhineland and in Austria, it had been possible for Hitler—without protest from decent Germans or a firm stand by Britain, France or the United States—to appropriate by blackmail the sovereign republic of Czechoslovakia; to declare war on Poland on a pretext so thin a child could see through it; to kill scores of thousands of handicapped Germans and Austrians of all ages; and to cover his extended Reich with a network of hundreds of concentration and labor camps where, mostly within sight of a blinded population, thousands of "disobedient" Germans (communists, devout Christians, Jews, Social Democrats) were whipped into compliance with the perfect police state to which later foreign slave workers were brought by the millions to serve Hitler's—and Speer's—war machine.

In a country where immorality and violence had been legitimized, with its Führer totally obsessed with Jewry, his secret order for the physical extermination of Europe's Jews, who were unwanted by anyone else and thus now entirely at his disposal, became an obvious final solution.

VIII

Unleashing Murder

Nuremberg, July 1946

FLÄCHSNER [final speech in Speer's defense]: The personal interrogation of the defendant and the cross-examination regarding his activity in the party have shown that Speer, by virtue of his position as an architect, exercised purely architectural and artistic functions even in the party setup. Speer was the Commissioner for Building on the Hess staff, a purely technical assignment.... Naturally [it was] purely for artistic reasons that the party took over responsibility for building ... nothing at all to do with any form of preparation for war....

BETWEEN 1933 AND 1937, much of the world admired Hitler's pioneering ideas. During his first four years as Chancellor, he expanded the health, social security and old-age benefits pioneered by Bismarck and later adopted by the Weimar Republic. His elaborate public works included a network of *Autobahnen*, innovations such as traffic-free city centers with strict pollution control, and he further developed the existing parks and green areas. Most important, as Joachim Fest wrote in *Hitler*, "he returned a feeling of security to Germans after years of traumatic fears and economic depression, however objectionable his methods." And John Toland wrote in his *Adolf Hitler*, "If [he] had died in 1937, he would undoubtedly have gone down as one of the greatest figures in German history."

This was the time most people now like to forget, when American expatriate writer Gertrude Stein thought Hitler should get the Nobel Peace Prize; George Bernard Shaw passionately defended him; the Swedish explorer Sven Hedin lauded his "indomitable passion for justice, breadth of political vision, unerring foresight and a genuine solicitude for the welfare of his fellow citizens"; and Britons such as Lord Halifax (in reports to the Foreign Office) and David Lloyd George conferred their stamp of approval. "Hitler is a born leader of men, a dynamic personality with resolute will and a dauntless heart, who is trusted by the old and idolized by the young," wrote Lloyd George in the *Daily Express* after attending the 1936 Olympics. He had visited Hitler at the Berghof and then attended the party rally as his guest. "*Heil Hitler,*" joked Lloyd George's daughter when he returned to Britain. "Yes, indeed, '*Heil Hitler,*' " he replied. "A great man."

At the same time, activists such as Oswald Mosley in Britain, Charles Maurras in France, Leon Degrelle in Belgium and Chiang Kai-shek in China set up organizations along the lines of the Hitler Youth (which had adopted elements both from the romantic German-Christian Wandervögel and the political Soviet Komsomol), while right-wing Americans such as Charles Lindbergh openly sympathized with the rowdy, racialist German-American Bund.

Dr. Theodor Hupfauer was one of the less-known passionate National So-

cialists of the early years, when the Nazis fought for and won power. As time
went on he became one of the party's most important administrative personalities and for the last year of the war, as Speer's right-hand man at the Ministry, was loyal to the end, and indeed for the rest of Speer's life.

In 1985 and 1986 I spent a good deal of time with Hupfauer and his wife.
They were then in their eighties and living in a book-filled flat in central Munich. Hupfauer had lost none of the sharp intelligence which enabled him to
re-establish his spectacularly successful life very soon after Hitler's defeat. In
many ways he was an archetypal modern organization man. His wife, though
apparently a classically complaisant German wife, did, as will be seen, turn
out to have had less benign functions under Hitler's rule.

The Hupfauers were disconcerting because although eager to talk and very
informative, they had much to hide. But it was rather refreshing to find them
making no secret of their early enthusiasm. "I was a convinced National Socialist," Hupfauer said. "I want nothing to do with all those people who now
claim they weren't, that indeed they were resisters. I really sometimes wonder
who it was who elected Hitler and fought and won all those battles for him.
All of Germany, it now appears, was nothing but anti-Nazis. Disgusting.

"In 1931," he said, "there were twenty-eight parties in the Reichstag; no
chancellor could have achieved a majority. In 1928 the SPD [Sozialdemo-
kratische Partei Deutschlands, or Germany's Social Democratic Party] had
154 seats—in 1932, with seven million unemployed, 200 seats went to the
Nazis.

"You have to think," he said, "that multiplying that 'seven million unemployed' figure by a conservative three to include families, there were then
about twenty million people in need, with no unemployment insurance and
only the most minimal social security benefits. When that earlier catastrophe, the inflation, struck, when a loaf of bread cost a million marks and butter and meat ceased to exist for millions of people, they grew to hate—really
hate—anyone who had money, thereby exacerbating the already profoundly
resented class system. Hitler's promises of a caring but disciplined socialism
fell on very receptive ears. [The unemployment benefit system instituted
under the Weimar Republic after World War I was virtually wiped out during the 1929–32 depression.]

"I remember it all very well," he said, "particularly because I was studying
in Switzerland in 1927–28 and found myself confronted with heartbreaking
contrasts every time I went home."

He had originally wanted to become a sports journalist, but when an
uncle, who after spending twenty years in the United States had returned to
Munich to become a famous lawyer, tempted him with an eventual partner-
ship, he agreed to study law. "I was fascinated by politics—an interest my

uncle didn't approve of," he said, "but I spent a lot of time attending the League of Nations sessions in Geneva, listening to people like [Gustav] Stresemann and [Aristide] Briand."

By 1933, when he was twenty-seven and had earned a good law degree, he had made plans to spend two years in the United States to improve his English and gain some experience in American jurisprudence. "But when the Nazis, coming to power in a country beset by union troubles but without an effective labor organization, first disbanded the unions and then created the Workers' Front [Arbeitsfront]," he said, "friends persuaded me to stay in Germany. The party was intending to change the whole concept of labor relations, based on the principle of co-determination and shared responsibility between management and workers. I knew it was utopian, but I believed in it with all my heart."

(On May 2, 1933, although the frightened unions had ordered their members to take part in Hitler's May 1 "Joy of Victory" celebrations, they were disbanded. Their buildings were occupied by SA and SS, and their leaders were arrested and sent to concentration camps.)

In the autumn of 1933, Hupfauer joined the central office of the Workers' Front, led by one of Hitler's early comrades, Robert Ley, and was put in charge of its most innovative initiative, the Office for Social Self-Responsibility.

"And, you know," he said, "this really did become perhaps the Third Reich's most significant success, for the transformation it brought about has endured to this day. They actually succeeded in imbuing management and labor with the awareness of a common purpose. And most important for this country, where labor had been bedeviled for centuries by class warfare, it brought about the abolition of the industrial class or caste system, which is much more significant for the functioning of any country than class differences in social life. The real signal change was that the class struggle in industry was replaced by solidarity."

The way this was done, he said, was to set up a small number of models. "Today you would call them social laboratories," he said, "which by trial and error worked out the best working and living conditions within the selected concerns; when, after a period of months or even years a functioning mechanism was found, proposals would go to the Labor Ministry recommending that it be applied to all of industry, by law.

"There were hiccups along the way," he continued, "because the fact is that not all organizations could reach these utopian levels, but at least the ambition was there to work toward them, and the functioning models proved that this new concept of living provided not only industrial peace and economic success, but above all human contentment."

As of 1935 he set up four thousand panels with ten members each selected by individual concerns, five on each panel representing management, five labor. (The "Beauty of Labor" [Schönheit der Arbeit] organization, to which Speer assigned Willie Schelkes in 1935, was another part of the same endeavor.)

"It was these panels who did the work," Hupfauer said. "When problems arose, it was their job to sit until a decision was reached. This virtually always meant a degree of compromise on each side, but because they were sitting together rather than, as under the union system, apart, they had no way of *not* reaching an agreement. The rule was that they sat until they agreed, and that was that. It created both a common interest and a common responsibility.

"It is true that to some extent," he said, "we did impose decisions, for when positive decisions were reached in matters which were demonstrably in the common interest of all industries, we recommended to the Minister to pass laws which would make them matters of law. But of course, these were freely arrived at by workers and management deliberating together."

(As I said in the Introduction, I am quoting exactly what Hupfauer said during our many conversations. Obviously I had many reservations about what he was saying, but some of the favorable things he said about the Nazi regime were true enough: for example, they did reduce class distinctions between workers and management, civil servants and the professional classes, and created at least a degree of community interest and responsibility. Nevertheless, as he in fact admits, decisions arrived at by management and labor were not by free negotiation, but by politically supervised deliberations which had to continue until a decision could be agreed upon.)

Under the general economic rulings, Hupfauer explained, all salaries—including management's—were fixed. "But, as you can see very clearly now, the way to affect people's lives is not only—or even mainly—by offering them ever more money. This merely serves to create a never-ending upward spiral of price increases. What has to be done is to enable people to live enjoyably, according to whatever they earn." It was the recognition of this need—as relevant and necessary today, he said (in 1985) as fifty years ago—which brought about the Volkswagen, cheap holidays and hotels and, above all, cheap and good housing to buy or rent.

"It was an incredibly creative and exciting period," he went on. "People of my age were given unprecedented opportunities, and we came to feel there was nothing we couldn't achieve."

We have to consider this global atmosphere when we retroactively question the motives and reactions of someone like the thirty-one-year-old Albert Speer. What the admirers abroad didn't know, or didn't wish to see, any more than anyone in Germany, was Hitler's real plans for Germany and Europe which, for those who had bothered to read the book, he had outlined clearly enough in 1924 in *Mein Kampf* and which, having brutally eliminated opposition within his party, he began to set in motion in 1937.

In 1936, in my last term at an English boarding school in Sandwich, Kent—I was thirteen and, coming from Vienna, had spent two years there— my favorite teacher, Lee Hindley, had given me *Mein Kampf* to read. "Anyone who comes from your part of the world needs to read this," she said. Although finding it hard going, I did read it, and from that time on did not understand how anyone could be in doubt about Hitler's plans, including the annexation of Austria and the elimination of the Jews from public life, though of course not their physical annihilation. "If anyone had thought he was planning on [that]," Speer had written to his daughter from Spandau, "he couldn't have been elected." He was probably right that most Germans, however anti-Semitic, would have been horrified at the thought of outright murder.

In Germany, not only after but during Hitler's time, there was a curious snobbism about the literary merits of *Mein Kampf*, which sold millions of copies but, according to most people I asked, remained unread on most bookshelves. ("Nonsense," said Willie Schelkes and his wife. "Everybody had it, everybody read it. They just don't want to admit it. A funny place to draw the line, isn't it?")

"We probably leafed through it," Speer had said when I asked him, and Margret had nodded her assent. "But I got into difficulties at Nuremberg when during pretrial interrogations I first said I had read it and then, questioned by the Russian prosecutor during the trial, had to admit I hadn't. It was absurd, but I felt embarrassed about it—I'm not sure whether I was embarrassed about not having read it or about what it was. The truth is that Hitler told me not to bother reading it, that it had been outdated by events."

That sounds right, for oddly enough Martin Bormann's son told me ten years later that his father had told him exactly the same thing during the war, when he was barely in his teens. Actually, both Hitler and Bormann were wrong. The book, in spite of its lack of literary quality, was illuminating in its unequivocal revelation that Hitler's plans for Germany could only be achieved through wars.

Given that soon there were at least some Germans who opposed Hitler's plans for war (by 1937, these included Field Marshal Werner von Blomberg and General Werner von Fritsch, Foreign Minister Baron Konstantin von Neurath and, up to a point, even Göring), how could it be that not only the majority of Germans but even those in Hitler's circle remained either ignorant of or morally indifferent toward his real program, first for the appropriation of sovereign nations, then for aggressive war and the subjugation of whole populations, and finally, entirely unassociated with needs or acts of war, the systematic murder of millions?

Already in October 1936, Hitler had told Mussolini's son-in-law, Count Ciano, that by 1939 Germany would be ready for war. Two months later Göring, now in charge of the Four-Year Plan, told a conference of air officials, industrials and top officials in Berlin that at the beginning of the New Year, "aircraft production [would be] increased as if mobilization had [already] been ordered."

By the summer of 1939, Hitler, while continually voicing both to the Germans and the Allied leaders his determination for peace, had annexed Austria (March 13, 1938), the Sudetenland (October 1, 1938) and Czechoslovakia (March 15, 1939). Despite desperate appeals from Vienna and Prague—and the Czech President Emil Hácha's heart attack when informed of Hitler's conditions—the Western democracies did nothing except lodge mild protests.

If little about the preparations for these acts, and worse ones like euthanasia and the murder of the Jews still to come, percolated as far as Hitler's intimates, then, according not only to Speer but many other members of Hitler's circle, it was because Hitler succeeded very early in imposing on those in his service a fetish for secrecy. This was formalized on January 11, 1940, in General Order No. 1 (*Grundsätzlicher Befehl Nr. 1*) which ordered that no member of a government or military agency was to be informed or seek to know more about secret matters than was required for the enactment of his or her duties. It was posted on the walls of every military office and communicated to all troops as well as party and government officials. Equally forbidden was the "thoughtless passing on of decrees, orders or information specified as secret."

In my talks with Speer he repeatedly emphasized the risks involved in any breach of this secrecy rule. "Hitler required us not only to compartmentalize our activities but also our thinking," he said. "He insisted that each man should only think about his task and not be concerned with that of his neighbor. Carried to its logical conclusion, and linked with his secrecy order, this meant much more than his wanting people to concentrate their minds—it meant it was dangerous not to."

But he himself, he said, for a long time didn't feel that this affected him. "For many years, really until well into 1943, I certainly felt in no danger from Hitler—on the contrary. And what's more, as I myself was basically only interested in my own work and wanted those who worked for me to feel the same way, I considered it the right—the efficient—way to govern. After 1943 I was in danger from others, though not yet from Hitler; as of July 20, 1944, there were indications Hitler no longer trusted me, and by 1945, yes, I felt in danger from Hitler too."

Hitler had never discussed his future plans with him, said Speer, except "in connection with building. In his closing speech at the 1937 Nuremberg Party Congress he emphasized his plan for 'a Germanic Reich of German nationals.' I happened to be present afterwards when his adjutant told him that Field Marshal Blomberg was so moved by this sentence, he had begun to cry. I saw how Hitler accepted this emotion as a confirmation of the Field Marshal's fundamental agreement with him in this matter.

"Very shortly after that evening in Nuremberg," Speer continued, "Hitler stopped me as we were going up the stairs to his flat in Munich. He told his retinue to go ahead, and when we were alone he said, 'We are going to create a huge Reich combining all Germanic people, starting in Norway and going down to northern Italy. I must still achieve this myself; nobody else has the experience or the will. If only I can keep my health. And your Berlin buildings will be the crowning achievement. Do you understand now the need for their huge dimensions—the capital of the Germanic Reich?'"

Goebbels's diary of March 14, 1937, shows how the whole atmosphere around Hitler was impregnated with these feelings:

> The Führer loves Berlin . . . more and more. Discussions with Speer about building projects, especially the new Munich Opera. . . . [This emphasizes the degree of Hitler's reliance on Speer for everything to do with his architectural plans, because Munich was not Speer's responsibility but had been given to his greatest competitor, Hermann Giesler, who profoundly resented Speer's special relationship with Hitler.]
>
> Excellent about Austria and Czechoslovakia. We have to have both of these to round off our territory. And we'll get them, too. . . . Those little states suffer from a kind of primitive megalomania. When their citizens come to Germany, they are bowled over by our size and power. We need to emphasize it more; this is also the reason for the Führer's gigantic building projects. . . .

I asked Speer on one occasion if he had not understood that such a Reich could only come about by force, through war.

"You don't understand," he said. "It is the same with what he said to me two years later, in the summer of 1939, when we stood one night in front of the model of the great meeting hall and its enormous dome. Hitler pointed at the drawing of the German eagle with the swastika in its claws on top of the dome, which was to be 290 meters high. 'This is to be altered,' he said. 'Instead of the swastika, have the eagle perched on top of the globe.'*

*The Great Hall, which Speer often called the "Kuppelhalle" (Dome Hall), was planned to have a height of 726 feet, a diameter of 825 feet, with room for 180,000 standing spectators.

"Of course I was perfectly aware that he sought world domination," Speer said. "What you—and I think everybody else—don't seem to understand is that at that time I asked for nothing better. That was the whole point of my buildings. They would have looked grotesque if Hitler had sat still in Germany. All I *wanted* was for this great man to dominate the globe."

If Speer had said this at Nuremberg, he could have been found guilty on all counts instead of only two, and would probably have been sentenced to death. But why hadn't he said this in his book? I asked him.

"I'm not sure," he answered, and told me that he had written it down in Spandau but that, for a variety of reasons, he had suppressed or perhaps changed his feelings when writing the book.

I asked if it was that, by the time he wrote the book, he couldn't admit or thought he couldn't afford to admit feeling anything positive about Hitler. He looked up sharply. "Perhaps. Don't forget, I couldn't write the book in a void. Sitting down to write it, my Spandau-concentrated mind was in a way a blank page which, very suddenly in this intoxicating new environment, was inundated with impressions, opinions and conflicting feelings. I know that several of my erstwhile friends, especially Rudi Wolters but also Arno Breker, felt I was finally too sharp, too negative about Hitler. [Breker was his old sculptor friend to whom, during the Third Reich, he had given many commissions.] But the truth is, throughout the twenty years in Spandau I *felt* very negative about him—and about myself in his service—and paid for it, I think, with isolation [from his fellow prisoners]. But perhaps—that is true—I did feel somehow liberated when back out in the world, especially among the young, I suddenly discovered I was not alone in these feelings, and outside Spandau I was free to be as negative as I felt."

When trying to understand the reactions—and evaluate the later inactions—of Albert Speer, it must be done in the context of the atmosphere he lived in from 1933 on, of the lives of the men and women who were subject to the same influences he was, day in and day out, and thus, in the final analysis (for everything revolved around this), of the various moves made by Hitler.

After knowing so many of the people who lived around Hitler, I have no doubt that he did in a sense lead a double life. He compartmentalized his life, leaving the awesome decisions he made with top advisors such as Goebbels and Himmler and with his generals strictly outside his small private circle. In Goebbels's diaries, and the particularly reliable Below memoirs, there is further confirmation of this complex compartmentalizing.

One of the key documents of the Nuremberg trials was the Hossbach *Protokoll*, the record which Hitler's then military adjutant, Colonel Friedrich Hossbach, kept of a "most secret" meeting Hitler had on November 5, 1937, in the Wintergarden of the Reich Chancellery. Present were Field Marshal

Werner von Blomberg, then Minister for War, Chief of Staff Freiherr Werner von Fritsch, Admiral Raeder for the Navy, Göring as head of the Luftwaffe, and Foreign Minister Konstantin von Neurath. This document provided the most damning evidence at Nuremberg of what the indictment called "conspiracy to wage aggressive war."

Speer—at that point only Hitler's architect—was not present, of course, and does not mention the meeting in his books. What is perhaps surprising is that Goebbels, who was Hitler's closest political ally and advisor, was not invited either. On November 6, 1937, he reports lunching with Hitler on the previous day. The subjects of their discussion were "restraint in propaganda," regarding the Czechs, and the churches. His only reference in that long entry to Hitler's crucial 4 p.m. conference that day is, "Führer has discussions with General Staff," and his subsequent notes make it clear that he was not informed of the subject matter of the meeting.

Luftwaffe adjutant Below, as a junior officer also not present, did find out about it a few days later when Colonel Hossbach, feeling a need for support from his military juniors at Hitler's court, asked him and Hitler's naval adjutant, Lieutenant Karl-Jesko von Puttkamer, to read—essentially to act as witnesses for—the "15- to 20-page handwritten" report he had written about the meeting.

In his memoirs, Below recalled his impression at the time that Hossbach felt this was "an extremely serious matter of fundamental importance which it was essential for us to know about." Colonel Hossbach's foresight in providing himself with witnesses for the 1937 report was justified when the original of his report, needed by the prosecution in Nuremberg to prove the Nazi "conspiracy to wage aggressive war," turned out to have disappeared. A photocopy which did turn up was introduced into evidence, giving rise to bitter defense arguments about its authenticity and validity.

However, Hossbach himself essentially authenticated it in his book, saying,

> I don't know whether the document used by the prosecution at Nuremberg was my handwritten original or the copy, and I cannot say with absolute certainty that the wording of this so-called "Hossbach *Protokoll*" is identical with my original of November 10, 1937. But, after a great deal of thought, I have come to the conclusion that in essence the document here printed is a legitimate representation of the original.

In his almost three-hour presentation, Hitler showed himself to be extremely well informed about Europe, both politically and economically, and highly realistic in his evaluations of the future which, he said, had to be based on the assumption of a vastly increased standard of living in all Western countries. Economically, he said, survival would only be possible through a linkage of the world market which was at present being seriously undermined by the Bolsheviks' destructive economic mismanagement. Rearmament could not be considered a viable basis for long-term economic stability.

Pointing out the problems in India and Ireland, he said he believed the British Empire to be no longer viable, France to be "inner-politically" corrupt and Italy and Spain to be driven by unrealistic territorial ambitions. Germany, however, he said, needed land. (Hossbach's own words, as quoted in Nuremberg, were stronger. ". . . It was [the Führer's] unalterable resolve," he wrote, "to solve Germany's problem of the *Deutsche Raumfrage* [Germany's living space] at the latest by 1943–45. . . . As history proves, Hitler said, this could only be achieved by confrontation . . . never without attendant risks. . . .")

In a three-page appendix to his book, Hossbach describes how the original report came to be written. Not schooled in shorthand, he said, he was unable to record the proceedings verbatim and therefore deliberately did not himself call his report a "*Protokoll.*" But he took copious notes, above all of Hitler's explanations, which were expanded from a sheaf of handwritten notes Hitler had brought along and took away afterwards.

Fully aware of his responsibility, Hossbach was reasonably certain he had recorded everything essential Hitler said, but he could not give the same guarantee for his account of the give-and-take in the sharp arguments that followed between Blomberg, Fritsch and Göring. Hitler, who listened without comment, could not have been left under any illusion, Hossbach said, that his political proposals had met with agreement and applause; it was clear that both generals were rejecting any confrontational policy that would lead to war. "I consider that before history I committed a sin of omission," wrote Hossbach, "by not recording fully the position Blomberg and Fritsch took, and therefore showing insufficiently the unequivocal bitterness of their arguments."

He had worked for several days on his handwritten report, completing it on November 10, when he dated and signed it. He showed it to General Ludwig Beck, the Chief of the Army General Staff, who had not taken part in the meeting and was "devastated" by the content. Beck wrote a long critical commentary on it which was probably at least in part the reason for his premature retirement from the army eleven months later. Before handing it over to Blomberg, Hossbach had twice asked Hitler to read it, but Hitler said he had no time. "I thought that that was strange," writes Hossbach, "as he had described his presentation that day as his 'political testament.'" Blomberg took possession of the paper a few days later. General Wilhelm Keitel, then Blomberg's principal advisor, told Hossbach that the Field Marshal had approved the content of the report, initialed it and ordered it to be put in safekeeping at the Ministry. Much later, Hossbach learned that as Hitler's and the Third Reich's end approached, an officer had had the document copied, and gave the copy to a relative who eventually handed it over to an Allied official.

In *Inside the Third Reich* Speer very briefly mentions developments of major importance in early 1938 which in fact are well documented elsewhere. On February 2 the career diplomat Neurath was replaced as Foreign Minister by the former champagne salesman Joachim von Ribbentrop, the critical General Fritsch (who had been falsely accused of homosexuality) by Walther von Brauchitsch as Chief of the Wehrmacht, and Hitler appointed himself as head of all armed forces.

And on March 13, 1938, came the long-prepared annexation of Austria. Speer wrote in *Inside the Third Reich* that he was in Hitler's apartment when these events were decided upon or took place, thus—providentially, he implies, as he was only Hitler's architect—a witness to them.

Given this fact, and that the realization of the importance the world accorded to these developments must have come to him later, it does seem extraordinary that both in his book and the "Spandau draft" he mentions them in the chattiest of tones, and without the least indication that in 1938, when they occurred, in 1953, when he wrote the "Spandau draft," or in 1969, when he wrote *Inside the Third Reich*, he was aware of their political or moral significance.

And yet, once again there is just that slight difference between the two versions in the way he describes the Anschluss. In the "Spandau draft" (and in the book) he speaks of sitting in Hitler's sitting room in Berlin with Hitler's adjutant and other guests—Hitler having retired to his study—listening to the radio when the Austrian Chancellor Kurt von Schuschnigg announced a plebiscite for March 13 in order to allow the people to choose an independent or German Austria. Schuschnigg ended his speech—during which Hitler's adjutant had taken notes—with the words "Austrians, the time [for decision] has come." The adjutant, grabbing his notes, rushed up to see Hitler, reports Speer, and shortly afterwards Göring and Goebbels hurried in, in festive garb—"it was the ball-season, and a few days later, the Germans marched into Austria."

In the "Spandau draft" he makes it quite clear that he knew immediately that this was the prelude to the annexation of Austria. In the book, however, he distances himself from these events. "A few days later the Germans marched into Austria" is replaced by "Once more enlightenment came to me several days later and via the newspapers . . . on March 13 when German troops marched into Austria," he writes, giving the impression that no such thought had previously entered his head—despite the fact that the Anschluss had been on the lips of everyone around Hitler for weeks, if not months, and that he had known exactly what Schuschnigg's speech would lead to.

There is yet another small and, on the face of it, unremarkable omission in the book. In the "Spandau draft," describing his own trip to Vienna ten days later in order to "prepare a hall for a grand Hitler rally," he wrote—with honest perception—"Wherever I went, the German car was recognized. Up to this day I am touched by the reception from the population: happy, hopeful, I would almost say virginally expectant. . . ."

In the book this has shrunk to "Everywhere in towns and villages German cars were cheered. . . ." It is such a very small omission one feels it is almost petty to mention it. And yet is it so trivial? For there is a difference. In Spandau in 1953, thinking back to this event, he admits to emotional involvement—"To this day I am touched. . . ."—and he uses emotional adjectives to describe the population: "happy, hopeful . . . virginally expectant."

Sixteen years later in Heidelberg, he rationalizes it: no emotion, no communicated joy with the "virginally expectant" Austrians. Here he represents himself as nothing more than a cool observer and—in order to drive home both his lack of involvement and, just in case anyone might not realize it, his own post-Hitler willingness for mea culpas—he asks at the end of the paragraph, "Did any of this concern me?"

ON MARCH 12, 1988, the fiftieth anniversary of the Anschluss, I wrote from Vienna for *The Times* (London) about it:

At 7:50 p.m. on Friday, March 11, 1938, Austria ceased to exist. At 9:30 p.m. Elfie, my best friend . . . phoned me. Could I meet her at the Johann Strauss statue in the park, she whispered. "Why are you whispering?" I asked her—idiotically, as I would find out. "Come," she said and hung up.

While I waited for Elfie in the deserted Stadtpark, I heard . . . that sound for the first time: that rhythmic shout of many voices, and then those words I had never heard before and couldn't quite make out from that distance: *"Deutschland erwache! Juda verrecke!"* ("Germany Awake! Jewry Perish!")

When Elfie arrived, we found ourselves standing stiffly in the dark, listening. Then she said, "My father—" and stopped.

"What's the matter with your father?" I asked.

"He is a Nazi," she said, her voice tight. "They told me tonight. He's been an 'illegal' for years." She cried. "He said I was never to speak to anybody at the school who was a Jew, and that anyway," her voice sounded dead, "the whole place will be 'disinfected' from top to bottom. What shall I do?" she sobbed.

Two days later, Elfie and I walked around Vienna all day. On the Graben, one of Vienna's loveliest streets, near my home, we came upon a scene of fear. Guarded by men in brown uniform with swastika armbands—with a large group of Viennese citizens watching, many of them laughing—a dozen middle-aged people, men and women, were on their knees scrubbing the pavement with toothbrushes. In horror, I recognized one of the cleaners as Dr. Berggrün, our pediatrician who had saved my life when I had diphtheria as a four-year-old. He saw me start toward one of the men in brown; he shook his head and mouthed, "No," while continuing to work his toothbrush. I asked the soldier what they were doing; were they mad?

"How dare you," he shouted. "Are you a Jew?"

"No, and how dare *you*?" I said, and told him that one of the men they were humiliating was a great doctor, a saver of lives.

"Is this what you call our liberation?" Elfie called out to all of them. She was a stunningly beautiful child, but her voice was already trained for singing, as clear as a bell. Within two minutes, the crowd had dispersed, the guards had gone, the "street cleaners" had got up and gone away.

"Never do that again," Dr. Berggrün said to us, sternly. "It is very dangerous for you." They gassed him in Sobibor in 1943.

I told Speer that I was in Vienna in March 1938 and asked whether he had seen any Nazi brutalities when he was there. "No," he replied. "I saw nothing like that; I wasn't there for long. I stayed at the Hotel Imperial, and did my work at the railway station, where the rally was to be held; I strolled along the Ring and the old streets of the inner city, and had a few good meals and lovely wine. And I bought a painting—that was nice. That's it." It was a startling demonstration of insouciance.

I asked him if he knew that when he visited Vienna a few days after the Anschluss, the first wave of suicides, mostly by older Jews, was sweeping the city, and both Catholic and Jewish patriots were being arrested in droves.

"I knew nothing about that," he said. "I still know nothing about that. Suicides? . . ." An afterthought: "Schuschnigg landed in a KZ [concentration camp], didn't he?" He did.

He gave as short shrift to the subsequent events in 1938 and 1939. The annexation of the Sudetenland in October is barely mentioned either in the "Spandau draft" or in *Inside the Third Reich*; the Kristallnacht, on November 9, has already been discussed; and finally the rape of Czechoslovakia in March 1939, though mentioned in both places, figures only as an afterthought.

This last event took place while the Speers and a group of friends, among them the Brekers, the Brandts and Magda Goebbels, were on an extended trip to the Doric temples of Sicily and southern Italy. For Goebbels's unhappy wife, whose husband was pursuing his love affair with the Czech film star Lida Baarova, the trip was an escape.

It would later be said that the intelligent and elegant Magda—a rare combination in that circle—had always been in love with Hitler and had married Goebbels only to be close to him. But although there were indications at the very end of her life, six years later, that this might have been true (and the von Belows among others always thought it was) Speer did not share this opinion.

For he had been witness to her profound love affair in 1939 with Karl Hanke. Their determination to marry was thwarted when Goebbels threatened to take the children away from her, and Hitler decreed that a divorce in his closest circle was out of the question. Speer acted as a mediator that summer; in the end Baarova was sent back to Prague, and Goebbels and Magda returned to their hearth and home. Hanke resigned and entered the army, but left it in 1941 to become Gauleiter of Lower Silesia.

About this time Hitler's young mistress, Eva Braun, who until then had divided her life between the Obersalzberg when Hitler was there and Munich when he wasn't, was given a bedroom in Hitler's Berlin residence. From then on Speer saw her almost every day. By this time an entirely platonic but affectionate friendship had developed between them.

In a curious way this friendship, her only one with one of Hitler's men, was to become another expression of Speer's special relationship with Hitler, who, totally controlling her life, let her off the leash to go to parties and skiing with the Speers, and even twice permitted her to accompany them on a trip abroad.

Speer felt that "Eva Braun has been much maligned. She was a very nice girl," he told me several times. He had been "discomfited," he told me, by Hitler's conduct toward the young woman. One night at the Berghof he heard Hitler say, as she sat next to him at table, that a highly intelligent man should always choose a primitive and stupid woman. On another occasion, when Speer was present at a dinner Hitler gave at the Hotel Vier Jahreszeiten in Munich, which Eva Braun had been permitted to attend, although sitting far away from Hitler, he saw her blush deeply when Hitler, walking by without speaking, handed her an envelope. Later she told him that it was money, and that Hitler had done this in public on other occasions. "I felt horribly embarrassed for her," Speer told me. "Almost for the first time, I began to have a twinge of doubt about Hitler."

Although, on the face of it, their friendship was a "family" relationship and, whether traveling or dancing, Eva Braun went with the Speers as a couple, Speer became her special confidant (she never talked about personal things to Margret). It was to him she would come in tears in 1943. "The Führer has just told me to find someone else," she sobbed. "He said he can no longer fulfill me."

"There were no two ways of interpreting this," Speer told me. "She made it quite clear: Hitler had told her that he was too busy, too immersed, too tired—he could no longer satisfy her as a man."

I wondered if she was tempted to take him at his word. "It was out of the question for her," he said. "Her love for him, her loyalty were absolute—as indeed she proved, unmistakably, at the end. She was very young, very shy and very modest."

Margret Speer, listening as we talked, had not found her so modest. "With us women, you know, she was quite aware of her position. On trips, she was very much the hostess. If Anni Brandt said, 'Let's go sightseeing,' but Eva Braun wanted to go swimming, it's swimming we went and that was that."

"Well, she *was* your hostess," said Speer, drily. "You never saw her behaving like that when she was out with us, did you? She was of course very feminine," he said, turning back to me. "A man's woman, incredibly undemanding for herself, helpful to many people behind the scenes—nobody ever knew that—and infinitely thoughtful of Hitler. She was a restful sort of girl. And her love for Hitler was beyond question."

Margret, on the surface so shy and vulnerable, tempted one to protect her, to shield her from one's own intrusive questions. But then the awareness of her almost unique position took over—these times I saw her, I felt, might be the last chance to hear direct testimony about an era, events and personalities whose few key witnesses were disappearing one by one. It was incredible to think that this shy and sensitive woman had for years seen Hitler as a private man day after day, had spent those twelve fateful years virtually in the exclusive company of the men closest to him—and their wives.

What was it like for the women who lived under Hitler's shadow? I asked her one day when Speer left us on our own while he dealt with urgent letters.

"Well, you know, it *was* heady living in that circle. He was always very gallant to women, very Austrian." Every sentence was interrupted by long pauses, reflections and retreats, to allow her, it seemed, to catch her breath. "One never . . . we all just chatted and we watched films." A question about having a serious or perhaps personal conversation with Hitler, during those many evenings around the fire at the Berghof, made her desperately uncomfortable. "Not *conversations*—it wasn't like that," she said, looking away from me. "He talked. We listened. You are looking for something that wasn't there. . . ."

I told her that I didn't seek to be indiscreet; I was only trying to get an impression of what life was like for the women who lived so closely to Hitler in those years. In retrospect, had she been happy?

"Yes," she said, "I think so. I didn't see much of Albert—he was always working—but I had the children and I liked the house in Berchtesgaden and"—her eyes lit up and her tone of voice changed as if by magic, suddenly sounding young and happy—"the skiing in the winter." She looked out of the window of their mountain farmhouse, where we were talking. "I could go out of the door and ski, just like here, every day."

Her best friend was Anni Brandt, who, exactly her age, shared her passion for sports. Anni had been introduced to Hitler in 1925 when, twenty years old, she had just won a German swimming championship, and she had remained one of his protégées from then on. She became engaged to surgeon Karl Brandt in 1932 and introduced him to Hitler the following summer. A few months later, Hitler appointed the personable Brandt his doctor-in-residence, and in March 1934 he was, with Göring, witness at the Brandt marriage.

Hitler's secretaries, Johanna Wolf, Christa Schröder, Gerda Daranowski (married name Christian) and Traudl Humps (married to Hitler's valet Hans Junge, who died in the war), sipped spritzers and sunbathed on the terrace with other Berghof intimates and guests. (So did his dietician-cooks Constanze Manziarly and Marlene von Exner, who was dismissed in 1944—"Regretfully," said Hitler—when she was belatedly found to have a Jewish grandmother.) But although the secretaries usually attended Hitler's suppers and film showings and, in the latter part of the war when there was no more social life, lunched with Hitler both in Berlin and at his various headquarters every day, there was a distinct social separation between them and the other regulars at Hitler's Berghof (which, curiously enough, never included the wives of his four principal advisors: Göring, Hess, Goebbels and Bormann). Whatever social life these women of the personal staff had was either with their families or, more frequently, with one another, seldom with "outside" friends.

The "elite" wives, Anni Brandt, Maria von Below and Margret Speer, constituted a circle of their own, unconnected with the women on Hitler's personal staff. Eva Braun had an ambiguous position as the Berghof's unofficial hostess, but was shunted away on formal occasions, excluded from any trips Hitler took and allowed only limited personal contacts "outside." She was thus curiously dependent on social crumbs from both groups of his intimates.

But did those women Margret saw all the time discuss what was happening? I asked. Politics? The war when it came? Perhaps some of the worrying things which were happening as of 1934?

She didn't answer for a long moment, and looked for hidden meaning in the questions. "Not really," she finally said. This was the only time I pressed her when she clearly didn't want to reply. Was she really saying, I asked, that the conversation among the elite women of the Reich was entirely restricted to "*Küche, Kirche, Kinder*" (kitchen, church, children)?

That stung. "Well, no. Of course one discussed daily events but not. . . ." Full stop. I waited. "You know," she finally continued, "one just talked about people, gossip really, and about plays, films, concerts—and a lot of talk about artists." She paused. "One talked about one's children."

Speer had warned me that she was horribly nervous that I might ask her questions about the Jews. I did intend eventually to do just that, but realizing her palpable anxiety, I thought I would approach the frightening subjects step by step. When things happened everyone knew about, I said, such as people being sent to concentration camps, was that never mentioned between them?

"I didn't know anybody who was sent to a KZ," she said. "We . . . we really did live very much on the outside. You can't imagine that, I think."

I said that, yes, I could imagine this golden circle, but was she saying they didn't know that there were concentration camps?

"Of course we knew," she said, almost angrily, "but if one thought about them at all, it was as prison camps, for criminals. I mean," she said, quite tartly, "you have no objection, have you, to criminals being sent to prison?"

She said she didn't know people were sent there for political reasons—people opposed to the Nazi ideas, such as priests, for instance. (I thought of but did not mention homosexuals sent to concentration camps for "re-education"—it was not a subject that readily lent itself to discussion with Margret Speer, or indeed anyone of her generation in Germany.)

Her husband had certainly known it, I said.

"I suppose so," she said, now beginning to sound weary. "But that wouldn't have been a subject for discussion between us."

There were things, I said, which much if not most of the German population knew about, such as the killing of the handicapped in 1940 and 1941. Did she and her friends really never discuss Hitler's Euthanasia Program and its moral and religious implications? And Bishop Galen's famous sermon against it at Münster Cathedral on August 3, 1941, which became so widely known?* Did all this bypass them altogether?

She didn't answer, looked past me out of the window at the snow-covered fields, looked at her tightly folded hands in her lap. I had now gone too far.

"Would you like some coffee?" she finally asked, her voice tremulous. I

*The courageous Bishop Galen's sermon is said to have forced Hitler to put an official stop to the program, though in practice and in even greater secrecy it continued until the end of the war.

shook my head no, but kept looking at her. After several minutes, she managed to meet my eyes. "I can't," she said. "I like you very much, but I can't."

In fact, it was not quite fair of me to use the topic of euthanasia as a pressure point with Margret Speer. For although, in her horror at the turn our talk had taken, she couldn't even make herself protest her ignorance, the fact is that, protected as she was, she might well not have known about the Euthanasia Program when it was carried out. The intention was eventually to present it to the nation as a decision Hitler had long hesitated over, and finally only arrived at because petitions had been received from so many parents asking that their desperately ill children be allowed to die. But in fact the idea had been in his mind for years, probably from the time the hereditary-disease-prevention law was launched in 1933. Certainly he told his Minister of Health, Gerhard Wagner, on October 6, 1935 (when the law ordering abortions when necessary to safeguard hereditary health was published), that euthanasia would have to await the beginning of war, as then "the Church will not be able to put up any resistance."

Hitler's Euthanasia Authorization, written in October 1939 but backdated to September 1 to associate it with the outbreak of the war, was addressed on the Führer's letterhead to Philip Bouhler, head of the Führer Chancellery, which handled Hitler's special interests. He was assisted by equally odious personalities, SS Oberführer Viktor Brack and SS Oberführer Werner Blankenburg. These three, and the appalling psychiatrist-doctors Hermann Paul Nitsche and Werner Heyde, were all eventually involved as well with the death camps in Poland. Hitler's Euthanasia Authorization is a unique document in that it is the only order for murder that he signed; all the others were issued orally. It is also the first time Dr. Karl Brandt was mentioned:

> Reichsleiter Bouhler and Dr. Brandt are charged with the responsibility for expanding the authority of physicians who are to be designated by name, to the end that patients who, in the best available human judgment after critical evaluation of their condition are considered incurable, can be granted *Gnadentod* [mercy death].
>
> Signed: Adolf Hitler.

By this time the organization of this undertaking had already been in full swing for months. The Führer Chancellery* would administer it. Lists of German (and Austrian) mental institutions had been prepared, and thousands of registration forms ordered for the institutions to fill out to enable selection boards to choose the victims. The first three of what would eventually be about a dozen Euthanasia Institutes (Schloss Grafeneck near Stuttgart,

---

*This was a separate, small suite of offices located in a carefully secured part of the Reich Chancellery, with its own entrance at Tiergartenstrasse 4; hence it became known by the cryptic designation T4.

Schloss Hartheim near the Austrian city of Linz and a former mental institution at Brandenburg an der Havel) were ready for their grim task. Nine psychiatrists, physicians and pediatricians, all reputable and even well-known men, had been appointed as early as July 1939 to head the organization. When a year later a euphemism was needed to protect the respectability of the Führer Chancellery, the euthanasia team was grotesquely renamed the Charitable Foundation for Institutional Care, a term which, with the gross cynicism the Nazis made their hallmark, would be extended two years later to the Aktion Reinhard, the SS group, staffed almost exclusively with euthanasia-trained personnel, that ran the four extermination camps built specifically for gassing in occupied Poland. (Auschwitz and Majdanek were huge labor camps with killing facilities in separate areas, and were not part of the Aktion Reinhard.)

The Nazis were selective in their choice of euthanasia victims. As Franz Stangl told me—he served as police administrator of Schloss Hartheim from November 1940 and was later *Kommandant* first of Sobibor, then of Treblinka—they reassured new staff that "four groups" with whom they might have emotional ties were specifically exempted: "The senile; those who had served in the armed forces; those who had been decorated with the Mothers' Cross, for women who had borne many children; and relatives of euthanasia staff." But there were other exemptions, above all of anyone with any possible connection to people around Hitler or to top people in the armed forces, who would have been shielded from such knowledge and therefore any necessity to take issue with it.

Such people thus either would not have known about it at all or, if they did (and perhaps, like many people, even agreed with the principle of euthanasia), would not have known the shocking details of the actual program, and indeed could have neither imagined nor believed their horror.

Margret herself was far removed from contact with it. What is very difficult to accept is that the wives of those directly and continuously implicated in these crimes—which of course Speer was not—could have remained in total ignorance. One of the most telling examples here is Karl Brandt, Hitler's personal physician, close friend of Albert Speer and husband of Margret's closest friend, Anni, who—except when Brandt accompanied Hitler to his field HQ—shared her husband's life throughout the war.

By all accounts, he was a fine surgeon and an attractive man with a first-class mind. And yet, as the record amply proves and his own testimony at Nuremberg in 1946–47 confirms, when Hitler appointed him Joint Chief of the Euthanasia Program in 1939 he applied all his talents to these tasks, without ever—as with considerable courage he admitted before he was hanged— questioning the morality of Hitler's and Himmler's orders. (He did, however, object to gassing the victims, on the basis that as it was a "medical program," they should be killed by injections, to be given only by doctors. He was overruled.)

Brandt under cross-examination at his trial said that sixty thousand insane people had been killed, and that "feeble-minded and senile patients were included."* The killing of the insane (adults) officially ended in August 1941, though it continued unofficially until the end of the war. The killing of children ended officially that fall, though in reality they were still being killed as late as April 1945—some by hanging (see Chapter XIX). Brandt, no doubt for administrative rather than humane reasons, resigned his authority on children in 1942, though he still intervened in special cases.

Brandt was also involved in some of the appalling medical research carried out on concentration camp inmates. SS Dr. Ernst Grawitz wrote to Himmler in 1943: "SS Brigadeführer Dr. Professor Brandt has approached me to help him obtain prisoners to be used in his research . . . into epidemic jaundice. . . . It is now necessary . . . to inoculate human beings with germs cultivated in animals. *Todesfälle* [deaths] must be expected."

In other experiments carried out by Dr. Grawitz and Dr. Otto Siewers, wounds were deliberately inflicted, then infected with mustard gas. "Arms . . . are badly swollen and the pain is enormous," Grawitz wrote. Hitler requested that they confer soon with Brandt. "On account of the urgency of the order given him by the Führer . . . details were reported to Karl Brandt."

Aware of Hitler's secrecy rule and the need to protect the peace of mind of families and friends, one can well understand that men such as Brandt—and many others in similar positions—would not deliberately have informed their wives and friends of the nature of their work. But it is extremely difficult to believe that wives could have remained entirely ignorant, given the intensity of the work and the emotional impact it must have had on the men.

Indeed we have many examples of this from other men gravely implicated in Hitler's murders. When I was preparing my book *Into That Darkness* on the Commandant of Treblinka, I spent several days in 1972 in Unterammergau, a beautiful hamlet a few minutes from Oberammergau, where the famous Passion Play is enacted every ten years. I was talking to SS Corporal Gustav Münzberger, whose job it had been to drive the Jews into the gas chambers at Treblinka and who had recently been released after twelve years in prison. "Did you know what your husband was doing?" I asked his wife, a big woman with no apparent sense of right and wrong. "Well . . . he wasn't supposed to say of course, but you know what women are," she replied, with a touch of pride. "I probed and probed and finally he told me. . . ."

*This contradicts what Franz Stangl had been told, above.

And in Brazil, I asked Franz Stangl's wife, Thea, if she had told anyone after she found out what her husband was doing as Commandant of Sobibor and Treblinka. "Nobody, oh, nobody," she said, "not for a long time, a year; then, because I couldn't stand it any longer—I just had to talk to somebody—I told our priest. He said he understood, and would have done the same in my husband's place. He absolved him. . . ."

In the middle of April 1945, two weeks before the end, Karl Brandt sent his wife and children out of Berlin to Thuringia, which was about to be occupied by the Americans. A few days later Hitler ordered him arrested and court-martialed for defeatism, for not moving them to the Obersalzberg. On April 23 Speer flew into Berlin, one of his goals being to spring Brandt from prison before—as had just happened to several other high-placed men—he could be summarily executed. On arrival in Berlin, however, he found that Himmler—"No doubt for his own good reasons," writes Speer—had already spirited Brandt away to the north.

He mentions his close friend Brandt just once in the 1,200-page "Spandau draft," on January 8, 1953, the day he began to write it. "Hitler appointed Goebbels, [Arthur] Axmann [Reich Youth Leader] and one other to sit as a court over Brandt," he writes, "and they sentenced him to death for no other reason than that he brought his wife to [the country] where she would be safe. Maybe though he had other reasons to do away with him. If I had known Brandt's [real] record I could have wished him to meet his end through Hitler: it would have been better for him."*

Did he consider it possible, I asked Speer one day in the mountains when he talked about Brandt, that Anni Brandt would have known nothing about her husband's activities? His answer was evasive. "Well, *I* knew nothing of that part of his activities," he replied. "I just knew that he was in charge of the Reich medical services."

I PUSHED FURTHER, asking again about Brandt's wife. "I think he would have kept these secrets very carefully," he said. "I really think he would have been more likely to drop a hint to me than to Anni, and he didn't. If he was involved in such dreadful things no one could have guessed this for a moment. He really did seem to be a man of excellence. Even if he acted out of conviction, as I suppose he must have, he would not have wanted his wife to know about it." He then said almost the same words Margret had used the day before: "It would not have been a subject for discussion between them."

---

*Brandt was sentenced to death in the Doctors' Trial at Nuremberg, one of several which followed the first major trial of the top men in Hitler's government. He was hanged at Landsberg prison in 1948.

Annemarie Kempf did not know about the Euthanasia Program. The subject came up quite soon after we began to talk in Hamburg in 1985. "I now think it is really strange that I didn't," she said, "because my older sister developed multiple sclerosis in 1942." At that time, she said, there was "a lot of talk" about the mercy-death propaganda film *Ich klage an* (I Accuse). "So you see, one did know that these ideas were about; not only that, I remember discussing the film with Wolters and with other colleagues in our office."

With Speer too?

"No, not with him. You see, we discussed the film, not something that was actually happening. Of course I can't be certain, but I have no reason to believe that he knew this was actually being done. You see, if one had known, one would have had to question it, one would have had to face the reality of it and—much more than when talking about it theoretically, as the subject of a film—one would have had to question one's own attitude toward it."

If Speer had known about the Euthanasia Program, I asked, would he in fact have discussed it? "Speaking speculatively," she replied, "I rather think not."

I tried to draw Annemarie out on this subject because it seemed important to understand more about the climate of opinion from individual memories, rather than official documents. What I always sought was raw data, personal and spontaneous, which might reveal more than what was commonly known.

"I did remember," she said, "though I paid no attention to it at the time, that at a certain point [during the Nazi time] many people took children away from institutions. There must have been talk about it for me to have become aware of it, and after the war, when it all came out, I realized that it was in order to hide them. So, yes, there must have been many people who knew."

As her sister's condition worsened, she was taken to hospital and stayed there for about six months. "We all knew it was progressive, and what would happen to her. She knew, too, but she lived another ten years." Never for a single moment, Annemarie assured me, did they fear that she was in danger from anyone. "It would have been unthinkable—she was just ill, to be looked after, helped, loved. You ask me did we have a 'buried suspicion.' But if we had really suspected anything, buried or not, even if the program had been officially stopped by then, our family would have had to face it, to confront it morally. I tell you, we didn't know."

Annemarie worked for thirty years with handicapped children, along the developmental principles of Rudolf Steiner. (Interestingly, these principles were also adopted by Speer's son Arnold and his wife in the practice of medicine.) When Annemarie died in 1991, she was vice-president of the German

Association for Curative Education and Social Therapy, which by then was caring for some four thousand young people. "However handicapped they are," she said, "the spirit is always there. I never realized, perhaps until we talked now, that my deep conviction of the essentiality of this has its origin in our past: in the narrowness within which people thought and acted in the Nazi time. . . . If people then had more dimension, one would like to think—" She stopped. "I spend my life with people many of whom have been associated with this sort of work for umpteen years. And yet, it is only now, when the clock is turning all the way round, that they seem to be confronting what happened in their homes and in their hospitals forty-five years ago. Even if the rest of us didn't know what happened, or only knew it subconsciously or marginally, how could they not have known or not have faced it?

"I have sometimes wondered what would have happened if I had found out then what they were doing to children exactly like these I'm taking care of now. I think I would have had to do something about it, but—and I don't know how to make you understand this—it wouldn't have made me reject National Socialism. The convictions we held were too deep, too deep to abandon or even to doubt. No, I think I would have thought that there were evil spirits at work, and I would literally have gone out, I think, to look for them."

Would she have thought then that Hitler couldn't know about such things, that it was others who were the "evil spirits"?

"I'm afraid that's exactly what I would have thought," she said bitterly, "the famous '*Wenn der Führer das nur wüsste*' ["If the Führer only knew this"] which people used to say about anything that went wrong."

I made a special point of asking Theo Hupfauer and his wife what they had known about euthanasia, for in February 1941 Hupfauer was named Commandant of the Ordensburg Sonthofen, an elite college for political education, on whose curriculum "hereditary health" and racial purity must have figured prominently.

"I was only the Commandant," he said evasively. "I didn't know about euthanasia. But let me add right away—I'm not against it. As you can see, it is now being discussed more and more."

It seemed inconceivable that as master of Sonthofen and high up in the German Workers' Front he would not have been informed about this program of fundamental importance for the New Germany.

"There was a notice on the wall of every office during those years," he said. "Did you know about that? It said 'Every man need only know what is going on in his own domain.' "

Sonthofen *was* his—and his wife's—domain as of April 1941. They had

proudly shown me a stack of beautifully printed *Sonthofen Hefte* (magazines). The first issue carried three patriotic proclamations: one by Hitler, the
second by Hupfauer as Commandant, and the third by Frau Hupfauer. She
wrote it herself, she said, proudly. And did she know about euthanasia? "No,
never," she said. "You know, I was busy with the house and children." She
and her husband looked at each other.

"We had an arrangement," said Hupfauer. "She looked after the family; I
looked after politics and the war. One of us in politics was enough."

"But I was a medical technician in the 1930s, you know," she suddenly
volunteered. "I saw a lot of children who I suppose were being kept alive to
enable doctors to experiment on them. I remember one little thing, about
eighteen months old, with an exposed spinal cord. It was dreadful, just
dreadful. What was the sense of letting it suffer like that? I remember very
well how I felt then—of course I felt it would be better off peacefully dead."

Dr. Hupfauer said again that in principle he was not against euthanasia.
"You can see that the whole world is slowly moving in that direction now,"
he said. "The question is only how and to what degree. Is there really such a
difference," he asked, "between the early-pregnancy tests done as a matter of
routine with the idea of termination if the fetus is abnormal, not to mention
the number of abortions now being performed for all sorts of reasons, and
what was done here forty years ago?"

But about his own feelings he was vague. "I don't know," he said, honestly. "You can believe me when I tell you that I was appalled, simply appalled, when I learned at Nuremberg what had been done in our name."

These two people had not changed. In 1940–41 they had believed in racial
purity and, I was sure, had not only known about the Euthanasia Program
but agreed with it. And now, with ever increasing arguments for some—
though less extreme—kind of legalized euthanasia, they feel that the world is
catching up with Hitler's ideas.

When I finally asked Speer why he had never mentioned the Euthanasia
Program in his books, I felt a sense of relief at his relative honesty. "I think I
did know about this," he said, "though of course not to the degree I learned
about it later—the extent to which it was abused. I vaguely recall Hitler describing mentally ill patients and talking about the horror of their lives and
how, merely vegetating, they were suffering. On the basis of that, I have to say
I wouldn't have been against the euthanasia measures. Quite recently [this
conversation took place in 1979] I visited a mental hospital—because it was
built by the famous architect Balthasar Neumann—and we saw some of the
patients, just in the corridors, you know. It was pretty terrible. Of course,
since 1945, I've read all the literature on what they [the Nazis] really did, so I

suppose I must be a little careful when I say that I wouldn't have been against euthanasia then."

He was backtracking. As he often did, while appearing to admit or commit himself to something, he was agilely changing to a less slippery path, and I tried to stop him. I asked if he knew at the time that the program included people, many of them children, affected by illnesses which did not affect the brain, such as multiple sclerosis and muscular dystrophy, for which cures are now increasingly being found.

Where his reply had initially been entirely open, when I added the dimension of children to what he had just admitted having known, he drew back. "No, I don't think so," he said tersely, a full stop in his tone at the end of the sentence. This he could not admit. The subject was closed.

IX

A Grey Path Indeed

Nuremberg, October 1, 1946, the last day of the trial

JUDGE FRANCIS BIDDLE, Chief Justice for the United States, announcing the verdicts: The Tribunal is of the opinion that Speer's activities do not amount to initiating, planning, or preparing wars of aggression, or of conspiring to that end. He became the head of the armament industry well after all of the wars had been commenced and were under way. His activities in charge of German armament production were in aid of the war effort in the same way that other productive enterprises aid in the waging of war; but the Tribunal is not prepared to find that such activities involve "engaging in the common plan to wage aggressive war" as charged under Count One, or "waging aggressive war" as charged under Count Two....

By acquitting Speer of these charges of planning or engaging in aggressive war, the Nuremberg court acknowledged that he would not have been in a position to know about, for example, Hitler's directive for the Wehrmacht's preparation for war in 1939–40, which included a paragraph on Fall Weiss (Operation White), the invasion of Poland, which had to be ready by September 1. The court also recognized that Speer had not been involved in the three General Staff meetings Hitler held on November 5, 1937; May 28, 1938; and May 23, 1939, in which his determination to go to war was clearly expressed—which first established and then confirmed the "common plan for aggressive war"—and Speer was one of only four accused to be acquitted on that charge.

Nicolaus von Below was present at two of these conferences and gave evidence for the defense. He did his best to help Field Marshal Keitel and General Jodl, the General Staff officers on trial, but his book four decades later provides insight into the psychology of witnesses such as he, torn as they were between loyalty to their friends and the duty to tell the truth.

As in the case of the Hossbach memorandum, notes about the later conferences had been found by the Allies and became key documents for the Nuremberg prosecution. These notes were kept by Hossbach's successor, Colonel Rudolf Schmundt, and were in the safe of General Walter Scherff, the military historian who had been entrusted by Hitler in the summer of 1942 with writing the history of his war. Below in his book discussed this second document:

> Understandably, several of the accused tried to introduce doubt about the authenticity of this document . . . and a number of its claims. Appearing as a witness, I attempted, if very carefully, to support them in this endeavor. But today [he wrote in 1980] there is no longer any reason to deny the accuracy of Schmundt's report. The participants he names, including Göring and Colonel Walter Warlimont [Keitel's deputy], were certainly present. . . .
>
> It is [also] totally out of the question [as was suggested by the defense in Nuremberg] that Schmundt could have drawn up his report much later,

like 1940 or 1941: I was familiar with Schmundt's awareness of the significance of such reports and his conscientious habit of recording such occasions as immediately as possible after they took place, [and I was also
familiar with] Hitler's thoughts. . . .

Speer, in Berchtesgaden with Hitler for most of that summer, although no
doubt unaware of dates or details, knew by the last week of August 1939, as
did the General Staff and everyone around Hitler, that war against Poland
was imminent. The date, originally set for September 1, was advanced to August 26, put off to August 27, and finally reconfirmed for September 1.

The main reason for Hitler's apparent indecision as late as mid-August
1939, less than two weeks before the scheduled launch of hostilities, was his
failure to achieve the nonaggression pact with the Soviet Union which he
desperately needed to ensure his freedom of action in Poland. If he finally did
succeed at the last moment, it owed less to the diplomatic skill of the German
Foreign Office which, offering ever-increasing inducements to the Soviets,
had carried on the negotiations for months, than to the belated and inept
efforts of an Anglo-French diplomatic team.

However, it is doubtful that anything would have persuaded the Soviets
away from the course they had decided on from the start. Their intention was
to get their hands on—and sovietize—a large part of Poland and the three
rich countries of the Baltic: Latvia, Estonia and Lithuania. To gain this prize
they had to go with the Germans.

Late in the afternoon of August 19, while in a different part of the Kremlin
the unsuspecting Allied delegation continued with their grudging offers, Soviet Foreign Minister Vyacheslav Molotov handed the German Ambassador,
Count Friedrich Werner von der Schulenburg, a draft of a nonaggression
pact and an invitation to German Foreign Minister Ribbentrop to come to
Moscow as soon as an economic agreement—extremely favorable to the
Soviets—was signed in Berlin. (Schulenburg, a diplomat of the old school
whom the July 20 plotters against Hitler earmarked as Germany's future Foreign Minister, was arrested after the failed assassination of Hitler and hanged
on November 10, 1944.) The drafts cabled to the Berghof that night were
barely skimmed through before, at 2 a.m. the next morning, August 20, Hitler hastily signed the trade agreement. At 4:35 p.m. that afternoon, he cabled
Stalin accepting the Soviet draft for the nonaggression pact, proposing only a
few minor modifications and, as the moment of crisis between Germany and
Poland could come at "any moment," urging utmost haste toward ratifying
the treaty. As much in need as Hitler of the economic advantages of the first
pact—and the breathing space the second would provide—Stalin cabled
back within hours inviting Ribbentrop to Moscow on August 23.

There was, of course, no question of any "moment of crisis" other than the provocations carefully planned by Hitler. The Poles, deeply sensitive to their military weakness, had no wish whatever for a confrontation. Given the behavior of Britain and France when Hitler, unimpeded by anything except feeble diplomatic protests and wringing of hands, took Austria in March 1938 and Czechoslovakia in March 1939, the Poles had little reason to put their trust in the West. In fact the Western Allies did finally live up to their promises to Poland, although Hitler too had never thought they would. He had therefore at the ready a number of scenarios which would permit him to lay the blame for the outbreak of war on Polish "atrocities."

The best known—it was actually carried out toward the evening of August 31—was the seizing of the radio station at Gleiwitz on the Polish border: SS men, dressed as Polish insurgents, were to storm the transmitter, broadcast a proclamation and escape. But another more complicated plan was also carried out that day and, like the incident at Gleiwitz, was promptly reported on German radio as a provocation by the Poles. Here too, a company of Polish-speaking SS dressed in Polish uniforms seized the German customs post at Hochlinden in a staged skirmish with the border officials. Six corpses of Sachsenhausen concentration camp prisoners, who were brought to the area dressed in Polish uniforms with soldiers' passbooks in their pockets, were left lying there as proof of the battle. It was to be years before the full story of these staged provocations became known and accepted. (Speer told me that he had believed until Nuremberg that the Poles were to blame for the Gleiwitz attack.)

During supper that evening of August 23, Speer had seen Hitler in an unprecedented state of excitement when he was handed a message from Stalin announcing the imminent signature by the Soviets of the nonaggression pact. He jumped up from his seat, banged the table so hard that the glasses rattled and, visibly losing control, shouted hoarsely, "I've got them! I've got them!"

But it was only after dinner, when the ladies had left them, that Hitler, who had little faith in the discretion of women, showed his entourage the signal. "To see the names of Hitler and Stalin linked in friendship on a piece of paper," writes Speer in his book (and in the "Spandau draft"), "was the most staggering, the most exciting turn of events I could possibly have imagined."

Speer had believed in Hitler's—and Stalin's—good faith. "I think now of course," he told me, "that it was all part of his political game and perhaps Stalin's too. But however difficult it is to believe this now, I assure you I didn't know this then. Not only that, I believe to this day that Ribbentrop, who certainly was in a position to have known better, also believed him to be in good faith."

In a way, Speer said, Hitler had always admired Stalin for his strength and for his ruthlessness. "Perhaps he really did think an entente between them through a division of Europe, or the world, was possible."

Of course, Speer would not have been privy to Hitler's words a mere two weeks before that fateful night when, on August 11, 1939, he had one of his many conversations *unter vier Augen* (under four eyes) in the course of which he is known to have communicated some of his most important decisions. This one was with Carl Burckhardt, a Swiss, whom, as League of Nations High Commissioner in Danzig, Hitler is believed to have tried to use as a conduit to the Allies.

Burckhardt, who shortly afterwards became head of the International Red Cross, described his meeting with Hitler in his book, *Meine Danziger Mission 1937–1939*. "Everything I undertake is directed against the Russians," he reported Hitler as saying, clearly intending his words—which were tantamount to a guarantee to the Western Allies—to be communicated to them. "If the West is too obtuse to comprehend this, I shall be forced to come to terms with the Russians. Then, after crushing the West, I will turn all my forces against the USSR. I have to have the Ukraine, so that they can't starve us into submission as happened in the last war."

In *Mein Kampf* Hitler had abundantly shown his determination to go to war against Russia. But even if Speer hadn't read *Mein Kampf,* as he sometimes claimed, how was it possible, I asked, that he and no doubt other intelligent Germans at the time could fail to see through Hitler's "divide and conquer" strategy? It must surely have been obvious that he was determined to isolate the Poles. By driving a wedge between the Soviet Union and the British and French, he could discourage the Western Allies from assisting them; by presenting the Soviets with irresistible economic and political alternatives, he could stop them from coming to Poland's rescue. How could Speer not have seen this? How could they not have understood that nothing could have made Hitler abandon his sworn battle against Bolshevism?

"I think," said Speer wearily, "that we saw only what we wanted to see and knew only what we wanted to know."

Putting his signature on the most cynical treaty of the century, Hitler achieved on August 24 his greatest diplomatic triumph. On the face of it, it was a fairly simple contract. Both countries were to abjure aggressive action against the other for a period of ten years, with an option for a further five. The nitty-gritty, however, was contained first in the trade agreement signed four days previously and also in a secret protocol in which Germany and the Soviet Union agreed to use Hitler's war against Poland, scheduled for one week hence, to carve up Eastern Europe between them. Finland, most of the Baltic states and Bessarabia were promised to Russia and, once Hitler's war in

Poland had started (the Russians were to support it by invading Poland from their side), so was all of eastern Poland: 77,000 square miles with 13 million inhabitants.

Speer had telephoned his head of staff at the GBI the morning of August 24 (he would return to Berlin with Hitler the next day) to instruct him to set up a technical team whose assistance for the construction of bridges, roads, airfields and bunkers he intended to offer to the Army High Command.

It didn't quite work out as planned. For while the team was duly ready for action when Speer returned to Berlin the next day, and General Friedrich Fromm, who was responsible for army mobilization, gratefully accepted his proposed help, Hitler—promptly informed by Bormann of Speer's independent step—immediately tightened the leash and forbade him to do anything except continue with building projects.

THEO HUPFAUER's career in the Workers' Front had developed enormously by that time. In 1938 he had been sent into Austria with the troops in order to set up Workers' Front organizations in what, in 1986 when we talked, he still called "the liberated areas." He felt that the Anschluss had been legitimate, both from a political and geographic point of view. "The 1918 Austrian State Treaty," he said, "specifically stated that Austria 'was part of Germany.'"

"I was amazed, though," Hupfauer said, "at the enthusiasm the Austrians demonstrated. Even though their economic situation was appalling and would obviously improve dramatically by annexation to the booming German economy, I had not expected that degree of enthusiasm."

He had remained in perfect agreement with Hitler over Austria and the Sudetenland. But when in March 1939, only months after the "peace in our time" agreements with Chamberlain and Daladier, it was Czechoslovakia's turn, he felt the first stirrings of discomfort.

"You mustn't think that we were unaware, or just sheep," he said. "We discussed this quite openly amongst ourselves. I always said that Hitler's greatest deficiency was his total ignorance of foreign countries and mentalities; after all, he never traveled. Except for his visits to Mussolini, later his trips to his military HQs first in the West and then in the East and his one quick trip to Paris, he never went anywhere. He simply was not a statesman," he said, repeating that Hitler's betrayal of the agreements had caused him "grave misgivings."

Nonetheless, Hupfauer continued in Hitler's service. Indeed, one of the proudest moments he remembered was when Hitler had been so impressed by articles he had written in the *Frankfurter Allgemeine Zeitung* on individual

social responsibility, that he instructed Robert Ley, head of the Workers'
Front, to have Hupfauer deliver the main speech at the ceremony awarding
medals for "model industries" for 1937–39. "At the end," he said, "Hitler
shook both my hands and said, 'This is the future,' and then—quite extraordinary—he delivered a fifteen-minute speech ad-libbing with perfect knowledge on the subject. He could do this, you know, about virtually anything.
The range of his knowledge was quite fantastic."

Four months later, in August 1939, he and five friends were on a long-
planned sailing trip in the Baltic intending to end up on the Isle of Man,
when their money ran out in Denmark, in the pubs of Tivoli, and they had to
turn back to Germany. Back at sea they met up with the German cruiser
Schleswig-Holstein, whose commander had formerly been Admiral Wilhelm
Canaris's deputy. Hupfauer had met him when he needed Canaris's authorization to visit certain army-controlled factories.

Asked aboard for a drink, the young vacationers asked the captain where
he was heading. "He answered evasively," Hupfauer said, "but when we told
him that we had originally intended to sail to Britain, he advised us to head
home as quickly as possible."

Did they understand what he meant? "Yes, of course we did. Hitler had
this idiot Ribbentrop as his advisor—it had to end badly. But I was really surprised when war came," he said. "None of us wanted it. It was stupid—at last
we had work and things were looking up. What could we possibly gain by
war?"

Did he now agree that it was Hitler, and not Poland, who had started hostilities? "Well, all right," he said, "but why didn't they just let him have Danzig—it was a legitimate request. . . ."

"It was a German city," his wife interjected. "I remember it well."

"The problem was that Ribbentrop had persuaded Hitler that Britain
wouldn't enter the war," Hupfauer said. "It all hinged on that. One cannot
know how he would have acted had he known—as certainly he should
have—that Britain would of course live up to her agreements with Poland.
They allowed Austria and Czechoslovakia to go, but traditionally their relationship with Poland was much stronger. And, politically, Poland was the
bulwark—the frontier against Russian incursion into, and domination of,
Western Europe. But these were all things Hitler was incapable of realizing.
This blindness was his doom."

Hitler's drive into Poland was already dramatically successful when, on
September 17, 1939, with German forces surrounding Warsaw, the Soviets finally performed a token incursion from the east which lasted less than a
week, at the end of which Stalin presented Hitler with new demands. On September 27, Foreign Minister Ribbentrop, hastily dispatched to Moscow,

agreed to the wily Russian's amendments. With Soviet troops already garrisoned in Estonia and Latvia under the terms of the original treaty, Stalin now offered Hitler a substantial extra bit of territory—all of Poland east of the Vistula—against a free hand in the last and most valuable of the Baltic states, Lithuania. This meant that the bulk of Poland's population, including most of the country's approximately two and a half million Jews, would come under German control.

Hitler, prepared to accept almost any conditions which would ensure Soviet neutrality and give him time to begin establishing his New Order in Eastern Europe, agreed. Not long afterwards, he also agreed to deliver to the Soviets RM 1 billion worth of military hardware, including planes, artillery and ships of the latest design, which, to the fury of his perplexed generals, gave the Soviets access to much of Germany's newest and most secret military technology. Hitler, however, was only too aware of Germany's shortages in raw materials (which, paradoxically enough, could have prevented him from carrying out his future plans in the East) and received as payment from the Soviets a million tons of feed grains, nine hundred thousand tons of oil, half a million tons of phosphate, half a million tons of iron ore and one hundred thousand tons of chromium ore. Another valuable concession was a guaranteed right of way overland through Russia for raw materials Hitler intended to purchase from Rumania, Iran, Afghanistan and the Far East.

It is curious how little the world knows even now about Poland's martyrdom during World War II. In eastern Poland, the USSR, intent on sovietizing their newly acquired lands, very quickly eliminated most of the Polish social and intellectual elite: judges, teachers, clergy, landowners and army officers, such as the fifteen thousand Polish officers murdered—it is thought, in May 1940—in the forest of Katyn, a crime only admitted by the Russians in 1990, after Gorbachev's *glasnost* had taken hold.

As Alan Bullock brilliantly demonstrates in his *Hitler and Stalin: Parallel Lives,* with the important exception of Hitler's mania about the Jews—the ferocity of which Stalin, though by no means pro-Semitic, did not share—the two dictators' goals almost coincided here. Both, while milking the Polish land and people and appropriating grain and minerals wherever they could, immediately put into practice long-held colonization plans, the Russians importing thousands of Soviet families, the Nazis—both more ambitious and far better organized—hundreds of thousands of ethnic Germans, mostly farmers.

It has so far been impossible to ascertain precisely how many Poles were killed by the Soviets or died in Siberia, though newly accessible archives may eventually enlighten us. One estimate is that one and a half million were deported, of whom about half perished. Even so, this number is fractional compared to Germany's slaughter of what is estimated to be about five and a half million people in Poland, including the two and a half million Polish Jews the Nazis gassed, shot or killed by working them to death. Geopolitically, Poland in a way served both the Soviets and the Nazis as a laboratory for the two dictators' plans for the future. As Bullock (who quoted the above figures) writes,

> Just as the eastern half of Poland was the first foreign country on which Stalin imposed the social and political revolution on the Stalinist model which he was later to export to Eastern and Central Europe, so the western half was the first area in which Hitler could try out the racial principles that he saw forming the basis of the empire he dreamed of conquering as far east as the Urals. . . .

The Nazis' program for their parts of Poland was two-pronged. Northwest Poland, renamed the Warthegau—including Danzig, Posen, West Prussia and a large part of Silesia (only half of which, incidentally, had been Prussian before the Treaty of Versailles awarded it to Poland)—was incorporated into Germany, the beginning of the *Lebensraum* in the East Hitler had promised the Germans for years. Here, even before Warsaw, the bitterly defended capital, had been taken, Himmler and his favorite vassal, Reinhard Heydrich, his new Chief of Staff for Security, for the first time unleashed their newly created special forces, the Einsatzgruppen (Action Groups). These consisted of a curious riffraff of (when at full strength a year later) about three thousand men, many of them early volunteers for SS information or police sections, others disaffected professionals—lawyers, dentists, even press or government information officials and diplomats. All of them essentially civilians, they were trained for murder rather than war—the Einsatzgruppen trials after the war demonstrated that their three-week training courses in Pretzsch, Silesia, included no tactical instruction. But fanatical Nazis one and all, the four groups of six hundred men each, eventually led by a large number of highly qualified SS officers, were to become the scourge and terror of the conquered territories in Eastern Europe.

The central part of Poland, with a population of eleven million and containing the country's major cities (Warsaw, Krakow and Lublin), was turned into an occupied province with its General Government headed by Hitler's former lawyer, Reichsminister Hans Frank. It was into this part of conquered Poland, essentially the only part of the country to be allowed to remain Catholic and Polish, that the Einsatzgruppen deported millions of Poles from the to-be "Germanized" annexed areas—the "Warthegau," where their farms and homes were handed over to ethnic German settlers imported from all over Central Europe and the East. By mid-1941, two hundred thousand *Volksdeutsche*, repatriates from the Sudetenland and points east, had been settled in the reconstituted Prussia and Silesia, whose language entirely reverted to German and where the influence of Polish churches and culture virtually ceased to exist.

The General Government, meanwhile, also became the dumping ground for the 1.9 million Jews who had lived in the now German northwestern provinces. At this point, and until after the beginning of the war against the Soviet Union, the policy toward them was largely isolation and containment; they were herded into the ghettos of the General Government's cities. These were soon desperately overcrowded, with their inhabitants suffering appalling deprivations. Still, to some extent the ghettos became self-governing enclaves where, with schools, clinics, places of entertainment and of worship somehow organized, a semblance of normality continued for a time.

A secret memorandum from Himmler in May 1940 specified that the former Polish state and its varying "races"—Poles, Ukrainians, White Russians, Jews—were to be broken up:

> . . . into the largest possible number of parts and fragments . . . the racially valuable elements to be extracted from the hodgepodge. . . .

The rest would be left to die. Within ten years, said the memorandum, the populations of the General Government "will be reduced to a remnant of sub-standard beings . . . a leaderless labor force capable only of furnishing Germany with casual laborers. . . ." Eventually "the Jews will be completely eliminated by a major deportation operation to Africa or some other colony," while the other people of the East should be driven further east, ceasing to exist as racial entities. (This suggests that in May 1940 the physical extermination of the Jews was not yet envisaged.)

In addition to eliminating the Polish educated classes, Himmler continued, their children would be carefully screened "so that those who are racially valuable" could be germanized, while the rest would be allowed only basic education, "not even being taught to read." His suggestions were well received by the Führer, as Himmler's chilling office note, headed "Special Train, May 28, 1940," shows:

> I handed my report on the treatment of peoples of alien races in the East to the Führer. [He] read the six pages and considered them very good and correct. He directed, however, that only very few copies should be made; . . . the report is to be treated with utmost secrecy. [After listing the officials who were to be informed, he adds,]

Everyone has to confirm that he has been informed of the fact that this
is to be considered as a directive, but that it shall never be laid down in an
order of one of the Main Offices: neither in the form of a mere excerpt nor
from memory.

There is no doubt that Himmler took his cue here from Hitler, who time
and again discussed his plans for the people of the East, above all from the
point of view of education for the young. His *Tabletalk** often records such
comments. For example, at dinner on July 27, 1941:

Nothing would be a worse mistake on our part than to seek to educate
the masses there. It is to our interest that the people should know just
enough to recognize road signs. At present they can't read, and they ought
to stay like that. [A year later, on July 22, 1942, he returned to the subject:]
Certainly no facilities for higher education: [which] would simply plant
the seeds of future opposition to our rule. . . . Instruction in geography
can be restricted to a single sentence: "The Capital of the Reich is Berlin. . . ." Elementary instruction in reading and writing in German. . . .
Arithmetic and such-like is quite unnecessary. . . . Yes, the cities we
build for our German settlers [these are the cities in the Occupied Eastern
Territories he had by then asked Speer to build] should be beautiful, with
wide streets, parks, and all facilities for leisure. As a special recompense
for work well done, groups of natives can be taken to these towns—
which ordinarily of course will be off-limits to them—to see how their
masters live. . . .

There was one group of Easterners who were taken to Germany long
before they could work, but even they went as a result of special selections.
These were the Polish—and later Ukrainian and Russian—babies and toddlers who, after being examined by "experts in racial science," were judged
worthy of being "germanized." The precise number of small children torn
away from their parents to be brought up as Germans has never been known,
but the search-and-find register at Arolsen, (then) West Germany, set up by
the Allied relief authorities at the end of the war, showed almost a quarter of
a million names of children sought by parents from Poland and the Ukraine.
It so happened that I became intimately involved with that particular aspect of the Nazi horrors when, as a child welfare officer for UNRRA—United
Nations Relief and Rehabilitation Administration—in the U.S. zone of Germany in 1945 I was in charge, for half a year, of a Child Tracing team. With

*Beginning in July 1941, Hitler's *Tabletalk* was recorded on Bormann's orders without Hitler's knowledge, because he felt that Hitler's discourses should be preserved for posterity. Although these quotations are dated after the Russian war began, Hitler was obviously saying much the same thing for
months and years before the record began to be kept. For a fuller discussion of *Tabletalk*'s history, see
Notes.

the help of some young Hungarian friends with good contacts among the population, I was able to locate about forty-five children, between three and eight years of age, who were living with German farming families in our area of operations but, according to local informers, did not belong to them.

Taking these children away from these families was one of the hardest things I have ever had to do. These foster parents, who had accepted the children as their own, loved them, and the children loved them in return. I took the youngsters to a special center we had prepared, and lived and worked there with them for months, for it took time even to begin repairing the harm of the double violence that had been done to them: first when the Nazis forcibly separated them from their parents, their homes and their language; and second when we—essentially not much more gently—removed them from what had become their adopted home and in most cases devoted adoptive parents.

It took even longer to find and reunite some of them with their real families. Of my group of forty-five, thirty-eight turned out to have been abducted from Poland, and in the spring of 1946 I took them—and about two hundred from other areas—back there. They were the first children to be returned, and just as I can't forget the pain of the German foster parents when they had to see the children leave, I will never, as long as I live, forget the welcome they received in Poland, never forget the faces of the parents, grandparents, uncles, aunts, brothers and sisters. The miracle of recognition of a long-lost child by those who love them is awesome to behold.

But given what happened next, I was almost thankful that by the time the Child Tracing program was abandoned some time later, only a fraction of the alleged 250,000 children had been found. Hundreds who were found and identified as having been taken away not from Polish but from Soviet parents, among them seven of my group of forty-five, had still another trauma awaiting them.

As a result of a political decision largely arrived at in Washington (and imposed upon the British), these children, unlike those from Poland, were never to be returned to their families. In one of the most high-handed decisions ever made by officialdom, the American and British governments, by now in a state of cold war with the Soviets, decreed that no children were to be returned to be brought up as communists. In one letter, replying to my protests, the U.S. State Department said they were acting entirely in the interest of the children, who could not be allowed to be subjected to the indoctrination they would no doubt suffer, and whose physical safety could not be guaranteed if they were returned to the Soviet Union. (The seven Ukrainian children then in my care were all under four.) I fought against this monstrous decision for months, supported every step of the way by Jack Whiting, the Director of UNRRA in the U.S. zone. But we lost, and these infants, psychologically doubly brutalized, first for grotesque racial principles by the Nazis and then for equally outrageous ideological reasons by their so-called liberators, were sent overseas, to America, Australia and Canada, to yet another strange land and a strange tongue, again to be adopted or fostered by strangers.

"May God preserve us from ideological maniacs, wherever they are," Georges Casalis said, when late one night in France I recounted this story.

THERE WAS NO REASON for Speer to know what went on in Poland in 1939–40. Up to a point he had obeyed Hitler's order, that first week of the war, to concentrate on building projects. In the winter of 1939 he installed field headquarters for Hitler and Göring on two feudal estates in the Taunus mountains, near the French border. Göring was delighted with Kransberg. "Only castles would do for him," Speer said. But Hitler rejected this outright and told Speer to find him "something small and simple. It is not fitting that I revel in luxury while my soldiers live in dugouts."

"Given the money and effort that had been expended, especially for the communication network that was required for Führer Headquarters," Speer said, "that struck me as fairly contrary even then, despite my infatuation with Hitler. I didn't think that any soldier would object to Germany's leader living according to his rank. But I now think my doubts about his motivation were rather unfair because, as it turned out, he was entirely consistent throughout the war in his insistence on spartan living, especially when in the field."

Even though Speer had had to withdraw his offer to build for the army, he later proposed the same to the Luftwaffe, though much more discreetly. Soon he was not only designing airports and putting up buildings for them all over Germany, but took charge of developing their installation at Peenemünde, later the experimental site for the rockets which were to plague London.

But even so, he spent most of that first year of the war perfecting the designs for the area around the projected Great Hall, to be the venue for Hitler's future speeches in Berlin; on Göring's new residence there; and on the 350,000-seat Nuremberg Stadium. His team of architects, a number of whom like Speer had been deferred from active service by Hitler's orders, also completed the plans for the university, museum and hospital district of the new Berlin which Hitler insisted, war or no war, had to be ready by 1950.

On June 23, 1940, a few days after the fall of Paris, Speer accompanied Hitler on his three-hour dawn sightseeing jaunt to the capital of defeated France, along with architect Hermann Giesler and sculptor Arno Breker.

A euphoric Hitler, returning that night to his field HQ in a farmhouse on the France-Belgium border, sitting at a wooden table in the kitchen, ordered Speer to stop refining plans and to start the construction of Berlin and Nuremberg.

"Wasn't Paris beautiful?" Hitler marveled. "But Berlin must exceed it [in beauty]. When we have it done, Paris will forever stand in its shadow." For the remainder of 1940, Speer commuted between Berlin and Berchtesgaden, with Hitler constantly inspecting the plans and reminding him of the 1950 deadline.

"During that wonderful hot summer," Speer told me, "it really sometimes seemed as if he had nothing else on his mind. Of course, all of us were, I can only say, in a state of rapture. I had no doubt whatever that he was the greatest conqueror of all times, comparable to the giants of antiquity or the Middle Ages. If he believed the war was as good as over and we could go back to building our future, then that was what I would do. And so, grotesquely as it turned out, that summer, my thoughts and those of my colleagues were entirely on building."

By that time, of course, the unbelievable had happened. Waging an unprecedented *Blitzkrieg*, largely conceived by himself in collaboration with the Wehrmacht's adventurous strategist, General Fritz Erich von Manstein, Hitler had overrun Europe. Secure in the knowledge that his army, having first taken Poland in little more than eight days and then Norway, Denmark, Luxembourg, Holland, Belgium and France in less than six weeks, he magnanimously—and incomprehensibly to all his generals—let the British execute their extraordinary evacuation of 338,000 men from Dunkirk with a motley collection of almost a thousand ships, destroyers, sailboats, ferries and motor launches. The energy Britain was capable of mobilizing during those extraordinary eight days, and the inability of Göring's Luftwaffe to halt the evacuation when Hitler, almost as if for sport, authorized it to give battle, should have given him pause. But he and his men saw only defeat in Britain's escape from the European Continent, and interpreted Churchill's addresses to the British people, as Goebbels put it with his inimitable elegance, as nothing more than "the yelping of a wounded dog." His diary entries during those weeks of triumph vividly describe the atmosphere:

May 27, 1940: . . . Calais in our hands; with that we have England by the throat. . . . May 28: In London they pray . . . all they can do. . . . May 29: Churchill speechifies, still impudent but sweating from every pore. . . . May 31: The English try to escape across the channel. Luftwaffe attacks successfully. . . . a wild rout. . . . June 2: The British are incredibly cynical, representing their defeat as a signal victory. . . . Their showing off gets on one's nerves . . . [but] things are going magnificently now with Mussolini on our side. . . . God bless our work. Life is beautiful. . . . June 16: The world can speak of nothing but our capture of Paris. . . . Since June 5, 200,000 prisoners. The German flag flies over Versailles. Triumph. It makes one's heart beat stronger. . . . The Führer calls to tell me about the capitulation of the French; he is deeply moved. . . .

As of June 20, when the British successfully bombed German industrial targets, his entries become slightly less ecstatic, and on June 25 he touches for the first time on the topic which was to puzzle all of Hitler's men over the next months:

Führer has not decided whether he wants to attack England. Thinks it is necessary to keep the Empire intact. . . . If it falls apart, it will only go into other hands. . . . He would agree to peace with them on the basis of agreement that Europe ours, colonies remain theirs [but] compensation is paid to us for what was stolen from us after the World War. We are already negotiating. July 1: There is only one question [on everybody's mind]: when do we start for England? . . .

Eight years later, Churchill described in *Their Finest Hour* Britain's appalling paucity in matériel and training at that point:

Our armies at home were known to be almost unarmed except for rifles. There were in fact hardly 500 field guns of any sort, and hardly 200 medium or heavy tanks in the whole country.

Had Speer ever heard Hitler indicate that he knew of Britain's poverty in arms? "Later when I became Minister, we of course discussed these matters," he said. "I don't know what he knew or didn't know in those earlier years. But what I, and many other people, did learn to understand was that whatever the tactical reasons he gave to the generals, the fact is, he really didn't want to wage war against England. I told you earlier—many of his decisions were based on emotion. Here, too, it was not strategy but emotion that ruled. Hitler liked and admired the British. 'They are our brothers,' he often said. 'Why fight our brothers?' And he was always sure—he said that often, too—that Britain would come around, would join him in the fight against Bolshevism. Of course, later, when he was forced to realize he had been wrong, he was very bitter, at the very end more bitter about them than about the Russians."

"They are our brothers" was a huge oversimplification by Hitler of his feelings about the British which, oddly enough, were shared for much of this century, until well after the end of World War II, by many Germans and Austrians, including Speer. Britons as people, rather than Britain as a country, represented excellence to them.

"I have always envied [Anglo-Saxons]," Speer said in a letter to Hilde on June 26, 1952, "their capacity for self-control." This was part of it, but by no means all. The British, men and women, were "gentlemen" in the eyes of the Germans, with all the connotations of the term: courageous, honest, "self-controlled" and—rightly, they felt, given Britons' obvious superiority—detached from and condescending toward lesser mortals. This may sound ridiculous now to the British themselves, but this emotional penchant, inexplicable or not, was a fact, one which enormously influenced Hitler's actions and therefore the course of the war and of history. For no one in Britain—Churchill least of all—was certain the country could have fought off a Nazi invasion in 1940.

Hitler made many mistakes, one of which was to present Britain with a year of breathing space with her army safely at home. This provided time for intensified production and training and immeasurable strengthening of her materiel and psychological alliance with the United States. Another error, after the shockingly rapid conquest of Yugoslavia and Greece, was the invasion of Russia, though even this was in his mind only a preliminary to greater things. He had asked the Wehrmacht to plan for an overland attack on India through Russia. A third and fatal misjudgment was his declaration of war on the United States.

Speer told me he was not aware of these daring visions: "Not so specifically." He pondered for a long time whether if he had known, he would have thought that Hitler was mad. "It's difficult to answer that, because from the perspective of today, of course I would or should have thought him mad. But thinking myself back into that time, I have to say I'm not certain. I think that in 1940–41 I thought him capable of achieving anything he wanted."

Speer's writing about his activities in 1940 and 1941—both in the "Spandau draft" and later in his books—is sparse, concentrating primarily on his continuing architectural work. He mentions only those commissions connected with the war which can be seen to be associated with his profession, such as (in the sequence he received these assignments) the assistance his organization, the GBI, provided for the Luftwaffe, building three huge factories in Brünn, Graz and Vienna for the production of their new medium-range dive bomber, the Junkers 88; the huge navy yard Hitler commissioned him to build in Norway in May 1941; the air-raid shelters he constructed across Berlin; and the armament factories he built all over Germany.

The tasks which, whether by intent or neglect, Speer doesn't describe in any of his writing happen to be those which either could be interpreted as having political connotations or might be considered as having put him in a position of learning about events of which he later claimed to have no knowledge. One such assignment began in the spring of 1939, when the launch of his Berlin building program required the clearance of whole streets and apartment blocks and the rehousing of thousands of people. To deal with this problem, Speer set up a new department in the GBI, the Main Division for Resettlement, headed by an administrator who had recently joined him, Dietrich Clahes, former Prime Minister of Brunswick. A few months later, when, after the beginning of the war and the bombings by the RAF, increasing numbers of people were made homeless and the GBI was made responsible for dealing with bomb damage in the capital, the tasks of this department would vastly increase.

But through this relocation work, the GBI, perhaps inevitably, became almost from the start associated with the measures against the Jews. On April 30, 1939, a new statute—the Tenancy Agreement with Jews—was added to the Nuremberg Laws. It decreed that any Jewish tenant could be evicted if "alternate lodging was available to him." Thousands of landlords across the land immediately gave notice to their Jewish tenants; Jewish welfare organizations were ordered to make lodgings available for them with other Jews; and "resettlement divisions" were set up within the regional housing authorities of most German cities to deal with registration, applications and complaints and liaise with both Jewish agencies and those effecting or enforcing the departure of Jews from their homes.

In Berlin, where the GBI already had a long list of people awaiting rehousing, this responsibility was assigned to Clahes's new Resettlement Department, working with the other agencies that were necessarily involved.

Most of this early resettlement work, whatever its consequences on various groups, including Berlin Jews, was purely administrative and it is unlikely that Speer himself, by now heading an organization of thousands, knew much about the details involved. This benefit of the doubt, however, cannot be extended to him for the next stage involving the Berlin Jews, two years later, in early 1941.

On March 20, 1941, by which time British bombing had begun to bite and Speer's responsibilities were considerably extended, a meeting was called at Goebbels's Ministry of Propaganda to discuss the problem of the remaining sixty to seventy thousand Jews in the capital. It was attended by both Adolf Eichmann and Clahes.

Leopold Gutterer, State Secretary at the Ministry of Propaganda, representing Goebbels, informed the group of a meeting between Hitler and Goebbels that week at which Hitler, though he had not yet decreed that the capital should be immediately cleared of Jews (mainly because about twenty-six thousand Jews were still working for armament production there), had "convinced Dr. Goebbels that the Führer will eventually be open to constructive suggestions about their evacuation."

Speer's representative, Clahes, remarked that twenty thousand apartments in Berlin still used by Jews "are needed for additional rehousing after further preparatory work on the urban renewal of Berlin and . . . as a reserve in case of major bombing damage." At the end of the conference, Eichmann was asked to work out a proposal for Goebbels for the evacuation of all Jews from Berlin.

It is impossible that Speer was not informed of the substance of this meeting—the evacuation of the Jews from Berlin. It is clear from his testimony at Nuremberg that there was no doubt in his mind that the sixty to seventy thousand remaining Jews in Berlin mentioned in this conference included the wives and children of the 26,000 men working in armament production. Under cross-examination on June 21, 1946, by the American Chief Prosecutor, Justice Robert Jackson, Speer pointed out that working in armament factories in 1941–42 enabled Jews "to escape the evacuation that was already in full swing. These Jews," he said, "were still completely free and their families still lived in their apartments."

One has to ask then, with this evacuation of Jews "in full swing"—except for those engaged in armament production—even if theoretically he might have told himself that Jewish men, like other non-Germans, were "merely" being shipped out to work, a point he made repeatedly to me, where did he think the women and children were being sent and for what purpose?

(According to Goebbels's diary in August 1941, only 26,000 of Berlin's remaining 77,000 Jews were "in employment." The Wehrmacht armament records of October 22, 1941, state that 18,700 were working in production for the armed forces. Although a Labor Office decree approved by Hitler was passed in December 1941 exempting families of Jewish labor conscripts from evacuation, Heydrich anticipated the decree by deporting between ten and twenty thousand—the exact number was never established—of their dependents to the East before it was confirmed.)

When talking with Speer, I was not yet aware of this documentation and therefore couldn't ask him about that specific testimony or series of events. But Speer refers himself to these evacuations in his last and in some ways most revealing book, *Infiltrations:*

> When I think about the fate of Berlin's Jews, I am overcome by an unbearable feeling of failure and inadequacy. In the course of my daily drive to my architectural office . . . I frequently saw crowds of people on the platform of the Nikolassee Railway Station. I knew this had to be Berlin Jews being evacuated. I'm sure that at that moment [of seeing this] I must have had a feeling of unease, a foreboding of dark events. But—impossible though it is to understand today—I was so wedded to the principles of the regime that phrases such as "Führer: command, we obey," or "The

Führer is always right," had a hypnotic effect, especially perhaps on those of us . . . in his immediate environment. . . . Perhaps too, our burying ourselves in work was an unconscious effort to . . . anaesthetize our conscience. . . .

To all of Speer's many critics these afterthoughts are only an inept attempt to claim that he had not been morally blind, only blinded. To me, though recognizing his by then familiar evasive technique of generalizing about specifics and admitting a little to deny a great deal, it was much more than that. His "momentary unease" (as he put it to me) when seeing the crowds of Jews at the railway station on his way to work in 1940 or 1941 had repeatedly come up in our conversations.

I pressed him as to why he should have had a sense of unease when he must have known that, normal enough in times of war, there were all kinds of movements of populations going on. What was so special about the Jews being moved?

By that time I was very familiar with that sudden sharp look from under those thick black eyebrows when he sensed disbelief (I always marked it in my notes). It was not only his look which became both hooded and guarded; his voice, on the whole invariably quiet, could also suddenly change. "I was blind by choice, as I already told you," he said coldly, "but I was not ignorant."

Here was not the reasoning Speer, my urbane host. Here was Hitler's great Minister who had ruled Germany's economy and the lives of millions. In the years I talked with Speer, there were only a few such moments of transformation, but in each case I was suddenly keenly and somewhat frighteningly aware—I can still feel my stomach muscles knotting—of the authority coiled inside this man, which, manifestly suppressed with constant deliberate effort, only burst out at moments of disappointment, intense irritation or weary anger. It never lasted long; he had a most extraordinary capacity for self-control.

"I did know, after all," he said, his tone back to its usual reasonableness mixed with gallows humor, "that the Jews were a special problem. Did you notice?" he added at once, back to his disconcerting habit of indicting himself before someone else could do so. "I said, *were* a special problem; even now I didn't say, *had* a special problem." He shrugged. "That shows you. . . ."

What in fact it showed me was that he didn't want to—or couldn't—answer the question. Much later in our talks he would again say that he had had a suspicion—or foreboding, a "sense"—about what was happening to the Jews. By this time I knew him much better, and he, I think, trusted me more.

"You say you sensed something," I said (the untranslatable word *ahnen* is more ambiguous but also stronger than "suspect"). "But you cannot 'sense' in a void; 'sensing' is an inner realization of knowledge. Basically, if you 'sensed,' then you knew."

He shook his head. "Thank God you weren't Robert Jackson," he said, a remark which he would repeat on other occasions.

Much of our evidence concerning Speer's knowledge about the Jews comes from the already mentioned *Chronik,* the office journal which Rudolf Wolters kept for Speer, first at the GBI and then at the ministry, from 1941 to 1944. This detailed record of Speer's activities in those four years is a basic source of information, especially in a period about which Speer himself wrote so little. For example, ten weeks after the conference at Goebbels's ministry, Speer himself was marginally involved in the question of Jewish property. The *Chronik* reports on June 12, 1941, that "after discussion with Herr Speer, instructions were given to set up a department as of July 1 that will examine all Jewish real estate up for sale in the western suburbs of Berlin, in order to ensure that the General Building Inspector's interest remains paramount. This will . . . prevent such properties being used for . . . official agencies."

Speer had always loathed bureaucrats and despised their greed, but they were a marginal concern for him, as was the persecution of the Jews. The sad truth is that he didn't care about the Jews then, any more than he would later care about the millions of forced laborers who slaved for him. When he needed something, he went after it, irrespective of human cost. What he needed at that point was housing, and housing he would have.

The history of this crucial document is complex. Toward the end of 1940 Wolters had suggested that, in view of Speer's ever-increasing responsibilities, he should keep a *Chronik* in which, using regular reports from all heads of sections in addition to those of Speer's activities he wrote up himself, he would record all important events. On March 19, 1980, Wolters in his memoirs described his role:

> I started my secondary activity as chronicler on January 1, 1941, and continued the monthly entries . . . containing dates and events I considered important . . . plus those I had witnessed myself . . . until December 1944. From then until the end of the war I had to limit my entries to those taken from my personal diary. . . . Speer [initialed each entry but] made no changes or corrections. . . .

When the end of the war approached, Wolters, who several months before had been instructed by Speer to prepare quietly for the future by setting up architectural offices in three towns not too far from Frankfurt or Cologne, made arrangements for the safekeeping of Speer's Berlin and Nuremberg models, photographs and copperplates, as well as the eight-hundred-page *Chronik* of which there were five copies, two complete and three covering the years 1942–43. Wolters distributed these to various colleagues for safekeeping; three were lost or destroyed in bombings and plane crashes. Part of another copy somehow ended up in the Imperial War Museum in London. One copy was returned to Wolters by friends who deemed it too dangerous to hold, and it (with some of Speer's speeches) was buried by him in his parents' garden in his hometown, Coesfeld.

This copy (to be referred to now as the "original") was safely recovered from its tomb in 1946, and became part of Wolters's very important and, until Speer's release from Spandau, very secret archive in the Coesfeld house. A copy of this "original" (somewhat re-edited) was among the mass of papers—including the 1,200 typed pages of the "Spandau draft"—which Wolters handed to Speer on the emotive occasion of Speer's visit to him in Coesfeld in 1966, ten days after his release from Spandau.

Speer told me that in working through the mountain of material Wolters had given him, it was some time before he got to the *Chronik*, the details of which he had no particular reason to remember. Therefore, not realizing this historic document had been amended and no doubt eager to prove his goodwill to an organization whose help he was going to need in the preparation of his memoirs, he photocopied it and passed it on in good faith, with many of his other documents, to Professor Wolfgang Mommsen, the director of the Federal Archives in Koblenz, to whom he wrote that he felt "it needed to be available to young historians as quickly as possible."

In 1969, two years after Speer had sent this copy of the *Chronik* to Koblenz, the British writer David Irving, who had examined it there, came upon a section of the *Chronik* at the Imperial War Museum in London. Noticing in this manuscript some details he did not remember seeing in Koblenz, he quite properly wrote both to Dr. Mommsen, at the Federal Archives, and to Speer in Heidelberg, drawing their attention to possible discrepancies between the two versions. Speer wrote to Wolters on January 1, 1970:

Dear Rudi,
    Now we are in the soup.... They found a copy of one year of the *Chronik* in London and, as the eager beaver writer David Irving tells me, they are now diligently searching for the rest. I got Irving to send me a photocopy in order to compare it to the text you gave me [in 1966]. Luckily, I note that the deviations, from the historian's point of view, are pretty inoffensive. Even so: don't you agree that it would be better if we now took the first step and I offer to replace the copy now at the Federal Archives with a photocopy of the original which (presumably) you have?

If you share my view, I would propose to quickly ascertain exactly what the differences are and inform you of what I find. . . . [Rudolf Wolters's wife, Erika, had just joined the Speers for a skiing expedition.] While Erika and I labor through snowdrifts, I hope you will see your way to let me thus set to rights whatever "drifts" the *Chronik* has suffered, not only in that one year's entries, but also the others. . . .

Wolters replied on January 10, jocularly titling his letter "Concerning: *'Bescherung'* " ("In the Soup"):

This business with the "drifts" which you now want to "set to rights" is of course a confounded nuisance. Before we consider what best to do, I'd like to explain in a few words how it came to this cleansing, which I did mention in passing when I delivered the manuscript to you. . . .

As I originally had only kept one [complete] copy of the *Chronik*, which, incidentally, I thought was the only one that had survived, and this was . . . in very bad condition, I decided to have the approximately 800 pages copied and equipped with an index. There was an obvious need to check the whole thing before it was copied, make some stylistic and grammatical corrections and delete a few things which were either just silly or irrelevant to contemporary history. As it was I who had selected what to include in the first place, I felt quite justified twenty years later in removing a few things I considered immaterial.

It is true, however, that I also felt obligated to take out a few—a very few—notes which, historically, are unfortunately not entirely unimportant. For instance: "In the time from October 18 to November 2, 1941, about 4,500 Jews were evacuated from Berlin. This provided one thousand further habitations for people affected by the bombings, which the General Building Inspector was able to make available [for them]. . . ."

This kind of thing, which occurred repeatedly, then culminated in a closing report by your associate Cl. [Dietrich Clahes] which concluded that 75,000 "persons" were "moved" with the result that 23,765 Jewish habitations were seized. That was of course an achievement!

Since just when I was reading these few but significant notes, some new witch-hunts had been launched against so-called "desk-perpetrators," I thought it right for that moment to consign these few remarks in the copies (not the original) to oblivion. For after all, Irmgard Clahes [Clahes's wife], who had to battle for a pension for years, was still alive looking after their children, and you, after all, were alive too and still in Spandau. I wouldn't have put it past the *Ludwigsburgern* [the lawyers at the West German Office for the Prosecution of Nazi Crimes in Ludwigsburg, near Stuttgart] to launch an additional prosecution against you on the pretext that this charge was not included in the Nuremberg Indictment.

I would now propose the following: that you ask Herr Mommsen [in

German, using "Mr." without the proper title of "Doctor" or "Professor"
is mildly insulting], to whom you so precipitately gave a copy, to return it,
so that the chronicler can reinsert the few things which have been taken
out. Of course, for you the original is at your disposal whenever you like; I
would only ask that it be returned to me intact. I would not welcome for it
to be passed on to Herr Mommsen, even photocopied, because in the
original the crossed-out paragraphs are clearly visible even when the pencil marks are erased. The method of correction I suggest can be explained
to the archive fellows as being simpler and cheaper than photocopying
800 pages.

Or if you like, just tell them "The fellow refuses to hand over the original." I'll be delighted to tell them my reasons. Aside from this you can rest
easy: I have made arrangements that the original is to be made accessible
to the public when no one can any longer be harmed by it. . . . Another
solution would be to say for the moment, that Marion [Riesser] has destroyed the original. . . .

Now over to you for decision, great Master of Armaments! (Sorry!)

Speer's correspondence with Wolters about the *Chronik* clearly demonstrates that it was not Speer but (for however selfless reasons) Wolters who
arbitrarily manipulated this historical documentation. It shows that while
Speer's first reaction, once it had been discovered, was that the only honorable thing to do was to come clean, Wolters, without refusing outright, implied that if Speer insisted on doing this, he would consider it an act of
disloyalty. And indeed it would have been, for once the Federal Archives became aware of what Wolters had done, this would inevitably have become
public knowledge, and in the political atmosphere in Germany in 1970 could
have created serious professional difficulties for Wolters, who as an architect
was primarily working for his home state.

It would have been even more embarrassing for Speer, whose *Inside the
Third Reich* had just been published to great acclaim. And when, although
conditionally falling in with the suggestion that they "come clean," Wolters
made it clear he was against it at that time, Speer readily enough agreed to
forward to the Federal Archives a pro forma letter Wolters would send him
stating (untruthfully, of course) that the original appeared to have disappeared. His letter to Wolters, written from his skiing holiday in the South
Tyrol, more than confirms this plan by both men to deceive the Federal
Archives:

Dear Rudi,
    You were quite right (for once!) in what you took out. Frau Irmgard
[Clahes] is coming to see me soon and she would certainly have suffered.
So I propose that the relevant pages cease to exist. However, contrary to

your suggestion, I think that they should cease to exist forever. Because a mere postponement to historically more propitious times seems to me a bad idea. For who then could take issue with a distorted interpretation which can only be strengthened by the fact of the pages having been withheld for years. As it stands now, anyone with any sense would consider your deletion of such pages quite legitimate. . . .

I hope that, despite the fog that surrounds us here, I am making myself quite clear. . . .

He did, as Wolters was to confirm on January 22, 1970, in a letter which is part lies and part truth:

Dear Albert,

Couldn't reply sooner to your letter from Selva as Marion and I spent all that time searching for the *Chronik* original. Without further ado: it has vanished without trace; it's gone; no longer here—it has ceased to exist. Well, I think it's just as well. Because if it did still exist, then, yes, one would have to hand it in as is. One certainly couldn't correct it again, for if that were discovered, it would be even more embarrassing. . . .

Having exercised my author's privilege of selection and editing in the first place, I had no hesitation to do so on the second occasion. But as a copy of the original [of the year 1943] apparently exists in London, I certainly would not wish to do it a third time.

So, as far as I am concerned, this is the end of this matter; I hope it is the same for you. If there are any complications, just blame it all on me—or Marion if you like: as an artist, meticulous organization of documents, understandably enough, is not her "forte." . . .

Three weeks later, Wolters repeated this letter, in more formal terms, for forwarding to the Federal Archives, which Speer duly did on February 13, 1970, with a covering note:

Dear Dr. Mommsen,

Unfortunately, my friend Dr. Rudolf Wolters has responded negatively about the *Chronik*. I enclose a copy of his letter of February 10. I'm sorry not to have been more successful in this matter: but hopefully, future historians will find the material that does exist in the Federal Archives valuable enough as it stands. . . .

In a closing paragraph, Speer offered Dr. Mommsen some historical film material he had rediscovered and, jocular as ever, wrote to Wolters by the same post: "I think Mommsen can be quite content now, given the films I sent him as a consolation prize."

Wolters had made a will in which he left his private papers to the Federal Archives in Koblenz, with access restricted to researchers approved by his son, Fritz, as his executor. (It was under this condition that I worked there in 1985–87.) But in October 1982, the year after Speer's death, Wolters changed his mind and handed over the first six volumes of the original *Chronik,* followed a few months later, shortly before his death, by his correspondence with Speer. In July 1983 Marion Riesser, whom Wolters had named his literary executor, offered the Federal Archives the balance of the Wolters collection, including the "corrected" version of the *Chronik.*

"I thought it was essential that they should have it," she said. She had been from the start very critical of Wolters's actions about the *Chronik.* "He started to work on it in 1964," she said. "I told him, 'You shouldn't cross things out—it isn't right. You are falsifying history.' But he said the *Chronik* was his creation: he was the author of it and as such had the right to do with it as he wished. And I think he got legal advice on it too."

AT SPEER's Nuremberg trial, his organization's (and his) involvement with this aspect of the persecution of the Jews never came up, and it might have remained buried forever if attention had not been thrown upon it forty-odd years later by the publication of a doctoral thesis by the young German historian Matthias Schmidt. In his *End of a Myth,* published in 1982 (the year after Speer's death), the author, making no claim of historical objectivity, frankly set out to prove Speer's iniquity, above all in his denial of knowledge about the fate of the Jews. He tried to achieve this by providing a selective account of the arrangements about the Berlin apartments belonging to Jews and the changes in the *Chronik,* claiming (with the information then available to him) that Speer had laundered the record about this event. He then concluded that these actions, although not legal evidence, were psychological proof of Speer's early knowledge of the planned murder of the Jews.

Although one can sympathize with the passionate conviction that engenders such a book, I am convinced that although Speer certainly knew by 1941 that the Berlin Jews were being deported, it is virtually certain he had no idea they were going to their death.

Annemarie Kempf, who does not lie and who knew Speer better than anyone else (including his wife), while remembering perfectly well the Jewish flats in Berlin, thought too much had been made of that episode later. We talked about it for hours, years after we first met, when I had studied some of the thousands of pages in the Wolters archive in Koblenz.

"Speer's responsibilities by then were enormous," she said to me in 1986. "This matter like many others would have been delegated; after all, he was particularly good at that: delegating. On the other hand, I don't think he would ever have realized that there *was* a moral aspect to this transfer of umpteen-thousand apartments. If he had noticed it, what he would probably have done is get rid of that particular assignment as being too troublesome, potentially embarrassing. He never looked to take on things which were likely to create problems for him. After all," she shrugged, "what he wanted was success.

"However, having said that," she continued, "I have to tell you that the drama, the tragedy behind these orders, simply never entered one's mind. It was purely an administrative matter. Knowing what we know now, one can say that it should have meant something, that we should have asked ourselves what exactly was happening, why all these flats were suddenly available, etc., but we just didn't. It simply didn't occur to us." In any case, she honestly didn't think, she said, that Speer personally had anything to do with these flats.

Well, she was wrong about that. What Speer didn't know at the time of the correspondence with Wolters, or even years later when he tried to prevent the publication of Schmidt's embarrassing book, was that three notebook pages, on which he jotted down questions to raise in meetings with his staff, had somehow slipped among the thousands of pages of documentation which Wolters eventually bequeathed to the Federal Archives, and would establish his personal knowledge of the Jewish-owned flats beyond a shadow of a doubt.

The first, page 48, bears a date of January 20, 1941, and contains, besides two notes for the architect Hans Stephan, one for Dietrich Clahes, Chief of Resettlement Department: "Cl: Couple [*koppeln*]* action on the 1,000 Jewish flats with preparation for emergency quarters for people made homeless through bomb damage." The other two pages are undated, both appearing merely to be reminders to himself to ask Clahes for reports: "Cl." he jots down, "Report about 1,000 Jew flats," and adds in the next line, still directed to Clahes, "& various other things I haven't heard anything more about." The third page note is only "Clah. Report about 1,000 Jew-flat action."

Whichever way one looks at the crossed-out *Chronik* entries and at Speer's aide-mémoire, one can be absolutely certain on a number of points: the first, that Speer, although he eventually came to accept Wolters's "cleansing," had nothing to do with these deletions, which Wolters made while Speer was imprisoned at Spandau. Second, Clahes's presence at the March 21 meeting at

---

*The word *koppeln*—a somewhat ambiguous term not quite equivalent to the verb "to couple"—indicates here Speer's apparent intention that the GBI's "action on 1,000 Jewish flats" should be seen to be linked (obviously for reasons of public relations) with the humanitarian provision of emergency housing for people made homeless by air bombardments rather than with the evacuation of the Berlin Jews—which had already become a matter of concern to sections of the public.

Goebbels's ministry shows that Speer's office, if not Speer actively himself, was indeed involved in the expulsion of Jews from their flats and the assignment of these properties to non-Jews who had been made homeless by bomb damage. And finally, the *Chronik* shows, and Speer confirmed in *Infiltrations,* that by October and November 1941, if not earlier, he was aware of the evacuation of Jews from Berlin and knew that men, women and children were being herded east. He regularly attended Hitler's meals where, as we can see in *Tabletalk,* the Führer made no secret in the second half of 1941 of his intention to "push all Jews to the East," though of course not their final fate.

The reason I describe this particular matter so fully is that although Speer had many critics, many just as passionate as Matthias Schmidt, this is one of only two instances in the fifteen years between his release from Spandau and his death when, with great determination and an enormous investment of energy, he took issue with specific accusations. (The second one will be discussed later.)

It is obvious that, given how many other things he was accused of and criticized for, his furious battle against these two accusations means that they were singularly important to him and therefore now require careful examination. While on the surface philosophical about criticism of his architecture, and almost humbly receptive to censure of his morality under Hitler, he fought bitterly to defend his stance of ignorance about the eventual fate of the Jews. I have no doubt that at the time of the events described above, Speer knew nothing of the impending (and in the last month of 1941 already functioning) plan to exterminate Europe's Jews.

But as Karl Hettlage said, "Nothing is just black and white." The path Albert Speer walked, starting in the late autumn of 1941, was neither black nor white, but very grey indeed.

X

A Moral Sore

Nuremberg, July 23, 1946

FLÄCHSNER: The activity of the defendant as Commissioner for Buildings was . . . relatively restricted and of minor importance. . . . It would be erroneous to try to deduce . . . any participation by the defendant in any Crimes against the Peace. The same is true of [his] other functions prior to and during the war up to his assumption of office as Minister. . . .

DR. FLÄCHSNER, as was his function at Nuremberg, was in retrospect being disingenuous about Speer, but really no more than Germany's military leadership had been during the years before the war.

Despite Hitler's impulsive nature, everything he did was rooted in long-held plans arising out of the political concepts he clearly announced in *Mein Kampf* in 1924. If his chiefs of staff were surprised by what he told them in the conference of November 1937, by his invasion of Austria the following March, of Czechoslovakia a year later and the outbreak of war in September 1939, then this is merely proof that they, who living in Hitler's immediate vicinity should have known better, were as blind as the rest of the world. Speer could therefore claim a degree of justification for professing his own ignorance of all these preparations and events, at least up to 1940.

For Speer, the second half of 1940 was almost entirely dedicated to his Berlin building projects. He gives little space in *Inside the Third Reich*—and none in the "Spandau draft"—to what must have been a disturbing experience for him in the last weeks of that year, when Hitler for the first time rejected a request from him.

He had asked Hitler to create a new position of NSDAP Commissioner for Architecture and City Planning. As Berlin's General Building Inspector, he not only already had the country's top job in architecture, but in addition enjoyed a unique "artistic-personal" relationship with Hitler. If his suggestion had been accepted, the appointment would automatically have gone to him. He would have become the czar of architecture in Hitler's Germany. But Hitler said no.

In the little Speer does say in *Inside the Third Reich* about this first defeat in his relationship with Hitler, he implies that he had only wanted this assignment for the general good. He wanted to bring order into the architectural chaos that had been created by Hitler's sudden decision to have more than thirty cities of Greater Germany rebuilt, rather than just those with a special significance to the party and to Hitler personally: Berlin, Nuremberg, Munich and Linz.

Speer also wanted to protect Hitler's town-planning vision by imposing some artistic hegemony over the local party authorities, who under Hitler's new plan would be in charge of commissioning the work. Besides, he felt that a central control was essential for the immense amount of money all this would require. Finally—as he says quite frankly—he was seeking to protect his own interests in Berlin and Nuremberg which, if materials were to be required for building projects all over Greater Germany, were bound to suffer.

If Hitler had proceeded with these huge building projects all over his New Germany—which of course he finally couldn't—a central authority such as Speer proposed would have been essential, so his suggestion was quite legitimate. However, it was not entirely or perhaps even mainly prompted by his concern for Hitler's peace of mind and the good of German architecture.

Speer's feelings about himself at that time were dominated by three factors. The first was his gnawing doubt from the very beginning about his architectural talent. The second was his very real emotion for Hitler, a mixture of hero worship, filial devotion and complicated feelings which he only came to understand much later. But it meant that his entire being was focused on this man, on every word he spoke, every motion he made (or at times did not make) toward him, and on his decisions. Between 1934 and 1942 Speer was not only professionally but, much more important, emotionally entirely dependent on Hitler. The third factor, his increasing ambition and growing desire—and indeed his need—for power, was necessarily entirely bound up with this relationship.

Most Hitler biographers are dismissive of his emotional capacities. The general trend has been to see him as cold and incapable of compassion. But while this certainly applies to his political self, more recent research suggests that he was neither cold nor indifferent toward those closest to him, and this certainly included Speer.

There is no record of Hitler's ever admitting to anyone that he had come to understand that Speer's gifts did not lie primarily in architecture, and it cannot be known when he first realized that Speer's genius for organization could and should be applied elsewhere. But the decisions Hitler made about architectural commissions in the two years before the war, and about Speer as of the latter part of 1941, would indicate an astute judgment of Speer's real potential.

Germany's best-known architects, Gropius and Mies van der Rohe, and a number of others of the world-famous Bauhaus group, left Germany between the time Hitler took over and the outbreak of war. But architecture had long been the profession of choice for many young Germans, and there were many men of talent to choose from when Speer staffed his offices in

Berlin. For young architects, in a promising but by no means yet blooming economic climate, Speer's setups were enticing. Through him as Hitler's favorite they had the most powerful and most lavish of patrons who provided them with dazzling opportunities. Speer was generous with money, praise and recognition.

Over the years, Speer and his group were not the only ones to receive commissions from Hitler, though others were generally assigned less ambitious projects. And these men had little or no direct contact with Hitler—except for Hermann Giesler.

Giesler's father and grandfather had also been architects, like Speer's, and he too received his architectural training in Munich, though at a different college. But they were very different men: Giesler's background was unpretentiously middle class and his family was close. Much more sure of himself than Speer, he was not as charming and not at all charismatic, but he was honest and direct. Seven years older than Speer, he had volunteered at seventeen to join the army in World War I, and both he and his brother, Paul, joined the Nazi movement at its very beginning.

Politics and politicians were central to the brothers' lives—not the case for Speer. Paul Giesler, also originally an architect, became an active officer in the SA and then Gauleiter of Munich. Hermann, unlike Speer, was not a man to swerve in his emotions or loyalties. When he became an architect—he was probably more talented than Speer—it was for life; when he became a National Socialist, with Hitler as his hero whose motives and decisions were beyond question, it was also for life.

It was to Giesler that Hitler turned at the end of 1938 for the rebuilding of Munich. If Speer was, without doubt, Hitler's and Germany's premier architect, then Giesler with this prestigious assignment certainly became number two.

He had already been involved in any number of architectural projects: in 1934, the Nazi Elite College at Sonthofen, which Hitler greatly admired; then, in 1936–37, important party buildings and historical reconstructions in Weimar and Augsburg with which Hitler, for the first time working with him, became personally involved. In 1937, he received the coveted title of Professor and in that year, like Speer, if for less spectacular designs, he won a Grand Prix and a Gold Medal at the Paris World's Fair.

At this point, Speer was very sure of his position with Hitler, so sure that he had suggested Giesler as one of twelve competitors for the Weimar projects. Perhaps he began to question the wisdom of this suggestion when Giesler not only won this competition and another soon after for Augsburg, but also received shortly afterwards the commission to design the German

Exhibition Halls for the projected 1942 World's Fair in Rome, which in 1937 had—with such spectacular success—been Speer's.

Speer may well have been concerned about his own status when Hitler awarded Giesler Munich, the birthplace of the movement, then a few months later approved Bormann's putting him in charge of all building at his beloved mountain retreat, the Obersalzberg. A year later, in 1940, he awarded him the reconstruction of Linz, the city where Hitler had lived as a child. Speer may well have seen Giesler as a rival over whom he had to gain control.

If the two men had always appeared to be friends on the surface, mutual doubts festered underneath. At the beginning of the war, Speer had obtained Hitler's agreement to centralize the administration of iron and steel distribution in the Reich through the GBI, which was already overseeing a country-wide Luftwaffe construction program. Giesler had been quite content with this arrangement, which was likely to save him and his Munich team a good deal of time. But he began to regret his ready acceptance of it after his return from France, in June 1940, when Hitler instructed him to begin construction in Munich immediately, just as he had told Speer to begin the building of Berlin. Giesler's requisitions for iron and steel, however, were so continuously ignored by Speer's GBI that, facing a virtual standstill of all work in Munich, he finally appealed for help and advice to Dr. Fritz Todt.

Todt, with his incredible successes as creator of the *Autobahnen*, his Organization Todt and now his immense responsibilities for the management of war materials, was one of Germany's most influential men.

By the time Giesler turned to him for help, Todt had for years been Inspector General of all construction, the most trusted advisor to Hitler on industry, and was about to be named by him Reichsminister of Armaments and Munitions. But Todt—who by background, education and even as a passionate skier and mountain climber, was much closer to Speer than he would ever be to Giesler—reaffirmed that Speer was the ultimate authority for the iron and steel quota system; he had initiated and reorganized it and, occasional holdups notwithstanding, it worked. Giesler would have to accommodate himself to Speer's schedule. Trying to mediate between the two men, Todt wrote to Speer on January 24, 1941, counseling restraint:

> Perhaps my own experiences and bitter disappointments with all the men with whom I need to work might be of help to you. . . . I have concluded that in our particular sphere . . . every act almost inevitably meets with opposition; everyone who is active rather than passive has rivals and unfortunately also enemies. Not because people want to be obstructive, but rather because they react differently to the particularly taxing pres-

sures and relationships of our working lives. Perhaps, being young, you have quickly discovered how to cut through all such problems, while I can only brood over them.

Having been rebuffed by Todt, Giesler remembered Hitler's advice in France to lay any problems he encountered onto Bormann's broad shoulders. Giesler and Bormann had already developed a very special relationship based on their unquestioning devotion to the party and to Hitler, and perhaps, too, on their mutual distrust and envy of Speer.

Although Bormann insisted that for the sake of the Führer's peace of mind, dissension and confrontations had to be avoided, he immediately obtained for Giesler the most urgent outstanding materials and told him, in strictest confidence, that the situation in his opinion required thorough investigation and an eventual decision by the Führer. Giesler was to let Bormann have, privately, a memo on the crisis in Munich brought about by the unreliability of the distribution process, i.e., of Speer and his organization.

The result of this conflict was Hitler's rejection of Speer's suggestion of a further centralization of all building authority. As Speer says in *Inside the Third Reich,* it was indeed Bormann who engineered this rejection, and Giesler's account of the sequence of events in his 1977 memoirs, *Another Hitler,* confirms Bormann's role.

Although Speer and Bormann were socially and intellectually totally incompatible, they could, each for his own advantage and for Hitler's sake, create a surface film of politeness for working purposes. But there could never be anything approaching a relationship between them. More than class and education, it was their fundamentally different personalities—Speer's deeply inhibited and reserved, Bormann's socially and emotionally grossly extroverted—which were bound to clash.

Giesler's description in his book of Speer, his character, his attitude at Nuremberg and his writings after Spandau showed that while Speer was afraid of Giesler's competition and did what he could to undermine it, Giesler disliked Speer—probably from the beginning, before there was any question of Speer betraying Hitler. When it was all over, when Hitler was dead and his ideas and plans discredited—most publicly and most effectively by Speer—Giesler came to loathe Speer; much of his book is a monument to this hate.

Rather than the duplicity which, although it was certainly part of Speer's character in those years, Giesler vastly exaggerates, the real reason for his detestation of Speer was probably that his own relationship with Hitler never became anything like the one Speer enjoyed for so many years.

After Speer was named Minister, three years subsequent to his first experience of a rebuff, it was Hitler's chats with Giesler about the reconstruction of Linz—the city to which Hitler dreamed of retiring—that would provide him with some relief from the war's pressures. And having become exceptionally close to Bormann, Giesler then had ever readier access to Hitler, even at his military headquarters. But comparing their pedestrian encounters, as Giesler describes them in his book, with the elation many of Hitler's circle observed in their Führer in the earlier years after his talks and walks with Speer, one can see that although Giesler was certainly Speer's rival in architecture, he could never take on that very special role Speer played in Hitler's emotional life.

Giesler, for Hitler, was a talented architect he could use. He readily listened to experts and endlessly lectured anyone at hand, but the people he liked to talk with were those who stimulated him, with whom at times he could even spar. Speer filled these functions, but quite aside from this, in the golden years, he was for Hitler someone for whom he allowed himself some human feeling.

Speer, trying to describe it, told the Nuremberg court that if Hitler had had a friend, he would have been that friend. I think that is wrong, because "friendship" has to be mutual and Speer himself would never have allowed himself to feel that he was Hitler's "friend."

In 1975, thirty-seven years after the perceptive remark by the financial expert Karl Hettlage about Hitler's feelings for Speer, Alexander Mitscherlich, one of Germany's most eminent psychoanalysts and social psychologists, as I mentioned earlier, discussed that relationship. Writing in the *Frankfurter Allgemeine Zeitung* about Speer's just-published *Spandau: The Secret Diaries,* he said, "In his own way, Adolf Hitler loved Albert Speer and in his own way Albert Speer loves Hitler." Mitscherlich described it as an infinitely complex "homo-erotic (not sexual) relationship, the result of needs each could uniquely fulfill for the other." Mitscherlich told me he saw the origins of this strange "friendship" very much as I did. The young, handsome and pure Speer, he said, represented for Hitler a dream he might have had of himself; and Hitler for Speer was not only the instrument of realization of all his fantasies—that would have been too simple—but the hero, the strong and powerful protector he had sought since childhood.

"Yes," Speer said when we discussed this article, "Mitscherlich came closest to the truth."

THE EUPHORIA of the victory in France and Speer's concentration on practical problems of construction contributed to his blindness to the beginnings of Hitler's evil. But it is clear that by 1941, by which time Poland had been under occupation for over a year and many thousands of Polish slave workers had been shipped to Germany, there were things Speer must have known and others which he "sensed." Soon we will learn what he refused—or couldn't bear—to see, and equally what others knew and didn't dare to tell him. But in any case reality inevitably entered his life, and indeed that of millions of Germans, with the invasion of Russia in June 1941.

We were sitting beside the big window in the Heidelberg house when I asked when he had first known that Hitler intended to invade Russia. The day after his trip with Hitler to Paris on June 28, 1940, he said to me, he heard the tail end of a conversation Hitler had with Field Marshal Wilhelm Keitel and General Alfred Jodl. As Speer walked up to them to make his goodbyes, he heard Hitler say that by comparison to what they had just achieved in France, a campaign against Russia would be nothing more than a game in a sandpit. (In the "Spandau draft" he explains that the Army General Staff conducted "war games" with little flags in a sandbox.)

In the renewed excitement over building for the rest of that year, and the peaceful atmosphere in Berlin and Berchtesgaden, he told me, he had forgotten those words. Over that "wonderful hot summer" of 1940 Speer was not the only one to feel it was a time of "rapture" for Hitler and his jubilant Germans. There were victories on land, the skies over Germany's cities were as yet quiet, and confidence reigned that all past, present and future opponents were weak.

A bare three months later, this had begun to change. The air war had begun in earnest and, against all of Göring's assurances of the Luftwaffe's superiority, by the latter months of 1940 the RAF had begun to wreak havoc upon German cities.

In July 1940 Hitler had told the Chiefs of Staff to begin work on plans for a sharp, short Russian campaign to start in the spring of 1941. And on December 18, 1940, by now convinced that the only reason Britain was not giving up was her reliance on Russia and the United States, his Directive No. 21 for Operation Barbarossa finalized his orders for war against the Soviets:

> The German armed forces must be prepared to crush Soviet Russia in a quick campaign even before the conclusion of the war against England. . . . Preparations requiring more time, if not yet begun, are to be started now and completed by May 15, 1941. The bulk of the Russian army in western Russia is to be destroyed by driving forward and creating deep armored wedges, and the retreat of units capable of combat into the vastness of Russian territory is to be prevented. . . . The ultimate objective is to establish a defense line against Asiatic Russia from a line running from the Volga River to Archangel.

> Then the last industrial area left to Russia in the Urals can be destroyed by the Luftwaffe. . . .

Only nine copies of this directive were distributed, but for the Wehrmacht Chiefs of Staff, everything from then on was to be subordinated to this overriding purpose.

All of Hitler's war plans were based on the *Blitzkrieg* strategy which had succeeded so spectacularly in the West. As his plans for Russia matured, all based on a campaign lasting no longer than five months, a few warning voices made themselves heard among his generals. The Chief of the Army General Staff, General Franz Halder, consistently tried to warn Hitler against false optimism about Soviet weakness, and Admiral Erich Raeder tried to convince him that the primary goal had to be the defeat of Britain before Roosevelt brought the United States into the war on her side.

It is perhaps understandable that not only Hitler but the rest of the world, too, so misjudged the likely resistance of the Russians. Stalin had, after all, killed many of his best generals and industrial managers in the purges of the 1930s. But certainly, all the intelligence services failed in their evaluations of the size of Soviet manpower, the determination and ruthlessness of the political and army leadership and, above all, the innate quality of the Russian soldier. The example of Napoleon's terrible defeat—the possibility that Russian resistance could last through the winter—appears never to have entered Hitler's head.

As Speer was to discover later, the German army's winter uniforms, though on his and General Jodl's suggestion redesigned by the Munich sport firm that had equipped the Himalaya expedition, turned out to be unsuitable for the arctic cold of Russia's winter. "Our new wool production process," he wrote in Spandau, "which produced a fabric easier to work on and less bulky to wear, had not taken account of the fact that it is precisely the grease that was removed to reduce weight that provides protection from humidity. The Russian soldiers with their old-fashioned thick coats and heavy blankets were much better off than our men, whose resistance was doubtlessly often fatally undermined by being continuously cold and wet." The Russian campaign was eventually to cost Germany 3,250,000 soldiers' lives; more than 100,000 of them froze to death.

But this was still in the future. At the beginning of 1941, Hitler was busily extending his group of allies. Mussolini had already hastily joined him when the *Blitzkrieg* against France was so successful. Then Hitler concluded pacts with Rumania (whose oil he had to have; his admirer, the military dictator Ion Antonescu, was to stand by him until the end of the war), Hungary and Bulgaria, which he had softened up by giving them each, with Antonescu's agreement, a portion of Transylvania, which had belonged to Rumania since the Treaty of Versailles.

He knew the traditionally pro-British Greeks would never join him peacefully, so the plans for Operation Maritsa, the invasion of Greece, were ready. When, early in 1941, his attempt to get Yugoslavia onto his side was blocked by an army coup, he invaded it as well as Greece, where Mussolini was mismanaging *his* invasion. Hitler's *Blitzkrieg* was again spectacularly successful, and he won that war in two weeks. By the end of April 1941, excepting the four neutral countries, Spain, Portugal, Sweden and Switzerland, all of Europe was in his camp—except Russia.

The feverish preparations for Barbarossa, the invasion of Russia, over the first months of 1941 were interrupted in May, six weeks before he launched the attack on Russia, by what Speer would describe to me as "the second-worst personal blow of Hitler's life," Rudolf Hess's flight to England on Saturday, May 10, 1941. (The first had been the suicide of his love, his niece Geli Raubal, in 1931.)

Hitler—we are told by Nicolaus von Below, who was as usual on duty—was still in bed on Sunday morning when Hess's two adjutants, Karl-Heinz Pintsch and Alfred Leitgen, arrived at the Berghof carrying the Deputy Führer's letter informing Hitler of his flight to Britain and his naive plan to persuade the British to get out of the war.

Once again, as so often at decisive moments, Speer happened to be at the Berghof, apparently waiting to show Hitler new designs. Hess's "pale and agitated aides," he writes with one of his not infrequent embellishments in *Inside the Third Reich*, putting himself more "in the know" than he actually was, "asked if I would let them see Hitler first: they had a personal letter from Hess to transmit to him." In the more factual draft (and in Below's memoirs) it is not Speer who allows them—or is asked for—precedence. The other guests, including Speer, are quickly herded up to the second floor, where they would wait for hours, in ignorance of the dramatic events downstairs. Hitler, having hurried down and perused the letter handed to him by General Karl Bodenschatz (Göring's liaison officer with Hitler), bellowed for Bormann, and ordered adjutant Pintsch into his presence. Hess's unhappy aides, having admitted that they knew the contents of the letter, were arrested and taken off to a concentration camp.

Hitler's immediate concern appeared to be that Churchill would use Hess's arrival to convince Hitler's partners, Italy and Japan, that Hitler was asking for peace. "Who is going to believe," Speer quotes him saying, "that he isn't going on my behalf, that the whole thing isn't a plot behind the back of my allies? It can lead to the most terrible problems with them."

The concern over Italy's and Japan's goodwill led Hitler to issue an announcement that night that Hess's flight to Britain was the result of a mental breakdown, the symptoms of which had been noticed for some time. "My God," wrote Goebbels in his diary that night, "and that was the second man in the Reich. What will the world think of us?"

Actually Hitler had to fear something considerably worse than the suspicion of his Axis partners and the mockery of "the world." This was the appalling prospect of Hess—voluntarily or by being drugged or otherwise coerced—giving away to the British the plans for Barbarossa, then scheduled for June 22, with which he was fully familiar.

"I don't know how far advanced the British were with truth drugs then," Speer told me, "but voluntarily Hess would never have betrayed Hitler, of that I am quite certain." In fact, in his letter to Hitler Hess had specifically promised silence, and he kept his promise.

Hess, though still formally Hitler's Secretary and Deputy, had come to be ever less welcome at Hitler's court, although meetings between them still occurred. He was pessimistic, and he was long-winded about it. Hitler had made it clear to Bormann, by then in charge of all appointments, that he preferred not to see too much of his depressing Deputy. Speer told me that Hitler complained to him, "Hess always brought up unpleasant matters and went on and on about them. Hitler hated being tackled on anything unpleasant." What was certain, he said, was that Hitler had neither sent him on that mission to Britain nor knew about it in advance.

Dr. Robert Kempner, who first assisted U.S. Chief Prosecutor Robert Jackson and subsequently became Deputy Chief Prosecutor under Telford Taylor for the remaining twelve war crime trials at Nuremberg, disagreed. Both Kempner's background and his position at Nuremberg were different from all other prosecutors'. Born in Germany in 1899, son of a distinguished Jewish family in Freiburg, he had become an eminent jurist, judge and professor of law by the time he emigrated to America in 1939. Between then and 1945, when he was named head of research for the U.S. Nuremberg prosecution, he had become a leading expert on legal, political, police and intelligence techniques of European dictatorships and foreign organizations in the United States, advising the U.S. Department of Justice, the Office of Strategic Services and the Secretary of War.

One of the most highly qualified men in Nuremberg, Kempner, as an ultra-distinguished German Jew, was also one of the most resented by many of the accused. Some defendants and many witnesses, however, readily collaborated with him when he questioned them prior to trials. One of these was Ernst Wilhelm Bohle, Chief of the NSDAP Organizations of Germans Abroad and State Secretary at the Foreign Office. Bohle, born in Bradford, Yorkshire, in 1903 and thus an *Auslanddeutscher* like Hess (who was born in

1894 in Alexandria, Egypt), was a protégé and confidant of Hess's. He told
Kempner that Hess phoned him on the evening of October 9, 1940, and asked
him to come to his apartment in Berlin. After making sure his door was
tightly shut, Hess told him he wanted to confide a very secret assignment to
him which no one, neither Hess's own family and staff nor Bohle's, must
learn of. "I chose you," Hess said, "because you speak English, know the
British and consider our war with Britain as much a mistake as I do." He
was working on a way to stop this war; was Bohle willing to help? "When I
immediately agreed, he told me that above all others, my chief, Foreign
Minister von Ribbentrop, must not hear even a breath of this intention as
he would sabotage it at once. Hess then explained that he wanted to write
to the Duke of Hamilton, whom he had met on the occasion of the Olympic
Games, and who had great influence in Britain, to suggest a private meeting
in Switzerland.

"He handed me the draft of the first part of a letter and asked me to translate it, right away, in an office next door," said Bohle.

Every few weeks after that until January 4, 1941, Hess called him to translate further drafts of the letter, the work of Hess's friend and political mentor, the professor of geopolitics Karl Haushofer, and his son, Albrecht.*
"Later I heard that Hess had made a first attempt in mid-January to fly to
England which, as well as the next one in February or March, he had to abandon for technical reasons," Bohle told Kempner. "I had no idea then that his
intention was to fly directly to England. In fact, having served as his interpreter at a dinner with the Duke and Duchess of Windsor some time before, I
had asked him to take me along to Switzerland where I thought he was going
to meet Hamilton.

" 'If your plan comes to pass,' I said to him, 'please suggest to the Führer
that I accompany you.' In his reply he didn't mention Hitler, but nor did he
say that Hitler knew nothing about the plan, and I have always been of the
opinion that Hitler was informed. I heard that Hess—who since the beginning of war seldom wanted to bother Hitler and thus saw him only rarely—
had had a four-hour-long private meeting with him at the Chancellery
shortly before he left. And on May 13 when Hitler received the 'top men'—
including me—on the Obersalzberg, he confirmed this meeting and said that
Hess had asked him whether he still stood by his program of collaboration
with Britain as stated in *Mein Kampf*. Hitler said he did. . . ."

One of the many things which supported his belief that Hitler had known,
Bohle told Kempner, was that he learned later that when, after the Hess
flight, Bormann had asked Hitler to sign the order for Bohle's arrest, Hitler

*Albrecht Haushofer was executed just before the end of the war, accused of participating in the July 20
conspiracy; his father later committed suicide.

refused to sign it. "This was incomprehensible if Hitler really was totally uninvolved. Even though I didn't know about the flight itself," Bohle said, "I did far more toward bringing it about than Hess's secretaries, chauffeurs, servants and others who were locked up. I was questioned for a long time on May 14 by Heydrich and Gestapo Müller,* but was told to go home. The only explanation I could think of was that Hess had told Hitler of the help I had given him, but had asked that I be let off if the thing went wrong and Hitler was forced to disavow him." (This kind of loyalty toward a colleague would not have been uncharacteristic for Hess.)

Another significant contemporary witness, however, was equally certain that Hitler did *not* know—Luftwaffe General Adolf Galland, Germany's ace fighter pilot and Commander of the Fighter Force. He has authored two books since the end of World War II and, though a passionate Nazi until he realized that Hitler's madness was going to lose Germany the war, ended up a highly paid figure on the U.S. lecture circuit, much courted by the media. He remained every inch a General, not only with visitors but one senses also with his staff. His office in Bad Godesberg where he received me was sterile rather than empty; there were books on shelves, but they looked unread; there were ashtrays, but one doubted that any visitor would dare use them; and all of the framed photographs were of airplanes with stiff figures beside them. As an informant, however, he was exceptionally useful for, with the trained memory of the flier, everything he recalled was precise; conversations, one suspected, almost verbatim.

I went to see him in 1987. He was just back from lecturing in the United States and was due to leave again in two days for other speaking engagements abroad. I knew from Speer that he had had enormous problems both with Hitler and with Göring, and asked whether people questioned him about them after his lectures.

"I don't talk about individuals," he said. "I talk about airplanes and air strategy."

His only interest in Hess had been his orders to kill him. "If Hess went with Hitler's knowledge," he said, "and I have no reason to think he did, then certainly Hitler didn't let Göring in on it, because Göring told me in no uncertain terms to take up a squadron of fighters to pursue him and to shoot him down. Hitler was an actor—a very good one—but Göring not at all; if he told me to shoot Hess down, it was because he thought Hess was up there against the Führer's orders or wishes, and that was that."

The idea of flying to England, Hess told Speer in Spandau, had come to

---

*Obergruppenführer Heinrich Müller had been a police chief in Munich before the Nazis took power. Heydrich made him chief of the Gestapo in 1935, where he was Adolf Eichmann's direct superior. He was last seen in the Reich Chancellery bunker on April 29, 1945, and is thought to have escaped abroad.

him in a dream. There had been no intention, he said, to defy or embarrass
Hitler in any way. What he wanted to get across to the British was what Hitler
had said countless times and (no doubt with Hess's editorial assistance) had
written in his second volume of *Mein Kampf,* which was that if Britain agreed
to give him a free hand in Europe, he would in return guarantee the continuing security of Britain's empire.

In many of our talks, Speer showed his concern for and his sincere liking for
Hess. "Officially," he said, "Hitler's attitude toward Hess, that he was a traitor
and would have to be hanged when the war was over, never changed. But
privately, I think, he was very attached to him. And you know, I never thought
he was a traitor—I didn't even think it when it happened. Of course, I didn't
know about Barbarossa then, but later, much later, the fact of Hess's absolute
discretion about this when he was in England seemed the best proof to me, not
only of course of his loyalty to Hitler, but really of his complete sanity."*

As it turned out, it was in the interest of both Germany and Britain to play
down the Hess affair. Hitler, as I said, announced that Hess was mentally disturbed; Churchill told Foreign Secretary Anthony Eden "to treat him as a
prisoner of war . . . but also as one against whom grave political charges may
be preferred." Thus Hess began his imprisonment which, following his sentence at Nuremberg five years later, he would continue in Spandau to the end
of his life.

ACCORDING to the Wehrmacht chronicler Helmuth Greiner,
who was responsible for the war diary, it was at a conference on March 3,
1941, that the generals were to find out how radically Hitler's concept of the
war in the East differed from theirs. In the Wehrmacht conference that day,
during which Hitler mentioned for the first time the "necessity of eliminating the political commissars," he established his goals clearly enough. "The
Jewish-Bolshevist intelligentsia," he said, "must, if at all possible, be eradi-
cated in the course of the military operations." In Hitler's mind "intelligentsia," "Bolshevists" and "Jews" were inescapably linked, as was to be their
"eradication"—by the army, together with Himmler's police.

"At this conference," testified Field Marshal Wilhelm Keitel at Nuremberg, "Himmler was given extensive plenipotentiary powers covering all police actions which would become necessary in the occupied territory."

Ten days later, on March 13, Keitel released the written preamble of the

---

*Churchill to Roosevelt, May 17, 1941: ". . . Hess was extremely voluble. . . . The British Empire . . . would
be left intact: . . . The old invitation to desert all our friends in order to save temporarily the greater part
of our skin. . . . Germany had certain demands to make of Russia which would have to be satisfied, but
[he] denied rumours that attack on Russia was being prepared."

Kommissar Befehl (Commissar Order) which would be communicated to the army two weeks later. The preamble said,

> In preparation for the political administration of the army's [future] area of operations, the Reichsführer SS [Himmler] by order of the Führer is charged with special tasks [*Sonderaufgaben*]* arising out of the conclusive and decisive struggle between two diametrically opposed political systems. Within the framework of these tasks, the Reichsführer SS acts independently and on his own responsibility.... The Army Chiefs of Staff are to settle details directly with the Reichsführer SS.

The only certainty the generals gathered from this apparently abstruse directive was that their authority was going to be usurped by the loathed Himmler and his SS. But two weeks later they would begin to know just what was meant by Hitler charging Himmler with "special tasks."

Hitler's orders for murder which, as Below was to recall forty years later, caused consternation among the generals and probably laid the seeds for the army's plot to assassinate him four long years later, were issued in stages, all basically before the campaign in Russia started. The wording of the Commissar Order—"by order of the Führer" and "Within the framework of these tasks, the Reichsführer SS acts independently and on his own responsibility"—though ostensibly applicable to political murders, was very soon applied to the assembly-line murder of the Jews, first by shooting and soon by gassing.

On March 30 in Berlin, Hitler, speaking for two and a half hours to the Wehrmacht General Staff, bluntly laid out the fundamental policy of his Russian campaign:

> ... Our task in Russia has to be to destroy the Red Army and to dissolve the Soviet state. It is a confrontation of two opposing ideologies. Bolshevism has to be seen as an association of criminals whose antisocial characteristics, infinitely dangerous to others, make them unfit for civilized human society.... We are going into a battle of annihilation. If we don't accept it as such, we may, being militarily stronger, gain a temporary victory now, but the enemy will then be able to re-emerge, ideologically revivified, a few years later.
>
> This is why, in the battle against Russia, our essential goal has to be the destruction of communism—through the annihilation of the Bolshevik commissars and the communist intelligentsia.... Commissars and communist politicians are criminals and must be treated as such. In the East, gentlemen, severity now is an act of kindness for the future.

*Since the Euthanasia Program, the prefix *Sonder-* (special) was the code word applied solely to operations connected with the different projects for murder: i.e., *Sonderkommando, Sonderbefehl* and—the most pointed—*Sonderbehandlung* (Special Treatment).

Later that afternoon, Keitel spelled it out for them. All political commissars who fell into the army's hands would have to be killed forthwith by the soldiers or, and there was an implicit threat here, handed over to the nearest SS or SD, the Security Service.

This was unprecedented in the annals of German military history. Notwithstanding accounts of German brutalities in Southwest Africa in the early twentieth century, and individual atrocity stories of World War I, the German army has traditionally far more often than not respected the law; German soldiers who committed offenses against either property or human life risked dire disciplining and even death. But Hitler's order threw over that whole concept; the pretext was—and would continue to be over the next years, when numerous laws governing the fate of war prisoners and the lives of occupied populations were revoked—that the Soviets had not signed the Geneva convention on military conduct in time of war. But the truth was something else and is of fundamental importance to history. With this Commissar Order, Hitler was setting in motion processes which, developing a fatal momentum of their own, would in a way change the world.

Absolutely essential to the carrying out of his awful vision, which was made inescapably clear in his address to the generals on March 30, was the fact that decent men were now to be directed to abandon all civilized rules of warfare and, restrained by nothing except their individual decisions and judgment, to commit political and ideological murders. For what has become abundantly obvious (though the soldiers, and for that matter the Wehrmacht generals in the field, would only find out gradually) is that the murder of commissars was only the beginning and, as can be seen from Hitler's words on March 30, was linked from the start to his two other and greater purposes—the elimination of the educated classes of Eastern Europe and the annihilation of the Jews.

In the Polish campaign, the soldiers had been left to fight the war while the Action Groups—the Einsatzgruppen—followed in their wake to attend to the civilian population. For the first year, the Jews were brutalized, but far more Christian than Jewish Poles were killed (a fact rarely acknowledged by either historians or the media). But to Hitler's fury, the Wehrmacht had soon protested against the "brutal and uncivilized" measures—the exact words to be found in several official protests—taken by Himmler and his men.

So the Russian campaign was planned differently from the start. Different from any other, this campaign was to be very specifically an ideological war in which no heretofore established rules applied. The Einsatzgruppen would virtually accompany rather than follow the troops; civilians in the stated categories would be dealt with by army and Action Groups together while military operations were being conducted. No soldier who killed under the circumstances outlined was ever to be called to account; in the Eastern theater of war, no individual was ever to be considered responsible for actions causing the death of anyone in those categories.

Hitler's speech of March 30 is on the record. Keitel testified at Nuremberg about his subsequent meeting with the generals and said that Generals Emil Leeb, Fedor von Bock and Gerd von Rundstedt demanded that General Walther von Brauchitsch, as Commander-in-Chief, lodge an urgent protest with Hitler. In Nuremberg Brauchitsch said he finally hadn't protested to Hitler because he believed he could invalidate the Führer's order by strict injunctions to the troops against excesses.

The record does in fact show that such injunctions were issued, and also, as mentioned above, shows protests by numerous officers of the lower echelons. But in the slaughterhouse that Eastern Europe was to become, injunctions and protests would turn out to be useless. What Hitler taught us—to an extent greater than anyone else in history, though we would become aware of it again in Vietnam—is that a license to kill creates a momentum which defies moral sensibility and discernment and destroys the capacity of the individual to distinguish between good and evil or, and this is perhaps even worse, to act against a recognized wrong. This emerges disturbingly from Nicolaus von Below's memoirs:

> . . . Hitler's concept of the Eastern campaign was radically different from the army's. While the Chiefs of Staff planned a traditional war, for Hitler it was a battle against the toughest and most ruthless of enemies. Indicative of this determination was Hitler's *Kommissar Befehl* in which he instructed the troops to shoot every commissar who fell into their hands without ceremony. This directive caused a great deal of alarm and I knew that, by individual commanders' decisions, it was withheld from many units.
>
> It caused the first widespread opposition against a *Führer Befehl* I had heard of. And this was when I realized for the first time that other Hitler orders could also end up being systematically suppressed. What contributed more than anything else to my realization of this was [General] Halder's manifest, though (unfortunately) [he] never openly expressed contempt for Hitler's orders and also for many of his ideas, causing great confusion in me; I was very aware how [this greatly admired general] continuously suppressed his feelings. . . .
>
> And thus we started out on a huge campaign, beset by divided loyalties and divided leadership—a great danger to a successful military operation.

However difficult it is to believe, Below, like Hitler's other young aides, his secretaries and all the intimate Hitler circle, knew nothing of the increasingly horrific plans for the civilian population in the East and for the Jews of

Europe. Strangely enough, they above all others were unlikely to be told by the few who did at that point know: Himmler, Heydrich, Göring and, later on, Goebbels.

Underrating Hitler has become a norm, less for historians of course than for the media, but it is the media which largely informs the public. It has never been quite clear why so many intelligent people find it more comforting to deprecate Hitler's manic gifts than to view them with awe. But he was by no means only manic—as already said, he could also be intelligent and considerate in his more personal relations. Certainly all those who lived around him were keenly aware of his exceptional capacity for compartmentalizing. Hitler would no more have had the ladies of his household—his four secretaries or the young wives of his aides, such as Below, and those of his closest associates, Speer and Brandt—disturbed with war horrors than he would have had the gentlemen of his court, and quite a few of them were indeed gentlemen, involved in his most secret of secrets.

I have asked a number of these people what they would have done if they had known of Hitler's plans for the murder of Poland's elite and of the Jews. It is a measure of their honesty that none of them simply said they would have departed in horror. I think several of them spoke the truth when they said that they would have felt horrified. But I believe that all of them would have tried to put it out of their minds: not because any of them were monsters, but because they were totally convinced that Hitler wasn't, and that therefore, whatever they might have heard couldn't have been quite as bad as it sounded—not "if the Führer knew."

The group I speak of here was, of course, very small and, with a few exceptions, such as again Speer and Brandt, lived in virtually cloistered conditions, as we have shown. It was only rarely, almost by accident, that they learned what had been the subject of Hitler's meetings "under four eyes."

Christa Schröder, Hitler's second senior secretary, told me of one such occasion when I talked with her in 1977. I mentioned that one of Bormann's former adjutants, Heinrich Heim (to whom he had entrusted the daily recording of Hitler's *Tabletalk*), had told me that *he* didn't think Hitler knew about the extermination of the Jews. Schröder laughed. "Oh, Heimchen—" she said, "he's too good for this life. Of course Hitler knew! Not only knew, it was *all* his ideas, his orders.

"I clearly remember a day in 1941, I think it was in early spring," she said. "I don't think I will ever forget Himmler's face when he came out after one of his long, 'under four eyes' conferences with Hitler. He sat down heavily in the chair on the other side of my desk and buried his face in his hands, his elbows on the desk. 'My God, my God,' he said, 'what I am expected to do.'

"Later, much later," she said, "when we found out what had been done, I was sure that that was the day Hitler told him the Jews had to be killed."*

When I told this story to Speer a year later, he considered it highly probable. "Himmler was a very paradoxical personality," he said. "I have read many memoranda in which, for instance, he regulated precisely the treatment for workers in concentration camps—so many calories, so many vitamins—and if they had received them, believe me, it would have been enough. The fact that they didn't get it had less to do with Himmler than with the stupendous corruption in all administrative areas, with countless people amassing fortunes for themselves.

"Certainly he was cruel and ruthless in his persecution of individuals," he said, "but he did have this other side, and I can perfectly visualize him coming out of Hitler's office after one of those 'under four eyes' conferences, and slumping down at a desk and saying, 'My God, what I am required to do.' Perhaps he wasn't saying it *to* Christa Schröder, but rather to himself, as a reaction to what he had experienced on the other side of the door. Yes, I can see him having just that reaction. . . ."

Hitler's youngest secretary, perhaps the one who would eventually come closest to liberating herself from Hitler's magnetism and to facing reality, was Traudl (Gertrude) Junge (née Humps), a twenty-two-year-old former ballet dancer when she entered Hitler's service in November 1942. Like so many who had lived near Hitler, she was very unhappy at the idea of talking about that time with strangers. It was several years, after many telephone conversations, before she finally invited me to her home, a small apartment full of pretty things, bright colors and nice smells, on a residential street in Munich.

About sixty-five when I met her but looking many years younger, she was tall, slender, well dressed in a relaxed sort of way, with a quiet voice. When we talked, she was very serious—the things we talked about did not really allow much humor. But I felt that this was really someone with whom I would have loved to laugh.

She was very young when she became Hitler's fourth secretary, and he treated her with great kindness, almost like a daughter. Six months later, urged on by Hitler, she married one of his two valets, SS Leibstandarte Obersturmführer (Lieutenant) Hans Junge, who had asked to be relieved of his duties on Hitler's staff in order to serve on the Russian front.

"He asked to be transferred to the front not because he disagreed with the Führer, or knew anything terrible, but because he felt he was living in a claus-

---

*Frau Schröder, appalled at her own indiscretion, which she feared, if published, could cost her the few friends she still had from the time of Hitler, later asked me not to use her account. I complied with her request during her lifetime.

trophobic environment. He told me, just before Hitler finally, after many
previous rejections, granted his request for a transfer to active service, that he
no longer knew the difference between what he really thought himself and
what Hitler, or those around him, thought. 'I need to get myself into a position of thinking for myself,' he said."

They hadn't wanted to marry so quickly. "I think finally *he* did want it,
firstly because he was going to the front—the usual 'not knowing' what
would happen—but also because Hitler talked him into it. But I, not at all—I
wanted to get to know this man slowly before making up my mind about my
life. But the Führer wouldn't have it. He was going to have us marry, or else. I
don't really know why. Certainly it couldn't have been because he wanted to
be surrounded by young widows. Perhaps he thought it would keep Hans at
HQ or because—you know, he really did care about all of us—perhaps he
thought it would make Hans happy, make him feel at peace and fight even
harder to stay alive."

During the subsequent years she would become very aware of the isolation
Hans had talked to her about. "Perhaps I was only reacting to what he had
said," she said, "or maybe I did become aware on my own of how deeply we
were under Hitler's influence; I find it difficult now, so many years later, to
be sure. Today the whole thing sounds almost impossible, the way we lived, I
mean. Here we were, in the middle of a most dreadful war, at the very center
of events and yet—I now know—we knew nothing, less even than people
outside. Many of them did finally hear Allied broadcasts, but we never did. If
they were perhaps affected by what their men, returning on leave from the
front said, this didn't apply to us. None of our friends, relatives or—yes, husbands—ever talked about horrible experiences or doubts. They just changed
and we didn't know why.

"In later years, after it was all over, some of the people from Führer HQ,
generals and others, told me of their meetings with Hitler, how they would
go in, fully prepared to tell him the truth of what was going on and the impending disaster. And then they would leave, having been overwhelmed by
his personality, his reassurances, his opinions, analyses and orders. They
found themselves unable to say a word to contradict him—it was as if he
hypnotized people."

The word "hypnotized," describing Hitler's ability to bend people to his
will, came up in almost every conversation about him. Even though many of
those who had lived in his immediate surroundings professed to deplore Hitler's crimes, there was not only a defensive but, curiously enough, an almost
pleasurable element in their descriptions of these hypnotic powers they had
been subjected to. It was almost as if the fact that they—so few among so

many—were in a position to provide such a description made them feel somehow proud. It was perplexing. And with the single exception of Traudl Junge, who had been the youngest member on Hitler's staff, none of them expressed a retroactive understanding that what he had hypnotized his people into was—however secondhand, however removed—participation in murder: of millions of Russians in POW camps, by starvation and exposure; of Jews and Gypsies, by shooting and gassing; of slave laborers and concentration camp prisoners, by overwork, hunger and torture.

Of all these untold murders—the estimates vary between the almost inconceivable figures of twelve million and twenty million civilians—the unique crime of the industrialized killing of the Jews has come to symbolize Nazi rule. The Nuremberg court would convict Speer almost solely for his use of slave labor and would virtually absolve him from any part in genocide. But he himself—and this is where he differed from the other accused—knew better. The murder of the Jews was central to his radical condemnation of Hitler, central to his awareness of his own guilt and absolutely central to his thoughts for thirty-five years. Starting, I believe, as a kind of hidden moral sore in the back of his mind well before the end of the Third Reich, by the time of the Nuremberg trial it would become his most intense problem of conscience. The extent of his knowledge was, as he once wrote me, the "cardinal problem of [his] life." It remained so until his death.

In order to understand how this "moral sore" came into being—not only in Speer but in a whole generation of Germans who, contrary to Speer, never took issue with it (and whose children and even grandchildren have had to face the consequences ever since)—we need to examine the sequence of decisions and events which led to the nightmare of the Final Solution.

Hitler's fantasies were certainly global, but his real perspective was always emotionally oriented and basically limited. The Jews he was primarily concerned with were for many years those in Germany and Austria. In *Mein Kampf,* so much of which is dominated by his loathing for the Jews, he does move toward a wider view of the problem but leaves an impression that he was paying lip service to the necessity of sounding world-minded, and that the real concern of this provincial man was always his province. However, he assumed for years that emigration was the answer. It was always the German and Austrian Jews he wanted to be rid of, from the very start—though in the early stages by emigration rather than by deportation, the limit of his intentions until well into the war.

Three developments between the late 1930s and the beginning of the war in Russia led him to the dreadful Final Solution of his problem. The first, recognized before the outbreak of war, was that, given the refusal of other nations to accept anything but minimal numbers of Jewish immigrants, an enforced total emigration of Jews from Greater Germany would be impossible. Alternative means would have to be found to get them out of Germany.

The second, the possibility of one huge Jewish settlement, such as on the often-mentioned French island of Madagascar or alternatively in numerous ghettos in the East from which Jewish labor could be drawn, arose with the conquest of Poland. But the size of the Jewish population in Poland itself—where, as already decribed, all "undesirables," whether Polish Christians or Jews, were crowded into the occupied zone—made that impossible, as Hans Frank, the Governor-General, soon explained to Hitler.

The third development, the eradication of the Jews under cover of the murder of the Kommissars, which Hitler had provided for in his orders to the generals in March 1941, was at that point merely theoretical but would be executed a few months hence when his armies moved into the Baltics and the Ukraine.

As new information has emerged the last few years, it has become clear that the fatal decisions were taken in the course of a series of meetings in Berlin in the spring of 1941, such as the "under four eyes" Hitler-Himmler conference Christa Schröder recalled decades later. It would have been unthinkable for Hitler's confidants in these private meetings to divulge what was said, so with a few exceptions the knowledge of them has died with the participants. On March 17, however, Governor-General Frank saw Hitler and was joined for only part of the meeting by Goebbels, who reported on the more harmless aspects in his diary the next day—the discussion about the Jews of Vienna, of Berlin and about Frank's "containment" policy in Poland:

> March 18: Vienna is almost cleared of Jews, and now it is the turn of Berlin; we discussed the details and also Frank's putting them to work in Poland where they obediently do as they are told.

Three days later, on March 20, 1941, the significant meeting which linked all these events took place. As we already know, the decisions of this Hitler-Frank-Goebbels meeting were communicated by Goebbels's favorite, Leopold Gutterer (who would become his Secretary of State two months later), to Speer's representative Dietrich Clahes, and to Adolf Eichmann, who would be charged with organizing the progressive evacuation of Berlin's Jews. Two days later, on March 22, Goebbels notes that there were annoying impediments to their evacuation plans:*

*The question of Goebbels's information on the Jews remains puzzling. Although he finally records their fate quite precisely on March 27, 1942 (see page 350), he later quotes Hitler on May 25 saying that "by preference he would like to settle them all [not in Siberia, where they would be toughened but] in Central Africa . . . in a climate that would [weaken] them and their resistance."

We have to go easy on the 30,000 Jews who work in armament production; we need them—who would have thought this could ever become
possible?

This "need" for the highly qualified Berlin Jews for war production would
endure for years, well into Speer's later reign as armaments czar, and was
helpful to him at Nuremberg.

The Germans had, of course, always known of the enormous number of
Jews in Soviet territory. Literally millions of them—the estimate now is two
and a half million out of the four million who lived in prewar Russia—would
manage to flee eastwards, but even this migration left one and a half million
within the advancing German lines. To Hitler's thinking, the Russian Jews,
like all others, were "destructive bacilli," and with the killing seed firmly
planted in the minds of his generals, he expected their troops and Himmler's
to deal with all of them as his troops advanced. All European Jews meanwhile
were to be transferred to the Occupied Eastern Territories, to work and to be
killed.

Toward that end, Eichmann's office in Berlin, IV B4 (administrative ab-
breviation for the Central Emigration and Jewish Investigation Office of the
Gestapo), dispatched a circular to all German consulates in France and Belgium on May 20, 1941, notifying them that Göring had banned emigration by
Jews from there. The official explanation was that if Jews who had fled there
managed to snap up some of the few available visas for overseas, it could
hamper emigration from the Reich. This deceptive explanation was in line
with many later euphemisms designed to hide the real fate of the Jews. Few if
any of the diplomats involved could have understood the meaning of the
closing sentence in this circular: "The Final Solution of the Jewish problem is
now undoubtedly close at hand."

They would not have known that the decision to liquidate physically the
Jews of Russia had now been made. It was communicated to the SS in April
and May. Obersturmbannführer Ernst Ehlers, a former civil servant, wrote
later,

As the Russian campaign approached, I was a member of Einsatzgruppe B. About April or May 1941 I was told that I was earmarked for
promotion as chief of Einsatzkommando 8 and that I was to report to the
police academy at Pretzsch [Silesia] where the Einsatzgruppen destined
for the Russian campaign were being formed. On the occasion of a staff
conference during which our duties were explained, we were informed
quite unequivocally that aside from combat against partisans, etc., we
would also have to carry through the liquidation of the Jewish population
in the rear. I could hardly believe this appalling disclosure . . . could hardly

believe that anything like this could be envisaged. . . . I finally decided to request a release from the proposed post . . . after which I was assigned, without ado, to HQ staff. . . .*

Speer was not alone in being kept in ignorance in 1940 and early 1941 of Hitler's military-political plans. The Gauleiter—Hitler's cadre of "Old Comrades" who were his political administrators, with enormous powers in their individual provinces—appear not to have known anything either. Even Goebbels, his most intelligent and politically his most indispensable vassal, who never showed any reluctance to confide all secrets to his diary though certainly explicit about getting rid of the Berlin Jews, is silent on Barbarossa until May 1941. He was obviously aware of it sooner, and on May 16 wrote, "It's supposed to start in the East on May 22—still depends on the weather."

The war against the Soviet Union began at 3:30 a.m. on June 22. Hitler, in the last days before it started, wrote Below, was "increasingly nervous and worried." It was only after midnight on June 22 that he heard him make a comment about the impending campaign. "It will be the hardest battle our soldiers will have to fight in this war," he said.

Speer, yet again near Hitler at a decisive moment, was invited to join him in his drawing room after dinner on June 21 to listen to a recording of a fanfare from Liszt's *Les Préludes*.

"Hitler told me this movement was going to be the victory fanfare of the Russian campaign," Speer wrote in his draft. "Hitler added, 'And we'll get ourselves all the granite and marble for our buildings we want.' "

In *Inside the Third Reich* Speer conveys the impression—without actually saying so—that he knew all about the invasion plan. In the draft which went to Wolters, who was well informed about the extent to which Hitler made Speer party to his plans, he adds, "You can see that I don't have that much to add to the historical record. I was as surprised as millions of other Germans the next morning that, breaking our treaty and without a declaration of war, we invaded Russia. . . ."

As soon as the Germans invaded the Baltic countries and then the Ukraine, they found that there were in these countries many wildly anti-Semitic locals thrilled to have a license to kill Jews. While this in no way diminishes Hitler's responsibility, it now seems probable that the first wholesale killing, particularly of women and children, began in the Baltics and was welcomed but not originated by the Germans.

It started the night of June 25–26, 1941, in Kovno, Lithuania's second city, four days after the Germans invaded. This was the first Baltic country they

---

*He may well have used relationships with superior officers to achieve this (see Münch, Chapter XVIII), but it shows once again that it was possible to avoid such assignments, without being punished.

entered after the basic decision had been taken in Berlin, though without precise plans as to how to achieve their goal of the annihilation of the Jews.

The information on the murders in Lithuania was meticulously recorded by SS Major General Franz Stahlecker, Chief of Einsatzgruppe A, and Karl Jäger, who commanded Group A's Kommando 3 and later became head of Security Police and SD for Lithuania, with his HQ in Kovno. Furthermore we have the testimony, at his trial in Riga in 1946, of SS Gruppenführer (General) Friedrich Jeckeln, the Higher SS and Police Leader of first the southern and then the northern Army Group. One of the most efficacious killers of Jews, he confirmed there all the reports from his field commanders and added many details.*

The most significant part of the Stahlecker field reports concerns the activities of Lithuanian anti-Soviet "partisans" immediately after the Germans arrived. He informed HQ that contact with the German occupiers had been immediately sought by a nationalist-rightist group, the National Labor Guard. It was they who "with encouragement but without German cooperation" launched the first post-occupation pogrom in Kovno that night of June 25, in the course of which the killing began. By the end of July 1941 these men had proved themselves so effective that the German command organized them into what ended up being twenty police battalions. About 8,400 men, all volunteers, were charged with the wholesale murder of the Lithuanian Jews, under the supervision but not necessarily active participation of the Eleventh Battalion of the German Reserve Police. These particular Lithuanian units were considered so outstanding that by the end of 1941, by which time all but a fraction of Lithuania's 265,000 Jews had been killed, they were posted on to Belorussia and then to Poland to continue their work.

Thus, most significantly, it was the Lithuanians on their home ground who, one might say, pioneered the killing of women and children. In Kovno, Stahlecker, taken aback by the ruthlessness of the Lithuanian units which, he reported, surpassed anything the Germans had so far envisaged, ordered films to be made of the Lithuanian actions so as to "make clear that it was the local population who spontaneously took the first steps against the Jews."

What he meant was that upon commencing the mass murder, the German troops did not know what the process actually involved—above all, perhaps, what the killing of women and children would feel or look like. The films could therefore serve not only as evidence of the enthusiasm the Final Solution met with locally but also for purposes of legitimizing Nazi orders and orienting their own troops.

The familiar "obedience to orders" defense advanced at Nuremberg has

*Jeckeln was hanged in Riga the day his trial ended in February 1946. Stahlecker would fall prey to Estonian partisans in March 1942. Jäger killed himself in prison after his belated arrest in April 1959.

been totally refuted by the virtually inexhaustible German war archives, which have over the last few years supplied diligent historians with many examples of successful protests and requests for transfer from the murder units. These objections came not only from officers and soldiers of the Wehrmacht, which was to be expected, but also, as already noted in the case of Ehlers, from the Einsatzgruppen themselves and from the Reserve Police battalions belonging to the Ordnungspolizei, the paramilitary "police army" Hitler first created in 1933 to bypass the disarmament provisions of the Treaty of Versailles, from which thousands of men—some middle-aged, some young volunteers—were drawn for occupation and killing duties in the East.

A General Staff adjutant of Army Group North, with the rank of Colonel, reported,

> When, in mid-morning of June 27, 1941, I arrived in Kovno, my car was held up by a huge crowd of people, among them many women who had climbed up on chairs and wooden crates or who lifted up their children to gain a better view. I supposed that the roars of applause, laughter and braying "bravos" were for a sporting event. But onlookers told me that "collaborators and traitors were at last getting their just deserts." When I pushed my way through, I witnessed what must be the most dreadful thing I have seen in two world wars. Using huge wooden clubs, they were beating men to death with them. . . . At GHQ [General Staff HQ] a little later I learned that the fact of these mass executions had been learned about with outrage . . . but were considered spontaneous acts on the part of the Lithuanian population, to be dealt with by local authorities without interference from the occupying German army. . . .

The General Staff Colonel avoids the word "Jews," and indeed during those first weeks of German occupation the Lithuanian nationalist gangs also murdered hundreds if not thousands of fellow Lithuanians who had collaborated with the Soviets during their period of occupation. A medic's report, however, made about the same time, was specific:

> About 150 meters from my quarters there was a fort, I think Fort VII. We didn't actually see any executions but a technical sergeant took pictures of the men, women and children who were brought to the fort from Kovno during the day to be shot in the night. As far as I remember, they were all Jews; at least, everybody said it was all Jews.

During the first weeks, only Lithuanians did the killing; soon it was on German orders, as the infamous SS Colonel Jäger, Commander of Einsatzgruppe A's Kommando 3, wrote in his final report which covers his unit's "executions" from July to December 1941. It is a detailed account, providing his superiors with a careful breakdown of who was murdered when, and demonstrating graphically the extent to which the two kinds of murders merged. The first two lines clarify the role played by the Germans:

> Executions carried out by the Lithuanian partisans upon my orders: July 4, 1941, Kauen [Kaunas, or Kovno]—Fort VII—416 Jews, 47 Jewesses, total 463. July 6, 1941, Kauen—Fort VII—Jews, total, 2,514. . . .
> Following the setting up of a mobile command consisting of 8–10 experienced men under the leadership of SS Lieutenant Colonel Hamann, the following actions were accomplished in cooperation with Lithuanian partisans. . . .

In the six-page list that follows, Jäger details the killings from July 7, 1941, to October 25, 1941, in his area of operations, which included about half of Lithuania, eventually extending into Belorussia. He presents total executions for each day, which are then separated into categories: male Jews, female Jews, "Jew-children." The vast majority of the 133,346 killed by his command (which was one of four) were Jews, but—a proportion which was similar throughout—there were 2,055 others, among them about 700 mentally sick, 2 murderers, 1 German communist, 17 Gypsies, 15 terrorists, 3 Russian POWs, and the remainder Lithuanian and Russian communists. He concluded,

> Amongst those dealt with by EK3 in the relevant three and a half months were 3,050 Jews in a Minsk Action [in Belorussia], for which a special EK3 commando was dispatched there. 4,000 more were liquidated by partisans prior to the assumption of security policing by EK3. . . . This brings the total to 137,346 and in my opinion, as far as EK3 is concerned, achieves the goal of solving the Jew problem in Lithuania. There are no more Jews in Lithuania except the approximately 34,500 work-Jews and their families. I wanted to finish them off, too, but was told off sharply by both the Reichskommissar and the Wehrmacht: these Jews and their families, they said, are not to be shot. . . . As it seems likely that these work-Jews will continue to be needed after the winter, I suggest beginning immediately now with the sterilization of the males; any Jewess who becomes pregnant before this program is achieved to be liquidated. . . .

The question of eradicating Jewry by sterilization (as had already been done to some Germans with hereditary diseases) had been discussed for some time. On March 28, 1941, Viktor Brack of the Führer Chancellery, who two years earlier had been one of the organizers of the Euthanasia Program, reported to Himmler on the completion of tests on mass sterilization by X ray. In his trial at Nuremberg he testified that by March 1941 the intention to kill the Jews "was no secret in higher party circles," but that he himself had advocated less extreme measures. Though there was from his corrupted point of view some truth to this claim, the court, having on hand his terrible correspondence with Himmler, sentenced him to death and he was hanged in Landsberg on June 2, 1948.

In his March 1941 report, Brack informed Himmler that, his investigations now completed, he could propose a method by which a one-time (two- to three-minute maximum) irradiation by means of two X-ray machines could sterilize "150–200 persons a day. This means that twenty such installations could deal with 3,000–4,000 a day." To carry out this process without the knowledge of the "persons thus dealt with," he proposed that special offices be set up to which these persons would be ordered to report to answer questions, and the machinery would be installed to carry out the irradiation "during the filling out of forms":

> The irradiation, invisible to the subjects, would be organized to take the necessary 2–3 minutes. We have found that men require a higher intensity, for a shorter time—two minutes—and women a lower intensity requiring three minutes.

As, for obvious reasons, none of the customary precautions could be taken, the subjects, noticing burns over the subsequent days and weeks, would necessarily become aware that X rays had been applied to sterilize and castrate them but this, he said, would have become irrelevant. He estimated that the X-ray equipment for each installation would cost between RM 20,000 and RM 30,000, to which had to be added the cost of the building and protective shielding for the officials on duty.

But eventually it was decided that this proposal, though worth considering for concentration camps, where the tests had been carried out and where the process, already used for years on people suffering from hereditary diseases, would be widely applied over the following years to Jews as well as recalcitrant Christians, was impracticable for the huge numbers the conquerors would be facing in the East, for whom the radical solution was the only possibility.

In the beginning of August 1941, a conference of unit commanders of Einsatzgruppe C in Zhitomir, Ukraine, had learned that Higher SS and Police Leader General Jeckeln had brought the instruction from Himmler (who had just visited him) that all Jews not working for essential German industries, and their families, were to be shot.

"For me this was a devastating order," testified Erwin Schulz, the leader of EK5, "and one I knew I could not execute." He asked for an urgent appointment with Reich Security Personnel Chief Bruno Streckenbach in Berlin, who agreed with him that what was happening in Russia was murder, but said it was impossible to put a halt to it. However, he would be released and reassigned to his former post at the police academy Berlin-Charlottenburg.

"I suffered no disadvantage whatever as a result of my intervention," Schulz said, and added that he was convinced these actions could not have been carried out if a number of commanders had, like himself, declared themselves unwilling to carry out the liquidations. "And I can't exempt the Wehrmacht officers in the area from responsibility. They were fully informed of the liquidations, and I have always been of the opinion that the avalanche could still have been stopped if [the command of] an army group had intervened. I do not know of any order, nor were there rumors of such orders, that anyone who refused to obey such orders would be destined for concentration camps."

The many reports by Higher SS and Police Leader Jeckeln, although not at all descriptive, confirm the sense of achievement the participants in these murders appear to have felt. One report, addressed to Himmler, covers specifically the activities from August 19 to October 9, 1941, of the five German police battalions he commanded in the Ukraine. (During this period, he also ordered, among untold others, the killing of 30,000 Jews of Dnepropetrovsk and the 33,771 Jews who would be remembered by the Russian poet Yevgeny Yevtushenko in his epic *Babi Yar*.)

There had been sixteen actions executed entirely by five Reserve Police battalions during that period, Jeckeln told Himmler, during which 37,783 Jews had been shot. Jeckeln had achieved in those three months probably the largest overall number of murders under one command, though he was closely followed by SS General Otto Ohlendorf, who would be one of the few accused in Nuremberg who, to Göring's fury, freely admitted their crimes. As commander of Einsatzgruppe D in the Caucasus and the Crimea during the year after the invasion of Russia, he testified, his men "liquidated approximately ninety thousand men, women and children, all of whom, except for a few communist officials, were Jews."

(Dr. Flächsner, Speer's counsel, described to me his surprise at seeing Ohlendorf called as a prosecution witness, just as "pleasant and suave" in court as he had been in the Ministry of Economic Affairs in 1944, when Flächsner, representing a bank director who was in trouble over some minor infraction, had visited him to ask for his assistance. Ohlendorf promptly helped him. "He really was a most pleasant man," Flächsner said. "Imagine my astonishment in court when, sounding no different than he had in his office that day, he said coolly that, yes, he had ninety thousand Jews shot in Russia but that he had made sure it was done 'humanely.' I sat there and felt as if I had been struck by lightning. 'Ninety thousand Jews shot,' " he repeated, with something like awe in his voice. "But humanely.")

Neither Jeckeln, Jäger or Stahlecker—or for that matter Ohlendorf in 1941—appears to have had any moral scruples, but, exactly as if dealing with an epidemic of rats, they contented themselves with factual reports on their elimination. Thus Stahlecker's account on January 31, 1942, reports that 229,052 Jews had so far been "eliminated" in the Baltic states and Belorussia. And he too concluded that "except for a few thousand work-Jews, Lithuania is virtually *judenfrei.*"

Later reports or requests provide evidence of some concern on the part of individual German occupation administrators, but always only about specific acts or actions, never the *principle* of murder. The German area commander in Slutsk, Belorussia, for example, who witnessed an action carried out by the Eleventh Lithuanian Police Battalion—the most infamous unit active in Lithuania in 1941 and Belorussia in early 1942—requested that this battalion never be deployed again in his district; his argument was not an objection to the murder of Jews—that was not questioned—but rather to the apparent German sponsorship of the methods employed by the Lithuanians, which were having a bad effect on relations with the local population.

By the same token, Wilhelm Kube, General Commissioner for Belorussia, wrote in the summer of 1942 to Hinrich Lohse, Reichskommissar for the Ostland, asking whether the intention was to have "the Reich Jews sent to the East also dealt with by the Lithuanians and Latvians whose methods the native population here [so] reject. I beg you to give clear directives with due consideration for the good name of our Reich and our party, in order that these, I know necessary, actions be executed in the most humane manner."

Hitler was perfectly well informed of these actions. On July 16, 1941, in conference with Göring, Hans Lammers (Chief of the Reich Chancellery), Alfred Rosenberg (Minister for the Ostland) and Field Marshal Keitel, he ordered the intensification of the "pacification program" behind the Russian front. Germany, he said, would never withdraw from its newly won Eastern territories; he would create there "a Garden of Eden." To accomplish this, anyone hostile to Germany would be exterminated. Naturally, this vast area must be "pacified as quickly as possible . . . by shooting anyone who even looks askance at us—the best method," he said.

On July 17, 1941, he received Croatia's Prime Minister, Marshal Slavko Kvaternik. "The Jews are the scourge of humanity," he told him. "The Lithuanians, Estonians and Latvians are now taking their bloody revenge on them. . . . If a nation for any reason whatsoever tolerates one single Jewish family remaining among them, it represents a core of infection that would bring about renewed decay."

On July 31, 1941 (by which time many thousands had already been killed in the Baltics), Göring as Plenipotentiary for the Four-Year Plan* formally

---

*Göring in 1936 had established the Four-Year Plan, in control of practically the whole economy.

instructed Heydrich to set in motion the "Final Solution of the Jewish question."

> ... herewith commission you to carry out all necessary organizational, material and financial preparations for an overall solution of the Jewish question in the European territories under German control. Insofar as this affects the jurisdiction of other central administrations, their interests are to be provided for.
>
> You are to submit to me as soon as practicable a summary of the organizational and financial measures already taken for the execution of the intended Final Solution of the Jewish question.

The primary reason for this document was bureaucratic. In January 1939, Göring had appointed Heydrich to supervise the emigration and subsequent evacuation of the Jews from the Reich, which was treated as an economic matter and therefore came within the province of his Four-Year Plan. Given the meticulousness of the German bureaucratic system and despite the fanatically controlled secrecy of the Final Solution, any extension of Heydrich's powers thus required his official imprint.

On August 7, 1941, when typhus had broken out in the Warsaw Ghetto, Goebbels wrote specifically for the first time about killing the Jews:

> The Jews have always been carriers of infectious diseases. One must either crowd them together in ghettos and leave them to it, or else liquidate them, failing which they will always infect the healthy civilized populations. . . .

Ten days later, on August 17, Goebbels visited Hitler. Below clearly recalled the occasion in his book forty years later:

> In August, on Hitler's invitation, Goebbels appeared for the first time at Field HQ. During his two days there, he had several meetings "under four eyes" with Hitler. We learned only later that the subject under discussion was the problem of the Jews. Goebbels and Heydrich urged a solution. Goebbels was eager to expel the 70,000 Jews still in Berlin and wanted to ensure Hitler's agreement. Hitler was not prepared to give it as yet and only agreed—as was published in the *Reichsgesetzblatt* on September 1, 1941—that the Jews were to wear in future a yellow star on their outer clothes. The fundamental settlement of this problem [of the Berlin Jews] was to await the end of the Russian campaign when it would be solved— we heard—in *"grosszügiger Weise."* [This term can be translated as either "generous manner" or "general manner." Below obviously took the first meaning.] The outrageous cynicism of this remark only occurred to me after the war when the whole horror of the annihilation of the Jews emerged. At the time, I had no idea that the order for wearing a distin-

guishing mark was simultaneous with the last preparations for the Final Solution, nor that the *Einsatzgruppen* of the SS and police were already killing huge numbers of Jews behind the front and that, as of December 1941, Jews from all occupied countries in Europe were being gassed in extermination camps in Poland. Nor did I know anything of the Wannsee Conference of January 20, 1942.

Of course, considering retroactively after the war and while I was in prison, evidence from the war years such as Hitler's increasing outbursts against Jews, or incidental remarks I overheard from high SS leaders, I realized it should all have given me to think. But like many others I thought that the deportations of Jews to the East—which of course were no secret—meant that they were being used there for war production, which, given all the other foreign labor that was being employed, seemed plausible enough. It was only afterwards that I realized how horribly I had been deceived. . . .

But certainly, there is no question whatever in my mind that, written instructions or not, it was Hitler who specifically ordered the extermination of the Jews. It is unthinkable that Himmler or Göring could have undertaken such a step on their own. Very probably Himmler did not inform him about every detail, but he would have acted with his approval and in total agreement with him.*

Two days after the visit by Goebbels which Below described, Goebbels, back in Berlin on August 19, recorded the gist of their conversations in his diary:

The Führer is convinced that his prophecy in the Reichstag [January 30, 1939] that, if Jewry succeeded once more in provoking a war it would end with their annihilation, is coming almost uncannily true. . . .

Continuing his diary report of his conversation with Hitler on August 20:

It is outrageous and a scandal that the capital of the Reich still has 70,000 Jews, mostly parasites, spoiling not only the looks of our city but its atmosphere. . . . [The yellow star] badge will help, but the only real solution is eliminating them, a problem we must approach without sentimentality.

Twenty-six thousand Berlin Jews were working for war production, but for Hitler it was not only the consideration of their useful work which differentiated the German and Austrian Jews from others. Even while the emotional Hitler reserved his most passionate hatred for the Jews of Austria and

---

*Below, writing in 1980, explicitly refutes claims by the British writer David Irving that Below had supported his thesis that Hitler was neither responsible for nor until 1943 even aware of the genocide of the Jews.

Germany, the politician Hitler knew very well that in Western Europe and in Germany in particular there were limits beyond which he could not go; many Germans and Austrians had known some "all right" Jews all their lives. As Himmler was to say later in a terrible speech addressed to his SS elite: "And then they come, eighty million worthy Germans, and each one has his own decent Jew. 'Of course the others are vermin, but this one is an "A1" Jew. . . . ' " (A1 is a German expression for excellence: A [first letter in the alphabet], 1 [first number].)

Everything that happened at this point in Germany itself concerning the question of the Jews needs to be seen in context with the developing situation in Russia, including the Baltics, and here the degree to which Hitler's "strict secrecy" Directive No. 1 of January 11, 1940, justified itself in those first months of the Russian campaign is truly astounding.

First, the German Army General Staff during the first six months of 1941 prepared the invasion of Russia by gradually assembling on the Soviet frontier the largest military force in history (more than three million men) without apparently arousing any suspicion in Stalin's mind. Then the stream of directives emanating from Hitler over those first seven months of 1941, beginning with the *Kommissar Befehl,* all unmistakably orders for political and ideological murders, became known very soon to both officers and troops. And yet, as we have seen, only in isolated cases did any of them protest or even less divulge to anyone "outside" what was happening. However outraged they were, however passionately they rejected the orders for themselves, they kept the secret.

Thus, one of postwar Germany's most distinguished public personalities, Klaus von Bismarck, a friend of mine for more than three decades, revealed in his memoirs, published in 1992, something he had never told before. A devout Christian and anti-Nazi, he elected active service at the front in preference to a staff appointment, and hardly returned to Germany throughout the war. Writing of June 21, 1941, when his regiment, poised at the Russian frontier, was awaiting the order to attack, he says that, having been aware for a long time of Hitler's megalomania, they sensed that the attack on Russia that night was likely to be the beginning of the end. And then late that evening the *Kommissar Befehl* was issued. In his book he described what happened:

> As the regiment's adjutant I had first sight of it. It said that the Soviet commissars, who accompanied each military unit, were . . . to be shot forthwith. . . . After repeated study of the text I knew that, whether the Soviets had accepted the Geneva Conventions or not, I would not execute such an order. As a Christian and as a human being . . . murdering people for no other reason than that they subscribed to different political con-

cepts . . . contravened everything I had been taught and was incompatible
with my conscience.

Before passing the order on to my superiors, I assembled a group of my
friends and told them that I was determined to refuse to carry out this
order. All of them, joining me in rejection of this order, agreed to have me
report our refusal to our commanding officer, with a list of our names.

This is what I did, and our commanding officer accepted my report
without comment. As far as I know, no "commissars" were shot by our
regiment to the end of the war, though many other Wehrmacht units appeared to have no hesitation to carry out the *Kommissar Befehl*.

Theo Hupfauer, who had known Speer quite well since 1934 and worked
closely with him as of 1943, was among those who had very early knowledge
of the events in Soviet territory. For this highly successful, thirty-three-year-
old industrial labor expert well up on the career ladder, it was patriotism that
motivated him to request leave from his safe job at the German Workers'
Front. He had been exempted from military service as indispensable to industry, but by 1940 he was tired of making speeches bucking up the morale of
factory workers and became desperate to join up.

"As the Wehrmacht wouldn't have me," he said, "I volunteered for the
Waffen SS, where I had friends. They took me on at once." He did his basic
training in Berchtesgaden, and was then sent to the SS officers' school at
Brunswick. After five months—"Just too late for action"—he went to France
as a Staff Sergeant and then to Holland "on invasion exercises [for Britain]—
all nonsense. Then I wrote to Ley [Robert Ley, head of the Workers' Front],
asking him to get me into the Leibstandarte because they got everywhere
first.* Dietrich took me on at once, and from then on I went with them, first
again to France, then through the Bulgarian, Yugoslav and Greek campaigns.
We went through Yugoslavia and Greece like a knife through butter," said
Hupfauer with glee when, during one of our many talks in Munich, he recalled the memorable occasion when they, a mere thousand men, coolly accepted the surrender of the Greeks' Epirus army of seven divisions. "What a
glorious moment," he said joyfully.

Soon after that they made their way east through Poland and, as the Russian campaign started, with the advance troops of the Wehrmacht, into the
Ukraine.

"Take it from me," he said, "the Ukrainians welcomed us with open
arms." But, remaining in the Ukraine until the end of 1941, he witnessed the
change in that popular acclaim. "The harm our civilian administrators did
there was incredible," he said. "They spoiled it all."

*The Leibstandarte Adolf Hitler began as Hitler's personal guard, then, still commanded by Hitler's old
comrade Sepp Dietrich, became an elite Waffen SS fighting regiment and eventually a Panzer division.

These German occupation administrators were called *Reichskommissare*, and one of Hupfauer's old friends, Klaus Selzner, had been named Area Head of the Ukraine. It had been Selzner who seven years earlier, in 1934, as organizational chief of the Workers' Front, had persuaded Hupfauer to join it rather than go to America to study the U.S. judicial and labor systems. "We would sit together for hours, throwing ideas to and fro," he remembered. "He had an incredibly open mind, a very impressive man."

Hupfauer was appalled to find Selzner posted as a Kommissar in the Ukraine. "How could this good man accept it?" he said. "We knew what these Kommissars were doing; without their mishandling of the population, the entire Ukraine would have been on our side. We lost them because the politicians were incapable of recognizing their goodwill."

Toward the end of 1941, a *Führer Befehl*—one of Hitler's personal commands—recalled Hupfauer to Berlin with orders to go wherever there was bomb damage in industry and take charge of reorganizing the workforce. Just over a year later, this led to Speer's putting him in charge of the workers in the all-important Ruhrgebiet, the industrial core of Germany.

When Hupfauer returned to Germany he knew, as he had told me, that the Kommissars in the Ukraine were politically "spoiling Germany's chances there." Was he telling me that he didn't also know then that the Einsatzgruppen were murdering people?

"Not Jews," he answered quickly. "I knew nothing about Jews."

Hupfauer, I believe, didn't like Jews any more when we talked than he had during the Third Reich. At the same time (even though he, like practically all Germans of that generation, contested the "figures which are bandied about"), for him too, while the killings of other civilians in the conquered East, whether Jews or non-Jews, were somehow legitimate acts of war, Hitler's gas-chamber murder of the Jews was the unsurmountable "moral sore" on his mind.

"How could they?" he asked, when that subject came up, briefly. "You tell me, how could they do such a thing?" But he quickly veered away. "The other day you asked why I didn't resign when I learned about the Einsatzgruppen. I have been thinking about that. Why didn't I? [He was by now tacitly admitting his full knowledge of the Einsatzgruppen murders.] What would have been the sense? There were many others only too ready to take my place."

By the early summer of 1941 the GBI had been renamed Baustab (Construction Authority) Speer. Even then Hitler would occasionally drop in to the basement to feast his eyes on the model of Berlin, to em-

phasize the need for a "martial look" in the future capital and to tell Speer to
increase the orders for granite from abroad for the Berlin buildings irrespective of the needs of the war economy. Speer paid lip service to his orders but
took them with a grain of salt.

For by then, certainly not without Hitler's knowledge, his Baustab was
working overtime—soon on twenty-four-hour shifts—to put up factories
for war production all over Germany and occupied Europe, to equip Berlin
with air-raid shelters and to repair bomb-damaged transport facilities all
over the new Greater Germany: the Altreich plus the appropriated territories—Austria, the Sudetenland and the germanized section of Poland.

On November 24, 1941, Hitler, closing his eyes to the fact that the Russian
campaign was rapidly becoming a catastrophe, asked Speer to head one of his
grandiose projects: the construction of splendid New Towns in the occupied
territories of the Soviet Union, which were to house Germans transplanted
into these rich lands as pioneers to oversee the workings of the land, the
mines and industry. This was not just a pipe dream; by mid-1942 thousands
of Germans, trained farmers and managers and their families, had been
brought to the Ukraine to transform the economy for Germany's benefit.

Speer had lobbied for months to get Hitler to put off any further work on
Berlin and other cities in order to devote the sophisticated construction apparatus he had created entirely to the war effort. "It was quite extraordinary
how adamantly he opposed this," Speer told me. "You understand, by this
time we knew that—quite contrary to us—Britain had fully mobilized, including, above all, putting women into factories and uniforms. It was totally
impossible, and remained impossible to the end, to persuade Hitler that in
total war women had to work in war production."

"The Baustab Speer," said Annemarie Kempf, during one of our early
meetings in Hamburg, "was given enormous official responsibilities. We had
organizational teams across all of Europe and in the Ukraine, and employed
by now tens of thousands of workers." By extending Speer's responsibilities
at the end of that fateful year well beyond architecture and beyond Berlin and
Germany, Hitler, whether by design or by intuition, prepared him for his
future.

Much more than what Speer understood—or didn't—about the Kristallnacht in 1938, what he might have known about Hitler's Euthanasia Program
in 1939–40 or the evacuation of the Berlin Jews in 1940–41, it was the Ukraine
in 1941 and afterwards that should have been the watershed for him and his
staff, as it should have been for the German generals, officers and soldiers in
the Eastern theater of war. For in those years they all became witnesses, or at
the very least *Mitwisser*—sharers, or participants of the knowledge—of horrific crimes.

By November 1941 the transport system in the East was threatening to collapse. Over the long front, the German army was entirely unprepared for the Russian winter which that year came exceptionally early. Tank engines and firing mechanisms froze, weapons became useless, and underdressed troops battled the frightening elements and well-equipped Russian soldiers who were used to the climate. Worst of all, the problem of resupplying the army had become virtually insoluble, for the Russians, while retreating all along the front (north, center and south), had proved themselves brilliant in the techniques of "scorched earth." Entirely indifferent to the fate of civilian populations, they had blown up hundreds if not thousands of bridges, roads and rail lines and destroyed rail yards, rolling stock, watering sheds and industrial installations.

In Speer's words, "What confronted the army, trying desperately to re-equip the front-line troops, was a frozen desert of destruction." Learning about the catastrophe from friends on the General Staff and top managers of the German railroad on his return from a brief art foray to Lisbon, Speer immediately proposed to Hitler to assign half his construction staff of sixty-five thousand men and his best engineers to repairing the Russian railway system. "It was extraordinary—" he told me. "Even then he couldn't bear to let me interrupt the Berlin building program. It took weeks before Fritz Todt was able to persuade him that his OT [Organization Todt] needed the expertise of our engineers to do the job. It is unbelievable to me now that even then, in full understanding of the catastrophic consequences of any delays, instead of being appalled by his indecisiveness I was touched by his attachment to our building plans."

Of course, the flagging war in the East was not Hitler's only problem then, for on December 11, 1941, four days after the Japanese attack on Pearl Harbor, he declared war on the United States.

Nicolaus von Below writes that he was "very alarmed by this step. It showed his total ignorance of America's potential which had, after all, already determined the outcome of one war in our century."

Hitler was not entirely wrong when, in his long speech to the Reichstag on the afternoon of December 11, he said that war between the United States and Germany had been inevitable, because Roosevelt had always wanted it.

John Kenneth Galbraith, now one of America's "wise men," a wonderfully elegant, classically American intellectual with a long, thin, craggy face, was part of Roosevelt's "think tank" at the time. How determined was Roosevelt to get into the war? I asked him in 1988, sitting in his study in Cambridge, Massachusetts.

"He was determined to help Britain absolutely to the utmost," he said. "After Austria and Czechoslovakia one knew of course what Hitler was about, and we were absolutely certain we'd have to get into it. Yes, I think it's true to say we were committed: committed to a way of life, of political and ethical morals in total opposition to everything Hitler seemed to—no, *did*—stand for. We knew this from *Mein Kampf,* from his speeches and of course from his actions. I suppose it is true that the fall of France was the decisive point: we could not allow France to remain 'fallen'—we could not allow him to rule Europe, with his kind of rule. But given the mood of some of the country, it was extremely difficult. When, immeasurably aggravating his own problem, he attacked Russia, it was, of course, an enormous step forward for us. . . .

"When Pearl Harbor happened, we were desperate. I remember, I left Washington and went to the country—to think. We were all in agony. The mood of the American people was obvious—they were determined that the Japanese had to be punished. We could have been forced to concentrate all our efforts on the Pacific, unable from then on to give more than purely peripheral help to Britain. It was truly astounding when Hitler declared war on us three days later. I cannot tell you our feeling of triumph. It was a totally irrational thing for him to do, and I think it saved Europe."

By the time Speer and I were talking about this, he had come to agree with Hupfauer about Hitler's fatal mistakes being due to his ignorance about foreign countries. But that hadn't been his opinion in the early years of the war. When I asked him about Hitler's declaration of war on the United States, he shrugged. "I realize it must seem strange that I didn't focus more on this in my book, but actually I think it reflects what I felt at the time. I think we had heard Hitler talk so often about Roosevelt's politicking to get his people to let him go to war against us that we expected it. Perhaps, stupid as we were, we were even proud that Hitler had stolen his thunder, so to speak. As he said in the Reichstag: 'We always strike first.' "

But he had not realized what it would mean to have America's huge industrial potential ranged against Germany, he said. "If I thought about it at all, it would have been, like Hitler, that Japan was going to keep Roosevelt very busy. But principally my mind was taken up with my enormous concern about what was happening to our army in the East and with what I could do to ameliorate the situation."

A conversation Speer had with Todt on December 27, 1941, the day Hitler finally agreed to move both Speer's and Giesler's construction teams to Russia, was prophetic. "I went to see Todt at his house near Berchtesgaden," Speer said. "Given his exalted position, it was a very modest place; he and his wife were very modest, very quiet people. I liked him so much. He was very depressed that day. He was just back from a long inspection trip to Russia, and he told me how horrified he was by the condition of our soldiers.

"Later I would remember his words and the utter sadness in his face when he said that he didn't think we could possibly win the war there. The Russian soldiers were perhaps primitive, he said, but they were both physically and psychologically much hardier than we were. I remember trying to encourage him. Our boys were pretty strong, I said. He shook his head in that special way he had and said—I can still hear him—'You are young. You still have illusions.' "

Todt assigned the Ukraine—logistically the most important area—to Speer, and the central and northern army regions to Giesler. The two men's problems and their experiences there would be identical, as no doubt were the impressions and the knowledge their frequent trips from then on provided. It is significant that neither Speer in his books and his drafts nor Giesler in his memoirs would have one word to say about the horrors they must have observed there.

Giesler and Speer were both Hitler's loyal vassals. They, too, without doubt, considered the Eastern populations an inferior species even though Speer would never have employed Hitler's gross term, *Untermenschen.* Except for occasionally noticing (and drawing Hitler's attention to) the blond "Germanic"-looking Ukrainian girls, as Wolters noted in his *Chronik,* the native population didn't exist for either of them.

The first time Speer saw his new area of operation was on January 30, 1942, when, getting a lift on a Heinkel bomber from Hupfauer's commanding officer, Sepp Dietrich, who was returning to his tank battalion at the nearby front, he flew to Dnepropetrovsk, where his team under the leadership of one of his top construction engineers, Walter Brugmann, had began work some weeks before.

On that first of many visits, he spent almost a week in this large industrial Ukrainian city. Later he would write how impressed he had been on subsequent trips after visiting the university complex the Soviets had begun to build there, "with facilities far beyond anything in Germany." But this initial stay, during which he confronted for the first time the freezing weather and the desolate conditions Todt had described to him a month earlier, was devoted almost entirely to working with his staff.

"Everything was under deep snow," he told me. "This had been a very important rail center, with many dozens of trains arriving and leaving every day; now only four trains a day came and went. My team was living and working on a train that stood on a siding. The station was now nothing but rubble. The Russians had destroyed everything including even much of their snow-clearing equipment, both for the rail yards and the airport, so even though the infrastructure had been re-created fairly quickly, all essentials, tools and machinery, had to be brought in. If you recall that it was August when the Russians retreated, you can see how farsighted their 'scorched earth' measures were."

The construction team had arrived only a few weeks before Speer came. "We had a few small trucks, a few jeeps and command cars," he said, "but except for work around the yards, nobody went anywhere. That winter the army had thousands of Ukrainians clearing the streets, but it was all but useless. All they had were shovels and brooms, and the snow was relentless; while I was there it never stopped."

BY THE TIME Speer came to Dnepropetrovsk, the city was, as SS Gruppenführer Friedrich Jeckeln had reported to Himmler around the New Year, "almost though not entirely *judenrein*." Of all the Higher SS Police Führers, Jeckeln was probably the most conscientious. "If I give a difficult order to my men, then I go with them when they execute it. That is my duty," he would say at his trial in Riga four years later.

He was with Einsatzgruppe C, Kommando 5, when they entered Dnepropetrovsk on October 5, 1941, fresh from Kiev and the murders at Babi Yar a week before. With him, at the head of his own very special command, was that most efficient killer of Jews, the former Düsseldorf architect, SS Standartenführer (Colonel) Paul Blobel, a drunk and a monster.

By the time the German army had conquered Dnepropetrovsk in the middle of August, only some thirty thousand of the city's thriving Jewish community of about one hundred thousand remained, most of them old people and young children who hadn't been able to leave with the retreating Russian army. And when, six weeks later, Jeckeln and his experienced butchers arrived, it took them a mere two days to kill those thirty thousand.

A young Czech, Majer Neumann, from Volove (a town in the part of Ruthenia appropriated by Hungary after Hitler's partition of Czechoslovakia in April 1939), was there with a detachment of Hungarian troops. Although he was Jewish, Neumann was protected by his Hungarian army status, and he survived and emigrated to Arizona after the war. When he was interviewed there later, he described the Jews of Dnepropetrovsk walking, eight abreast, through the autumnal streets of the city whose population had been ordered to remain in their houses. But nobody could have remained ignorant of what happened, he said. The Jews carried their babies and bundles, and for two days machine-gunning could be heard from the antitank ditches the Russians had dug on the outskirts of the city which the Germans used for the killing and burying.

Over the next five months, until March, Jeckeln reported to Berlin, they "wiped up stragglers": small groups of people who had managed to hide and who, when caught, were conveniently dealt with—an imaginative touch—in the Jewish cemetery.

On that first January trip to the snowed-in, destroyed city, there might have been little reason for either Speer or his people to have heard about killings which had largely taken place four months before. But the fact is that later he went there repeatedly, as well as to many other cities where similar horrors had taken place. Was it possible that then, too, neither he nor his staff ever heard about any of these murders?

Six months later, in June, several of his top people accompanied him on a week-long inspection of Organization Todt installations in "Russia-South"; among them were his chiefs of administration, personnel, supply and information—Gerhard Fränk, Erwin Bohr, Walter Schrieber and Rudolf Wolters—and of course Speer's private secretary, Annemarie Kempf. They traveled all over the southern army area and spent two days in Dnepropetrovsk.

It was in Alpbach, a beautiful village in the Austrian Tyrol, where Annemarie and I, walking through a snowy wood, came to speak about Dnepropetrovsk. She was appalled by the story I told her of the murder of the Jews there. Standing stock-still on that forest path, she was totally silenced by the account, and it is inconceivable that her horror was anything but real.

"It is not possible," she finally said, "simply not possible! You see, Speer wasn't alone there—we were with him. He might have seen various of the top commanders and administrators on his own, but we saw other people, lots of people. And nobody, not one single person, mentioned such events. As you were talking about it, I tried to revisualize the place, to recall the two days we spent there. And it remains inconceivable."

She kept coming back to this the following days. She had meanwhile re-checked Speer's book—which she had brought along—to see what he said about the Ukrainian trips and had found that he did not mention the one in the summer of 1942, and hadn't said much about the first one either. (Only in the first "Nuremberg draft"—his very first attempt at recording his reminiscences which later developed into the "Spandau draft" and then into *Inside the Third Reich*—was there a longer description of the January trip.)

"You said they buried them in shallow graves in antitank ditches on the periphery of the city. But, you know, when we were there it was unbelievably hot; we stayed at the House of Culture, and I remember washing my dress and hanging it out of the window to dry; fifteen minutes later I could put it back on. Dnepropetrovsk was not a big city, you know; if they really buried

thirty thousand people there in shallow graves, can you imagine what would
have happened, even months later, in that heat?"*

"Of course," she said, "if this really happened, not that long before Speer's
first trip there in January, and then intermittently until March, that would
have a very special significance for us, because it would mean that a whole lot
of people we knew must have deliberately hidden it from us."

I had of course discussed Dnepropetrovsk repeatedly with Speer, and he
always said that he had never heard anything about murders of Jews there or
in other Russian cities. "To me this is not surprising," he said. "Even my own
people—if they knew, and I doubt that they did—would not have felt in a
position to discuss it with me. I remember, in Dnepropetrovsk I dined one
night with the District Governor [Selzner]; he didn't tell me anything either.
But then, how could they have told me?" he asked. "Everybody knew how
close I was to Hitler. How could they have risked speaking to me—me of all
people—about the unspeakable?"

*Yes, I could imagine: Years before, the onetime Chief of the Church Information Branch at the Reich
Security Office, Albert Hartl, had told me of a summer evening—that same hot summer in 1942—in
Kiev when he was invited to dine with the local Higher SS Police Chief and Brigadeführer, Max Thomas.
A fellow guest, SS Colonel Paul Blobel, had driven him to the general's weekend dacha. "At one moment—it was just getting dark," said Hartl. "We were driving past a long ravine. I noticed strange
movements of the earth. Clumps of earth rose into the air as if by their own propulsion—and there was
smoke; it was like a low-toned volcano; as if there was burning lava just beneath the earth. Blobel
laughed, made a gesture with his arm pointing back along the road and ahead, all along the ravine—the
ravine of Babi Yar—and said, 'Here lie my thirty thousand Jews.' "

XI

A Fatal Appointment

Nuremberg, October 1, 1946

From the preamble to the verdict: On February 15, 1942, after the death of Fritz Todt, Speer was appointed Chief of the Organization Todt and Reichsminister for Armaments and Munitions [after September 2, 1943, Armaments and War Production]. The positions were supplemented by his appointments in March and April 1942 as Plenipotentiary General for Armaments and as a member of the Central Planning Board, both within the Four-Year Plan.

It was purely a coincidence that Speer found himself at Hitler's Eastern Field Headquarters at Rastenburg, East Prussia, on February 8, 1942, which was to become the most fateful day of his life.

That morning at 7:55 Hitler's Minister of Armaments, Fritz Todt, who for months had been telling Hitler that the war in Russia was unwinnable and had to be stopped, died in a plane crash that would forever remain unexplained. Five hours later, Hitler named Speer Minister of Armaments in Todt's place.

Speer and I talked many hours about this day which sealed his fate for years to come, with consequences for the rest of his life. But although he readily gave a detailed description of the days which led up to February 8, of Hitler's attitude toward him then and afterwards, and of the changes which occurred in his life from that moment on, he said very little about the mysterious death of Todt, a man he had greatly admired.

According to his original schedule, he should have been back in Berlin that day, for by February 6 he had spent six days in Dnepropetrovsk with his construction team, had completed his inspections, and a Russian tank battalion was closing in on the city. "I knew my people would be glad to see the back of me," he said, telling this story of the snowed-in Ukrainian city under attack with relish; he found an almost childlike enjoyment in the description of dangerous situations. "I was anything but a hero," he told me frankly, "so I got myself onto a hospital train leaving that night."

A few hours out of Dnepropetrovsk—Speer was sleeping soundly in a bunk he had been given—the train was stopped by ten-foot snowdrifts and returned to the city, arriving at dawn. Two hours later, the pilot of Sepp Dietrich's plane, Luftwaffe Captain Hermann Nein (who shortly afterwards and until the end of the war would be assigned as Speer's personal pilot) offered him a lift as far as Hitler's HQ.

"I was only too glad to accept," Speer said. "The Russians [who in fact did not then succeed in regaining Dnepropetrovsk] were at that point only ten kilometers from the airport. Anyway, I had never yet been to HQ East and hadn't talked to Hitler for weeks, so I was rather hoping he'd want to see me."

In the "Spandau draft" he described his long flight on February 7 from Dnepropetrovsk:

> After leaving Kiev behind us we fly for hours over the uninviting Pripet marshes and finally, at last land at night at Rastenburg, which after my few days in Russia seems quite beautiful. . . .

After he reported his presence by phone, a car from the Führer motor pool picked him up, and at HQ he went straight to the mess hall to have his first real meal in days.

> Hitler is not present. Dr. Todt, at HQ to report, is dining with him in private. Late in the evening he emerges from the long and, it appears, trying discussion looking strained and exhausted. I sit with him for a bit while he drinks a glass of wine.

In *Inside the Third Reich* he adds a few details: "He wore a depressed air. I sat with him for a few minutes while he silently drank a glass of wine without speaking of the reason for his mood."

At the end of what Speer describes here as a "rather lame conversation," Todt offered him a lift to Berlin in his plane early next morning, and Speer accepted.

There is a curious difference between Speer's various descriptions of his conversation with Hitler when he was invited to join him in his quarters around 1 a.m. that night. In his Nuremberg draft in 1946 he mentioned only talking about their building projects in Nuremberg and Berlin. In the "Spandau draft" in 1953 there is no mention of buildings, but a long conversation about the Russian situation:

> He gets me to tell him of my impressions in southern Russia. I tell him as much as I can. He seems very interested and helps out with careful questions. We talk about the problems of reconstruction down there; the incomprehensible strategy of the Russian tank corps; and I tell him about the soldiers' evenings, with those sad songs. . . . I remember more and more and we talk about everything. Hearing about the soldiers' songs, he asks what the songs are about, and as it so happens that I have some texts in my pocket I give them to him to read. He becomes very silent.

After the war, Speer heard that Hitler had ordered those responsible for the printing of the songs to be court-martialed, and he comments on Hitler's "typical . . . mistrust and suspicion. . . . He was always sure . . . his clever questions . . . would allow him to come to important conclusions." And, he continued in Spandau:

> [Before going to bed at 3 a.m., after leaving Hitler] I informed Todt's flight captain that I was too tired to join the flight that was due to take off

in five hours. What I needed was a good night's sleep. In my little bedroom I pondered what impression I had left with Hitler—who didn't do
this after spending two hours talking with him? I was content.

In *Inside the Third Reich,* he combines the two themes, with the main emphasis, however, on the building plans, which "clearly relaxed and revivified
Hitler who visibly brightened," until finally Hitler asks him (briefly) about
his impressions of Russia. This emphasis on the Berlin and Nuremberg
building plans only developed in the fourth—and final—draft for the book
as published.

His statement in the "Spandau draft" that he "was content" clearly referred to his relief that his relationship with Hitler was still secure. But by the
time he worked on the final draft of his book, it was far more than that. Now
he conveys the impression that most of the conversation had been about future buildings, anything else having only come up in passing:

> I was content, my confidence restored that we would be able to carry
> out our building projects, a matter I had begun to doubt in view of the
> military situation. That night our dreams were transformed into realities;
> we had once again worked ourselves into an illusionary optimism.

Having warned Todt's flight captain that he would not be coming along,
Speer went to bed just after three o'clock. A few minutes after 8 a.m. he was
awakened by a call from his friend Dr. Brandt, who told him that Fritz Todt's
plane had crashed after taking off: Todt was dead.

"This was sad news, for me too," he wrote in Spandau and, he says more
dramatically in the book, "From that moment on, my whole life changed."

Well, yes, indeed. But was that really all he thought when he learned that
this man he had liked so much—and with whom he would have flown that
morning had he not at 3 a.m. changed his mind—had died?

While everyone in the dining room at Hitler's HQ that morning was
speculating who would be appointed Todt's successor, Speer continues in his
book, he was perfectly aware that an important part of Todt's tasks would
come to him. Already in the spring of 1939, Hitler had told him in the course
of an inspection tour of the West Wall that "if anything should happen to
Todt, you would be the man to carry out his construction assignments." And
a little over a year later, in the summer of 1940, the Führer received him "officially" at his Chancellery Office to tell him that since Todt, whom he had just
appointed Minister of Armaments, was overburdened, Speer was immediately to take over all his construction work, including the fortifications along
the Atlantic.

Certain that Todt would have been deeply offended by such a step, Speer wrote, he had persuaded Hitler to abandon that idea. But remembering this occasion on that tragic February morning at Hitler's HQ, he was prepared to be given precisely that assignment when he was summoned to Hitler's office as the first caller of the day.

However, "thunderstruck," he found himself instead appointed Todt's successor "in all his functions. . . . For the soldiers as well as for the party and industry," he wrote in *Inside the Third Reich*, "I was a typical outsider. Hitler, as usual (by turning an architect into a Minister) was recklessly obeying his intuition without considering the risks. Really the same risks he took by appointing [Joachim von] Ribbentrop, a former champagne salesman, as Ambassador to Britain and then Foreign Minister, and [Alfred] Rosenberg, the party philosopher, as Minister for the Occupied Eastern Territories. . . ."

IN THE "SPANDAU draft," as well as in his book, Speer reported that Hitler ordered an Air Ministry Commission of Inquiry to be set up, chaired by Field Marshal (and Air Ministry State Secretary) Erhard Milch. His description of Hitler's attitude at the time varies with each of the four drafts he prepared for the book, as well as between the German and English editions. I have copies of the relevant pages in all the drafts and the many different handwritten versions, with numerous sentences crossed out and rewritten, demonstrate how Speer agonized over how he should present the story.

The 1946 mini-draft at Nuremberg has nothing at all on investigations following Todt's death. The 1953 "Spandau draft" is terse: "Immediately after Todt's accident, Hitler ordered Milch to investigate the causes. He had a suspicion that there was something odd about it." He adds a long note, which recurs in all versions, about what the investigation concluded.

In 1967, in the first of three post-Spandau drafts, his initial instinct, as at Nuremberg, was not to write about it at all, but he soon changed his mind. A much-corrected page was inserted, which expands the Spandau version: "Upon Hitler's orders—as he suspected something odd about the accident—the Air Ministry undertook an investigation whether my predecessor's crash could have been due to sabotage . . . they came to the conclusion that sabotage could be excluded. . . ." He then crossed out a mention of his friend Milch and the remark that "without having an explanation for this mysterious event, Hitler soon ordered the investigation dropped."

The next manifestly much-pondered addition is drawn from the official result of the Air Ministry inquiry, and can be found in all editions (German and foreign) of the published book: "Judging from the examination of the wreck, it certainly seems reasonable to suppose that the plane (which according to the Commission of Inquiry had a self-destruct mechanism) exploded at low altitude." However, in his next-to-last draft he excised the next words: "But how, by whom and due to what was the mechanism activated? It is a question which allows latitude to all—however fantastic—speculation." He was still not sure how far to go in accusing Hitler, and only hinted at it by asking questions.

In the fourth and final draft, apparently written in 1968, he wrote, then crossed out, then reinserted, "Hitler seemed to treat Todt's death with the stoic calm of a man who must reckon with such incidents as part of the general picture." But then, still only in the final draft, he brings up a new theme: ". . . [Hitler] thought it was a successful act by the secret service of our enemies [i.e., the Allies]. But then, it is doubtful that he would have expressed to me any other conjecture. . . ."

In the German edition of the book this became ". . . he thought it was a successful stroke by the secret services . . ."—without specifying which—the British, the Americans or his own.

In the English edition (which he carefully checked, according to his editor) the role of the "secret services" changes diametrically: ". . . he was going to have the [i.e., his own] secret services look into the matter."

In all published editions of the book Hitler's suspicion of "foul play" and the secret services is followed by this passage: "This view, however, soon gave way to an irritable, often indeed distinctly nervous reaction when the subject was mentioned in his presence. At such moments Hitler might remark, sharply, 'I want to hear no more about that. I forbid further discussion of the subject.' Sometimes he would add, 'You know that this loss still affects me too deeply for me to want to talk about it.' "

Hitler might have forbidden any further mention of the incident in his presence, but that did not end the mystery. Both the commission and Speer thought it necessary to mention two points: one, that the plane Todt was flying in, a Heinkel 111 converted for passenger use, "had been put at Todt's disposal for this trip by his friend, Field Marshal Hugo Sperrle, as his own plane was undergoing repairs. . . ." and, two, that "this plane, like all courier planes, was fitted with a self-destruct mechanism which could be activated by pulling a handle between the pilots' seats whereupon the plane would explode."

The fact is that neither of these points was correct. Todt's eighteen-year-old fighter pilot son proved within months that there was no self-destruct mechanism on the plane. Thirty years later, Nicolaus von Below who, as the ranking air force officer at HQ, was closely involved with Todt's plans that day, remembered the plane, Todt's schedule and finally the Commission of Inquiry very differently in his memoirs:

The plane Todt had in Rastenburg was the new two-engine HE-111 he had obtained at the end of 1941 for his travels [author's italics]. As Hitler had forbidden the use of two-engine planes by any of his top people, I found myself forced to draw this to Todt's attention and to forbid him to fly the plane out. He was absolutely livid and said that Hitler's ban didn't apply to him.

Shortly after he and Hitler had sat down to dinner on their own in Hitler's bunker, I was called in and Hitler asked me to explain myself. I told him that I had merely followed his strict instructions. He [understood, but] allowed himself to be persuaded by Todt and ordered me to see to it the next morning that the plane was made ready.

But Below continued to be concerned about the safety of this small new airplane and, evidently still that night, gave an order which now adds to our mystery.

I arranged that *the plane was to be taken up for a trial spin before Dr. Todt's departure,* and . . . was got out of bed by the flight captain of the Führer-courier squadron, who told me that Todt had just crashed, shortly after starting. I dressed and hurried over to the airfield. I found nothing there except still smoking wreckage; all occupants of the flight were dead. After Hitler got up, I reported the crash. He was very startled and was quiet for a long time. Then he asked me what the cause was, but I had no explanation. The weather was not good, the sky and the snow-covered ground equally grey, the line between conceivably invisible. I suspected human error by the pilot, who wasn't as yet sufficiently familiar with the plane in difficult weather conditions. . . . A thorough investigation of the accident was carried out by the Reich Air Ministry *and the SS,* but provided no explanation [author's italics].

So Below, who had to know, mentions no self-destruct mechanism, says the plane had already been up once that morning and brings the SS—Speer's prime suspect—into the investigation. His failure to refer to the Commission of Inquiry's obviously wrong final report, about the explosion sixty-five feet in the air, or the discussion of possible sabotage, can only be explained by his reluctance to enter the controversy about Todt's death.

But not everyone was so discreet. Wolters wrote to Speer on March 16, 1953 (in a "black," i.e. smuggled letter), to discuss the first three chapters of the draft which had just arrived, and went on to discuss the Todt mystery.

I have given [the third chapter] the working title "Assumption of Power." It is quite outstanding, immensely better and much more lively than your Nuremberg version.

What is particularly important and revealing are your observations about Dr. Todt's misadventure.

Clearly in association to his word "misadventure," Wolters then refers to a book by Jürgen Thorwald, about seven well-known men, including Todt, all active in German military or political life during the latter period of the Third Reich, who died more or less mysteriously.

You will remember that I mentioned Thorwald's *Unresolved Cases* in a previous letter and that he finally considered that of the seven, only the Todt affair remained unexplained. Thorwald says that Todt, on the eve of his death, had explained to Hitler that the continuation of the war against Russia, especially after his inexplicable declaration of war on the United States, was bound sooner or later to lead to catastrophe, and that a new offensive in the East was materially impossible.

Wolters's letter said further that Thorwald's book suggested that those suspected of having brought about Todt's death were first Hitler, then Göring and "then (of course) Speer, whose nomination as Todt's successor was to be accomplished with such haste that the thought was unavoidable that Hitler had already for weeks considered a separation from that troublesome warner [Todt] in favor of a younger, technically less knowledgeable but more daring man. . . ."

Speer implied in his book that Todt might have had some premonition of trouble:

Incidentally, not long before his death, Dr. Todt had deposited a sizable sum of money in a safe, earmarked for his personal secretary of many years' service. He had remarked that he was doing this in case something should happen to him.

A postscript to this story can be found in a note Wolters made twenty-five years later. On January 7, 1978, he lunched with Fritz Todt's widow at her house in Munich. It was Ilsebill, then fifty-six years old, who opened the door to Wolters that day.

She took me into a beautiful large room with a southern exposure over a small garden which borders directly onto the Leopold-Park [one of Munich's loveliest parks]. Ilsebill's face has something particularly soft and endearing. An occasional wisp of obstinacy in her character manifests itself with humor rather than aggression, such as when I ask her whether she was inclined to believe that Speer was to blame for the crash of her father's plane. She smiles knowingly. "I think he is capable of anything," she said. It is impossible to persuade her away from her strong antipathy to Speer. . . .

("She visited the Federal Archives a few times," said a former archivist in Koblenz. "And she spit poison about Speer.")

Given how Wolters himself felt about Speer by then, it is of course doubtful that he would have attempted to "persuade her away from her . . . antipathy." Between the lines of all his notes of that time one can sense his reassurance when he found his own opinion about Speer echoed by others, who in turn felt supported in their rejection of Speer by the agreement of his former best friend.

This is clearly expressed in a letter Ilsebill had written to Wolters after their first meeting, to express her and her mother's pleasure in "at last getting to know you personally. I regret again," she wrote, "that fate, instead of leading you to my father during those years, brought him this *'Pappenheim'** whose guiding artistic and creative spirit, I feel sure, you were all along."

The day before his lunch with the Todts in Munich in 1978, Wolters had visited Xaver Dorsch, then seventy-eight years old, who had been chief of the Organization Todt under both Todt and Speer. Dorsch, a brilliant construction engineer, was yet another considerable personality in Speer's and, finally, also Hitler's world. Though also deeply anti-Speer and about to enter hospital, he was more than willing to talk with me when I telephoned him in 1986, and we had a long and enlightening conversation over the phone. Sadly, he died soon afterwards.

After the end of the war, Dorsch had made a spectacular career, as had most of Todt's and Speer's men. At the time of his meeting with Wolters he was working with a Swiss firm on creating a net of motorways in Saudi Arabia, which, on the principle of Todt's famous *Autobahnen,* were designed to be lined by trees and flowering bushes. Interestingly, some of his work in the Near East was done in collaboration with Speer's eldest son, Albert (born in 1934), by then a highly successful Frankfurt architect.

Dorsch's primary loyalty—he told me this with admirable frankness as soon as we began to talk on the phone—had always been to Todt, whom he deeply admired. Not surprisingly, though Speer had considerable respect for Dorsch's great capacities, they clashed from the start. To Dorsch, who had been Todt's most trusted man, Speer was not only a new broom and an interloper, but an amateur in a field which desperately needed professionals. Dorsch knew, probably better than Speer, Todt's despair about Hitler's war in the East at the time of his death.

Nonetheless, Wolters wrote, despite his attachment to Todt, Dorsch did not hesitate to express his appreciation of Speer. Todt and Speer, he told Wolters, shared some very important qualities. Both (contrary to so many others in Hitler's world) had lived simply, loathing any kind of pretension.

*One of Speer's ancestors was a Baron Pappenheim, but Ilsebill Todt was using the term ironically: in German, a *Pappenheimer* is an unsubstantial individual.

He thought Todt was more sensitive and "human" and devoid of the vanity Dorsch had certainly sensed in Speer, but he had found Speer exceptionally good at negotiation and at creating good relations with his staff.

Dorsch recalled an occasion toward the end of the war when Speer and he had been sitting together during a break at a conference, and Speer had suddenly brought up Dorsch's lack of trust in him. "You've never been able to stop thinking of the loss of your former Chief," he had said, sounding sad. And Dorsch had suddenly felt sorry for the long disharmony between them. He said that when Speer had left Spandau after those long twenty years, he had written him a conciliatory letter, but Speer had never replied, and he was sorry about that too.

Wolters, however, manifesting here the ambivalence in his feelings about Speer which was to plague him to the end of his life, was unimpressed by retroactive compassion from people who had "sat comfortably in their mouse holes for those twenty years without caring a hoot about the fate and problems of Speer and his family." Nor, however strongly he felt himself, did he have much time for petty criticisms of *Inside the Third Reich*. "Everybody has something to say against it," he writes. "Most of it isn't worth mentioning; what do they know? What have they suffered by comparison with Speer?"

Dorsch said that Todt, on his return from a previous tour of the Russian front, had indicated to him that the war could no longer be won by force of arms, only possibly by negotiation. "It appears," writes Wolters, "that he and Hitler had their third confrontation about this the evening before Todt's death."

As Todt's son had done before him, Dorsch also refuted the long-held thesis that either the pilot or Todt himself might have accidentally released the plane's self-destruct lever. "He said that this small plane wasn't equipped with this provision," said Wolters, "therefore [it] couldn't have been accidentally released. He also said without hesitation [contrary to the opinion so quickly proposed by the Commission of Inquiry Hitler set up] that the crash may indeed have been due to sabotage. . . . One must at least presume [Dorsch said to Wolters] that Hitler would not have wanted Todt dead."

These various factors—Todt's mysterious plane crash, Speer's fortuitous presence at Führer HQ that morning, his long talk with Hitler the previous night followed by his cancellation of his trip home on Todt's plane, and then Hitler's swift appointment of him as Todt's successor—had led, as we have seen, to speculations about his possible involvement in his predecessor's death.

When we were talking about his appointment, I asked if he had known of these rumors. "Not at the time, no," he said with a weary smile. "I still had my illusions then. In 1942 it would never have occurred to me that anyone could suspect me of such a terrible thing. Later—" He shrugged. "Well, people always talk, don't they? For most of them, gossip, the more malicious the better, is the spice of life."

When I then asked him directly about the other rumor I had heard—that Hitler might have had Todt eliminated, or knew who did—he shrugged and didn't reply. His many changes in the drafts and his description of Hitler's "distinct nervousness" are perhaps enough. What we will never know is whether it was Hitler, during the two hours he chatted with Speer that night while Todt slept, who suggested that Speer not join Todt's flight a few hours hence, but stay at HQ the next morning. It is the something Speer—however innocently he might have followed such a suggestion—could never have admitted, even to himself.

XAVER DORSCH had been one of the earliest *Mitwisser* of Hitler's treatment of populations in the East, and judging from at least one letter, he and Todt had discussed it. On July 10, 1941, less than three weeks after the German invasion of the Soviet Union, Dorsch found himself in Minsk, the capital of Belorussia, and from there, after "consultation with Reichsminister Dr. Todt," sent the following report to the Minister for the Occupied Eastern Territories, Reichsleiter Rosenberg.

Subject: Prison camp in Minsk.

The prison camp Minsk, approximately the size of the Wilhelmsplatz [a large square in Berlin], contains about 100,000 POWs and 40,000 civilian detainees. The prisoners, crammed into this tight space, can hardly move and are forced to relieve themselves wherever they happen to stand. The security of the camp by one company of soldiers [between 100 and 200 men] can only be effected by brutal force. The problem of feeding the POWs being insoluble, they have largely been without nourishment for six to eight days and . . . are almost manic in their need for sustenance. The civilian prisoners are males from Minsk and surrounding districts aged between fifteen and fifty. Those who have families in Minsk are receiving food; their relatives crowd the gate in endless queues. But during the night, the other inmates assault and often kill them for a piece of bread or a bone.

The guards who are on duty day and night can only deal with this impossible situation by making indiscriminate use of their weapons. Given the army's priority on transport and supplies, there seems to be no possibility of redressing this chaotic situation. . . .

Anyone even marginally familiar with Todt's personality will realize the extent to which such conditions—however carefully worded Dorsch's letter might be—must have aggravated the doubts he, with his knowledge of Germany's logistic capacities, no doubt entertained from the very start of the Eastern campaign. It is of interest that, instead of having Dorsch send his report on Minsk to the Ministry of Defense, the authority responsible for prisoners of war, he evidently instructed him to send it to Rosenberg, of whose own qualms about the treatment of Russian prisoners, which were to be expressed a few months later in a surprisingly frank letter to the Army High Command, he may well have already been aware. Rosenberg wrote on February 20, 1942, to Field Marshal Keitel:

> Of 3.6 million prisoners of war, only a few hundred thousand remain capable of working. Many have died of starvation, others from typhus. Although, given the immense numbers, supply problems were bound to be inevitable, a proper appreciation of our policies could have avoided this extent of loss. Thus, while a few sensible camp commanders facilitated the provision of food by local inhabitants, most of them prohibited it, preferring to let the men die or (on many occasions) even shooting them. In many camps, even in snow and ice, there was no covered accommodation and not only were there no latrines, but not even tools to enable the prisoners to dig holes. The result of the commonly employed maxim, "The more croak, the better," is that typhus has spread not only to the civilian population and German troops, but even into Germany. . . .

He points to the total political ignorance demonstrated by the execution in many camps of "Asians"—prisoners from Transcaucasia and Turkestan— "who in fact are known to be deeply anti-Bolshevik and thus are potential allies for us." All efforts by his ministry, he writes, to explain to the relevant military authorities that it was shortsighted to mistreat Eastern populations who, having gone through the horrors of Bolshevism, were passionately opposed to it and considerably more prepared to cooperate with their German liberators than the sophisticated countries of Western Europe, had been in vain and by now had cost the "Reich . . . the German economy and the armament industry well in excess of three million willing workers. . . ."

It is likely but not certain that Speer, in his review of his predecessor's files after his nomination as Minister of Armaments, would have seen Dorsch's July 1941 letter to Rosenberg, but there can be no doubt that he received a copy of Rosenberg's letter to Keitel which was written less than two weeks after his appointment. But while it is necessary to note this for the record, it is basically immaterial. For it must be assumed that Speer had long been aware of the practical applications—and misapplications—of Hitler's population and prisoner-of-war policies in the East.

Of course, as stated earlier, Speer played no role whatsoever in Hitler's first

East European colonization experiments in Poland. But his involvement in the Russian campaign, first in his role as GBI, later as Hitler's Minister, began from the time Operation Barbarossa was launched, and lasted until the bitter end. And here, his persistent later claim that despite frequent trips to the front and the Occupied Eastern Territories during the next years, and despite his increasingly wide circle of friends among the Wehrmacht command, he never knew anything of the horrors being committed there is entirely untenable.

At the time when he had figured mainly as Hitler's premier architect and favorite leisure-time companion, his contacts with that other elite of Hitler's Germany—the industrialists and above all the army—had been very limited. But with the expansion of his field of activity, first before and then to an immeasurably greater extent after his nomination as Minister, his circle, going considerably beyond the politicals such as Göring, Goebbels, Hess and Ley, whom he had known by then for years, became dramatically extended. Men such as rocket scientist Wernher von Braun; industrialists such as Alfred Krupp von Bohlen and Walter Rohland (referred to as "Stahl (Steel) Rohland"); officers such as Field Marshals Milch and Keitel and Generals Jodl, Kurt Zeitzler and Friedrich Fromm were different men, of different backgrounds—basically, as Speer would very quickly realize, much closer to his own.

I asked Speer repeatedly if he felt that associating from then on with these culturally much more familiar men changed him. It was a question he found particularly troubling. It was to be many months before he really answered it.

"You asked whether what was essentially a change of environment as of late 1941 changed me," he said. "I've been thinking and thinking about this. You see, in a way, yes, it changed things for me because it widened my perspective. But it is only now that I realize this, only now that I understand, that contact with these very different men created a conflict in me. Unfortunately, though, at the time it happened unconsciously. Now I can recall it—even, if you like, refeel it—but at the time I don't think I was consciously aware of it at all."

His tragedy, and theirs, he felt now, was that, although these men had more capacity for detachment, they too were for a long time committed to Hitler's dream, though less passionately than he to Hitler as a man.

"I'm not trying to justify myself by saying that others were as committed as I," he said. "How can I, when my blindness endured far beyond the time some of these men fully realized the fatality of his actions and put their lives on the block in an effort to stop him?"

The assassination attempt of July 20 was also very late, I said, and in a way for the wrong reasons.

"With that," he said, "you prove that you cannot understand. You cannot understand because you can't empathize with that absolute commitment to country which is—or perhaps was, as today's young Germans don't seem to feel this—a characteristic of Germans of my and earlier generations. When a minute ago I mentioned our 'tragedy,' it was that in those earlier years Hitler and Germany were one, for those men as well as of course for me. By mid-1944, when I was still battling with—oh, call it whatever you like—my loyalty or whatever to Hitler versus the interest of the country, the men of the Twentieth of July had made their choice: Germany, which to them decidedly was no longer Hitler."

He felt that this "commitment to country"—at that time personified by Hitler—did mean unquestioning acceptance or obedience to Hitler's orders, but only up to a point. "If only one had known more, one might have realized Hitler's danger the moment when he overturned the age-old army regulation which allowed soldiers to protest against what they considered illegal or immoral orders. Obviously, he did that because he was about to issue precisely such orders. Of course, no one knew this outside the Army Chief of Staff. But given what we know now about ourselves, heaven only knows whether, if we had known, anyone *would* have protested."

When outrageous orders *were* then issued, he said [he was referring to the *Kommissar Befehl*], as the Nuremberg trials showed, a number of generals, for instance Rundstedt, Bock and Leeb, did have serious reservations, but, in line with traditional discipline, expressed them not to Hitler but to their superior in the hierarchy, Field Marshal von Brauchitsch, who did nothing.

"But of this I cannot speak from my own knowledge," Speer said. "And anyway, who am I to criticize others?" And he told me that he was present in 1937 when Hitler ordered that Pastor Martin Niemöller, who despite warnings had delivered yet again a sermon critical of the Nazis, be sent to a concentration camp and kept there indefinitely. Speer didn't feel that was wrong. Niemöller had been warned and hadn't heeded advice. Nor, he added, did he feel he was wrong six years later, when he did nothing to help Hans and Sophie Scholl, the young brother and sister who were the founders of the Christian student resistance movement The White Rose. "I only heard about them by chance," he said, "because a colleague had imprudently talked about them on a train and got into trouble. I got him out of it, but I admit they didn't interest me very much—I didn't know any details, certainly not their age [twenty-five and twenty-two years]. But you must understand—for me they were traitors, just like Niemöller. [They were found guilty of treason and beheaded in February 1943.] True, had I known their age and that they would be executed, I would have been against that. But even then, I can't now honestly say that I would have done anything. I would have agreed that they should be neutralized, put where they couldn't do any more harm."

When I asked if he felt now that this was a lack of civic courage, a lack of morality, he pondered for a long moment, got up to fix a curtain that didn't hang straight, and for quite a while looked out at the dark night. On his way back he straightened some books on a table and put another log on the fire. "If I just answered that question with 'yes,' " he said, "it would be too simple. For of course, *now* I think it was immoral. But what does that mean? Nothing. How can it help our understanding of those times, which is what you and I are trying to do here, I presume, for me to say yes, yes, mea culpa.

"Yes, of course, mea culpa, but the whole point is that I *didn't* feel this, and why didn't I? Was it Hitler, only Hitler, because of whom I didn't understand? Or was it always a deficiency in *me*? Or was it both?"

Speer's fifty-nine-page profile of Hitler, written when he was in custody at Eisenhower's HQ near Frankfurt in 1945, remains, I think, one of the most authoritative analyses that has been done of Hitler.

"One thing is certain," he says there. "All those who worked closely with him were to an extraordinary degree dependent on and servile to him. However powerful they appeared in their domain, in his proximity they became small and timid." This effect Hitler had on the people around him would preoccupy Speer for the rest of his life. He wrote in the Nuremberg draft:

> In the autumn of 1943, after a visit to Führer HQ, Dönitz and I once discussed this hypnotic quality of his. And we realized that both of us had reduced our attendance at Führer HQ to once every few weeks for the same reason: to maintain our inner independence. Both of us were certain that we could no longer function properly if, like Keitel for example, we were continuously near him. We were sorry for Keitel who was so much under his influence that he was finally nothing but his tool, without any will of his own. . . .

This, he wrote in *Inside the Third Reich*, applied not only to Hitler's so-called Old Comrades but even more to those in Hitler's immediate surroundings who were subjected daily to the intensity of his opinions.

> All of them were . . . mere puppets in his hands . . . without any will of their own. During my activity as his architect, I noticed that being near him for any length of time made me feel weary, exhausted and empty, as if it paralyzed any effort to act or think independently. It was because of this that, when he named me Minister, I tried to schedule my discussions with him two or three weeks apart, thereby maintaining detachment from him. . . .

Paradoxically, in the matter of daily or marginal decisions, he wrote, Hitler was immensely subject to influence from people who understood how to handle him. He wrote some of this in *Inside the Third Reich*, but more fully in the "Spandau draft":

He had one extraordinary deficiency, if one can call it that. He himself was not really manipulative, not in the accepted sense of the term. After all, he totally dominated his environment—he did not need to manipulate: he ordered. Thus, though he was certainly suspicious of others, he had no understanding of, no feeling for the game of manipulation, indeed no suspicion that anyone could slowly, steadily work on him and manipulate him so cunningly that he would finally be convinced that he, and he alone, had changed a long-held opinion. Göring, Goebbels, Bormann and up to a point Himmler, too, were masters at this game. It was Hitler's lack of awareness of this kind of subtle deception that helped these men to obtain and maintain their position of power.

What he had seen many times, which applied both to others and to himself, he told me later, was Hitler's absolute refusal to listen to bad news. "He never wanted to hear that anything was wrong with the state of the army, or the war. On the other hand, what I can confirm is that during situation reports which I attended after I was named Minister, general officers, such as for instance Jodl, frequently did question Hitler's ideas and decisions. Most of them, you know, were not sheep but superbly trained technicians. When they thought Hitler was wrong they told him so. And what's more, he always listened and was quite capable of changing his mind. He had a great respect for experts.

"When I said 'if they thought Hitler was wrong,' " he explained, he wasn't referring specifically to moral issues, though, he added, "who is to say that military questions, involving the life or death of thousands of soldiers, are not also moral matters? Furthermore," he said, quite testily, "immorality in the pursuit of military goals was not restricted to the Germans."

He quickly pre-empted a point he thought I might have been about to make. "I know what you mean. Of course there were moral issues entirely particular to us and to that time."

Like many other Germans, by no means only of his generation, Speer was always convinced, with much justification, that any mention of "morality" by foreigners was bound to refer to the crimes against the Jews. It was never helpful to point out, to him or to other Germans of his generation, that this was their own feeling, a reflection of their own horror quite as much as that of many people in the world who associated Hitler's criminality mainly with what he did to the Jews. Speer—and others—could no more believe this than they believed that there were many people, such as myself, who felt that however unique the crime against the Jews had been, this was a too limited interpretation of Hitler and of the catastrophe and tragedy he brought about.

Of course, he did feel now, he said, that his change of professional environment wrought changes in him, that it removed some blinkers from him, and by distancing him—even more than had already been the case, by his own choice—from the politicians he so despised and disliked, it had in a way returned him, he said, "to a culturally more familiar world. Of course," he added quickly, "I knew very little—really nothing about military matters. I had to learn everything. But, yes, they spoke my language, literally and figuratively."

I asked if, particularly in the last months of 1941, the generals he had now begun to hobnob with told him what was happening in the Eastern theater of war, and what they were ordered to do.

"Never," he said, repeating what he had said many times before. "Nobody ever told me anything. They would not have dared. I was too close to Hitler."

XII

An Irresistible Challenge

Nuremberg, June 19, 1946

FLÄCHSNER: Can you briefly tell me . . . the extent of your task?

SPEER: I can best show you the development by dealing with the numbers of workers under my authority. In 1942, I took over the armament and construction programs with altogether 2.6 million workers. In the spring of 1943, Dönitz gave me the responsibility for naval armaments as well and at this point I had 3.2 million workers. In September 1943, in agreement with the Minister for Economics, Herr Funk, the production side of [that] ministry was transferred to me. With that I had 12 million workers under me. Finally, on August 1, 1944, I took over air armament from Göring. At that point, the total production of the Greater Reich, not counting that in occupied countries, was marshaled under me with 14 million workers.

July 30, 1946

From the final statement by the Chief Prosecutor for the Soviet Union, GENERAL R. A. RUDENKO: Speer was not only aware of the methods . . . employed for the forcible deportation into slavery of populations from occupied territories . . . but took part in decisions on the abduction of millions from their countries [to Germany]. Speer worked closely with Himmler; Himmler delivered to him [concentration camp] prisoners for labor in armament works; [and] branch-camps of concentration camps were established in many factories which operated under Speer's control. . . .

This is the true face of the accused Speer, and the real role he played in the crimes of the Hitler clique.

SPEER HAD EXPECTED that "an important part of Todt's tasks" would come to him after Todt's death, but his staff at the Baustab Speer in Berlin were stunned on February 9 when they heard about his nomination. His closest collaborators, among them Wolters and Annemarie Kempf, met him at the railway station when he returned from Rastenburg early the next morning. They both found him looking anything but elated. "I was overcome by anxiety," Speer wrote. Wolters confirms this in the *Chronik* and also mentions it later, in his letter to Spandau on March 16, 1953. In his diary, which was later incorporated into his reminiscences, he noted,

> He was clearly pleased to see our little reception committee, but he looked pale and exhausted. What apparently worried him more than the mountain of unfamiliar tasks awaiting him was the address he would have to make the next day at the ministry to Todt's staff. "Above all, don't listen to it," he told me. "It would put me off. I think I'll have them assemble in the courtyard when it's dark and I'll talk to them from the window above."

"You were over the moon when it went down with a bang," Wolters wrote to him in Spandau in 1953. "Dorsch told me that even before you spoke you had [already that first day] made short work of various attempts by people to snap away some of your new functions. . . ."

On the morning of February 12 Fritz Todt was laid to rest, with a tearful Hitler delivering the funeral oration. This "great National Socialist," he said, "was a man who had no enemies."

That same afternoon Göring, who had been Todt's bitter enemy, fighting Todt's incursions upon his economic power as head of the Four-Year Plan almost to the day he died, summoned Speer to his office in Berlin.

Four days earlier, arriving posthaste at Hitler's HQ only hours after Todt's death to claim the Ministry for himself, Göring had only with difficulty suppressed his fury upon learning from Hitler, in Speer's presence, that Speer had already been appointed Todt's successor. Now, in his office that afternoon of February 12, he informed Speer that he expected him to sign an agreement identical to one Todt had signed with him, which stipulated that procurement for the army could not infringe on areas covered by the Four-Year Plan. He would send the document for signature to Speer's office.

Speer now understood at least some of the difficulties under which Todt had operated. The Four-Year Plan embraced the entire economy, and it was obvious that if Speer signed such an agreement, his hands too would be tied. Fundamental—indeed almost revolutionary—changes would have to be made in the armament-procurement machinery and, novice though he was, he already had clear ideas as to what had to be done.

Armament production would have to become an entirely separate entity, removed from Göring but also, perhaps an even tougher nut to crack, to a degree from the army's competence. And, if his authority was to be clearly established, it needed to be done at once, with Hitler's open support. The very next day, February 13, Field Marshal Erhard Milch, State Secretary at the Air Ministry, was chairing a long-scheduled major armament conference for representatives of the three branches of the services and the major industries, which Speer in his new function would have to attend. Luckily he and Milch had been on friendly terms ever since Speer's Baustab had begun to build for the Luftwaffe much earlier in the war. Although it was too soon to submit the program that was by then half formulated in his mind, he would have to use the occasion to establish his authority once and for all. Hitler had told him that he would have access to him at all times and at short notice if he met with trouble or needed urgent support, and Speer went to see him shortly after leaving Göring.

The conference, Hitler agreed, would be decisive for Speer's future standing and for whatever changes he wished to bring about to increase production. If, as was more than likely, he found himself in difficulties there, he was to interrupt the proceedings and invite the participants to attend Hitler in the Cabinet Room, the venue for his formal occasions. "I will then tell these gentlemen whatever is necessary," he said.

Thirty men attended the conference, among them General Friedrich Fromm, now head of the Reserve Army; Lieutenant General Ernst Leeb, head of the Army Ordnance office; Admiral Karl Witzell, Armaments Chief of the Navy; General Georg Thomas, chief of the War Economy and Armaments Office of the OKW (High Command of the Wehrmacht); Walther Funk, Reichsminister of Economics (who after Nuremberg would become one of Speer's co-prisoners in Spandau); two top representatives of industry; and a number of Göring's officials from the Four-Year Plan.

After Field Marshal Milch, with Speer on his left and Funk on his right, told the group that they had come together to try to solve the untenable problem of conflicting demands from the three services, Albert Vögler, general manager of the United Steel Works, demanded that the chaos be resolved by placing the power of decision making in the hands of one man; industry didn't care who. When Funk (on Göring's instructions, as he told Speer later) rose to nominate Milch, the Field Marshal, already informed by Speer in a whisper of Hitler's instructions, declined the honor and told the conference that Reichsminister Speer had an immediate invitation for them from the Führer.

The Führer, said Speer, wished to see the participants in the Cabinet Room as soon as they could all get there. The conference would then reconvene in five days, February 18, "at my ministry," he announced, leaving no doubt in anyone's mind who was now in charge.

Shortly afterwards, having been briefed by Speer, Hitler, speaking for about an hour, made it even clearer. Göring, he said, could no longer look after armaments within the framework of the Four-Year Plan—it was too much for one administration to handle. This task would be turned over to Speer, who had proved his capacity for imaginative organization as head of the Baustab Speer, which had achieved astonishing feats in construction.

There was no mention of the "one man" rule industry had requested; that wasn't the answer, and both Hitler and Speer knew it. But in Hitler's salon before Speer took his leave, Hitler, with Martin Bormann standing by, advised Speer to concentrate on industry for help. "It was once again extraordinary," Speer told me thirty-six years later. "He couldn't know what I was going to do because I didn't quite know it myself, not enough anyway to put it into words. And yet, I felt he did know. It was uncanny."

Speer, aiming his remarks at Bormann as head of the party secretariat, told Hitler that he was indeed planning to draw on people from industry, but that, as many industrialists had always kept aloof from the party, he would have to have a free hand to use anyone he needed regardless of the extent of their political involvement.

"Agreed," said Hitler in the terse manner he employed on such occasions, and instructed Bormann to make sure Speer was not troubled by "petty interference."

Speer had won his first major battle, but he now had five days before the group reconvened to put together a program which would not only be acceptable to all the services and industry but, on an individual level, galvanize people into the enthusiasm and exceptional efforts needed to make it work.

Annemarie Kempf told me that Speer had immediately asked her to come with him to his new job. "But I couldn't make that decision," she said, "so I went on holiday to Carinthia, to ski. I loved skiing—it blew the cobwebs out of my mind. Near the village was an OT office, and two or three weeks into my stay, a messenger came to tell me to meet Speer in St. Johann, in the

Tyrol, where new snow-clearing equipment was being tried out for the Russian campaign. The message said Speer needed me there, so I went. I suppose that by then I must have made up my mind to go to the Ministry—perhaps I always knew I would in the end. The fact is that once the message came, I just packed and went. And then I went back to Berlin with him. The Ministry was next door, at Pariser Platz 3, and I moved into his outer office there. He used to say, 'Just think of it as a door that opened between us.'

"He was a *Lebenselement* [indispensable] for me," she said suddenly. "It would be easy to say I admired or loved him, but that's too simple. Though it's true: others such as Rudi Wolters, who was a *'Du'* friend, used to tease me and say I was in love with him, but I wasn't, not in the usual sense. It was more, and then again less. But he certainly had the power to hurt me. Do you remember what I told you about his ignoring my father's death? I suppose in those years when our team was so close, with none of the usual hierarchical limitations, I did sometimes feel bitter about this one-sided relationship, me so totally wrapped up in his life, his thoughts, ideas and problems, while he appeared oblivious, not of me, but of my life outside of him."

As a kind of revenge, she didn't tell him when she became engaged. "Everybody in the office knew, except he. Finally Willy Liebel told him, and said to me afterwards that Speer was speechless for a moment and then said, sounding thunderstruck, 'And she didn't even tell me?' Childish of me, but I was glad he noticed."

After a wedding party her colleagues gave her (Speer came, "looking a bit miffed," she said), she and her devoutly Catholic young husband, who had refused to become an officer in Hitler's army, went off on their short honeymoon. On March 9, 1944, he was reported missing in Russia.

Speer had kept on Todt's former private secretary, Edith Maguira, and she and Annemarie would work in tandem. "It was a golden rule with him never to let anyone go who had experience, but to use them," she said. "I moved into her office with her and an aide called [Karl] Cliever, and she and I shared out the work between us. Except for a small clique—Dorsch, Haasemann [Todt's personal assistant] and a very few others—most of Todt's people had no doubts whatever about Speer.

"Even so, at first the atmosphere was tentative," Annemarie continued, "but then, one wouldn't have expected anything else. Speer and Todt were very different people. Todt had been in the habit of having his aides and assistants brief him on all situations. Speer never did this; he always got his information directly. He was a delegator par excellence, but he always remained in immediate contact with all those to whom he delegated. This was very different from virtually every other official office. All ministers were protected by assistants and aides who decided who their chief would see, and who not. Speer wouldn't have this. He opened the doors; there was complete access to him. Of course, as he often told me when I suggested that perhaps he could hold back a little, have a little more private life, he had to make himself available if for nothing else than to learn his job. 'Where do you want me to get all this information I need,' he said, 'except by opening myself to all of it, from anybody?'

"But for all those who had worked with Todt for years, this approach was very new. For those of us who had worked for Speer all along, it had become quite usual, for instance, for him to take his team along when he went to show Hitler his architectural plans. But the ministry people were stunned, simply stunned, when he told them he wanted them along on his armament conferences with Hitler. *He* didn't care," she said. "He accepted whoever Speer wanted to bring."

Speer's concept for his ministry was supremely simple. The administration of war production would be taken out of the hands of the huge army bureaucracy that had run it under Göring's lackadaisical supervision, and would be entrusted to industries, factories and industrialists on a basis of individual responsibility. The manufacture of each product, large or small, planes, submarines, tanks, guns—or the manifold components for each— would be concentrated in single plants, benefiting thereby from steady quantity production and avoiding the dispersion from which it had so grievously suffered heretofore.

Both in *Inside the Third Reich* and before that in the "Spandau draft," he readily gave credit for the concept of industrial "self-responsibility" not only to Todt but also to the "great Jewish organizer of the German economy in World War I," Walther Rathenau. The "Spandau draft" reflects vividly the excitement and creativity of those first ministerial days and weeks. His long letter to Wolters dated March 14, 1953, shows how his mind worked:

My dear friend,
   I'm afraid what I'm about to write will be pretty boring. I recently read a book by Stefan Zweig about Casanova, in which he says that Casanova would never have produced his lively prose if he hadn't been forced to spend the last years of his life in a philistine little town that offered no intellectual stimulation. . . . If he had been able to recount his adventures in a Parisian salon, says Zweig, he would have talked them to death and would never have been forced—or able—to put them down on paper. Well, although I am no Casanova, I feel somewhat like that.
   The structuring of the ministry would be totally uninteresting to anybody, if the Americans, after the war, had not been overcome with admiration about our "phenomenal" successes in armament production despite the bombardments. Very flatteringly for me, they ascribed it to my

genius for organization. Well, although "genius" is going rather far—it is true that the changes were quite simply due to proper organization. . . .

The authoritarian state not only doesn't admit criticism, but doesn't know what it is. Mistakes can be made for years without any opposition. . . . The needs of the army were in the hands of two enormous bureaucracies [one for weaponry and the other for war production].

When I studied architecture, it emerged very clearly that the students were fairly evenly divided into two groups: those who longed only for the day when they could become free and independent architects, and then the others whose goal was to exercise their profession in the service of the state until, at the appropriate age, they were eligible for pensions and security.

I'm not making a value judgment. It is simply that they were diametrically different people with different needs, the ones needing stability and security, and the others longing for responsibility, risk and a chance to compete.

Thus for instance, a man who chooses a military career is more likely to want to lead his troops into battles than to sit at a safe desk dealing with paperwork. So if officers ended up in war production they actually felt themselves to be failures, with resulting self-contempt and resentment. And basically, the more people resent what they do, the less considerate they are likely to become of others, and the less capable of constructive or creative thinking.

Now free enterprise, in which people choose their work rather than being assigned to it—as must happen in the military, the civil services and ministries—provides a very different scope. But the idea of getting industrial "technicians," as I will call them, to take over the leadership of armament production, was not mine. Todt had already begun drawing on them, and the real originator of this idea of industrial "self-responsibility" was Rathenau, who, charged by Hindenburg during World War I with the procurement of raw material, carried out this task not with functionaries [the despised *Beamten*] but high-powered industrialists. One of Rathenau's "old men" sat in Todt's ministry and played a considerable part in the changes already begun by Todt. . . .

Speer's letters from Spandau were quite descriptive and lively, showing how observant and reflective this "rational man par excellence," as Hettlage described him, had become. He often recorded interruptions by guards, fellow prisoners, the prison timetable, or breaks for rest, a period of reading or thought. While these interpolations do not show up in *Inside the Third Reich,* many of them reappeared in his second book, *The Secret Diaries.* Already in his private letters to his children, as well as here, he minutely and often humorously depicted the nature, duration and effect of interruptions, thereby providing not only a unique picture of the four-powers-controlled Spandau, but what is probably one of the most vivid and telling evocations ever of long-term prison life.

Thus he described, time and again, the changing light in his cell, or the sounds of the guards' steps and their carefree voices chatting in the corridors. ("I'm sure our prisoner voices never sounded carefree, even when—rarely enough in those first years—we did talk to each other," he said to me later.) Carefully noted are the duty visits of the prison directors, so different one from the other, depending not only on nationality but also on their time of service at Spandau. The French were from the start almost invariably lenient: "a tolerance born of indifference," he said once. The Americans were easygoing, curious about their charges and benign; he called it "the benevolence of plenty." The British were the most disciplined and formal, he said, "but always fair." He liked the American guards (and later, strangely enough, the Russians) best, but had the greatest respect for the British. The Russian directors and guards were in the first years the most difficult—angry, suspicious and wedded to rules—but then with the passage of years increasingly showed shy friendliness, and their family snapshots.

"When they were awful," he told me once, "I'd remind myself of what I had seen of the desolation of their lives. And when they were, yes, kind, it always reminded me of one icy winter day in Dnepropetrovsk, when my face had begun to freeze, and a street cleaner, taking his own clean handkerchief, helped me by massaging my face. I couldn't even remember what 'thank you' was in Russian; I said, '*Danke*,' I think, and walked off. Afterwards I wished I had said something."

In many letters to Hilde—and in those to Wolters—he wrote about the music the chaplain played for them after the service on Saturdays, and about the books he read. Thus he continued his letter to Wolters about his innovations at the Ministry after an hour's interruption while the Russian duty guard "swanned about," controlling the cells through the peepholes. He said he had used the time to read about Pharaoh Ikhnaton, "a remarkable man in ancient Egypt." The interruption had given him time to remember that he had read somewhere that already in the French Revolution the Minister for War, Lazare Carnot, had successfully reorganized production by putting nonpolitical technicians in charge:

> . . . demanding and receiving assurance, incidentally, that they would be protected from any interference by "politicals"!! I don't suppose Rathenau knew about this precedent any more than Todt or I did when we followed the same path.

As you can see, the idea was not at all new. But the point about ideas is actually to translate them into action. And this—nothing whatever to do with "inspiration," "genius," and so on—just demands an incredible amount of spadework and understanding of details. But the obstinate preservation of essential details is precisely what architects, who are constantly having to deal with fickle-minded patrons, need to be good at. Anyway, thanks to Hitler's unconditional backing, I was able to go much further in assigning responsibility to industry. His support made me far freer than Todt had been to eliminate interference.

Göring—once he had accepted the principle—wanted the organization to be handed over to the great industrial bosses—[Wilhelm] Flick, [Hugo] Stinnes, [Alfred] Krupp. "Why don't you commission them directly?" he often asked me, and he couldn't understand that the qualifications of these industrial giants were purely commercial: entirely useless to me.

The fact was that neither *Beamten*, the military, nor businessmen could cope with the gigantic task at hand, only the "technicians" of industry who had battled with production on the ground—the factory floor—for years. Then, as long as we could provide the maximum support in supply of raw materials, labor force and transport facilities, and as long as we concentrated production of any one item onto one plant in optimum quantities, it had to work, and as you know—who better?—it did.

Of course for development of new tanks, guns, ammunition, etc., we did also set up mixed commissions of representatives of the army (later also navy and air force), and leading industrial designers and engineers. But invariably, they were not chaired by generals but by the most eminent specialists available in industry. Thus, the development of new tanks was put in the hands of [Ferdinand] Porsche [the creator of the Volkswagen], and that of guns in those of Krupp's famous industrial designer, Professor [Karl] Müller.

I've often been asked what the incentive was for these industrial aces— the technicians who became our consultants. ["They were really very much like Roosevelt's 'Dollar-a-Year' men," Speer said to me later.] After all they received no pay, always working only part-time for us while continuing with their regular jobs, which was of course part of the concept: only constant contact with their home base—their plant—could keep them in touch with what I would call the "feel" of the reality of it. So I don't know what their incentive was, except perhaps satisfaction? Pleasure in something that worked? In any case, all the success was due to them: I was only a layman who knew how to smooth their path and protect them from interference.

It is amusing to think that while the war forced the Americans and other democracies into setting up rigid and authoritarian industrial structures, we succeeded by doing just the opposite—i.e., by loosening the authoritarian fetters away from bureaucracy into an organization based on—yes—democratically conceived commissions and committees. Pondering here in prison about this excursion of ours into democracy is sort of fun. Of course there was no vote as such, and final decisions lay with the presiding chairmen, but—and this was entirely new within the system—they were duty-bound to listen to arguments. The discussions often lasted several days, with everyone free to contribute, without difference between officers and civilians, or regard to status.*

Although Speer's Industry Organization included more than 10,000 "Dollar-a-Year" men by the end of the war, the Ministry itself never grew beyond 220. It was essentially organized into four main sections, each headed by a top man but all working under Speer's eagle eye. He wrote in Spandau:

I eliminated from the start the usual buffer job of a State Secretary to stand between me as Minister and basically everyone who wanted to see me. Traditionally there are two perfectly good reasons for this civil service institution: first of all, because normally ministers come and go but the civil servants remain to provide continuity. And secondly, theoretically the State Secretary looks after the daily hullabaloo in order to give the Minister peace and quiet to ponder fundamental decisions. Well, that wasn't at all the ticket for a workaholic such as me, so I split up the work in five or six sections, to the head of each of which I was freely available.

While soon bringing over to his ministry a number of his principal members of staff from the Baustab Speer, as a "new boy" he had no choice but to keep on many of Todt's experienced top people, many of whom were old party men, well known to Hitler. This was to prove a mixed blessing. "For some of them," he says mildly in the draft, "it was more difficult than for others to understand and accept my approach."

This applied particularly to Xaver Dorsch, the head of the Organization Todt. Probably the most brilliant engineer in Germany after Todt, he would necessarily retain this job. Although Speer tried to forestall his anticipated hostility by the gesture of adopting the OT uniform for himself as well as for three of his top men from the Baustab Speer whom he prudently inserted into the OT, Dorsch would nonetheless succeed in turning the Organization Todt into a separate small empire.

Another close associate of Todt's who had often accompanied the former Minister to his conferences with Hitler was Karl Saur, whom Speer, in a political gesture he would come to regret, confirmed as head of his technical section. Speer saw this section as playing an essential coordinating role between the Ministry and the industrial commissions which in his new setup made the decisions on new products. But Saur, with the aggressiveness of the

*See Hupfauer's description of this, Chapter VIII, p. 181.

born yes-man, could not accept these limitations of functions, and his frequent interference with the industrial commissions' privilege of "self-
responsibility" for development and completion required Speer to intervene
time and again. His greatest problem with Saur, however, was that as head of
the technical section he was—as he had been under Todt—responsible for
statistical reports. It was he who in the last year of the war, with almost daring fantasy, put together the production figures which were reported to Hitler almost daily.

"What this meant for me," Speer told me, "was that I could make Hitler
happy by standing by Saur's figures, which particularly in the last months of
the war were wildly inflated because he based them on orders, not on what
actually survived after our immense losses through bombardments. Or I
could make Hitler unhappy and provoke his anger by contradicting Saur,
who with these crazily optimistic reports had gained a very secure foothold in
Hitler's esteem. Of course, the closer we came to the end, the more anxious
Hitler was to accept anything that appeared to indicate hope. One was constantly walking a tightrope between telling him the truth and risking not just
being thrown out (which could have been a blessing) but being shot, or else
going along with his fantasies in the hope of saving *something* for the German
people."

It was mainly Saur and Dorsch who in 1944, while Speer was ill, would intrigue against and succeed in ousting three of Speer's closest collaborators,
and who would come close to toppling Speer himself. Nonetheless, to a considerable degree, Speer protected both Saur and Dorsch at Nuremberg and, if
certainly condescending toward Saur as he had always been, was comparatively kind about him in the "Spandau draft," where he wrote (though not in
any of his books):

> Even though rather loud, under his rough shell he had no doubt a good
> heart, which prompted him to intervene frequently for prisoners and for-
> eign workers, though this was outside our competence. The fact that with
> increasing proximity to Hitler he became somewhat of a megalomaniac
> was not really his fault. It was par for the course for most of those around
> Hitler. . . .
> Well, that's how our great Technical Ministry came to be. Of course, it
> meant, sadly, saying goodbye to architecture until I could complete my
> ministerial stint—my war job—and, as Hitler had specifically promised
> me, could return to my profession. . . .

"His unpretentiousness was incredibly attractive," said civil engineer
Ernst Görner, who, in a comparatively lowly function, was to see a great deal
of Speer after he became Minister. Görner was a tall, thin man, himself ex-

ceptionally modest. "I wasn't really anybody," he told me in 1987, when I went to spend a day with him in Rodenkirchen, a small town near Cologne. He had been working in the research department of the Society of Civil Engineers when Todt, just two weeks before he died, appointed him to take notes of all his meetings. "Todt was a very modest man, too—a huge *Respektperson* for me," Görner said. "It really was strange for a man such as me to end up in the proximity of two such remarkable personalities."

"Görner was in fact a highly intelligent man who somehow fell between two stools," said Annemarie, who was a friend to so many of Speer's men. "He was knowledgeable about a lot of things, but not an expert at anything that could serve the war effort. But in a curious way, he had distinction—he was, very clearly, a man of integrity and discretion. I think Speer felt this the moment he met him."

"The first day he came to the Ministry," Görner said, "I was just sitting in my little office where Todt had installed me, next to the *Grosse Saal*, the Minister's office, feeling sort of lost, when Speer opened the door. 'What are you doing here?' he asked, and I told him that I'd been taking notes for Todt. 'Well, that's all right then,' he said. 'You can do that for me too.' And that very afternoon I was called in to record his first ministerial conference."

We were sitting in a sort of covered arbor he had built in the garden of his house, overlooking a small swimming pool: small house, small garden, small arbor, small pool, mostly for the grandchildren's use by the time I met him.

He didn't keep a verbatim record, he said. "That was done when necessary by one of Speer's secretaries in shorthand. No, my job was to produce a kind of digest, outlining the content of meetings as fully as possible, but at the same time describing the atmosphere. It really did become terribly interesting." Unfortunately, most of the protocols he wrote, both in Berlin and on trips with Speer, perished in Dresden, where he had deposited them for safekeeping at the beginning of 1945. All that is left are partial notes from March and April 1945, and a few earlier ones which Wolters had incorporated into his *Chronik* but, apparently wishing the historical record to show only his own reports, later crossed out.

"When I met Speer first," Görner said, "he impressed me as a very normal man who never spoke down to anyone. Well," he said, smiling, "I suppose 'normal' was exactly what he was not, or perhaps he was an abnormally normal-seeming man. We were both rather silent people, do you know what I mean? He looked at me that February day, and I looked at him, and I think we both knew we could manage together."

Görner, who had decidedly not been a Nazi, was the first person I met in Speer's environment who admitted to having read *Mein Kampf.* He had found it very interesting when he first read it. "Exciting? Oh, I suppose so, at first, but it palled, oh, dear, it palled." He said that of course Speer would have read *Mein Kampf*—"Everybody read it." But it was music he and Speer truly had in common, he said. "We managed to hear a lot of music together. Given how compulsively he worked, I really don't know how, but we did."

Wolters, among other things, also shared music with Speer, as he marked in his diary on March 3, 1942, just three weeks after Todt's death and Speer's appointment:

Last night with Speer at the Philharmonic. In his box Frau Speer and Ilsebill Todt, the eighteen-year-old daughter of the late minister, who so resembles him in her facial expressions. Speer wants to help her to study interior design. He has asked me to find a suitable school.

Speer said that he already feels quite at home with his new job. . . . He said that when a few days after his appointment he . . . explained his ideas about the standardization of the armament industry to the assembled army and industrial leaders, no one budged when he asked whether there were any objections, so he had them all signify their approval by putting their signatures on his proposal. They only realized what they had done when they got home. Then they picked up the phone and complained to Göring that they had been tricked into signing. When the Reichsmarshal rang to tell him about these complaints, he explained what he was trying to do, whereupon Göring virtually made him his deputy on the Four-Year Plan then and there.

"With this," Speer told me at the Philharmonic that night, "I already have more power now than Todt ever had."

Late that night, Speer invited his ten leading architects and his closest collaborators from the GBI—Stephan, Schelkes and me—to supper at Horcher's [Speer's favorite restaurant]. He told the group that he was already feeling quite at home in his new position . . . and that he thought he would be able to make himself useful there, especially as the Führer had assured him of his full confidence. Regretfully, he would have to leave them to their own devices, at least for two years; by then he thought he would have the problems licked. While of course taking on the whole spectrum of armaments, he intended to concentrate first of all on tanks, and had already thoroughly familiarized himself with the new Russian ones—he had driven one for four hours the previous day. . . . He thought that architects rather than engineers would be the future leaders and managers of technology. After the war he, Speer, would presumably be put in charge of a new Ministry for Construction.

"He was cock-a-hoop," said Annemarie Kempf. "He was on top of the world."

XIII

A Maelstrom of Intrigues

Nuremberg, December 11, 1945

THOMAS J. DODD (U.S. Deputy Prosecutor): We shall show that the Defendants Sauckel and Speer are principally responsible for the formulation of the [forced labor] policy and for its execution: . . . that the Defendant Speer, as Reichsminister for Armaments and Munitions, Director of the Organization Todt, and member of the Central Planning Board, bears responsibility for the determination of the numbers of foreign slaves required by the German war machine, was responsible for the decision to recruit by force, and for the use under brutal, inhumane and degrading conditions of foreign civilians and prisoners of war in the manufacture of armaments and munitions, the construction of fortifications, and in active military operations. . . . We say this system of hatred, savagery and denial of individual rights, which the conspirators erected into a philosophy of government within Germany . . . followed the Nazi armies as they swept over Europe—the Jews of the occupied countries suffered the same fate as the Jews of Germany, and foreign laborers became the serfs of the "master race" and they were deported and enslaved by the million. Many of the deported and enslaved laborers joined the victims of the concentration camps, where they were literally worked to death in the course of the Nazi program of extermination through work.

July 27, 1946

HARTLEY SHAWCROSS: Speer has admitted that his responsibility for conscription of labor helped to bring up the total number of workers under him to 14 million. He stated that when he took over office in February 1942, all the perpetrations or violations of international law of which he could be accused had already been realized. Nevertheless he went on to say: "The workers were . . . brought into Germany against their will. I had no objection to their being brought to Germany against their will. On the contrary, during the first period until autumn of 1942, I certainly used all my energy so that as many workers as possible should be brought to Germany."

June 20, 1946

FLÄCHSNER: The Prosecution alleges that you approved of the use of force and terror. Will you comment on that?
SPEER: I had no influence on the method by which workers were recruited. If the workers were being brought to Germany against their will, that means, as I see it, that they were obliged by law to work for Germany. Whether such laws were justified or not, that was a matter I did not check at the time. Besides, this was no concern of mine. . . .

SPEER'S VERY FIRST months as Hitler's most important Minister already ensured his eventual fate in Nuremberg. But, extraordinarily enough, given his postwar awareness of Hitler's criminality, the aspects of his work because of which he stood before that court—the deportation and forced labor of millions of men and women in factories he largely controlled—still appeared to be of marginal importance to him thirty-six years later. What he happily described to me for many hours was the energy he succeeded in generating in all those who worked for him by the innovations he suggested and which Hitler fully supported. Of these, his new system of self-responsibility was, he thought, the most important and productive.

"To be responsible makes people feel free," he said, "and for our workers, and managers, this was a very new feeling."

In *Inside the Third Reich* he does his best to minimize a rather different kind of early help he requested—and received—from Hitler. "Over the objections of the Minister of Justice," he writes, "I had established the principle, right at the beginning of my job, that there would be no indictments for sabotage of armaments except on my motion."

This sounds like a more innocent description of this early move than the one he gave to the General Staff on February 19, 1942, and in a subsequent press conference, when he explained the absolute necessity to protect at all cost the labor interests of armament production. Already, he announced, he had ordered the removal to a concentration camp of two works managers who had in their domestic employ workers who should have been working for war production. That day he sent Hitler a draft for a Führer Decree for the Protection of the Armaments Industry, which Hitler signed on March 21, 1942:

In the deployment of existing manpower, absolute priority is to be given to the requirements of war. The same applies for the distribution of raw materials and products essential to the war economy.

ARTICLE I

1) Whosoever makes intentionally false declarations about the requirement or availability of manpower [and/or] about the requirement or reserves of raw materials, products, machinery or equipment essential to war production and thereby endangers the requirements of armament production will be punished by penal servitude [and] in grave cases by death.

ARTICLE II

Whosoever has made himself liable to prosecution in the sense of Article I will be pardoned if false declarations are rectified within three months of publication of this decree. . . .

ARTICLE III

Jurisdiction for prosecution is in the hands of the People's Court [the infamous party court, which imposed the most savage punishments], except for culprits who come under the authority of the Wehrmacht. . . .

Prosecution is solely at the discretion of the Minister of Armaments, also acting as General Deputy for Armaments within the Four-Year Plan.

ARTICLE IV

This decree becomes effective within three weeks after its proclamation [and] applies to the entire territory of the Reich and the General Government [in occupied Poland].

Signed: The Führer, Adolf Hitler
Reichsminister and Chief of the Party Chancellery, Dr. Lammers
The Chief of Staff of the Wehrmacht, Keitel

On April 25, this awesome edict was declared applicable to the management of raw materials, and three days later Speer extended it to the construction industry.*

Speer was almost immediately caught in a maelstrom of conflicting interests and intrigues. "Of course, I had by then been a member of Hitler's 'court,' so to speak, for years," he told me. "But I cannot tell you to what extent it suddenly felt different. First of all, of course, our relationship changed, from the moment he appointed me. While during my years as his architect it had always been not just warm but almost intimate—well, let's

---

*"It would hang, until the end of the war, like the sword of Damocles over the heads of [industry]," writes Gregor Janssen in *The Speer Ministry*, and adds in his Notes that Speer, in a personal communication to him, had claimed that this decree had been issued for no other purpose than a "fictitious shock maneuver" and had never been applied. Janssen says that Ministry records cite no examples of the application of the decree, thus apparently confirming this, but Matthias Schmidt, in *End of a Myth*, describes three cases in 1944, one of which was dropped. The result of the other two is not recorded.

say as intimate as any relationship with him ever was—as of that morning of February 8, he became distant and cold. There was no longer any informality or, of course, lightness whatever. Although when he was in Berlin, or I at HQ, I continued to see him almost daily, for quite a while our meetings were entirely formal. He would ask for my report on events of the past twenty-four hours and any comments I wished to make; he would then respond, very quickly—he was always very quick drawing conclusions and making decisions—and then he would give me leave to go. There was none of that familiarity that had developed between us over the years.

"It was very painful for me, until I understood that it was deliberate. He kept me at a distance until he was sure I had learned the lesson of how a Minister behaves. When he thought I knew, we returned to a somewhat easier relationship."

Annemarie Kempf, who was very observant, said that she never noticed Speer's concern over a change in Hitler's attitude toward him. "He wouldn't have talked about it specifically," she said, "but I would have felt it. One of the most remarkable things about Speer was his imperturbability, his nonchalance; it was the first thing almost everyone noticed about him. But when one knew him well, one came to recognize the cracks in this composure, and they occurred invariably in connection with something Hitler did or said." She thought that the "painful change" in Hitler's attitude Speer mentioned to me must have assumed a greater significance retrospectively than at the time, or perhaps was very brief.

"By the time we met in St. Johann [in March 1942]," she said, "he was full of the job and triumphant about Hitler's wholehearted support. And, as I saw when we got back to Berlin, they saw each other or were in touch every day, quite aside from the necessary production conferences. But he became very quickly aware of the atmosphere of intrigue around Hitler and quite soon found himself in the unhappy position of having to waste time making sure it was not directed against him."

When we discussed the question of these intrigues in Hitler's environment, Speer first said that before he became Minister he hadn't really known about them, then he hedged. "Well, there was one person early on who personally intrigued against me [Giesler], and, of course, Bormann never liked me, or I him. But in those years before the war, I personally felt pretty secure. I was very much part of his inner circle, his 'family' if you like, and this continued to apply up to a point after he named me GBI; probably because, even when it began to involve construction for the Luftwaffe and later facilities and New Towns in the occupied territories, it was still in a way architecture.

"His interest in and response to architecture was never limited to Berlin, his office or normal working hours. More than anything else, it rested and stimulated him, and most of our meetings, talks and decisions concerned with building took place at night, both in Berlin and the Obersalzberg.

"After he made me Minister, the whole environment changed. Certainly for the first months I saw him virtually only formally—at his office, and at lunch in Berlin or at Führer HQ, where he was surrounded by his staff, rather than as before, over supper and afterwards with his 'family,' who had no need to engage in intrigues. It was in this formal environment that he was surrounded by intrigues, people vying for his favor, for assignments, for jobs and for acceptance of plans and projects, one always in opposition to another and to the detriment of others. He himself was fairly naive about it. He either didn't recognize, or else simply didn't accept, the reality of these court intrigues. Although, very annoyingly, he would often deliberately duplicate assignments, forcing people to compete, I don't think it was an *emotional* game, playing people off against each other, such as many rulers in history have done. Not because he might not have enjoyed it, but rather because—as I have said before—he simply didn't understand the nature of intrigue. Just as, although he loved to laugh, he didn't understand anything but practical jokes—those could make him laugh until he cried."

(An example of Hitler's simplistic sense of humor is Speer's description of an occasion in 1943 when Ribbentrop's Foreign Office colleagues wanted to present their Minister for his fiftieth birthday a beautiful handmade casket filled with photocopies of all the treaties and agreements he had concluded. "We were thrown into great embarrassment when we were about to fill the casket," Speer quoted Ribbentrop's liaison man at Führer HQ, Ambassador Walter Hewel, as saying to Hitler. "There were only a few treaties that we hadn't broken in the meantime." Hitler's eyes, Speer wrote, filled with tears of laughter.)

A few weeks after taking office, Speer had a meeting with the two generals who would become his closest allies and supporters, Erhard Milch and Friedrich Fromm. They agreed that the war in the East had to be won before October, and therefore with the weapons already available rather than counting on those yet to be produced. Essentially they agreed with what Todt had so desperately tried to convince Hitler of before he died: that unless the Eastern campaign was won before the onset of another Russian winter, the war was lost.*

At least partly as a result of this meeting, Speer made two radical suggestions to Hitler. Fortunately for the Allies, he failed with both of them. The first and most important was to convince Hitler of the necessity for total mo-

---

*On September 7, 1942, *The Times* in London printed an article titled "The Speer Plan in Action" which "with stunning accuracy," as Speer described it to me, summed up the conclusions of the March meeting with Milch and Fromm.

bilization of the German labor force, including women. The second was to
reorganize the whole economy to put it on a war footing comparable with
that of the British, beginning with a suspension of all building projects not
connected with the pursuit of the war.

There were two fundamental reasons why he lost these essential battles at
the very beginning of his new responsibilities. First, the whole country and,
more important, Hitler and his closest minions were so used to easy victories
that the idea not just of possible defeat but of a conflict over many years to
come was inconceivable to them. No armament reserves, nor any production
plans, looked beyond the next six months because the whole of the German
military economy was geared to Hitler's *Blitzkrieg* strategy—heretofore so
brilliantly successful.

Second, as far as the civilian population was concerned, Hitler was determined that they were not to feel the war: as far as possible, they were to have
everything they needed and, thanks to the conquest of so much of Europe
with all its human and mineral wealth, in greater plenty than ever before.

Speer, however, almost from the day he took office, opposed this easy option. Total war, he told Hitler, required sacrifices and discipline from all Germans, whoever they were. But with these demands he came up against the
personal interests and pet ideas of Nazi Germany's most privileged men, the
Reichsleiter and Gauleiter—all Hitler's "Old Comrades." They immediately
lobbied against using women in war production—an offense, they said,
against the sacred nature of German womanhood—and against any interference with their pet building projects, planned for their own or their provinces' benefit.

The principal culprit here was Martin Bormann, Chief of the Party Chancellery (and in 1943 officially named Hitler's Private Secretary), with his
never-ending rebuilding of the Obersalzberg, which he, as administrator of
the Führer funds, considered his private fiefdom. Though Hitler temporarily
accepted Speer's suggestion for a construction moratorium, Bormann soon
convinced him that construction at his mountain retreat had to continue.
("It looked like one huge building site, to the end," Speer said. "When the
Americans occupied it, they still found work crews beavering away at new
villas and bunkers ordered by Bormann.")

All the other Gauleiter and party bigwigs followed Bormann's example.
Thuringia's Gauleiter, Sauckel—one of Hitler's favorites—insisted on carrying on with his Party Forum at Weimar; Robert Ley, head of the German
Workers' Front, experimenting with pigs on his model farm, needed a mammoth new pigsty; the Gauleiter of Posen needed a new residence and renova-
tions of Posen Castle and the principal hotel. (More than a year later, Speer
and Goebbels, attending a Gauleiter conference there, would angrily com-

ment on the [prohibited] use of bronze for the doorknobs at the hotel.) Ley, Keitel and a number of others had to have luxurious private trains; and with the increasing bombardments, all the Gauleiter, Göring and Hitler himself wanted more and safer personal bomb shelters. Hitler also wanted the representational Schloss Klessheim near Salzburg renovated, and Himmler had acquired a property near Berchtesgaden for what he called his "second family"—his mistress, Hedwig Potthast, who had been his secretary, and their two children.

(It was here that, late in the war, fourteen-year-old Martin Bormann, Bormann's eldest son and Hitler's godchild, had an experience that would plant the seeds in him for what was eventually to become a very different life. He was, of course, a passionate young Nazi, immensely proud of his "strict but just" father and of his Führer—his family and Hitler's circle, significantly enough, called young Martin *Krönzi*, for Crown Prince.

Martin was sixty when we met first in 1990, when I attended a therapy group composed of children of high-ranking Nazis. A former priest who had become a teacher, he was a tall man with iron-grey cropped hair, an ascetic face and—although he could be very funny and both he and his wife, Cordula, love to laugh—an essentially grave mind. It was at this group meeting, part of a project initiated by the Israeli psychologist Dan Bar-On to help the children of Nazi "perpetrators" come to terms with their background, that Martin told an appalling story which we repeatedly discussed later.

That day in 1944, he was at home on the Berghof for holidays from his Bavarian boarding school at Feldafing. In the morning he was busy as usual during holidays, running errands for his father and Hitler, carrying films, photographs and maps to and fro. One afternoon, however, Frau Potthast invited his mother to bring him and his younger sister Eike to her new house for tea. He remembers the house as standing "in a wild sort of garden. She gave us chocolate and cake; it was nice."

Later, Frau Potthast said she would show them something interesting, a special collection Himmler kept in what had become his special lair. She led the way up to the attic.

"When she opened the door and we flocked in, we didn't understand what the objects in that room were—until she explained, quite scientifically, you know," Martin said, his voice now toneless. "It was tables and chairs made of parts of human bodies. There was a chair . . . the seat was a human pelvis, the legs human legs—on human feet. And then she picked up a copy of *Mein Kampf* from a pile of them—all I could think of was that my father had told me not to bother to read it as it had been outdated by events. [Speer had told me that Hitler had said exactly the same thing to him.] She showed us the cover—made of human skin, she said—and explained that the Dachau prisoners who produced it used the *Rückenhaut*, the skin of the back, to make it."

He said they fled, his mother pushing them ahead of her down the stairs. "Eike was terribly upset," he said, "and I was too." It hadn't helped them much, he said, when his mother, trying to calm them, told them that their father had refused to have the book in the house when Himmler had sent him a similar copy.

Not much more than a year later, when it was all over, Martin, now a penniless fifteen-year-old refugee on a mountain farm in Austria who didn't know where his family was and whether his mother and siblings or his father were alive, saw photographs in a Salzburg newspaper of the horrors that had been discovered in the concentration camps. "People said that the photographs had to be fakes, but I knew it was all true," he said, his face red with stress. "After what I had seen in that attic I had no doubts at all, ever. . . ."

"The swine," said someone who was present as the story was recounted.

"To call those people swine," said Martin Bormann's son, "is an insult to swine.")

LATE THAT SPRING of 1942 Speer realized that dealing effectively with the Gauleiter was beyond him, and that if he wanted their help in the procurement and distribution of labor, he needed one of them on his staff to help him. He suggested to Hitler that his old mentor Karl Hanke, now Gauleiter of Lower Silesia, be appointed to that role. But here again Speer failed: Hitler said that Hanke had not been Gauleiter long enough to wield sufficient influence. He had discussed it with Bormann and he was going to appoint Fritz Sauckel as Commissioner General for the Allotment of Labor—he was the right man for the job.

"Do whatever you can for the Minister for Armaments," he adjured Sauckel two days later when, in Speer's presence, he handed the document of nomination to his "Old Comrade." There were 250 million people now available to the German labor market in the countries occupied by the Reich, he said; Sauckel should have no problem.

Even so, Speer, well aware of Ernest Bevin's radical war-labor program in Britain, under which not only all men but also millions of women not on active service were mobilized for production and moved about wherever they were needed, tried to impress Sauckel with the need to recruit labor from the huge available ranks of German women. Sauckel and Göring, on whom he called for support, flatly refused. Sauckel, with Göring nodding enthusiastic assent, recited the Gauleiter credo—factory work could be morally harmful to German womanhood, possibly even putting at risk their ability to bear children. (Speer, describing this period in Spandau, added a bracketed comment to Wolters, "When German women read this, they will praise Göring and Sauckel and be furious with me.")

After getting Hitler's agreement, Sauckel informed his fellow Gauleiter of this fundamental decision: "In order to provide the German housewife, above all mothers of many children, with tangible relief from her burdens, the Führer has commissioned me to bring into the Reich from the Eastern territories some 400,000–500,000 carefully selected, healthy and strong girls."

(By 1943, Speer writes in his Notes to *Inside the Third Reich*, Britain had reduced the number of female domestic servants by two-thirds, from 1,200,000 in June 1939 to 400,000. Over the same period in Germany, it was brought down by a mere 140,000, from 1,582,000 to 1,442,000.)

Attempts were made almost immediately to persuade young people in the occupied East and West to volunteer for work in Germany. At the Nuremberg trial, the court was shown copies of placards which had been distributed in Poland and the Ukraine offering all kinds of inducements—money, good housing, medical care, regular holidays at home, and aside from this apparently paradisaical existence for themselves, extra food and clothes rations to volunteers' families at home. It should have worked, but it didn't, because however effective the propaganda was at first, particularly in Poland but also in the Ukraine, the number of volunteers was almost immediately too small and therefore had to be increased by other less benevolent means. Furthermore, although (contrary to public assumptions after the war) there were many factory and farm managers in Germany who did their best for their foreign workers with extra food and time off, many of these good intentions could in the end not keep pace with the official rules. These specified that the foreigners were not "guest workers" (as later generations of imported labor were called in postwar Germany) but *Untermenschen*. As Erich Koch, Reichskommissar for the Ukraine, said in a speech in early 1943 to party members stationed in Kiev: "We are a master race, which must remember that the lowliest German worker is racially and biologically a thousand times more valuable than the population here." And Himmler told the leaders of the Hitler Youth seven months later:

> Whether [Eastern] nations live in prosperity or starve to death interests me only insofar as we need them as slaves for our culture, otherwise it is of no interest to me. Whether ten thousand Russian females drop from exhaustion while digging an antitank ditch or not interests me only insofar as the antitank ditch for Germans is completed.

Although Speer's twenty-year sentence at Nuremberg was essentially imposed for his use of slave labor, he writes very little on this in *Inside the Third Reich*. When he does refer to it, it is to blame either Sauckel—who was hanged for having carried out assiduously (and largely for Speer's benefit) the job Hitler gave him—or Himmler, who with equal zeal supplied concentration camp labor for armament production.

The only admission in the book of his co-responsibility for these crimes is in a footnote: "I must share the responsibility for Sauckel's dire labor policies. Despite differences of opinion on other matters, I was always in basic agreement with his mass deportations of foreign labor to Germany." But in a classical Speer tactic to divert attention from any admission of guilt as soon as it has been made, he immediately calls the reader's attention to a book, *Foreign Labor in Nazi Germany*, by Edward L. Homze, which "gives exhaustive details on the little war that soon developed between Sauckel and me . . . these internal enmities and clashes [being] typical."

Once again he was far more sensitive in his draft, prefacing his description there with the sort of personal remark to Wolters one wishes he had retained for the book. He had started on this chapter on March 21, 1953, writing fourteen pages of technical details and anecdotes followed by a two-day break, before getting to what he described as the "gloomy section" on March 23:

> Well, I'm trying to put in as much as possible—it's always easier to cut than to add. Besides, the breadth of my descriptions actually corresponds to the range and scope the job entailed. Added to which, I don't want to omit the negative aspects. If that means bringing up unpleasant memories even now for those who read me, and (you may think) risks harming me, well, then we must put off publishing until all this is only of historical interest. A book such as this may then only find a few thousand readers, but that doesn't matter as I *don't* wish to make money with it. On the contrary, if I do at all well professionally [in architecture] I intend not to use any money these writings make for myself, because I feel it is actually unclean to profit financially from them.

> I am now getting to a pretty gloomy section which, from whatever way one looks at it, throws a heavy shadow over my part in the war effort; nevertheless, there is no way it can be erased because of it.

Sauckel, "the new master of labor allocation," he wrote, had promised him and Hitler that he would dispose of all their worries and solve all labor problems.

> And I did everything to support him and his new authority. Of course, he had promised a great deal. Under ordinary peacetime circumstances, every year produces a new generation of six hundred thousand young

men to take the place of the old or dead. But now that the Wehrmacht took virtually all of these, and several hundred thousand more every year from the ranks of those in industry who had originally been exempted, we had a quite unbelievable shortfall—of about one million a year . . . which Sauckel unhesitatingly promised to replace.

And to begin with, he was surprisingly successful with volunteers from the Ukraine. I was told that their trains to Germany were decorated with flowers and banners. I didn't see this myself, but it was perfectly possible. People I knew who went East found the population there to have such a low standard of living that the incredible [to them] wealth of our soldiers must have given them an impression of enormous riches in the West.

But when the volunteers' trains arrived in Germany they were soon disillusioned: upon the order of the SS, their quarters were like prison camps behind barbed wire . . . to prevent them from spreading communist propaganda. One can easily see why, among the many things forbidden to them, they were also barely allowed to write home!

Sauckel, it has to be said, was appalled by these rules, imposed by others than himself, not to speak of how I felt. I told Hitler as soon as I learned of this, and he did immediately order the removal of the barbed wire. But that wasn't all by any means: when some weeks later I visited the Krupp works in Essen, I found out that the Russian workers' rations were so minimal that they couldn't work properly. Again I told Hitler, who ordered that they were to be better fed. Of course, all this wasn't really my business, but at that point Sauckel was glad to have my help—and I to give it.

"Sauckel and I actually got on quite well," Speer would tell me later. "In fact, in some ways I got on better with him than with Saur. At least he had no pretensions; he was what he was, a simple, rather primitive man. His family was rather nice; we went to see them once in Weimar—he had many children, and they were *very* nice. He was of course not up to this huge job; his experience had been political, not administrative or organizational. Thuringia, where he had been Gauleiter, was the province where Bormann had his political beginnings—hence his loyalty to Sauckel. If one wants to understand Hitler's Germany, one must never underrate the importance of the 'old fighters' in the scheme of things," he said. "In many ways they were not only Hitler's most faithful servants, but his emotional backbone too.

"Hitler was a chameleon, you know. He changed 'color'—i.e., personality, expression, behavior, above all his manner of speaking—depending on the group he was with, the place, the time of day . . . but it was almost always calculated. That was part of his genius, but also part of his need. He relaxed with only two kinds of people: his Berghof 'family' and the 'old fighters.' Of these, Sauckel was one of his favorites. In earlier days he often went to visit him in Weimar, staying at the old Hotel Elephant which Sauckel had had specially renovated for him. In public Sauckel could be very angry, irascible, but in private he was actually quite pleasant. . . ."

I asked how he had felt when Sauckel was sentenced to death. "I don't know how to reply to that," he said, and then tried all the same to find an answer. "So many were sentenced to death, one's feelings were blurred, except that, yes, there was that awful, that shameful relief that it wasn't oneself.

"The time I felt really badly about him," he added after a few moments, "was earlier on, during the trial, when out of the blue he suddenly said to me one day that he was sorry about the difficulties we had had. I mumbled something about it having been Bormann who had created the difficulties, which was true but meaningless in the context of his friendly remark. And that's what I thought of first when I heard about his sentence: that he had said something generous to me, and that I had not known how to return the kindness."

His lack of response was another example of that "wall" between himself and others he had pointed out before, and confirmed here by those last sad words. In the "Spandau draft" he continued,

> A little later [in 1942] a new problem arose when the Russian workers discovered that they were getting only a fraction of the salary paid to Germans. This was actually in consequence of a decision by Hitler and Göring long before workers were imported that, given the low living standards in the East, prices and salaries there were to be kept radically low after occupation, in order to reduce the cost of production there for us. At a conference which I attended with Sauckel, Göring did finally raise salaries for those of the Russians who came to Germany voluntarily, but even so, their salaries remained much lower than those of Germans.

Hitler, at dinner at his Rastenburg headquarters on May 4, 1942, had made the same point:

> The integration of twenty million foreign workers at cheap rates into the German industrial system represents a saving which . . . is greatly in excess of the total debts contracted by the State. A simple calculation— which curiously enough seems to have escaped the notice of most of our economic experts—will show the correctness of this contention: the foreign worker earns approximately a thousand marks a year, compared to two thousand marks for a German worker. Work out what this comes to in toto, and you will see that the final gain is enormous.

Speer continued, in the "Spandau draft":

> Of course all these initial mistakes were fatal to getting the Easterners to come voluntarily—though in my view that would have been impossible

anyway in the numbers we needed. Added to all this, we very soon had other complaints, this time from the plant managements. Did we realize, they asked, that we were introducing thousands of potential saboteurs into sensitive war production? And how exactly did we think they could deal with this number of foreigners, without interpreters, foremen who spoke their languages, or any social or health provisions whatsoever?

This was evidently around the time when Speer suggested (in vain) the full mobilization of German women. He continued in Spandau:

> After this Sauckel lost all restraint and ordered the civil and military authorities in the East to proceed at any cost and by the use of ruthless methods with the procurement of the necessary labor force. Despite all this he entertained the extraordinary illusion that all these foreigners, having had a taste of our paradise, would return to their homes as propagandists for National Socialist thinking. . . .

Countless documents were presented at Nuremberg which testified to the "ruthless methods" Speer mentions here. The American deputy prosecutor, Thomas Dodd, in his presentation on slave labor on December 11, 1945, had made the position crystal clear. He said that the Nazi foreign labor policy, for which Speer and Sauckel were mainly responsible,

> . . . was one of mass deportation and mass enslavement . . . carried out by force, fraud, terror, arson . . . unrestrained by . . . any considerations of compassion. [It] was also a policy of underfeeding and overworking foreign laborers [and] of subjecting them to every form of degradation, brutality, and inhumanity. It was a policy which compelled foreign workers and prisoners of war to manufacture armaments and to engage in other operations of war directed against their own countries . . . a policy . . . which constituted a flagrant violation of the laws of war and of the laws of humanity.

One of the first of many documents Dodd submitted in evidence was a communication from Sauckel to Rosenberg, Minister for Occupied Eastern Territories, dated April 20, 1942; the second quoted here was a statement made in Kiev on March 5, 1943, by the already cited Erich Koch, Reichskommissar for the Ukraine. (Speer never claimed, for the record, that he was unaware of these documents at the time.) Sauckel wrote,

> The aim of this new, gigantic labor mobilization is to use all the tremendous sources conquered and secured for us by our fighting armed forces under the leadership of Adolf Hitler for supplying armaments to the forces, and also for the supply of food to the fatherland. The raw materials as well as the fertility of the conquered territories, and their human

labor potential, are to be used deliberately in their entirety for the profit of Germany and her allies.

The demands for additional millions of slaves from the East came with increasing frequency. In the early spring of 1942, as has been shown, Sauckel was told to bring in two million men and "400,000–500,000 healthy girls." On March 17, 1943, in another letter to Reichsminister Rosenberg, he demanded another million men and women from the Eastern territories, to be delivered within four months. These requests for the dispatch to Germany of millions of slaves continued with increasing brutality until very late in the war—indeed, as will be shown, well beyond the point when most of the Army High Command, the industrialists and Speer knew perfectly well the war was lost.

The conditions under which these men and women who were forcibly brought to Germany worked is illustrated graphically by a list of regulations, issued as early as mid-1941 by the Minister for Finance and Economy for the state of Baden, titled "Directives on the Treatment of Foreign Farm Workers of Polish Nationality."

The workers, the document said, had no right to complain, leave their place of employment, use bicycles, attend churches, visit places of amusement or take part in any cultural activity, engage in sexual intercourse, use trains, buses or other public conveyances, or change employment for any reason whatever. There was to be no established limit to working hours, which were entirely at the employer's discretion. Workers were to be housed away from German households, "in stables, etc.," and "Every employer has the right to administer corporal punishment [other documents provide revoltingly precise descriptions on how] if persuasion and reprimands fail."

Sauckel's directions to housewives a year later about their employment of domestics from the East echoes these already established rulings: "Domestics do not have the right to request time off; if their work is satisfactory, they may leave the home for three hours once a week, until the onset of darkness; however, they are prohibited from entering restaurants, cinemas, or churches. The duration of their service is indefinite. . . ." For them, too, sexual intercourse was forbidden; an infringement of this order was punishable by transfer to a concentration camp.

Sauckel's report to Hitler on April 15, 1943, on the completion of one year as his Plenipotentiary for the Allocation of Labor, clearly denotes success: ". . . I can report that 3,638,056 new foreign workers were distributed to all sectors of the German war economy from April 1 of last year to March 31 of this year. . . . [Of these,] 1,568,801 were assigned to armament production. . . ."

• • •

IN THE SPRING and early summer of 1942—with Western and much of Eastern Europe increasingly harnessed to Germany's plough, and Russia apparently well on the way to being "blitz-occupied" like the rest of Europe—hopes for an early victorious end to the war ran high in Germany. In his *Tabletalk* between April and July 1942, Hitler hardly mentions the war, and the newspapers of the Reich, as Speer writes in the "Spandau draft," reported the latest offensive in the East as if no further Russian resistance was to be expected.

General Fromm, with whom Speer was in the habit of lunching once a week in a private room at Horcher's restaurant, was not so optimistic. The only chance of still winning the war, he told Speer on one of those occasions in late April, was if Germany created a dramatic and uniquely effective new weapon. He was in touch, he said, with a group of scientists who were capable of producing something that could annihilate whole cities—possibly put the whole of the British Isles out of action. He proposed that Speer should come with him to see these men, who in fact were not under his or Speer's authority but that of the Ministry of Education, which had been keeping them on the tightest leash.

"You must understand," Speer said to me, "I knew next to nothing about science, and also I wasn't that interested. This was supposed to be part of Göring's job; technical things were more my thing. On the other hand, meeting these incredible people that day in May 1942 did suddenly make me aware of possibilities I hadn't even thought of before."

Speer's account in the "Spandau draft" of his feelings about the production of an atom bomb, and the actions he took after several meetings with the physicists of the Kaiser Wilhelm Institute, including the Nobel Prize winners Otto Hahn and Werner Heisenberg, is much terser and once again subtly different from the description he gives in his book. The change in emphasis demonstrates clearly the effect that freedom, and exposure to the feelings of young people in the world of the late 1960s, had on his thinking.

In Spandau he recalls being staggered by the first meeting with "these fantastic people," and although his account is very short, he was obviously determined to encourage and assist the physicists toward the production of an atom bomb.

Their group, Heisenberg told Speer, had been in the forefront of nuclear research after Hahn's discovery of nuclear fission in 1938, and some useful work had been done with the support of the military after the outbreak of war. But they had never received the total support required for such difficult and costly research and were therefore now no doubt far behind the Americans, who were apparently devoting enormous resources to atomic research. Additionally, the scientists said quite openly, the Americans were profiting from the forced departure from Germany and the emigration to the United States of some of Germany's greatest scientific brains.

Replying to Speer's question as to what they would need in money, materials and additional staff in order to proceed, they said a few hundred thousand marks, some of the young scientists who had been drafted, some barracks and small amounts of restricted metals: steel, nickel, etc. Their first step would be to build a small cyclotron.

Speer, surprised by the modesty of their demands, said that as Minister of Armaments he could easily give them many times that, but Heisenberg replied that their research was too far behind to make greater resources useful at that point. They couldn't bypass the interim experiments which were essential in the approach to "the big one."

Hitler's knowledge of atomic science, Speer wrote, was limited to his disapproval of anything that appeared even remotely associated with Einstein, for whom he had conceived an irrational hatred. It was therefore Hitler's rejection of what he called "Jewish physics" which had led to the Ministry of Education's shortsighted suppression of support for the atomic scientists. Candidly admitting his wartime attitude, Speer wrote in Spandau in 1953,

> Thanks to the insane hate of the leadership we allowed ourselves to lose a weapon of decisive importance. If, instead of backing the—in the final analysis—ineffective rockets with hundreds of millions, we had devoted them to supporting atom research from the start, it would have been more useful for the war.

As it was clear that no results could be expected for a long time even with the support he would now provide, he wrote, he carefully avoided telling Hitler about these fantastic possibilities. He knew only too well that once Hitler's enthusiasm was aroused, he would ignore all problems and, in almost total ignorance of the requirements of science, would blindly insist on immediate results. For the same reason Speer had tried for months—though unsuccessfully—to keep Hitler away from any personal contact with the other "miracle weapon," the rocket.

But as he needed support against the Ministry of Education, which had failed to stop the mobilization into active service of the valuable young scientists, he suggested to Göring (thereby flattering him into helping him get these young men exempted) that he should take the war-oriented development of science under his wing. "Of course, egocentric as he was, I couldn't tell him about the atom bomb any more than I could Hitler," he wrote, "but my suggestion did briefly get him out of his [lethargy] and he did in fact help me in getting several hundred young scientists released. Heisenberg and his team were delighted."

"It took me a long time before I got used to all this secrecy business," he told me. "Later it would become second nature, but during those first months it was difficult to know to whom it was safe to speak openly. I got on very well with Goebbels then and really for a long time afterwards, and I nearly blundered there. When I told him that in theory there was a possibility of miracle weapons, he wrote a lead article with a big headline, 'Miracle Weapons on the Way.' *That* taught me a lesson."

But with all this, Speer, in the "Spandau draft," leaves no doubt that, understanding perfectly well the potentially devastating military application, he was extremely eager to support the atomic research and, indeed, hoped against hope that the Americans would not be as successful as he suspected they were likely to be.

It is evident that in 1953, writing his "Spandau draft," he had no intention of denying this stand. Indeed, he demonstrates this by one of his little parenthetical side remarks to Wolters, which often assumed particular significance later. Here, writing that "the small cyclotron they succeeded in building is still in Heidelberg," he adds in brackets a remark he did *not* use in his book: "I do hope Heisenberg is not now claiming that they tried, for reasons of principle, to sabotage the project by asking for such minimal support!"

Heisenberg did in fact try precisely that after the war, when he told the Allies that he had had reservations about building a bomb, but the record shows that the facts were quite different. In a conversation in German-occupied Copenhagen in September 1941 with the Danish Nobel Prize–winning physicist Nils Bohr, which Bohr subsequently reported to his associates at the Nils Bohr Institute, Heisenberg had made his political stand crystal clear.

His team, he told Bohr, had gone some way toward discovering a way to produce an atom bomb. Germany was going to win the war, probably quite soon, and Bohr should join them now in their efforts.

Bohr was apparently staggered—it is not quite clear whether by the fact that a bomb was being discussed as a real possibility or because the *Germans* might be producing it. But he was a Danish patriot and also, quite aside from that, an anti-Nazi. Soon afterwards, he left occupied Denmark for Sweden and England, where he was welcomed at Cambridge. Heisenberg would claim later that Bohr had misunderstood him in 1941, that he had come to him to get his help in setting up an international front of physicists united against the production of an atom bomb. This discrepancy has been a matter of dissension among physicists for many years, most recently in Thomas Powers's book, *Heisenberg's War*. Powers accepted some of Heisenberg's claims which are now shown by Speer's Spandau account to be false.

But Speer's various versions of events also differ. In *Inside the Third Reich* he stated unequivocally (thereby adapting himself to the then accepted scenario) that the nuclear physicists informed him in the autumn of 1942 that an effective atom bomb could not be counted on for three or four years, and that the project was therefore scuttled in favor of an energy-producing uranium motor for propelling machinery, which was of interest to the navy and might be available in time to be useful.

Fifteen years earlier, however, in the "Spandau draft," on July 3, 1953, still in ignorance of what the German physicists were claiming, he wrote that *it was only around the time of the Allied landings in Normandy, in June 1944,* that the atom scientists came to see him to admit there was no hope of an atom bomb for several years. They therefore suggested, and he accepted, that they should work instead on a nuclear engine. This timing is borne out by his discussion with Hess, on December 2, 1962, which he reports in *The Secret Diaries,* written five years after *Inside the Third Reich.* Hess was astonished, he writes there, that Speer had on his own responsibility switched the scientists' efforts toward a motor instead of a bomb. "You mean to say that you didn't send up a query about the bomb?" he interjected, dismayed. Speer said no, he decided on his own—"At the end it was no longer possible to talk with Hitler." "*At the end*" could not have referred to 1942, as he said in *Inside the Third Reich.*

SPEER NEVER FELT that either in his books or in conversation with journalists or historians he ever quite succeeded in explaining the extent of the power struggle around Hitler. The profiles of the men around Hitler which he produced three months after the end of the war were probably his best analysis of that struggle. These were written, as already mentioned, before the Nuremberg trials began, at the suggestion of a British Intelligence officer named Hoeffding, who helped him by asking questions.

"The battle for Hitler's favor was almost something out of the Borgias," Speer said to me in 1979, as we discussed the individuals in these profiles. "This was doubly strange in that the men principally involved in this— Himmler, Bormann, Lammers—really had none of the 'qualities'—in quotes—which are historically associated with such figures. How can I tell you? These three were—bourgeois hardly describes them. They really were very gross men. Goebbels and Göring, who of course also played at intrigue, were not gross in that sense; they were very intelligent. Göring was corrupt, but perhaps his corruption had its origin in his sickness, his morphine addiction. How can we know? Goebbels was never corrupt, just horribly dangerous."

Bormann, he said, was "definitely the most dangerous of them all. He came to have quite unique power over Hitler's life. From very early on, 1935 I think, when he was on Hess's (Führer Deputy) staff, he very carefully administered Hitler's finances: his income from *Mein Kampf,* which was of course enormous, the buying and selling of land on the Obersalzberg and—a brilliant financial coup—the royalties Hitler received for the use of his picture on postage stamps.

"Hitler was punctilious about paying his way from his private funds. For instance, he paid his housekeeper and the rent for his Munich apartment, contributed to the domestic staff at the Berghof, and he paid for all the furniture in his private residence at the Reich Chancellery *(Reichskanzlei).* Of course, not for the state apartments later, but anything that was for him personally, he paid for."

That also applied to paintings he bought. Heinrich Heim, who on Bormann's orders took down most of Hitler's *Tabletalk,* and who was an expert in graphics and paintings, was sent on several art-buying trips to Italy and France, and it was well known that Hitler paid the bills. Heim confirmed this to me later, during several talks in Munich in 1985.

"Of course Bormann's power grew immeasurably after Hess's flight to England in 1941," said Speer. "Long before then, he had succeeded in virtually eliminating Hess from contact with Hitler, which was no doubt one of the reasons for his crazy trip. After he had gone, Bormann (who, incidentally, then behaved appallingly toward Hess's wife) very quickly, really within days, took over his functions and had himself appointed Führer Secretary, which meant that he was in charge of Hitler's environment and thereby really controlled his daily life. He was always with him or near him, the only one who was in such continuous and permanent contact."

That didn't mean that other people, including Speer, could not see Hitler privately. "In the final analysis," he said, "Hitler was his own man; Bormann's control—and power—only went as far as Hitler allowed it to go. Hitler trusted him implicitly but, although Bormann was always there, he had no personal relationship with him. He valued him immensely for his quite incredible diligence and as a totally loyal vassal, but always as a vassal. In all my years near Hitler, and the countless days and evenings on the Berghof, I don't think I ever heard Hitler make a private remark to him."

Possibly except for Göring, he said, who—until his physical deterioration and Bormann's manipulation of Hitler against him sharply reduced his influence—was indeed for many years the number-two man in Germany, all these political men who were closest to the power center, Hitler, functioned not as single entities but in groups.

The most powerful of these, as of the spring of 1942, was the trio of Bormann, Lammers and Keitel. Bormann's power, quite aside from his proximity to Hitler, stemmed from his dominance of the party as head of the Party Chancellery, a position he had held since 1933; Lammers was head of the Reich Chancellery, thus the top bureaucrat in the government; and Keitel was a Field Marshal and Chief of Staff of the Wehrmacht. "They eventually closed a ring around Hitler," Speer said, "Bormann controlling access by the party, the 'old fighters' and the Gauleiter; Lammers by Ministers and other bureaucrats; and Keitel, of course, the military."

The one who, despite being close to Bormann, remained outside this, and essentially an independent force to the end, he said, was Himmler. "These relationships of the leading men can only be fully understood if one realizes that all of it was no more and no less than a battle for succession."

He never felt that Goebbels had this particular ambition. "He was without doubt the most intelligent of all these people," he said. "He was a university graduate, as one could clearly deduce from his vocabulary and his diction. Contrary to Göring, Himmler and Bormann, he had a facility for detachment from daily events. He was not egocentric either; nor was he a coward. He told Hitler his views, including when he felt the war was over, and Hitler always listened to him. He was, I think, a genius in propaganda, and I think one can say that he made Hitler as much as Hitler made him. His was a very complex personality—totally cold."

Speer didn't think Goebbels had any thought of succeeding Hitler. "Though in 1944," he said, "when essentially there was no hope left and he was probably the only one who continued to have ready access to Hitler, he did become very active both in political and military policy making. But one felt it was then *faute de mieux,* because he felt there wasn't anybody else to take it on."

All this made Goebbels sound rather benign, I said.

Speer smiled at that idea. "Yes, it is dangerous, isn't it, to say anything positive about people of that time? Because inevitably it sounds like admiration or approval. In retrospect, no, I don't think Goebbels was in the least benign; in the very worst part of Nazism—the measures against the Jews in Germany—he was the moving spirit. And he was 100 percent in agreement with Hitler's other ambitions. But I only learned to understand all this fully much later. At the time, and for quite a long time, Goebbels and I became allies, allies in understanding what most of the men around Hitler didn't—or didn't want to—understand: the forces which were ranged against us, the strength of Britain's commitment, the historical strength of the Russians at war, the industrial strength of the Americans and the absolute necessity for our committing ourselves to 'total war' if we were to have any chance at all.

"Bormann was Hitler's catastrophe," he said. "He understood nothing except Hitler's magic and Hitler's power. And as we can see from Lenin-Stalin and I suppose also Hitler-Hess, diligent, devoted and ambitious Secretaries did become Deputies, and in Stalin's case, successors. Certainly, after Bormann had essentially eliminated Göring from power—or Göring had eliminated himself—he and Himmler were in the forefront, and for a long time they worked hard to maintain a cordial working relationship."

Neither Bormann nor Hitler, Speer said, had any understanding of the dynamics of foreign policy, or of the world, but "inner-politically" they were in charge.

Speer felt that nobody had really understood or adequately described Himmler. "He was of course in a way mad, but he was very, very effective and he came very close to achieving his aim, which was to set up a state within a state."

When we spoke in the summer of 1979 Speer had begun work on *Der Sklavenstaat* (in the United States titled *Infiltrations*) which was to be his last and least successful book. It dealt with Himmler's efforts to set up a parallel SS state within—perhaps even to replace—the Nazi government. Different from the others, like Göring or Bormann, Speer told me, Himmler had a whole concept that from the start, "and particularly," he specified, "from the time of the Röhm Putsch, was based on succession. The title Reichsführer SS, which he had adopted already in 1929, clearly predestined him as successor of the Führer of the Reich. It *is* difficult to characterize or really describe Himmler, which is no doubt why most writers have failed in the attempt. It is difficult because he did seem, as many of them have said, such a very insignificant and pedantic little man. But in fact, he was anything but 'little,' and he had remarkable qualities: the quality of patience to listen; the quality of long reflection before coming to decisions; a talent for selecting his staff, who on the whole turned out to be highly effective people. So you see, in the end that doesn't indicate an insignificant personality.

"There was, of course, that other side to him, which in the eyes of more sophisticated people—and there were those, you know—just made him ridiculous. But precisely because romantic mysticism appeals to the German character, this had an enormous effect and was very attractive, especially to simple minds and the already brainwashed young: his determination to emphasize the value of the race—of German stock; excavations he ordered all over Europe to find proof of old German cultures; anthropological research he funded in Japan and Tibet with the goal of discovering—or confirming—the Germanic origin of these admirable Asian nations."

But people were not fools, I said. How could anybody believe this nonsense?

"As history shows, many did. I myself knew very little about any of this, until quite late. Essentially I think he will always remain something of a mystery. One explanation for his success might well be found in the very quality many people have mocked," he said. "He looked and talked like a schoolmaster, which is what his father was. And"—he smiled—"Germans like professors. When Himmler addressed his young disciples, we can be sure he didn't rant and rave; the enormities he said will have been pronounced firmly but quietly, in middle-class German—very effective. He was, of course, a very reserved, no, more than that, a very closed man, I gather, even to those close to him. There was little social contact between him and Hitler, or of course any of us. I think his secret was that he was a perhaps unique mixture of a clear-sighted realist, who knew exactly what he wanted and how to get it, but also to an extraordinary extent a 'dreamer'—of dreams which, as was after all horribly proved, *did* have an enormous appeal to Germans.*

"What affected *me* after I became Minister," Speer said, "were the practical aspects of Himmler, his determination to insert his SS into every area of German life, and his incredible success with this. As I said, he probably effectively started this after Hitler eliminated Röhm, in 1934, but he laid the foundations even before then. By the time I became really aware of him, he appeared to have on his staff a well-trained man for every single field of activity, by no means only areas commonly associated with the SS. What it came to mean was that wherever there was a gap, Himmler had a man ready to fill it. His aim, quite clearly, was to have available a leader generation whose talents and training could be applied—universally."

Historically, he said, the mistake has been to think of Himmler's "apparatus" in terms of a series of organizations—the SS, Waffen SS, the Police or SD, the Gestapo and so on. "That wasn't it at all," he said. "There was only one structure which embraced all of it, and that was the SS, to which everything else was subordinated and which thus controlled it all. Interestingly, while all this involved hundreds of thousands of people, very few of them became known as individuals; it was as if his own bent for anonymity was impressed or imposed on them."

One of Himmler's closest associates, he said, was his childhood friend orthopedic surgeon Dr. Karl Gebhardt, Gruppenführer in the SS and head of Hohenlychen, a hospital where this eminent physician conducted particularly atrocious human-guinea-pig experiments on concentration camp prisoners (the specific crime for which he was hanged in 1947) and where Speer—convinced that Gebhardt had been told to kill him—nearly died in 1944.

Himmler's closest aide was his personal assistant, Gruppenführer Rudolf

---

*The German word he used for "dreamer" was the disparaging *Phantast*.

Brandt (not to be confused with Hitler's doctor and Speer's friend, Karl Brandt). His principal liaison officer with Hitler (at times also with Speer) was his Chief of Staff, Obergruppenführer Karl Wolff, who after a short stay in prison lived happily in a charming house in Bavaria overlooking Lake Starnberg until he died in 1984.

Speer certainly knew, but chose neither to speak nor more than marginally write about, the man Himmler considered for many years his own Crown Prince. Obergruppenführer Reinhard Heydrich, arguably the darkest personality on the Nazi firmament, was certainly a very talented man, whose ambition it was, without any doubt, one day to follow in the steps of or to supplant his chief.

Blond, handsome, vain and ragingly ambitious, he was, paradoxically, a fine musician, a champion skier and fencer, a fearless pilot and an outstanding organizer. At the same time, though married, and by all accounts devoted to his children, he was a virtually friendless loner. In 1931, when he was twenty-seven, Himmler named him Chief of the SD (Security Service); by 1934, his SD had become established as the party's Intelligence Service. By 1939, now chief of RSHA (Reich Security Main Office) which also encompassed the Criminal Police (*Kriminalpolizei*, or *Kripo*) and Gestapo, Heydrich was probably the most dangerous man in Germany, intensely feared by the few who knew him, or knew of him.

(Judith Holzmeister, beautiful daughter of one of Austria's finest architects, was an immensely talented student at the Reinhardt-Seminar in Vienna when the Germans marched into Austria in 1938, and became one of the finest actresses on the German-speaking stage. She came home that fateful night of March 11, 1938, to find her one-year-older brother listening to the Chancellor, Kurt von Schuschnigg.

"Except for the radio, the flat was all dark," she told me in Vienna, when we were exchanging memories of that day fifty years later. "My mother was in Paris, my father in Turkey [where he would remain]. I didn't turn a light on either, just stood next to my brother as we heard Schuschnigg say his goodbye in that heavy voice—'May God protect Austria.' We knew in that second that our life was torn apart—that the future was empty."

She had been in love for several years with a young communist. "So you see, I knew what the Nazis were; he'd taught me. I had no illusions." Her friend had fled Austria that very day but was sent back in 1941 on a mission. "They caught him," she said. "He was beheaded."

Judith went back to school when it reopened a few days after the Anschluss, but otherwise stayed home until one night an actress friend persuaded her to come out to dinner with her and a "nice young German" she had met. "She said he was going to bring a friend."

The two German officers the girls dined with that night were pleasant enough, both exceptionally handsome and—especially the one Judith mostly danced with—knowledgeable about music and theater, the main subject of conversation until the end of the evening.

And what did she think about the Anschluss? he asked her, smilingly, when he drove her home. "You may be a perfectly nice man," she said, "but I think the Nazis are bandits who have no business stealing other people's countries, and your Brownshirts are disgusting brutes."

He roared with laughter. "Well, we'll have to change your mind about that, won't we?" he said.

Unexpectedly, her mother had returned from Paris that evening, and she and Judith's brother were waiting up for her. They listened to her account of the outing and that final exchange with the handsome young officer. What was his name? her mother asked. "Reinhard Heydrich," she replied. "Oh, my God!" said her evidently well-informed mother.)

IN 1941, HIMMLER, eager to put some distance between his ambitious subordinate and the center of power in Berlin, got Hitler to name Heydrich Reich Protector of Bohemia-Moravia (Czechoslovakia), replacing the ineffectual diplomat Konstantin von Neurath (later the oldest prisoner at Spandau).

Heydrich's brief governorship, during which he managed to persuade a surprisingly large number of Czechs to cooperate with him, was triumphantly successful. Indeed, so much so that on May 27, 1942, two young Czechs were sent from London to assassinate him. They fired at him and threw a grenade into his open Mercedes as he drove the twenty kilometers from his residence, the castle of Jungfern-Breschan, to his Prague office in the Hradcin Palace. Although Himmler brought Hitler's doctors, Brandt and Morell, and his friend Gebhardt to Prague to look after him, gangrene set in and Heydrich died a week later. The revenge followed swiftly. On June 9, the SS surrounded the village of Lidice, on the pretext that it had provided refuge for the assassins, and it was razed; 199 adult males were shot; 191 women were sent to Ravensbrück concentration camp, where 50 of them were to die; and the village's 98 children were deported to Germany, where only 25 survived.

But this atrocity was not Heydrich's most terrible legacy to this century. For it is Heydrich, allegedly part Jewish himself* and fanatically anti-Semitic, who is credited with the concept of the extermination camps, and in particular the creation of the Sonderkommandos, groups of strong young Jews who

*Heydrich allegedly ordered his birth records removed from the Halle registry, and erected a new tombstone in Leipzig for his maternal grandmother, omitting the name Sarah.

on arrival in the killing centers were temporarily kept alive to clean, sort the victims' possessions, burn the corpses, bury the ashes and efface the traces until, burnt out or at the Germans' whim, they too were gassed. Heydrich boasted that he had drawn the idea from his study of Egyptian history, where a similar necessity to preserve the secrets of the tombs of the Pharaohs found the same solution: the immediate death of all those who had built them.*

On January 20, 1942, Heydrich chaired the Wannsee Conference in Berlin, the intra-ministerial meeting at which the organizational and bureaucratic details of the Final Solution were agreed. In June, a few weeks after his death, Himmler named the organization in occupied Poland, which administered the four extermination camps in which two and a half million Jews were to be gassed over the subsequent sixteen months, the Aktion Reinhard in his honor.

Heydrich's nephew and godson Thomas, a well-known cabaret artist who sings and recites, mostly from works by Jewish poets, was eleven years old when his father's much-loved older brother was killed. "I was very angry because at that time I was of course a passionate *Pimpf* [junior Hitler Youth]," he told me, when I met him in 1990 at the same group meeting where I met Martin Bormann. "He was a hero to us; we didn't know anything about politics, we only knew that he was a fantastic sportsman. And of course he was always in the papers, standing next to our idol, the Führer. I was sad because I knew my father would be very unhappy. My uncle was a very good, tender father," he said, thoughtfully. "It's almost a cliché now, isn't it, about these appalling men? But that doesn't make it any less true. One just doesn't like to think of it. Can you imagine? 'Tender'? " He repeated the word bitterly.

Thomas Heydrich's family lived on the exclusive Prinzregentenstrasse in Berlin when he was small. The large house next door—"It had lovely big steps on which I played as a child"—belonged to Jews. "It was burned down during the Kristallnacht," he says. "I watched furniture being thrown out of a window, including a piano—imagine, a *piano!* I remember wondering why anybody would do this rather than calling the fire brigade. I mean, our family was musical, and I knew those neighbors were too. I asked, but was told to hush."

Very shortly after that, he noticed placards on shops and park benches: *Juden Verboten* (Jews Forbidden). Again Thomas was told off when he asked questions. He despises the Nazi generation of Germans who insisted, to the end of their lives, that they knew nothing, saw nothing and even suspected nothing reprehensible during the Nazi time.

"I saw all this, and everybody else did too. They are all liars," he said, "a

---

*One of Heydrich's intelligence officers, Wilhelm Höttl (writing under the name Walter Hagen), tells this story in his memoirs, *Die Geheime Front.*

generation of liars." He thinks his father, who was a journalist, began to have doubts in 1941. "He suddenly asked for a posting to the Eastern front as a private in an army information unit," he said. "He was by nature a very happy, jolly sort of man. I adored him. Every time he came home on leave after this, he was more depressed. My mother often asked why he was so sad, and he would invariably answer, 'We'll talk about it after the war.' "

Thomas thinks his father only found out the worst things his uncle had been responsible for after Reinhard Heydrich's assassination.

"There is a photograph of my father at my uncle's state funeral in June 1942, standing in his sergeant's uniform between Hitler and Göring. Later that day an officer came, bringing my father a thick letter from my uncle that had been found in his safe. He took it and went to his study. Hours later he came out, ashen-faced, with this sheaf of pages.

"He went into the kitchen, which still had an old wood stove, and burned them one by one, very slowly, almost like a ceremony. There must have been a hundred pages. We all stood there watching, and at the end, when he looked as if he was about to drop and my mother put her arms around him and asked him what was in the letter, he said, 'Don't ever ask. I can't talk about it, ever—not until it's all over.' "

Thomas feels sure that in the letter his uncle explained to his father everything he was planning and offered justification for everything he had done. Thomas's conviction stems from the fact that his father became as of then an active anti-Nazi, using the printing facilities available to him to produce passports and other papers to spirit people—most of them Jews—out of Germany. In late 1944, believing himself discovered, he wrote a goodbye letter to his family and shot himself.

The family never learned about his father's anti-Nazi activities until after the war, when a man who had worked with him told them. "We never knew whether he'd really been discovered," Thomas said, "but a prosecutor had come that evening and they'd spent all night in his study, talking. Soon after the man left, he killed himself." A trade-off, Thomas thinks: the suicide and the family's safety, rather than a scandalous treason trial of Reinhard Heydrich's brother.

Very similar to the young Martin Bormann, a few weeks after the end of the war Thomas read what had been done and saw the photographs. As of that moment "and forever," he says, he carried his family's guilt. "I was, if you like, deputizing for all the others," he said, "my aunt, who, inconceivable as it is, felt proud of her husband; his three children, who, incomprehensibly to me, claim to feel nothing; my mother, who, having always instinctively disliked my uncle, was able to hide comfortably behind that early rejection.

My father, who would have helped me shoulder this guilt, was no longer there. *Somebody* had to feel guilt for the devilish things my uncle had done."

IF HEYDRICH barely figures in Speer's books, Himmler of course does, but as a negative political, rather than moral, entity. During all this time, Himmler, the official coordinator of the education of Germany's young elite for murder, determinedly continued to lay his plans for the creation of a "parallel state." In the pursuit of this goal, he had already conferred honorary ranks upon almost all government ministers and offered Speer almost as soon as he became Minister the highest commissioned rank in the SS, Oberstgruppenführer, or Colonel-General. Speer barely mentions this in *Inside the Third Reich* but wrote a little more in the "Spandau draft":

> I told him that I had already refused similar honors from the party and the army, but in order to placate him, and I meant it of course as a joke, I added that I would gladly accept a rank of simple SS-man. I was sure that would end the matter, but to my surprise, his liaison man at Führer HQ [Wolff] two years later rather sheepishly offered me an ID in precisely that rank. I declined.

Speer's sense of humor was lost on Himmler, who went busily to work trying to get Speer into the SS, apparently without informing him of what he was doing. An investigation into Speer's and his wife's Aryan ancestry was put in train, and a thirty-seven-page *Ahnentafel,* or genealogical table, was prepared, going back six generations, to 1750. On July 25, 1942, Himmler's office submitted it to the Chief Office for Race and Settlement, but specified that it was not to be brought to Speer's attention. It read (author's translation):

Der Reichsführer SS   Berlin W35
                                             July 25, 1942

To: Chief Office for Race and Settlement
Concerns: Admission of Reichsminister Albert Speer, born 19.3.05 [March 19, 1905], into the SS.
Herewith, with request for further action and verification, the family tree of Reichsminister Albert Speer. By order of Reichsführer SS, Reichsminister Speer was, with effect from 20.7.1942 [July 20, 1942], attached [*aufgenommen*] to the Personal Staff RFSS as SS-Man No. 46,104.
Reichsführer SS does not wish Reichsminister Speer to be inconvenienced at this point about these very incomplete enrollment documents [author's italics indicate how cautious Himmler was being with Speer]. You are

thus instructed to address yourself directly to the relevant offices (regis-
tries, parishes, etc.) in order to obtain the necessary documentation
in support of the family tree. You are requested to inform this office
upon completing verification so that the SS Suitability Certificate can be
endorsed.

A curious series of mistakes by the official Nuremberg translators could
well have led to fatal consequences for Speer. Ralph G. Albrecht, for the U.S.
prosecution, setting out on January 8, 1946, specific charges against various
defendants, submitted in evidence a faulty official translation of this letter
from Himmler's office, but read out only the first sentence, which appeared
to him to be sufficient:

> "Reichsminister Speer by order of the Reichsführer SS was enrolled
> [*sic*] as an SS man on the personal staff of the Reichsführer SS under SS
> Number 46104 with effect from the 20th July 1942." I think, [Albrecht
> added] except to draw to the Tribunal's attention that a questionnaire at-
> tached to this document demonstrated that Albert Speer was in the SS
> since the autumn of 1932, that is all I need to read from that letter.

A two-pronged misunderstanding here, and the fact that defense counsel
Flächsner hardly spoke English, could have had extremely serious consequences for Speer, which purely by luck were avoided.

First, Albrecht was mistaken in his reading of the "questionnaire" he mentioned. While it is true that Speer had joined the SA in 1931, his affiliation to
the SS was purely nominal and not by choice. He had joined the NSDAP
(Nazi Party) Motorists Association, a minor party group which, as often happened, was at one point automatically attached to the SS.

Second and more important, Speer's position before the court might have
been seriously impaired if it was established that he had sought or even
agreed to accept SS membership in July 1942. It was here that the mistransla-
tion of the SS documents could have played a disastrous part for him. The
tribunal translators had understood the German word *aufgenommen* to
mean "enrolled"—which conveyed the impression that Speer had formally
applied to join Himmler's staff, while the correct translation of "attached"
would have established that it happened on Himmler's initiative, without
Speer's desire or even his knowledge.

Flächsner knew Speer might be in serious trouble about this. He had a
photocopy of the original SS documents and knew that they showed that
Speer had been a member of the SA, which, although not as perilous as membership in the SS, was also dangerous for his client, though it had so far not
been mentioned. But he was unaware of the faulty translation and had no
way of appreciating what Albrecht was saying in English in his presentation.

It might have been pure luck, or perhaps trial fatigue on a late afternoon, that led the court to accept his long-winded argument that while it was true that Himmler wanted Speer in the SS, the appointment document which General Wolff had been ordered to hand over to Speer had never reached him. "Therefore," he argued, "there can be no question of Speer having been a member of the SS, which anyway [he added, somewhat tactlessly] in terms of the charges in the Indictment, is a very minor point."

Later I found in the archives another letter which explicitly established Speer's non-membership in the SS. Strangely enough, it had been overlooked or ignored by the tribunal researchers, and Flächsner too was not aware of its existence.

Dated October 6, 1942, and attached to the completed documentation, it was addressed to the SS Registration Office. It says, "Herewith we are returning the documentation of Reichsminister Speer with the endorsed certificate." Despite the endorsement, the letter continues, the certificate was not valid as "all personal details, including the obligatory medical for hereditary health, are lacking. As according to instructions from the Reichsführer SS direct contact [with Speer] is prohibited, the matter is ordered shelved."

If more emphasis had been laid on Albrecht's mistaken interpretation of Himmler's letter, together with the true allegation—that Speer had in fact joined the Mannheim SA in 1931—it could easily have tipped the balance against Speer and gotten him sentenced to death. Speer himself was confused about his status. He wrote in *Inside the Third Reich* that in 1942, when offered a high SS rank by Himmler, he refused but "volunteered to reactivate [his] former ordinary membership in the Mannheim SS—not suspecting that [he] had not even been listed as a member there."

Although Himmler's attempt to get Speer under his authority failed, he did succeed in another direction which again could, and in a moral-judicial sense perhaps should, have had fatal consequences for Speer. Within a short time of Speer's appointment, he suggested that armament factories should be built within or near the major concentration camps, and that the prisoners should work there under the supervision of the SS.

"There has been some testimony about your relation to concentration camps," said Justice Jackson in the course of his cross-examination of Speer in June 1946. "As I understand it, you have said to us that you did use and encourage the use of forced labor from the concentration camps?"

"Yes," replied Speer, "we did use it in the German armament industry."

"And I think you also recommended that persons in labor camps, who were slackers, be sent to the concentration camps, did you not?" asked Justice Jackson.

"That was the question of the so-called *Bummelanten*," Speer said. "By that name, we meant workers who did not get to work on time or who pretended to be ill. Severe measures were taken against such workers during the war, and I approved of these measures."

Did Speer agree, Justice Jackson asked, that part of the usefulness of concentration camps was to make people afraid and to keep them at work?

"I would not like to put it that way," Speer said stiffly. "I assert that a great number of the foreign workers in our country did their work quite voluntarily once they had come to Germany."

(Speer's last phrase made an interesting distinction. Fritz Sauckel, at a meeting of the Central Planning Board on March 1, 1944, while Speer was away ill, said, "Out of five million foreign workers who arrived in Germany, not even two hundred thousand came voluntarily.")

Speer also agreed that four hundred thousand prisoners of war were employed in armament production. "But two hundred thousand or three hundred thousand of them were Italian military internees and Russian prisoners of war to whom the regulations of the Geneva conventions did not apply."

Did that make it better? I asked him more than thirty years later, and he shrugged. "Not 'better' in the sense you mean, but it meant that it wasn't illegal under international law. The others, French and Dutch and so on, worked in sections which certainly did not contravene the convention. My duty as Minister of Armaments was to put to use for war production as many workers as were possibly available, and in that sense I considered it proper to use prisoners of war and concentration camp prisoners."

By mid-1942, he said, they needed every able-bodied young German for the army who could somehow be replaced by women or foreigners. "As you know, they didn't allow me to mobilize German women, but in fact girls from the East turned out to be good at precision work, and they were clean and conscientious." But there were areas, he said, where he had to have workers who were already specialists.

"For instance," he said, "we couldn't have run the coal mines without the Russian prisoners of war, many of whom had previously worked in mines. You have to remember," he added—one of the rare occasions when he showed impatience—"I was running a country's war machine, not a church bazaar." Two years later, he said, the total workforce for which his ministry, by then in charge of all of Germany's production, military and civilian, was responsible was twenty-eight million workers. "Six million of them were foreign, two million of these worked in the armament industry, about sixty thousand were concentration camp prisoners."

At Nuremberg, I said, he had claimed that the treatment of these and all other slave laborers was not strictly his concern but that of other authorities. He had also said there that his understanding was that these authorities—

Sauckel, the relevant factory managements, and even Himmler and his labor administrator, Oswald Pohl, the SS parallel appointment to Sauckel—were as aware as he always was of the need to keep the workers fit so they could work. He had also told the court that if the foreign workers were dissatisfied, they could complain through their elected spokesmen; a machinery had been set up for this.

Was he still claiming now that these six million slave workers were adequately housed and fed and that they had civil rights which allowed them to complain and receive satisfaction?

"That was what I was told at the time, and yes, in principle—and in many places—this was adhered to. What has been almost entirely forgotten—or suppressed—as a result of the dreadful things which emerged after the war," he said, "is the very real solidarity many German workers manifested with the foreign workers; almost all complaints which did reach labor authorities, we now know, originated with German workers. Many of them—again we only learned this when it was all over—shared their food rations with the foreigners, especially the Russians and women. Many, too, made friends among them, though admittedly this applied more to people working in agriculture and other parts of the economy where they lived close to the civilian population. Here again, we now know, many friendships and relationships have endured to this day. Of course," he said, sounding resigned, "that kind of information wasn't dramatic, it wasn't the stuff for war crime tribunals, nor was it, in those years, what people wanted to read in their papers."

What he said here was certainly true. But so was the almost universal denial, by Germans who had been in authority at the time, of knowledge of the appalling suffering of the slave laborers. Speer was by no means the only one to emphasize the efforts which were made, by himself, by Hitler, by Sauckel and the management of the factories where the slave workers toiled, to improve their lives. "I remember being told that many of the Russians were virtually skeletons when they arrived," he said at Nuremberg, "and that before they could be put to work they had to be put on regular weight-gaining diets." Unconvincing though this was, Speer was after all on trial for his life. What was almost more amazing was how one of Speer's great industrialists, Walter Rohland, head of the Third Reich's steel industry, remembered the "foreign workers." He wrote in his autobiography, published in 1978,

They were usually lodged in residence blocks; apart from the living barracks and necessary appendages—WCs and washrooms—most camps had: leisure rooms, often with facilities for putting on shows; radio facilities, canteens; their own showers and bathrooms, although those belonging to the works were also at their disposal; hairdressers and barbers; laundries and ironing rooms; shoemakers and tailors. It goes without saying that the air-raid shelters were shared by all workers, German and foreign. . . . Women worked primarily on "light work"— kitchens, storerooms and small machines. The working hours of foreigners were no longer than those of Germans and their rest periods were the same; foreigners received food and tobacco bonuses for special achievement. Salaries, fixed by law, were the same for Western workers as Germans, about fifteen percent less for Eastern workers.

Rohland also mentions the Russian prisoners of war who needed to be fed properly before being put to work. "It usually took about eight to ten weeks of improved diet, though even then they were given light duties until they were quite well." And he goes on about the excellent medical facilities at their disposal, the roast meats and desserts on Sundays and holidays, and the theater and variety troupes the factories brought in for their entertainment.

This is an extraordinary representation of conditions which everyone by now knows caused the death by starvation and overwork of literally hundreds of thousands of slave workers. The Nazis in fact had a name for it: "Extermination through Labor."

One report entered in evidence at Speer's Nuremberg trial, for instance, stated that on February 16, 1942, twenty-three Russian POWs were assigned to work in the boiler shop of a locomotive construction factory. The food ration was three hundred grams of bread each, issued between 4 a.m. and 5 a.m., which had to last them to the end of their working day at 6 p.m. Then they received a bowl of watery soup made with root vegetables and often rotten potatoes. When German workers protested against such conditions for fellow workers, they were sharply reminded that Russian POWs were "Bolsheviks who were soulless people, and if one hundred thousand of them died, another one hundred thousand would simply be brought in to replace them."

Such accounts are legion and not limited to the Russian POWs, nor did they originate only from anti-Nazi factory physicians and workers. The conditions the foreign workers were going into, soon known in the East, made recruiting for work in Germany progressively more difficult. On October 25, 1942, Otto Bräutigam, an aide to Rosenberg, Minister for the Occupied Eastern Territories, sent him a top-secret memorandum:

> . . . After countless prisoners of war who could have been used for work have died like flies of starvation [in the POW cages in the occupied East] we now have the grotesque experience of having to recruit . . . millions of laborers from the Occupied Eastern Territories in order to fill the gaps

Above: Speer loved driving in open cars, and here takes his (then) five children for a spin in his Mercedes. *Left:* Speer and Eva Braun, Hitler's mistress, liked each other, and he deplored Hitler's callous treatment of her. Her role was hidden from the public until Hitler married her hours before their suicide in 1945.

Left: Maria von Below, whose husband was Hitler's army adjutant from 1937 to 1945, usually lived at the Berghof.
Below: On the terrace of the Berghof, Eva Braun (left) talks to a friend and Sepp Dietrich, commander of the Leibstandarte Adolf Hitler. The Speer and Bormann children in the group include Hilde, who often looked unhappily at the camera.

Nicolaus von Below was almost constantly at
Hitler's side for eight years. In his memoirs, published in 1980, a year before his death, he provides
a thoughtful record of those years from the point
of view of a professional army officer.

Left: Karl Hanke, who became State Secretary in the Ministry for Propaganda, was Speer's first patron, obtaining commissions for him from Goebbels and the Party. Later, as Gauleiter of Lower Silesia, he allegedly warned Speer to avoid Auschwitz, where "terrible things are happening." *Below:* Fritz Todt (left), the great engineer who conceived the *Autobahnen* and the West Wall. Minister of Armaments as of 1940, his plane mysteriously crashed in 1942, after he had repeatedly begged Hitler to stop the unwinnable war. Hitler appointed Speer to all of Todt's posts, including that of Minister.

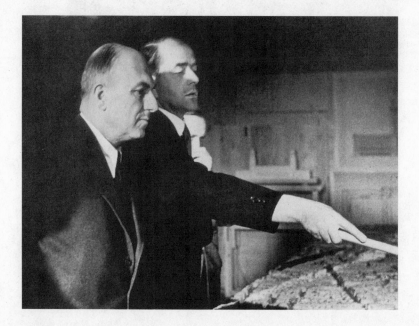

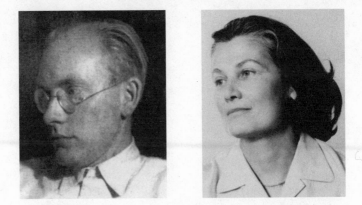

Above left: Rudolf Wolters, Speer's faithful friend and chronicler, who cared for Speer's family and writings during his twenty years in Spandau, only to break with him later, partly over Speer's criticisms of Hitler. *Above right:* Marion Riesser, a young (half Jewish) graphic designer, was Wolters's love and assistant. She transcribed tens of thousands of Speer's handwritten missives. *Below:* Annemarie Kempf, Speer's secretary until the end of the war, remained his friend and helper. For the last thirty years of her life, she devoted herself to the care of handicapped children.

Hitler during his dawn tour of Paris, three days after the signing of the armistice in June 1940, with Speer (left) and the sculptor Arno Breker. Speer's rival architect, Hermann Giesler, was with the party but, being farther away from Hitler, is missing in the photograph.

Above: Hitler gives instructions to Speer, with Martin Bormann as usual in attendance. *Below:* Berlin, February 9, 1942: the dramatic moment when Speer, newly chosen as Todt's successor for all his functions, addressed the staff, assembled in the Ministry forecourt, in a snowstorm.

Above: Speer inspects in 1943 the Atlantic Wall against an Allied invasion. Xaver Dorsch, behind him, was then regional head of the Organization Todt, and later a hostile department head in Speer's ministry. *Right:* Fritz Sauckel recruited the slave labor that Speer needed, and later was hanged for it. *Below:* Dr. Karl Brandt, a friend of Speer's, is shown here on a visit to the front. He was Hitler's physician but also was involved in dreadful medical experiments. He too was hanged.

that have arisen in German production. With the usual limitless disregard for the Slavic people, "recruiting" methods are used, a precedent for which one would have to go back to the blackest periods of the slave trade.

Although Rosenberg himself, a boring and physically unprepossessing man, frequently pleaded for better attitudes toward and conditions at work for his Slavs, this did not help him avoid the gallows at Nuremberg, as he had predicted in a postscript to the memo when forwarding it to Sauckel on December 21:

> Even if I in no way deny that the numbers of workers required by the Reich Minister for Armaments and Munitions, as well as by the agricultural economy, justify unusual and severe measures, I must, as the responsible authority for the Occupied Eastern Territories, emphatically request that, in filling the demanded quotas, measures be excluded the toleration and consequences of which will some day be held against me, my colleagues and the German people. . . .

When Speer told the Nuremberg court that he—and even Sauckel—did everything they could to see that foreign workers were properly cared for and that those he saw, including concentration camp and prisoner of war workers, appeared healthy and content with their lot, what did this mean to the court? Was it possible they believed that the true condition of these millions of men, women and eventually child workers, too, remained hidden from him? And what about Walter Rohland's *Memoirs,* published in 1978, when there was no longer any danger whatever in telling the truth? Was Rohland simply lying? Or is the answer to be found in what the great Dutch Protestant theologian W. A. Visser 't Hooft suggested, which I suspect applies to many people including—to a large degree—Speer: that "people cannot find a place in their consciousness . . . their imagination . . . or finally have the courage to face (or allow themselves to remember) unimaginable horror. It is possible," he said, "to live in a twilight between knowing and not knowing."

"I KNOW you don't believe that I didn't know about the Jews," Speer once said to me, sadly. "I don't know whether Jackson did or not, but perhaps in Nuremberg they did come to understand what my life was like. Perhaps that is what saved me."

"I think that is right," Annemarie Kempf said to me, when I mentioned what he had said. "I thought it was very clever of Flächsner to build up his case for Speer as he did. He was greatly underrated, not least by Speer. I think he did succeed in conveying to the court a picture of Speer's life in 1942 and 1943, and a sense of the pressures upon him in those years. I think he

managed to get them to see that until the moment he finally collapsed, in
January 1944, Speer worked like a demon. Whether he was in Berlin, at
Führer HQ; on his endless inspection trips to the Eastern front; to the defense constructions in the West [where forty thousand men, many of them
forced laborers, were working on the Atlantic Wall]; to factories in the Ruhr,
the North, the Ostmark [Austria], France, Czechoslovakia, Poland—his day
always started before dawn, never ended until deep in the night, which from
the very start of his ministerial appointment, he very often spent in his office
when he was in Berlin, sleeping perhaps three hours on a cot.

"He very rarely saw his family," she continued. "The Speers had a small
town house in a residential suburb, Berlin-Schlachtensee, which he had built
in 1935, but when the family stayed there, he basically never saw them—especially not the children. They would be in bed when he got home in the middle of the night, and in the morning he would practically always be out
before they were up. So finally he saw them only if they happened to be in
Berchtesgaden when he went to the Berghof for meetings with Hitler."

"The children hardly knew him," Margret Speer told me one day. She had
started this conversation—a rare occurrence—without being asked, after I
had remarked on how worried her husband had been about her the previous
evening when she ran a temperature. She was in bed with flu that day; I sat
with her while she ate some soup I had made for her. "Perhaps he did know
the four older ones a little," she said (Albert, born 1934; Hilde, 1936; Fritz,
1937; and Margret, 1938). "Before the war, he did sometimes take a day off or
something. But the two youngest [Arnold and Ernst, born in 1940 and 1943],
practically not at all. For all intents and purposes, the children didn't have a
father."

But what about those trips abroad and the skiing holidays he told me
about? I asked. Didn't the children ever go along?

She laughed out loud at my naiveté. "Good heavens, no. His 'team' went;
Eva Braun went; Magda Goebbels. Sometimes his friends."

His friends? I asked. Were they only his friends, not hers?

"You think I am unfair," she said, and added thoughtfully, "perhaps I am.
I did like some of them, but you know, except for Anni Brandt, I had hardly
any '*Du*' friends. Sometimes—" she paused. "Sometimes in, oh, bad mo-
ments, I imagined myself saying '*Sie*' to Albert." She giggled, without mirth.
"I imagined myself telephoning him"—again that rather shrill little laugh—
"Herr Speer," she mocked herself, "this is Frau Speer."

It was one of the few really revealing remarks she ever made, and the saddest, and I stopped her from talking any more that day.

•   •   •

WANTING TO KNOW if Speer discussed what he saw on his trips abroad during the war—his impressions of the people in the East, the conditions under which people worked in the Ruhr, his one visit to a concentration camp, Mauthausen—I asked Annemarie Kempf.

"When he went abroad, some of us were, of course, often with him," she answered, "and there, yes, he would describe some of the things that had impressed him when he went on his own for those drives which scared us to death. But he talked mostly about buildings then and churches he had visited; he made it sound like touristic outings. But, yes, he told us about Mauthausen that one time he went there; he said it was much better than he had feared. I especially remember that, because I remember how relieved we were. Now of course, we know that what they showed him was all fake—what they called their 'VIP treatment': a couple of good barracks with, for God's sake, vases with flowers; shiny kitchens with tasty food on the stove; immaculate shower rooms; and clean, robust-looking prisoners who declared themselves well satisfied with their imprisonment. No wonder he said it wasn't so bad. How could he know? How could anyone expect him to have known that it was all put on? That this was not food that the real slave workers ever saw and that these were 'special' prisoners, office workers and *Kapos,* who never saw the work sites where men and women keeled over dead every day and who, by telling VIP visitors that things were just dandy, were paying their dues? Now that you ask, except for one or two occasions, no, he didn't speak to us about what we now know were 'bad' things.

"Later in the war, he would talk a lot about the results of the Allied bombardments, and he would of course always dictate for the record who he had seen, what was discussed and decided. But. . . ." She paused. "I know what you are asking," she said then. "And yes, in the East, when we traveled together, he did often draw our attention to the poverty of the people, and also their extraordinary warmth; but no, with a few rare exceptions, he never talked about 'impressions' the way you mean: about having been *told,* or having *seen,* or *feeling* that wrong was being done. I don't believe anybody ever *told* him anything—they wouldn't have dared. And I doubt that he ever *saw* anything. I now think, like in Mauthausen, he would have been prevented from seeing wrong being done. *We* certainly didn't see anything. Or perhaps. . . ." She stopped. "Perhaps some of the men saw things and didn't tell us."

"Wolters?" I asked, and she nodded slowly. "Yes, yes, now I think that's possible."

Wolters wrote in his diary on May 31, 1942:

Russia-South
We leave Lemberg [Lodz] at 10 a.m . . . via Tarnopol, cross the Russian frontier at Wolotschik . . . beautiful rich hilly countryside . . . road lined

with wonderful ancient trees, just passable though full of holes. . . . All along our German OT men supervise troops of foreign workers, hard at work repairing it. Our chaps say that qualitatively the Jewish details are first-class; they apparently work double shifts, partly voluntarily. They know the alternative. . . .

"But in the final analysis, the main point about Speer was—" said Annemarie Kempf, "there was no time for him to think about anything that didn't have to do with work."

And no time to feel either? I asked.

She shook her head. "No time to feel," she said.

Speer himself was more realistic, for it wasn't only the lack of time or imaginative capacity that stopped him from thinking about the slave workers' conditions, and he admitted it frankly. "The truth is," he told me, "my responsibilities were such that my estimate of the importance of slave workers and their conditions of life would have been minimal. If one reads my ministry's *Chronik* one can see how very minor a matter were sixty thousand concentration camp workers or two million foreigners among the six million armament workers and eventually the twenty-eight million workers altogether. I'm not happy to face it," he added, "but in the context of my life then, these workers' only significance was what they could produce toward our war effort; I didn't see or think of them as human beings, as individuals."

XIV

A Blinkered Commitment

Nuremberg, June 21, 1946

MR. JUSTICE JACKSON: You . . . knew of the policy of the Nazi party and the policy of the government towards the Jews, did you not?

SPEER: I knew that the National Socialist Party was anti-Semitic, and I knew that the Jews were being evacuated from Germany.

JACKSON (citing a letter from Sauckel of March 26, 1943): "At the end of February, the Reichsführer SS, in agreement with myself and the Reichsminister for Armaments and Munitions, for reasons of state security removed from their places of work all Jews who were still working freely and not in camps, and either transferred them to a labor corps or collected them for removal." There is no question that they were put into labor units or collected for removal, is there?

SPEER: That is correct . . . [but] I must point out to you that, as far as I can remember, it was not yet a question of the Jewish problem as a whole. In the years 1941 and 1942 Jews had gone to the armament factories to do important war work and have an occupation of military importance [thanks to which] they were able to escape the evacuation which at that time was already in full swing. . . . These Jews were completely free and their families were still in their homes.

THE OBSESSION of Speer's life after Nuremberg, as I have pointed out, was Hitler's murder of the Jews. The ambivalence, however, was that while he sincerely grasped every opportunity to reiterate his sorrow and his pain at having been—the automatic formula he used—"a part of a government that committed such crimes," he was totally incapable of saying that he had known about them at the time.

Because he was so desperately preoccupied with the subject, a droplet of apparent admission at times escaped him. But it was invariably followed by a veritable torrent of denials, and often quite convincing rationales for them.

It was one of the extraordinary phenomena of Speer's trial at Nuremberg that although objections were raised to some of his statements about slave labor—though perhaps none as strenuous as might have been expected—no one, neither Justice Jackson, responsible for much of the judicial preparation for the trial, the brilliant British prosecutor Hartley Shawcross, nor the tough French and Russian prosecutors, challenged Speer either on what he said in court or on the documents about the Jews produced in evidence. We know now, even if the Nuremberg court didn't, that he was aware of the evacuation of Jews from Berlin years before. But in Nuremberg there was this one moment when he appeared to indicate wider knowledge of the intention to make Germany *judenrein* by shipping all Jews out of the country, as quoted from the record above—"It was not yet a question of the Jewish problem as a whole." Even so, no detailed questioning followed.

There were three occasions during the months of presentation of prosecution evidence which the defendants, talking afterwards to their defense counsel and the two psychiatrists who were present throughout, referred to as "black days."

The first was November 29, 1945, when the Americans, without prior warning, had shown a documentary of Nazi concentration camps as the U.S. troops had found them. Seven of the twenty-one defendants had cried afterwards; all (except Göring, who declared that all films made by the Allies were fakes) claimed to have been horrified; every single one said they had known nothing of such conditions. Speer, speaking with Dr. G. M. Gilbert, the

American psychiatrist, shortly after the session ended, said only that what he had seen confirmed his belief that the Nuremberg trials were essential.

The second "black day" was February 19, when it was the Russians' turn to show a documentary, this time of atrocities in the East. Dr. Gilbert described it as showing "acres of corpses of Russian POWs murdered or left to starve; the torture instruments, mutilated bodies, guillotines, and baskets full of heads; bodies hanging from lampposts . . . the ruins of Lidice; raped and murdered women, children with heads bashed in; the crematoria and gas chambers; the piles of clothes, the bales of women's hair at Auschwitz and Majdanek."

Göring, refusing to watch, pretended to read throughout the showing; Frank, who had been in on the planning of atrocities in Poland from the start, appeared distraught and blamed it all on Hitler and Himmler; Hans Fritzsche, a middle-rank official at the Propaganda Ministry, who was only in court because the Russians caught him and who would eventually be one of only two defendants to be acquitted, was devastated by the American film and again by the Russian one. Also talking to psychiatrist Dr. Gilbert, he said, "I have . . . the feeling . . . I am drowning in filth. . . . I'm choking in it . . . I cannot go on . . . it is a daily execution."

The third "black day" for the defendants was eight days later, on February 27, when Soviet Chief Counselor L. N. Smirnov questioned three survivors of the Nazi genocide.

The first was a survivor of the Vilna ghetto, where two SS actions, the first in the summer of 1941, the second in 1943, had killed all of this beautiful Lithuanian city's eighty thousand Jews, except six hundred of the strongest who survived in the sewers. He told the court how all babies, including his own, were killed at birth. It was always the children survivors talked about first.

The second witness, a Russian woman slave worker, though pregnant on arrival, had survived Auschwitz. She described the treatment women and children received there: babies born in camp, she said, were taken away immediately and never seen again. "In the name of all the women of Europe who became mothers in concentration camps—" she suddenly cried out, all movement in the courtroom stopping dead. "Tell us, you German mothers, where are our children now?"

Then Samuel Rajzman was called to give testimony about Treblinka, the biggest of the four extermination camps in occupied Poland. He was one of fewer than sixty people to survive this camp where more than a million men, women and children were gassed. Twenty-five years later, when I was preparing my book *Into That Darkness*, I went to see him in Montreal, where he had settled. He was a reserved and quiet man, not given to exaggeration or to externalizing his feelings—except when talking about his child, a small daughter who was killed. When he told me how that happened, how he and his wife, also subsequently gassed at Treblinka, tried to save the child and some others the day she was taken with other young children as they played in the street, and how they eventually failed, he cried. "Ever since," he said, "I cannot bear to look at any child, especially German children. I know that is wrong in me; it is not their fault, but when I was in Germany to testify, every time I saw a little girl, I thought of mine. . . ."

The tenor of the questions he was asked that day in court showed how shamefully little this court, assembled there to judge the Nazis' crimes, knew about this—the worst of all of them. He described how men, women and children, separated by sexes, had had to undress after arrival at Treblinka, and how women had to have their hair shaved off "before they went to the gas chambers."

"Why was their hair cut off?" he was asked.

"According to the ideas of the masters," Rajzman replied, "this hair was to be used in the manufacture of mattresses for German women."

The whole process between beginning to undress and walking to the gas chamber, he said, lasted eight to ten minutes for the men, and, because of the haircutting, a little longer—about fifteen minutes—for the women.

Lord Justice Lawrence, the president of the tribunal, was obviously staggered by this—as a lawyer, thinking literally, he appeared unable to believe it, his skepticism emerging clearly in the tone of his question. "Do you mean that there were only ten minutes between the time when they were taken out of the trucks and the time when they were put into the gas chambers?" he asked.

"As far as men were concerned, I am sure [the process] did not last longer than ten minutes," Rajzman answered.

"Please tell us, witness," asked the Soviet prosecuting counsel, "were the people brought to Treblinka in trucks or in trains?"

"They were nearly always brought in trains," replied Rajzman. "Only the Jews from neighboring villages and hamlets were brought in trucks. The trucks bore inscriptions, *Spedition* [Shipping or Transport] *Speer.*"

This was a most startling testimony to come upon when studying the Nuremberg transcripts after Speer's death—it is the only mention of his name in association with the extermination process in Poland.

Knowing Rajzman, it was impossible to doubt his words; moreover, they were so specific that no error in transcription or translation could account for them. Many months later in my research, I came upon some documents in the U.S. National Archives which provided some explanation. These were transcripts of pretrial examinations of Speer by members of the U.S. prosecution in Nuremberg. During one session the interrogator raised the subject of the "Legion Speer," and Speer explained that it was part of the Transport Corps of the Organization Todt.

In the course of the trial, in connection with quite different matters, Speer had in fact told the court that trucks from his Organization Todt had "operated in the East under my ministry's authority."

The answer to this riddle therefore appears to be that such trucks were indeed sometimes used for the terrible purpose Rajzman had described, though the logo may have been *Legion Speer* rather than what Rajzman remembered, *Spedition Speer*. This said, there is no reason to think that Speer would or indeed could have had any knowledge of every use the huge arsenal of transport operating under the aegis of his ministry was put to.

But the court simply bypassed the problem. It seems almost inconceivable, but not a single member of that Nuremberg court picked up this mention of a defendant's name by a dignified prosecution witness. No one asked a question of Rajzman or of Speer, or asked that it should be further investigated, or commented on it in any way.

DESCRIPTIONS of Hitler's genocide of the Jews abound; one is therefore reluctant to add to this wealth of accounts. And yet, the apparent void in Speer's consciousness of the violence that was being enacted upon the conquered people of the East, apart from his constant awareness of the gassings in Poland, can only be evaluated in the context of the developing events.

By the beginning of winter 1942, Europe had become an ocean of death. Already Barbarossa had cost the German army 371,000 dead and (according to a Russian document found by the advancing Germans) the Soviets more than 11 million dead, injured and missing.

A few months later, Stalingrad was to demand the lives of another 200,000 German soldiers. In addition, of the 91,000 prisoners taken there by the Soviets, fewer than 6,000 would eventually return to Germany, years after the war was over. But the toll among Soviet prisoners of war in German hands was even worse. By mid-year 1942, 3 million Russian POWs, out of the 4 million the Germans had captured in 1941, had died of exposure and starvation in atrocious open compounds.

And then, of course, there were the "civilians" who had come into Nazi hands in the East. According to the Nazis' own figures (Heydrich's statistics and the reports of the Einsatzgruppen commanders), about a million Soviet Jews and non-Jews, including hundreds of thousands of Balts, had been shot by the end of 1941. Ten months later, by the onset of winter 1942, an additional 14,257 Soviet "partisans" and 363,211 Soviet Jews were reported as having been subjected to *Sonderbehandlung*—special treatment, that is, killed—in Russia.

In December 1941, the gassing operations were started in Chelmno (Kulmhof), the first of the four extermination centers of the Aktion Reinhard which the Nazis set up within the subsequent five months in isolated localities in occupied Poland, for the sole purpose of killing the Jews of Europe. The killing of 100,000 Jews in gas vans there (which had previously been used for killing comparatively small numbers of Jewish Serbs) showed insurmountable difficulties when applied to large numbers. One alternative method, gas chambers using diesel exhaust fumes for the killing, was chosen for the other three planned extermination camps of the Aktion Reinhard. The use of Zyklon B cyanide gas was a parallel technique, used only later in the gas chambers of Auschwitz, and on a limited scale in Majdanek, both of which were primarily labor camps, with added extermination facilities.

By the end of October 1942, when Chelmno had been closed, these three Aktion Reinhard installations, all within a 150-kilometer radius of Lublin (Belsec as of March; Sobibor as of May; and Treblinka, the largest, as of June), had already eliminated with terrifying efficiency nearly three-quarters of a million men, women and children. By Christmas, it would be more than a million.

This assembly-line genocide—primarily of the Jews*—was a unique phenomenon in the world's history of cruelty and violence, even within the Nazis' monstrous overall program for murder. The huge losses in human lives from many other causes on both sides were terrible, but somehow conventional. The gas chambers remain unique, an unbearable memory of what human beings can do to other human beings.

The enormous historical, literary and dramatic material produced over nearly half a century about the Final Solution has created a kind of resistance. But it would be perilous if we allowed this "compassion fatigue" to make us forget the singularity of this horror. As all surviving reports demonstrate, and Himmler confirmed in some of his terrible speeches late in the war, *two-thirds* of the victims were women and children. That, probably more than anything else, is the origin of the Germans'—and Speer's—"moral sore" I spoke of in an earlier chapter, and the essence of the trauma, not only for Jews and Germans, but for us all. It is equally important to record, however, that it was at least in part the fervor of West Germany's reaction to this horror after the war which restored morality and gave rise to the renaissance of

---

*It must not be forgotten that the same methods were applied to one other group of men, women and children from both Western and Eastern Europe: two hundred thousand Gypsies, or Romanies, who died in the same concentration and extermination camps as the Jews, but in whose memory only a few voices have been raised.

civic responsibility, establishing West Germany as one of the most stable democracies in Europe and, for well over forty years, as the world's leading refuge for the persecuted and the poor.

In spite of these positive reactions, there has been an extraordinary failure for almost fifty years now, both in Germany and in the rest of the world, to consider the genocide of European Jewry in its whole context. By some curious process of psychological selectivity, the two huge acts of mass murder, in Russia by shooting and in Poland by gassing, until recently have been treated as separate and different phenomena. As a result, for most of the world, including most Jews, the term "Final Solution" has mainly or entirely been identified with the gas chambers in occupied Poland or, even more narrowly, those in Auschwitz. For almost half a century, the murder by shooting of between one and a half million and two million Jews in the occupied Soviet territories has somehow been treated differently. Grotesquely, more often than not, these murders by shooting have been neatly classified as "acts of war," an extraordinary misconstruction of history which plays straight into the hands of the so-called revisionists, who in the pursuit of their nationalist political goals must somehow whitewash Hitler. Realizing that the gas-chamber murders have made him historically unacceptable, they find themselves driven to pretend these never happened, that the gas chambers never existed.

Various arguments about the number of Jewish dead, by no means restricted to neo-Nazis or revisionists, stem primarily from a misunderstanding of how the figure was arrived at. True enough, six million people could not have been gassed in the six extermination camps (four of the Aktion Reinhard in Poland, plus Auschwitz and Majdanek) in the comparatively short time they existed. Even adding those who died in Germany's concentration and forced labor camps, from epidemics, overwork and starvation, could hardly achieve that number.

But what finally explains—or approximates—this six million figure, which has so often been strenuously denied or doubted (and which, according to Russian experts, may have to be increased by as much as an additional million once precise Russian figures become available), is the huge number of people the Nazis shot in Russia and the Baltics.

ACCORDING TO the report titled "The Final Solution of the European Jewish Question," submitted to Himmler on March 23, 1943, by Richard Korherr, his Inspector for Statistics, there were, in 1939, 10,500,000 Jews on the European Continent. Of these, 4,600,000 lived in the Soviet Union and 3,300,000 in Poland. In the preface to his sixteen-page analysis, a slightly edited copy of which survived, Korherr says that his figures were accurate as of January 18, 1943, and should be seen merely as a preliminary account. He suggested, in the euphemistic terms used by the Nazi bureaucrats when dealing with this touchy subject:

> It would perhaps be best to supplement the attached with a meticulously worked-out final and consolidated report on the numerical development of Jewry to be undertaken in stages, say, on July 1, October 1, and December 1, 1943. . . .

As Korherr confirmed when I spoke to him in 1977 during my research into David Irving's book, *Hitler's War,* he and his SS masters knew by autumn 1942, when he was preparing his report, that by the end of 1943 the main part of "the work" (as he called the gassing of the Jews) would be completed.

However eager most Germans were to deny any possible knowledge of the worst actions, I have found that direct participants in these murders—and Korherr ranks high among them—were extremely eager to convince me of the opposite, that "everyone knew about the gassings of the Jews." Korherr, true to form, said bitterly that by the time he was preparing his report, "Everybody in Germany knew about the gassings. Good heavens," he exclaimed, "the sparrows were whistling it from the rooftops. Let no one tell you differently."

This was of course not true. At that point, almost no ordinary people in Germany knew of the *gassings* (as opposed to the widespread knowledge in the German army of the shootings). Hardly anyone outside the minute inner circle of administrators and perpetrators, local inhabitants in the Polish villages who knew better than to talk and, as we will see, a few very special men who tried very hard to spread the news but failed, knew about the gas chambers in occupied Poland.

This seems of course unbelievable when one reads Korherr's devastating figures: 2,419,656 European and Eastern Jews had so far been "evacuated," he told Himmler in his January 1943 report. This figure is made up of two categories: "Total evacuations (including Theresienstadt and *Sonderbehandlung*), 1,873,549; or without Theresienstadt, 1,786,356. Further: evacuation from the Russian territories and the Baltics since the start of the campaign in the East, 633,300."

The first total mentioned above excludes the Theresienstadt figures, because it was the Nazis' "model ghetto" in Czechoslovakia, set up as a transit camp for Czech Jews on the way East, and for aged members of the German Jewish elite, considered potentially useful for purposes of "sale" or exchange. By the end of the war, the camp register showed 109,126 entries, 16,000 deaths in the camp and 43,879 "evacuated East."

But the euphemism Korherr used—*Sonderbehandlung* (shooting in Russia and gassing in Poland)—was no longer considered sufficiently innocuous, and Himmler's instructions as to changes in the text were issued on April 10. But basically he was satisfied with the report, as he wrote on April 9, 1943, in disgustingly gross terms to Ernst Kaltenbrunner, who had succeeded Heydrich as Chief of Security Police and SD:

Reichsführer SS Field HQ   April 9, 1943
Top Secret!

To the Chief of the Security Police and SD Berlin:
I have received the Inspector of Statistics' report on the Final Solution of the Jewish Question.
I consider this report well executed for purposes of camouflage and potentially useful for later times.
For the moment, it can neither be published nor can anyone [outside the restricted circle] be allowed sight of it.
The most important [matter] for me remains that whatever remains of Jews is shipped East. All I want to be told as of now by the Security Police, very briefly, is what has been shipped and what, at any point, is still left of Jews.

HH

The following day, Obersturmbannführer (Lieutenant Colonel) Rudolf Brandt, soon to be promoted to Lieutenant General by his grateful chief, passed on to Korherr Himmler's instructions which, as he was to testify before being hanged in Landsberg in 1948, he had received orally:

Field HQ Reichsführer SS
Personal Staff   April 10, 1943

To the Inspector for Statistics
Pg [Party Member] Korherr
Berlin
The Reichsführer SS has received your report about the Final Solution of the European Jewish Question. His instruction is that the word *Sonderbehandlung* is to be eliminated from the report. Thus page 9, point 4, is to be amended to read as follows:
Transport of Jews from the Eastern Provinces to the Russian East: . . .
Sluiced through the camps in the General Government: . . .
Through the camps in the Warthegau: . . .
No other wording is permitted. I am returning the copy already initialed by the Reichsführer SS, which you will be good enough to amend as directed and return.

[Brandt]
SS-Obersturmbannführer

From a historical point of view, it is lucky that these two letters exist. For only two versions of the Korherr report survive: one is a copy of his sixteen-page original, with page 9 amended as ordered, i.e., "sluiced through" replacing *Sonderbehandlung*. The other is a seven-page digest of the report, which Korherr was ordered to prepare for Hitler.

These letters, in contradiction to Korherr's remark about widely available knowledge, demonstrate the determination of the Nazis to keep these particular murders hidden; Himmler's mention of "for purposes of camouflage" indicates that the intention may well have been to extend this secrecy indefinitely.

Certainly, for official references to the subject—if eventually not, as will be shown, for the military and political elite—they maintained to the end the camouflage of euphemisms; the terms "evacuation" and "resettlement," endlessly quoted later by apologists for Hitler, proved all the more effective as so many hundreds of thousands of men, women and children apart from Jews—German settlers, East European slave laborers and eventually, too, Germans fleeing their destroyed houses and cities—were indeed being shipped, evacuated and resettled, thereby lending some apparent credibility to the contemporary and postwar claims about the essential similarity between these consequences of war and the transports of Jews.

Having said what the majority of Germans did *not* know, it is necessary to look at what *was* known, in order to consider what Speer might or should have known. At least a dozen high-ranking German officers of the General Staff and an even greater number of top Nazi officials knew of the plans as early as the spring of 1941. (On April 2, 1941, for example, Alfred Rosenberg noted in his diary after a two-hour private conversation with Hitler that the discussion had turned on plans ". . . which I do not wish to record on paper but will never forget.") There was the three-week SS orientation course in Pretzsch near Leipzig in May 1941, at the end of which a number of officers who had been appointed leaders of the Einsatzgruppen destined for Barbarossa, horrified by what they learned, managed to get themselves transferred. And of course, barely two months later, in Russia, while some courageous, decent men (such as Klaus von Bismarck's regiment) refused to obey Hitler's *Kommissar Befehl*, many thousands of ordinary German soldiers and officers not only knew about but took part in the murders there.

Ever since the end of World War II, a clear distinction has been created between the crimes committed by Himmler's SS and the "war actions" taken in the East by German soldiers. This image of unsuspecting German soldiers fighting bitter battles at the front while the SS and its Einsatzgruppen, unbeknownst to them, committed mass murder in their footsteps, was determinedly fought for at Nuremberg, not only by the military but also by others, including Speer. The generals accused at Nuremberg admitted culpability with regard to the *Kommissar Befehl* (and Hitler's later Commando Order which required the German armed forces to execute Allied commandos without trial). Keitel, who was sentenced to death by hanging, died at least partly for this crime. But all of them denied any association with, knowledge of or guilt for the murder of the Jews which began in that fateful last week of June 1941 in German-occupied Lithuania and swiftly spread throughout the Baltics, Belorussia and the Ukraine. That, they stoutly insisted, was an SS affair, nothing to do with the Wehrmacht.

By early 1942, subsequent to Speer's appointment, the second stage of what was now assembly-line killings had begun. Although there is ample confirmation of the Nazis' attempts at dissimulating their actions, there is also considerable proof of official knowledge.

First of all, there are the fourteen participants of Heydrich's organizational Wannsee Conference in January 1942, two of whom (Georg Leibbrandt of the Ministry for the Occupied Eastern Territories, and State Secretary Friedrich Kritzinger of the Reich Chancellery), interrogated in 1947 by U.S. Special Prosecutor Kempner, uneasily demonstrated how thoroughly informed they were of the Jews' fate. (Their evidence, painstakingly elicited by Kempner, disproves the claims, still made by Hitler apologists, that Wannsee had nothing to do with genocide.)

KEMPNER: Did you have occasion to go to Wannsee . . . to a conference organized by the RSHA?

LEIBBRANDT: Yes, they did hold some conference there, a luncheon. I think Heydrich hosted it, as far as I can remember.

KEMPNER: What was discussed there?

LEIBBRANDT: As far as I know, all kinds of things. . . . The whole war in the East was discussed.

KEMPNER: What did that have to do with Heydrich? [Leibbrandt remained silent.] Did it also have something to do with Jews?

LEIBBRANDT: That was probably also discussed.

KEMPNER: The truth is, is it not, that you were taking part in a decisive meeting about the Final Solution of the Jewish Question? I have the minutes.

LEIBBRANDT: About the Final Solution of the Jewish Question?

KEMPNER: Yes; if you will read the second line in this document of January 20, 1942, what do you see?

LEIBBRANDT: My name. . . . It was a routine discussion, without knowing precisely what it was all about, and then they wrote minutes.

KEMPNER: What it was, was a coordination of the project, laying down the role for each Ministry, was it not?

LEIBBRANDT: Impossible.

KEMPNER: Don't you still get cold shudders running down your spine when you think back on this conference? Were you appalled or not?

LEIBBRANDT: . . . You can say I was.

KEMPNER: . . . Did you tell anyone of your shock?

LEIBBRANDT: I told the Minister [Rosenberg] at the first opportunity that I didn't agree with this madness and that the proposals . . . were totally unacceptable.

KEMPNER: Then why didn't you want to recall the conference? Did you want to block it from your mind? . . . You are an intelligent man: reflect back on the discussion, the plan for murder, and the men you talked with. . . . Not one of you stood up and said "Here I am; I can't agree to this." Am I right? [Leibbrandt remained silent.]

Not long afterwards, on March 11, 1947, Friedrich Kritzinger, less restrained or more courageous, provided Kempner with detailed information on the conference. He died a few months later.

We know from Goebbels's diary entry on March 27, 1942, that at least by then, if not before (he gives no precise indication of when their relevant meeting had taken place), Hitler had informed him of the Aktion Reinhard's brief in Poland. He demonstrates here not only his own complete knowledge, as of then, of the genocide of the Jews, but Hitler's responsibility for this "radical solution."

Beginning with Lublin [he wrote], the Jews are now being removed from the General Government, to the East. . . . [By "East" he means the short distance between Lublin, the headquarters of the Aktion Reinhard, and the camps a few dozen kilometers "east" of the city for which the transports were destined—Treblinka, Sobibor and Belsec.] The procedure employed here, not to be described [on paper], is pretty barbaric; there won't be much left of the Jews. In general one can say that only 40 percent can be put to work; 60 percent of them will have to be liquidated. The former Gauleiter of Vienna [Odilo Globocnik], who is carrying out this action, is doing his best to make the procedure as inconspicuous as possible. The punishment the Jews are being subjected to, though barbaric, is entirely deserved. The Führer's prophecy [of September 1939] is being realized in the most dreadful way. One can't allow oneself to be ruled by sentimentality in these things. If we didn't act against them, the Jews would destroy us.

No other government, and no other regime, was able to solve this problem. Again it is the Führer who is the pioneer and constant champion of a radical solution now made possible by circumstances and thus inevitable. Thank God the war offers us possibilities which would have been barred to us in peacetime. These we must now use. As the ghettos of the General

Government are emptied, they will be refilled with Jews removed from the Reich, the process then being repeated. . . .

A few days before Goebbels made this entry, Hitler, on Speer's suggestion, had made a vitally important new appointment. Within weeks of becoming Minister of Armaments, Speer had become aware that one of his gravest problems in the East was transportation, and that the Minister for Transport, Julius Dorpmüller, although a particularly likeable man, was not equal to the task.

Months before, in Dnepropetrovsk, Speer's attention had been drawn to Theodor Ganzenmüller, a young railway official who was showing great ingenuity in overcoming the appalling railway problems there. Later, he had talked with him at length in Berlin.

"I suggested to Hitler in March that he should gently ease Dorpmüller sideways and let Ganzenmüller become the de facto head of the railways. I told him he was the right man for the job, and he believed me," Speer told me. "The formalities took a while, but on May 25 he officially named Ganzenmüller Undersecretary of State for Transport. At the same time, to give the young man the necessary immediate support, he temporarily made Milch and me traffic czars."

In relation to what Speer would know or not know, this seemed a very significant development. Ganzenmüller was his protégé; rail transport for armaments for the front was a top priority for Speer; the surviving records, including Wolters's *Chronik,* show that the two men worked together closely, meeting several times a week, sometimes daily.

By that time about ten thousand people a day were being shipped to the two extermination camps then functioning, Belsec and Sobibor. (Chelmno had been closed, and Treblinka was ready two months later.)

On July 28, 1942, twelve days after receiving an urgent telephone enquiry from Himmler's top aide, SS General (Obergruppenführer) Karl Wolff, Ganzenmüller replied with a letter which, if a war crime prosecution against him could have been completed, might have proved fatal:

> With reference to our telephone conversation on July 16, I am able to inform you that since July 22 one train a day, with 5,000 Jews, is going from Warsaw via Malkinia to Treblinka; and also two trains a week with 5,000 Jews from Przemysl to Belsec. . . .

Wolff's reply came two weeks later:

> My warm thanks, also in the Reichsführer SS's name, for your letter of July 28. I was especially delighted to learn from you that already for a fortnight there has been a daily train, taking 5,000 of the Chosen People to

Treblinka, thus enabling us to carry out this movement of populations with increasing tempo. . . .

Robert Kempner, whom I visited repeatedly during the 1980s, was very bitter about Ganzenmüller. "We felt very chuffed when finally, years after the war, we managed to get Ganzenmüller into court in Essen," he told me when we talked about that infamous exchange of letters. "But it was a short-lived triumph. Of course he said at once that he had been a mere cog in the wheels and had only obeyed orders.

" 'Really?' I said. 'Are you saying that you, as the top executive of one of the most important government ministries, blindly obeyed every and any order? Meaning that, although responsible for all railways, all trains, all stations and personnel, you were totally unaware of the purpose for which your trains were used, and what 'cargo' they contained?' He gulped a convincing 'Oh, oh!' clutching the area where most people have a heart. His defense counsel shot up, demanded a doctor who said he had a heart attack, and that was that. The case was over. The court in its so-called compassion decided he was unfit to plead: a man guilty as sin, who, as you know is alive, kicking and no doubt laughing at the lot of us to this day. A catastrophe for justice."

Speer knew that I was familiar with the Ganzenmüller-Wolff correspondence, which I had used in *Into That Darkness*. "But if you were the czar in charge of the Eastern railway system when all that was happening? . . ." I asked him, leaving the question hanging in the air.

"Only for about a month," he said at once. "After that, Ganzenmüller no longer needed any propping up. Nonetheless," he went on, "I asked myself that very question long before I met you, after reading in your book where the Polish stationmaster of Treblinka village actually provides authentic figures of the numbers of people transported on those trains. I figured it out. We were responsible during those weeks for 145,000 rolling stock, of which I suppose one might say 2,000 were used to transport these victims. Do you feel it is unreasonable to say that the man in charge in Berlin would not have been aware of the details of 2,000 railway cars out of 145,000?"

I had not in fact supposed that as traffic czars he and Milch would or could know any details, but rather that in general terms he might have learned then of the nature of this "movement of populations," not least from Ganzenmüller, who for the next three years was one of his closest collaborators. What surprised me, however, was that having read the figures in my book before he ever met me, he would have gone to the trouble to work out an answer to a question he couldn't possibly know anyone would ever put to him.

Wolff, Himmler's Chief of Staff, was like Ganzenmüller a "catastrophe for justice." A very intelligent man with charm and suave manners, he was surprisingly successful in his efforts to represent himself to the Allies, and later to some gullible journalists and pseudohistorians, as innocent and indeed ignorant of all the horrors. And yet, there could hardly have been anyone who knew more about the horrors than Himmler's closest adjutant, a fact which was confirmed even before his exchange of letters with Ganzenmüller, when in mid-April 1942 he received a letter from SS Colonel (Standartenführer) Harald Turner, from Belgrade.

After thanking Wolff for his help in a dispute between the Wehrmacht and the SS, he "took the liberty to use the occasion" to remind him of a letter he had addressed to Himmler on January 15 and to which he had not yet had a reply. Turner wrote,

I did not want to press the Reichsführer SS . . . as I know that such matters require time. But as I am aware of your interest in these matters, and as the problem could become acute very soon, I thought I would draw your attention to it now. . . .
[His "problem" was to obtain, through Himmler's intervention, the release of Jewish Serbian POWs from the German army camps where they were under the protection of the Geneva Convention. In order to kill them, he needed them under his control.]
Already several months ago, I had whatever Jews were available in this area shot, and Jewish females and children concentrated in one camp. With the help of the SD, I obtained a "delousing car" [Turner's quotes: the SS euphemism for "gas van"] with the help of which the camp will now be completely cleared in between two and four weeks. . . . We will then reach the point when, whether we like it or not, the [Serbian] Jewish officers who are at present under the protection of the Geneva Convention in POW camps will discover that their relatives no longer exist, which could conceivably lead to complications.
Of course, if those in question are released, and thus under our authority, this matter will be settled once and for all by making sure that their liberty will only be momentary, lasting no longer than that of their racial brethren. . . .

Wolff, already promoted to SS General in 1943, was put in command of the SS troops in northern Italy in 1944. With Himmler's agreement he entered into early negotiations with Allen Dulles, the amazed and delighted OSS head in Switzerland, for their surrender. Without much difficulty he persuaded Dulles to accept him as a man of honor. When Wolff was tried after the war, he served only a very short prison sentence. In 1966, however, he was tried again, largely on the basis of the Ganzenmüller correspondence, for complicity in the Treblinka murders, and was sentenced to fifteen years, of which he served five. The formerly occupied countries of southern and Eastern Europe were not as forgiving as the Americans, and Turner was sentenced to death and hanged in Belgrade in March 1947.

Speer had known Wolff well: "It was inevitable—he was Himmler's liaison officer with Hitler." Three more of Speer's wide circle of acquaintances—none of them dishonorable men—recalled later having early knowledge of horrors in the East. As early as October 1941, Walter Frentz, for whom Speer, two years earlier, had obtained the plum assignment of movie cameraman at Führer HQ, apparently found himself the witness of a mass execution while traveling to Minsk with Himmler, and caught it on film. Back at HQ he consulted Hitler's aide Rudolf Schmundt, who advised him to destroy the film and "not to poke his nose into matters that did not concern him."

Almost a year later, in October 1942, Nicolaus von Below became involved in a similar experience when a young lieutenant of the communication corps sought him out at Hitler's HQ in Vinnitsa, in the Ukraine. "He told me," Below writes in his memoirs, "that while working on a cable transfer nearby, he had come upon a troop of SS who, standing in a trench, were shooting men and women. He said he had been so horrified by this, he felt he had to report it."

The naiveté of Below's reaction shows his own ignorance of the true situation. He writes that he went to discuss the matter with (of all people!) Himmler's then liaison officer at HQ, Wolff. "I asked him to investigate and get back to me. When, not having heard from him, I got in touch with him again a few days later, he gave me a very ambiguous answer, pointing to probable sabotage acts in those areas. But he also asked me to refrain from further enquiries. . . ."

In a recent documentary film, *The Restless Conscience: Resistance to Hitler Within Germany, 1933–1945,* screened on public television in New York on December 30, 1992, Captain Axel von dem Bussche, a Wehrmacht career officer, gave an almost identical description of a murder action he witnessed near Vinnitsa fifty years ago.

Von dem Bussche's disgust at what he had seen led him to join—like several other officers from his regiment—the army resistance to Hitler which led finally to the July 20, 1944, assassination attempt by Claus von Stauffenberg. Already in October 1943, von dem Bussche had volunteered to set off a bomb which would kill Hitler at the cost of his own life. This was one of many attempts which narrowly failed through last-minute changes of Hitler's schedule.

Another of Speer's later friends, the already mentioned General Adolf Galland, Nazi Germany's greatest fighter pilot, told me in 1987 about something he had experienced. I had asked him if he thought Speer knew about the extermination of the Jews, or was it possible that he didn't?

"Whether it was possible, I can't say, but likely, no," he replied. "Everybody knew about concentration camps. Speer, too, of course—after all, that was where many of his foreign workers were kept. But the Jews, gassings, extermination—no, I never knew that. The first indication I had, which made me think seriously of genocide," he said, after a moment's thought, "was while flying over Russia, around March 1942, with Himmler and Speer—anyway, the Minister of Armaments. That was already Speer, wasn't it, in March 1942? Anyway, Himmler pointed down where we could see a lot of people moving about, and he said, 'Last year we had decided to kill them all—this year we need them for the *Rüstung* [armament production].' That remark jolted me. I thought, what does he mean '*kill* them all'? And of course, if it was Speer who was there with us, then he heard that too."

Speer, like Galland, might have become generally suspicious through such events, but he could hardly have had any inkling of the most dramatic of all the disclosures about the gassings. This was given on August 21, 1942, on the Warsaw-Berlin overnight express to a young Swedish diplomat, Goran von Otter, by a tortured young SS officer, Obersturmführer (Lieutenant) Kurt Gerstein, who had that week witnessed the gassings in two camps. He would later become the central figure of a world-famous play and several fine books.

Baron von Otter was seventy-six when I met him in Paris in 1981. He was to appear as a witness in a libel case against French revisionist Robert Faurisson, who claimed that Kurt Gerstein was a liar and that there had been no gas chamber murders of Jews by the Nazis. It became clear, as we talked, that his experience with Gerstein had marked this distinguished Swede for life.

Otter had already been in the Swedish Foreign Service for seven years, stationed in Vienna and Budapest, when he was posted as First Secretary to the Swedish Legation in Berlin in 1939, where he stayed for five years.

"I was very interested indeed in Speer during the war," he said, and added bitterly, "as you know, my country had frequent cause to communicate with his ministry [Sweden supplied steel to Germany]. The whole Berlin diplomatic community, which by 1942 was not so large, was interested in Speer when it became known what he was achieving at his ministry. He was, you know, quite stupendously effective."

He didn't remember seeing Speer at any party German functionaries attended; he couldn't recall anybody in the diplomatic community mentioning having met him, and he had certainly never met him himself. "You asked me whether Speer could have heard about what Gerstein saw and what he told me," he continued. "You know, it was very, very dangerous knowledge for Germans. . . . As Gerstein told me himself later, he did talk about it. But those he spoke to in Berlin were mostly, or perhaps entirely, members of Christian groups he had always been in touch with. You ask about Speer: I have to say that unless Speer shared the very special commitment of that very special group—and I cannot believe he would have—no, I don't think he could have heard about Gerstein. For them, you see, Speer would have been"—he shook his head—"exceptionally dangerous."

Gerstein's life is perhaps the most significant testimonial to the presence of moral convictions and heroism in the midst of the Nazi monstrosities. It is almost impossible to convey the complexity of his personality, or the conflicts which bedeviled him—conflicts between his love of his country (which led him to become a member of the Nazi Party in 1933) and his passionate Christian ethics which, when he heard rumors of monstrous, officially condoned crimes—euthanasia—finally induced him in 1940 to apply to join the SS to try to find out the truth. Amazingly, although he had twice been arrested for anti-Nazi statements and spent short periods in concentration camps, he was immediately accepted. Thereby (as the Protestant Pastor Otto Wehr, a friend of his for many years, would testify in 1949 at the Doctors' Trials in Nuremberg) he entered "the realm of the demon."

As Speer had said when he was telling me about joining the party, the Nazis desperately needed university graduates to join their ranks. Thanks to Gerstein's degrees in engineering, mining and medicine, he rose swiftly in the hierarchy and, in January 1942, was put in charge of the SS Sanitation Service, which included the control and distribution of poisonous substances "for hygienic purposes."

In this capacity this devout Christian, then thirty-seven, whose only motivation in joining the SS was to discover and eventually reveal its members' crimes, found himself drawn into the very heart of the crimes. He was entrusted with Nazi Germany's darkest secret in 1942 in Lublin, where he had been ordered to deliver one hundred kilograms of Zyklon B, which had become the favored means of gassing in Auschwitz and Majdanek. (He promptly sabotaged the shipment and declared it defective, as he did repeatedly over the subsequent years.) He was also taken to see gassing actions in two other camps, Belsec and Treblinka, where the killing was done not by Zyklon B but by diesel fumes from old tank engines.

The next day, August 21, 1942, in the corridor of the overcrowded night express train to Berlin, Gerstein met the tall young Swedish diplomat. Otter had been in Warsaw to visit four Swedish businessmen, who had been imprisoned by the Germans for acting as couriers for the Polish resistance. Like

Gerstein, he had no reserved seat and was going to have to spend the night sitting on his suitcase.

"The train left Warsaw late in the afternoon," Otter told me that day in Paris. "I noticed that this SS officer kept darting looks at me. He was pale, looked very nervous, very tense. We didn't speak, but I was curious about him; it was obvious he wanted to talk to me. I wasn't expecting anything extraordinary." He smiled briefly. "Perhaps I just thought it might be a little feather in my cap if I got some information from an SS."

Less than an hour from Warsaw, the train stopped in open country. "We both got down to get a breath of air. I offered him a cigarette. He refused but immediately whispered, 'There is something terrible I have to report. Can I come and see you at the legation?' I realized then that he must have asked the conductor who I was.

"I said, 'Why not now, on the train?' He nodded, but even before we got back on he said, 'I saw something dreadful. . . .' It was strange—my immediate reaction was to say, 'Is it the Jews?' And he answered, 'Yes, it is—I saw more than ten thousand die yesterday.' "

Otter said that it had been known in Sweden since the beginning of 1942 that Jews were being systematically murdered. Reports had come from German military sources, probably Wehrmacht people who had seen the Einsatzgruppen at work in Russia. Some courageous Swedish newspapers, he said, had tried to publish this but, while not officially censored, had found such attempts frustrated by sudden distribution problems. "So you see," he said, "it must have been in the back of my mind."

Back on the train, the two men settled down to talk. "At the beginning, the words tumbled out of him," said Otter. "He looked desperate, almost ill. After a while, he became more composed."

Later, after Gerstein had finished the awful description of how he had watched thousands taken to the gas chambers in Belsec and Treblinka, he told Otter that it was all part of an official policy which had been decided at Wannsee.

Otter had not known about the Wannsee Conference at that time. "Gerstein hadn't attended it, but he certainly knew all about it," he said. "Even before this, I had asked to see what papers he had, and he showed me his identity card, some papers mentioning Zyklon B crystals, some technical designs, and he drew a sketch of Belsec for me."

They talked for almost six hours. "Finally he said that what he wanted me to do was to get word to the British of what was happening. They could then, he thought, drop leaflets over Germany. He was sure that once the German people knew what was being done in their name, they would not stand for it.

And he told me he was going to visit the Papal Nuncio in Berlin and the Swiss legation." Later Otter heard that the Nuncio had refused to see Gerstein, because he had come in SS uniform, and that the Swiss had also rejected his approaches.

At first Otter, too, had not believed him. "It was all so dreadful, so unbelievably awful," he said, his own face, as he told his story now, as strained, as pale as I imagined Gerstein's to have been that night. "But in the end, with all the details, and, yes, the way he looked, the way he suffered—he spoke, you know, very much as a Christian—yes, I believed him."

At Otter's request, Gerstein gave him several references, including the anti-Nazi pastors Otto Dibelius and Martin Niemöller, who was in a concentration camp. "Obviously I could not meet Niemöller until much later," said Otter, "but Dibelius, whom I saw almost as soon as I got back to Berlin, immediately and unreservedly guaranteed Gerstein's integrity."

Otter immediately reported the conversation to his minister in Berlin. "I was off shortly on leave, to Stockholm, and he advised me, rather than putting it on paper, to report directly to the Foreign Ministry. I did so, a few days later, to the head of the Political Department. He said it was difficult," Otter said sadly. "Sweden was in a very difficult position, the Germans on one side, Russia on the other. Also, although this was the first precise, detailed and firsthand report, as I told you, the *fact* that Jews were being killed was already known—not only to us but to the Allies and the Vatican. So . . ." He stopped. "Well, after enumerating all the problems, he told me to go away and forget it, enjoy my holiday, leave it with him. He would do the necessary. Later— much later—I found out he did nothing. And I . . . I . . ." He turned away from me for a moment. "I went to have my holiday. . . ." His face when he looked up was ravaged.

A few weeks later—"It may even have been months," he said—back in Berlin, he met Gerstein again briefly. "One day when I came out of the Legation, I heard 'Psst, psst' from across the street, and there he was, hiding behind some bushes in the Tiergarten. We walked in the park for about fifteen minutes. He looked dreadful, and he was very depressed. This is when he told me about his failure to see the Nuncio and the Swiss minister, and he asked me what I had done. I told him, but even as I spoke, I wished—no, I knew— it should have been more. Even then I knew that for me it was the beginning of a trauma that might never end.

"When VE-day came at last, I wondered what I could do. I realized that as an SS officer, involved, yes, even implicated—however unwillingly—in this terrible crime, he could be in great difficulties."

He paused for a long time, and then he described his efforts to help a man in Germany who at almost unimaginable personal risk had tried, actively and from the start, to stop Hitler's genocide. Otter had finally decided that his best means of getting the information to the new War Crimes Commission, just set up in London, would be via a close friend at the Swedish Embassy there. "It took me two months to come to that decision," he said heavily. He had no idea that Gerstein had given himself up to the French in late April, or that after a few weeks of open detention in a pleasant hotel in Rottweil, Germany, his fortunes radically changed when he was sent to the Cherche Midi prison in Paris. There, after severe questioning over many days, he was charged, according to "Order No. 1171," with "murder and complicity to murder during his service as SS *Oberscharführer* [*sic*]. . . ." (He was actually an SS Lieutenant, that is, Obersturmführer.)

"I wrote my friend a long letter on July 25," he said, "giving him all the details of what Gerstein had tried to do to save the Jews." Later he learned that Gerstein, apparently losing all hope after being charged as a war criminal, had killed himself two days before, on July 23.

I wondered what more could have been done for him. "How can one know?" he said. "It *was* a most difficult and ambiguous case, and feelings ran very high then. For the French, who themselves had so much to regret, so much to hide, he was a tremendous catch. The first people who held him in Germany that April, both the French and the Americans, were part of the fighting troops; they had a different attitude. But once he got into the hands of the police, the political bureaucracy in Paris. . . ." He shook his head. "It is almost unimaginable: that man in a Paris prison, alone, with no one around who could possibly understand either him or the extraordinary circumstances under which he acted. It was hopeless."

Again he shook his head. "I can't forgive myself for that. I could have helped. I shall regret to the end of my life not to have written my letter earlier. If I had, perhaps he would not have died. . . ."

BY THE TIME Gerstein communicated his desperate knowledge to Otter, virtually the same information had become available to the Allies through another rare act of courage and moral conviction by a German. However, virtually duplicating the reluctance of the Swedes to pass on the tragic information, here, too, the informants came up against appalling manifestations of prejudice, racism, indifference and economic self-interest on the part of individuals in the highest places in the governments of the United States and Britain and in the Vatican.*

In July 1942 Dr. Gerhardt Riegner, a brilliant young German refugee law-

---

*This story has been told fully by Arthur Morse in his book, *While Six Million Died;* by Walter Laqueur and Richard Breitman in their book, *Breaking the Silence;* and in my own *Into That Darkness.*

yer working as legal counsel for the World Jewish Congress in Geneva, heard from an incontrovertible source that a leading German industrialist with access to Hitler's HQ had learned that Hitler, many months earlier, had ordered the physical annihilation of all Jews in "countries under German control." In cables to Washington and London, Riegner said it was planned, according to the German informant, that "from three and a half to four million, excluding Jews in the Soviet Union, should after deportation and concentration in [the] East be exterminated at one blow to resolve once and for all the Jewish question in Europe."

Although the slight exaggeration "at one blow" unfortunately exacerbated the credibility problem Riegner encountered, the mention of "excluding the Jews in the Soviet Union" should have convinced the recipients of the astonishing extent of the German informant's knowledge. The fact that the Nazis by this time considered the Soviet Jews under their control as having been disposed of, and, as a result of their experience there, were turning to a completely different method of killing the remainder of European Jewry, could only be known to Hitler's closest collaborators in the plan.

I have talked with Dr. Riegner many times over the years, in London, Munich, Paris and Geneva, where he still lives. Born in 1911, he is a charming and usually sparkling sort of man, but his voice trembled and his face became drawn when he recalled that day fifty years later. "Yes," he said, "I was told this; it was the worst day of my life. I had heard rumors for months and didn't believe them. But then, on the promise of total secrecy, I was told who the German industrialist was, and then I knew it was true. No one, except finally under duress the American Minister in Switzerland, learned that name from me while he lived . . . but now he has been honored by the Israelis, and what's more he is dead, so his name can and should be told."

Their informant, a passionate anti-Nazi, was Eduard Schulte, Director General of Giesche (in Breslau), one of the largest metal factories in Germany, part of the International Zinc Combine which included important Swiss interests—no doubt the reason for his comparative freedom of movement. Soon afterwards he defected and lived abroad to the end of his life, first in Switzerland and later in California.

(Robert Kempner had mentioned Schulte to me years before his name became public. "He was one of ours, one of the most important men the OSS had in Germany. His second wife was Jewish—perhaps that had something to do with his motivations. But perhaps not; perhaps he just understood evil when he saw it. It was he who among other things told us the date of Hitler's planned invasion of Russia, 'Barbarossa,' more than a month before it happened.")

Schulte's exceptional standing with the Allies was indicated to Riegner when he sought reassurance of his credibility before passing on this unbelievable information. The cable he then sent was addressed to Stephen Wise, the Chief Rabbi of the United States, and sent via the U.S. State Department. "Even so, I must have had a presentiment," Riegner said, "for I took out insurance by sending a copy to the Foreign Office in London. There was no reaction from Washington, and when I pressed for information I was devastated by the reply. The State Department had suppressed the information, on the basis, so I was told, that it came from an unreliable—meaning a Jewish—source. Almost a month later, after constant urging from me and others, the copy I had sent to the Foreign Office was forwarded to Rabbi Wise, but even then the State Department persuaded him to refrain from any public announcement until they could obtain 'official confirmation.' "

This was to take another two months. In mid-October a Commission to Investigate War Crimes was finally set up in the United States, but even then it took a further two months before, on December 17, 1942, the Allies issued an official condemnation of the Nazis for the extermination of the Jews. "Five months," said Riegner, "five months during which they gassed a million people."

HITLER'S HATRED of the Jews—as can be seen from his last will and testament "to the German People," dictated shortly before he killed himself—was an obsession central to his being, and finally the core and driving force of his pathology.

"I have thought and thought about it," Speer told me, "and you know, even if all the people who had been close to Hitler during one or another period of his life were alive and available for questioning by the many historians and psychologists who have tried to come to grips with Hitler's personality, I cannot think of a single person who could have explained it."

I was curious if he had ever discussed that aspect of Hitler with Hess, in Spandau. "I discussed Hitler's anti-Semitism with him, of course. But given that he entirely rejected that Hitler could have had anything to do with the murder of the Jews, and that in my opinion Hess himself was totally innocent even of knowledge about it, it would have been insensitive to discuss it in any but a purely intellectual and historical basis. Equally, however, he and I were rather isolated from our co-prisoners, he by his own choice, I by theirs. I think we both knew that to a degree we depended on each other; when he was ill, as happened often, I tried to help him; when I was ill, which happened too, he helped me. We"—he reflected for a moment—"we were careful of, no, careful *for* each other. Neither of us ever tried to challenge the other or score points. We did not argue; we talked. Of my six co-prisoners, except for von Neurath, Hess was the only one I would have hoped to see again, later. I said this to him once and he answered, very wisely, 'I don't think so. Outside we would fight.' "

Over the four years I knew Speer, it was always he who brought up the subject of the Jews. In our original conversations, when the purpose was to look at all of his life, it came up often enough, but as I've said, I was determined to put off the full confrontation with it he seemed continually to seek until near the end of our three weeks together. In our many talks after that, however, I never sought to avoid it, and he brought it up time and again, on one pretext or another such as when talking about Hess.

Neither Hess nor he, he said, had been what he would call "conscious anti-Semites." He laughed briefly, mocking himself. "I suppose both of us would have considered that infra dig." But both of them, he said, however aware or unaware, had grown up in a society riddled with anti-Semitism. "It was simply *there*," he said, "even where, like, God knows, in my family, it was never overt. Indeed, I don't think my father ever had such feelings. As you know, as boys we had a governess who was Jewish. Later I vaguely recalled remarks against Jews owning this or running that, and I suppose that—just like Hess—I was preconditioned to the anti-Semitic rantings in Hitler's earlier speeches. True enough, I became immune to what was gross or violent in them; I suppose because I didn't want to see him that way. But even so, nothing I ever heard him say made me think, even for one moment, that he had any intention of *killing* them. Killing," he repeated, with awe in his voice, "that was unthinkable. Now we know that he ordered this to happen, first in Russia, then in Poland. I don't suppose he had much to do with the technical aspects, but even the *decision* to proceed from shooting to gas chambers would have been his, for the simple reason, as I know only too well, that no major decisions could be made about *anything* without his approval."

Summing up, he said once more that Hitler's anti-Semitism in the early years, directed against the disproportionate influence of Jews on Germany's economic and cultural life, even though "discomfiting when it became shrill," was at least politically or propagandistically "understandable. But if you are asking me what it was in Hitler that could issue such an order for the murder of a people, then I can only tell you again, I don't know, and I'm quite convinced that no one else understands it either."

Annemarie Kempf said, on one of the many occasions that we discussed this subject, "I, of course, have come to believe that human beings can be taken over by evil spirits." She smiled, almost apologetically. "It isn't the sort of thing you could say to Speer. Although I think that is the only explanation for Hitler, in a way I too resist it. Because if, in one's inability to understand otherwise, one says that Hitler, who after all started out by doing wonderful things for us, must have been taken over by the devil or whatever, then in a way one frees him of responsibility. One sets up a basis for compassion, and that has to be wrong. He has to have been responsible for what he did, just as we were responsible for what we failed to do, even if, closing our eyes to it, we did not 'consciously know' what it was."

It is this "conscious knowledge" I sought in Speer. And I have become convinced that in 1942, even though thousands of German soldiers by now knew something of the murders of Jews and non-Jews in Russia, and even though a number of men working closely with him knew what was being done, first in Russia and then in Poland, Speer was not yet "consciously aware" of Hitler's genocide of the Jews.

WHAT ALMOST entirely occupied Speer's thoughts as the spring and summer of 1942—the hottest in Europe in living memory—ended and the cold autumn inexorably turned into icy winter and Stalingrad loomed was how to increase war production to replace the prodigious losses the German army soon began to suffer in the East.

November 1942 was the real beginning of the end of Hitler's war: first Rommel's defeat at El Alamein, then the Allied landings in North Africa and then, on November 19, the launch of the Soviets' huge winter offensive, incomprehensibly entirely unexpected by Hitler who, rejecting all advice from the General Staff which didn't agree with his opinions—or his wish-dreams—had put himself by then virtually entirely in command of the army.

But did the generals not see what was coming? I asked Speer. And moreover, what about him? He was by now close to many officers on the General Staff and at the same time close to Hitler. Could he not have made him aware of the realities of this desperate situation?

"The central problem," he said, "was between Hitler and the generals. Except for Keitel, who was 'his' man and only told him what he wanted to hear, and Jodl, whose activities were soon severely curtailed precisely because he showed some independence of thought, he accepted information but never tactical advice, and was increasingly surrounded by what I came to call *Nickesel* [nodding donkeys]."

As of late November 1942, these yes-men, Speer said, were increasingly the only ones permitted into Hitler's presence by the three men who virtually took charge of his life: Bormann, as Secretary of the Führer, thus virtually his deputy; Keitel, whom he had named Chief of Staff of the Armed Forces; and Lammers, Reichsminister and Chief of the Reich Chancellery, administratively in charge of domestic political affairs.

"As military production was of course at the top of Hitler's priorities,"

Speer said, "I continued to have access to him and in fact, except when I was away, saw him at least twice a week, and often daily when he was in Berlin or we were both on the Berghof. But as of that November he became a changed man. He was never the apoplectic personality people later invented for him; all that nonsense about carpet-biting—a silly American invention. Until that awful winter of 1942, I had rarely heard him rage, or even raise his voice in arguments. In fact, he was most dangerous when his voice was softest. But now, visibly exhausted, his body bent over with fatigue and his voice hoarse, his anger and bitterness toward the generals became quite awful, and it was all he would talk about, in that awful rasping voice. Everything was their fault; it was they who had betrayed him, lied to him. [Kurt] Zeitzler, one of the best Chiefs of Staff the army had, tried desperately time after time to get him to see the true catastrophe of Stalingrad, and the need to allow [Field Marshal Friedrich] Paulus and his two-hundred-thousand-strong Sixth Army to retreat westward, to abandon their heavy armaments and to dig in at defensible positions where we could drop supplies and send in reinforcements. He virtually accused him of cowardice. Stalingrad, he decreed, even when the city was totally encircled and the troops nearly out of food and munition, had to be held. Zeitzler, in protest, cut his own food rations to the same level as the Stalingrad troops, and within two weeks had lost twelve kilos, more than twenty-five pounds. Hitler, informed by Bormann, ordered him to return to a normal diet, but banned the serving of champagne and brandy at HQ "in honor of the heroes of Stalingrad."

Speer wrote about this period in Spandau:

Just before the time when the situation in Stalingrad became completely hopeless, thinking some music might help to clear my brain, I accompanied my wife, who like everybody else still suspected nothing untoward in the Eastern war, to a performance of *The Magic Flute* at the opera. But sitting in our box, in those softly upholstered chairs among this festively attired audience, all I could think of was that same kind of crowd at the Paris Opera when Napoleon was retreating in Russia, and of the now identical suffering of our own soldiers. I suddenly felt violently ill with palpitations and fled to the ministry, back to work, where I tried to suppress my horrible feelings of guilt toward my brother, who as a private in the Sixth Army was caught at Stalingrad, and where I tried to hammer into my brain Hitler's order, "Think of nothing except your own sphere of activity—there is no such thing as collective responsibility."

In *Inside the Third Reich* Speer only briefly mentions his own family's loss at Stalingrad, but he wrote more personally about it both in the Nuremberg and the Spandau drafts. At Nuremberg he wrote,

In the middle of it, panic-stricken calls from my parents: my brother Ernst, serving in an advance observation unit, is caught at Stalingrad. They have alarming letters from him: he has the Sixth Army disease, jaundice, and is lying in a primitive field hospital with fever, swollen legs and kidney pains. There is little food and a minimum of drinking water. . . . The "hospital" is in a horse-stable, only partly roofed and without walls; no heating, the wind and snow blow in; the men die of hunger and exhaustion.

"My mother, who never showed her emotions," he told me later, "sobbed into the telephone. 'You can't do this to him,' she said, as if I was doing it, and then my father, sounding like a broken man, added, 'It is impossible that you, you of all people, can't do something to get him out.' "

His Nuremberg account continued,

I had seen my brother last the previous summer when he was home on leave. He came to see me at the office but I had people waiting, an official lunch, meetings scheduled. Even so, going against Hitler's rules which prohibited people holding high rank in government from extending privileges to their relatives, I promised that I would get him out of Russia at the end of this campaign and get him into a construction battalion in the West for the remainder of the war.

Later he told me the rest of that story. "Sitting beside me in my office, phones ringing, people running in and out, he saw I was pressed for time," Speer said. " 'Ah, well, thanks,' he said, and standing up automatically came to attention, to my embarrassment. 'Goodbye then,' he said, and then he was gone before I could even stand up. After a moment I did rush out trying to catch him. I was going to walk out on the luncheon and take him out. But he was gone. I hadn't even shaken his hand."

Göring's planes were incapable of supplying the Stalingrad troops, but they did bring mail in and out. Ernst's next-to-last letter told his parents that he couldn't stand it at the field hospital, couldn't stand to see all the dying. Somehow he had managed to get himself back to his unit and, although all his limbs were now swollen to twice their size and he could no longer walk and felt weak like a baby, he felt better for being with his comrades.

Speer continues in *Spandau*:

In mid-January Hitler, having at last realized Göring's incapacity to act, finally ordered Milch to try to save the day. I drove to the airfield with him when he left for the Luftwaffe HQ south of the encircled city from where he would direct whatever rescue operations were still possible and he promised faithfully to try to find my brother. Despite the Russians' dreadfully effective air defense, he did manage to fly in a few supplies of food and medicines and, more extraordinary still, flew out another few thousand wounded. But he couldn't find my brother—the unit was searched for but it, and he, had disappeared. Like hundreds of thousands of other soldiers, my brother was declared missing, presumed dead.

"Dreadfully enough," Speer told me years later, "no doubt thanks to Milch's planes, my parents had one more letter from him, desperate about life, angry about death, and bitter about me, his brother."

GERMANY, IN THE second half of 1942 and all of 1943, was a country in the grip of schizophrenia. Nothing demonstrates this more clearly than Speer's almost manic drive to help Hitler win his war, which was already lost, and to achieve his goals though he increasingly recognized them as evil. Himmler, Goebbels and of course Nicolaus von Below continuously note their reactions to the success of his efforts. Below wrote,

> It was very clear to all of us [as soon as Hitler appointed Speer] that this had to bring about a fundamental change in the management of armament production. And indeed, we could observe this change very quickly, in an astonishingly positive direction.

And Goebbels's diary entries show his increasing enthusiasm for Speer almost from the moment of his appointment:

> [He is] the only man capable of replacing—and, one hardly likes to say so—even outdoing the great Todt. [An entry a few weeks later:] Speer is not only approaching his huge task with the finest sense of idealism, but immense expert knowledge. He is beginning to rationalize the apparatus; will get rid of all the far too many dilettantes . . . streamline the whole operation. . . . What luck to have Speer; we work splendidly together—at last a kindred mind.

Within a few short months, this wily politician, perhaps the first in Germany to see in Speer a possible successor to Hitler, would draw him deeply into his political net. Speer, fascinated by Goebbels's flair, didn't realize then—or, as we will see, later—the extent to which this link-up with Goebbels would affect his life.

Hitler's individual communications were always on a carefully selective "need to know" basis, and he now spoke in Speer's presence of matters he would never formerly have mentioned in front of him. Partly this was, of course, because Speer's position was now a political and not an artistic one. Equally, however, Speer's ready collaboration with Goebbels—and their open appreciation of each other—put him into a different category.

Hitler's categorizing of people was essentially simple, and always primarily intuitive. Thus during the years when the relationship with Speer had been based on their mutual passion for architecture, he regarded him not only as one of his "Berghof family"—who, like the "ladies" and "gentlemen" of his court, was entitled to his protection—but also as someone whose sensitivity, which Hitler felt they shared, set him apart.

In this role, he would have kept Speer—and indeed did keep him for years—at arm's length from unsuitable or unpalatable matters. This, of course, included all his plans for murder.

In view of the events to come, it can be assumed that Hitler's attitude toward or—as Karl Hettlage so clearly explained—feelings for Speer were deeply enough ingrained that even now, when Speer's position appeared to have so drastically changed, he would only have hinted at the worst of his plans: the physical annihilation of the Jews.

But in the world within which Speer now moved, directives were issued which, even if he didn't see them, in the final analysis, he had to know about, or sense their consequences. For instance, on October 2, 1942, Himmler issued a directive to five SS agencies regarding Jewish workers, with three copies to the General Quartermaster of the Army. Although designated "Secret," they could not have failed to become fairly widely known, and Himmler's last sentence is crystal clear.

The first item in the directive was about "so-called armament workers," who were occupied exclusively in tailor, fur and shoe workshops. These people, said Himmler, were to be put into concentration camps in Warsaw and Lublin:

1) The army can then channel their orders through us and we will guarantee delivery. I have given orders that those who oppose our plans on the pretext of supporting armament interests, but who are really merely looking out for the Jews, are to be dealt with without mercy.
2) Jews who are really working in armament installations, i.e., munition factories, automobile repair shops, etc., are first of all to be segregated within factories or workshops, and secondly to be sent in working groups to concentration camps where they will join the relevant work sections.
3) The Jewish workers will be replaced by Poles while a few large concentration camp workshops will for the moment carry on in the General Government camps. *Eventually, however, in line with the Führer's instructions, these Jews too will disappear.*

[Author's italics. In practice this meant that Jews still busy in workshops or factories were first to be segregated within these establishments, then moved "east" to labor camps such as Majdanek or Auschwitz, or would "disappear" into the gas chambers of Treblinka, Belsec or Sobibor.]

Two months later, on November 26, 1942, Sauckel implemented this order. Addressing his directive to the presidents of the *Land* (province or state) Labor Offices, he said, "In agreement with the Chief of the Security Police and the SD, those Jews still in employment are to be evacuated immediately from the territory of the Reich, and are to be replaced by Poles who are being removed from the General Government. These are to be sent to the Reich without families . . . to work in armament factories replacing the Jews . . . , or to be put into concentration camps if . . . 'asocial.' "

Either Speer himself or his ministry liaison man with Sauckel must have seen Sauckel's directive; at this point they must have known what would happen, in accordance with Himmler's orders of two months before, to the German Jewish workers Sauckel ordered "evacuated" to join their fellow sufferers in Poland.

Nor can this be considered in isolation from the other events in Speer's life. As we can see in Goebbels's diary notes from the time Speer's close association with Goebbels began, Hitler, often receiving them together, time and again brought up the subject of the Jews—the need to "get them out of Germany," "to eradicate their influence" and, then, a large step further, "to liquidate them from Europe's life."

"This is when I should have begun to realize what was happening," Speer said to me. "This was the point, I now think, when, had I *wanted* to, I could have detected hints."

And if he had found out, I asked, what would he have done?

"Don't you know that this is the question I have asked myself a million times, continuously hoping that I would be able to give myself an answer I could live with?" He rested his head in his hands (half covering his face, my notes say). "My answer to myself is always the same," he said, his voice dark and a little hoarse. "I would somehow have gone on trying to help that man win his war."

Speer's moral corruption had its seed in his emotional attachment to Hitler—he likened it to Faust's fatal bargain with Mephistopheles. Achievement and success rooting it ever deeper over the years, he lived—almost addictively—in an increasingly vicious cycle of need and dependence.

And now Hitler's cleverest and totally amoral disciple, Goebbels, "the most stimulating man around," as Speer described him to me, who understood perfectly the extent of Speer's subjugation to Hitler and saw himself as a kingmaker par excellence, would try to tempt him totally over the edge, by holding out to him dizzying temptations and so far undreamed-of prospects.

XV

The Unbearable Truth

December 20, 1945

MAJOR WARREN FARR (for the U.S. prosecution): On August 5, 1943, Himmler directed: ". . . that all young Ukrainian or Russian female prisoners capable of work are to be sent to Germany for work. Children, old women and old men are to be collected and put to work in . . . women's and children's camps established . . . on the borders. . . ."

Further, a statement on record from the defendant Speer: "We have to come to an arrangement with the Reichsführer SS as soon as possible, so that POWs he picks up are made available for our [labor] purposes. The Reichsführer SS gets from 30,000 to 40,000 of them per month."

June 21, 1946

ROBERT JACKSON (cross-examination of Speer): Now, the foreign workers who were, for example, assigned to Krupp . . . they were housed in labor camps and under guard, were they not?

SPEER: I do not believe that they were under guard, but I cannot say. I do not want to dodge giving information here, but I had no time to worry about such things on my visits . . . to factories. In all my activities as Armaments Minister, I never once visited a labor camp and cannot, therefore, give any information about them.

"AT FÜHRER HQ in early 1943," wrote Speer in Spandau, "the two shorthand-writers whose duty it is to record every one of Hitler's words* ... are looking paler and paler as [their idol] continues to pour dishonor on the army. The fact that Stalingrad, with 108,000 soldiers prisoners of the Soviets, the others missing and presumed dead, was entirely a result of his orders, appeared entirely forgotten: day after day he rails against the 'lazy,' 'cowardly,' 'unimaginative' generals who are to blame for that defeat, for those in Africa, and, as that awful winter went on, for the continuing setbacks in the ice and snow of Russia. . . ."

It is true that 1943 was a decisive year for Hitler, militarily and politically. It was the year Rommel began to lose in North Africa, the Allies won in Tunisia and landed in Sicily, and in Russia Manstein lost the great tank battle for Kursk. In Italy Mussolini was ousted and much of southern Italy joined the Allies, while in Germany itself carpet-bombing reduced Hamburg to ruins, killing seventy thousand people—a shattering blow to Germany's morale. In the course of that year a number of diplomats and generals would advise Hitler to seek an end to the war, and although he refused all such suggestions (by Milch, Ribbentrop, Manstein and, finally, even Goebbels), unofficial feelers were put out via Zurich, Stockholm and Geneva.

I asked Speer at one point whether he had been among those who advised Hitler to seek a negotiated peace. After all, he had known, perhaps better than anyone, what Germany's chances would be in a war which was already on three, and would shortly be on four, fronts.

"To each his own," he replied airily. "I left that to the generals."

This seemed an extraordinarily evasive reply. Was it really possible by that time to departmentalize the handling of the approaching catastrophe in this way?

He gave me one of those penetrating looks. "Well, not quite," he said after a moment. "But there were ways and ways. Hitler—never forget—always acted on impulse, inspiration and emotion. He readily listened to experts,

*This refers to the verbatim record of Hitler's situation conferences (*Führerbesprechungen*) from autumn 1942 to the end of April 1945, not to be confused with his *Tabletalk*.

but in the end the only people who could really affect his decisions were those closest to him—and they really had no ideas of their own and only mirrored his.

"If one was close to him," he continued, "there were ways of changing his mind, but it had to be done very subtly. The men who were in that position during and after Stalingrad were only yes-men—there was no possible subtlety there. I did try to bring about a change after Stalingrad."

Extraordinarily, it was not only in *Inside the Third Reich* but already in the Nuremberg and Spandau drafts that Speer emphatically downplayed the importance of 1943 in his own life. It was the year when it became clear to him that a number of politicians and generals, and finally apparently even Hitler himself, were considering him as a possible successor. It was not a possibility he had envisaged before, but once it was in the air it had, I believe, an enormous effect both on his actions and on his inactions.

For this was also certainly the year when he was brought face to face both with the slaughter of the Jews in Poland—if almost certainly not the method of their murder there—and the horrors suffered by the slave laborers. To acknowledge the reality of these crimes, first within himself and then to Hitler, would without a doubt have brought about a radical change in his life. Given the unique nature of his relationship with Hitler, the inexplicable emotional side of it might just have survived such a confrontation. As he was by now indispensable to Hitler, I doubt that he would have been harmed, and indeed might even have retained his job. But to identify as crimes what Hitler considered to be legitimate political acts would certainly have cost him Hitler's intimacy—and with it any possibility of the succession which was suddenly dangling before his eyes.

In his writings Speer gave little indication of the momentous discoveries he made in the second half of 1943, but he did discuss the "change" he had tried to effect after Stalingrad, change in the personal conduct by Germany's political leaders, and changes in the authority of the army command.

Since the winter of 1942, which had led toward the defeat at Stalingrad, Hitler was almost exclusively under the influence of what came to be known as the Committee of Three: Field Marshal Wilhelm Keitel, whom Hitler had made Chief of Staff of the army when he himself assumed overall command of it in 1938; Hans Lammers, Chief of the Reich Chancellery; and Martin Bormann. In December 1942 Goebbels decided that the hold of what he called "this evil trio" had to be broken, and soon turned to Speer for support.

"He really did seem to me," Speer told me when we came to talk of this, his first real attempt to enter the arena of active politics, "the clearest head and the cleverest mind." Goebbels manifestly had the same high opinion of Speer. In his diary of February 5, 1943, he noted,

Speer and his wife to dinner at my house last night. . . . He and I get on extremely well; he is one of the few men around who responds to—and thus can help me toward the realization of—my ideas. And what stupendous things he has achieved so quickly. Bitter though it sounds, one must agree with the Führer in a way that Speer was a very advantageous swap for Todt. In the final analysis, Todt was too much of a soldier, eternally at attention before all generals, which of course in no way applies to that essential civilian, Speer.

Compared to what one must now admit was a primitive armament industry a year ago when he took it over, the production figures now are positively startling: he is an organizational genius. . . .

Having agreed from the start that the influence on Hitler of the "evil trio" had to be eliminated, Goebbels and Speer recruited two others they thought sympathetic to their ideas: Minister of Economics Walther Funk and the Chief of the German Workers' Front, Reichsleiter Robert Ley. Furthermore, they hoped to bring Göring, who when at his best was still a force to be reckoned with, onto their side. The intention then was to set up a Council of Ministers which would advise Hitler, administer the country's inner political affairs and restructure the defense policy. For the sake of the country, they felt, Hitler, manifestly exhausted, now needed responsible support. "What we have," said the ever-realistic Goebbels, "is not a leadership but a *leader* crisis."

Their main aims, in the order of priority, were, first, to put the country at last on a total-war footing (Goebbels, testing the waters, publicly proposed this to frantic applause on February 18, 1943, in an address at the Palace of Sports); second, to recapture the dangerously dwindling faith of the people by dealing ruthlessly with the corruption on all levels of government and administration and by abolishing the system of privilege the top echelon of the party—the Gauleiter—so openly enjoyed; and third, above all else, to work closely with the army, traditionally Germany's most respected body of men, in order to return to the Army High Command the autonomy without which an army cannot function.

In essence, although planned in a spirit of loyal service to the head of state they all still revered, it was a revolution. The four of them, as yet without Göring, had begun to meet at night at Goebbels's Berlin residence in order to lay their plans. He wrote in his diary, February 13, 1943:

> Evening at my house, Speer and Ley. . . . We are entirely of one mind on all fundamental questions. . . . February 27: Speer, Ley and Funk at the house—we talked about everything until 2 a.m. . . . Speer & Funk . . . feel, however, with Göring now so lethargic and resigned . . . I should take over leadership of Council [of Ministers], on the face of it as his deputy. I [tell them] I am quite prepared to do this but we would at least nominally need

his agreement. He is at present . . . yet again . . . vacationing. . . . Speer offers to get on his plane in pursuit, in order to persuade him to agree. If we get him on our side, I have no doubt we'd very quickly get the Führer's backing and . . . could begin work. I would propose a group of ten leading personalities with whom I would then govern, i.e., set up a structure of inner-political leadership. All of us know there will be problems, but on this evening it is perfectly clear to us that if there was ever to be a repetition of events such as we witnessed this past winter on the Eastern front, we would be facing a most severe crisis of public confidence. . . . Our only reason for fear is the never-to-be-thought-of possibility that we could lose the war . . . but the time to consider this danger and take all measures against it, is now.

The discussion this evening was incredibly productive. What a relief to talk with true National Socialists such as these three.

Throughout this important entry one can read between the lines Goebbels's skillful manipulation of the group, above all of Speer who, although now perhaps no longer entirely a novice at high-level politicking, knew as yet virtually nothing about intrigue as practiced by a master of the art like Goebbels.

True to his offer, Speer flew to Berchtesgaden the next day where Göring, feeling ill used by Hitler's criticisms of his leadership of the Luftwaffe, was sulking at his palatial country house near the Berghof. He received Speer, his face rouged and fingernails lacquered, wearing a trailing dark green velvet robe adorned with a huge golden brooch, in its center "a diamond of rare beauty."

It is strange—and indicative of Göring's fundamentally strong personality—that someone as deeply conservative as Speer was able to take seriously this ludicrous figure. In Nuremberg, where of course he was daily faced with a reborn version of the man, detoxicated, slimmed down and openly admired by the defendants and their German lawyers, as well as the German people who listened to the proceedings on the radio, he wrote that he had found him exceptionally open-minded that day in Berchtesgaden:

He viewed the situation exactly as we did and he was particularly struck when I told him that we were sure Bormann was seeking to succeed Hitler. I was able to present him with a number of details supporting this view. That certainly activated his juices! We reached complete agreement and decided to ask Goebbels to fly up the next day for a second conference.

By the next evening everything was decided: we would set up the Council of Ministers as a joint instrument of power; Goebbels and I would be appointed members.

We set a date for a third meeting in Berlin [with Funk and Ley] after
which we would proceed together against Bormann and his group. We
would stand together, supporting each other in the decisive meeting with
Hitler. All was agreed: a small conspiracy.

Speer talked to me about this period with great animation, communicating thirty-five years later the elation they had felt. Almost nothing in our
dicussions so clearly showed me the chasm in his thinking in those years, the
ambivalence which, given the excitement the memory of these events
aroused, I thought might well have endured.

Even accepting for the sake of argument, I said, that he was at that time
still in some ignorance of Hitler's basic monstrosity—his worst crimes—and
of Goebbels's obvious connivance in them, how could he even conceive of
helping to set up a group with or under Göring, a man steeped more deeply
than anyone else in the very corruption they were dedicating themselves to
wiping out? And having just seen Hitler sacrifice without a further thought a
whole army group—incidentally including Speer's own brother—how could
he co-plan this "revolution," which was intended not to free Germany but
basically to continue and intensify an insane war?

"In order to get rid of the terrible trio that was fencing Hitler in," he explained, sounding patient and rational, "we had to offer him the strongest
possible alternative. Despite his recent disappointments over Göring, we
knew he remained attached to him as he invariably was to all his early comrades. He always saw men as they had been, never as what they had become,
so psychologically if not in reality, Göring, almost until the end, remained
one of his mainstays and of course, don't forget, until the end of April 1945
his official successor.

"I have to say that I too had a weak spot for Göring. I had known him as a
charming and highly intelligent man, and even now saw him more as an in-
dividualist, an eccentric, if you like, than as sick or evil. I myself was by then
profoundly linked to the army, their interests and their points of view. At
Führer HQ the men who were close to me were Colonel von Below and General Rudolf Schmundt, Hitler's principal military adjutant. [Schmundt died
in August 1944 from injuries sustained in the July 20 attempted army coup
against Hitler.] Outside, the men I saw not only most often but most gladly
were Zeitzler, Fromm and Milch. At that particular point, and ever since
before Stalingrad, although I considered Hitler ill with exhaustion and hardly
compos mentis, he had humiliated and dishonored the army, and this could
not be allowed to stand. I'm trying to explain to you not what, seen from the
perspective of now, would have been rational and right, but what I felt then.
Once a situation could be created in which the army would regain their

proper place in the scheme of things, and thus their honor, then the next step would be considered."

And would the next step have been ending the war? I asked.

He was trying to be honest. "I'm not sure how quickly," he said. "There was, after all, Hitler. I did not know then that assassination of Hitler was already being considered within the army and indeed, that three attempts on his life—all unsuccessful—were about to be made. But I *am* sure that ending the war was in the minds of the generals long before the Twentieth of July."

The political conspirators decided to strike on April 12, 1943, using as a pretext the pressing need to confront Sauckel, Bormann's man of confidence in Speer's ministry, with a discrepancy of about a million workers between the figures he reported to Hitler and those the industrialists provided for Speer.

"That meeting, held in the Berghof building built specifically for use by the Berlin Chancellery," Speer told me, "essentially finished our plans before they could ever begin."

The conspirators not only found themselves confronted by Bormann, Keitel and Himmler (who of course had not been expected), but worse still, deserted by Goebbels, who sent a message that he was down with a kidney attack. "Later I realized," Speer said, "that he must have learned—quite possibly from Bormann himself—that we had been outmaneuvered; so he stayed home!" In Spandau he described the fiasco:

> Göring showed his true colors at once. Instead of calling Sauckel to task as he had promised, he immediately launched a violent attack against his own Undersecretary of State, Field Marshal Milch, who by prior arrangement was the one who raised our objection to Sauckel's labor-bookkeeping. How could Milch accuse that good party comrade Sauckel, who worked so hard for the Führer, of wrongdoing, Göring thundered. Ironically, it was he who only two days earlier had proposed our strategy of spearheading our general attack with an objection to Sauckel's fantasy-figure reports to Hitler.
>
> And Himmler immediately joined the stifling of our initiative. "Isn't the most likely explanation for the million missing bodies that they are dead?" he asked equably. It was only when I learned in Nuremberg of the numbers of dead in the concentration camps that I understood what he meant.

"If it had not been so sad," Speer told me later, "it would have been funny. Before the meeting started, Göring took me aside and warned me against Milch: 'He is totally unreliable, and if it is to his advantage, he will drop any friend like a hot iron.' When I repeated this to Milch later, he laughed. 'That's exactly what he told me about you,' he said.

"And much later, in Spandau, Funk said that I had been mad ever to trust Goebbels. 'He was never honest with you,' he said. 'How so?' I asked him. 'Because he was not an honest man,' he replied. 'But who was, in those times? I, after all, went along with it too.' Well, I suppose he was right. The very next day, Goebbels, miraculously recovered, let Bormann know that from then on he would use him as the conduit for his communications with Hitler and would be grateful if, on the other hand, Bormann would see to it that his requests got prompt and favorable attention."

Thus ended their attempt to bring about changes, Speer said. "Except for two things, which had consequences for me later. The first was when Himmler, running into me at Führer HQ a few weeks later, threatened me for the first time. 'I advise you never to try again to recruit the Reichsmarshal [Göring] for your goals.' I wasn't intending to, but still, that was when Himmler began to alarm me personally—the first time I suddenly found him sinister.

"The other development had in fact started when I had first become friends with the three generals, Milch, Zeitzler and Fromm, and they began repeating to me laudatory remarks Hitler allegedly made about me. Already some months earlier Zeitzler had said gleefully that Hitler had told him how glad he was that in 'my person,' as he put it, 'a new sun had arisen next to Göring's.' And only days later, he had said in several generals' hearing that with me, 'a new personality was on the scene who represented hope for the future.'

"Zeitzler had found that very significant, and although I asked him not to repeat it to anyone, I couldn't quite forget it myself. Especially when, a few days after that, when as it happened Himmler and I entered the situation room at HQ together, Hitler exclaimed, 'Ah, here are the two equals. I enjoy it when I can see you side by side.'

"Himmler didn't like that at all. It was only much later, in Nuremberg, talking to Goebbels's former Undersecretary of State [Naumann]," Speer said, "that I realized the importance given to this kind of occasional quip by Hitler. He told me that in the course of 1943 most people had come to assume that I was Hitler's successor-designate."

What had given him most food for thought, however, Speer said, was when shortly after the abortive meeting at the Berghof Chancellery office, General Schmundt sought him out during one of his next visits to Führer HQ. "He sat down next to me, looked around, quite obviously making sure he was not overheard, and then said, 'I'm hearing your name mentioned a great deal these days. The army is entirely behind you. Keep it in mind.' And then he got up and went away, leaving me flabbergasted."

It meant, however, that he was not entirely unprepared when, following a meeting with the three generals not too long afterwards, Milch asked him straight out whether he had thought of himself as a successor to Hitler.

"I shrugged it off, with a joke I suppose," said Speer. "But from then on, it was in the air."

The thought of the succession, it appears, remained on Speer's mind. In October 1943, probably the most important milestone month for Speer, as will be discussed, he himself initiated a conversation on the succession with one of the leading men in his ministerial cabinet, Hans Kehrl, the ministry's head of planning, who reported on it in his own memoirs, *Krisenmanager im Dritten Reich* (Crisis Manager in the Third Reich). At the end of a long discussion about who of Hitler's leading men could succeed him, and agreeing that Himmler, Goebbels, Bormann and Göring were out of the question, Kehrl writes that Speer asked him point blank whether he thought that Hitler was considering him. Kehrl did think so; no one else, he reports his own reply, shared so much with Hitler, including artistic interests, or had such a close personal relationship with him. And then, of course, everyone knew that Hitler was immensely impressed with his achievements as his Armaments Minister. Speer, wrote Kehrl, appeared pleased.

But why had he always denied it, including at Nuremberg, I asked Speer. He smiled. "Don't be naive. How could I not deny it there?"

But having said it once, fairly explicitly, in the Nuremberg mini-draft, I said, why didn't he admit to it in print later? Why did he skate around it in *Inside the Third Reich*?

"It seemed wiser to leave it by the wayside, so to speak," he answered. "Let sleeping dogs lie, no? Finally, it wasn't important, was it?"

In fact, it was, of course, immensely important. For where a man engaged in the hopeless task of keeping a war machine functioning for a war he knew was lost might well seek ways to end his commitment, the prospect—however unrealistic at that point—of appointment to the highest place in the state might equally well persuade him to hold on, shutting his eyes to wrongdoing until he himself could take over the reins.

Time and again Germans from that period have said that no one who hadn't lived under that dictatorship could understand what it was like. To a degree this is true. The life and thoughts—and thus finally, too, the reactions and acts of individual human beings—are immensely affected by their environment and their emotions. Therefore, when considering and evaluating the reactions and acts of Speer in those years, it is important to always remain aware—more consciously aware perhaps than *he* was at the time—of the background against which his actions and reactions took place.

A number of documents describing events in 1943, though possibly demonstrating more Speer's determined ignorance than his knowledge, cer-

tainly laid him open to questions. Two of them, both much discussed by
Speer's critics, stem from him or concern actions taken by him. At Nuremberg, where some questions were perfunctorily asked, he parried them with
ease and the court accepted his explanations. Other documents quoted here,
while not directly linked to Speer, are immensely indicative of the atmosphere within which those in leading positions in Hitler's Germany had to
function.

The Reichsminister   Berlin, February 1, 1943
for Armaments and Munition
GB.-II/B Gr. Aussendienst [external service]

To the Reichsführer SS

Dear Party Comrade Himmler,
   I am informed that a large resettlement drive is about to be undertaken
in the district of Bialystok. Following the evacuation of about 40,000 Jews
from the district's ghettos, 40,000 White Ruthenian peasants, who if left
in place could support partisans active in the areas, are to be transferred to
the habitations left by the Jews. As the available space is considered insufficient for their needs, application has been made to me for building
materials for a barrack settlement for 20,000.
   While fully appreciating these measures, I fear priority for building materials in these times of scarcity must be given to housing for armament
workers and victims of enemy bombardments at home. I must therefore
ask you to have these people settled without further demands on our limited building supplies.
                                        Heil Hitler
                                        Yours, Speer
[Himmler replied on February 9 that he entirely agreed and that instructions had been issued accordingly.]

Though in retrospect hard to accept, it is in fact quite possible that Speer,
at that point, even though doubtless aware of the large-scale shootings behind the front in Russia (which he, like so many others, will have convinced
himself was part of "the war"), still believed that the "evacuation" of Jews
from some areas and their "resettlement" in others meant exactly what it
said; the foreign workers he and Sauckel were bringing into Germany by
the millions were, after all, also in a manner of speaking being "moved" or
"resettled."
   I was curious whether, writing these lines, Speer gave any thought at all to
where these forty thousand Jews, families rather than men capable of work,
were being taken. He always expected questions about the Jews, although
perhaps not as specific as this, and readily replied to them.

He had no memory of this letter, he said. "Do you really think that I personally drafted all my letters?" he asked. "Dozens of applications for building materials arrived every day; dozens of letters went out approving them or disapproving them. And all of them came to me for signature."

He didn't read them?

"Barely," he said. "Certainly not with sufficient attention to analyze their content."

What if he *had* read this particular letter with attention? Would it have provoked questions in his mind?

He shook his head, almost sadly. "I'm afraid not. I'm afraid I really wouldn't have cared. My mind was entirely on getting labor, on keeping production going. If anything, however illogically, I would have associated the removal of these Jews with the needs for security, and for labor."

When years later I asked Annemarie Kempf about the letter, she looked at it and said immediately that the GB indication meant *Generalbau*, a section of the Ministry. "If Speer had dictated this, this heading wouldn't be there—it would have on the right 'SP/' and the initials of the person who took the dictation."

The Bialystok letter, she went on, showed Speer's determination to give away nothing to Himmler. Such a letter would have been one of many "contingency" letters; one wouldn't even have looked at the details. "Now of course, when I look at this," she said, "I think we should have sensed something wrong, and we should have asked ourselves the same questions you are asking. But we *didn't*, and it was normal enough not even to think about it."

SPEER WOULD never have seen the train schedules issued daily between July 1942 and October 1943 by his protégé Ganzenmüller's *Ostbahn* directorate. Perhaps even Ganzenmüller, busy with higher matters, did not see them.

Hundreds of these "railway orders," meticulously filled out, have been preserved. They carry no "Secret" stamp; they must have gone through many hands. What is marked here, day after day, and page after page, is the departure from various Polish cities and towns of "Resettlement Special Trains" *(Umsiedlersonderzüge)*, each carrying thousands of people; the arrival of the *Vollzug* (full train) in Treblinka in four to eleven hours, depending on distance; and the departure of the *Leerzug* (empty train) four and a half to ten hours later, depending on how full they had been.

The "Special Instructions" attached to daily and sometimes weekly schedules are explicit:

1) Weight: Full: 800 tons; Empty: 600 tons.
2) Both Special Train and empty train to be run to schedule in order to maintain the proper rhythm of loading and unloading. . . .
3) In Treblinka the trains are to be cleaned by camp workers.
4) Empties not to be put on sidings at any time.

The reason for that last order was that the returning trains, while empty of passengers, were not empty at all. As is shown in a copy of a Wehrmacht cargo certificate dated September 1, 1942, the train, traveling from Treblinka via Siedlce to Lublin (where it would be directed to its ultimate destination), was to carry: "No officers or officials; no civilians; no service dogs; no horses; no Wehrmacht cargo in open wagons, [but]: non-commissioned officers and men, and 50 covered wagons carrying *clothes for Waffen SS*" (author's italics).

This did not mean that the SS intended to dress their soldiers in clothes taken off by the victims before they were killed, but simply that the SS controlled the distribution of all goods taken off them. Clothes, as we will see, went to needy foreign workers and "resettled" ethnic Germans; the food many of the victims brought on their journey toward death—often preserves of jam and honey—was distributed among camp staff. Jewelry and money, of which there was a good deal in gold and every kind of foreign currency, ended up, as the Railway Instruction sheets duly state, "via the SS/HQ Lublin and the 'Führungs Hauptamt,' " in Berlin [they meant the *Führer Kanzlei*, which included T4, the administration of the Aktion Reinhard], in the coffers of the Reichsbank, administered by Minister of Economics Walther Funk.

There was, as I said, no reason for Speer to have seen these train schedules, but if he had, he might have learned what happened to the forty thousand Jews of Bialystok in February 1943: from February 9 to February 13, five trains (Pj 127, 129, 131, 133 and 135) took them to Treblinka, arriving each day at 12:10 p.m., the "empties" leaving at 9:18.

On February 6, 1943, SS Obergruppenführer Oswald Pohl, head of the SS Office of Economic Administration and thus Speer's opposite number in the SS (Pohl was sentenced to death at Nuremberg on November 3, 1947, and executed June 8, 1951), reported on the "Utilization of Textiles: Used Clothes from the Jewish Resettlement":

An attached list shows the amount of material so far obtained from the Jewish resettlement in the camps in the Lublin area, and Auschwitz. Please note that usable material, particularly for men, is much diminished by the fact that many clothes are rags. . . . We are encountering great difficulties in obtaining the necessary transport, especially to the Ukraine where ethnic Germans are in great need of [winter] clothing. However, with the help of the Reich Production Ministry, which has promised continued assistance in this matter, we have been able to obtain a large number of railway cars to transport this material out of the General Government and toward the recipients.

It would be absurd to hold either Funk, at that date Minister of Economics, or later Speer personally responsible for such assistance. But there had to be officials in Funk's and Speer's ministries with whom such a request from the SS had to have been discussed in some detail.

I showed this document too to Annemarie Kempf after I found it in the files of the Federal Archives in Koblenz. "I have never seen this before," she said, visibly horrified by what she read. "But then, you see, Pohl would not have presented this to anyone in our place, or Funk's either, in this manner. He would have said he needed transport to get 'winter help' to needy people in the East and, of course, if it was possible, our office would respond to such a request."

On April 9, 1943, Pohl, busy as ever, wrote to the head of Himmler's personal staff, Dr. Rudolf Brandt, to get Himmler's instructions about rations for pregnant Gypsies and their children in Auschwitz.

> The camp administration asks me for authorization to distribute increased rations . . . because the Reichsführer SS apparently has special plans with these Gypsies. What they are requesting would mean that these people's rations would be equal to Germans'. Could you ascertain the Reichsführer's wishes on this matter? An alternative could be to give these Gypsy women prisoners' rations but with certain additions; or we can put them on a par with female Eastern workers, again with supplements, although please note that these are not available to pregnant Eastern workers; or finally we can assign them the same rations as to German pregnant mothers.
>
> Are we to feed the children according to rations for German children, or perhaps here too choose a middle way between this and Eastern workers?
>
> Warmest greetings,
Heil Hitler
Pohl

The reply arrived six days later: the Gypsies, pregnant women and their children were to receive the same rations as female workers from the East.

Though there is no specific connection, and the documents do not show what Himmler's "special plans" were for the Gypsies, the above gains a sinister significance in light of a previous letter about "special plans" addressed to

"Kamerad Brandt" in the winter of 1942 by the administrator of *Das Ah-nenerbe*—one of Himmler's most disgusting agencies for racial research. This worthy gentleman, who no doubt died peacefully in his bed, wrote,

> As you know, the Reichsführer SS has given instructions that SS Captain Prof. Dr. Hirt is to be given all possible assistance for his research. For certain anthropological examinations, about which I have already informed the Reichsführer SS, he now needs 150 skeletons of prisoners: i.e., Jews, which are to be put at his disposal by the KZ [concentration camp] Auschwitz. What is still required, however, is an official order from the Reichsführer SS to the Reichssicherheitshauptamt [Reich Security Main Office].
> Attached: draft for letter to Reichssicherheitshauptamt.

Some months later a decision was apparently taken to do the "preparatory research" on designated victims in Auschwitz before killing them. On June 21, 1943, an SS physician, Dr. Bruno Berger, reported, this time to Eichmann in Berlin, that, owing to the danger of epidemics in Auschwitz, he was interrupting his work there:

> We have altogether worked on 115 individuals, of which 79 are male Jews, 2 Poles, 4 Asians [from the USSR] and 30 female Jews. The prisoners, separated by sexes, are at present in quarantine, lodged in a hospital building.
> In order to carry on the work, it is now essential that they are transferred as quickly as possible away from the danger of epidemics at Auschwitz to the KZ Natzweiler [the concentration camp closest to Strasbourg, where Hirt had his institute. "To carry on the work" meant concluding the physical examination of the living prisoners, then killing them to use their skeletons for "anthropological research"].

While we can be certain that Speer had absolutely no idea of these terrible pseudoscientific experiments on human beings, it is unlikely, Annemarie Kempf's loyal assurance to me notwithstanding, that he was as ignorant as he claimed about the conditions in concentration camps.

On March 30, 1943, Speer paid his one and only visit to a concentration camp—Mauthausen, near Linz, where, as Annemarie told me, he spent about forty-five minutes being given the so-called VIP tour which carefully protected visitors from seeing anything that might shock their sensibilities. It was no doubt under the utopian impression this tour provided that he wrote five days later to Himmler protesting against the "lavish building projects" he noticed at the camp. Given the extreme shortage of steel, wood and manpower for building armament factories desperately needed to supply the front lines, he felt that despite the admittedly important tasks for the war ef-

fort assigned to concentration camps, the SS really could not continue building along such generous lines:

> We must therefore carry out a new planning program for construction
> within the concentration camps, which, while allowing for the maximum
> success for present demands of the armament industry, will require a
> minimum of material and labor. The answer is an immediate switch to
> primitive construction methods.

He proposed that one of his senior colleagues, together with a representative to be appointed by Himmler, "should inspect all concentration camps *in
situ.*" Pohl reacted to this a week later with a livid three-page epistle addressed to Himmler, via his personal assistant, Rudolf Brandt:

> Reichsminister Speer claims that we are engaged in luxury construction
> in the concentration camps, without adding that he was not only in-
> formed of every single building project, but that indeed he had authorized
> all requests for materials himself, with his signature, on February 2, 1943.
>   It is entirely unrealistic to suggest an immediate switch to primitive
> construction. The Minister appears not to realize that we have 160,000
> prisoners and are constantly battling against epidemics and a dispropor-
> tionately high death rate, both largely due to impossible sanitary condi-
> tions. It is my duty to warn you that a change to primitive construction
> [temporary wooden walls without plastering] is likely to result in a huge
> increase of the death rate in the camps.

Two months later, in early June, Himmler wrote Speer, mildly reprimanding him for making up his mind on the "inefficient use by the SS of prisoner
labor" on the basis of seeing only one camp rather than viewing, or at least
studying the figures for, all of them. Himmler may have been deliberately
creating a false record, for by the time he wrote this letter, he had known for
two months that Speer was sending two young men from his ministry, accompanied by Himmler's own chief of SS construction, Brigadeführer Hans
Kammler, on an inspection tour of all major concentration camps. As Annemarie Kempf would tell me forty years later, many letters were written for the
record, to "cover their backs," not unlike the same kind of letters, one might
think, written by government ministers in all countries every day.

The tour actually took place in May, and on May 30, 1943, Speer wrote offering to provide about 2,500 tons of structural steel for various construction
purposes in "the concentration camps, particularly Auschwitz."

Although the three men sent to visit the camps were no doubt again spared
the worst of the sights, they presumably saw more than Speer. For in *Infiltrations,* about Himmler and the SS, Speer wrote that "they discovered catastrophic sanitary conditions in Auschwitz which really did alarm me."

He added—an odd mistake—that "a hand-written postscript in Pohl's report to Hitler appears to indicate that the report I received from my men
confirmed that 'the inspection of the other concentration camps provided an
absolutely positive impression.' " The fact is, however, that the postscript he
quotes was not in Pohl's report, but at the end of his own May 30 letter to
Himmler, written in his own hand.

SPEER AND HITLER were certainly on good terms all that spring
and summer of 1943, during which production figures rose enormously even
while Germany and Italy suffered defeat after defeat in North Africa, Russia
and Sicily. During that unhappy spring and summer, whenever Speer visited
Führer HQ, he was invited to share Hitler's solitary lunch, "which, taken in
almost complete silence," he wrote in Spandau, "was an hour of torture."
Hitler, having wordlessly spooned his soup, would finally remark on the
weather while waiting for the next course to be served, after which the conversation was limited to his praise for his vegetarian-diet cook. Toward the
end of the meal, there would be the usual outburst against the military.

"Believe me," Hitler often said, "I would be happy to take this grey uniform off for good—today rather than tomorrow." And he would then come
back to his old dream of years before, to give up the leadership as soon as
possible, to leave it to a successor, and to retire to Linz, to the house Giesler
was building for him there. How he wished he could have been an architect
rather than the politician he became against all his inclinations, he would
sigh.

Speer described Hitler's mood in Spandau (though not in his books): "I
think he was so tired and depressed in those months that he really regretted
having become the Führer."

Talking to me about Hitler's depressive state during that first half of 1943,
Speer remembered one occasion, just after one of the situation conferences
he attended at Führer HQ, when, with several of the military still present—
Keitel, Jodl, Warlimont, Below—the windows had been opened to let in
some air.

"Hitler went to stand at the open window while the rest of us remained
standing behind him," Speer said. "I remember—and I don't know why—
the room was very silent. And suddenly he said, still standing at that window,
his back to us, 'Gentlemen, the bridges behind us are burnt.' He said it very
quietly, almost matter-of-factly—no drama, no emphasis. And I felt a cold
shiver go down my back; I remember very clearly, I had a dreadful foreboding, a sudden sense of something awesome. . . . I now think," Speer continued, after a moment, "that he meant what had been done to the Jews."

Around that time, in early summer 1943, Speer was able to change Hitler's mind about one dreadful order Sepp Dietrich had told him he was about to issue. It had just been discovered that Soviet troops had killed German prisoners, and Hitler had announced then and there "a thousandfold retaliation in blood." In the new offensive about to be launched, no prisoners were to be taken.

Speer wrote in *Inside the Third Reich:*

> For months we had been trying in vain to close a gap of hundreds of thousands in the supply of labor. I therefore took the first opportunity to reason with Hitler on this score. It was not difficult to persuade him . . . he gave me the impression of being glad to give way. That same day, July 8, 1943, he had Keitel prepare instructions to the effect that all prisoners must be sent into armament production.

Three weeks later, from July 25 to August 2, the blanket bombing of Hamburg, which reduced much of that wonderful old city to rubble, put the fear of God into Speer. Six more such attacks on German cities, he told Hitler three days afterwards, would bring armament production to a standstill. Hitler merely said that he was sure Speer would manage. And in fact, Speer did manage. "Not because we were so clever," he told me, "but because, luckily for us, the RAF didn't follow it up with similar raids on other cities, and the Americans, who two weeks later tried and failed to destroy our ball-bearing plants at Schweinfurt, made similar tactical mistakes. If they hadn't, we would have been finished, Hitler's confidence in me notwithstanding."

Over the next critical weeks, when the fate of Mussolini was in the balance and the King of Italy negotiated with the Western Allies, Speer took part in the top-level deliberations at Hitler's field HQ in Rastenburg which, by early September, resulted in SS flying ace Otto Skorzeny and his paratroops spiriting Mussolini out of the mountaintop hotel where the King had exiled him, and most of Italy being occupied by the Germans.

Goebbels wrote on July 27, 1943:

> The Pope is playing games. The Italian aristocrats and their monarch show their true ungrateful colors. . . . What best to do? Everybody at HQ is confused. Except the Führer, who, always in his element at a crisis, shows total calm and inner superiority, demonstrating time and again his complete mastery of the situation. . . . He proposes that we take over Rome. . . . Ribbentrop and I manage to persuade him of the inadvisability of occupying the Vatican. . . . The situation is too sensitive. . . . It would be dangerous to explain too much to the people . . . there are those here, too, who might decide to take advantage of it. . . . By the evening, the Führer is exhausted and dines alone, while at our table it emerges clearly that virtu-

ally none of our leading brains assembled there—Ribbentrop, Rommel, Dönitz, Keitel, Bormann—has any concept of the scope of our problem here . . . except Speer, with whom I have a long talk after dinner. Of all the leading men in Germany, he is one of the few whose analysis of the situation is hard, bold and totally realistic. . . .

On September 2, having shortly before named Himmler Minister of the Interior (which did not, however, save his predecessor, the bureaucratic Wilhelm Frick, from the gallows at Nuremberg), Hitler extended Speer's area of responsibility to all of Germany's production. His official title was now Reich Minister for Armaments and War Production (instead of the previous Armaments and Munitions). Even though the new title specified "War Production" as a sop to Göring's possessiveness over his Four-Year Plan (which Speer was anyway controlling through his Central Planning Board), Speer was now in fact in charge of all of the country's production, including all consumer goods. Speer's plan, with which both Hitler and Minister of Economics Funk were in agreement, but to which Bormann, representing the interests of the Gauleiter, took bitter exception, was to turn all of the country's large consumer-goods factories into armament plants, while transferring the bulk of the production of consumer goods to factories in occupied Western Europe, starting with France.

At a conference in Paris in July, he had proposed to the French the setting up of "protected factories" which, producing armament components for Germany, would be made immune from Sauckel's dreaded levies of French workers. The fear of being drafted for forced labor had driven thousands of workers to flee their factories, at least some of them joining the French underground. Now, two months later, Speer understood—with the help of France's young Minister of Production, Jean Bichelonne, a professor at the Sorbonne—that notwithstanding the frankly pro-German faction in the Vichy government such as Premier Pierre Laval, the workers of France would always balk at producing armaments for Germany. But producing only civilian goods for Germany, while offering the workers the same guarantees against deportation, was more acceptable. Shortly after the new addition to his title, he issued a formal invitation to Bichelonne to come on a state visit to Berlin.

Bichelonne, a man his own age who shared many of his ideas, was probably the first foreigner with whom Speer really communicated. "I liked Bichelonne very much," he told me. "He was a passionate nationalist but very sympathetic, as I was, to Pan-European ideas; you may remember that my father was already very interested in [the concept]. Of course, when Bichelonne and I played with the idea of a European Economic Union, we thought of it as Utopian. But"—he laughed—"it wasn't all that Utopian, was it?"

It sounds as if with this youngish, like-minded Frenchman, Speer found some lightness of spirit. "We agreed that in the future we would avoid the mistakes of the First World War generation, who were now at the helm. Irrespective of national frontiers, Europe had to be economically integrated; for this, I told him, I would happily oppose Hitler's present plan of carving up France—giving Alsace-Lorraine back to Germany, for example—which I considered entirely unnecessary."

It was treason to say that to a foreigner, he said, "but I trusted him; I think if he had survived, we would have been friends." (Bichelonne died in early 1945, after an operation in Germany for a pulmonary embolism, carried out—extraordinarily enough, as will be seen, on Speer's recommendation—by Himmler's friend Professor Gebhardt.)

Having received Hitler's agreement prior to Bichelonne's arrival, Speer suggested to him the formal creation of a German-French production planning council which could eventually be expanded to much of Western Europe. The last part of their talks took place over the weekend at a country house near Berlin belonging to a friend of Speer's, the sculptor Arno Breker. And here he and Speer agreed on the specifics of this new German-French collaboration: Speer would tell Sauckel that, instead of importing French labor for German factories, his staff in Paris were to persuade French workers to volunteer for the "protected factories" where they would be guaranteed security from deportation. The plants could be given the necessary support in money, transportation and food, while Speer could concentrate all German production on armaments.

The success of this daring initiative, which resulted in the creation of ten thousand new factories in France working for German production, and was then extended by Speer to Holland and Belgium, infuriated Sauckel but delighted Hitler. "He always enjoyed driving a wedge between his people," Speer told me. "It was a childish pastime which he mistook for shrewd management. Aside from this, however, he knew a good thing when he saw it. If we could get Western Europe working for us without the trouble of forcing laborers to come to Germany and housing and feeding them, it was tremendously to our advantage."

What Speer had to do now was to persuade the Gauleiter to collaborate with his "total war" measures. They considered the loss of consumer production and the conversion of these factories into armament plants not only a gross interference with their personal authority but also an immense economic loss to their districts. He was scheduled to address them on the subject on October 6, at a Gauleiter conference in Posen, but he knew their attitude

and that words would no longer suffice. And so on October 5, the day before
the conference, he entered into a formal agreement of cooperation between
his ministry and the SD, Himmler's Security Service. In the morning of that
day, he had flown back from the Ruhr, where, accompanied by Theo Hupfauer (recently appointed as his special liaison official with the Ruhr workers), he had spent all of October 4 inspecting the bomb-damaged factories.

("He came on flying visits," Hupfauer said, "sometimes several times a
week. He would arrive just before bombardments, stay through them and
walk around afterwards. It had an enormous effect on the workers. He
seemed oblivious to danger. It wasn't even courage really; it was foolhardi-
ness. But he said, 'Repair those plants,' and that's what we did. Do you have
any idea what it meant to rebuild bombed factories to the point where they
could function again, sometimes in as little as a week?")

Wolters reported in the *Chronik* that Speer spent most of the night of October 4 watching the bombardments from a hilltop house belonging to one
of the industrialists:

> On his return to Berlin [in the early evening of October 5] he had a
> meeting of several hours with Admiral Dönitz about new U-boats . . . and
> then addressed a meeting attended by 100 officials of the SD. On this occa-
> sion the Minister, SS Brigadeführer Ohlendorf and Gauleiter Hanke [act-
> ing for Himmler] signed a formal agreement between the [newly set up]
> economic department of the SD and the ministry.

This assurance of SD support was directed first against Sauckel and his
staff, who in Speer's opinion were going the wrong way about getting workers from abroad and equally wrong in their treatment once they were in Germany; and second, against the Gauleiter with their lackadaisical attitude
toward "total war," whom, now with Himmler behind him, he intended to
tackle in Posen the next day.

THE ASSEMBLY of the Reichsleiter and Gauleiter in Posen on
October 6, 1943, was part of Hitler's determination to make sure that his supporters were all implicated in the catastrophe he was bringing on Germany.
Hitler had told his closest army advisors months before that the "bridges behind us are burnt," but now he charged Himmler with making the most
faithful in the party privy to the guilty knowledge. The Allies had already announced in October 1942 their intention to proceed against war-crimes suspects, and in December linked this to the German government's "bestial
policy of extermination of the Jews of Europe." Himmler's orders from Hitler would have been to draw everyone in the upper ranks of Nazis into the

net, so that no one could henceforth dare to break ranks, claiming innocence or ignorance. The first group to be initiated in Posen were high SS officers on October 4. Himmler's second address on October 6, virtually identical to the first, was, as already mentioned, to the Reichsleiter and Gauleiter. In January 1944 it was repeated to a group of the highest-ranking Wehrmacht generals.

Notification had been sent from Bormann's Party Chancellery Office at Hitler's HQ on September 30, 1943, to all Reichsleiter and Gauleiter, the Reich Youth Leader Arthur Axmann and two Reich Ministers, Speer and Rosenberg. A special train would leave Berlin's Friedrichstrasse station for Posen at 9:32 p.m. on October 5, arriving back in Berlin October 8 around 8 a.m.

Participants intending to travel from their bases via Berlin were requested to confirm their requirements by telex or phone. Dress would be "Uniform, white shirt, breeches, boots." The train had seven sleeper cars. Forty-six beds were assigned: Speer's was in car 4, compartment 13/14, although it is not known whether he used it or went by car. As the surviving sleeper list shows no reservations for Speer's five associates—one ministry official and four industrialists from his "Dollar-a-Year" group, who would be addressing the Gauleiter before Speer's own speech—they must have made their own way to Posen, by air or road.

Himmler's speech would be the main—and last—address of the conference, late in the afternoon. But the program started at 9 a.m. with brief talks by Speer's industrial experts, the last by Walter Rohland, Germany's steel czar. Goebbels wrote that night in his diary,

> They didn't say much that was new for me, but . . . their black on black descriptions of the state of the war . . . and war production . . . were a good introduction for Speer's own fifty-minute address. . . . Based on solid facts and figures, he demonstrates as clearly as can be that nothing will now help . . . except . . . total effort for total war . . . as—for all the good it did—I already said in my speech at the Palace of Sports [in February]. . . .
>
> Speer told them very bluntly that no protests and no arguments would deter him [from converting all plants to war production]. He is, of course, right: The Führer has ordered him to transfer a million workers into armaments at once and, furthermore, to release sufficient young men from the armament industry to form about twenty divisions. The Gauleiter are screaming holy murder, for of course it means the end of most of their flourishing industries. But they'll have to go along with him. . . .

What Goebbels—in total sympathy here with Speer—didn't mention in his diary, was the last sentences of Speer's speech, which caused an uproar in the sumptuously renovated Golden Hall of the romantic Posen Castle, where the meeting was held. Speer quoted his own speech in *Inside the Third Reich:*

> You will please take note of what I'm saying. The manner in which some of the *Gaue* have hitherto obstructed the shutdown of consumer goods production will no longer be tolerated. . . . I can assure you that I am prepared to apply the authority of the Reich Government at any cost. I have discussed this with Reichsführer SS Himmler, and from now on districts that do not carry out within two weeks the measures I request will be dealt with firmly.

The Gauleiter, Speer wrote in his book (as he had at greater length but otherwise identically in the "Spandau draft"), were incensed, interpreting particularly his last sentence as threatening them with concentration camps. Taken aback by their furious reaction, he asked Bormann to let him return to the platform to clarify his meaning. But Bormann, "hypocritically friendly," Speer wrote, told him there was no need. Soon afterwards, however, Hitler gave him to understand that he knew of the Gauleiter's anger against him, and said that it was "unfortunate" that he did not know how to handle them. "Bormann had at last found a way to undermine my standing with Hitler. . . ."

Speer commented bitterly in *Inside the Third Reich* on the Gauleiter's excessive drinking after the conference, but did not mention Himmler's speech to them in the afternoon, which gave Hitler's political leaders good reason to drown their trepidations that night of October 6, 1943.

Himmler arrived at 3 p.m., listened to speeches from Admiral Dönitz, Field Marshal Milch and the new Chief of Staff of the SA, Schepmann. Then, from 5:30 to 7 p.m. he delivered his ominous lecture. It was almost an hour—seventeen typewritten pages—before he arrived at the core of his message. Himmler said,

> I want to speak now, in this most restricted circle, about a matter which you, my party comrades, have long accepted as a matter of course, but which for me has become the heaviest burden of my life—the matter of the Jews. You all accept happily the obvious fact that there are no more Jews in your province. All Germans, with very few exceptions, realize perfectly well that we couldn't have lasted through the bombs and the stresses of the fourth, perhaps in the future the fifth and even sixth year of war, if this destructive pestilence were still present within our body politic. The brief sentence "The Jews must be exterminated" is easy to pronounce, but the demands on those who have to put it into practice are the hardest and most difficult in the world.

You see, of course they are Jews; obviously, they are only Jews. But think for a moment how many people—including party comrades—have addressed one of those famous petitions [to us] in which was written that of course all Jews are pigs, but so-and-so is a decent Jew who should be exempted from whatever was being done. I daresay that according to the number of such petitions . . . there must have been more decent Jews in Germany than there were Jews altogether. I'm only mentioning this because you will know, each one of you, that in your own province there are good respectable National Socialists, each of whom knows one decent Jew.

I ask that you only listen but never speak of what I am saying to you here today. We, you see, were faced with the question "What about the women and children?" And I decided, here too, to find an unequivocal solution. For I did not think that I was justified in exterminating—meaning kill or order to have killed—the men, but to leave their children to grow up to take revenge on our sons and grandchildren. The hard decision had to be taken to have this people disappear from the face of the earth. For the organization which had to carry out this order, it was the most difficult one we were ever given. . . . I think I can say that it has been carried out without damaging the minds or spirits of our men and our leaders. The danger was great and ever present. For the difference between the two possibilities . . . to become cruel and heartless and no longer to respect human life, or to become soft and succumb to weakness and nervous breakdowns . . . the way between Scylla and Charybdis is appallingly narrow.

The immense fortunes we requisitioned from the Jews have been handed over to the last penny to the Reich Minister for Economics. My position has always been that while we have done our duty here, toward our people, our race . . . and our Führer who this once in two thousand years has been given to us . . . we do not have the right to keep one penny of this requisitioned Jewish wealth. My order has been from the start, that any SS man who steals even one single mark, is to be put to death. And I can tell you that I have signed about a dozen death sentences precisely for this in these last days. . . .

I considered it my duty to speak to you, who are the highest dignitaries of the party, of our political order which is the Führer's political instrument, for once quite openly about this question . . . to tell you how it was.

By the end of this year, the matter of the Jews will [also] have been dealt with in the countries under our occupation. . . . You will not doubt that the economic aspect presented many great difficulties, above all with the clearing of ghettos: in Warsaw we fought street battles for four weeks in the ghetto, four weeks of clearing seven hundred bunkers, one after the

other. Because that ghetto produced fur coats and textiles, we were prevented from taking it over when it would have been easy: we were told we
were interfering with essential production. "Halt!" they called, "This is
war production!"

[Then came a remark, apparently addressed to Speer himself:]

Of course, this has nothing to do with party comrade Speer: it wasn't
your doing. It is precisely this kind of so-called war production enterprise
which party comrade Speer and I will clean out together over the next
weeks. We will do this just as unsentimentally as all things must be done
in this fifth year of the war: unsentimentally but from the bottom of our
hearts, for Germany. . . .

And with this I want to finish about the matter of the Jews. You are now
informed, and you will keep the knowledge to yourselves. Later perhaps
we can consider whether the German people should be told about this.
But I think it is better that we—we together—carry for our people the responsibility . . . responsibility for an achievement, not just an idea . . . and
then take the secret with us to our grave. . . .

Even in this dreadful speech, as in the others he delivered on this subject,
Himmler carefully avoided describing the method of these murders—the
words "gas chamber" never appeared—and the probability remains that all
those who heard him, most of whom already knew about the shootings in
Russia, thought that this continued to be the way the Jews were killed. The
existence of the gas chambers, in which half of these millions died, and which
the so-called revisionists have so busily denied ever since, was apparently un-
mentionable even for Himmler, Hitler's master of death.

Himmler's speeches revealing to the Reich's leadership the genocide of the
Jews are of course part of the historical record. No one who has studied the
period can fail to have read them (parts even survive in recordings made at
the time) and to realize that here, on Hitler's orders, the Rubicon was
crossed.

I had always believed that, given Speer's presence in Posen that day, his
presence at Himmler's speech was inevitable. But I had specifically planned
to avoid this necessarily disturbing subject, and the whole question of his
denial of knowledge about the Jews, until the last few days of our first concentrated three weeks of conversations.

When he brought it up, the last morning of our second week together, it
was, curiously enough, the first day when there was no sun and, with snow
falling thickly and covering the window, the kitchen where we sat was
strangely dark.

We were going to Munich the next day where a book entitled *Albert*

Speer, Controversies about a German Phenomenon, edited by Adelbert Reif, with contributions from writers around the globe, was to be launched.

Had I heard of the Gauleiter conference in Posen? he asked. I said, yes, I had, but why not talk about this after our return from Munich?

He shook his head. I reached out to turn on a small lamp on the table, but he stopped me. "Leave it for a bit," he said and added that he wanted to tell me about something before we went to Munich; it was a controversial subject and as there was something about it in the *Controversies* book, he thought it was likely that it would be brought up by journalists at the launch.

Six and a half years earlier, in October 1971, a Harvard historian, Professor Erich Goldhagen, had launched a bitter attack on Speer in the American magazine *Midstream.* In an article titled "Albert Speer, Himmler and the Secret of the Final Solution," Goldhagen had claimed that Himmler's direct address to Speer in his Posen speech was clear proof that he was present when it was given, thus giving the lie to his continuing claim of ignorance about the murder of Europe's Jews. Goldhagen said it established his full complicity and the hypocrisy of his admission of generalized rather than specific guilt at Nuremberg and ever since. In the notes section at the end of his article, Goldhagen added what purported to be an additional sentence from Himmler. "Speer," he quoted Himmler saying, "is not one of the pro-Jewish obstructionists of the Final Solution. He and I together will tear the last Jew alive on Polish ground out of the hands of the army generals, send them to their death and thereby close the chapter of Polish Jewry."

Speer's face had gone deep red and then very pale as—not knowing that I had long known about this attack—he told me about the *Midstream* article. I got up to get him a glass of water, and I opened the window to let in some fresh air. He was sitting on his straight chair, for a moment resting his head on his hands and then turned toward the open window breathing deeply.

"You see, I *was* in Posen the day of that speech," he said then. "I addressed the Gauleiter that morning. But I could not for the life of me remember hearing Himmler's speech. And yet, I immediately looked it up in the archives and it was true; he had given that speech, except for that last sentence Goldhagen quoted. That I couldn't find."

I now told him that I had read Goldhagen's article, among the many cuttings I had studied before I came to see him, and that I, too, checking it against Himmler's speech, hadn't found that last devastating quote. I told him that I had telephoned Goldhagen at Harvard to ask him about it. He told me that this had been an unfortunate mistake. "In the note," he told me, "I merely wished to clarify further what Himmler meant. The editor of *Midstream* mistakenly put it in quotes, and I never got around to correcting it.

But if you read Himmler's speech carefully," he had added, "you'll agree with me that that was his meaning."

I told Speer then, as I had told Goldhagen on the telephone weeks before, that I didn't agree and that it seemed a rather daringly dramatic interpretation, whether in or out of quotes.

Speer was almost speechless when I told him this. "Oh, my God," he finally said. "My God . . . I can never, never, thank you enough for that." His voice had suddenly gone hoarse. "For me," he said, "reading Goldhagen's article was devastating. Do you know that for two days I really thought I had gone out of my mind? I kept thinking: Was I mad? Had I really sat through this, but succeeded in pushing it out of my mind, to the extent of honestly not remembering myself in that situation?" He paused. "It was my worst two days in many, many years. And then, quite by chance, I talked to an old friend, Walter Rohland, a steel magnate during the Hitler time. I told him I was having this trouble, and he said immediately, 'But you weren't *there*. Don't you remember? You left with me immediately after your speech, before lunch, and we drove to see Hitler at Rastenburg.' He happened to remember it particularly vividly because a year before he had described the drive and that meeting with Hitler in an outline for a book of his own memoirs."

Subsequent to this, Speer said, he had also received a letter from the man responsible for the organizational side of the conference, the Posen Gauleiter's administrative aide, Harry Siegmund, saying that he remembered their leaving. And furthermore, General Milch had also told John Toland, then working on his book *Adolf Hitler*, that Speer had left the meeting at lunchtime.

He went to his study to get the two affidavits these men had given him. By the time he returned, his hair brushed and his face pink, the snow had stopped, and the sun was out. Margret came into the kitchen. "Come on, get those papers off the table," she directed. "Go and sit outside in the sun for a bit—do you good the both of you. I'm getting lunch."

The atmosphere had totally changed. My help in the kitchen rejected, Speer and I, both of us wearing anoraks and armed with apple-juice spritzers, went outside. He cleaned the snow off the end of their big refectory table in front of the house, and we sat in the suddenly brilliant midday sun, talking about skiing and about our shared love of mountain walks. By the time Margret's soup was on the table his eyes were clear, his skin smooth. The emotional storm I had witnessed less than an hour before might never have been.

After lunch we parted, as always, for a rest. Would he mind, I asked, if I took the two affidavits upstairs to read? He handed them over without a word.

Both were formal documents, signed under oath and witnessed. Rohland confirmed that he had addressed the Gauleiter that morning of October 6, just before Speer's speech:

> As the Gauleiter were scheduled to confer with Hitler in Rastenburg the next day and Speer feared that by that time the effect of our addresses would be dissipated, we drove to Hitler's HQ that same day in order to convince him of the urgency of our demands and the need for him to be tough with the Gauleiter.
> This is what I wrote a year ago, without having communicated with Speer about it in any way. Our trip took place in Speer's fast Mercedes which he drove himself. We left Posen after a snack and arrived at Hitler's HQ just after dark.

This was the only address Rohland ever gave to the Gauleiter, he concluded. It was also the only time he drove with Speer to Rastenburg. Error was thus impossible.

> I declare under oath that the above information, given from my best recollection, is the truth.
> Signed, at Ratingen, July 6, 1973

The second statement under oath, by Harry Siegmund, seemed as convincing. He wrote,

> I remember clearly that Speer left [Posen] in his car shortly after lunch. A number of conference participants were accommodated at the Hotel Ostland where we had the reception and the lunch. As I was responsible for organization and protocol, I was in constant touch with the hotel's director to make sure that everything would go off smoothly. I was therefore informed about all arrivals and departures.
> I also recall that when, in the course of a conversation on a later occasion with the liaison officer of the local army command, Prinz Reuss XXXVII, we compared Speer's cool presentation of the armament situation with the ominous rumors about Himmler's speech, Prinz Reuss emphasized that Albert Speer was not present during this speech.

Himmler, he stated, was exceptionally shortsighted:

> I would therefore doubt that Himmler during his speech could have noticed who was present, especially since, considering the "Romanic" style of Posen Castle, bright lights were avoided.
> I declare on oath that the preceding statement, made from my best recollection, is the truth.
> Badenweiler, October 22, 1975

The two statements were indeed persuasive. By the time Speer and I met again, as every day, at 3:30 that afternoon for coffee, I had had ample time to reflect upon that morning's emotion, so extraordinary a display for that cool, cool man.

Margret always joined us for the afternoon coffee and cake, after which she withdrew to her room while we remained at that comfortable kitchen table. Around 7:30 p.m. it would again be cleared for our cold supper—cold cuts, cheese, fruit and a glass of wine—after which we repaired, sometimes all three of us, sometimes only Speer and I, to the lovely big room he called his studio, where he lit a big fire, played records from his huge classical collection, and we had coffee, wine and more talk.

I told him that afternoon, after Margret had withdrawn, that I had read the statements. Given all these confirmations, I said, I could accept that he wasn't there the afternoon of Himmler's speech. But did it really matter? Sixty Gauleiter were there, including three of his friends.

"Yes," he interrupted, "Kaufmann [Gauleiter of Hamburg] told me that Himmler had used my name. . . ."

Exactly, I said. And yet he would have us believe that neither Karl Kaufmann, nor his old friend Hanke [Gauleiter of Lower Silesia], nor anyone else told him in what context Himmler had used his name? Was that likely, or even possible? Baldur von Schirach, I said, wrote later in *his* book that everyone was so depressed after Himmler's speech that "when Bormann offered us a snack after the end of the speech, we sat wordlessly, avoiding each other's eyes." (Though Schirach described the speech accurately, he misdated it to May the next year.) So his friends had been "deadly depressed" about this enormity but said nothing, absolutely nothing to him the next morning, or ever? He didn't answer, only shook his head.

And what about in January 1944, I asked, when Himmler addressed the generals in almost the same words, although he added that "whatever our uniforms, we are all soldiers, and I obeyed a superior order," obviously referring to Hitler, his only superior. This time, I said, it was his military friends who had listened to this horror. Was he saying that they too kept their counsel, told him nothing—asked him nothing?

"At that time," he answered, now sounding very weary, "I was on sick leave; I wasn't around."

IN THE CONTEXT of our talks, of the manner in which he told me about his reaction to Goldhagen's article and responded to my challenges, of the sworn affidavits by Rohland and Siegmund he showed me and of Goldhagen's unfortunate mistake, I found myself inclined, on balance, to accept Speer's interpretation of these events. But by that time I had decided anyway that whether he had actually been present at this speech or not, he had to have known about the genocide of the Jews by shooting, though conceivably not about the gas chambers.

However, in researching this book, the Himmler speech and Speer's degree of knowledge of it had come to seem to me absolutely central to an understanding of him. Every aspect of it was crucial—his reaction first to whatever he knew during the remaining year and a half of Hitler's rule, then when talking with Georges Casalis in Spandau, then in 1971–72 to Goldhagen's article, in 1977–78 when we talked of it and finally in his last years until he died in 1981. In my years of research, therefore, I repeatedly checked every aspect and every document connected with this episode.

In 1978 I had studied Speer's "Reply," as it was printed in *Controversies,* edited by the young German historian, Adelbert Reif. But nine years later I found in Koblenz his draft for it, at thirty-six pages twice as long as later printed. It clearly shows the research time he invested, but his digressions, trying to prove how his ministry fought to keep Jews working for armament production rather than allowing them to be taken away, are irrelevant to the issue of his presence at Himmler's speech.

When Speer cut this draft for inclusion in Reif's 1978 book, he added three more arguments to the statements of Rohland, Siegmund and Milch. He wrote,

1) It is impossible that I could have gone by air to Rastenburg after Himmler's speech, at about 7 p.m., because according to a declaration on oath by my former pilot, Lufthansa Captain Hermann Nein (ret.), in order to fly I would have had to leave Posen shortly before 4 p.m. as the Rastenburg airport was not equipped for night landings.

2) It can be assumed that I covered the 430 kilometers between Posen and Rastenburg on straight roads virtually free of traffic in about five hours. Thus Dr. Rohland and I could have arrived at Hitler's HQ between 6:30 and 7 p.m.

3) Hitler's appointment list [*Terminkalender*] shows no fixed dates between 5 p.m. and 9:10 p.m. on October 6, 1943, except for 9:10 with two permanent members of his HQ staff. . . . There were thus, including supper, about two hours available for Hitler's meeting with Rohland and me.

4) I spoke twice to the Gauleiter in Posen, on October 6, 1943, and on August 3, 1944. Both times I went to Hitler's HQ at Rastenburg after my speech: once with the Gauleiter's Special Train as I described it in *Inside the Third Reich* and once in my car. When I wrote my book, I mixed up the two journeys. . . .

Each of these desperate arguments unfortunately fails. First, there is the denial that he could possibly have flown *after* Himmler's speech. Hitler's personal pilot, Hans Baur, told me it was total nonsense to say one couldn't fly into Rastenburg at night. "I won't say it was easy," he said, "because it wasn't. It's true that the airport was not specifically equipped for night flights. For night flights we put up temporary lighting, and therefore preferably used a larger airport nearby. But I certainly flew into Rastenburg at night."

Second, Speer's argument that Hitler had time between 5 and 9:10 to see Rohland and himself is based on an uncharacteristic mistake. Speer thought the *Terminkalender* was an appointments list, but in fact it was a record kept by Hitler's valet Heinz Linge of Hitler's activities during the day, written up last thing at night after Hitler had retired, never before two a.m. This meticulous diary records Speer's presence at supper and tea only on the next evening, October seventh, but not on the night of the sixth, when he claimed to have talked with Hitler.

Third, his agonized last-minute claim that he had confused the two Gauleiter meetings is totally unacceptable, for there was an enormous difference in atmosphere between those two conferences. He had written in his book in 1968 that the hung-over Gauleiter arrived late for the speeches in the morning, were furious that he had "threatened them with concentration camps" and were drunk that night when they got on the train that took them to Hitler's HQ.

"I and a few other sensible people," he continued (in the draft), "were appalled at the example given by the party's leaders in a public place, and I appealed to Hitler the next morning to say a few words on 'temperance' to his political associates. But he protected the feelings of his 'Old Comrades.'"

It is impossible that he could have mixed up this 1943 meeting with the one on August 3, 1944, because his situation vis-à-vis the Gauleiter was then entirely different. After the failed coup of July 20, 1944, when his name was found on a list of proposed ministers in a new government, his position seemed briefly in danger, but not for long. Within a few days Bormann invited him again to address the assembled Gauleiter.

Goebbels reported in his diary on August 2, 1944, the night before this conference, that Speer and he had a long talk during which Speer informed him of the entirely felicitous themes of his planned speech to the Gauleiter the next day, including the progress of the new A-4 rockets (later called V-2s) which would soon plague London. Writing as usual in the night after the event, Goebbels described the atmosphere at the August 3, 1944, conference,

. . . which simply cannot be compared with the last one [October 6, 1943] . . . In the afternoon Speer speaks for two hours . . . giving them for the first time the detailed new production figures which cause a sensation: his achievements, of which the Gauleiter really had no idea, are very impressive and *have a calming effect on them.* . . . Later Himmler . . . [about] the Twentieth of July with shocking details . . . which we must not allow the public to hear. . . . *At midnight I travel with Speer to headquarters* [author's italics].

In 1944, thus, he traveled with Goebbels; in 1943, apparently, with Rohland. Although it is thus impossible that Speer had simply confused the two Gauleiter meetings in Posen, his despair about Goldhagen's article, which brought back to public notice that landmark date of his life, October 6, 1943, was very real.

"The Posen speech was a trauma for him," Koblenz archivist Hedwig Singer told me. "He sent me Goldhagen's article, I think late in 1971, and asked me to start looking where there might be proof that he wasn't there."

In a long handwritten letter in January 1972, he asked Frau Singer whether the Himmler speech was in the Nuremberg files. "If so," he wrote, "why didn't they use it against me? The fact that they didn't could be important." At the end of January, after hearing that Himmler's speech—though among the background documents—had not been discussed in court, he wrote again. "If what Goldhagen writes is true, all I can think is that the prosecution looked into it, and must have decided that Himmler's sentence contained no proof against me."

Hedwig Singer is an intelligent and perceptive woman who, despite her liking for Speer, always managed to retain an objective detachment. She is the best witness about his work in the Federal Archives during those years. "It did sound to me," she said, "as if his search was honest. Certainly his horror about Goldhagen's article was. . . . During that year, and well into 1973, he spent a lot of time here. He looked through all the files that might have provided some answers; he searched for a long, long time. He was an enormously careful researcher, very thorough."

It was a cold November day in 1986 when Frau Singer and I discussed this matter over tea in her apartment. I told her what Speer had told me, that Walter Rohland had reassured him within two days after reading the Goldhagen article that they had left Posen together early that October 6, and that therefore he wasn't there during Himmler's speech. I saw her look of surprise. "Rohland told him that?" she repeated. "When?"

I repeated, "two days" after he had read Goldhagen's article. I then read her Rohland's sworn statement in 1973. "He told him in 1971, and then wrote that statement in 1973," Singer said thoughtfully. "Well, all I can say is that during the time Speer spent here in 1972 and 1973, he went to see Rohland quite often. Of course Speer might have told me about Rohland, and I could have forgotten. But if he had that testimony in 1971, why did he go on looking?"

It looked as though Rohland had simply come to the aid of an old friend. But to add to the complexity, one important bit of evidence appearing to support Rohland's story turned up later among the Nuremberg trial documents. Rohland stated during interrogation on May 20, 1946—twenty-five years before Goldhagen's attack—that he and Speer had a conference with Hitler, *before* the Führer's speech on October 7 to the Gauleiter: he did not specify then, however, *when* they talked with Hitler. In his memoirs, published in 1978, by which time it seemed no doubt important to support Speer's stand, Rohland expanded on the theme by describing the cold supper he and Speer were served at Hitler's table that night (the sixth), and the small talk with which Hitler entertained them.

But there is another possibility. Linge's *Terminkalender* shows that Hitler had a relaxed morning on October seventh—Dr. Morell at 11 a.m., a walk with Bormann at 11:30, breakfast at 11:45, his barber at 12, and his usual situation conference at 12:30. Lunch at 13:35 with the Gau- and Reichsleiter was followed at 14:35 by time to draft his speech to them, which he delivered at 15:15.

There were thus several gaps when Hitler could have had a brief talk with Speer and Rohland (without Linge necessarily noting it) "before [his] speech to the Gauleiter," just as Rohland stated in Nuremberg. The "expansion" of his account—Hitler's small talk over a cold supper—was written long after Speer's trauma over Goldhagen in 1972 and helpfully fleshed out his story. This seems to me the most likely explanation: he was a good friend.

By 1986, when I was carrying out research into this question, it had begun to be difficult to find former Nazi witnesses to check other points in Speer's account. They had either died or they shied away from talking, especially about Speer, the despised "traitor."

But the author of the second affidavit, Harry Siegmund, who had stated that he recalled distinctly Speer leaving in his car "shortly after lunch," was alive and did talk with me, though only on the telephone. I asked how he came to volunteer this helpful statement.

He laughed out loud. "Volunteer?" he asked. "I didn't volunteer anything. Speer pursued me with I don't know how many phone calls, so I finally gave him what he wanted."

I said I was interested in his mention of "ominous rumors" about Himmler's speech. "I have nothing to say about Himmler's speech," he said.

Had Prinz Reuss attended it?

"Certainly not; whatever makes you think so? He was *army*."

I said I understood that. But if he didn't attend it, how did he know that Speer didn't, and how did the subject arise between them? Herr Siegmund hung up on me then.

Traudl Junge, Hitler's youngest secretary, and I discussed this whole subject for a long time. She had understood very well how important it was, both historically and for Speer personally. She was sure that Linge's record was the best evidence. He was physically, she said, the closest person to Hitler: the first to see him in the morning and the last to see him at night, when he saw him to bed. And (somewhat like Goebbels for his diary) it was always then—late at night—that he wrote out the *Terminkalender,* the day's events in retrospect.

We checked my photocopies of Linge's diary for the evenings of the sixth and seventh. On the sixth, the situation conference at 9:30 p.m. was followed by a few minutes with Below and Ambassador Hewel, and at "11:50: Tea with Frl. Wolf, Frau Junge, Professor [Dr.] Morell, Lieutenant Frentz [camera-man], Lt. Col. von Below, Hauptsturmführer Pfeiffer.

"2:30 a.m. End, Signed //Heinz Linge SS-O-Stuf."

"There was a rota for us [the four ladies]," Traudl Junge explained. Whichever two of the secretaries attended Hitler at lunchtime would then also be required for the afternoon tea session; the other two would be on duty for supper and the late-night tea. This schedule of course, she said, was elastic. If Hitler wanted to lunch or dine alone, or with one guest, they were free. But attendance at the nightly tea, she said, was normally obligatory until the end of his life. Hitler needed these *gemütliche* late-night gatherings—to comfort and distract him.

When we looked at the evening of the seventh, after Hitler's speech to the Gauleiter, the difference in atmosphere was obvious. Neither Below nor any of the ladies were present. The guests, both for supper at 9:00 and for "tea" at 11:30 p.m., were Ministers Speer and Rosenberg (Eastern Occupied Territories); Bormann and Himmler's liaison man, Karl Wolff; and Gauleiter Hanke (Lower Silesia), Sauckel (Forced Labor), Hofer (Innsbruck) and Rainer (Carinthia). All those present at tea that night had been present at Himmler's speech. Within this trusted circle, the discussion was bound at least to touch upon Himmler's revelations in Posen.

The fact is that the more Speer tries to explain away awkward facts, the clearer it is that he is trying desperately to avoid facing the truth. There is simply no way Speer can have failed to know about Himmler's speech, whether or not he actually sat through it. I believe that this was the turning point in his relationship with Hitler, even though it took a long time for it to be a complete reversal—if it ever was.

．　　．　　．

A CAREFUL COMPARISON of the "Spandau draft," private letters from Speer on this period, and the relevant pages in *Inside the Third
Reich* shows the stress he was under in the latter part of 1943, and the increased ambivalence in his relationship with Hitler. He told me during our
talks in 1978 that he saw Hitler only once between October 6, 1943, and his
long sick leave which began in mid-January 1944. He was trying to emphasize
to me the beginning of a separation between himself and Hitler, but this was
not true. Between the *Chronik* and Linge's *Terminkalender* seven meetings
are recorded between Speer and Hitler; on four of these occasions Speer
spent the night at Führer HQ after the late-night tea gathering.

In his memoirs, he mentions only one of these occasions, on November 13,
1943, at HQ when, he writes, Hitler reprimanded him "in a tone he had never
used toward me before." In yet another of Hitler's "hold out to the last man"
commands, he had ordered the army to hold Nikopol, the center of manganese mining, "at any cost." Chief of Staff Zeitzler had phoned Speer in despair to say that an immediate retreat was the only way to avert another
Stalingrad. After consultations with his steel experts, Röchling and Rohland,
Speer writes, he had sent an explanatory memorandum to Hitler and cabled
a copy to Zeitzler, saying that sufficient stocks were available in the Reich for
eleven to twelve months.

"What got into you," Hitler snarled, "to give the Chief of Staff your memorandum on the manganese situation?"

"But, my Führer," Speer replied, "it's good news."

"You have no business to give Zeitzler any memo whatever. Any information you have is for me and me alone. You have put me in an intolerable
situation. I have just given orders for all available forces to be concentrated
for the defense of Nikopol; at last a reason to force the army group to fight.
And then Zeitzler presents me with your memorandum, which makes me
out a liar. If we now lose Nikopol, it's your fault. I forbid you once and for all
to address any memos to anybody but me. Do you understand me? I forbid it."

It would be the only time Hitler became almost hysterically angry with
him. But Speer had long noticed a real change in his attitude, he writes. Until
the summer of 1943, Hitler had telephoned him at the beginning of every
month to ask for the latest production figures and, as they were usually outstanding, greeted them with exclamations of praise. When, with affectionate
messages to Margret, the call came to an end, Speer would thank him, saying
goodbye with the usual *"Heil, mein Führer."* Hitler—as he certainly never
did with anyone else—would frequently reply jokingly, *"Heil Speer."*

From that autumn on, however, Speer writes in *Inside the Third Reich*—
not in the draft—the telephone calls ceased and Hitler called Speer's deputy,

Saur, instead, who like Dorsch was an ally of Bormann's. "I gradually began to feel insecure in my own ministry."

Wolters commented on this in his *Segments of a Life:*

> ... Opposition to Speer by then was by no means limited to the Gauleiter, but also made itself felt more and more in his own working sphere, above all at the OT where Dorsch resisted any cooperation with the three of us whom Speer had installed in the top echelon; [Gerhard] Fränk as business manager, Bohr as head of personnel, and me in charge of public information.
>
> In order to stop once and for all the constant quarrels, Speer withdrew us at the end of 1943 from the OT and reintegrated us within the Ministry, with instructions however to keep a careful eye on the OT operations. . . .

Speer had one more shock that year of 1943. On December 10, four months after the rocket factories at Peenemünde had been destroyed by Allied bombs, he traveled to the Harz Mountains, not far from Buchenwald, to visit the underground installations (called "Dora") where Wernher von Braun's V-2 rockets were being produced.

It is astonishing that Speer was ever allowed to see this. "I virtually forced my way in after my ministry's medical director told me it was Dante's *Inferno,*" he told me. It is to his credit that in this case, not having been able to bring himself to write about it in the "Spandau draft" (of course addressed to his friend Wolters, who was already showing discomfort at Speer's constant criticisms of Hitler), he finally decided to write about it in *Inside the Third Reich.*

In Nuremberg Speer was to tell the court that he had never visited a labor camp, and this, possibly the most hellish of any, was apparently the only one he ever saw. (Mauthausen, of course, was a concentration-*cum*-labor camp.)

The creation of this underground camp was a direct result of a meeting in Rastenburg between Hitler, Speer and Himmler on August 22, 1943. Himmler had arrived that morning with an offer. He would undertake to guarantee complete secrecy about the rocket production if the work would be entirely produced by concentration camp prisoners, all of whose contact with the outside world would be eliminated. He offered to provide all the necessary technicians from among the prisoners. All industry would have to provide would be the management and the engineers.

Speer writes in *Inside the Third Reich,* "Hitler [who after initial skepticism was now convinced that the rockets were the miracle weapon which would win the war] agreed to this plan." Speer—and Saur—had no choice but to agree, as they had no alternative to offer. The man Himmler cannily chose to handle the rocket program was the previously mentioned SS Brigadeführer Hans Kammler, in looks and ruthlessness almost a reincarnation of Reinhard Heydrich.

The factories, Kammler proposed, would be built in the caves of the deep Harz Mountains; there they would be safe from Allied bombs and prying eyes. The workers would be drawn from the nearby Buchenwald concentration camp and would be under the authority of the SS.

The Peenemünde scientific team under its head, Colonel Walter Dornberger, and its most famous scientist, Wernher von Braun, would be responsible for the technical side; Speer's ministry would bear the financial responsibility for the project; Kammler and his SS construction apparatus would be in charge of building.

On August 23, 1943, the day after this initial meeting, the first one hundred prisoners from Buchenwald were brought to the site and construction was started that very morning. Two and a half weeks later, on September 10, Hitler formally approved the mountain complex and gave it its name: Central Works, code name Dora.

Jean Michel, a French slave laborer at Dora (Speer met him in Essen in 1947, when he and Wernher von Braun were called as witnesses at the war-crimes trial of Dora guards), was born in Paris in 1906. He was thus one year younger than Speer, thirty-eight to Speer's thirty-nine in 1943, when Speer came to inspect Dora.

"It was a cold day in December when I went there," Speer told me. "I was entirely unprepared; it was the worst place I have ever seen."

It was the morning after our conversation about October 6. Again Margret had gone skiing; again we sat at that comfortable kitchen table; again, immediately and impossible to fake, his face went pale; again he covered his eyes for a moment with his hand. "Even now when I think of it," he said, "I feel ill." The prisoners, he said, lived in the caves with the rockets; it was freezing cold, humid.

Jean Michel described it in his book, Dora:

> The missile slaves . . . from France, Belgium, Holland, Italy, Czechoslovakia, Hungary, Yugoslavia, Russia, Poland and Germany . . . toiled eighteen hours a day . . . for many weeks without tools, just with their bare hands . . . ammonia dust burnt their lungs . . . they slept in the tunnels in cavities which were hollowed out: 1,024 prisoners in hollows on four levels which stretched for 100 yards. . . .

"I was outraged," Speer told me. "I demanded to see the sanitary provisions. . . ."

No heat, no ventilation, not the smallest pail to wash in: death touched us with the cold, the sensation of choking, the filth that impregnated us. . . . The latrines were barrels cut in half with planks laid across. They stood at each exit from the rows of sleeping cubicles.

One of the SS guards' favorite jokes, Michel wrote, was to watch the slaves sit on the plank, laugh and push them into the barrel.

We all had dysentery. They laughed and laughed when we tried to get up and out of the shit. . . .

"I walked past these men and tried to meet their eyes," Speer said, despair in his voice. "They wouldn't look at me; they ripped off their prisoners' caps and stood at attention until we passed." From *Dora:*

The deportees saw daylight only once a week at the Sunday rollcall. The cubicles were permanently occupied, the day team following the night team and then vice versa . . . no drinkable water . . . you lapped up liquid and mud as soon as the SS had their backs turned. . . .

"I demanded to be shown their midday meal," Speer said. "I tried it; it was an inedible mess." After the inspection was over he found out that thousands had already died. "I saw dead men . . . they couldn't hide the truth," he said. "And those who were still alive were skeletons." He had never been so horrified in his life, he said. "I ordered the immediate building of a barracks camp outside, and there and then signed the papers for the necessary materials. . . ." Michel in *Dora:*

It was not until March 1944 that the barracks were completed. At Dora, the work was as terrible as ever, but we could at least leave the tunnel for the six hours of rest allowed. . . .

Eventually, thirty-one subcamps surrounded the Dora complex deep under these mountains, Jean Michel wrote, and added bitterly that no one could convince him that General Walter Dornberger (who after the war became a missile consultant to American aviation until he peacefully retired to Buffalo, New York) and his Peenemünde team of scientists, above all Wernher von Braun, who equally harvested financial and scientific glories in the United States, did not know who built their rockets and under what conditions. All these men, he says, collaborated with historians and writers after the war and indeed wrote books and papers themselves. "The word 'Dora,' " he wrote, "does not appear in any of those writings." It was, he says, as if that hell on earth had never been. Sixty thousand men were deported to Dora; thirty thousand of them died.

When I asked Speer what he had felt at Dora, it was the only time he admitted feeling something for the slave workers. "I was appalled," he said. "Yes," he repeated, almost as if in retrospect he was surprised at having given way to feeling, "Yes, there I *was* appalled."

TWELVE DAYS LATER, he and his closest associates—of course Annemarie Kempf and Wolters too—left Berlin for Christmas with soldiers and OT workers in Lapland, taking along a famous violinist, Siegfried Borries, and a magician named Kalanag to entertain the troops. Perhaps Speer thought that listening to a Bach partita played around a huge open fire in a primeval forest, nocturnal ski tours to Lapp encampments and sleep in a reindeer-skin sleeping bag in the icy open air could cleanse his soul. "I didn't want, I couldn't face, Christmas at home," is all he said by way of explanation. With six children, including the latest baby, Ernst, born that September, and Margret, who could not be told anything at all, and in his state of mind, it was hardly the moment for a happy Christmas at home.

Speer's brief description in the "Spandau draft" of his return trip from Finland to Hitler's HQ accompanied by violinist and magician—in a plane sent by Hitler—is very different from the book, and I have no explanation for this discrepancy.

In the "Spandau draft," he and Hitler meet amicably, and Hitler, hearing of the presence of the magician, invites him (though not the violinist) to perform for him and a small group of guests.

In *Inside the Third Reich*, however—and in Speer's account to me—there is nothing about a friendly post–New Year's get-together. His first visit to Führer HQ in the New Year, he wrote there, was to attend a major conference on the labor program for 1944. The meeting, with all the relevant ministers present, led to further furious confrontations with Hitler, who again—Speer wrote—called him to order, told him he would not tolerate his trying to force his ideas on a conference, and reminded him that *he* was in charge of the meeting, and that it was *he* who would decide at the end of it what was to be done. After asking all the ministers present how many workers they thought they would need in 1944, he added up the sum and, turning to Sauckel, asked him whether—"yes or no"—he could obtain four million workers for 1944. Sauckel assured him he could, but when Speer protested that the majority of these millions could very well be found in Germany itself, Hitler cut him off sharply. "Are you responsible to me for the labor force or is Party Comrade Sauckel?"

"Bormann and his cohorts had won, all down the line," Speer told me. "Four million more workers were to be dragged in, the nightmare of Dora was in my mind, and I was in disfavor with Hitler." There is little doubt that Speer's mind magnified some of Hitler's anger and some of his responses, but essentially it was true enough.

(Memory, one knows, is not immune to the influence of emotions and therefore can play strange tricks, magnifying and dramatizing some experiences and diminishing or moderating others. It is too easy to accuse Speer simply of lying—about his knowledge of the fate of the Jews, about his involvement in the horrendous maltreatment of the slave laborers and about various aspects of his relationship with Hitler and of his work. Many of the facts do suggest that he lied and most of his critics have accused him of it for what is now fifty years.

The truth, of course, is that lies are not necessarily simple, nor are the motivations which bring them about. Speer's lies, I think, as they reflect his life after that key date of October 6, 1943, are a demonstration of his ever-increasing need to schematize his life into an alignment of feelings and fears he could live with. "How can a man admit more and go on living?" said his daughter Hilde, who herself, I am convinced, would rather die on a rack than lie.)

A few days later Speer collapsed and on January 18, 1944, entered hospital, suffering from exhaustion, depression and an inflamed knee.

In the subsequent ten weeks, during which a palace revolution at his ministry in Berlin nearly toppled him from power, during which he became convinced that Himmler wanted him murdered, and during which he had an extraordinary experience of "dying," Hitler's magic began to wane for him. "I found something and lost something," he told me.

Found himself? Lost Hitler?

"A little of both and not enough of either," he said.

XVI

"It Was Not Yet My Time"

Nuremberg, March 11, 1946

FLÄCHSNER: Witness, you have already told us that the Defendant Speer was a sick man in 1944. Could you tell us approximately when his illness began and when it ended?

FIELD MARSHAL ERHARD MILCH: His illness started in February and I think lasted until about June.

FLÄCHSNER: Do you know anything about this long illness being exploited in order to severely undermine his . . . authority?

MILCH: It is very difficult for me to name here the individuals who probably hoped to succeed him. . . .

DURING THE LAST months of 1943 Speer had finally realized the real nature of Nazi crimes he had previously only suspected or sensed. ("*Ahnung*" for "sense" was the word he would repeatedly use to describe it to me.) During the first months of 1944, the traumatic effect of this inner—never open—admission allowed him a first understanding of the degree of his bondage to Hitler, the first step toward freeing himself from it.

It would not be possible to exaggerate the extent of Speer's exhaustion when he entered hospital that January, or the aggravation of the underlying illness while he was in the care of Himmler's close friend, Dr. Karl Gebhardt.

It was, of course, entirely consistent with his character that he did not give way to it for a long time. Later he would say that he had been medically mismanaged, and the medical records appear to bear this out. But whatever was wrong with the treatment he received, there can be no doubt that his insistence, for the first twenty days, on conducting—and controlling—the affairs of his ministry from his sickbed did not improve his state of health.

The intrigues at his ministry—basically emanating from those primarily loyal to the party (Dorsch, Todt's former personal assistant; Konrad Haasemann, whom Speer had recently replaced as personnel chief; Fritz Sauckel, in charge of forced labor; and later the ambivalent Karl Saur)—had simmered throughout the last months of 1943.

"The hyenas," he told me, "had only waited. When my position with Hitler suddenly seemed vulnerable, they made ready to pounce."

Bormann, backed by Himmler, had already used Speer's absence at Christmas to dispose Hitler further against him; Hitler's open rejection of him at the January 4, 1944, labor meeting in Rastenburg had encouraged his opponents. And when they then heard that he was gravely ill, "there was no holding them," Speer said.

He had originally asked his friend Dr. Karl Brandt for advice about his increasingly swollen leg, and it was he who insisted that he should consult Dr. Gebhardt, a leading orthopedic surgeon with a state-of-the-art hospital at Hohenlychen, outside Berlin. "I knew Gebhardt was a personal friend of Himmler's," Speer told me, "but that, of course, wasn't a medical disqualification. Until I learned it at Nuremberg, I had no idea that his hospital belonged to the SS or that, much worse than that, [deep freezing] experiments were carried out there on concentration camp prisoners."

Speer went to see Gebhardt in his hospital consulting room on the morning of January 18. He was immediately given a room in the hospital's north wing and ordered to bed. "On admission, January 18, 1944," Gebhardt's clinical notes say, "the patient appeared exhausted. Exceptionally taut swelling of the left knee joint. We immobilize the leg and apply arnica poultices. Diet: vegetarian and fruit."

When there was no improvement after five days, he ordered massive doses of sulfa. Eight days after admission, although Speer now showed general cold symptoms—bronchitis, hoarseness and nasal catarrh—and although the consultant's registrar suspected pleurisy, Gebhardt stuck to his diagnosis of rheumatoid inflammation of the left knee.

Although a retrospective study of Gebhardt's clinical reports clearly establishes that he misdiagnosed his patient, who either already on arrival had the beginnings of an embolism or developed it in the course of that week, it is highly doubtful that, given Speer's determination to continue working, any physician could have done much better.

"In Hitler's Germany," Speer told me, "it was not advisable for a Minister to get ill. First of all, nobody believed it. Because if Hitler, who hated sacking people, did fire one of his higher officials, it was invariably attributed to 'ill health.' The paradoxical result was that if you were *really* ill, you had to pretend to be well in order to avoid rumors of impending dismissal."

He therefore requisitioned three extra rooms in the private wing, had a direct telephone line connected to the Ministry switchboard and moved his two private secretaries, Kempf and Maguira, to Hohenlychen. He instructed the head of his Planning Department, Willy Liebel (who would be one of the first victims of the brewing palace revolution), and Liebel's deputy, Karl Hettlage, that all correspondence would continue to go out over his signature.

"We all tried to persuade him to rest," Annemarie told me, "but he was as if driven. I know what he has told you, and I know that you think that October 6, the Jews, Dora and all that was the cause, but I honestly can't say that my impression then was that specific. Yes, he was depressed, which was unprecedented for him, as indeed was this terrible fatigue. And even though we knew nothing about Himmler's terrible speech in Posen, of course he had told us about Dora, and we had seen for ourselves the effect that experience had, both on him and on those he had taken along.

"But I would be lying to you," she said, "if I said now that this was what I attributed his depression to at the time. No, I thought (naively, I know now) he was desperate—and desperately angry—about the intrigues against him at the Ministry, with people attempting to come between him and Hitler. These played havoc with the effectiveness of our work at a time when, more than ever before, everything—the whole war—depended on meticulous organization of production."

I asked if she thought then that he still believed in the war.

She shrugged. "That wasn't the point, was it?" she said. "What he could not bear—I think *really* could not bear—was to cease believing in Hitler, because of things like Dora." She hesitated for a moment, and then went on. "And I agreed with that, one hundred percent. Can you not understand that? If we couldn't believe in Hitler, what was there for us?"

She believed that the palace revolution at the Ministry was simply the attempt of the party to get into the one ministry where they had never been able to gain a real foothold. "It really is very difficult to explain the nuances," she said. "Yes, we were loyal National Socialists, certainly by conviction, even those who were not party members—and a lot of us in the Ministry weren't."

I asked how a man such as Dorsch, for instance, from a not entirely dissimilar background to Speer's, with at least some similar interests and talents, differed from Speer. She looked at me, momentarily surprised.

"First of all," she said, "Dorsch was an ideologue and Speer was an idealist. But more important, the difference was of course Hitler. Speer's idealism from the start had been focused, as countless others' were too, on this one man. But where it became different for Speer was when Hitler focused on *him.* This was when, I suppose you could say, Speer became his, body and soul. There really was nothing else—nothing unconnected with Hitler—in his life. Nothing can compare to the intensity of his feelings for Hitler, of their relationship. I wouldn't know how to describe to anyone Hitler's apparent lightness of spirit when they were together in the earlier years, or the quality of Speer's concern for him—concern even when he felt impatience or anger, later."

Everybody else she could think of among the leading personalities in the Third Reich, she said, however devoted they were to Hitler or to his cause, had other dimensions to their lives: their women, their children, their homes, other role models (such as Todt had been for Dorsch, she said) or even, as was the case for the army officers, other ideals. And for those who were totally dedicated to Hitler—such as Bormann, Goebbels and others, like Giesler—there was still the enormous difference that Hitler felt little or nothing for them.

Goebbels often commented in his diaries on Hitler's affection for him, I said.

She shook her head. "From what I read, or saw—never without a conditional remark such as 'I *think* the Führer is fond of me' or even 'I'm so happy; he does *not try to hide* his affection for me.' " She laughed out loud. "Can you imagine Speer writing things like that? For him," she said, "it was all inside. He had no emotional lightning rod. There was no . . . no 'safety net' for Speer. So when he began to doubt, illness was his only answer, his only possible escape."

She was with him all the time at Hohenlychen but didn't notice any overt change in him. "Nothing was so . . . direct," she said. "How could it be? He was so ill, and anyway, I didn't have that kind of perceptiveness, not then. In a way, I was a lot like him: I didn't like sentimentality. It made me uncomfortable to ponder or talk about feelings, my own or other people's. I preferred facts, rationality. So what I saw most of all at that time was that people wanted to harm him. I still thought that 'harming' him meant setting Hitler against him. I was not clever enough to understand all the game playing that was going on.

"I never saw that basically it was about the succession, until months later, many months later, when Speer did things against Hitler for which any other man in Germany would have been executed. And when Speer saw Hitler for"—she paused briefly—"what he really was. . . ." Again she paused. "Can you imagine that I am *still* finding it difficult to say that? Anyway, when he understood that, and yet so obviously still couldn't abandon him. . . ." She paused once more, "They couldn't really give each other up, could they? That's what it was all about. The people who tried to turn Hitler against Speer didn't know that, didn't understand that. Who could?"

When, lying in his hospital bed, Speer learned of the extent of the palace revolution being waged against him in Berlin, he first orchestrated a thorough investigation of all the circumstances and people involved. He telephoned his closest associates or brought them to Hohenlychen to see him, then wrote letters to the three main agitators against him.

To Dorsch he issued an ultimatum of virtual dismissal if he didn't toe the line. To Haasemann he explained his wrongdoings (and then had him arrested). To Bormann he wrote assuring him of his conviction that he ("who I know would consider it beneath your dignity to have anything to do with such backstairs intrigues") would be as appalled as Speer was by the disgusting means employed by disloyal employees. And on January 31 he wrote to Goebbels to inform him of the disloyalties in his ministry while he was incapacitated, asking for his active support on his return.

At the same time, he was not going to let Sauckel get out from under his control. On January 25 (by which date Gebhardt's clinical notes report a puzzling deterioration of Speer's general health), he dictated two letters to Sauckel:

I'm informed by Thyssen [armaments firm in the Ruhr] that in a transport of 509 just-arrived workers from the East were 161 children from 1 to 14 years old, and 49 men and 69 women incapable of performing work: it seems pointless to assign family groups to factory work for which, obviously, only young and unattached workers are suitable. The others, if anything, would surely be more useful on the land. . . .

In his second letter he informed Sauckel that it was impermissible to allow armament workers in the Hamburg area to have fled their vitally important jobs because of the bombardments.

My understanding is that 40,000, who apparently just wandered off, remain unaccounted for. It is essential to proceed very sharply indeed here; they are to be brought back from wherever they are and put to work in the places they were assigned to.

And finally he wrote a seven-page letter to Hitler—the first of three he would send from hospital—in which he summarized his efforts since he took over his ministerial assignment and the assistance Hitler provided for him. Without the total authority Hitler had vested in him from the beginning, he wrote, it would not be possible to maintain the flow of armament production. But here, for the first time, there was an indication of withdrawal:

I do not have to emphasize to you, my Führer, that I never had ambitions for a political career, either during or after the war. I consider my present activity purely as war work and am looking forward to the time when I will be able to dedicate my life as an artist to tasks more suited to me than anything of a political nature. . . .

Speer's many critics, both underestimating his involvement and overrating his prescience, attributed these letters on the one hand to Speer's fear of losing power and, on the other, to a clever tactic of taking out insurance against the perils of the future. The truth, I think, is simpler: Speer's conflict, as Annemarie Kempf so rightly said, was anxiety not about his power but—though certainly not unrelated to it under the circumstances—about his relationship with Hitler.

Indeed, his next unprecedentedly emotional letter to Hitler, two days later, in a way begs for recommitment. Never had he bothered Hitler before with small problems, he said, but as his illness prevented him from taking the necessary measures himself, he saw himself forced to report two instances of disloyalty which could not go unpunished. Goebbels, whom he had asked to act as an ombudsman in this matter, was entirely of his view that in the National Socialist state, intrigues behind the backs of Ministers were impermissible. He added,

He and I both feel that any personnel problems, including those of a political nature, must be dealt with by the relevant Minister himself, who is the only one in a position to draw the consequences. . . .

There are two curious aspects to this letter. On the one hand it is an almost pathetic cry for help. On the other, however, his assertiveness borders on rudeness. He was going to have to insist, he continued, on an official investigation and the severest penalties, including a period in a concentration camp for the guilty. Almost challenging Hitler, he wrote that a copy of this letter was being sent to Reichsleiter Bormann, "who I know would wish to be helpful in this matter."

Except for information from Margret, his secretaries and from the doctors that Hitler (who had from the beginning ordered his own physician, the dubious Dr. Theodor Morell, to report daily on Speer's condition) was continuously asking about him, Speer received no answer to his letters. Instead there were additional indications every day that his ministry had been seriously infiltrated both by Bormann's party spies and Himmler's SD. In addition, all of Hitler's top men—Bormann and Himmler, but also Göring and finally Ley—were vying for Speer's power and, in the case of Ley, unashamedly for his job. Göring had linked up with Dorsch and Saur, taking them along to his meetings with Hitler and always singing their praises. Bormann and Himmler meanwhile continued to throw suspicion onto Speer's closer associates, in some cases going so far as to plant evidence of anti-party activities against them.

"I can't tell you what it was like," Annemarie Kempf remarked to me. "The going and coming, the tension in his hospital room, the constant telephone—it was worse than anything had ever been at the office. And with all this, I could see that he was getting ever more ill, and I could not understand how it was that Gebhardt, who saw him at least twice a day, didn't see it."

And then, one day, "I can't remember the date exactly," she said, "but it was around the eighth or ninth of February," Himmler had come to Hohenlychen, and she overheard a conversation between him and Gebhardt.

"It was one of the most shocking, most frightening moments of my life," she said. Several times by then Speer had told her he had a bad feeling about Gebhardt. "I took it for a sick man's fantasies. You know how it is; when one feels physically weak, the imagination can begin to play tricks."

"Twice, after one of Gebhardt's visits, Speer said, 'I think he's trying to do me in.' And I had said that what was doing him in was he himself with his stubborn insistence on conducting affairs of state from his bed. But then I heard that conversation.

"I was in the room we had been given as an office; it was after Speer's lunch, and as he was having a rest I had decided to lie down for a moment myself. And I heard these voices right outside my door."

Recognizing one of them as Gebhardt's and hearing Speer's name mentioned, she tiptoed over to the (locked) door and listened. "Then I realized the other man was Himmler. I came too late to hear the beginning of a sentence, but I heard him say, 'Well, then he's dead.' Then Gebhardt said, 'But—' and Himmler cut him off, saying, 'That's enough. The less said, the better.' "

I said that there was a curious resemblance here to a story Funk allegedly told Speer in Spandau, and which Speer had mentioned in *Inside the Third Reich.* Apparently, in the autumn of 1943 at a Leibstandarte drinking party, Funk's onetime aide Horst Walter, who was then Sepp Dietrich's adjutant, had heard Gebhardt tell some SS officers that Himmler considered Speer dangerous and that he would have to "disappear." She shrugged. "Gebhardt drank like a fish, like the rest of them," she said, contemptuously. "In his cups, he might have said anything.

"Of course," she said, going back to her memories of Hohenlychen, "I wasn't given to hysterics. If Speer hadn't made these remarks to me, and if I hadn't been so worried about what certainly seemed to me a curious minimum of treatment for an obviously very sick man, I think I might have ignored it. After all, it could have meant anything—or nothing. But at that moment it frightened me to death. I went straight to the phone and rang Margret Speer."

"I had never heard Frau Kempf sound like that," Margret Speer said when we came to talk about Speer's illness in 1978. "I remember it very distinctly, though all she said on the phone was that she was very worried about my husband and could I come. So of course I went right away."

She didn't share Annemarie's fears, though. "That is, I didn't think anybody was deliberately trying to kill Albert, but I did think—as did Frau Kempf—that he was being wrongly treated, and I also saw that he himself was extremely unquiet and that he had lost all confidence in Gebhardt. So we called Brandt and asked him to get us a second opinion. He said immediately that he would send Professor Koch, a close friend of his and principal assistant to Germany's leading surgeon in internal medicine, Ferdinand Sauerbruch." (This version of events, which is also Speer's, has been challenged by a number of Speer's critics who, I think rather naively, accept Gebhardt's own account, that it was *he* who called in Koch, who, he claimed, had been working for some time both with him and for Himmler.)

Koch arrived in the late evening of February 10. His notes say that he found Speer extremely ill, with severe back pains, an excruciatingly painful cough, accelerated pulse, sweating and in a state of complete lethargy.

Brandt, who was not only Hitler's surgeon but Commissioner for Public Health, immediately ordered Gebhardt to have a room prepared for Koch and to hand Speer's care over to him.

The crisis came within hours, when Speer's temperature went up and traces of blood appeared in his sputum. In the night from February 11 to 12, his pulse went up to 120; his skin went blue, he hemorrhaged repeatedly and was in severe pain.

"We were all there," Margret said. "Koch took me outside and said I needed to prepare myself for the worst. Gebhardt hovered around until Koch more or less told him to go away. Those three days, from the eleventh to sometime on the thirteenth, he was hardly conscious," she said. "He looked dreadful. I thought he was dying."

Describing his illness in his book Speer merely said that while the doctors apparently feared the worst, he had been in a state of euphoria. But, he told me late one night, it had been much more than that.

"I have never been so happy in my life," he said. He was "abo looking down at himself in bed. "I saw everything very clearly. and nurses hovering, and Margret, looking sort of soft and sl small and pale. . . ."

I had never heard him speak of her like that; even the vocabi ferent from his usual words. "She sat on one side of the bed and a corner of a handkerchief around a finger. I felt myself smiling warm about her, and wondered whether she knew it. . . ."

"Did you see him smile?" I asked Margret later. "Of course not," she tersely. "It was all in his mind."

"What Professor Koch and the nurses—two of them—were doing," Speer continued, "looked like a silent dance to me. The room was so beautiful. I can still visualize it very clearly now as I saw it then. It was really quite a small room, you know, with white varnished military wardrobes. Well, they changed into beautiful armoires. And the plain white ceiling was suddenly magnificently inlaid. All of it was big and white and airy, an airiness that also surrounded me where I was, quiet and light and wonderfully happy, happier than I ever was before or have ever been since."

He smiled at the memory. "I was not alone; there were many figures, all in white and light grey and there was music. . . . And then somebody said, 'Not yet.' And I realized they meant I had to go back and I said I didn't want to. But I was told I had to—it was not yet my time. What I felt then was not something I know how to describe. It wasn't just sadness, or disappointment—it was a long feeling of loss. . . .

"Since then I've read books about this. In a way it was reassuring to read that other people have had such experiences. But although they sound very much alike, I'm somehow sure that they are actually very different. To this day I think that I felt things in those hours which the man I know myself to be cannot feel, or see, or say. I tell you one thing: I've never been afraid of death since. I'm certain it will be wonderful."

The morning after he told me this I asked Margret whether he had told her about that strange experience. Margret, a very no-nonsense sort of person—she had that in common with Speer—laughed out loud. "Yes, yes, he did," she said, a small note of mockery in her voice. Sitting nearby as we talked, Speer had heard her laugh. "She always laughed about it," he told me a little later when she had gone. "I think it embarrassed her."

Was it so surprising, I asked, that Margret should find something embarrassing that he himself had treated with considerable restraint in his book?

"Well," he said, now mocking himself, "I was supposed to be that super-rational man, you know, writing a definitive book on this terrible history of our time. What do you think readers would have said if in the middle of that book I had suddenly written that I am sure, sure to this day, that I died that night and came back to life? Can you imagine the fun the critics would have had with that?"

Nothing Speer wrote or said, to me or others, about the course of his illness was essentially untrue. The facts as he reported on them in the Nuremberg and Spandau drafts, and in his books, may differ slightly in insignificant details but otherwise coincide. What he saw in a different perspective, in retrospect, are his feelings.

The facts are plain enough. His last night sleeping in the freezing open air in Lapland reactivated an old knee injury, which had occasionally given him trouble ever since his youth. "If I had just taken the weight off my leg and rested until it recovered," he told me, "that would probably have been the end of it. But as you can imagine, that was impossible."

There is no doubt that the inflammation which put him in hospital on January 18, 1944, developed from this old familiar trouble. On two previous occasions overstrain of the troublesome knee had led to a need for bedrest and anti-inflammatory drugs.

What was different here was that this basically simple medical problem was almost fatally aggravated by his state of mind. This was an escalation of the pattern established many years before, in his childhood. As he told me, when his unhappiness about his parents' indifference and his brothers' cruelty became unbearable, he would become "terribly hot, then very cold and then, boom," he would faint. Twenty years later, when Hitler called him the great architect that he knew in his inner being he was not, his terror of being

"found out" and abandoned by his idol brought on "tremors, pins and needles; I would feel ice-cold and panic-stricken and be forced to lie down so as
not to fall."

Both when a child and later as Hitler's favorite, he could never externalize
to others or even articulate to himself the reasons for his pain and fear. Now
it was even worse, for this time he knew—the gradual realization growing
over many months, from Stalingrad, to Posen, to Dora—that the man he
worshiped, and who had invested him with unique power, was mad and his
purpose evil, and it was causing his body, fusing with his mind to escape the
unbearable reality, to give up.

He fought it, he minimized it to those around him, he blamed his visible
anxiety on the acts of disloyalty in his ministry, and by a frantic working
rhythm in the midst of physical and nervous collapse perhaps invited oblivion. "I think, finally, I did want to die," he told me.

I believe that on some levels of his unconscious he did then want to die
and that this was the explanation of the "out of body" experience he described to me. The fact, however, that this dream, feverish fantasy or—who
knows—perhaps really a precognition of dying ended with a denial of death
was, I believe, because of his innate strength, not of morality, but of an intrinsic determination to win.

In Hohenlychen that February 1944, after four days of complete rest, the
crisis was over. "An astonishing recovery," noted Koch on February 15:
"temperature still at 38 [100.5° F], but pulse down to 80–90, breathing normal, bleeding stopped. Patient's mind clear, shows appetite, need for sleep
and manifests interest in his environment. Leg and knee suddenly normal,
no sign of phlebitis, no other physical symptoms." The origin of the inflammation, first of the knee, then of the left lung, "remains a mystery," he concluded and added pointedly, "certainly not due to a physical trauma." He
prescribed ten to fourteen days "strictest bedrest; after that at least four
weeks of complete convalescence and quiet."

One of Speer's oldest friends, onetime industrialist Robert Frank (who,
a declared anti-Nazi, had relinquished his top managerial post soon after
the party came to power and had been protected by Speer ever since), visited
him at Hohenlychen not long afterwards. He told Speer that Gebhardt had
tried to persuade Koch to perform a lung puncture. Koch had told Frank in
confidence that this surgery not only was unnecessary but in Speer's perilous state would have been life-threatening. Asked by Speer later, Koch
replied evasively, merely saying that he and Gebhardt disagreed on
Speer's treatment and that he was under the impression that Gebhardt,
acting under Himmler's control, was playing "political games." Gebhardt,

he added, had even suggested that Koch needed to be a "more political doctor."

"Professor Koch stayed at Hohenlychen for the five crisis days," Annemarie told me, "but afterwards, too, he came by almost every day." As soon as he put Speer back on a normal light diet, the Speers' housekeeper, Clara Samuels, was brought in to cook for him.

"I was given a room, and Herr Speer said I was to prepare every single thing on his diet starting with breakfast," she told me in 1986. "He wouldn't eat anything I hadn't cooked. He thought they wanted to poison him. Everything I brought, he would say 'Did *you* cook it? Are you quite sure?' And I always assured him I had prepared it all with my own hands." But she hadn't really believed that anyone was trying to poison him. "I myself ate what the hospital cooked for him. I was working in the same kitchen where they cooked, and after he told me, I kept my eyes open," she said. "They would have had to be pretty fast on their feet to fool around with the food I watched them ladle out, and then immediately took away. Anyway, a bit later Frau Speer told me just to alter the food a bit, you know, make it *look* as if I'd cooked it. So then I did that.

"Frau Speer didn't say anything," she went on, "but I concluded that she didn't share her husband's fears. Anyway," she said comfortably, "all men, even giants like Herr Speer, become childish when they are sick. I've noticed it all my life."

She stayed at Hohenlychen for four weeks. "The Brekers [the sculptor Arno Breker and his wife] lived nearby, and Frau Breker often came with good things to eat," she said. "And then, I think it was mid-March, we left, first for a few days at Salzburg, and then we stayed for six weeks at a wonderful castle near Meran. The whole family came—the children too. We got Herr Speer really well there."

Speer told me that they left for Meran, via Salzburg, on March 18. Normally Speer would have stayed at Schloss Klessheim, the official government residence in Salzburg. But the Hungarian regent, Admiral Miklós Horthy, was there for meetings with Hitler, so Speer and his party were given the Kleeblattschlösschen, a beautiful baroque pavilion in the Klessheim park built by Fischer von Erlach.

This was the Hungarian regent's last visit to Hitler before the Nazis, furious about his refusal to hand over Hungary's Jews and afraid that he might turn to the Allies, virtually occupied Hungary. A year earlier, on April 17, 1943, also at Klessheim, Horthy, when reproached for his "coddling" of the Jews, replied that as he had already deprived his country's Jews of practically all means of making a living, he couldn't very well "beat them to death." Ribbentrop replied, "Certainly: they either have to be killed off or sent to concentration camps." After this, Hitler, lecturing the Hungarian head of state in an academic tone of voice, made his one public admission of the massacre of the Jews:

> In Poland this state of affairs has been . . . cleared up: if the Jews there did not *want* to work, they were shot. If they *could* not work, they were treated like tuberculosis bacilli with which a healthy body may become infected. This is not cruel if one remembers that even innocent creatures of nature, such as hares and deer when infected, have to be killed so that they cannot damage others. Why should the beasts who wanted to bring us Bolshevism be spared more than these innocents?

Now Horthy was told there was no more room for discussion. An air raid was faked, and all telephone communication with countries to the East was cut, forcing Hungary's head of state to remain at Klessheim for twenty-four hours, the time needed to move in occupation troops virtually to ring the Hungarian capital, and for Himmler to get his SD and SS organizers and Einsatzgruppen to Budapest to begin the deportation of Hungary's eight hundred thousand Jews.

Speer told me he had known nothing of the subjects being discussed with Horthy, though the potential usefulness of the many well-trained Hungarian Jews for German armament production had of course repeatedly arisen in past months. He thought the March conference with Horthy was primarily caused by Hitler's determination to keep Hungary on the Axis side.

Following the events in Posen on October 6 and at Dora on December 10, this was, to put it mildly, a disingenuous reply. It is unlikely that he did not know about German demands for Hungarian Jews for road building as early as October 1942, and the shameful agreement in March 1943 under which the Hungarian government sent thousands of foreign-born Jews into horrific labor battalions on the Eastern front.

Even though the Hungarians had been slow to agree to radical deportations of their own Jews, Hitler's ruthless handling of Horthy at Klessheim that March day in 1944 (the fragile regent suffered a minor heart seizure there) quickly bore fruit. Within days a Jewish Commissariat was established in the Hungarian Ministry of the Interior, the dreaded Arrow Cross (Fascist Party) was given liaison power between the Hungarian police and German security services, ghettos began to be established in all major Hungarian towns (except, at first, in Budapest), and the order was given to deliver 50,000 Jews for labor in the Reich in April and 50,000 more in May. The success of these orders exceeded expectations, and by May 6, six weeks after

Klessheim, 200,000 people had been deported. By May 15, that number had grown to 320,000.

More relevant to Speer, and his less-than-candid reply to me in 1978 on this question, was the fact that Field Marshal Milch was one of his few associates who had regularly visited him at Hohenlychen, Klessheim and Meran, and kept him informed of all developments. This certainly applied to the construction of huge underground bunkers for airplane construction, the so-called Jäger Program, which had been under discussion for months, though opposed by Speer. Milch was told by Hitler on April 9 that he had instructed Himmler to find one hundred thousand Hungarian Jews to build the bunkers. Not only is it impossible that Milch would not have discussed this order with Speer, but his complete awareness of this plan from the start is documented in his recorded conference with Himmler's supervisor of the Jäger Program, SS Gruppenführer Hans Kammler, six weeks later, on May 26.

In reply to Speer's question, Kammler informed him that the Hungarian Jews were "on the way," and that the first two transports would be ready for the bunker sites within days. When these transports from Hungary via Auschwitz did indeed arrive at the work sites, it was found that they were all yet again (as Speer had complained in his letter to Sauckel four months earlier) children, women and old men. This led to Speer's order—which was to give him considerable trouble at Nuremberg—that a further ninety thousand Eastern workers already in Germany were to be taken into "protective custody by immediate special action" by Himmler's SD. This meant that men from Poland and the Ukraine, many of whom had come voluntarily to work in factories and on the land and had been in Germany for years under the comparatively benign authority of the German Workers' Front, were arrested on faked pretexts or none at all and sent to concentration camps. There they came under the control of the SS, to be assigned to the backbreaking construction labor in the underground bunkers.

Some of these events were, of course, still in the future when Speer came to Klessheim on March 18, 1944. Nonetheless, the basis for them already existed and, together with his memories of what he heard and saw on October 6 and December 10, could not fail to be in Speer's mind when he came to Klessheim.

"By that time the children hadn't seen hide or hair of Albert for nearly four months," Margret told me. "It was going to be his birthday the next day, on the nineteenth, so I brought them down to see him. But even that day they could hardly spend any time with him; he saw people from morning to night—Hitler, Saur, Himmler, von Below, that awful Morell, God knows how many generals—and then of course the usual crowd, his team: Frau

Kempf, Wolters, Görner, Hupfauer, endless. By the time we left for Meran, he was worn out."

"That's true," Speer said. "But I'm not sure it was because I was seeing everybody there; I had after all been having daily meetings for weeks in Hohenlychen too." (The *Chronik* records them: four on March 1; six on March 2; three on March 3; seven on March 6 and 8; three on March 10; Dö- nitz on March 11; Ley, Hupfauer and two others on March 12; six on March 13 and 14. And on March 16, the night before he left, he threw a party for the hospital staff, with a recital by his friend, the pianist Wilhelm Kempff.)

"Meeting Hitler again was a shock," he said. Not wishing to add to Wol- ters's discomfort about his criticisms of Hitler in the "Spandau draft," he waited until he wrote *Inside the Third Reich* to describe the effects of this shock, expanding on it when speaking with me.

"Hitler came over to see me that first evening. I remember it as if it were today: I was resting, half stretched out on a chaise longue in the drawing room, when my adjutant ran in to say that Hitler was on his way over— Annemarie Kempf had just seen him from a window walking through the woods from the *Schloss*.

"I stood up as he entered the room. He came up to me very quickly hold- ing out his hand. But even as I stretched out mine, I had an extraordinary sense of unfamiliarity. Of course, I hadn't seen him for almost ten weeks, but that wasn't it. It was his face: I looked at it and thought, 'My God, how could I never have seen how ugly he is; this broad nose, this sallow skin. Who is this man?' And as these thoughts flashed through my mind, I had a sudden sense of fatigue such as I had not remembered feeling before."

Hitler, by no means unperceptive, had evidently noticed something amiss. For not more than half an hour later, Margret, invited over to the castle for a glass of champagne, heard him remark to Bormann and Keitel that it didn't look as if Speer would get back to normal. (Hitler's actual remark, *"Speer wird nicht mehr,"* has usually been translated as meaning that Speer was dying, or at least not going to recover. Speer's own interpretation, however, that it didn't look to Hitler as if he would be up to the demands of the job in the future, was probably nearer Hitler's meaning.)

Speer was justified in believing that Gebhardt was spreading false rumors about his state of health, for on the nineteenth Göring, phoning to congratu- late Speer on his birthday, commiserated with him on his "bad heart," which Gebhardt had just told him about. When Speer protested that his heart was fine, Göring said that they had probably wanted to spare him from hearing the truth.

Did he think at the time that it was possible his real condition was being hidden from him? I asked.

"No, I didn't. Koch had done every possible test, and all vital signs were entirely normal. No, what it showed me, and believe me the very thought made my heart sink, was that the intrigues against me had anything but abated. The party—Bormann and company, and their man Dorsch—distrusted me. Himmler quite rightly considered me a threat to his plans and would have had me killed, or let me conveniently die if he could have—and Hitler, well, Hitler had been under tremendous pressure for months from all of them to let me go."

But he himself was deeply discouraged with the whole situation. Obvious questions arose: Why didn't he just use the illness as a convenient and safe pretext to leave? Why didn't Hitler who had, at the very least, come to feel uncomfortable about him, just pension him off with good wishes?

When I put these questions to him, he shook his head as if bewildered. "You are right," he said. "Logically it is inexplicable, from either him or me. This morning, I reread what I wrote about it in my book. It is quite childish, isn't it? Here he had come to see me three times in those five days—at Klessheim that first night, then on my birthday with a huge bunch of flowers, and yet again on my last day to say goodbye—and all I could do in my book was complain about his apparent lack of appreciation for what I had done for him in the past as an architect and Minister. I think I was terribly dependent on him, even then. Not for power, as my critics have written. That really wasn't the point."

I interrupted him, to point out that he himself had told me that power was a major factor.

"It was a factor," he said, "but I now think that Hitler's main effect on me, from the start, was that he gave me faith in myself."

Was that all it was? I asked.

He smiled at me, a real smile. "No, you are quite right; that wasn't all," he said. "There is a lot I have learned to understand since, above all that for some mysterious reason neither he nor I could give each other up. I know now, as long as he lived, I would have been drawn to him. And I suppose as long as I lived, there was something about me he needed."

IN *Inside the Third Reich*—again very different from his "Spandau draft"—he has little positive to say about that long, happy holiday in Meran. On the other hand his story about Gebhardt's presence in Meran, both in the draft and in the book, conflicts curiously with surviving historical documentation.

Gebhardt, he wrote (in both places), had resisted for weeks Speer's plans to leave Hohenlychen and convalesce in South Tyrol. It was finally only when

Koch in early March insisted in a telephone call to Himmler that Speer's re-covery required a long stay in the healthy Meran air that Hitler gave the go-ahead for the move.

"He ordered, however," Speer wrote, "that Gebhardt was to take over the responsibility for my safety in his capacity as an SS Gruppenführer, and for my health as a physician. Thus Dr. Koch was officially excluded from my case. Instead it was Gebhardt who was in charge, with an SS squad which he posted to my residence to protect me. . . . Of course, I didn't let them get away with it: I invited Koch along as my personal guest." On April 19, Geb-hardt, supported by Himmler, made what turned out to be his final move against Speer by ordering Koch, in the name of the Reichsführer, to leave.

Against Speer's account, however, there is a letter from Professor Geb-hardt to Himmler dated several weeks earlier, February 21, 1944 (a letter I saw only after Speer's death). In it he informed Himmler that Speer

> . . . intends to leave Hohenlychen in one or two weeks . . . and has re-quested that [the Gauleiter of South Tyrol] find him a large property at an altitude of about 1,500–1,800 meters, with 16–20 rooms. Furthermore *the Reichsminister has asked me to accompany* [*him*], *with my family, in order to look after him until he feels he has adapted himself to the change of climate* [author's italics]. Although I have provisionally agreed to his proposal, could I please have the Reichsführer's decision on this. . . . Above all, could he let me know how, once there, I am to establish communication with General Wolff.

He is thus asking Himmler how, when staying with Speer in an unfamiliar and uncontrolled environment, he is to "establish communication" with Himmler's principal liaison officer, Wolff: that is, to report to Himmler on Speer's activities.

Himmler replied on February 26 that he considered it "very desirable" that Gebhardt and his family should accompany Speer to Meran, and subse-quently telexed "Wölffchen" that "our friend Karl Gebhardt—who sends you his best regards—is accompanying Reichsminister Speer . . . to Italy and has been charged by the Führer with the medical responsibility for him, and with his security." He instructed Wolff to have the locality 100 percent secured, "not only from the point of view of state security but also against air raids."

Speer was right to have feared Himmler at this point. Speer's increasing dominance over German production, his ever-closer links with the army, and, above all, in spite of Hitler's momentary disfavor, his strong place in the succession represented immense threats to the man who, by now heading a state within a state, firmly intended eventually to replace Hitler's government with his own SS administrators, and himself to succeed Hitler.

Though almost inconceivable in light of these circumstances, Gebhardt's letter to Himmler indicates that Speer had initiated the invitation to this dreaded doctor to go along to Meran, even though he was certain Gebhardt had been charged by Himmler to use the unexpected opportunity of his illness to get rid of him. No less puzzling, Gebhardt would write Speer a profuse letter on April 28, thanking him for "everything you did for my family [and] for your understanding and comradeship toward me. . . ." And six weeks later, Speer wrote to "warmly congratulate" Gebhardt on a high decoration Hitler had bestowed upon him. "I am all the happier for the recognition this confers on you," he wrote, "as I myself benefited from your great skill. . . ."

A year later he recommended Gebhardt's surgical proficiency to his friend Bichelonne, who, as already mentioned, died of the operation. In one of our discussions, I asked Annemarie how one should interpret these paradoxes.

"It's impossible to understand the games they played," she said, "games they *had* to play in order to lull each other into a feeling of security. I honestly think it was more complicated than in the times of the Roman Emperors or the Popes. I don't know how Speer's invitation to Gebhardt came about; I never talked with him about it. But it is certainly true that he had to have a doctor along; I can only imagine—and this is certainly in line with the way he operated—that he thought the devil he knew was preferable to someone new they would have planted on him, as they would most certainly have done. As it was, on the pretext of giving Gebhardt and his family more privacy, they were lodged several kilometers away in the town of Meran, while Speer, his family and friends—among them as you know, for days at a time, Professor Koch—took over a charming castle up in the hills and hardly saw them. I remember Speer giving instructions for cases of wine to be delivered to Gebhardt and remarking that that would keep him quiet."

Speer wrote in Spandau,

> Meran was a very special time for me. It was really the first time I had with the family since I became Minister. It is dreadful to think what I allowed myself to miss in those years. It's only here, in my isolation, I can appreciate it. . . .

"Well, yes, it was nice," said Margret, when I mentioned it one afternoon, "but of course it wasn't the kind of quiet convalescence Koch had envisaged and kept reminding him of. Albert was incapable of that."

Guarded day and night by twenty-five SS men who were lodged partly in the house and partly in tents in the gardens, he received streams of well-wishers and hosted several large parties.

For the first two weeks or so, Margret said, he did spend some time with the children. "But after that he was again up to his neck in conferences and dictation. As of then, he saw more of Milch and the others who came than of us. Still, it is true, at least for the first time in years, we were all living in the same house for a prolonged period and we even had some meals together."

I asked her if they discussed the children, as parents do, how they did at school, what their talents seemed to be, and all that.

She laughed. "No, we didn't have time for that, but anyway, you know, first of all, the children were all very young—Albert not yet ten and Hilde still only seven—but also, discussing children that way is really very new; I hear our grandchildren now being discussed endlessly by their parents, but in our time, or at least in our family—" She shrugged. "I can't even imagine Albert talking to me about a child, in those days. Later of course, in Spandau—*then* he thought about the children; *then* he had time."

Wasn't that a bit unfair? I asked.

"Perhaps," she said, with spirit. "But *you* try being married to a man like that."

Within days of arriving in Meran, Speer learned that Hitler, disregarding his advice, had decided on the already mentioned major building program of six huge underground industrial sites. Each was to be an area of more than one million square feet, to which the main airplane factories were to be transferred to escape the bombs. On April 14 Hitler summoned Dorsch to HQ to discuss design. Dorsch promised ("ridiculously," Speer told me) to have them ready in six months.

On April 19 Speer wrote Hitler the first of what over the next few months would become a stream of ever more defiant memorandums. "In a way," he told me, "I found myself through them. I would never have thought it possible that I would speak so openly, and when I found I could, it gave me an incredible sense of liberation."

In the first letter, he warned Hitler seriously against undertaking this project; the only building the country could afford at this point, he told him, was quick reconstruction of bomb-damaged plants and workers' housing. In production, priority had to be given to armaments, which, even at best, were running short. Knowing Hitler's intransigence, however, and his resistance to pressure of any kind unless it was exerted in person and with the utmost diplomacy, Speer declared himself willing to compromise. If, despite his own doubts, Hitler considered the underground construction absolutely necessary, he would assign one of Todt's former assistants, Willi Henne, to this task, while Dorsch would "continue to use his invaluable experience in the occupied territories." And he suggested appointing his best construction engineer, Walter Brugmann, whom Hitler knew well from the building projects in Nuremberg and Berlin, as overall director of construction.

Gerhard Fränk, a longtime colleague of Speer's and chief administrator of a Ministry section, who had been staying with him in Meran, delivered the letter into Hitler's hands that evening, April 19. Hitler's senior secretary, Johanna Wolf, told Speer on the phone later that night that Hitler had been furious about it. "Even Speer has to realize that there is such as a thing as political tactics," he said.

("Hitler rejected this proposal," Speer wrote in *Inside the Third Reich*. "Five weeks later, on May 26, 1944, Brugmann was killed like my predecessor Todt in an unexplained plane crash." Speer was being a bit naughty here, for it was an accident, not an "unexplained crash." Wolters in his *Segments of a Life* wrote that "Brugmann's plane, flying low through a mountain pass in foggy weather, collided with treetops and exploded on impact.")

Speer immediately telephoned General Milch, who had just arrived on the Obersalzberg in preparation for Hitler's birthday the next day, and asked him to tell Hitler that he was resigning.

"By the next morning, extraordinarily enough," Speer said, "my offer to Hitler to resign had got around like wildfire. First Göring phoned me to say that I couldn't do that—except, of course, for reasons of health. And then, even before lunch that April 20, Walter Rohland arrived. Was I out of my mind? he asked. How could I even conceive of leaving industry in the lurch, at the mercy of those who might follow me? And then he brought up the specter of a desperate Hitler ordering wholesale destruction of the country's living potential, as Stalin—so admired for it by Hitler—had done so efficiently in Russia. If for no other reason, Rohland said, I would have to stay to do what I could to prevent the worst. Nobody else could."

This was not the first time he and Rohland (or he and Milch) had admitted to each other that the war was lost. "But it was somehow the first time that anyone suggested the madness of 'scorched earth,'" Speer told me. "And somehow that gave me suddenly a different perspective. I don't know how to explain it, but for the first time, I think, I stopped thinking of myself and thought only of our country—of the people. You know, all those terrible months in 1943, when on my many trips I saw so much destruction, can you believe that I never thought of people then? Of what it was doing to them? I only thought of my damned factories. It was as if imagination had died in me—do you know what I mean? Well, that day, as I sat in the garden with Rohland, the unending waves of unopposed Allied planes overhead in that blue sky, my children's voices from where they played and Margret's and Clara's [the housekeeper] in the kitchen, suddenly, for the first time in years,

I had a sudden vision of physical destruction—not of buildings, but of people."

Of his own children? I wondered.

He shook his head as if to bar that image. "I don't know whether it was so direct, but perhaps it was." He tried to laugh. "I'm being soppy, aren't I? Funny how the feelings come back."

Late the same night, about one o'clock in the morning, Milch, Fränk and Saur arrived straight from the Obersalzberg, bearing—Milch had announced in a significant tone of voice on the telephone—"a message from the Führer." Years later, after Spandau, Milch would admit to Speer that he had pressured Hitler. He had told him that production would collapse without Speer; it was too late for a change. Speer had to be persuaded to stay, and, in order to achieve this, Hitler had to make him feel indispensable. But the personal message Hitler then sent had surprised Milch. "Tell Speer that I'm as fond of him as ever." (In German this is considerably warmer: *"dass ich ihn weiter lieb habe."*)

"He can kiss my . . . " Speer, who was never vulgar, heard himself say, quoting Goethe's famous *Götz von Berlichingen.*

"You are not big enough a man to say this about the Führer, even as a joke," Milch admonished him, sternly.

Even before his long talk with Rohland and with Saur, who at Hitler's suggestion had come along, Speer had decided to withdraw his resignation, but he let it appear that they slowly persuaded him. His condition, however, he told them, was that Hitler restore Speer's authority over construction in Germany, including the planned six underground sites, and over Dorsch.

Hitler's three peace negotiators flew back to Berchtesgaden at dawn with a directive Speer had drafted during the night. Hitler, receiving them immediately after breakfast, signed it (as Milch would say later) virtually unread.

Three days later, however, Speer decided he had been overhasty. The underground factory project—above all, its completion in six months, as Dorsch had promised—was doomed to fail. If Speer was officially in charge of it, industry would end up blaming him for giving it priority at the expense of armament production, and Hitler would finally blame him for the inevitable failure to complete it. On April 24 he flew to the Obersalzberg in order to propose a new idea to Hitler: a total separation between war production and construction, with Dorsch appointed Inspector General for all building, both in Germany and the occupied territories, so that Speer could concentrate on armaments.

"It was very strange to be back there," he told me. What was strangest was that he felt curiously detached. "It was as if nothing could happen to me, almost as if I was free."

Only minutes after Speer had arrived at his empty Obersalzberg house, Hitler's adjutant phoned to invite him to accompany the Führer and his circle on the customary afternoon stroll to the teahouse. "And, unprecedented in my and probably anybody's experience, I found myself declining; I said that I needed to see Hitler officially and alone."

About two hours later, to his surprise, he found himself being formally received by Hitler, wearing cap and gloves, awaiting him like a foreign state visitor on the steps of the Berghof. (In June 1953 in Spandau, he told Hess about this formal reception. "Hess recalled, with visible pleasure, that he, too, on just one occasion, had been received by Hitler in this manner. He didn't want to tell me what the occasion was, but he said that it remained a milestone in his life.")

"When this meeting was over," Speer said, "I had won, but so had Hitler. He was still a master at understanding human nature. He knew that—just as Hess showed years later—no one could fail to react to him if he showed them special regard; so he 'won' because he wanted and needed me back in his corner, and he got me. He even made it seem a compliment when he rejected my new suggestion, saying that he wouldn't entrust building, which, as I knew, meant more to him that anything else, to anyone but me. From this moment on, he said, he would approve anything I suggested for the building sector, sight unseen.

"I 'won,' too, however, because later that night at the tea gathering, when for the first time in five months I sat in front of the fire with him, with Eva Braun next to me, openly delighted at my return, he made his favor very clear." Looking back at that night now, he added, he felt astonished at the depth of his relief then. "A relief which I now know had very little, perhaps even nothing, to do with the political victory I had undoubtedly gained. As I sat there surrounded by the usual faces, uttering the usual inanities, to the sound of Hitler's usual preferred music—in this case *Die Fledermaus*—I felt a profound sense of peace, and safety. Not safety of my person," he said—and stopped. The words were obviously impossible to say, but his meaning was clear. It was emotionally that he felt back in safe harbor.

Once again, Nicolaus von Below's memoirs provide the other side of the coin—Hitler's feelings about Speer in those months:

> There can be no doubt that even though Speer, in his innermost being, had withdrawn from Hitler and, from the time he returned after his illness, frequently quietly ignored his orders, it was immensely important to him not to lose Hitler's trust. Hitler was aware of the change in Speer—he knew that Speer was no longer convinced of our victory. But, in the many conversations he drew me into, particularly during those comparatively

quiet [spring] months . . . he said repeatedly that despite Speer's diminishing faith in victory, he was the only one capable of understanding the
complexity of the armament sector. "Given our urgent needs now," he
said, "Speer is the only one who can deal with it." And the fact is, that
once Speer had taken it all in hand again, the old close relationship between him and Hitler was quickly restored and there was not a trace of
distrust on either side.

Speer knew he had also won a huge power struggle over Bormann,
Himmler and Göring, and the reaction not only of these three men but also
of all those around them, he said, showed they knew it.

"Over the subsequent two weeks," he said, "back in Meran, I had letters
and phone calls from men I hadn't talked to in months; my wife got flowers
from people she'd barely met; and on the occasion of my next visit to the
Obersalzberg soon afterwards, Bormann invited me to his house where, just
as he had never been to ours, I had never been. Embarrassingly, he suggested
we should address each other from then on with the familiar *Du*." (Speer
avoided this by pointedly addressing him the very next day with the usual
formal *Sie*.)

On May 8, 1944, Speer returned to his desk in Berlin and within four weeks
two major Allied moves foreshadowed the end of the war. On May 12, the
American Eighth Air Force sent 935 bombers on a daylight attack of the fuel
plants in central and eastern Germany, and destroyed in that one day more
than half of Germany's capacity. His only hope, Speer wrote in the "Spandau
draft," was that the Americans, as had happened a year before when they had
bombed the ball bearing plants at Schweinfurt, would fail to repeat the attack. But it was a vain hope.

"After the war," Speer said, "when I met [Paul] Nitze, [George] Ball and
[John] Galbraith, I understood why it had been hopeless. Rather than being
only advised by military strategists, the American air force had economists
and agronomists telling them what to bomb."

("The British, less successfully," Speer said on another occasion, "allowed
psychologists a look-in. They were as mistaken about their forecasts on German morale as we were about the effects of the rocket attacks on London.")

Sixteen days after the first attack, when Speer and the OT had just
managed to put the factories back together "more or less with glue and sta-
ples," he said, the American bombers came again, this time for two days,
with four hundred planes. By the time it was over, production capacity of
synthetic fuel had been reduced by 90 percent. "Our only chance now of
even partial reconstruction," said Speer, "was if we pulled something like
half a million men out of armament production to rebuild the hydrogena-

tion plants. Short of that, we were virtually entirely dependent on our re-serves, which under such conditions, as I told Hitler, would be exhausted by September."

It was to take him dozens of conferences and three beseeching memoran-dums to Hitler to get at least a partial green light. "For months he kept saying that he couldn't let me denude armament production of workers because then he would have fewer tanks. I simply could not get across to him that it was pointless to have tanks if we had no fuel to run them. It was a blind spot in his mind—he couldn't take it in."

It was finally only the Allied invasion of Normandy on June 6 that shocked Hitler into agreement with Speer. At this time Hitler was largely conducting the war from the Berghof. In February he had had intelligence information from Stockholm that an officer from the General Staff had been selected to assassinate him. Security was immediately increased, and the decision was made to strengthen the ceiling and walls of the Führer bunker in Rastenburg against attacks from the air. During the construction, Führer HQ would be moved to the Berghof. After the eventual return to Rastenburg (in July), se-curity would be sharply reinforced by examining all visitors' briefcases and files. Below wrote,

> We suggested to Hitler that visitors should be subjected to body searches, too, but he was opposed to such extreme measures . . . and really, security-wise, while we stayed on the Obersalzberg, nothing much changed.

Ernst Görner felt that security had been incredibly lax at Führer HQ. "I had to go there once, sometime in 1943, I can't quite remember when, to bring Speer a file he had forgotten," he told me when we talked in 1987. "The blockhouses were sort of spread all over the place in a big wooded area. I asked a young man where I could find Minister Speer, and he pointed ahead where there was a small cluster of buildings and said, 'Just go over there and look around; you'll find him there.' So I went into the first of the houses and somehow found myself in a bathroom. A dark-haired man—I think it was Bormann, I never met him before or afterwards—asked what I was doing there. I said I was looking for Speer and he just said, 'Wrong place; this is the Führer billets,' and then he showed me where to go. But it seemed extraordi-nary to me; there were no guards, no security at all."

Hitler had always detested security measures. At the Obersalzberg before the war, he regularly went for walks without anyone guarding him. Later, ac-cording to Bormann's son, Martin, there were guard posts to the approaches to the Berghof, but no one remembered it being a fortress, as it was some-times described later.

This still applied to early 1944. However, if little had changed in precautions against visitors—or possible assassins—a great deal of work had been done to make the Obersalzberg generally more secure for Hitler and his immediate team. A number of large air-raid shelters had been tunneled into the mountain, not only for the Berghof but equally for the houses of some of the other principals, such as Bormann and Göring. "Not mine," Speer told me. "I thought it was outrageous to use badly needed workers for our own protection."

Carpeted and comfortably furnished throughout, the bunkers had been equipped with sophisticated communications and huge provisions of food. ("I had no doubt later," Speer said, "that intelligence information the Allies received about these installations led to their mistaken belief in the existence of an alpine redoubt.") The Berghof itself was covered with camouflage netting which from then on, as Speer put it, "made even a sunny morning seem like a dark late afternoon."

It was there on June 4, when, according to Below, nobody thought the invasion was even close, that Rommel—on a twenty-four-hour visit before going on holiday in southern Germany—repeated a warning he had already given at the end of 1943 in Rastenburg, when Hitler put him in charge of the western coastal defenses. The Allies, he said, must not be allowed to establish a beachhead. When the invasion came, they had to be defeated on the beaches. And it was there, too, in early June, that Speer and Milch, perhaps at least marginally profiting from Rommel's constant reminders to Hitler that the war would be won or lost in the air, finally persuaded Hitler to transfer the responsibility for aircraft production from Göring's lethargic Air Ministry to Speer.

The probable site of the expected invasion had been argued at Rastenburg and at the Berghof for months. Most of Hitler's logistics experts held that a large invasion could only succeed if the opponents gained possession of at least two harbors. The most likely place for this attempt, with the best harbors, was in the Pas de Calais, and it was here that Dorsch's (and Speer's) OT that spring had worked twenty-four-hour shifts making fortresses of all the harbors along that coastline, and it was here that the main army reserves were grouped.

But German intelligence had failed all along the line. For when the Allies landed at dawn on June 6, it was 150 kilometers west, on the comparatively unpopulated Normandy coast, halfway between Le Havre and Cherbourg. Speer learned of the invasion on arrival at the Berghof at 10 a.m. that day. Hitler, he was told, was still asleep and, no, would not be woken up to hear the news. "The Führer always gets the latest news *after* he has had his breakfast," the duty adjutant apparently said, tranquilly.

When Hitler joined his staff for the situation report at noon, Rommel's warnings were forgotten, and there was general agreement that these landings, along a coast where there were no harbors, were an Allied feint to trick Hitler into deploying his forces away from the site of the real invasion, the Pas de Calais. The best strategy therefore, Hitler decided, was essentially to wait and see.

But there was another catastrophic failure of German intelligence. They had not learned of the Allies' technically brilliant stroke, the Mulberry Harbors, about which, under the heading "Most Especially Secret," Winston Churchill informed Stalin on June 7, in reply to the Soviet leader's news that the Soviet summer offensive would begin within the week. His cable said,

> We are planning to construct very quickly two large synthetic harbors on the beaches of this wide sandy bay of the Seine estuary. Nothing like these has ever been seen before. Great ocean liners will be able to discharge and run by numerous piers supplies to the fighting troops. This must be quite unexpected by the enemy, and will enable the buildup to proceed with very great independence of weather conditions. We hope to get Cherbourg at an early point in the operations. . . .

"Hitler and Stalin were very alike in some dreadful respects," Speer told me, "but there is one fundamental point in which they differed absolutely. Stalin had faith in his generals and, although meticulously informed of all major plans and moves, left them comparative freedom. Our generals, on the contrary, were robbed of all independence, all elasticity of action, even before Stalingrad. All decisions were taken by Hitler and once made were as if poured in cement, whatever changing circumstances demanded. This, more than anything else, lost Germany the war."

At no time since Hitler's strategically insane orders which led to the disaster of Stalingrad can that have shown up more clearly than in those months of June and July 1944, when Hitler idled while the Western Allies firmly established their base on the Continent, and while in the East the Soviets triumphantly swept the German army ahead of them out of Belorussia and the Ukraine.

By June 17, when Hitler met Rommel and von Rundstedt in France for a conference, the Allies had landed more than six hundred thousand troops and were well on the way to capturing Cherbourg on June 26. Exactly two months later, Charles de Gaulle triumphantly entered Paris. The Soviets had launched their offensive on June 10 with more than a million men on four fronts, and in one week captured four strong points Hitler had designated as areas "to hold at all cost." By August 1, they recaptured Vilnius, Lublin and Brest Litovsk, as well as all of Estonia and Latvia, and, having cleared the whole of Russian territory of the invader, they arrived within four hundred miles of Berlin. The long delayed launching of the first flying bombs (V-1s) on June 12 was a dud, and even when they became operational were disappointing in their minimal effect on British morale. The V-2s, finally ready in September after long delays, would cause more damage but again would not succeed in breaking the spirit of London's hardy inhabitants, including, from the first day of the war to the last, Britain's royal family.

Speer, when talking to me, said time and again that there was a pathologically self-destructive element in Hitler's insistence on issuing orders the only resultant "glory" of which could be death.

Almost the same thing could be said about Speer himself, who, however reunited with Hitler, was by this time not only aware that the war was lost, but also of the penalties likely to be imposed by the Allies on individual Germans who had committed war crimes. One must, for example, wonder how he could have approved a communication issued on June 12, 1944, by the Ministry of the Occupied Eastern Territories; as it involved the Organization Todt, over which he had ultimate responsibility, he could not have been entirely ignorant of it:

> Army Group Center [the area where the Soviet offensive had begun two days before] has the intention to apprehend 40,000–50,000 youths of the ages of 10 to 14 who are in the army territory and to transport them to the Reich.
>
> . . . It is intended to allot these juveniles primarily as apprentices to the German trades, to be used after two years' training as skilled workers. This is to be arranged through the Organization Todt which is especially equipped for such a task, by means of its technical and other set-ups. . . .
>
> This action is aimed not only at preventing a direct reinforcement of the enemy's military strength but also at a reduction of his biological potentialities as viewed from the perspective of the future. These ideas have been voiced not only by the Reichsführer SS but also by the Führer.
>
> Corresponding orders were given during last year's withdrawals in the Southern Sector. . . .

The last sentence shows that the order was being issued in full awareness and expectation of the forthcoming withdrawals from that central region. We don't know whether this obscene plan of adding 50,000 more children to the 250,000 already stolen from the Occupied Eastern Territories was carried out—there are no further documents in the files about it. Probably not, for within five weeks the Soviets had destroyed or captured the approximately twenty-eight German divisions—350,000 men—of Army Group Center, and regained Minsk, the capital of Belorussia, where the Nazi administrators of the region had their headquarters.

. . .

THE FIRST WEEKS after the invasion in Normandy, Speer said, were among the most extraordinary ones he remembered. On the face of it, one catastrophe had followed another, but at the Berghof, camouflage nets notwithstanding, life returned to its customary cozy superficiality. Generals and politicians came and went but hardly interfered with the normal early summer on "The Mountain." Hitler slept late, hardly ever appearing before noon for the situation report. The ladies, Eva Braun, the secretaries and the intimates' young wives—Margret Speer, Anni Brandt, Maria von Below—took the sun on the terrace. During luncheon Hitler, never a word of present disasters passing his lips, remembered past glories. Even the afternoon walks to the teahouse were resumed, if now under the eyes of guards posted at regular intervals, at a discreet distance from the path. And at night, though films had been forbidden for the duration, there was the usual late tea with music and chitchat around the fireplace, the air scented by the slowly burning logs and the smell of cut grass from the open windows.

"As you can see," Speer said, "it was not only I who lived a schizophrenic existence. We all did, Hitler perhaps most of all."

Nicolaus von Below's description of the strangely unruffled atmosphere at the Berghof in those catastrophic months of June and July is very similar to Speer's. Four weddings were celebrated that spring, in three of them the marriage ceremony performed by Himmler.

Below's wife, Maria, stayed with him at the Berghof from February until Hitler went back to Rastenburg in mid-July, and most evenings Hitler, taking their arms, would take her and Margret Speer in to dinner. Eva Braun, taking Speer's arm, or in his absence, Bormann's (whom she was said to detest), would always sit on Hitler's left, the other two alternately on his right.

"He was actually very good at conversation," Maria von Below told me. "How shall I put it and not be misunderstood? He was very warm, very personal. It is true—though I only realized this later—there wasn't much variety in his personal conversations with us. With me, or Margret Speer or Anni Brandt, he would ask about the children, be quite interested, I thought, in little stories about them, respond with laughter or understanding nods. In my case he often asked me how things were going for my parents who were running their largish estate. I remember once, without meaning to complain or anything, I said they were running short of oil. Later that night, without telling me, he told Bormann to get some supplies to them. He was thoughtful that way.

"He was very, very concerned about the young people around him—you know, like us young wives. He didn't want us to be worried about anything.

It is hard to talk or even think about him so personally now, when I have my own terrible doubts and my own sadness—as Klaus had too, until he died—about what we lived for, and didn't, couldn't do. But for anyone who wasn't there, who didn't share this experience then and therefore our inner conflicts later, it must be entirely unacceptable to have me speak of him like an ordinary man. I know it has to be unacceptable to my children.

"But we were of course quite isolated. We depended entirely on each other, socially and emotionally. Anni Brandt and I went to Salzburg a few times, but even that so rarely that now, after all these years, I remember each occasion. You see, when you stayed at the Berghof, you didn't treat it like a hotel. You were always a community: Hitler's cook cooked for you, his maids took care of your clothes, your mending—you *lived* there and, like in many families, you were never really on your own except in your bedroom."

I asked if her husband told her about decisions that were made, about what Hitler planned.

"Up to a point, yes," she said. "It really wasn't possible to have secrets between us, especially when we were living at the Berghof for extended periods. We hardly saw each other except in Hitler's company, so Klaus and I would really only talk about such things, or talk at all, in our room."

Did they lower their voices, whisper? I asked. She looked at me, surprised. "Whisper? No, we didn't whisper," she said, and then smiled to take the sting out of her tone. "Klaus and I were always pretty quiet, so you know, we just talked. It would never have occurred to us that anyone would try to listen. I assure you, nobody ever did—nobody in that house would ever have listened at doors." She shrugged and then smiled again as if mocking herself for the thought. "Or looked through keyholes. I mean, it's unthinkable; it was all terribly proper, terribly homey."

Homey? Even during those months in 1944?

"Extraordinarily, yes, even then. We were all so glad to be together. . . ."

XVII

The Twentieth of July

Nuremberg, June 20, 1946

FLÄCHSNER: Herr Speer, you also figured as Armaments Minister on the [government] list drawn up by the men responsible for the [coup d'état] of July 20 [1944]. Did you participate in the attempted assassination?

SPEER: I did not participate, nor was I informed of it in advance. At that time I was against assassinating Hitler.

SPEER'S ROLE in the assassination attempt has always been a matter of debate. His enemies within the Hitler circle would always believe that he had been part of it, but Hitler never did. Speer himself has always insisted that while in sympathy with the conspirators' aims, as he learned of them later, he had not collaborated with them and indeed had not even known of the plan.

"Rationally," he told me, "I had realized for months, if not longer, that only Hitler's death could save us from catastrophe. But psychologically, or emotionally if you like, I could not have been party to it. I proved this again to myself seven months later when I actually thought of a way to eliminate him but realized that I could never have done it."

It was understandably prudent but also perhaps very perceptive of the conspirators, many of whom were Speer's friends, that, certain he would intrinsically be on their side, they jotted down his name as a possible member of their future government but, equally aware of his ambivalent feelings toward Hitler personally, did not in fact draw him into the conspiracy and left a question mark against his name—which may have saved his life.

During the long weeks of false calm at the Berghof, a large group of army generals and other high-ranking officers, plus leading public and religious personalities, convinced that nothing could prevent a huge catastrophe for Germany except the removal of Hitler, was setting up the operation which would culminate in the assassination attempt on July 20.

Over the years, there had been an astonishing number of previous attempts, including six within the past twelve months by young army officers who had remained miraculously undiscovered. All of them had failed because of last-minute changes of plans by Hitler. This time a much larger group of conspirators not only intended to make sure of the dictator's death but had carefully worked out plans to arrest the other principals, and to eliminate the political and armed apparatus of the Gauleiter and the SS.

The moving force in the conspiracy as it now developed was thirty-seven-year-old Count Claus Schenk von Stauffenberg, who, terribly wounded by a mine in the African campaign—he lost one eye, one hand and part of the other—was reassigned to Berlin, first as Chief of Staff to General Olbricht, Commander of the General Army Office, and subsequently in the same role to General Friedrich Fromm, head of the Replacement (or Home) Army, both with their offices at the Bendlerstrasse HQ of the Chiefs of Staff.

Stauffenberg, together with his friend Peter Yorck von Wartenburg (a member of the "Kreisau Circle," the anti-Nazi Christian think tank started years earlier by Count Helmuth von Moltke), had become convinced that huge political changes needed to be effected in Germany and that nothing could be done until Hitler, with whom neither the East nor the West could possibly negotiate, was dead. He and most of his friends were disgusted with ineffectual German conservatives. But it is particularly significant here that almost all these young aristocrats, although all committed Christians, both Catholic and Protestant, and many of them people of considerable intellectual caliber (several of them had been Rhodes scholars), had originally been sympathetic to National Socialism and Hitler. However, although a number of them, such as Wartenburg, Adam von Trott zu Solz, Fritz Dietlov von der Schulenburg and Hans Bernd von Haeften, held high office in the party or in the Foreign Office, none of them were ever close to Hitler and therefore, unlike Speer, not exposed to his "hypnotic" personality. It is also true that they had the one protection he "fatally" lacked, as Speer would write later to Hilde; even if they had been exposed to Hitler's magnetism, they, contrary to him, were immunized against its effect by their strong religious faith.

Following the last vain attempts on Hitler's life by two of the earliest younger resisters, Major General Henning von Tresckow and lawyer Fabian von Schlabrendorff, and profoundly discouraged both by the political squabbles and the caution continuously displayed by the older conspirators, Stauffenberg finally decided he would kill Hitler himself.

His first attempt to take a bomb into a Situation Report at Hitler's Rastenburg HQ was planned for December 26. The meeting, however, like others before, was canceled at the last moment. It was now that he developed a new plan with General Olbricht, more comprehensive than anything yet planned. Rather than only killing Hitler, his assassination would be followed by a deployment of Fromm's Replacement Army to control strategic points, above all in Berlin, and to prevent any action by the SS. A contingency plan codenamed "Valkyrie," drawn up long before in case of a rebellion by the millions of foreign workers and involving the use of these troops, provided a ready-made framework for quick action. Field Marshal Rommel and General Karl Heinrich von Stülpnagel in France would control the occupied countries in the West.

General Fromm, to all appearances devoted to Hitler, had always been a problem for the conspirators. When Stauffenberg's transfer to his staff was mooted, he decided characteristically to meet this difficulty head-on. He informed Fromm face to face that he was involved in the preparation of a coup d'état against Hitler. When Fromm received this information without comment and confirmed him in his appointment, the conspirators' belief that Fromm shared their views seemed well founded, and Stauffenberg was now in precisely the right place to carry out their plans.

By early July, everything was ready. The elderly Field Marshal Erwin von Witzleben and former Chief of Staff General Ludwig Beck, deeply at odds with Hitler since the invasion of Czechoslovakia in 1938, were now titular heads of the conspiracy, but there were many others, both officers of the General Staff in Berlin, at Hitler's HQ and at the fronts, as well as leading personalities in German public life. Carl Goerdeler, former mayor of Leipzig, who had opposed the Nazis from the start, was to head an interim coalition government, part military and part civilian.

The plan was that Stauffenberg would again get himself invited to Hitler's Situation Report on the decisive day. He would leave a time bomb to blow up Hitler, Himmler and Göring and would then, having alerted Olbricht in Berlin to start Valkyrie, fly back to Berlin to take charge.

He tried four times. The first two occasions were at the Berghof, but were aborted because either Göring or Himmler was not present. On the morning of July 14, Hitler flew back to Rastenburg, and Stauffenberg followed on July 15, taking a bomb in his briefcase. He telephoned the Bendlerstrasse to say he was planting it, but Hitler left the conference even as Stauffenberg made his call, and again the coup had to be aborted.

On July 17 the conspirators learned that the Gestapo were about to arrest Goerdeler—who immediately went into hiding—and that Rommel, vital to their plans, had suffered grave injuries in an Allied air attack in France. It was now decided that they could put it off no longer: there were too many people involved, too many in the know, the impetus too difficult to maintain. And so, in the early morning of July 20, even though the conspirators could not count on the presence of Himmler and Göring, Stauffenberg, duly invited to attend Hitler's noontime Situation Report in Rastenburg, left Berlin in a small plane and took a light brown briefcase containing an already-armed bomb into Führer HQ.

The conference was being held not in the usual "situation" room, which OT workers were still reinforcing, but in Speer's blockhouse, which was the only other barrack to contain a conference room. Field Marshal Keitel's adjutant, John von Freyend, trying to be helpful to the famous war-wounded visitor, after lending him his own room to freshen up, insisted on carrying his briefcase into the room where the noontime conference had already started, and placed it under the map table across from Hitler's seat. Stauffenberg, following him into the room where Hitler briefly bade him welcome, pushed it with his foot until it was about six feet away from Hitler. It was timed to explode five minutes later, and Stauffenberg, making his murmured excuses, left the room to join his fellow conspirator, Signals Commander General Erich Fellgiebel, in the OKW [Army High Command] signals office a few blockhouses away. They heard the tremendous explosion and knowing where the bomb had been placed, Stauffenberg was certain that Hitler was dead. He bluffed his way through two guard posts and flew to Berlin.

The return in Stauffenberg's small Heinkel 111 took just under three hours. As the plane's radio was for much of that time out of range from Berlin, Stauffenberg could not know that his attack had misfired. Colonel Heinz Brandt, senior aide to General Helmuth Stieff—both part of the conspiracy, but like others there not informed that this was the day—finding the briefcase in his way as he was trying to lean across the table to consult the map, picked it up and moved it away, to the other side of a heavy table support. His action effectively shielded most of the twenty-four people present, but put him in line with the worst of the blast. Although most of them, including Hitler, suffered burns and concussions, and several would be forced to take sick leave, only four people were seriously wounded (though Below says eleven in his memoirs). Two of them died: Colonel Brandt and General Schmundt.

A few days later, when Hitler was informed that both Colonel Brandt, whom he had had posthumously promoted to General on July 22, and Major General Henning von Tresckow (one of the army's finest young generals, who, in a clearing near the Rastenburg HQ, feigning an attack by partisans, had shot himself on July 21 and who, like Colonel Brandt, had already received a solemn burial), had both belonged to the conspiracy, he ordered them disinterred and their ashes disposed of in an unknown place.

Hitler himself, although laid low the next day with burst eardrums and a minor concussion, would not allow his immediate injuries—splinters in both upper legs, a sprained elbow and superficial wounds on his right hand—to stop him from taking a walk and chatting reassuringly with Organization Todt men completing their security-enhancing work on the site. He had lunch with his astonished secretary, Christa Schröder, to whom he talked with animation throughout. And at 2:30 p.m. as scheduled, he welcomed Mussolini, who arrived by train for an afternoon's discussions—as it turned out, the last they were ever to have.

Stauffenberg in the meantime arrived at the Rangsdorf military airport near Berlin to find no one meeting him. When, telephoning Olbricht, he heard that a rumor that Hitler had survived had caused total confusion at the

Bendlerstrasse, he assured him that he was dead and that the agreed orders had to be given at once. Nonetheless, when he reached Bendlerstrasse an hour later, he found that Olbricht had awaited his return and further confirmation that Hitler was dead before activating Valkyrie, thereby losing the vital first hours to neutralize the political leaders and the SS. Field Marshal von Witzleben, disgusted with the shambles he had found when he arrived there early on, had walked out hours before, to return to his country estate, where he would be arrested a few hours later. The only one who precisely followed the previously laid plans to disarm the SS, put guards on all members of the SD and cut off all communication with Berlin, was General von Stülpnagel in France. Unhappily, and fatally for him, the result was that as his own correct orders cut him off from contact with Berlin, he became the very last to hear that the coup had failed.

Only in one other place were Stauffenberg's orders obeyed to the letter: it happened in Vienna, where a small group of staff officers had long formed a nucleus of resistance within the XVIIth Army Group in charge of Vienna. Major Carl Szokoll, a friend of Stauffenberg's for years, was in direct communication with him. As soon as he received the information from Rastenburg that Hitler was dead, the three ranking staff officers, Colonel Heinrich Cordé, Colonel Robert Bernardis and Colonel Rudolf Graf Marogna-Redwitz (and Major Karl Biedermann), ordered the occupation of the two buildings housing the Police Command and the Gestapo, the arrest of the Gauleiter (Sanitzer), the Police President and the head of the Vienna Gestapo and put on alert the troops under their command.

Of these five men, three were to be hanged—Bernardis and Marogna-Redwitz that summer, together with all the others sentenced by the despicable "People's Court," Biedermann months later. Cordé was sent to a concentration camp and never heard of again.

Carl Szokoll has survived, and with him, perhaps, the last words we know of from Claus von Stauffenberg. For Szokoll had been given his direct dial number in Berlin and rang him that dreadful night from July 20 to 21 when the resistance group in Vienna heard the rumor that Hitler was alive. Stauffenberg, it appears, picked up the receiver. "What's going on?" said Szokoll. "Is it true that Hitler's alive?"

"So you too are quitting," said the tired voice in the Bendlerstrasse in Berlin and hung up. Szokoll rang back almost at once, but there was no reply. When he rang again three minutes later, a strange voice replied and this time Szokoll rang off.

Fromm, who had only been reluctantly involved, changed allegiance the moment Hitler's death was in doubt. As soon as Stauffenberg arrived at the

Bendlerstrasse insisting that Valkyrie had to be activated whether Hitler was finally dead or not, Fromm demanded that Beck, Stauffenberg and Olbricht shoot themselves; the conspirators thereupon confined him to a locked room, but it would not save them or, eventually, him either.

No one, of course, has survived who could have said what went through Stauffenberg's mind during these last hours of his life. Four times this extraordinary man had fought his way through to the decision to kill the tyrant; four times he had himself carried a bomb on his damaged body. What we do know is that even in those final moments, he tried to infuse others in the Bendlerstrasse with his spirit, his energy and his courage.

WHEN THE BOMB exploded in Rastenburg, Speer was in Berlin, in the Propaganda Ministry's beautiful banquet hall completing a morale-bolstering speech to his fellow ministers, two hundred of their top officials and a group of journalists selected by Goebbels. A few minutes later, he was enjoying a drink with Funk in Goebbels's office when a telephone call from Rastenburg informed them of the failed assassination attempt.

Goebbels's (and Hitler's) first thought was that one of the Organization Todt workers could have smuggled in a bomb, but this idea was soon abandoned when it was realized that the bomb had been the signal for a military Putsch in Berlin and in France.

Speer's description in his writings, and also later to me, of his own first hours—and his feelings—after the news of the assassination attempt is oddly disjointed. In his writings he says only that after a few minutes with Goebbels, they both returned to their "ministerial routines"—a strange thought on that particular day, but apparently true, as Annemarie Kempf told me later. He kept a lunch date in his private dining room with a front-line commander, Colonel Gerhard Engel, Hitler's former army adjutant, and the two had a long discussion about a memorandum Speer had just sent to Hitler about better liaison between his ministry and the Wehrmacht. After lunch, Speer wrote in *Inside the Third Reich,* he discussed the "safeguarding of Rumanian oil" with a Foreign Office official, until in the middle of that meeting Goebbels rang and asked him to come to his private residence at once.

I had read all this in Speer's book with some astonishment and, when we talked for the first of many times about the Twentieth of July, told him that I could hardly believe this story. Surely everyone's concern that morning in Berlin had to be the danger Hitler had been in and what it all meant.

"You would think so, wouldn't you?" he answered. "I've often wondered about it myself. The only way I could explain it to myself was that perhaps our very shock made us escape into routine." After that call, he said, he spent the rest of the day with Goebbels, first at his office and then at Goebbels's residence.

"That's quite right," Annemarie said. "He had been due to attend the funeral of Leni Riefenstahl's father that afternoon; I recall he asked me to phone and make his excuses. Early that afternoon our ministry was suddenly ringed by soldiers, but I remember that it was from his own office, not Goebbels's, as he later thought, that he tried to reach General Fromm. When Fromm [then still held incommunicado] was said to be unable to accept his call, Speer asked for General Olbricht, to whom I then heard him angrily complain about the soldiers who were stopping people entering and leaving both our building and Goebbels's ministry. I can still see his face literally go pale at Olbricht's reply," she said.

Speer had told me about that phone call. "Olbricht apologized," he said. "He said that in the case of our ministry it was a mistake; he would put it right in a moment. I was really shaken. If he was in a position to say that guarding *my* ministry was a 'mistake which he would put right in a moment,' it meant not only that he, a top officer at the Chiefs of Staff, was part of the conspiracy, but that they thought I was too. Where would this end? Above all, where did Fromm stand? How wide was it and how high did it go?"

At this point, he said, he had no idea that the highest echelons of the army, active and retired, in Germany, the occupied territories and at the front were involved, but he was extremely worried about Fromm. Nor did he know—as he would find out later that night—that his name, fortunately with a question mark, was on a ministerial list the conspirators had drawn up.

Speer told me (and wrote in *Inside the Third Reich*) what had happened three days earlier, on July 17—an event which in retrospect he would consider very important. Fromm, he said, had sent Colonel Stauffenberg to invite him to come to the Bendlerstrasse on July 20 for lunch and an after-lunch meeting. As he was to deliver his big speech that mid-morning however, he hadn't felt like following it up with what he was sure would have been hours of talk at the Bendlerstrasse and therefore had declined. Stauffenberg—uncharacteristically, he thought later—had been quite insistent and said Fromm needed urgently for him to be there. But Speer said he couldn't.

"I've never had any doubt," Speer told me, "that during that lunch, while in Rastenburg Stauffenberg was placing his briefcase containing the bomb under the table in Hitler's temporary situation room, Fromm had intended to find out whether that question mark next to my name should be replaced with a confirmation. When he was arrested I tried to help him, but not very effectively, I fear."

Early that afternoon (according to Annemarie, just after Speer's telephone conversation with Olbricht), Goebbels phoned to ask him to come at once to his house. It was only on arrival there that Speer was told of the extent of the coup. Goebbels had been charged by Hitler with the re-establishment of the legitimate authority in the capital and told Speer he wanted him to stay with him from then on for consultation.

"He had moved there from his office," Speer said, "because it was more secure. At this point nobody knew anymore who was for or against." Earlier on Goebbels had discovered that the commander of the Berlin troops guarding the government buildings was a Major Otto Ernst Remer, said to be a loyal Nazi.

"It is extraordinary to think," Speer said, "that it was finally almost entirely due to this one basically insignificant young officer that, with one clever stroke by Goebbels, the army coup was essentially over."

Ordered by Goebbels to call off his soldiers, Remer had replied that he was acting on superior orders because Hitler was dead. When Goebbels told him that he had been misinformed and got Hitler to speak to him on the telephone, Remer had sprung to attention.

"*Jawohl, mein Führer. Jawohl!*" Speer heard the young officer say, his voice breaking with emotion.

Hitler told Remer that his superior, General [Paul] von Hase, evidently part of "the small clique of traitors," would immediately be put under arrest. In the meantime Remer was to assume command over all Berlin army troops and take his instructions from Goebbels.

At eleven o'clock that night, by which time Fromm had long been released by officers loyal to Hitler and had promptly put Beck, Olbricht, Stauffenberg and their aides under arrest, Speer and Goebbels learned that Fromm was about to hold a summary court martial.

In *Inside the Third Reich,* Speer claims he hurriedly drove to the Bendlerstrasse, taking Major Remer in his white Mercedes, because he thought that such an act would seriously incriminate Fromm, and furthermore that "Hitler himself should decide what was to be done with the rebels."

I asked Speer why he wanted to stop Fromm. Surely the conspirators' fate was sealed anyway. Under the circumstances it had to be almost an act of mercy for Fromm to have them shot before they could be tortured, as they undoubtedly would have been.

"I was sure Fromm was implicated," he said. "And I thought, as it turned out, rightly, that such a court martial would result in his being suspected of having wanted to silence them before, under torture, they might have given him away."

So he thought that this suspicion led or contributed to Fromm's arrest? I asked.

"It certainly didn't help him, did it?" he replied drily. "The fact is, of course, that they kept him alive for months because they never found real proof against him, nothing on paper, as with so many of the others, and no accusations against him under torture. Otherwise they would have executed him sooner."

Speer's reasoning here may well have been right, but the fact is, as I would discover many years later when I studied the "Spandau draft," that it was not just the court martial or concern for Fromm which brought him to the Bendlerstrasse that night. The story, as he tells it there, is very different. Here he describes the measures which are discussed as he sits with Goebbels in his office at his residence. Rumors abound, coming by telephone or messengers: Himmler has disappeared, Himmler has gone over to the conspirators, large numbers of troops which have joined the rebellion are marching on Berlin. Here is the "Spandau draft":

> Toward evening new excitement. A tank unit coming from Potsdam stood at the ready [in the center of the city] waiting for orders from Guderian, their chief commander, the only one they would obey.
>
> "And who knows which side *he* is on?" I say to Goebbels. "He's always been rather hot-blooded." But I was wrong about that. A colonel well known to me from my work with the Tank Corps people was in command of this unit, and I managed to get in touch with him. The tanks, he told me, were not part of the rebellion, and shortly afterwards he joined us in Goebbels's house to be informed about the situation. Meanwhile it had become clear that the center of the rebellion was Bendlerstrasse . . . and an action against them was initiated with the tanks.
>
> It was dark outside by the time we received the report that the building had been taken. I drove over with the tank colonel. . . . [In his book he took Major Remer.] At the gate I found Kaltenbrunner [head of the Gestapo] with a number of SS leaders. He told me that the SS thought this was an army matter, to be settled by them, and that therefore, as any participation by the SS would only lead to ill-feeling, his people had been forbidden to enter the building. I thought it was a sensible attitude, though as it turned out, it didn't last long.

Telling me again about his drive to the Bendlerstrasse that night, he said that Berlin was of course blacked out, but the HQ building, located on the fringe of the Tiergarten, was lit up by searchlights. Even as he and Major Remer (he didn't mention the tank colonel to me) got out of Speer's white Mercedes, a tall figure came toward them through the trees.

"It was Fromm in full formal uniform," Speer said, "looking devastated."

Fromm's voice was hoarse as he told Speer that it had been his duty to hold a court martial of those of the participants in the coup who had been members of his own staff. "He said that General Olbricht and his Chief of Staff, Colonel von Stauffenberg, had been shot in the courtyard, and added, unnecessarily I thought, 'They are dead.' "

Fromm then insisted on immediately being taken to Goebbels's office so that he could speak to Hitler himself. At the Ministry of Propaganda Goebbels had him wait in another room while he himself spoke to Hitler. A few minutes later Fromm was put under arrest.

It is clear that Speer had mixed feelings about Fromm. They had been friends, or as near to being friends as Speer was capable of. Certainly during the crisis of his illness, when he felt himself abandoned by most of those around Hitler, Fromm (with Zeitzler, Guderian, Milch, Dönitz and Funk) had been the only "power figure" who remained entirely loyal to him. Speer clearly thought Fromm was part of the conspiracy, and also thought—probably at first with resentment—that he had tried to draw him into it. Indeed, one suspects that his rush to the Bendlerstrasse, that night of July 20, was not so much to stop Fromm from harming himself, as to make sure he would not harm Speer.

This said, however, Speer's documented offer to appear as a witness for Fromm at his trial in March 1945, a gesture made at a time when people were being executed left and right on mere suspicion of disloyalty, was an act of considerable courage and went a long way toward erasing the ambivalence of his attitude.

Though doubtless not in words at the time, in all his later writing there was never any ambivalence about his liking for Stauffenberg—he makes a point of it both in Spandau and in *Inside the Third Reich*. "He was a very special, gentle man," he told me, "an almost mystical figure. I liked him exceedingly. It was Schmundt who had recommended him for his appointment to the Chiefs of Staff. It is a tragic irony that Schmundt died from the injuries he suffered from Stauffenberg's bomb."

The "Spandau draft," almost entirely contradicting Speer's later stance, emphasizes what Speer already said in so many words in his Nuremberg draft—he was against the coup because its first and principal aim was Hitler's death. "That is not the right way," he wrote in Nuremberg. "To have done away with those around him, yes, but Hitler himself. . . . I don't think that's right."

What emerges very clearly and disturbingly in the "Spandau draft" where, his only reader being Wolters, he tells the story as it was, is the extent of his active collaboration with Goebbels in suppressing the rebellion. In *Inside the Third Reich*, having by then gained some understanding of the psychological developments in Germany and the profound rejection of Hitler—particularly by the younger generation—while he was in prison, he carefully changes the emphasis. Between the lines he indicates that even though he was not officially part of the conspiracy, his sympathy for it was clearly demonstrated by the fact of his name being on the ministerial list for their new government. The restraint toward him afterwards by Hitler and those around him, he writes, confirmed their suspicion of him.

There is no doubt that his name on the list put him under a cloud for the first few days after the coup. At first neither Goebbels nor he himself took it very seriously. He was with Goebbels late that night of July 20 when the list was discovered in the safe at the Bendlerstrasse. Wilfred von Oven, Goebbels's personal chronicler who was present, would write later that both men had laughed when they saw Speer's name, and that Speer would have had to be a brilliant actor if "his hearty laughter" was a sham.

But although Speer already sensed a certain precautionary distancing by a number of people on the day itself, he felt it more the next day when he and all the top ministers were convoked to Rastenburg. He alone of all of them was requested to bring his two deputies, Dorsch and Saur, to whom, he felt, Hitler showed considerably more warmth than to him. Everybody close to Hitler, he thought, avoided him—people falling silent when he entered a room, or even pointedly walking out, as did Gruppenführer Schaub, Hitler's oldest and principal adjutant, but not before "hissing" at him (he writes in the "Spandau draft"), "Now we know who was behind the assassination attempt."

He reported no further dramas during his three-day stay at HQ, and indeed, before returning to Berlin on the twenty-fourth, insisted on dropping in on the dismissed General Zeitzler, who, he told me, "was shunned like the plague by everyone, including his fellow officers," and was preparing to leave his nearby headquarters. "I felt I had to say goodbye to him. I couldn't believe he had been part of it, and, of course, again it was never proved. I did wonder why he told me that his adjutant [Lt. Col. Günther] Smend, who came in when I was there, and who a few weeks later was among those who were hanged, had just been to Berchtesgaden to 'clean out' the General Staff's safe there. It worried me, because it either meant that Zeitzler was innocent but foolish, or that he indeed had been part of it and thought I was too. It was very worrying.

"A few weeks later," Speer went on, "a friend on Hitler's staff got me a copy of Kaltenbrunner's report of his interrogations. And there was a copy of a letter young Colonel Smend had written to Zeitzler from prison in which he thanked him for all his kindness to him during his posting as his adjutant, and begged him to forgive him for having followed the dictates of his conscience by joining the conspiracy, thereby, no doubt, putting him at risk. It was one of the most touching letters I have ever seen, from this attractive young man, who of course knew then that he was going toward a horrible death. Of course, he could conceivably have written it to save Zeitzler, but I didn't think so. It added to my original conviction that Zeitzler had no part in it."

He was relieved to find, he wrote already in the Nuremberg draft, that his own name did not appear in Kaltenbrunner's report, and even more to realize that the conspirators had after all been loyal Germans:

> What clearly emerged was that there was no indication whatever of any connection or communication between the conspirators and the enemy. . . . It was quite clear, that these accused men who were on the General Staff, or serving officers of the Home Army or at the front, in no way forgot or neglected their duty to their country. What emerged was a clear division between their commitment to the coup, and the awareness of their obligation to maintain the army's will to fight. . . . They manifestly intended to continue the war in the East, hopefully in collaboration with the Western Allies with whom they would doubtlessly have negotiated better conditions for peace. It is important to state for posterity that these men were not traitors to their country. . . .

On the evening of July 24, when he had returned from the stressful days at Rastenburg, his body had once again reacted to his state of mind. "I just made it to my little flat," he told me.

Since his own Berlin residence had been bombed months before, he had been camping in a modest three-bedroom apartment in his (also badly bomb-damaged) ministry, previously used by one of the chauffeurs.

"My always vulnerable left leg had swollen up to twice its size," he said. "It hurt like blazes."

Annemarie told me that Dr. Brandt had given her anti-inflammatory pills for him late that night. "But he also gave me 'Baldrian drops' [a homeopathic sedative]," she said, "of which he said Speer was to take a double dosage that night and again in the morning." She said she now thought that perhaps Brandt, too, had thought his leg troubles were at least partly psychosomatic.

It was here, lying on his bed the next morning, that Speer received the head of the Gestapo, Kaltenbrunner. He came with an "air of cordial menace," as Speer put it, to show him the document which had been discovered in the safe in the Bendlerstrasse. "You are down on the list as Armaments Minister," he said.

In *Inside the Third Reich,* Speer describes this event as though this was the first time he heard of being on the ministerial list. But in fact, as we have seen, he had known about this since the document was first found. Thus forewarned, he was able to point out to the Gestapo chief at once that his name on the list was followed not only by a question mark but a notation, "If he accepts after successful coup," thus proving that he had been entirely ignorant of this matter.

In the "Spandau draft"—where he sounds both less surprised and less concerned than in the book about his cool reception at Führer HQ—he first wrote perfectly frankly about his previous knowledge of this document in Goebbels's office. But by the time he got to Kaltenbrunner's visit, he was already having editorial afterthoughts about the value of drama for the eventual book. He put in a remark in brackets addressed to Wolters: "Better leave out first part of this minister story (the bit in Goebbels's office); it's more effective this way."

Annemarie laughed when I told her about this. "I told you before: he wanted success, and I guess that didn't stop in Spandau either! The leopard doesn't change his spots, does he?"

I asked Speer what he would have done if the conspirators had invited him to join them.

"I can only thank God that they didn't," he answered at once. "I would have been desperate."

Desperate that they wanted to kill Hitler?

"No," he replied after a long moment, "desperate that I didn't, that I couldn't have."

Ernst Görner, whom Speer had taken over after Todt's death as his private "recorder," and who admired Speer to the day he died in 1991, had still another, and slightly different, impression of Speer and July 20.

"A few days before July 20," Görner told me, when we talked four years before his death, "I went with Speer to Berchtesgaden, where he said he had to attend an army meeting at the [Hotel] Platterhof. Of course I didn't go in. But I know that one of the generals there was later hanged, and so were two younger officers who were there. One of them was Zeitzler's aide, Smend."

The meeting, Görner recalled, lasted for several hours. "I remember, I went to have breakfast with Leni Riefenstahl and Speer's aide, Karl Cliever. When Speer came back to the car he told us that 'the officers had been surprised' to see him. I remember distinctly thinking that was odd, as he had told me specifically that that meeting was the reason we were going to Berchtesgaden. If he had been invited, why should they have been surprised to see him?"

I asked what he thought Speer could have meant by it.

"I thought later that it had been a precaution, that he was taking out insurance by emphasizing his 'outsider' role to us. He was quite careful, you know, the sort of man who not only thought way ahead but who could see around corners. I have always believed that he knew about the Twentieth of July.

Certainly, afterwards, when it had gone so dreadfully wrong, he gave me the impression of being desperately worried."

Speer talked to me for a long time about the consequences of July 20. "What could be ruinous," he said, "was rumors, and there was an avalanche of them, including about me, about people being arrested, having disappeared, fled, committed suicide or being shot."

Annemarie, who was a witness to Speer's activities and the recipient of information for him about these rumors, confirmed how dangerous they were. "We were almost immediately aware of the consequences," she said. "It was amazing, by comparison, how silent our telephone became in those first days. And we ourselves, long convinced that not only our phones but our offices were tapped by Himmler's snoops, found ourselves chitchatting about inanities with grotesque false cheerfulness."

She never thought for a moment that Speer was part of the conspiracy or, contrary to Görner's opinion, that he even knew of it. "I would have known, believe me," she said. "It is true that he was very close to some of the generals, and it's true too—I often heard them—that all of them endlessly criticized the orders coming from Führer HQ. But from that to actually informing Speer of their plans would have been a vast step. Even at that point, after his illness and the disillusionment you suspect, and although he certainly shared their conviction that the war could no longer be won, they couldn't have risked informing him of a plan that involved first killing Hitler.

"But afterwards . . ." Annemarie, usually so calm, was angry now. "How many people high in Hitler's government dared to stand up for colleagues and friends as he did? Don't forget, I was there; on his instructions, I took down his telephone calls and his letters to Hitler; to Himmler; to Kaltenbrunner; to Thierack, the Minister of Justice, asking for help and clemency for men he knew from our ministry, from industry, from public life, and of course the army. And for their wives and children, whom they imprisoned—whole families were taken. And he sent packages to all of them in prison and in concentration camps, with food, clothes, medicines; we packed them. They came to be referred to as '*Speer Pakete.*' Who else high up in the government took the risks he took? I'll tell you, nobody. And he paid for it."

By "paid" Annemarie did not mean Speer's eventual Nuremberg sentence of twenty years at Spandau. She, more aware perhaps than anyone of what he described to me as his "schizophrenic existence" when he returned to Berlin after his illness, was talking of his fears then, which she, more than anyone else, came to share.

"There is no point pretending that I wasn't afraid," Speer told me. "As I told you before, I really am not a hero. So whatever else I felt, fear was a large part of it. First, physical fear of Himmler and his minions, who I knew wished me dead; then fear—emotional fear—of Hitler's disfavor. And then, for months after the Twentieth of July and the terrible fate suffered by so many, a really grinding fear, above all in the night, in my dreams, of physical pain."

He was thinking of the tortures, which, it was common knowledge, suspected men were being subjected to.

"During the day I could suppress this fear with work," he said, "but in my dreams the blood and gore was always there. It was unlike me. I am really," he laughed briefly, "well, a quiet dreamer, even when my dreams reflect painful memories. But in those months . . ." He stopped.

In those months for the first time, one must believe, he had to confront violent acts: not what war did to anonymous thousands, but acts perpetrated by men he knew personally, on men whom he knew terribly well—of whom in many ways he had wanted to be, had become, and felt, a part.

During the first weeks following the coup, as the Gestapo interrogations of the main conspirators went on day and night in the cellars of their Prinz Albrechtstrasse headquarters, and more and more people were arrested as a result—or on the pretext—of statements under torture, the city was awash with whispers. The first trial by the so-called People's Court, though filmed for posterity, was closed except to a chosen few party bigwigs. But the news about the vulgarity of the proceedings; the gross language used by the presiding judge, Roland Freisler; and the appalling appearance of the accused quickly spread through the corridors of official Berlin.

That first hearing on August 8 was of eight men. The faces of these scions of some of Germany's oldest families, household names of the proud German army, were changed almost beyond recognition. They wore crushed civilian attire without collars, socks or belts, and clutched their trousers which, when the court ordered that they stand at attention, repeatedly slipped down around their ankles. On one such occasion, the court—and the judge—erupted in guffaws when the victim, not permitted underclothes, stood there, his thin trembling flanks exposed, his face rigid with horror. "So that is a hero of Germany's brilliant Chiefs of Staff," Judge Freisler cried, "not even capable of holding up his pants."

"This was a man I had dined with not much more than a month before; a bearer of the highest decorations our country could bestow," Speer told me. "It was . . . inconceivable."

There would be many victims of Hitler's rage, army officers of all ranks, and civilians. Those who knew there was no hope and who managed in time committed suicide. Most of the others, after being put through unspeakable tortures by the Gestapo, would also appear before that dreadful People's Court to be humiliated and finally sentenced to death.

Some of those who died were general officers such as Beck, Erich Fellgiebel, Hase, Olbricht, Hans Oster, Rommel, Helmuth Stieff, Stülpnagel, Tresckow, Eduard Wagner. There were brilliant younger men, officers and diplomats, such as, of course, Stauffenberg, his adjutant Werner von Haeften and Haeften's brother, Hans Bernd, who was chief of personnel at the German Foreign Office and a leading member of the previously mentioned Kreisau Circle.

Tresckow had shot himself in Rastenburg as soon as he learned the day of the attempted assassination that Hitler had survived. Stauffenberg himself was shot on Fromm's orders that night, but most of the others would eventually be hanged. This also included Helmuh von Moltke, the founder of the Kreisau Circle, diplomat Adam von Trott zu Solz and Peter Yorck von Wartenburg, all devout Christians and early resisters. Wartenburg had been on the conspirators' cabinet list (as was Speer) and was among the first eight to be hanged, as was the journalist Julius Leber, who, a socialist member of the Kreisau Circle, was the intended Minister of the Interior if the coup had succeeded. And then of course, there was Erwin Rommel, that most famous of German generals after his victories in North Africa, who on October 14, 1944, after recovering from the injuries he had suffered when his car was strafed by Allied planes on July 17, killed himself when offered the choice of committing suicide and being granted a hero's funeral—and his family his pension—or an ignominious trial as a traitor.

Stülpnagel, blinding himself when attempting to commit suicide, was judged sufficiently well to be hanged on August 30. Kluge took poison, leaving a letter protesting his loyalty to Hitler, though Speer wrote in Spandau that he was probably only trying to protect his family; documents found later appeared to bear out this suggestion.

General Beck, to whom Fromm in consideration of his advanced years had handed a pistol on that fateful night at the Bendlerstrasse, tried twice to shoot himself and twice missed. He was finished off by a sergeant. Fromm, himself arrested within hours, was like many others executed eight months later, in March 1945, only weeks before it all ended. Canaris and his Chief of Staff, General Hans Oster, although immediately arrested, were hanged in Flossenburg concentration camp, on April 8 or 9, after Admiral Wilhelm Canaris's diary, recording his and Oster's many contacts with the Allies, had been found in the rubble of his bombed office. That same spring, also in Flossenburg, the Nazis executed some of Germany's most distinguished and determined resisters: the Protestant pastor and theologian Dietrich Bonhoeffer; his older brother, Klaus, a jurist; and their brother-in-law Hans von Dohnanyi (in Canaris's Abwehr); and their lawyer, Rüdiger Schleicher.

According to Maria (Missie) Vassiltchikov (in *Berlin Diaries 1940–1945*), who was a friend of many of the longtime anti-Nazis, Trott's death sentence came when the Gestapo discovered records he had unfortunately kept of his negotiations abroad with the Allies. Canaris and others were similarly victims of their own diaries.

The two most remarkable survivors of this large group, both of whom had themselves attempted to kill Hitler on earlier occasions, were Axel von dem Bussche, who luckily for him was in hospital on July 20, recovering from a war injury, and Fabian von Schlabrendorff, whose interrogation by Judge Roland Freisler was just beginning when an Allied bombardment scored a direct hit on the People's Court, killing Freisler and destroying von Schlabrendorff's file, which the dreadful judge had been holding in his hand.

There are many different estimates of the number of those executed in connection with the July 20 plot. According to Nazi sources, about 7,000 were arrested immediately after the coup. The official total number of executions in 1944 and in the four remaining months of Nazi rule in 1945 was 5,684. About 200 of those executed had been directly implicated in the coup. They included 21 generals, 33 colonels and lieutenant colonels, 2 ambassadors, 7 senior diplomats, 1 Minister of State, 3 Secretaries of State, the head of the Criminal Police, Count Helldorf; his deputy, Count Fritz Dietlov von der Schulenburg and his seventy-year-old uncle, Count Friedrich Werner von der Schulenburg, former German Ambassador to Moscow. More than 5,000, including many wives and children, were sent to concentration camps.

Today, exactly fifty years later as I write, the Twentieth of July remains a subject of controversy, in Germany and elsewhere. How was it possible, people ask, that the cream of Germany's General Staff and the German Foreign Office had so misjudged the situation that the coup was almost bound to fail? How could they not know the extent of loyalty Hitler still commanded? How, above all, could they so grievously misinterpret Churchill's and Roosevelt's attitude of total condemnation not only of Hitler but of Germany, and (at that point still) admiration of the Soviet war effort? How, Germans and others ask fifty years later, could any well-informed German at that time believe that a German conspirators' government could succeed in persuading the Western Allies—as Speer believed was the intention—to side with a German army freed of Hitler in a continued war against the Soviets? It is unlikely that these questions, asked now with retrospective wisdom and ardor, can ever be answered. But certainly, these were desperate and courageous men and their purpose was honorable.

For Speer the single most devastating incident was to see photographs lying on Hitler's desk a few weeks later, of men, dressed in striped convict suits, unrecognizable in their death agony, hanging from meat hooks. One of these, an SS officer told him, inviting him to a showing that night of a film of the hangings, was Field Marshal von Witzleben. Speer declined the invitation. "The very thought made me sick," he wrote in Spandau. "Many SS leaders attended but no army officers."

When I asked him about it, he said, "As far as I knew Hitler never saw the film, and I have always said so. It was not his nature to want to see a thing like that. I doubt, too, that he looked at the photographs any more than I did."

Historian John Toland quoted (from a 1971 *Playboy* interview) Speer saying that "Hitler and his guests attended a screening," and that "Hitler loved the film and had it shown over and over again: it became one of his favorite entertainments."

"I didn't say that," Speer told me, and added, mildly, "I think a number of misquotes were probably due to linguistic misunderstandings, no doubt my fault—my English was not that good." He shrugged. "It happens often."

Below, who was at headquarters throughout, in his memoirs agrees with Speer: "I declined to look at these photographs. And Hitler would have found no more pleasure in looking at them than in seeing photographs of destroyed cities. He literally closed his eyes if forced to see the consequences of his orders. . . ."

XVIII

Scorched Earth

Nuremberg, June 20, 1946

FLÄCHSNER: Herr Speer, were orders given to destroy industry in Belgium, Holland and France?

SPEER: Yes . . . Hitler had ordered [at the beginning of July 1944] a far-reaching system of destruction of war industries in all these countries. . . . Army Command West was responsible for carrying out these orders. . . . I informed [the commanding general] that as far as I was concerned this destruction was senseless . . . and that I, in my capacity of Armaments Minister, did not consider [it] necessary. Thereupon no order to destroy these installations was given. By this, of course, I made myself responsible to Hitler for the fact that no destruction took place. . . .

FLÄCHSNER: With regard to the other occupied countries . . . did you use your influence to prevent destruction?

SPEER: From August 1944, in the industrial installations in the Government General, the ore mines in the Balkans, the nickel works in Finland; from September 1944, industrial installations in northern Italy; beginning in February 1944, the oil fields in Hungary and industries in Czechoslovakia. . . .

FLÄCHSNER: At the beginning of September 1944 when enemy troops approached the German boundaries from all sides, what were Hitler's intentions . . . for the preservation of the means of existence for the . . . population?

SPEER: He had absolutely no [such] intention. On the contrary, he ordered the "scorched earth" policy with special application to Germany. . . .

As of the late summer of 1944, traveling through the industrial regions of the country, encouraging industrialists and workers and negotiating with the generals, Speer was hardly in Berlin for any length of time. By now Hitler had issued the first of his many orders to destroy industrial installations, first in the occupied territories as the Allies advanced, and then in Germany.

Until the first month of 1945, craftily using Hitler's own continual predictions that he would reconquer the lost territories, Speer had succeeded in persuading him to replace his "scorched earth" orders, which he first issued in August 1944, with shutdowns of the plants. If they were totally destroyed, Speer argued with deliberate hypocrisy, they would be useless for the production of armaments for years to come; if merely temporarily immobilized, he could get them back into operation as soon as the areas were regained. For those first months he succeeded with this tactic.

One important change in Speer's life after his return from his illness in May 1944, and one which enormously aided him in his fight to bypass Hitler's orders, had been the appointment of thirty-four-year-old Major Manfred von Poser as his liaison adjutant with the Chief of the General Staff.

A veteran of the French and Russian campaigns, Poser was to become almost his constant companion during those last dangerous months of the war, and Speer's choice of this distinguished young officer for this role was a kind of statement.

"I realized as soon as I met him," Speer told me, "that this was a man who in his inner being—more than 'unpolitical'—had to be 'against.' We didn't talk about it when we met, and we never talked about it later, not even after Spandau, but the feeling he gave me, because of that, was one of relief, and of . . . cleanliness. I knew I was going into ever more difficult times. This was a man I wanted at my side."

The fact is that Poser had not always been "against." When I first went to see him and his wife, Carola, in 1986, they, like several others I spoke with whose lives became closely involved with Speer, made no secret of their early sympathy for the Nazis. We talked in a house full of light and quiet comfort, in a small town northwest of the Ruhr where they had settled after the war. Although by nature reserved, they laid bare much of their younger years in order to help me understand the Germany they loved, lost and finally regained.

"I don't know anyone from my world in those early years of Hitler's rule who was against the Nazis," Manfred von Poser said, "although perhaps this applied primarily to the young. My parents, for instance, and Carola's parents too, were against them."

"I joined the BDM [Association of German Girls] like everybody in my class at school," said Carola, "but my parents made me get out. They wouldn't have it. I don't think they knew anything specific, just as we, later, didn't really *know* anything for a long time." She too used that untranslatable word *"ahnen"* with which Speer had tried to describe his "sensing" that there was something dreadful going on about the Jews. "One 'sensed' there was something wrong. But you see, sensing isn't knowing. One hears things which make one feel uncomfortable, without being able to put one's finger on anything specific. It's almost an atmosphere—a way people talk or speak, their conduct, or perhaps their gestures or even just their tone of voice. It is so subtle. How can one explain it to anyone who hasn't experienced that time, those small first doubts, that kind of unease, for want of a better word? We couldn't have found words to explain what we felt was wrong. But to find out, to look for an explanation for that . . . that 'hunch,' well, that would have been very dangerous. . . . One did know very early on that there were dangers in knowledge."

When I met the Posers I was already well aware of what army people who served in Russia necessarily had to have known about the murders there. Not only because the *Kommissar Befehl* and the subsequent verbally transmitted orders told them, but because it was impossible not to either see what was being done or, at the very least (as was the case for many officers on the Chiefs of Staff), hear it described.

In an ideal world, honorable men such as this would rebel, leave the country, or perhaps opt out, leave the army, put up a moral barricade to separate their private world from such horrors. But realistically, few men will risk all—their wives, their children, life itself—for morality. Realistically, the choices for men such as this are limited.

The Posers were "army"—in the traditional sense of German army families: solid, with landed but not necessarily titled family backgrounds, conventionally religious, owning perhaps some land but no fortunes, for younger sons little or no money aside from their army pay. In Nazi Germany older army officers, morally reluctant to take the oath for Hitler, could find a pretext to take early retirement and eke out life on their pensions—General Beck was a good example, and there were others. But young army officers, whatever their reservations about political events, could not; their profession, for honorable men entirely linked to their country, was not a readily salable commodity.

The men in the Poser family have been in army forever, and they married the same kind of girls. Poser's great-grandfather was a general, his maternal grandfather was in the Hussars, as was his father, who died in 1946 in a Russian POW camp. His brother, who also died in the war, was in the air force. "I think I may have ended up with Speer," he said, "because my parents requested my release from active duty after my brother was killed; it was customary in the army when only one son was left. But they never told me whether they did that." And—typical of his generation—he never asked.

"He was a find for me," Speer had told me, referring to Poser's arrival. "I think we clicked," Poser said. This was in late May 1944, by which time Poser had been attached to the Ministry for three months. "I was called in, in February 1944, and told that I was being assigned to the Speer Ministry as liaison officer between Speer and the General Staff. I didn't like it at all. To me that meant the party, but of course there was no way of refusing. When I got to Berlin, Speer wasn't there [he was ill in Hohenlychen], so they attached me to Saur, who was acting as his deputy."

Poser's brief was to facilitate the exchange of ideas between various departments of the General Staff and the Ministry, short-cutting as far as possible the tortuous bureaucracy.

"But of course, as soon as Speer got back, it became much more than that," he said. Technically, Saur was very well informed, very able, he said. "That's what impressed Hitler, of course. He always had a lot of time for experts. It was why, if Speer hadn't come back, Saur would certainly have got the job. But in every other way, in any wider sense, he couldn't get within shouting distance of what Speer could achieve.

"What Speer had was an almost incomprehensible ability to oversee the totality: the needs of the army, navy, air force, the workers and the civilian population." He shook his head. "Originally, of course, these jobs were held by five different men, each supported by a staff of bureaucrats. Until, obviously, Hitler realized that here was that one man who could take all of it on, and do it better. So he gave it all to him—it's as simple as that."

Poser noticed very soon, he said, even before Speer returned, that there was a very special atmosphere in Speer's ministry, that for all intents and purposes there were no imposed politics in that building. "I heard people say things in those offices I wouldn't have believed possible in Nazi Germany," he said. "Like everywhere else, there were people there who were devoted to Hitler's cause. But Speer didn't care where anybody stood politically; he was only interested in what they could contribute. Anybody he took on could feel absolutely sure that Speer would stand up for him, come what may. Believe me, in those times that was a remarkable reputation to have.

"On one of those trips, quite early on, before I really knew him," Poser said, "he suddenly asked me whether I thought the war could still be won. What do you say to Hitler's first minister, supposedly his friend, when he asks you a question like that? All those thoughts raced through my mind, but then instinct, I think, made me decide to just tell him the truth. And I said that with the Dnieper already lost in the East, with the Allies having gained mastery over the skies, and with many hundreds of thousands of Allied troops firmly anchored in the West, I didn't think so. Typical for him, as I soon learned, he shrugged his shoulders and said something inconsequential like 'Ah, well . . .' For heaven's sake, he knew—no one better—that it was all over. He was just trying me out. . . ."

Poser would realize very soon that Speer had considered the continuation of the war senseless from the time of the Allied invasion. "He was one of the few public personalities," he said, "if indeed not the only one, who at that point over a period of many months told Hitler time and again how he saw the true situation and the extent to which he disagreed with his views. As the year went on, his one goal became to preserve not only Germany's but Europe's economic potential for the future."

While it is true that Hitler ruled absolutely and few people dared to contradict him, the fact is, although Speer was finally the only one who dared to *act,* he was never the only man in Hitler's circle who openly disagreed with him. Years earlier there was Todt, who may have died for it. Of the party personalities, Schacht, Hess, von Papen and von Schirach are known to have contradicted him at times. And Goebbels, though perhaps the most faithful disciple, was also the one most readily prepared to argue with his Führer. Hitler invariably listened and often followed his advice. Perhaps, in the final analysis, Hitler's relationship with Goebbels, whom he respected for his sharp intelligence and whose loyalty he rightly trusted absolutely, was stronger than with anyone else. With Speer in earlier years he had shared his better dreams. With Goebbels he shared his awful reality.

Among the generals, too, there were some who spoke up, however fruitlessly in earlier years, such as Beck, Witzleben, Halder, Blomberg, Fritsch and even, at times, the formalistic Brauchitsch. And, as Speer said, during the war, Zeitzler, Fromm, Milch and some others also tried. And finally there was General Jodl, who, although unhappily for him, he was never sacked or transferred, very often spoke his mind and, particularly in the last months, went through long, harrowing periods of the kind of disfavor Speer experienced, when Hitler, although insisting on his presence, would pretend he wasn't there.

("He would come home, late, late in the night," Jodl's wife, Luise, a woman of great distinction then and now, recalled when we talked, "his face exhausted, his voice hoarse. He didn't have to say anything: I knew that he had again tried, again failed to influence Hitler. All I could think of was how to ease his despair, how to help him just to rest. So finally, one would talk about practically nothing. You know, the weather, the dogs; just things of little importance, gentle things.")

Nicolaus von Below in his book cites numerous occasions when he heard visitors contradict Hitler and when he himself argued with him. Thus, only days after the July coup attempt, Air Force Commander General von Richthofen, visiting Hitler upon his return from sick leave, begged him to end the war. Below wrote,

> I was appalled when I heard him. I knew that Hitler was less prepared than ever to discuss this subject. But perhaps because of his great respect for this German hero, or perhaps because there was no one else present, he appeared open to it.
> He *had* put out feelers here and there, Hitler told him, but all in vain. He saw no possibility of achieving peace at tolerable terms. . . . The very frank discussion went on for a long time. . . .

Speer also knew of Hitler's attempts to placate those who were arguing for peace while he maintained the full war effort, as he testified at Nuremberg: "From the summer of 1944 on [Hitler] circulated, through Ambassador Hewel of the Foreign Office, definite statements to the effect that conversations with foreign powers had been started. Jodl has confirmed this to me here. In this way, for instance, the fact that the Japanese Ambassador repeatedly called on Hitler was interpreted to mean that we were talking to Moscow via the Japanese." Other envoys, he added, were reported to have initiated negotiations with the United States via the Balkans or Sweden.

Below either didn't realize or didn't want to discuss in his book the fact that whether Hitler "put out feelers" or not was immaterial. Whomever he might send as his envoy, it was he himself who was entirely unacceptable to the Allies, even as the instigator of talks. "This was a fact neither Hitler nor Himmler, who also later 'negotiated,' ever faced," Speer told me.

A few days after Richthofen's visit, Below collapsed from the effects of his ignored concussion from the July 20 bomb, but as he insisted on remaining at HQ (though in bed), he received frequent visits from Hitler. He wrote,

He was now clinging to a new plan, a huge new offensive on the Western front with fresh tank divisions and new fighter squadrons. I thought this was quite wrong, and I think anybody else in Germany would have thought the same. I said right away why not use all these fresh troops against the Russians instead? He replied that he could do that later, but not if the Americans got to the middle of Germany. First, he said, he had to secure the Western borders. [Below argued that surely the first priority was to hold the Russians beyond the old German frontiers] . . . but Hitler didn't agree with that: he gave me to understand that he feared the influence of the Jews in America much more than the power of the Bolsheviks.

In the aftermath of the July coup, Hitler, abandoning even the last vestiges of reliance on the army, had appointed Himmler commander of the Replacement Army (replacing Fromm) and Goebbels Reich Commissioner for Total Mobilization of Resources for War. But within less than two months, Goebbels, eagerly supported by the party fanatics Bormann and Ley, and by Himmler, vastly expanded his domain, basically taking on the functions of a defense minister, for which he was entirely unsuited.

Passionately adopting Hitler's own blind spots, Goebbels now made his obsession the enlargement of the armed forces. As his diary entries demonstrate, this put him on a collision course with Speer:

September 2, 1944: Speer rings from HQ [where Hitler had ordered that all services, including the armament industry, had to supply men for the army] complaining once again. . . . He tells me the Führer wants 300,000 men at once. . . . Göring will give us 100,000 from the Luftwaffe, Speer says he [can only find] 50,000. But I intend to persuade the Führer not to let Speer pick the raisins out of the cake.

September 3, 1944: . . . The Führer has decided: Speer has to give us 100,000 men, now.

September 20, 1944: . . . Conference with Speer who brought Field Marshal Milch along for support and becomes very stubborn. I try again to explain to him that the choice is not between having ammunition *or* soldiers, but to have arms *and* soldiers. Without soldiers the war can't be carried on . . . and the armament industry is now the only place where we can find large numbers of deferred men. . . . What we are calling up now only covers the most essential needs of the Wehrmacht. We have no intention to confront the enemy with unarmed soldiers. . . . Speer's function is to make sure that the new divisions we are creating are properly equipped. . . .

Speer still hasn't learned: I, in any case, will now be more reserved with him. I think we have allowed this young man to become too big. . . . I'm not impressed with his constant talk of historical responsibility and his threats to resign . . . it is entirely un–National Socialist behavior.

Goebbels's quarrel with Speer was to continue for several months, until in early 1945 even Goebbels became extraordinarily critical of Hitler's indifference to the fate and indeed survival of the German people, and returned to a degree of collaboration with Speer.

THE CLOSEST SPEER came in *Inside the Third Reich* to confessing knowledge about the fate of the Jews came after a passage discussing his guilt feelings about his own disregard of the human beings enslaved by the system he served. In the summer of 1944, he wrote, his friend Karl Hanke, Gauleiter of Lower Silesia, had come to see him in Berlin and, sitting "in the green leather easychair in my office," appearing confused and speaking "falteringly with many breaks," had advised him never, under any circumstances, to accept an invitation to inspect a concentration camp in Upper Silesia, which Speer said he later realized was Auschwitz.

He had seen something there which he was not permitted to describe and moreover could not describe. I did not query him. I did not query Himmler, I did not query Hitler, I did not speak with personal friends. I did not investigate—for I did not want to know what was happening there. Hanke must have been speaking of Auschwitz and then *during those few seconds, while Hanke was warning me, the whole responsibility had become reality again* [author's italics]. Those seconds were uppermost in my mind when I stated to the International Court at the Nuremberg trial that as an important member of the leadership of the Reich, I had to share the total responsibility for all that had happened. From that moment on, I was inescapably contaminated morally; from fear of discovering something which might have made me turn from my course, I had closed my eyes. . . . I still feel, to this day, responsible for Auschwitz in a wholly personal sense.

When we talked of this first, in 1978, I asked Speer if he was really saying that for Hanke the fact that Jews were being killed in Auschwitz was shocking news in the summer of 1944? After all, as Gauleiter of Lower Silesia (the Jews of Breslau, its capital, had been deported to Auschwitz in March 1943, making the old city officially "Jew-free"), Hanke had certainly attended the Posen conference in October 1943.

"I can only cite what he said to me," Speer answered, his voice both edgy and weary, as it always became when this subject arose. "What more could I do in the book, or in Nuremberg, than accept responsibility for all of it?"

This was a response almost impossible to argue with. On the face of it, he had voluntarily accepted a moral responsibility for *all* crimes committed by the government he had served. What more could he have done? Nobody else had done it, no individual in legal history, before or afterwards, had elected to declare himself guilty in principle, even for criminal acts in which he had had no part and of which, by implication, he had had no knowledge.

My skeptical question about Hanke's knowledge, I decided later, was perhaps unfair. It was possible that Hanke *could* have received a shock in Auschwitz that early summer. For although he would certainly have been familiar with this nearby installation, Germany's largest labor-*cum*-concentration camp, it is very probable that he had never seen Birkenau, Auschwitz's death camp, which was certainly not on the program for visiting VIPs. And although the smell of burning bodies spread "for miles around," all labor camps had a great many dead bodies to deal with, and crematoria to burn them. It is also conceivable that Hanke, while aware of the murder of Jews by shooting, working and starving them to death, had not known about that unspeakable horror that not even Himmler could pronounce: the gas chambers.

But between May 15 and June 30, 1944, 380,000 Hungarian Jews arrived in Auschwitz. More than a third of them were sent to work in the armament industry's new underground factories—the "hundred thousand" Himmler had promised Hitler (and Speer) a few months before. About 250,000 of them—useless for work—were gassed (or when the gas chambers proved insufficient, shot) at the rate of 6,000 a day. To prepare for these huge transports, new commandants had been assigned, both to Auschwitz itself and to Birkenau—Richard Bär and Josef Kramer, crude, ruthless men who could be relied on to dispose of this last mass of Eastern Orthodox Jews from the Hungarian countryside.

Other *Sonderaktionen* (special actions) over the preceding two years had been routinely carried out in Birkenau, fifteen kilometers away from the main camp, but these sudden immense movements of people could not be camouflaged. For their arrival a special branch line of the State Railway—the Reichsbahn—had been laid, with the debarkation point within two hundred yards of the gas chambers and crematoria. Selections were carried out within sight of the women's barracks in the main camp. Not only the one hundred thousand slave laborers and their thousands of SS guards knew about the Hungarian Jews, but so did the railway personnel and the German armament workers, many of them friendly and helpful, next to whom the foreign slaves, both Christians and Jews, worked in the I.G. Farben and Krupp factories in the main camp.

In this situation it is entirely possible that Gauleiter Hanke, on a routine visit to Auschwitz during those weeks, could indeed have received the kind of shock that Speer described. He was not, after all, a brute—Speer said elsewhere that Hanke "had shown himself a man of compassion and directness." Below was also a friend, and wrote, "I valued Hanke . . . we had talked together a great deal over the months, and I was aware of the profound serious-ness of his mind."

But questions still arose. Why would Hanke suddenly warn Speer against a situation at Auschwitz most people would assume he already knew about? And finally, why did Speer bring up this painful subject at this point, when we had been focusing on the period between the Allied invasion and the July 20 coup attempt?

It was when I neared the end of my research, long after Speer's death, that I realized that this story, and Speer's way of presenting it, went to the heart of what Casalis had called his "inner torture" about the Jews. It was Speer's own despairing knowledge that for the "different man" he had wanted to become under Casalis's guidance in Spandau, his generalized acknowledgement of a moral mandate had only been an elegant ploy; behind it lay a nightmare of unavowed knowledge, a mine field of unalleviated guilt. In that paragraph in his book, he had tried to say so: "I still feel, to this day, responsible for Ausch-witz in a wholly personal sense."

IF SPEER FOUND morality unattainable at that time, an extraor-dinary young German doctor, Hans Münch, had fought another battle of conscience, worth relating here to show how a kind of morality could be maintained even in the hell of Auschwitz.

When I talked to Münch in 1982, his wife and he were living as they did before the war, in a small, peaceful Bavarian village, a skiing resort in the winter. The windows of his living room looked out over ski lifts and practice runs, but the feeling inside that comfortable house, which also contained his busy consulting room, was anything but peaceful. There was a deep rift be-tween this bearded elderly man and his wife, and between him and his three grown children.

But here, remarkably, the difficulty was not because of the husband's crimes under the Nazis and his later denial or silence about them, but, on the contrary, because of his comparative courage during those times, and his need ever since to question publicly the limits of that courage.

His father had held the chair in biology at the University of Munich, but never got involved with the Nazis—"He lived on a different planet," said Münch. "And my mother was in perpetual opposition—against the Prus-sians because they were Prussians, the French because of Alsace-Lorraine, and the Nazis because they were louts. I was a party member from university days—otherwise one couldn't study—but not a Nazi. That would have been against my whole family background. When I qualified, I chose to practice in the country to be out of the political brouhaha.

"I was and am, however, a German," he added. Although assigned early in the war to take over two older doctors' practices, by late 1942 he felt embarrassed to be safe when others were serving in the forces. One day in Munich, he said, he bumped into a former classmate who was in the Waffen SS. "He told me he could get something for me pretty quickly in his outfit, in one of my specialities, pathology."

Within weeks his friend got him an appointment, and after a brief basic SS training course he was posted to Rajsko, a medical institute which was part of Auschwitz. He was told (quite correctly) that he would be conducting research into the control of epidemics. "I was so ignorant," he said, "I let my wife travel with me as far as Auschwitz station; we had a meal there, and then she went back. I just didn't know I was going to a concentration camp."

He certainly found out in a hurry. Apart from one other SS pathologist, the whole staff in the installation he now headed—seventy-one men and a few women—were Auschwitz prisoners. Many of them had been eminent scientists in Poland and France, and 90 percent of them, he was soon told, were Jews. "I wouldn't have known the difference," he claims, and he certainly got on with them well enough.

"He treated us as human beings," one survivor said on German TV later. "He shook hands with us on arrival, and addressed us as '*Herr Doktor*' or '*Herr Professor*'—it was unheard of."

By June 1943, typhoid and typhus epidemics were ravaging the prisoner population (about one hundred thousand people, mostly working in armament factories nearby) and beginning to endanger the seven thousand SS guards. The task of Münch's hygienic institute, about fifteen kilometers from the main camp (as were many of the thirty-one subcamps), was to find effective mass immunization methods. He does not deny that he experimented on prisoners at Auschwitz's infamous Block 10, the barrack where the abominable Dr. Mengele carried out his sterilizations and obscene experiments on twins and others. "But my injections and vaccinations," said Münch, "were totally harmless. On the contrary, the patients got supplementary rations."

He was aware of the other experiments that were being carried out, and soon found out about the gassings at nearby Birkenau, where his patients would end up when he had finished with them, extra rations or not. "One was always aware of the smell of burning," he said. "Everyone for miles around knew about it. I have always been mystified that I had not known about it before. Perhaps because Auschwitz was so huge, with the main emphasis always on getting the maximum of work out of the prisoners, the details of the actual killings in Birkenau, a comparatively small installation, didn't go far beyond the district." But despite the constant enjoinders for secrecy, it would have been impossible not to know about them, he said.

He had refused to watch gassings, but he had seen victims being pushed into the gas chambers and, on one occasion, passing by, he had heard their death moans. "A sound like no other," he said. "Very soft."

All the SS officers, particularly the doctors, talked endlessly about the Final Solution, he said, "more openly, much more freely than on the outside." He was speaking in a kind of monotonously recitative tone that somehow accentuated the horror, not only of the words but—I had no doubt of it—of his own feelings enunciating them. He had said most of this many times before, but one sensed his need, the pressure on him from within, to say it again, and then no doubt again and again. "Many of the officers, while acknowledging the necessity of removing the Jews from Western European society, deplored the gassings and would have preferred resettlement in remote areas."

I asked if he himself "acknowledged" such a "necessity"?

"I knew you would ask that," he said, sadly. "I would like to say no, but I don't think I can. You see, thinking about that had not been part of my earlier life at all. I have no excuse, I seek no excuses, except I think I can say that even if I had theoretically agreed, as so many others did, I think I somehow would not have associated it to people, to human beings. But I was there, and did take part, I cannot—I don't have the right now to—answer your question with 'no.' "

But Münch also appeared unable to condemn the monstrous Mengele, who, to him, was not a monster. "He was exceptionally knowledgeable about medicine," he said. "From the scientific point of view, he was the only SS doctor there of quality." He paused. "For me, he was very worth talking with," he said with a resigned kind of honesty.

"He was an ideologue, body and soul," he said. "Never any emotion; he showed no hate or fanaticism. And in this way he saw the gassings as the only rational solution, and as the Jews were going to die anyway, he saw no reason not to use them first for medical experiments."

He didn't agree with this monstrous reasoning, he said, yet again added with that extraordinary frankness, "but he fascinated me. He was entirely unique. I found his mind irresistible. I have to admit that I wanted to be with him, sought him out, so I cannot now claim that I didn't like him."

In mid-1944, by which time the brutish new commandants, Bär and Kramer, had taken over, he was finally forced to take a stand. It was decided that since, with the arrival of the Hungarian Jews, all the SS doctors were overworked, the two Rajsko research physicians had been sufficiently coddled, and would now have to take part in the selections. "I took the night train to Berlin that very evening," said Münch, "and I told my department chief that doing that was against all my ethical principles and that I refused.

He said he, too, had children and would have refused, that certainly I didn't have to, and he telephoned Bär then and there and told him so."

A few weeks later Münch's young assistant, Dr. Hans Delmod, fairly recently arrived from an SS elite college, also refused. "But they finally, quite gently and subtly, tricked him into it," Münch said. "First they agreed to excuse him if besides his institute work he took double shifts on the camp roster. Then, when he was exhausted by these triple shifts, they invited his young wife, a beautiful blonde, to come and stay at Rajsko. With some help from her he was talked around, and in the end he agreed to take part in the selections." Delmod committed suicide as soon as the war ended, and one senses a deep sense of guilt in Münch at Delmod's fate.

At the end of the war forty Auschwitz doctors were arrested by the Russians and handed over to the Poles. The trial in Krakow, Poland, ended on December 22, 1947, with twenty-three of the accused sentenced to death, six to life imprisonment and ten to prison for between three and fifteen years. Münch alone was acquitted. Nineteen former prisoners had testified in his favor.

Since then he has not ceased to question himself and to lay himself open to questions from others, even though his wife begged him to stop. "I can't stand it anymore," she said to me. "What is the point of his torturing himself?"

Was she sure that it wasn't an unavoidable need for him, rather than a torture? I asked.

"Well, perhaps," she said. "But then it's self-indulgence, and it is torture for *me*. Do you think it's nice for me to hear about this day after day? And the children—he owes something to us too."

"I know she feels like that," Münch said. "But how can I stop? To stop talking about it is the same as to stop thinking about it. But I have to think about it; I have to understand. How could I stand it?" he said. "I could have left; I could have deserted, gone to Switzerland. True, I would have had to leave my family behind. I couldn't have got us all across. But even so, how could I, as a human being, bear to stay?"

In an eerie echo of Speer, he added, "I cannot understand myself, and somehow I must understand. I must find the answer, before the end."

BY THE AUTUMN of 1944, all but the most benighted of the Nazi leaders had seen the writing on the wall. Even Himmler, first via General Karl Wolff and then through contacts in Sweden, was using the Hungarian Jews as bait to enter into negotiations with the Western Allies. The worst horrors were nearly over.

The three remaining extermination camps of the Aktion Reinhard, directed from Lublin, had finished their terrible work by the autumn of 1943, and were dismantled by October that year. Majdanek, though an appalling place where many thousands died, some eventually by gassing, was mainly a labor camp and survived until the Russians occupied Lublin in July 1944.

When the Russians announced what they found when they overran Majdanek and the other extermination camp sites, one month after the last of those 250,000 Hungarian Jews who had arrived in May and June were gassed at Auschwitz, Himmler virtually stopped exterminations. The last transports arrived in Birkenau in September 1944; the last selection for the gas chambers was at the end of October. On November 26, he ordered the Auschwitz crematoria to be destroyed. By this time the evacuation of the remaining inmates—a terrifying *Völkerwanderung* (mass migration) on foot in the freezing cold of initially about 30,000 men, women and children to concentration camps further west or south—had long been under way, ending in the deaths of many thousands of them. On January 18, 1945, eight days before the Russians arrived, the last 64,000 Auschwitz "walking" inmates were set en route for camps in the German interior. The Russians upon arrival found only some 3,000 invalids.

The final accounting for the tragedy of Auschwitz includes many hundreds of thousands of slave laborers of all religions and from many nations, not primarily Jews, who died in Auschwitz of starvation, overwork, maltreatment and disease. Gerald Reitlinger, in his classic book, *The Final Solution* (1968), estimated that 800,000 Jews were gassed in Birkenau. Recent figures (1993) from the Polish authorities indicate a total death toll in Auschwitz-Birkenau of between 1,100,000 and 1,500,000, about 90 percent of them Jews.

BY THE END of 1944 Speer was working at full stretch in two almost diametrically opposite directions. On the one hand, even though he knew that the end was imminent and that Hitler's program was evil, he continued his efforts to produce arms for his war. He undertook three trips to the West, combining bolstering visits to industrial centers and conferences with the generals at the front, whom he urged to "clean up" (regain or protect from Allied incursion) areas vital to continued production. He wrote to Hitler on November 11, after returning from the Ruhr:

> However problematic the situation now is and however hopeless any improvement may seem, we must absolutely persevere. We will do the utmost to win this battle for the Ruhr, decisive for the fate of our Reich.

On November 15, he flew back to the Ruhr, visiting Krupp in Essen, Dortmund, Bochum, the fuel plants at Scholven and Geisenberg, the power plant at Goldenberg, nitrogen and piping plants near Cologne and Düsseldorf and bomb-damaged areas nearby.

"How can one describe it?" Hupfauer said. "He cajoled, he reassured, he urged them to hold out and advised them how to go about it. I never understood it, but he carried us all along—the generals, the industrialists, the workers. He gave people the feeling that they were winning in defeat. I think he saved our self-respect." He smiled briefly. "I don't think anybody would have described Speer as an endearing or lovable man. He was too . . . lofty for that. But in those months, people, *all* of us, felt something akin to love for him."

Speer's recruitment of Hupfauer as head of his ministry's Central Planning Board (replacing Speer's friend Willy Liebel, who had collapsed under the strain) brought in a colleague he knew well and trusted. This appointment to a key position had an additional advantage: Himmler, determined to introduce a highly placed SS spy into Speer's camp, had been lobbying both with Bormann and with Hitler. Hupfauer, who had remained commandant of the SS elite college Sonthofen (where his family lived until the end), was now a full colonel in the SS. Speer enjoyed describing his political masterstroke in the "Spandau draft," though carefully never mentioning Hupfauer's name:

> It was a great worry to me. I pretended to listen seriously to the impossible suggestions from the SS and then had the sudden brainstorm to offer the job to [Robert Ley's] best man who, over the months of increasing military deterioration, had closed ranks with me, consistently proving himself extremely sensible. After a long and very frank discussion, we agreed to join forces. I rang Bormann and asked him whether he approved my choice and he was so startled he immediately said yes, and undertook to clear it with the party authorities.

Speer, always at odds with the "bourgeois vulgarians" of the party, was delighted to have stolen away one of their most valued men. But more important, he needed all the support he could get from the Gauleiter for his next and most ambitious project. For even as he was encouraging arms production with one hand, he was determined to block Hitler's successive moves to make the German people—who had failed him—pay for their failure.

First Hitler ordered that all rail transport be reserved for the transport of armaments; then the food industry (butchers, bakers, cheesemakers) was to be stripped to provide manpower either for the army or to produce armaments. The population west of the Rhine would just have to manage for food as best they could.

"He told me this one day in November," Speer said to me, "and I told Göring the same evening that I simply couldn't obey that order. Göring, matter-of-fact as he was, said that as long as I drew a salary as Hitler's minister I had to obey his orders. When I said again that I couldn't do this, he said, 'Well, then, you'd better get out, get abroad.'

"I told him that I couldn't do that either, but that I wouldn't do what Hitler ordered. The people of the Ruhr were going through hell as it was. It was our duty to provide for them as far and as long as we could.

" 'Well, then, do what you must,' Göring said. 'Nobody is going to hear about it from me. I'm not an informer.' I was really impressed by that—that was elegant," Speer said. "Despite his dreadful decline, he did have character, and style. I never forgot that."

Poser felt that whatever Speer had failed to do earlier, as of this time he showed unique civic courage. "He was outraged by that Hitler order," he said, "and he didn't only not obey it, but a few weeks later, when the Ruhr was virtually encircled by Allied troops, he sent provision trains 'blind' into the zone, with orders to go as far as they could. That food bridged the crisis when the Allies finally got in, when otherwise there would have been famine in that huge province."

Food for the Ruhr was only one of Speer's problems that autumn. He also prevented a further dreadful extension of the war the party fanatics Goebbels and Ley were demanding.

On June 21, 1946, Robert Jackson, the chief U.S. prosecutor in Nuremberg, questioned Speer about Goebbels's and Ley's attempt to persuade Hitler to authorize gas warfare in spite of the Geneva Convention. German chemists, Speer replied, under conditions of utmost secrecy, had produced two new combat gases, tabun and sarin:

> They were both quite extraordinarily effective. There was no respirator or any other protection against them that we knew of; soldiers would have been unable to protect themselves in any way and it killed in seconds or certainly minutes. We had had three factories manufacturing these gases for some time and, entirely undamaged by the aerial attacks, they worked at full capacity until November 1944.

A few weeks earlier, Hitler had suddenly appointed a special commissioner, responsible only to him, to oversee a hugely accelerated program of gas mask production. In October (Speer wrote in his Nuremberg draft) Robert Ley suggested the use of these gases, at least against the Russians.

Speer told me that Hitler said, at a situation conference, that if he ended up ordering their use, it would "of course" be restricted to stopping the Soviet advance.

He hadn't believed Hitler's assurances, however, he told the court, and after writing one of his memorandums to Hitler, saying that as cyanide and methanol, both basic ingredients of these gases, were in extremely short supply, medical requirements for them would have to be given priority. When Hitler rejected his appeal and ordered him to bend all his efforts toward the production of the poison gases, he simply ignored the order. He stopped the production of both tabun and sarin that November. He told the court,

> What I did was to . . . stop altogether the production of preliminary supplies essential to the making of these gases, and reserve all cyanide and methanol for the use of the wounded and sick.

"Your reasons, I take it," said Jackson, "were the same as the military's, that is to say, you realized it was certain Germany would get the worst of it if [they] started that kind of warfare. That is what was worrying the military, wasn't it?"

"No, not only that," Speer replied. "It was because at that stage of the war, it was perfectly clear that under no circumstances should any international crimes be committed which could be held against the German people after they had lost the war. That was what decided the issue."

I suggested to him in one of our talks that this was a rather limited interpretation of "international crimes." What in his view was the essential difference between the crime of killing civilians by shooting, or gassing, or working them to death, and the crime of gas warfare against soldiers? How was one crime more "international" than the other?

In Nuremberg, he answered stiffly, Jackson's question referred to gas warfare and it was that question he had answered.

A critical point of change, both for Speer and for Hitler, had arrived. Even while Hitler was preparing the Ardennes offensive, his last major battle* which was planned to start on December 1, Below heard him for the first time say, "The war is lost." This beginning of the end was the moment when he began to despise—perhaps even to hate—the Germans who "wouldn't, couldn't, didn't have the strength," he told Speer, and Below, to win.

"Until then, yes, even then," Speer told me, "Germany and Hitler had been synonymous in my mind. But now I saw two entities opposed to each other. A passionate love of one's country could no longer be reconciled with obedience to a leader who seemed to hate his people. It was a point the men of July 20 had reached months or years earlier."

"Speer was outraged by the Hitler orders to destroy everything," Poser said. "He had always been a 'direct action' man, but as of that autumn, not only disobeying but specifically countermanding Hitler's orders, he was quite

---

*After this, the only large military action Hitler initiated was in February 1945 when he ordered Sepp Dietrich to "liberate" Budapest in the so-called "Plattensee Offensive." When it failed in early March 1945, the road was open for the Russians to take Vienna.

literally taking over. Without making any attempt to hide his actions, every order he altered or gave was one more step undertaken to save what could be saved of Germany, for the people, for the future."

I asked what he meant by "taking over."

"The reins, responsibility. . . ." He shrugged. "Call it what you will: leadership. There was nobody else to take it on."

Speer's (and later West German Chancellor Adenauer's) financial advisor, Karl Hettlage, who had so astonished Speer in 1938 with his suggestion that he was "Hitler's unhappy love," was equally perceptive, fifty years later, I thought, in his analysis of Speer.

"I'm sure that in the last year of the war," he said, "Speer felt morally in a void, with no firm ground under his feet. His decision finally to sabotage Hitler's 'scorched earth' orders was, I am sure, an ultimate expression of his despair and disillusion. And from this also came his dream—for that is all it ever was—of killing Hitler. This was for him the point of no return—it simply couldn't be allowed to go on. Others felt this, too, you know, but he was the only one who *acted,* and perhaps the only one who *could* act."

Certainly, Speer was the only man in Hitler's government who organized an active resistance to the "scorched earth" orders. But, besides his closest allies in this endeavor—Poser; Hupfauer; and his secretariat, Kempf, Cliever and Edith Maguira, Todt's former secretary—there were many others who took enormous risks by following his lead. This applied not only to the army officers who did not carry out Hitler's command to "reduce the land to ashes" as they retreated but equally to countless civilians—industrialists, factory laborers, fire fighters, and communications and public utility workers, all of them upon Speer's orders issued with arms—who stood ready to oppose any attempts by the party to destroy their places of work and their land.

Hupfauer, as Speer had hoped, was invaluable in dealing with the Gauleiter. To me Hupfauer had limited the description of his war to the admission of having joined the Waffen SS in order to go on active service. Like so many others, upon his return to Germany he "blocked" from his mind whatever he had seen in Russia, blaming the "messy situation" in the East on administrative stupidity and lack of vision. But, different from Speer's, Hupfauer's own evasions, rather than inspired by a wish to protect Hitler or by moral shame, were largely prompted by a realistic acknowledgement of how the world was turning. He was, until his death in 1993 at an advanced age—I had visited him that summer—a very realistic man.

Nonetheless, toward the end of the war he showed considerable courage and was immensely useful, both in Berlin and even more during the months after January 1945, when the "scorched earth" pressure was at its worst. He spent most of his time traveling, with Speer and Poser when joint persuasion on the spot was indicated, but also frequently on his own. Putting himself at considerable risk, he used his personal reputation and, just as Speer had hoped, his close contacts with the party administrators to help him stem Hitler's avalanche of destruction.

On December 1, 1944, Speer gave his last speech to the heads of the armament commissions and his ministry, pretending an optimism he certainly couldn't have felt. A week later, having himself overseen the transport to the front of almost ten million liters of fuel wrested from plants temporarily repaired between bombings, he addressed the soldiers at the front in similar terms of reassurance.

By the beginning of January, however, the Ardennes offensive lost, he finally accepted that it was over. Speer and Poser spent the last week of the year at the front, where they found that even the stalwart Sepp Dietrich had lost faith in Hitler. Their return to headquarters on New Year's Eve was nightmarish—constantly taking shelter from fighter planes, it took them twenty-two hours to drive the two hundred miles to Ziegenberg, now HQ for Field Marshal Gerd von Rundstedt, Chief of Staff West.

They were given rooms three miles away at Göring's castle, Kransberg. At 2:30 a.m. at Felsennest, the modest Western headquarters Speer had built when Hitler rejected the lavish Castle Ziegenberg, he found the usual intimate circle assembled. "Adjutants, secretaries and doctors," he said, "all with champagne glasses in hand which had obviously been refilled many times, all valiantly trying to appear to celebrate the turn of the year. The atmosphere was somehow made even worse by Hitler's histrionic optimism and everybody's desperate attempt to appear to believe him." ("The contrast between this grotesque performance," he wrote in Spandau, "and what I had seen over the past days at the front was truly eerie.")

Already for weeks Hitler's moods had been totally unpredictable. Below wrote that around Christmas, anticipating the Ardennes defeat,

> Hitler had been in a state of despair. I stayed with him late one night [because] I had never seen him in such a state before, nor ever again either. He talked about killing himself; that the last chance had gone; that the Luftwaffe and Wehrmacht had betrayed him. I know the war is lost, he said. The other side is too strong, we cannot match them. . . .
>
> A little later he made a 180-degree turn—it was frightening. We would never capitulate, he said. We might sink, but we'd take the world with us. I've never forgotten that night, have never mentioned it to anyone until I'm writing this now. This was when I realized for good that he would never compromise and that he would take everyone down with him. . . .

"That New Year's night," Speer told me, "he seemed to react with an almost hysterical exhilaration to that awful gloom around him. As you know, he never drank—but that night he seemed drunk."

In the armament conference which began January 3, Speer made one more try. When Hitler, enthusiastically seconded by Bormann and Goebbels, said that this was the right moment for total conscription, for putting every male capable of holding a gun into the army, Speer said that that would simply mean bringing all remaining industry to a dead stop. If Hitler wanted to continue the war, industry, the railroad, communications and their workers had to be kept as intact as was humanly possible.

He lost. What was needed was *soldiers,* they said, and if Speer couldn't see that, screamed Goebbels ("Hitler nodding, his eyes glistening," was Speer's description to me), then he would bear the blame for a lost war. "After that," Speer said, "I gave up. I just sat there, and Hitler directed his irrational remarks to Saur."

It was Saur, unfailingly compliant, who would attend the increasingly pointless armament conferences from then on while Speer ("I avoided Führer HQ like the plague," he said), appalled by Hitler's ever more radical orders, traveled from one end of the not yet conquered areas to the other, concentrating on preventing the orders for destruction from being carried out.

On January 19, 1945, reminding the Party Chancellery in a letter of his orders of months before, he succeeded once more in deflecting the destruction of industry in favor of immobilization. But Goebbels was making good propaganda use of the drastic Morgenthau Plan,* and after the Yalta Conference on February 4, when the Allies confirmed their determination for unconditional surrender and announced their intention to break up Germany into three zones (later four) of occupation, Hitler countered with the announcement of all or nothing: Germany must win or be obliterated. From now on, he said, when Speer handed him yet another memorandum telling him that the war was lost and that there was no alternative to negotiation, such an utterance would be considered treason and punished accordingly.

Within weeks, Hitler would decide on a gigantic evacuation program. All Germans, East and West, were to be taken out of the endangered areas. During the last weeks, Goebbels in his diary would question time and again the feasibility of that order:

---

*The plan drafted by Henry Morgenthau, the U.S. Secretary of the Treasury, and initialed by Churchill and Roosevelt, was to convert Germany after defeat into an agricultural country with a minimum of industry, so that it could never again threaten the peace of the world.

March 2, 1945 . . . Evacuation now proceeding in a semi-orderly manner. The question is whether we can actually transport great masses of
German refugees to Denmark, as the Führer wishes. . . .

March 3 . . . In the Reich, overall, some 17 million people have now been
evacuated . . . a really horrifying percentage. . . . Some 800,000 people
[moved] . . . largely by sea since the Soviets had already cut the roads. The
Reich has now become fairly constricted. We have therefore decided to
carry out no more evacuations from the west . . . people must look after
themselves. . . .

But Hitler overruled Goebbels's realism and insisted until the end that the
populations, not only of the Eastern provinces but in the West too, had to be
moved out, by whatever means—not in order to save them, but to prevent
the Allies from making use of them as manpower. "The men can walk," he
said. Goebbels wrote in his diary:

March 13 . . . The Führer has now decided that, notwithstanding the
extraordinary difficulties, evacuation is to continue in the west. But [his]
decision, as I can see from a situation report from Speer after a trip to the
west, is based on false premises since the people simply refuse to leave
their towns and villages. Speer studied conditions exhaustively and
reached the conclusion that further evacuation is impracticable.

He is very critical of these measures. His viewpoint is that it is no function of war policy to lead a people to a heroic doom . . . and points out
that the Führer explicitly stated this himself in *Mein Kampf*. . . .

Weeks before that, at the beginning of February, one of Germany's top industrialists and a friend of Speer's for many years, Friedrich Lüschen, head of
the German electric industry, had given him a slip of paper on which he had
copied the paragraph from *Mein Kampf* Goebbels mentioned. Did he know,
he asked Speer, that this passage was being continuously cited now by the
public? It read,

The task of diplomacy is to ensure that a nation does not heroically perish, but that measures are taken to preserve it. Any means that achieves
this purpose is entirely proper and any failure to pursue this end must be
considered a criminal neglect of duty.

When he had read it, Lüschen, without comment, handed him a second
excerpt from *Mein Kampf*:

Authority of the state cannot exist as an end in itself since otherwise
every tyranny on earth would be sacred and unassailable. If, by means
government has at its disposal, it leads a people to destruction, then the
rebellion of every single member of such a nation is not only a right, but
a duty.

That very night Speer decided to kill Hitler. About a week later, during a heavy air raid on Berlin, Speer found himself alone in a ministry shelter with Dieter Stahl, his "Dollar-a-Year" industrialist in charge of munition production. Not long before, he had had occasion to intervene in his favor when Stahl, who had been deeply critical of Hitler for years, was charged by the Potsdam Gestapo with making defeatist statements in public. Speer described the meeting in the "Spandau draft":

> The tension of the raid no doubt contributed to the frankness of our conversation about the catastrophic policies pursued by the Reich Chancellery. I asked him whether he thought he could get hold of some of the poison gas Tabun for me and when, not surprisingly, he looked at me questioningly, I told him that I wanted to try to introduce it into the Reich Chancellery bunker. He seemed neither surprised nor alarmed.
>
> A few days later he told me that he had talked to his people and found out that Tabun only became effective on explosion. Although they told him that, if required, it could be introduced into artillery shells which his own factory produced, we both realized that, as this would have shattered the thin air ducts of the bunker, it meant that this method was unsuitable for my purpose.

Stahl gave an identical description of this event in his written interrogatory at Nuremberg. He ended his statement:

> To my total surprise, I found here for the first time a man in a leading and responsible position who saw the situation realistically, prosaically and clearly, and had not only the courage to initiate such really dangerous conversations, but was determined to act.

Over the next fortnight the two men discussed the possibilities each time they could meet in Berlin. Speer became increasingly convinced that the only way to put an end to it all was to kill not only Hitler but with him Bormann, Goebbels and Ley. His plan was to aim for one of the now frequent late-night get-togethers of the four men, when no one else would be in the room. "In my opinion," he wrote in Spandau, "those three could become even more dangerous without Hitler than with him."

Stahl agreed to get him some of the "normal kind of gas." At the same time Speer suggested to Henschel, the chief engineer of the Reich Chancellery, whom he knew well from his building days, that the bunker's filter system should be renewed, on the pretext that he had heard Hitler complain about bad air. A few days later, when this work was being carried out, he accompanied Henschel on an inspection of the ventilator shaft in the Chancellery garden and discovered that while it had previously been at ground level, it had been altered to have the air intake come in ten feet high, on top of a chimney-like structure.

"That put an end to it," Speer told me, "and you know, I was very relieved. It was an impulse of despair, but I would never really have done it. I couldn't have."

I asked if that was because of his feelings for Hitler, or because of the danger?

He thought for a long moment. "Both, I think." There was a small, uncertain smile I had noticed before when he found himself confronted by a question the answer to which he hadn't really worked out. "I think I was afraid, for myself and also for my family. But I'm not sure that that was the primary reason for my relief. You see, the curious thing, throughout those two weeks when I thought of little else, was that whenever I could get back to Berlin I almost particularly sought Hitler's company. At the time perhaps I thought it was a safety precaution. But later I didn't think that was the answer. I think I *needed* to be near him; his nearness and his death were in some way"—he suddenly laughed briefly, that nervous laugh I often heard when he was embarrassed hearing himself say something high-flown or emotional—"fused together." He shrugged. "It's again that same thing, isn't it? That division in myself, my"—again that laugh—"my schizophrenia about him?"

I suspect that the weeks he was pondering this fantasy was a very low point for Speer. And it was during this period that he went on a particularly strenuous trip taking in Hungary, Czechoslovakia, Danzig and Silesia, in all these places mustering support for his anti–"scorched earth" measures.

At the end of this trip, perhaps at the limit of his strength, he made another trip, which appears neither in the "Spandau draft" nor in *Inside the Third Reich*. This was to Landsberg in Bavaria (the town where Hitler was imprisoned in 1924), where, as an extension of the Dora Jäger Program in the Harz, an engineering miracle had been accomplished with the creation of a series of underground factories for the production of the Me-262 turbojet.

Rudolf Neuhaus, a slight man with an almost aggressively neutral personality, was one of the building engineers in charge of this unprecedentedly sophisticated monster construction. "They called us to Munich in May 1944 to meet with Dorsch, executive head of the OT, Professor Franz Dischinger, the inventor of shell construction, and representatives of the building industry," he told me in Landsberg in 1987. "They told us we were to build three underground factories, the first, in Landsberg, to be ready by November. The five-floor bunkers were to be 27 meters high, 400 meters long and 84 meters wide. Each bunker would require the removal of more than a million cubic meters of earth and used 372,000 cubic meters of concrete, 130,000 tons of cement and 7,500 tons of steel reinforcement. The OT, we were told, would provide ten thousand German and ten thousand foreign workers.

"The word 'Jew' was not mentioned there," he said stiffly, when I queried him. But within weeks, when the expected thousands of Italian workers had not materialized, the SS brought in Jews, first from the Czech and remaining Baltic ghettos, and a little later the first of the 100,000 Hungarian Jews Himmler had promised Hitler—and Speer.

"The skilled workers lived in dormitories," said Neuhaus, still using euphemisms forty years later. (For "skilled workers," read "Germans.") "The Jews were billeted in barracks and tents, first all of them—men, women and children—together; later they moved the women and children to a women's camp. It was grotesque. Most of these Hungarians were intellectuals, professionals—lawyers, doctors, professors or merchants. What could they do? Most of them had never touched a hammer or a shovel in their lives; they had white hands. The women were 'ladies.' " He said the word with contempt.

One day, he said, he found that the SS had surrounded a camp and were going to remove the children. "I protested," he said. "They asked whether I was a friend of Jews. I said not particularly, but that everyone had a right to their children. But they went on loading them on trucks. I insisted on being connected with Dachau, who were officially in charge of them, but they said the decision would have to be made higher up. That was one of the worst things I ever saw. But if you are told the job you are doing will effect a turnaround in the war, what can you do?"

So the children were taken; I asked if he knew what happened to them. "Now I know. Then I didn't," he said.

Until then the SS had guarded the perimeter of the camps, but inside the prisoners had been able to organize themselves. Shortly after taking the children, however, they brought *Kapos* from Dachau (usually German criminals) who moved into the camps.

"I was never inside a camp," Neuhaus said defensively, "but I was told that their provisioning was in line with war conditions, no better and no worse than our POW camps in Russia."

I asked if he knew that hundreds of thousands of POWs, both on the German and Russian side, had died of starvation. "I know it now," he said again. "I didn't know it then."

But he could see the Hungarian Jews' physical condition, couldn't he? In his opinion, then, were these men and women capable of thirteen hours of hard labor, with one break of ten minutes and a diet of a bit of bread and two spoonfuls of watery soup a day?

"Well," he said, rather desperately now, "one day I was called to the station when a train arrived for the [labor] camp, and I saw that almost half of the people were dead. I was horrified. I demanded that the train be held there until I could find out what had happened. Telexes went to and fro, between us and Dachau, and then us and the Ministry [Speer's]. Everybody said it was not their fault or not their business. . . . Finally I went back to the train and asked the Jews whether they wanted to go back wherever they had come from. They said, then they would all be dead. So they were taken off the train and over my protests sent to Camp 4, where thirty people were dying every day of typhoid. I knew that; the SS doctors had told me when I enquired about the many absent workers. Organization had simply broken down. We were short of food, medicines, clean clothing and above all, delousing powder. So when a few weeks later, I got a phone call to say Speer was coming to see us, I hoped he'd get it organized, changed.

"He arrived with a whole string of cars following him; we welcomed him at the gate. He immediately noticed an enormous amount of explosives stacked up under the trees. 'What idiot gave the order for this?' he asked. I said 'Dorsch,' and I thought he would immediately order the construction of fortified store rooms, which I had asked for and been denied for months. But he didn't. He seemed quite extraordinarily uninterested."

(Three months later, on May 5, 1945, Kurt Weiller, a German-born industrialist who had emigrated to the United States in 1936 and was posted to Germany as a corporal in U.S. Army Intelligence, wrote a letter to his cousin Max Hermann in the United States. Weiller had been sent to find a reputedly large number of German ordnance depositories in the area of Landsberg. In his letter he first reports coming upon what he called a *"Vernichtungslager* [extermination camp] for Russian, Hungarian and Czech Jews." Almost all Allied soldiers at that time referred to all camps as "extermination camps," but the camp Weiller found had clearly been one of the labor camps Neuhaus had described, to which people were sent to work rather than to be killed immediately, but where many died. His letter continued,

. . . Then two [former prisoners] told me about a plant where they had worked and indicated the way. You wouldn't believe it, but I almost passed it without noticing it. . . . I know this sounds strange, but let me try to describe it: it comprised an area of about 20 square miles and looked like a dense forest of tall pines. . . . The thing was built by . . . the Organization Todt; Todt was the mastermind who built the West Wall. There are several plants at some distance from each other and most of the buildings are underground with tall trees growing on top of them. . . .

If anybody told me about it without my seeing it myself, I would say "Hell, man, you are crazy. That sounds like one of those Orson Welles Martian fantasies." But it was no fantasy.

What they had needed was underground installations where they could construct their planes in peace, and surely, no bomb could ever penetrate that place. . . . They first dug a hole in the ground deep enough—4 stories [*sic*; it was actually 5] into the ground to be exact; it is a little higher than the dirigible hangar in Akron, Ohio, to give you a rough idea. Its roof thickness is a mere nine and a half yards of concrete, and on top of that is another 16 yards of earth, and in that they planted or replanted those tall pine trees. . . . The length of the hall is 940 yards: yes, 940 yards! The concrete . . . wasn't put up there by trucks or hand or anything like that. Trains pulled into a separate mixing plant about a mile away . . . and from there . . . they "piped" it to the hall. It's the most wonderful piece of large scale engineering you could ever see . . . a project even surpassing the Boulder Dam. With all the ordnance shops—not 200 as my people thought, but 1,500 throughout the plants—the whole thing, including the three main bunkers, contained about 1,600 buildings. Fine concrete roads running through the entire area, but all of it invisible—camouflaged by that incredible pine forest. . . .

Just this very minute, the news came over the radio that the Krauts have surrendered to the 7th Army. Well, well . . . I'll get myself drunk now and start sweating out the Pacific War. . . .

I don't think there is any doubt that Speer knew that February day in Landsberg who the workers were who were building those planes.

"As we drove from one installation to another," Neuhaus said, "I told him that it would be impossible to meet the deadline for the completion of the building work. Parts of the plant had of course been finished for the first due date, end of November, and planes were streaming out from there. But I told him that it would take three or four months before we could hand all of it over to him. He didn't say a word. So then I said that the prisoners they sent us as workers were ill and starving—that we had no means of dressing or feeding them. So he said to an officer in the car, 'Get in touch with Himmler; see what can be done.'

"That sounded to me like the usual 'passing the buck,' so I asked how the people in Berlin thought we could work with these half-dead people, many of them women and almost-children? I said 'people in Berlin,' but of course I meant *him.* He didn't react except to ask about morale: I presumed he meant ours, not the workers, so I said that we worked thirteen days with one day off, and then another thirteen days; no reaction to that either.

"When we approached the next bunker, he said, 'Is it the same kind of hole as the other one?' *Hole?* I just nodded, dumbfounded, and he told the driver to turn around. It had been obvious from the start that he wished he were elsewhere. I didn't understand why he had bothered to come. Also, though, he gave me the impression of a sick man."

· · ·

WHATEVER those two weeks of pondering Hitler's murder had done to him, by the end of February Speer had recovered his equilibrium. His main goal now was not only to provide the areas about to be occupied with foodstocks but, with equal secrecy, to supply their industries and agriculture with the components for the repair of agricultural and railway machinery and with the means for the immediate return to production, as soon as the war was over.

His first step was to put virtually all of the Armaments Ministry's huge reserve of lorries at the disposal of agriculture for the otherwise imperiled work on the land. The second step was to ask Hitler, on the pretext of armament production needs, for new powers to reorganize the collapsing railway system.

Manfred von Poser's record of his trips with Speer between mid-February and the end of April shows a dizzying schedule: eighteen trips in February with thirty-five meetings, thirty-one trips in March with thirty-five meetings and finally nineteen more trips in April with twenty-eight meetings.

"Yes, we did manage to stop at least some of the destruction," Speer told me. "Not everywhere; not all the Gauleiter or for that matter all the generals agreed, but on the whole, where we couldn't stop it entirely, at least they agreed to standstills rather than destruction. But I fear that even if I hadn't had this very specific purpose, I think I would still have kept up this schedule. I simply couldn't sit still, couldn't bear staying in Berlin, didn't want to think, eat, sleep."

Poser's travel notes—neatly typed up later, he told me, by Speer's secretaries—provide only an occasional laconic word which calls to mind the mind-numbing violence and chaos in the midst of which these thousands of kilometers by car—or on rare occasions by plane—were accomplished, usually under the cover of night.

Throughout their January 19–22 trip, for example, to the disintegrating northeastern front at Oppeln and to Silesia, they evidently drove—as Poser notes—on "pure ice." On this particular journey, on which they were never away from the sound of guns or farther than a few kilometers from the rapidly advancing Russians, a collision with a truck on sheet ice on a bending narrow street in an evacuated village twisted the steering column and crushed Speer's chest. He was left pale and gasping for air, sitting on the steps of the deserted village tavern. "You look like a cabinet minister after a lost war," was apparently Poser's dry comment. Then he broke into the tavern and found a telephone which—one of the miracles of the last weeks of Germany's war—was still working. Surprisingly, his call quickly produced an ambulance.

Next to other entries on Poser's three-month travel record appear words, always in brackets—reminders for him, evocative for us a half-century later—such as "fighters!!" (above them), then "fighter escort" (protecting them) and the occasional comment on destruction they came too late to prevent: "dreadful" or, commenting on the orders from a particularly eager Gauleiter, "even *private* houses" and "anything of any value." Finally there were bitter remarks where they had obviously failed: with Himmler's friend General Wolff, "hopeless!"; with three Gauleiter who accused them of disloyalty, "sickening"; with Field Marshal Model, "evasive"—he would commit suicide a month later; about Hitler's order on March 18 for complete evacuation of the Saar, "impossible"; and finally, when on March 26, they learned that two of Speer's industrialist friends who had been cooperating with him for months had been arrested, "Dear God."

In the "Spandau draft" Speer describes in considerably more detail than in *Inside the Third Reich* both Army Chief of Staff Guderian's helpfulness to him personally and the efforts made by other people to assist the population. "Bormann's Secretary of State, for example," he writes, "had a brochure prepared and widely distributed which provided information on edible roots, berries and mushrooms in the forests, and the Wehrmacht distributed all their foodstocks before retreating."

A few weeks earlier, he writes, Guderian had tried in vain to dissuade Hitler from his mad decision to continue the hopeless battle for Warsaw. And when two officers on the Chiefs of Staff, who on their own responsibility had ordered the city to be given up to the Russians, thereby saving the lives of tens of thousands of German soldiers, had been arrested on Hitler's orders and sent to a concentration camp, Guderian had only with difficulty been stopped from killing himself. He also tried, with considerable force but with equal lack of success, to persuade Hitler to let him evacuate an army corps by sea. "But Hitler appeared curiously intimidated by his vehemence," Speer wrote, and added that without Guderian's unstinting cooperation he could not have saved any of the Rhine bridges from destruction. Nevertheless, the general's entirely fearless opposition to Hitler was to cost him, only a few weeks later, his job.

Since Speer's protective actions for the populations—although decided on and prepared in secret—were certainly highly visible when carried out, it was obvious that Hitler was aware of them, and his knowledge of Speer's activities would be confirmed a few weeks later. One might speculate therefore that his surprise move at the end of February, appointing Speer Minister of

Transport, may also have been influenced by what in the final analysis might have been admiration—perhaps even a kind of inverted envy—for the very few men around him in whom he sensed integrity, and the energy and determination he himself no longer had.

Certainly, Hitler's conduct toward Speer during the last two weeks of March, the decisive ones for his "scorched earth" prevention, and then the last week of April, the final days of Hitler's life and the Third Reich, can only be explained by some such complicated and contrary feelings. They are in fact confirmed by Nicolaus von Below, who had been Speer's official "man of confidence" on Hitler's staff since the previous May when, in the euphoria over Speer's return, Hitler had readily agreed to his request to have Below named Speer's personal liaison officer at HQ.

Goebbels, though essentially now again in agreement with Speer, remarks repeatedly in his diary during those days that Hitler now appeared more impressed with Saur and "hardly paid any attention to Speer." Below disagrees:

> Speer asks me to give Hitler his latest report on the March–April state of the economy. . . . He provides in these pages a frank and clear picture and states what in his opinion the consequences must inevitably be.
>
> Although Speer's reports by then contained nothing but bad news, Hitler always took them along to his bunker and read them when he was alone. In this particular paper, Speer said unequivocally that it was our obligation to the last moment to "maintain the people's basis for living, even if in the most primitive form. We have no right in this phase of the war to undertake destructions which can affect the people's survival and it is our duty to leave them with the potential which will secure for them a new life and a new future."
>
> Hitler allowed Speer greater latitude than anyone else. Their long collaboration in better times had brought them so close that Speer was probably the only person who could say things like this to Hitler, without having to fear for his life.

As it turned out, Below was right, and Speer, remembering himself as being somehow more excited than frightened those last weeks, was, as he had told me once before, aware of this strange bond between himself and Hitler which kept him safe.

"I think he was the only one who thought he was safe," Annemarie told me. "*We* thought he was crazy. That night of March 18 [1945], he went over to Führer HQ carrying an extra copy of his memorandum which he was going to hand to Below for Hitler. 'Can't hurt to make sure,' he joked as he left. I was terrified."

After asking Below to warn Hitler in advance about what the long memorandum contained, he told Julius Schaub, Hitler's adjutant, that he would like to have a photograph of Hitler with a dedication for his fortieth birthday the next day, on March 19. He would attend the late-night situation conference on the eighteenth, he said, before flying that night to confer with his staff at Königsberg, hard pressed by the Russians.

The conference that night was about the Saar, where Field Marshal Albert Kesselring had reported that afternoon that the population wanted the battle to stop. Local representatives were begging his officers not to destroy their villages by defending them against the Americans.

Hitler did not hesitate for a moment. He told Keitel to write an order to Kesselring and the Gauleiter which he would sign at once. The entire population was to be forcibly evacuated. One of the generals tried to argue that it was impossible to evacuate hundreds of thousands of people, without trains, without food, without prepared shelter on the way. "That can't be our concern any longer," Hitler said. "Get them out."

It was past midnight, and Speer's birthday had begun. He asked Hitler whether he could see him for a moment. Hitler handed him the red leather case, stamped with the Führer emblem in gold, in which he usually presented his silver-framed photographs, and congratulated him warmly while apologizing for his handwriting. It was hard for him to write these days with his trembling hand, he said. (He had developed this as a result of his injury in the July 20 bomb explosion.)

Speer opened the case to read the inscription which, though almost illegible, was couched in unusually warm terms, thanking him for his work and assuring him of Hitler's enduring friendship.

Speer thanked him and said that he had decided to drive west that night instead of flying to Königsberg, to see whether he could help Kesselring. Only moments later while, still at the Führer Bunker, he was telephoning for his car and driver, Hitler had him recalled. He had decided, he said, the warmth of the previous minutes gone as if it had never existed, that it would be better if Speer took one of his cars, with Erich Kempka, his own chauffeur, to drive him. ("Speer was appalled," Poser told me. "He was sure Hitler was sending his faithful Kempka, an SS Colonel by then, to spy on him.")

As Speer turned to leave after at least managing to get Hitler to agree to the compromise that he could take his own car, with Kempka sharing the driving, Hitler said icily, "This time you will receive a written reply to your memorandum. If the war is lost, the people will also be lost [and] it is not necessary to worry about their needs for elemental survival. On the contrary, it is best for us to destroy even these things. For the nation has proved to be weak, and the future belongs entirely to the strong people of the East. Whatever remains after this battle is in any case only the inadequates [*Minderwer-tigen*], because the good ones will be dead."

Speer received Hitler's written reply the morning of March 20, during a late breakfast with Field Marshal Model, in a village inn in the Westerwald. Since 4 a.m. on the nineteenth, sharing the driving with Kempka as agreed, he and Poser had driven from Berlin to the Saar to see Kesselring and Stöhr, the local Gauleiter, and then back to the Ruhr to negotiate with Model about the preservation of the railroads. While Kesselring refused to disobey Hitler's orders, the political officer on his staff, the Gauleiter and, some hours later, the SS commander of the northern region of the Palatinate had agreed that an evacuation could not be carried out.

"This concerns you," Model said to Speer, looking embarrassed, when an officer came to the inn and handed him a message.

"I don't think I'd ever seen Speer as surprised as when he read that," Poser told me. The order was that "all military, transport, communication and supply facilities, as well as all material assets in the territory of the Reich," were to be demolished. "It was point by point, deliberately and explicitly, the opposite of everything Speer had suggested in his memorandum," Poser went on. "And if their orders had been carried out, then areas of Germany would have been ruined for years after the war. Furthermore, in this edict, Hitler stripped Speer of all authority in these matters, and revoked all his orders for the preservation of industry. It was a huge shock for him.

"We immediately started for Berlin," Poser said. "I remember, at one point, during a rest stop, he [Speer] and I walked across some fields and climbed a hill. It was misty but sunny; we sat down, the earth around us smelling richly, and looked across the hills and that beautiful countryside. It was to be the only time I ever saw Speer give way to deep depression. 'How can he do it?' he said, drawing a semicircle with his arm. 'How can he want to make a desert of all this? It can't be,' he said then. 'I won't let it be.' We got back to Berlin at dawn."

Speer and Hupfauer were sharing the small flat in the half-destroyed Ministry. "I think it was 5 a.m. when he came into my bedroom," Hupfauer told me. "He turned on the light and sat down on a chair next to my bed. At first he said nothing, just stared at the wall, looking bleary eyed and played out. And then he said, 'Hitler is a criminal.'

"That was somehow really shocking. You see, he didn't say, 'The Führer is a criminal'—somehow that would have been, how shall I put it? more personal, less sharp, almost . . . warmer. But this '*Hitler* is a criminal' was said by Speer, about whom one was never unaware that he was Hitler's favorite, someone he almost looked upon as a son. Well, he'd woken me up out of a deep sleep; his appearance, the way he—whom I had never seen with a hair out of place—was slumped in the chair, unshaven, his uniform creased, his shirt grimy. What he said then really alarmed me. When I told him that he mustn't be so brutal with me, he handed me the Hitler order, without saying anything. And then I understood. And I agreed—the man who had issued this order *was* a criminal."

"On the twenty-third," Poser said, "we drove back to the Ruhr. Speer simply ignored Hitler's restriction of his own powers, and of course the industrialists were all with him, and finally so were the generals."

With the Americans advancing on all fronts, both Kesselring and Model now decided against any more destruction, but the Gauleiter, still convinced by Goebbels's propaganda that an all-powerful new secret weapon was about to win Germany the war, was harder to persuade.

"I repeated so often, to so many different people, that there *was* no secret weapon, that it was all over," Speer told me, "I began to feel like a parrot. And with our peculiar German talent for technical improvisation, the Gauleiter had managed to get together a damned good plan for destruction of the Ruhr industry. Thank God, they couldn't put it into practice without explosives, and those were under my control."

With the help of Speer's friend Walter Rohland, it was arranged to throw all dynamite, blasting caps and fuses into the sumps of the mines. And to make the transport of explosives entirely impossible, a squad of reliable drivers was recruited to drive all the Ministry and OT trucks out of the Ruhr.

Before returning to Berlin, Speer did a last service to his hometown, Heidelberg, where he stopped over to see his parents. The Americans were less than twelve miles away when he sent a message to SS General Paul Hausser, who a week earlier had proved helpful to him in the Saar, and asked him to declare Heidelberg a hospital city, to be surrendered without battle. He then spent the rest of the night talking with his parents. It was to be the last time he would see them. His father died almost exactly two years later, in April 1947, his mother in June 1952. When, thirty-three years after that goodbye, he told me about his unrequited love for them as a child, it was the first time in his life, he said, he had talked about it. It was also the first and only time he allowed himself to admit this unhappy childhood to himself.

"But as a man," he told me, "I was allowed to love them. And that dawn in Heidelberg when, after my father had quickly come up to the car once more, taken my hand and silently looked into my eyes, they stood at the front door of our house watching me leave, I think they loved me then."

XIX

"I Stand Unconditionally Behind You"

Nuremberg, June 23, 1946

FLÄCHSNER (from his final plea in Speer's defense): Hitler had especially forbidden that third persons should be informed about the true situation of the war. Nevertheless, after the severest orders for destruction had been issued by Hitler, Speer informed the Gauleiter and the commanders of various army groups that the war was lost and thus helped prevent, in part at least, Hitler's policy of destruction.

Hitler declared to Speer on March 29, 1945, that he would have to take the consequences customary in such cases if he continued to declare that the war was lost. In spite of this, Speer traveled two days later [*sic*], on April 1, 1945, to [Arthur] Seyss-Inquart [Reich Commissar for the Netherlands] in order to explain to him, too, that the war was lost. . . . This conversation with Speer . . . led to Seyss-Inquart requesting a meeting with the Chief of the General Staff of General Eisenhower, General [Walter Bedell] Smith. This led finally to the handing over of undestroyed Holland to the Allies.

WHEN SPEER had left his army friends in the Ruhr and, two days later, his parents in Heidelberg, he told me, he felt virtually certain this was the last time he would see any of them. He knew that his main task on returning to Berlin would be to get his family and then the remainder of his own staff out of the city, to the safety of northern Germany which he knew was designated by the Allies as a British zone of occupation. "Aside from that," he said, "I was going to have to play it by ear, live from day to day—I remember saying that to Manfred von Poser as we drove into Berlin. And I told him to make sure, that very night, that his own family was safe."

Speer arrived in Berlin from the Ruhr at 1 a.m. on March 29,* to find in his *Vorzimmer* (outer office) Annemarie Kempf, Edith Maguira, his assistant Cliever and Görner, waiting up to tell him of momentous developments which had taken place. During his absence Hitler had made three fundamental changes in the command order. Putting SS Gruppenführer Kammler, Himmler's Heydrich-clone and now his most important associate in Berlin, in charge of aircraft production, he had demanded both Speer's and Göring's countersignature to this decree, which demoted them both. (They both signed: "Göring fumed; I was hurt," Speer told me.) At 4 p.m. on March 27 Hitler had issued yet another "scorched earth" order, supplementing that of March 19. It ordered the "total annihilation, by explosives, fire or dismantlement" of all of the railroad system, the waterways, the whole of the communications system, telephone, telegraph and broadcasting and of all masts, antennas and stocks of spare cable and wireless parts. Equally, all switching and cable diagrams—any drawings which could assist in repairs—were to be destroyed. And finally, he had let it be known that he intended to appoint Himmler Inspector General for War Production, with Armaments delegated to Saur.

Annemarie was spending a weekend with my husband and me in London, when we began to talk about Speer's dramatic return to Berlin that night and

*In his book Speer dates his return to Berlin on March 27 and his meeting with Hitler on March 28, but other documents show he was one day off.

his desperate efforts over the next weeks to preserve the necessities for people's continued existence before the inevitable collapse.

By now she and I had been talking, off and on, for almost three years: in
Hamburg, where she worked; in Munich, where my husband and I had lived
for three years when I began the research for this book; in my favorite mountain village, Alpbach in the Tyrol; and now finally in London, which she had
longed to see and where, arriving that afternoon from frozen Hamburg, she
was astonished to see blooming daffodils.

As we began to talk after dinner that night, we were sitting in front of the
fireplace in our large living room, with windows across both ends looking
out on gardens. It was a very quiet and peaceful house. "It's eerie," she said.
"When all these things I'm telling you about were going on, we thought London was destroyed, with its government and virtually its entire population in
flight from our rockets; that's what they told us, no doubt to emphasize"—
she laughed, bitterly—"how wonderful Berlin was by contrast, in ruins but
still functioning."

By the time Speer and Poser got back at 1 a.m. on that night at the end of
March, to find his small personal staff waiting for him, their office telephones
had been very quiet for twenty-four hours. "To all appearances," she said, "it
seemed that Hitler—we thought, pushed by Himmler and Bormann—was
neutralizing Speer. And frankly, when we saw him arrive so tired, so dispir-
ited, there were moments when I thought, 'Well, thank God; he'll be out of
it,' out of the awful end we all knew by now was rapidly approaching.

"But we talked until early morning, and he kept coming back to the same
point. Who would do what he was doing, what had to be done, if he went?
Years later, there were journalists, historians—all these people wise after the
event—who wrote, 'He should have left, he could have quit, it was his duty
to,' or, even worse, 'All he wanted was to retain his power.'*

"Well, I'd like to know what they would have done, any single one of these
desk-moralists. What did they know of what it was really like? Even so, I cannot simply say, 'No, he didn't,' or 'Yes, he did,' " she said. "Yes, it's true he
didn't want to lose his power. But no, it was not his *position* he was protect-
ing, not in the sense they meant: only in the sense of preserving his ability to
be effective."

But Speer himself had told me, I said, that after it was all over, it was extremely difficult to find himself suddenly powerless.

*Geoffrey Barraclough in the *New York Review of Books*, January 7, 1971: "If any proof of Speer's hypocrisy is needed, it has to be that famous double-headed interview with Hitler on March 27 [1945]. In his
book [*Inside the Third Reich*] he represents himself as the only man willing to tell Hitler the truth, to risk
his life to save Germany's future. The truth is that, Hitler having turned away from him to his deputy
Saur, he saw his power wane and therefore the purpose of his life removed. . . ."

"Of course, *then,*" she said and suddenly laughed, a moment of real joy as she remembered the changing tone in his letters. "It took him five whole years at Spandau—until 1952—until he regained an inner sense of self-value, which you might also call the potential for power. I was quite relieved when he started to boss me again." And then the laughter stopped. "That last month, if he sought 'power,' it was not *Macht* in the sense of dominance, but *Vollmacht,* in the sense of authority to do what he felt, what we all felt, had to be done."

Around 6 a.m. they finally managed to get Speer to lie down for a few hours. "He said to wake him up at eight, but I finally woke him with breakfast at nine. Schaub's call came at noon; he was to see Hitler after the situation conference late that night."

Speer had unending phone conferences all that day, while he waited for that meeting. "I remember he talked repeatedly to Guderian, whom Hitler had just sent on so-called sick leave, though he was perfectly healthy," said Annemarie, "and then to a whole series of generals. The people who had been *with* him in stopping the destruction remained with him, naturally, and it was with some of them he talked that day, and that included some of the more sensible Gauleiter. I remember Speer said that Guderian, with funereal laughter, advised him 'not to lose his head.'"

"When I got to the Bunker," Speer told me, "it was the third time that I encountered that frigid atmosphere from those I met on the way. You know, none of the usual 'Good evening, Minister.' Funny how people express embarrassment by their eyes suddenly busily focusing on the ceiling, the walls or the floor."

Hitler was standing as taut as a bowstring when Speer came in, and it shook him. "He went straight on the attack," Speer said, "without any warning. His voice was very low, but his speech very formal, without any of that Austrian inflection. This, I knew, was when he was most dangerous. Bormann had informed him, he said, that I had told the Gauleiter that the war was lost and that they were no longer to carry out his orders. Was I aware, he asked, what had to follow from such treasonable conduct? And then, abruptly changing, he said in a mild, almost gently reprimanding tone of voice—yes, now with the Austrian modulation—that if I were not his architect, I would have to suffer the usual consequences."

Speer, "exhausted and fed up rather than particularly courageous," he told me, replied that Hitler should act as he saw fit, without consideration of his person.

"And then, the accomplished actor as ever, sounding even warmer and giving me the impression that this was the course he had decided upon in advance, he said with a curiously persuasive voice that I was obviously ill.

'You have worked too hard,' he said, and that he had therefore decided that I was to go on leave at once. 'Somebody will deputize for you at your ministry,' he added indifferently, which was not surprising as there was virtually nothing more to do at my ministry, most of which I had evacuated to the country weeks before.

"In those few seconds," Speer said, "I realized—I suppose you could say yet again—that he didn't want to harm me, he wasn't going to hurt me. I said that, no, I was perfectly well and had no intention to go on leave. If he didn't want me anymore as his Minister, then he would have to dismiss me. He said that he didn't want to dismiss me and repeated that I was to start my leave immediately.

"I suddenly felt somehow sorry for him and heard myself say, 'I can't, my Führer,' the first time that night that I had addressed him in this otherwise obligatory manner. He said I had no choice, that there were a number of internal and external political reasons why he couldn't dispense with me.

"So I told him that by the same token I couldn't leave; and as long as I held the office of Minister, I would *be* the Minister."

All this was of course true on both sides. As long as Hitler maintained his fantasies of a continuing war, Speer was necessary to him. "Speer is still the best we have," he would say two days later to Funk. As for Speer, paradoxically, without Hitler's apparent authority he would not be able to continue defying him, as he had been doing for months. But in the final analysis, their reactions that night and the next were not dictated by politics or rational needs, but rather because neither of them could leave—or let go of—the other.

"There was a long pause then," Speer said. "He sat down, and for the first time ever, I think, so did I, uninvited."

And then followed what can only be described as an entreaty by Hitler that Speer demonstrate his faith in him. If he could assure him of his conviction that the war could still be won, he could carry on in his office. Speer said, gently enough, that he couldn't do that. "The war is lost," he said. Then Hitler spoke, for hours it seemed to Speer, of the past, the terrible problems he had faced and mastered by exercising patience, energy and fanatical belief in his cause. "He went through everything—everything I had heard before, but there it was again—the early party struggles, the terrible war winter of 1941–42 and then my own successes: overcoming the transport catastrophe and achieving miraculous increases in armament production. There was something hypnotic in his even, persuasive tone. In words, it was very much the same thing between us as that day so long ago when I played that childish eye game with him, which—do you remember?—I won."

Speer said he just kept looking at him, saying nothing, and suddenly Hitler reduced his demand. If he could just *believe* that the war could still be won, everything would be all right. "This was so sad," Speer said, "he almost got to me then. But then I remembered the words in his latest 'scorched earth' order and I said that I couldn't, and added, childishly I think, that I didn't want to be like the pigs around him who assured him of their faith in victory without believing in it for a minute."

After reminding Speer of Frederick the Great, who was saved from defeat at the very last moment, Hitler said, "If at least you could *hope* that we aren't lost; surely you must be able to hope? I'd be satisfied with that."

There was another long pause when Speer still didn't answer, and then Hitler stood up abruptly. It was 2 a.m. Speer had twenty-four hours to think it over, he said; then he was to let him know whether he hoped that the war could still be won. "Without a handshake I was dismissed," Speer wrote.

I have always felt it was extraordinary that, even retrospectively when writing his book, he should have expected a handshake after this, and I said as much to Speer.

"Perhaps," he said. "I never thought of that; perhaps I shouldn't have expected it, but I did." Here was that strange childlike need he manifested so often, of a physical affirmation of Hitler's unfailing attachment.

Speer had been exhausted by his confrontation with Hitler, Manfred von Poser said to me many years later. "He was ashen when he came back. When we heard what had happened, we knew, of course, that that night had been the crisis point: Hitler had offered him a way out, and he had rejected it. Hitler had, yes, begged him to accept a compromise, and he had refused. And then Hitler had given him an ultimatum. . . ."

In Spandau Speer wrote,

> When I returned to my ministry with the 24-hour ultimatum, I needed above all to be alone. I lay down on the bed in my little backstairs apartment and, feeling very spent, allowed my mind to cast about aimlessly. . . .

"I didn't know what to do," he told me. "It obviously wasn't possible to do nothing and expect him to leave me in charge so that I could undo his terrible orders; at the same time, I couldn't lie, in the sense of allowing him to believe that I had any hope for victory."

Why couldn't he? I asked. Surely it would only have been one more lie to add to many he had told over the past months, in the service of a good cause.

He looked at me for a long moment. "That is true," he said. "I lied about him, and about his orders. But now I found I couldn't lie *to* him. I suppose it was again that curious something, that feeling between me and him, or him and me. *He* couldn't have me executed, even though I had certainly, in his sense, committed treason, and he couldn't even bring himself to dismiss me when that was obviously what—in his sense—he should have done. Well, *I* couldn't lie to him. The war was lost; I had said so time and time again, and this had to stand."

Because it had to stand, he wrote that night yet another letter to Hitler, his last one, twenty-one pages long.

In the letter he wrote what his inner lack of composure had prevented him from saying to him, to his face, that night: above all, that leaving his post at this decisive moment, even if it were by Hitler's command, would to him be an act of desertion. He would happily and proudly continue to commit himself to work for him and Germany as long as Hitler entirely understood his inner attitude, irrespective of the consequences this could have for Speer.

He then told him that if—as Hitler had said that night—he had been successful in the task Hitler had confided to him, it was because he had confronted it not in the capacity of an expert but as an artist, with faith in imaginative solutions and with the inner integrity without which art was unthinkable.

(To reach Hitler at the level which he knew was most precious to him and on which they had come closest to each other, he had related his achievements as minister—with a daring jump—to their common quality as artists.)

As such, he continued, he believed in the future of the German people. "I believe in a just and inexorable Providence and thus I believe in God."

Speer said this to me during the third week of our conversations in 1978, but while, over the subsequent three years he would hardly ever talk again about his life with Hitler (and indeed wrote me once that he didn't want to talk about it anymore), he would bring up these very last weeks time and again; they were his last memories, and he could not bear to let them go.

We were sitting, as usual, in the kitchen of the Allgäu house when he read out this last letter to Hitler. "Heavens," I interrupted, "where I come from, this is called romantic waffling."

He looked startled, and then said, "I suppose you are right. It is rather *Quatsch* [twaddle], isn't it? And rather disconnected at that. Well, it's how I felt: terribly emotional and very disconnected."

When I asked if at that time he really believed in God, he paused again for a long moment of thought. "I don't think so." Suddenly there was a small teasing smile, gone almost as soon as it had come. "Forgive me, I can't really be intellectual about this. I don't know anymore why I said this or the other, though I expect I had a purpose—then. Still, when I finished, I thought it was a pretty poor effort, as obviously you think now."

In the second part of the letter, he told Hitler about his despair years before when he came to realize the extent of corruption, "the lack of inner standards in the leadership," he called it, meaning above all the Gauleiter. Nonetheless, he tried to console Hitler. In this most technical of all wars, fate, he wrote—the terrible weather for the Russian campaign, the blue skies for the Allied invasion in the West—played a decisive part in the unhappy military developments. Even so, until only a few days before he had been certain that that same fate would somehow permit them to save their brave people, who with unprecedented heroism had fought this war on the fronts and at home.

It was on March 18, he wrote, when Hitler had made it unequivocally clear that with the war lost he considered maintaining the basic elements for the people's survival to be pointless, that he had shaken him to the core.

"No, I cannot believe in the justice of our cause if, at this decisive moment, we systematically destroy our people's future," the letter continued. "If we commit such a terrible wrong, then fate will punish us. And thus, I can only continue to serve you with faith and conviction . . . if you, my Führer, will commit yourself, as you have in the past, to the protection and preservation of the people. . . ."

This last letter to Hitler would be the first he would end with the words, "God protect Germany."

Having dictated the illegible handwritten pages to Annemarie on her ordinary typewriter, he called Hitler's senior secretary, Johanna Wolf, and asked, as he had often done in the past, whether she could type it out for him on the special "Führer typewriter" (with outsize letters). Shortly afterwards she rang back. Hitler had forbidden her to accept any letters from him. He wanted his reply orally. And shortly after that an aide rang to say he was to come to see the Führer at once.

"Already in his memorandum of March 15," Poser told me, "Speer had said things that no one else had ever dared say to Hitler, and we were extremely worried how he would take it. [Hitler told Guderian that he had put it away, unread, but Below said in his memoirs that was untrue.] This latest one, however, really left us petrified."

Even while he wrote memorandums to Hitler which "petrified" his closest staff, and traveled frantically east and west to stop destruction in all the areas about to be occupied, he also, even at this ultimate moment, played the most extraordinary political games to try to divide the Allies.

As he reported in the "Spandau draft," just about the time when the German forces in the Ruhr capitulated, he sent a message to Julius Schnurre, one of Ribbentrop's favorite negotiators with the Russians, who had wisely reported he was sick during a recent trip to Stockholm and stayed there. He told Schnurre that there had been a remarkable change over the past weeks in the Americans' bombing tactics; they were now concentrating almost exclusively on factories producing fine instruments and electric components located in the Eastern part of Germany, i.e., those about to be taken by the Russians. And he sent Schnurre (whom in his draft he mistakenly calls "Schnurer") an extract from the past month's damage reports, suggesting that someone at the Soviet Embassy in Stockholm might like to forward it to Stalin to let the Russians know what were now the Western air strategists' preferred bombing targets.

"I cannot understand the ambivalence in myself at that time," Speer said when I questioned him, not about this particular act (which I didn't know about until I read the "Spandau draft" after his death), but about similar ones he committed during those weeks. "Other people, considering these events in retrospect, look for rational explanations for what were so obviously irrational feelings and actions. If I can't explain myself to myself, why should others?"

"We [his personal staff in the outer office] had of course waited for him to come back from seeing Hitler in the middle of the night," Annemarie told me. "And he told us his conversation with him, word for word. He said he had no idea what to tell Hitler in twenty-four hours; he'd try to sleep on it. And then he had gone to lie down. We had of course been there all day and much of the previous night too. But as we didn't think he'd sleep and suspected he might need us, we took alternate shifts in the office, catching cat-naps on the bunks in our air-raid shelter. Around noon he called us to his apartment; he looked just dreadful. I got him to lie down again; Edith made us all some coffee and he read us his letter. I thought it was heartfelt, and I understood why he had to say it all. But I didn't think it would change Hitler's mind. After all the dreadful orders he had issued, how could he rescind them? Afterwards he slept for a while; we went to wash and change. Later, just as he told you, he called Frau Wolf; she called him back. Then Schaub called and at midnight he left for Hitler's bunker.

"I remember that moment as if it were yesterday," she said. " 'Na, also . . .' [Well, then . . .] he said, gave us a brief wave and was gone. I thought it quite possible that he wouldn't come back, that this time he had gone too far. We were quite desperate."

It was very late—but Annemarie obviously wanted to go on. I put on a Schubert tape and went to make tea. "Oh, how nice," she said, straightening up when I came in. "It is so strange, isn't it, to sit here, in London of all places, and talk about those terrible days.

"When I remember our little group sitting there together that dreadful night of March 30," she continued after a moment, "I don't think there was anyone who didn't agree with Speer in what he had been doing and what he had still to be done—it was essential. We all knew what we too were risking. But, yes, I suppose when we thought about it we *were* afraid.

"I often wish now that I could say that I had by then unequivocal feelings of hatred for Hitler. But it wouldn't be true; it was never so clear-cut. It was very ambivalent, very complicated. One's feelings about him had been too deep; life became too confusing, too violent, loud, ugly. One couldn't really think. We—our little group—existed by holding on to each other; we were very close and that helped."

"When I drove those few hundred yards to the Chancellery," Speer had said to me, "it was well before the twenty-four hours were up. But it made no difference. I didn't know what to say then, and I wouldn't have known any better two hours later." In Spandau, where his description was fuller than in *Inside the Third Reich,* he wrote,

> When I got down to the Bunker Hitler stood waiting, now looking weary rather than tense. "Well?" he asked—just that one word—and so I lied, and yet again at that moment did not lie; anyway, the answer came to me instinctively. "My Führer, I stand unconditionally behind you." His eyes brimmed and he held out his hand, which he had not offered when I came in.
>
> I caught hold of myself within seconds and said, "But then it will help if you will immediately reconfirm my authority for the implementation of your March 19 decree."
>
> He complied at once, still visibly moved, and told me to draw up a document for him to sign immediately. I am sorry to have to admit—here again that split within me—that I was deliberately lying. I had no intention whatsoever to carry out any further destruction.

It was 1 a.m. Upstairs in the Chancellery Speer first telephoned his office and told them to get every motorcycle, car, driver and orderly they could find to the Ministry, and to fully staff the telephone and Teletype offices and open up the Ministry printing plant.

"He wouldn't say any more over the phone except that he'd be back within an hour," Annemarie told me. "But I could of course tell from his voice. He'd done it. We couldn't think how."

The document Speer drafted, an addendum to Hitler's "scorched earth" decree, restored to him the sole authority to carry it out and thereby to block anyone else from acting. He merely added three points: "1) Implementation will be undertaken solely by the agencies and organs of the Ministry of Armaments and War Production; 2) The Minister of Armaments and War Production may, with my authorization, issue instructions for implementation."

And—an important concession—"3) Although bridges and other transportation installations must be destroyed to deny the enemy their use for a prolonged period, with industrial installations the same effect can be achieved by crippling [immobilizing] them. . . ."

Speer continued, in Spandau,

> Hitler signed the paper, in pencil, almost without discussion, insisting only that everything important—to be listed by me—had to be destroyed. Of course, I was deceiving him. . . . Indeed, there would never be such a list. . . .
>
> But then again, perhaps it wasn't really deceit, as . . . he signed in full knowledge that his orders for destruction would only be conditionally carried out. And I think he was finally relieved. . . .

After the paper was signed, Speer told me, they talked for a few moments. "He asked whether I wanted tea. I said, no, I would have to go. He had them bring in a glass of wine for me which, believe me, was welcome. And then he said very calmly, that anyway, a 'scorched earth' policy had little point in Germany, and was only really useful in vast spaces such as Russia. This was of course totally illogical but I drank my wine and kept my mouth shut."

SPEER'S SINGLE sentence in reply to Hitler's "Well?" that night presented his critics later with rich pickings. From their point of view, it was true he had written the challenging twenty-one-page letter but, luckily for him, Hitler had not accepted it. By the time the ultimatum was up, they claimed, Speer had changed his mind. He was determined to keep his power, and the only way he could do that was by "unconditional surrender" to Hitler's will.

This is nonsense—at this moment of Hitler's apocalypse, what possible use was any "power" conferred by him except, as for Speer, to use it against him?

"Of course I was dishonest with him," Speer told me, "but only relatively. It was necessary for me to do what had to be done. But at the same time, I think—and Eva Braun would confirm this to me a few weeks later—he wanted me with him just as much as, in the final analysis, I wanted to be with him. And that was not dishonest."

"That night was unbelievable," Annemarie said, her voice suddenly quite different, almost joyful. "He came back from the Bunker almost bursting with new energy. Our print shop had been waiting for him. Within half an hour several hundred copies of Hitler's new signed order were ready."

"We sent them out by car, motorcycles and, within Berlin and surroundings, even on bicycles," Speer told me, still sounding delighted with his own initiative thirty-three years earlier. Bormann's State Secretary Gerhard Klopfer, already for months an ally in the prevention of destruction, learning of these dramatic developments as if by osmosis, had arrived at Speer's ministry in the night and on his own authority had the executive decree officially distributed to the Gauleiter, via the Party Chancellery's powerful communications system.

Speer's next two weeks were even more hectic than the previous ones. Now, often splitting his team—he and Poser going in one direction, Hupfauer accompanied by Speer's junior military liaison aide, Siebert, going in another—he attempted to prevent all "scorched earth" acts, or to stop them where they had already been started, for this process entirely disregarding Hitler's order that each individual decision had to be approved by him.

(Speer's junior aide, Siebert, wrote an account of his wife's getting a lift into Berlin with Speer on one of these trips. At one moment when the Russian artillery sounded particularly loud, she asked him what he would do if they were suddenly faced with Russian troops on the road.

"I'd encircle them," said Speer.

"That's what he was like," said Siebert, "cool as a cucumber, a joker even then.")

Speer's instructions to industry, the army and the party authorities, many of whom had now openly joined his efforts, were precisely opposite to Hitler's of March 19. They were to safeguard all industrial installations, public utilities and food plants. It was now that he dispatched over a dozen food trains "blind" into the already encircled Ruhr, as Manfred von Poser remembered; persuaded the SS general in charge of Wehrmacht clothing and food supplies to distribute all his reserves to the civilian populations; instructed his representative in Upper Silesia (which would shortly be entirely occupied by the Russians) to prevent the destruction of any of the remaining bridges; and in Oldenburg, on the Dutch frontier, met with Seyss-Inquart, the Reich Kommissar for the Netherlands.

Seyss-Inquart, an Austrian lawyer and longtime Nazi sympathizer, was appointed Chancellor of the Ostmark [the Nazi's name for Austria] after the Anschluss in March 1938, then served as Hans Frank's deputy in Poland and went to Holland in May 1940. The Nuremberg court would sentence him to hang.

Under his governorship of Holland, a greater proportion of Dutch Jews were to die in extermination and forced labor camps than in almost any other West European country. As Airey Neave (who as a major in the British War Crimes Executive was detailed to assist the court at Nuremberg) reports in *Nuremberg*, out of 150,000 of Holland's Jews (a number of them German refugees) about 120,000 died in Sobibor, Auschwitz, Belsen and Mauthausen. Twenty-five thousand of them were alive, hidden by friends, at the end of 1942—among them, of course, the young Anne Frank and her family. But by the end of the war, only 8,000 of these still lived.

Seyss-Inquart, writes Neave (who met and had occasion to talk with each of the twenty-one accused at Nuremberg when he served them with the indictment), was proud of his "step by step" achievement against Holland's Jews. He had first removed them from all professional life and then (long before they were deported) confiscated their property, allowing them to keep only wedding rings, four pieces of silver (a knife, a fork, a soup spoon and a teaspoon) and about $45 a month of their own money to live on.

Later, as the particularly active Dutch resistance became increasingly successful, hundreds if not thousands of Dutch hostages were executed. Seyss-Inquart claimed proudly in Nuremberg that he had tried to keep the number down to "humane proportions," the ratio he exacted being six hostages for every dead German, or Dutch collaborator, instead of the more usual ten to one as in other occupied West European countries.

Speer told me that before he heard Seyss-Inquart testify at Nuremberg, he had known little about him except that he was an excellent administrator. "A rather mild man, I always thought," he said. "Seemed rather civilized. To me he talked mostly about art; he loved old Dutch houses, Dutch craftsmanship and the Dutch painters. He had joined my anti-destruction efforts as early as September or October 1944, when I visited him in Holland. He agreed then that even when the enemy advanced into Holland, he would not order any destruction, including of course that most catastrophic one already ordered by Hitler of the breaching of the dikes, which would have flooded and thus ruined Holland's agriculture and most of its economic potential." Speer wrote in Spandau,

> This was one of Hitler's men but I had no hesitation whatever in speaking openly to him: I had had many indications of his standing up to the SS for "his" Hollanders as he referred to them, and people I trusted had assured me of his trustworthiness.

The consequences of nationalist and racialist ferocity are no strangers to us in the 1990s. We have witnessed them in the Near and Far East, in Africa, in India and, most painfully to many of us, in the former Yugoslavia. Whether those who suffer are Jews, or Kurds, blacks or whites, Arabs, Muslims, Orthodox, Protestant or Catholic Christians, we know that there is no end to intolerance, and yet in practice there is an end, though it is rarely either honorable or lasting. It comes, not when the people involved become politically wiser, spiritually purer or emotionally calmer and more enlightened, but simply when they find themselves stopped by stronger forces, or they run out of steam. Then conveniently forgetting their own horrible feelings only just felt, or horrible deeds only just committed, they may become willing, indeed eager, to negotiate, accommodate, mediate. And this act of ready accommodation not only allows them to feel like—but suddenly presents them as—civilized men.

Seyss-Inquart is a very good case in point. For on April 2, 1945, when he met with Speer in Oldenburg, he readily informed him that, using a Dutch "middleman" by the name of Hirschfeld, he had been in contact with the Allies for "some time." (Both Seyss-Inquart and Mynher Hirschfeld were to confirm this in Nuremberg.) Speer got his agreement to transmit via this middleman his offer to the American High Command of a compassionate exchange: German coal against American potatoes for the population of the Ruhr. Equally, however, he wanted the Western Allies to be informed that he was doing all he could to hand over Western Europe's industry unharmed.

He described this in Spandau, though not in *Inside the Third Reich*:

> These offers were in fact communicated to Eisenhower's Chief of Staff within days. Although they had occupied most of the Ruhr by then, it gave proof of my goodwill and that I in no way stood "unconditionally" behind Hitler, but was trying to help as much as I could.

On his trip back he stopped in Hamburg to get the agreement of his friend, Gauleiter Kaufmann, not to destroy the wonderful Hamburg bridges or the dockyards as ordered by Hitler. "It was a strange experience," Siebert, who had accompanied Speer on this trip, told me. "Kaufmann was extraordinarily security-conscious; I'd never seen anything like it. For instance, the external doorknobs on the door to his private office had been removed. No one—not even his secretaries—could go in unless he himself opened the door from the inside."

IN THE "SPANDAU draft," contrary to his statement in Nuremberg and in *Inside the Third Reich,* Speer leaves no doubt of Hitler's awareness of his anti-destruction activities and speaks freely of his failures. In the final analysis, despite all his efforts, many factories, rail installations and bridges—including the lovely old bridge over the Neckar in his hometown of Heidelberg—fell prey to the determination of party fanatics. To his own mind, his last real success, almost entirely due, he says, to the enlightened help of General Gotthardt Heinrici, Commander-in-Chief of Army Group Vistula, then standing east of the Oder where the Russians were massing for their main attack on the city, was largely to stop the destruction of the Berlin bridges. This had been planned by General Helmuth Reymann, whom Hitler had appointed commandant for the battle for Berlin. He had said he would follow Hitler's orders to the letter: Berlin was to be defended by all possible means, and therefore all bridges would be destroyed.

"I decided that he was probably sufficiently deluded for me to use my old trick once more," Speer told me. "So I asked him whether he believed in our victory and, as expected, the poor fool, sounding miserable, said, 'Well, yes.'

"I asked him how in that case he could justify leaving a destroyed Berlin whose people after victory could not survive—could not get food or get to work—without bridges?" Speer said. Reymann then agreed to General Heinrici's compromise of destroying only the outlying bridges, which could conceivably slow down the Russian advance, but leaving all those over rail and road approaches and in the city center intact. (This strategy was to save 866 of Berlin's 950 bridges.)

But anyway, Heinrici told Speer after Reymann had left that he had no intention of allowing a prolonged battle for Berlin. "We must hope they can get in quickly enough to take the Führer and his staff unawares," he said. And Speer—reporting this in the "Spandau draft," but not in the book— replied that the illusionary optimism at Führer HQ might well lead to such a surprise. "If I can do anything to bring it about, I will."

As of then, events progressed with great rapidity. Sometime in April, Poser told me, they obtained an Allied map showing the planned zones of occupation. But the battle positions of the four powers had indicated long before who was likely to be where later. Speer mobilized fleets of trucks, accompanied by armored cars, to transport Germany's gold bullion (along with that "appropriated from" France and Belgium, Speer said) worth billions, and as many of the Berlin Museum art treasures as possible, to the West, all of it to long-prepared shelters deep down in mines. A second fleet, equally protected, took millions in currency to southern Germany in order to maintain the economy there if it should become the last redoubt.

Already on February 8 Speer had sent Wolters on a voyage for the future. Wolters wrote in *Segments of a Life,*

> His plan was to start, together with a small number of the architects of his Baustab, an architectural firm which would introduce prefabricated housing on a large scale. Rather than use our obsolete building industry to produce these prefabs, he planned to turn to experienced airplane manufacturers such as Heinkel and Messerschmitt.
>
> He himself, he said, was unlikely to be available to this future project for the first few months after the war: he was pretty certain the Allies would wish to use his expertise for the country's reconstruction. . . .
>
> He had wanted my friend Schlempp, one of his top Baustab managers,

to accompany me on this trip, but as Schlempp was still busy supervising factory construction for the V-2 rockets, he told me to take Schlempp's deputy, a man called Lübke. . . .

Westphalian Heinrich Lübke, surveyor by profession and socialist by conviction, who fourteen years later would become President of West Germany, was one of those who, vulnerable because of their past, had found refuge in Speer's Baustab early in the war, first setting up the rocket station at Peenemünde and then working on the Jäger project.

Speer's idea for this postwar architectural enterprise was to open three offices in the future British zone, in towns far enough apart to enable his new firm to cover the expected huge demand for this relatively new kind of housing for the whole zone.

"This was manifestly a brilliant idea," Annemarie commented to me. "He was going to take us all along, with three other architects, Apel, Schlempp and Wolters and a surveyor named Berlitz. And as Lübke then appeared on the scene, Speer would have taken him on too. But the extraordinary thing was that it never occurred either to him, Rudi Wolters or any of us, that he might not be in a position to open an architectural firm when it was all over. We really did live in the clouds, didn't we?"

On April 7, back in Berlin, Wolters spent a long evening with Speer, which he described the next day in a long letter to Marion Riesser. They talked for hours about Speer's memorandums, Wolters wrote, and his meetings with Hitler in March.

> When I asked who was having this destructive influence on Hitler, Speer replied that it was Hitler himself. I suggested then that we shouldn't forget that when everything was going swimmingly, we went happily along with Hitler's intransigence; now that things were critical, we were proving to be pretty weak in our support for him. When Speer asked how I had found the mood among the people, I told him that . . . it was pretty bad: people couldn't understand why nobody stopped Hitler or bumped him off. When Speer answered, "Well, why have none of *them* ever tried?" I said that surely nobody was in a better position than he himself. He took a pistol out of his back pocket and wordlessly laid it down on the table.
>
> He then told me all about his measures for opposing the Führer's "scorched earth" order. . . . Finally he told me that if necessary, i.e., if Hitler so ordered, he would stay in Berlin. Running away, he said, was pointless and wrong. But he ordered me to leave Berlin, taking Lübke and Berlitz, and to keep out of anybody's way until it was all over and then to make for our prepared postwar offices where, if it was possible, he would join us. . . .

(Marion told me what had happened at the end of the war to the rest of Speer's people. Wolters had sent Marion Riesser to the safer "north" in March, and she joined him and Lübke in Höxter in May. "Three days after we opened our office there," she told me, "Lübke, who knew the town mayor, got us our first job: to reconstruct the town bridge which—contrary to Speer's orders—had been dynamited the previous week. From then on we were in business." In the autumn, when Wolters went to visit his parents in his native Coesfeld, much of which had been destroyed, he was given the mammoth commission of reconstructing the town, and they moved to Coesfeld.

"Lübke and Apel left us then," Marion said. "It was just as well because the situation had become difficult." She smiled at the memory. "The Höxter office had been all chiefs and no Indians. Can you see those three, all of whom had been heads of huge government departments in Berlin in charge of work involving thousands of people, suddenly sitting in a tiny office all giving orders? It was a shambles. Luckily they parted before wringing each other's necks.")

By April the Ruhr was entirely encircled by American troops who, to Speer's delighted surprise, appeared to wish to leave the huge industrial area of Dortmund, Essen and Duisburg intact, an intention finally acknowledged by Field Marshal Model who, pretending total ignorance of a stream of signals from Hitler promising (an imaginary) new German offensive to relieve him, sent him a radio message saying, "I'm still here. Where are you? Model," and then capitulated to the Americans. (Model committed suicide afterwards.)

The same evening Speer also received a radio message from his friend steel czar Walter Rohland, who was his honorary representative in the Ruhr: "The Ruhr bids you goodbye. We will always be in your debt."

("I cried," Annemarie told me. "He said, 'We'll wait and see.' ")

His name was now repeatedly mentioned on foreign radio stations, and a leading Swiss newspaper carried a report that the only peace negotiators who might be acceptable to the Allies were Brauchitsch, Hitler's onetime Chief of Staff, and Speer.

All ministries had long been evacuated from Berlin, Speer's under Saur's deputyship to the Harz Mountains. But in these last weeks new plans were made in case Hitler decided to go south, and all Garmisch hotels were reserved for the ministries. Speer wrote in Spandau,

I booked for us the Sporthotel, 2,800 meters up on the Zugspitze. I explained to my chief of planning [Hupfauer] that all we had to do there to have peace and quiet was to stop the funicular. Then we could do a little skiing, lie in the sun and rest up for the future.

"It was a very unreal time," Speer said, "but somehow we were frenetically busy, I can't quite remember why."

But life had changed: Hitler had moved entirely into his Bunker, only coming up occasionally to his half-emptied office in the half-ruined Chancellery for special meetings. Eva Braun, who had arrived from Munich at the end of March, moved into the room next to his and declared she was there to stay. Below wrote,

> She adapted herself entirely to life in the Bunker. She was always neat, beautifully dressed, and, invariably warm and helpful to everyone; she never wavered to the end.

"I tried repeatedly to persuade her to get out of Berlin," Speer told me. "I liked her so much; I wanted her to be safe." He offered her on three different occasions a seat in the ever rarer planes out of Berlin. "She persistently refused and finally told me, with a big smile, to stop pestering her. But despite my friendship for her, sadly, one now had to be rather careful of what one said to her."

In early April, Hitler's surgeon Dr. Brandt had evacuated his wife and child to Thuringia, where the arrival of the British was imminent. When Braun quite innocently told Hitler, he thundered to her horror that this was treason, and ordered that Brandt be court-martialed and sentenced to death. Speer wrote in Spandau,

> We were appalled. Johanna Wolf, who had been his senior secretary for twenty years, sobbed, "I don't understand him any longer." Luckily, there was a missing witness and Brandt's execution was put off awaiting his return. Himmler—of all people—assured me privately that this witness would "not be found."

Speer had his own problem with this. A few days before, probably just about when Brandt moved his family away from Berchtesgaden, he had done the same. Now it was a crime.

Hitler, he knew, intended to divide the country into two commands, with Field Marshal Kesselring in charge of the southern half and Admiral Dönitz the north.

"I had a terrible feeling that even if he did finally decide to go south rather than stay in Berlin, he would create a *Götterdämmerung* at the Berghof," Speer told me. "So I had been determined to get the family north, to the potential British zone and Dönitz's sensible command sector, but it wasn't easy. Eva Braun asked me every day where they were."

He finally decided to play on Hitler's well-known family piety and told him that, until his final decisions were known, he wanted his family nearby and therefore had arranged for them to stay on a friend's estate, about an hour from Berlin.

"When he got used to that, I quietly moved them all to the estate of my parents' old friend Robert Frank, on a peninsula on the Baltic, where until it was all over they lived under a pseudonym."

"Speer had discovered that Bormann, Himmler and Ley went off to the country at night after Hitler retired," Hupfauer told me later. "And using this information, he worked out a plan with his pilot friends Galland and Baumbach to kidnap and put them under arrest before they could have anybody else killed, or for that matter kill themselves. But then my friend Klopfer [Bormann's State Secretary] told me to warn Speer to be careful at all times what he said and to whom he said it. He said mysteriously that 'things were known.'"

"About this time General [Wolfgang] Thomale, Chief of Staff of the Armed Forces, took me out for a drive," Speer continued, "and told me to give up all these fantasies. 'What you have to do,' he said, 'is survive,' and he assigned me an escort of four heavily armed young army officers. From that moment on, they moved into my tiny apartment and accompanied me wherever I went, excepting the Bunker."

OF ALL OF SPEER's memories of these last weeks of the Third Reich, three have remained in his mind as if hewn in granite. The first is the final concert given by the Berlin Philharmonic, the second his last meeting with Hitler and the third the day he learned that Hitler was dead.

Earlier that year, he had advised the Philharmonic's conductor Wilhelm Furtwängler, whom he knew to be in bad odor with the party chiefs, not to return to Germany from an impending concert tour in Switzerland. "But how can I do that?" Furtwängler had exclaimed. "How about my orchestra?"

The orchestra would have to return, Speer told him, but he would see them safe to the end. He kept his word. When he learned in early April that Goebbels had ordered all the musicians to be drafted at once into the People's Militia for the defense of Berlin, he dispatched Poser to remove all the musicians' cards from the files of the Berlin draft board. He also told the orchestra's manager to schedule a series of last concerts. "When I would ask them to play Bruckner's Romantic Symphony, I told him, it meant the end was near and the musicians should get ready to leave Berlin."

The Philharmonic Hall was filled to bursting the afternoon of April 12. Nicolaus von Below wrote of the occasion,

> It was unforgettable. I sat with Speer and Admiral Dönitz and listened to Beethoven's Violin Concerto, the finale from the *Götterdämmerung* and Bruckner's symphony. Can there ever have been such a moment, such an experience? Silently the three of us walked afterwards across the totally destroyed Potsdamer Platz back to the Reich Chancellery.

"Electricity was of course strictly rationed by then," Speer told me, "but I had it switched on for this occasion. Absurd, I know, but I thought that Berlin should see that lovely hall, miraculously still intact, just once more fully lit."

"What those who didn't attend didn't see," said Annemarie, "were the baskets offered to spectators on the way out—cyanide capsules. Speer was just horrified. We never found out who organized it, but doubtlessly the party. The baskets were offered by Hitler Youths in uniform—children."

"The subject of suicide was being constantly discussed ever since Hitler had declared his intention to kill himself if the war was lost," Annemarie went on. "We heard that everybody around him said they would follow him. Speer said it was not only madness, but cowardly."

"We knew, of course, from listening to the BBC and the American broadcasts in German which everybody heard by then," Speer told me, "that the Allies were totally unforgiving. There had been the Morgenthau Plan and then the British Eclipse, both proposing to reduce Germany to the status of an agricultural nation with only the most basic industries, in order to reduce forevermore her potential for war. And we knew they were determined to hold trials. And I thought that was right; it was why, before I was talked out of it, I had wanted to detain the terrible trio—Bormann, Himmler and Ley. I thought then—and as you know, I never changed my mind—that such trials might offer a chance to deflect the hate and anger away from the German people onto those who really deserved it. Strangely, it never occurred to me that, except perhaps as a witness, I would be—indeed, of course had to be—part of it."

(Later, I would find that he had expressed some of these thoughts, which never found their way into his book, in the "Spandau draft.")

April 12, 1945, was also the day Hitler learned of Roosevelt's death. "He thought it was a sign from heaven," Speer said. " '*Now* we will win,' he told me, and a couple of days later Goebbels suggested that as it appeared that I was the only one with any credibility in the eyes of the Americans, perhaps I should get on one of our new long-range planes and fly to see Truman. I said I didn't think it was a good idea."

"I really think that for most of us the worst shock was to learn that Goebbels intended for his wife and their six young children to die with him in the
Bunker," Annemarie told me. "It seemed just totally unreal, impossible.
Speer said he just wouldn't have it. So a few days before Goebbels moved
them all into the Bunker, he sent me to see Magda Goebbels, at her country
residence near Berlin. He had been there the day before and failed to persuade her. He thought that speaking to her as a woman I might have a better
chance. He had worked out a way of getting her and the children out of Berlin by water. He had a houseboat prepared for them, quite a substantial craft,
fully crewed and standing ready near the landing stage of their house on the
river, in Schwanenwerder. It could have taken them off right there from their
own dock. The pilot's orders were that, traveling in the night with Frau
Goebbels and the children hidden below deck, he was to take it up to a tributary on the western side of the Elbe. There were enough supplies to keep
them safe there if necessary for several weeks.

"But Frau Goebbels said no," Annemarie continued. "One knew she
would; one knew her closeness to Hitler. Many people thought she had always been in love with him, though Speer didn't. He had got to know her
very well during her passionate love affair with Hanke; he was her confidant
then, as he was and would be to the end for Eva Braun. *That* always surprised
me—I could never imagine what they found to talk about.

"Magda Goebbels was a different matter. She really was an extraordinary
woman, you know, very beautiful, very much a 'lady,' at the same time an
experienced woman of the world. There weren't that many around. Speer
liked her a lot and I did too. I always knew she'd say no to me as she did to
Speer, but the children—it was intolerable, unbearable. One had at least to
try.

"The children came in, to say hello." Annemarie suddenly cried, without
warning, as if these were tears held back for a long time. "I cannot tell you
what nice children they were: five girls and a boy, all their names—ridiculous—starting with H. The oldest Helga, a grave sort of child, I thought;
she was twelve. The boy, Helmuth, ten, seemed very shy to me, almost
withdrawn."

(It is very doubtful that Annemarie consciously evaluated the Goebbels
children this way on that harrowing visit, but this was how they had been
"filed away" in her mind. And now, quite instinctively, when suddenly
brought to talk about them, she saw them in the context of her twenty-five
years of working for children in the Rudolf Steiner Home. Later I would see,
in Goebbels's diaries, how perceptive she had been. For Goebbels, who to all
appearances was a devoted—or certainly sentimental—father, constantly
gabbling about the "adorable lights of my life," never mentioned his son's

existence until one and a half years after he was born. The boy was nine before his father, at least in the diary, indicated any interest. "Helmuth shows at last some signs of becoming a boy," he wrote then, sternly.)

"The youngest," Annemarie continued, "was Heidi, five, a real funny bunny. They were brought up to be very polite, you know: the girls curtsied; Helmuth bowed, rather stiffly. All firmly shook my hand and looked me straight in the eye.

"Except Heidi—she sort of patted my hand as she whirled by, and then made a funny production of curtsying, a sort of deep though a bit wobbly court reverence, holding her skirt out at each end; and then, laughing fit to burst, with everybody laughing with her, *boomps*, before I could think, there she was, on my lap with her arms around me. She was just—an enchanting child." She picked up the handkerchief she had been holding in her hand, and wiped her eyes, angrily. "How in the world was I going to talk to their mother about not killing her children?"

HANKE, WITH whom Magda Goebbels had had that long passionate relationship just before the war, had told Speer in January when he came through Breslau that he would defend the city to the last man, allowing his recently renovated *Gauleitung*, a beautiful building designed by Schinkel,* to burn down before he would allow the Russians to get their hands on it. Speer argued with him, he wrote in his book, until he thought he had convinced him that vandalizing a beautiful city was unlikely to be of service to Germany. But he had been too optimistic. In the end Hanke, behaving more brutally to the population than any other Gauleiter, defended his fiefdom exactly as he had said he would.

Four months after Speer had tried to persuade him not to sacrifice Breslau, while Hanke was still holding on in the burning and now starving city, Speer wrote him on April 14 a particularly warm goodbye letter, presumably communicated by Teletype. At that point he believed Hanke was intending to die with his city, and saw no point in raking up the argument about saving Breslau. Although they both used the familiar "*Du*," they addressed each other by their last names, as was the custom. He wrote,

Dear Hanke,
You have given me a great deal in my life [and] I admire your character, your loyalty and steadfastness as much today as I did when we first met.
You have already done a lot for Germany by your exemplary defense of

---

*In the German edition of *Inside the Third Reich*, Speer credits not Schinkel but Langhans with this building.

Breslau. One day your achievements will receive the recognition reserved
to only very few real heroes in Germany's history. At this time, when a
whole leadership has failed the people, you stand as a shining example and
by your conduct bear witness, loud and clear, against these others.

Germany will not perish! Though desperately struck by fate, it will survive and one day regain its honor.

The *people* were uniquely brave and loyal; it is not the *people* who failed.
And all those who have betrayed this *Volk* will one day suffer the consequences. May God protect Germany.

I, dear Hanke, thank you once more with all my heart for all you have
done for me. It was to you I owed my first decisive successes and owe
equal gratitude now for standing by me later, as my faithful friend.

But I will not pity you: you are going toward a fine and worthy end of
your life.

> Most affectionate greetings,
> from your friend, Albert Speer

The relationship obviously remained warm at least as long as the Third
Reich lasted. But a footnote to his report in *Inside the Third Reich* shows a
radically changed opinion about his old friend, which, as it does not figure
at all in the "Spandau draft," he presumably arrived at only after leaving
Spandau:

> A few months later [after he thought he had convinced Hanke about
> saving the Schinkel building] he waged the battle of Breslau without re-
> gard for human lives or historic buildings, and even had the mayor of
> Breslau, an old friend, publicly hanged [for defeatism].
>
> Then, as I later heard, shortly before the surrender of Breslau, he flew
> out of the besieged city in one of the few existing prototype helicopters.
> [Breslau surrendered a week after Hitler's death, when Dönitz finally
> signed the unconditional surrender.]

"We never quite knew what happened to Hanke," Annemarie told me.
"Some said that he was killed by his own people when they caught him trying
to get away. But perhaps that wasn't true; perhaps he did get away. Quite a
few people did, and information was often spread that they had been killed
and the bodies had never been found in the confusion, and so on. Decades
later they emerged, safe abroad. But with some of them, as you know, one
never knew; perhaps Hanke was one of those. His wife, whom he married
well after the beginning of the war, got married again later, so she must have
thought or known by then that he was dead. . . ."

Her impression, reinforced by Hanke's help, given at considerable risk to
himself when Speer was ill, had always been that, fundamentally, their
friendship had survived. I asked if she had been surprised by Speer's bitter

footnote in his book. She shrugged. "Speer's writing in his book," she said, "was of course not unaffected by his bitterness about the rejections he suffered from some of his former so-called friends after he came out of Spandau. The most vituperative came from people belonging to the former Hitler circle, which included people close to Hanke. That's one thing. As far as Hanke himself is concerned, however, I know it sounds absurd, but I think he was somehow disappointed, disillusioned if you like, when he heard reliably that Hanke, instead of dying the hero's death everyone had expected and accepted, had not only behaved monstrously toward his own people during the siege, but in the end had allegedly left everyone else to die and flown off God knows where."

She shrugged again. "So he put in this footnote. Speer was capable of great restraint. After Spandau, to my amazement, he could sometimes be quite humble—not a word one would normally associate with him! But then he could be very sharp too, particularly if he felt betrayed. He was not an angel, you know."

Speer had by now two hideouts prepared for him by friends. One was on an estate sixty kilometers north of Berlin, "where, if necessary, I could have walked," as he described it to me. Another, a hunting lodge much farther north, belonged to Prince Fürstenberg.

There was also the escape to Greenland he had planned with his friend and pilot, Werner Baumbach. "It was a fantasy, but fun while it lasted," Speer continued. "We had prepared the plane with skis, kayaks, fishing tackle, some delicacies, some good wines and lots of writing paper. I saw myself romantically writing my memoirs in snow and ice and after finishing them—I was thinking in terms of a few months—flying to England to surrender to the British. By that time the dust would have settled, I thought. All nonsense, of course, which we realized even before the plane was bombed to smithereens in an Allied raid."

APRIL 20, HITLER'S fifty-sixth birthday, was the last time the top government people visited him. Göring, Ribbentrop, Himmler, Kaltenbrunner, Speer, Admiral Dönitz, the generals—Keitel, Jodl, Krebs and Burgdorf—and about a hundred other officials came to congratulate him in the Bunker, just before the noon situation report. Most of them begged him to leave on the one road still open from Berlin to the south. He refused, but said that at this point all those not on his immediate staff who wanted to leave could leave, and about eighty of the remaining Reich Chancellery staff left that night and the next morning, as did Himmler, Ley and Kaltenbrunner.

"Ribbentrop stayed, surprisingly," Speer told me. "He said Hitler might still need him."

Göring said immediately that he had urgent business in the south, and departed to an icy goodbye from Hitler. Only Dönitz, who left on Hitler's orders to represent him in the north, received a warm farewell.

In mid-April, against the advice of everyone around him, Hitler had decided that Berlin was after all to be defended street by street, and had ordered the mobilization of all Hitler Youths in the city aged fourteen to sixteen. And in the afternoon on that last birthday, Hitler went out of doors for the last time. In the park of the Chancellery, a few steps from the Bunker entrance, he pinned the Iron Cross on the now dirty Hitler Youth uniforms of some fourteen-year-old boys who had been fighting with the militia. The last photograph taken of Hitler shows him looking old and exhausted, clearly making an enormous effort to exert that old magic of looking people straight in the face. He stroked the cheek of one small boy, and, astonishingly, the photograph shows the faces of these children still lit up as if warmed by his presence.

Later that night, as Below and Hitler's secretaries report in their memoirs, he and Eva Braun received the intimate circle—adjutants, secretaries, Bormann and the doctors—in his small living room in the Bunker for a schnapps. Just before this, Hitler had dispatched his naval adjutant, Admiral Karl-Jesko von Puttkamer, to the Berghof to begin the destruction of his official papers there. (Two days later, his faithful Schaub would be sent to burn the private papers.) He had then told Johanna Wolf and Christa Schröder that they, too, had to leave. When they cried and begged that they be allowed to stay, rather than the younger secretaries, he told them that, no, they were the most valuable to him; he would need them in the south as he intended to start a resistance movement from there.

"The younger ones," he added, "will always manage," and he even managed a weak, macabre little joke on the subject of his attractive and worldly secretary number three, Gerda Daranowski Christian. "Frau Christian will certainly manage," he said, one imagines with a tired wink, "and if one of them in the end doesn't, well, then that's fate."

He retired unusually early that night, and a few minutes later Eva Braun took the whole group up the many steps into the still undamaged drawing room of the Reich Chancellery. The only remaining piece of furniture, a large round table (of Speer's design), had been festively laid. "Everybody came," Traudl Junge told me, "even Bormann and Dr. Morell [Hitler's personal physician, whom he would also send south two days later]. We drank champagne and danced to the accompaniment of a single record somebody had brought. People laughed hysterically. It was horrible; soon I couldn't stand it and went back down, to bed."

Although Speer had been present during the ceremonial part of the day, following which Hitler had shaken hands with all those who were going to leave, he had not said goodbye to Hitler.

"I could never explain this to myself later," he said when I questioned him on that curious omission. "It must be that I knew—though certainly not consciously—that I would see him again. Though it could of course also have been that I simply couldn't bear to say goodbye to him—like that." With "like that" he meant as one of many, rather than privately.

That morning he had given Hupfauer, who three days earlier had been at Sonthofen to say goodbye to his family, his final orders.

"He handed me a letter with precise instructions," Hupfauer told me. "It said—and he repeated all this when we talked—that Hitler had not made the final decision whether to stay in Berlin or go north or south, but that whichever it was, Speer himself would stay with him. If Hitler—and Speer—went north, I was to stay in the south; if Hitler and Speer came south, I was to somehow make my way north. Anyway, I was to take over wherever Speer would not be.

"One thing is certain, though," Hupfauer said. "Speer was sure he would be needed by the Allies. I said, 'For heaven's sake, we are going toward complete annihilation; nobody will want any of us.' But Speer said, 'Yes, they will need me—they will need my knowledge.'" Manfred von Poser agreed. "He was always sure the Americans would call on him for help," he told me.

Speer had known for some time that Dönitz was going to establish his headquarters in Plön on the Bay of Kiel, and two days earlier he had sent his aide Cliever north, to locate space nearby where he could set up his own HQ.

"Cliever's wife was already safe, staying with the Speer family in Kappeln on the Baltic," Annemarie remembered during another evening in London. "That night of April 20, when he came back from the Bunker, he told us that he and Major von Poser were leaving at dawn and that we, Edith Maguira and I, were to leave too."

"I think they suspected what, as I said before, I certainly didn't consciously know at that time—that I would come back to Berlin," Speer said. "My own fault probably, because of my confused statements in my letter to Hupfauer—no doubt he had told Frau Kempf about that. They said, stubbornly, that they were going to stay. I sat Maguira down at her empty desk, dictated a travel order for them addressed to the head of our motor pool, and told them that I expected to find them at the Hotel Atlantik in Hamburg (where he had

had for some time a permanent suite of rooms) when I got there. And after that I went to lie down."

"I woke him up at 4 a.m., as arranged," Poser told me years later. "On our way to Hamburg, we were planning to watch the beginning of the last battle on the Oder."

Years before the war, Speer had bought a tract of land from his friend, Arno Breker, part of the estate Breker owned not far from Berlin, to build a country home for his family. He never got around to building his house, but from a dugout he had had prepared on a hill overlooking the Oder, he and Poser, armed with binoculars, tried to follow the battle across the river.

"There was impenetrable fog," Poser recalled. "We saw absolutely nothing, and as far as I remember, Speer hardly talked."

"It was weirdly silent," Speer told me. "I felt sort of embarrassed, I think, to be 'sightseeing' on this tragically useless battle. We couldn't see anything except the by then rare sight of some Russian planes; they seemed to be dropping bombs on some woods in which, as far as we knew, there wasn't anybody. We stayed there a few hours. And then one of the gamekeepers came and said our people were retreating all along the line and that the Russians would be there soon. So we retreated too, on back roads to Hamburg. Oddly, the back roads around Berlin stayed open for a long time: understandably, perhaps, the Russians preferred Todt's beautiful *Autobahnen.*"

"Before leaving, I remember he stopped the car at Breker's empty house," Poser said. "He got out, and wrote his name on the wall and the date—April 21, 1945."

IN HAMBURG that afternoon, where some navy fanatics still wanted to dynamite the Elbe bridges and destroy the docks, Speer and Kaufmann managed after many hours to dissuade them. "That was when, to our horror, we had actually seen demolition charges exploding all along an important shipping installation," Speer said. "We were too late to do anything about that one. But I knew of Hitler's, Bormann's and Ley's insane plans for continued resistance, even after defeat, and of course Ley's idiotic 'Werewolf' plans [for a resistance movement, largely by Hitler Youth]. This fantasist, like all the others, was allowed to run amok in those last weeks and had actually set up a fully staffed secret radio transmitter, over which orders for continued destruction were to be broadcast. I wanted to speak out against all this nonsense, but of course it was dangerous while it was all still going on. Even my friend General Heinrici strenuously advised against trying to record it in Berlin."

Kaufmann, however, had surrounded himself with a protection squad of university students, armed to the teeth. "They are a match for any SS," he said, and invited Speer to stay in Hamburg. "We'll get you some of my students," he said, "and you'll be as safe in the Atlantik as a baby in its mother's lap."

A week earlier, sitting on a tree stump during a short break on his last anti–"scorched earth" journey with Poser, Speer had written a speech to be broadcast to the German people when Hitler was no longer alive. In Hamburg late that night he recorded it in a studio of the Hamburg Rundfunk. He instructed police and militia to prevent all demolition, by force if necessary. All political prisoners were to be released forthwith, no executions whatever were to be carried out, and POWs were to be freed and afforded all possible help to return home. He ended by appealing to the people to conduct themselves with dignity toward the occupying authorities, and to concentrate on rebuilding their devastated country and rehabilitating Germany's honor before the world.

Even if his speech had been broadcast immediately, it was already too late to affect one atrocity. For on April 20, with the British virtually within shouting distance of Hamburg, the war as good as over and Hitler as good as dead, some of his worst henchmen committed a horrifying crime.

Just about the time when Hitler was stroking a small Hitler Youth's cheek in the Chancellery garden that afternoon of April 20, a column of trucks coming from the Hamburg concentration camp Neuengamme delivered their loads at the door of an empty school building on Bullenhuser Damm in the north of the city: twenty-six men, two women and twenty-two children.

The children, boys and girls of mixed nationalities but all Jews, between four and twelve years old, had been used for medical experiments in Auschwitz. A few months earlier, when Auschwitz was evacuated, they had been transferred to Neuengamme, which was considered suitable for continuing and if possible completing the experiments.

But time had run out. The Neuengamme SS knew that, alive, these children represented the most terrible evidence of their crimes. So on that April afternoon they took them into the large gymnasium of that Hamburg school, which had been equipped with looped ropes placed symmetrically two meters apart, and they hanged them. When they had finished with the children, they hanged two French doctors and two Dutch nurses who had looked after them, and twenty-four Soviet prisoners of war who had shared their ward.*

*Like so many other of the worst crimes the Nazis committed, this incident was never brought up at the principal Nuremberg trial, nor were the relevant British trials in Hamburg publicized by the Allied-controlled German press. It is in fact a crime that remained virtually unknown until 1988, well after Speer's death, when one of Germany's most remarkable documentary filmmakers, Lea Rosh, who has for years focused on the Third Reich, made an extraordinary documentary about it—which was never shown to English-speaking audiences.

A year later, when the British tried some of those involved, a Polish doctor claimed that he had given the children morphine injections to reduce their suffering. But the court found no evidence of even that degree of compassion, and he, as well as a number of others who took part in these murders, was sentenced to death. Insufficient though it was, this was the closest anyone could get at the time to dispensing justice.

Mercifully perhaps, Speer never learned of this ultimate horror. Kaufmann may have known, but didn't tell him. The Hamburg newspapers, which continued to publish almost to the end, may have heard rumors about it but of course didn't print them. Besides, those last two weeks before Speer managed to get it named an open city, Hamburg was living through its own *Götterdämmerung*.

XX

He Is the Dream

Nuremberg, June 21, 1946

SPEER (replying to Mr. Justice Jackson in cross-examination): On April 23 I flew to Berlin in order to take leave of several of my associates and—I should like to say this quite frankly—after all that had happened, also to place myself at Hitler's disposal. Perhaps this will sound strange here, but I was still so beset by conflicts about what I had done and wanted to do against him, and about the things he had done . . . I somehow needed to clarify my feelings and my relationship with him, and that is why I flew to see him. I didn't know whether he knew of my "doings," nor did I know whether he would order me to remain in Berlin. But I felt that it was an obligation not to run away like a coward, but to face up to it once more.

WHEN SPEER DECIDED to return to Berlin, only twenty-four hours after he had joined his team waiting for him in Hamburg, it was, he would tell me, because he felt himself irresistibly drawn back. What he had said at Nuremberg was true enough; he did need to clarify his feelings and his relationship with Hitler, though certainly he couldn't have said that so explicitly in April 1945. But also, he told me, it was that he couldn't bear to be "on the outside," as he put it. "Somehow I had to be in, on the end."

Annemarie Kempf was appalled when Speer told them on April 22 that he was going back. "When he had arrived in Hamburg the previous day," she told me, "apparently so relieved to be with us, I thought that now he was at least out of Bormann's clutches—after all, Hitler had told him that night of March 29 that Bormann had told him all about Speer's 'treasonable conduct.' And now this. He said something about wanting to try to get Brandt out, but I thought it was a pretext. I didn't really know why he wanted to go back, but I was sure it wasn't Wagnerian dramatics. I . . ." She hesitated. "Well, yes, it did occur to me that perhaps he had a death wish. Anyway, I was dreadfully sure he wouldn't get back."

Speer's second adjutant, Siebert, recalled that Speer had asked him and Poser who wanted to go with him. "Frankly, I didn't want to go," he said. "It was madness. I said, 'Minister, my rank is too modest for such a responsible assignment.' One could say that sort of thing to him and be understood."

Poser said to me that he also was told he didn't have to go, because Speer wasn't sure he'd get back. "But I said I was his liaison officer, and it was my job to go with him wherever he went. Later on that day, I can't remember exactly where, he told me that he wanted to say goodbye to Hitler. He said, 'However funny that sounds, just *because* we've had so many conflicts since March, I feel I must see him again, even if it means that in the end I don't get out.' "

In Berlin that same day, Hitler had sent an aide to ask the four women left in the Bunker to join him in his apartment. By that time Elsa Krüger, Bormann's secretary; Constanze Manziarly, Hitler's dietician; Gerda Christian and Traudl Junge had been in the Bunker, fifty feet underground, for ninety-six days. When he called for them, Manziarly was cooking Hitler's lunch, and the others were sitting with her, drinking strong coffee.

"Constanze took the food off the burners," Traudl Junge remembered the moment decades later. "We had a terrible premonition, all of us at the same time." Walking through the small waiting room next to Hitler's quarters, they saw several officers standing pale and silent. "Hitler looked terrible: white, thin, old," she said. He told them all, including Eva Braun, who had finally come in with them, that they were to get ready right away—a plane would take them south in an hour. It was the end, he said, there was no hope left.

"We had expected it," Traudl Junge said, "but now that it came, we were struck dumb."

She and I talked three times, always in her pretty Munich flat, but unlike almost everybody else I spoke with, our meetings, though friendly, were never long. She hated to talk about it all. In the late 1980s, after being beleaguered by historians and the media for years, she finally entrusted her notes about her time with Hitler to two French journalists she took a liking to, who, combining what she had written with additional interviews, wrote *Last Witnesses in the Bunker*. "I hoped that would be the end of it," she sighed when reluctantly—I think mainly because she liked Speer—she agreed to see me once more in 1990. She has pondered deeply about those times and turned out to be very important to my understanding of the relationships between Hitler and his circle.

"When I finished talking to the Frenchmen," she said, "I drew a line under the subject. Forgive me, but even now it is so difficult. One would think, wouldn't one, that after all these years I could have come to terms with it, could have forgotten the feelings, especially of those last days." She shook her head. "It doesn't work. It's inside me: the memory of the Goebbels children; that deep fear I felt of death, which I was sure was coming; that awful guilt—I didn't know for what; that tearing feeling of pity, yes, for Hitler too. Even today, when I know of his terrible crimes, I can still think of him affectionately, for what he was to me."

When Hitler told the women that early afternoon of April 22 that they had to leave, Eva Braun walked over to him, took his hands in hers and said, gently, that he *knew* she would never leave him. Why did he even bother to ask her to? "He looked at her," Traudl Junge said, "and then, ignoring us, kissed her fully on her lips. It was the first and only time we saw him touch her like this."

She and Gerda Christian then said almost simultaneously that they were staying too. "When he then ordered us to go, we both together said, '*Nein.*' "

Then Constanze Manziarly also said she wouldn't leave, and Elsa Krüger did too. "He got hold of my hand with one of his, and Gerda's and Con-stanze's with the other and held them tightly, and then he said, 'If only our generals had been as brave as you.' "

Later that day he sent Generals Keitel and Jodl to join Dönitz in the north, and his personal adjutant Schaub to the Berghof. Schaub had been busy all day burning the contents of Hitler's safe in the Bunker; now he was to do the same with his private papers in Berchtesgaden.

"Schaub actually only left the next evening, the twenty-third," Frau Junge recalled. But Hitler had now authorized everybody else to go. The only ones to stay were Generals Krebs, Burgdorf and Mohnke with their adjutants; Ad-miral Voss, the liaison to the Naval Command; SS Major General Ratten-huber, head of Führer security, and his deputy, Axmann, head of the Hitler Youth; Captain Baur, Hitler's personal pilot; Press Chief Heinz Lorenz; the military adjutants Below and Johannmeier; Hitler's personal aide Günsche; and two surgeons, Stumpfegger and Haase, who looked after wounded sol-diers in a neighboring bunker.

"And Linge stayed," Traudl Junge said, "and so did Hitler's chauffeur, Kempka, three orderlies, the kitchen personnel and telephone operators."

In fact only one telephone operator, Rochus Misch, stayed, and with him the chief engineer and electrician Henschel: the same man with whom Speer, two months before, had discovered the rebuilt ventilation shaft which ended his fantasy of killing Hitler.

Misch was a strange man to find in the Leibstandarte, and so close to Hit-ler for years. He was just twenty-three in 1940 when, having been wounded in the Polish campaign, he benefited from the German army rule which pro-vided that an only son is released from active service. In his case he was the only grandson, for his parents had died when he and his brother were babies, and his grandparents had brought them up; his brother died at the beginning of the war.

He is tall, the required SS height of 1.80 meters (5 feet 9 inches), a simple honest man, with a friendly, attractive and articulate wife. He is a Catholic, always was. "No, I never gave it up, and no one asked me to, just as no one asked me to become a member of the party."

We were talking in 1983 in their small house on the outskirts of Berlin, where they have lived for years and where they brought up their two chil-dren. His wife, born in 1920, came from a family who had been Social Demo-crats for three generations. "I remember the first few months after the Nazi Party came into power," she said. "My parents hardly ever undressed at night; they were always expecting that knock on the door. But after a while Hitler ordered an end to what was called the *Blutkrieg* [blood war], and then they felt safer. But I learned very early to dissimulate, to be one thing at school and another at home."

She said that as a young girl she didn't feel as enthusiastic as all the others did about the Nazis. "Not really—the home influence did count," she said. "But of course, when Rochus was put on Hitler's staff, that *was* interesting." During the war she was a secretary at the Ministry of Economics, and after the war became headmistress of a girls' school and an SPD deputy on the Berlin Council.

In May 1940, Misch received a telephone call and was told to report to the Reich Chancellery, and was assigned to the "Führer-Begleitung," Hitler's personal staff. "There were eighteen of us boys from the Leibstandarte in the Führer's retinue," Misch said, "always near him wherever he went. Four of us were on duty at any one time. We had to just be around, act as his valets, run messages and all that. I found myself, to my utter amazement, in Hitler's presence within days of arriving. That day I was told to go to his bedroom. My God, his bedroom! What was I—just I—doing there? I couldn't believe it. I wasn't anyone special; lots of others had been wounded in Poland too. I never did understand what made them choose me.

"Anyway, that first time I was called in was just four days after I started. He handed me a letter to take to Vienna, for his sister. His aide, Brückner, gave me RM 150 and told me that a room had been reserved for me at the Hotel Imperial. When I got there, I stood in the street in front of it and couldn't make myself go in; you know, I saw that big hall through the revolving doors—I mean, *me*, how could I? Finally I just went back to the station, got on a train to Berlin and spent two days with my grandmother."

During those years he spent in Hitler's close proximity, he told his wife about various things he saw or heard. "Well, not secret things he heard," she said quickly, smiling.

"Quite aside from it not being allowed," Misch said, "that would have been dangerous for her." He too smiled. "But I told her small things, you know, gossipy things which couldn't hurt. And she was very, very discreet."

"He did tell me once," said his wife, "very early on, quite soon after he began there—we were engaged but not yet married—that he had overheard [Reich Press Chief] Dr. Dietrich reporting to Hitler that there was bad news about Count Bernadotte's negotiations, we thought with the British."

"Yes, I remember that," Misch said. "The man acting as his valet that day—I can't remember who it was—came out and told me that Hitler had said, 'My God, what more can I do? I can't get down on my knees, can I?' "

"Yes, that's what you told me," she said to him. "And you said that England was his bugbear."

"That's true," Misch said. "I heard him talk about England so often; he always thought they would come in with us, against the Russians. 'Churchill is no communist,' he said."

That first year he was in the Führer retinue, Misch said, he saw a very different Hitler from what he became after the beginning of the war against the Russians. "He went out, saw musicals, watched movies, he joked, he spent long hours with people. But afterward, less and less, and by the end he only saw people when he had to. He even saw Speer, who was so special to him, much less then. Before, he was always delighted when Speer came."

He himself had not liked Speer, he said. "He was so arrogant. Some of the higher-ups would talk to us, even Göring did. But Speer, never."

Hitler, Misch said, also liked to see Goebbels. "We often said amongst ourselves, 'He should be his confidant, not Bormann.' Bormann was a bull, a workhorse. Although he was very nice to me when my wife had a baby. It was after I had sent her out of Berlin, and he offered that if I wanted, his driver could bring her and the baby to visit me. That was pretty nice."

On that fateful April 22, when Hitler told everybody they could leave if they wanted to, Misch knew he must stay: "Nobody told me to, but it was obvious. By that time I had been in charge of the switchboard for a long time, and they had to be able to make and receive telephone calls. Henschel knew he had to stay too, just like me; he was responsible for electricity and air-conditioning. How could they do without him?

"And it was all right," he said. "The family was safe at the Berghof, so my mind was at rest about them. Until that day we really had thought Hitler would go there too. Of course, I could always talk to my wife when the switchboard was quiet. In those last days I called her often—one of the babies was sick, so I was worried.

"The day before, I had managed to get a suitcase for them onto one of the last two planes that left—a very important plane carrying lots of big wooden cases. We understood they contained the steno records of all the meetings over the last months. Hitler had put his favorite valet, Willie Arndt, in charge. Willie was there when I came up with my suitcase. He said, 'We already have so much stuff.' But I told him they could manage just one more case. Of course, my wife never got it. It was terrible—that plane was lost.

"You see, at my board, I could hear everything: Hitler's rooms were just a few steps away. And when General Krebs came to report to him that the plane was gone, I heard Hitler call out, 'Oh, no, not Arndt; why just that plane?' We too were very sad—not only Arndt but a whole squad of our boys were on it, we assumed to protect those important cases. . . ."*

*In 1982 that plane and those "important cases" were to become famous when the German magazine *Stern* claimed they had contained the "Hitler Diaries," which turned out to be forgeries.

• • •

"NOT TOO LONG after that," Traudl Junge told me, "Goebbels came and told us that his wife and children were about to arrive. The day before, the orderlies had cleared out a box room and had put up three double-tier bunks for the children. Their parents were given what had been Dr. Morell's room. Goebbels asked us girls to help look after the children."

Lunch that day, which the secretaries took with Hitler and Eva Braun, was, she said, quite extraordinary. The conversation calmly turned to the most convenient and least painful way of committing suicide. Hitler had said that the best way was to put the barrel of a revolver in one's mouth and pull the trigger. "The skull is shattered and death is instantaneous," he said. Eva Braun had been horrified; she wanted to be a beautiful corpse, she said. She was going to take poison, and Hitler had agreed that that was painless and quick. "So Gerda Christian and I asked whether he would give us each one of the cyanide pills Himmler had brought. And after lunch he came and handed us each one of them. He said he was sorry he couldn't offer us a better farewell present."

Right after lunch the Goebbels family arrived and Traudl Junge was put in charge of the six children, who were thrilled to see Uncle Adolf and soon filled the Bunker with their noise and laughter.

"We knew that their parents were going to kill them," she told me. "Of course, *they* didn't know. One of them told an orderly who played with them that they were all going to have an injection so they wouldn't get sick. So you see, they had prepared them."

"All that day," Rochus Misch said, "Hitler was around. I mean, everything was just entirely different. He walked aimlessly from one room to another talking about his suicide, or else he sat on a bench in the corridor near my switchboard, cuddling one of the puppies his dog, Blondi, had had a few days earlier. I mean, it was as though he was a different person."

"Eva Braun told him she was sure Speer would come," Traudl Junge told me. "She said he was Hitler's friend, a real friend; he wouldn't stay away."*

IT WAS AN ABSOLUTELY beautiful day in the Allgäu when Speer and I decided to take a long walk in the snow which we had promised ourselves for days. "It's the best time for it," Speer had said at breakfast that morning. "If I'm going to tell you about that trip to Berlin I don't need any documents to remind me, and you can make your notes when we come back.

*The direct quotations from Traudl Junge are from conversations with me, but a few descriptions are taken from *Last Witnesses in the Bunker*, Galante and Silianoff, 1989.

I'll check them for you to make sure you don't misquote me," he joked. After unremitting days indoors, I was punch-drunk with the need for fresh air and exercise, and so was he. "Oh, this does one good," he exclaimed, directing me firmly toward a steep hill. I looked rather doubtfully at the deep snow. "You don't think perhaps . . . ?"

"I'll talk," he said. "You just breathe, deeply."

"The Minister has spoken," I said rather feebly, and he laughed as I hadn't heard him laugh before; he loved that silly joke. "That's right," he said, and laughed some more. "Forward, march!"

Finally he didn't quite get away with it, as I told myself later. Used to daily skiing or hiking tours, he was considerably more fit than I, but the battle with the deep new snow took his breath away, as it did mine. So it was only when we reached the plateau at the end of that forest path, and sat down on a bench the Allgäu tourist authority had thoughtfully provided, that we could talk. Using his country hat he cleared the snow from the bench and then told me about that last trip to Berlin.

He had been not only unsure but puzzled for many years about what made him go to Berlin that day. "Of course it was irrational to go," he said. "It just came about by my inventing for myself a number of justifications. Perhaps Berlin was somewhere in my mind as a possibility, but basically I was just restless, I couldn't sit still. Because there was nothing more for me to do, I felt myself on the edge of a depression. Of course, that would have been normal; I was going against nature by forcing my body to reject fatigue, but I couldn't do otherwise; I had to be active.

"I heard in Hamburg that Hettlage was in Sigrön, an estate halfway between Hamburg and Berlin I had rebuilt for friends years before; my family and I had often been guests there. That telephone line was out, and I told myself Hettlage needed to know that Sigrön was scheduled to be in the Russian zone—silly of course, because he would have worked that out for himself long before.

"But off we went to Sigrön and there, quite by chance, was one of Brandt's top men. He knew exactly where Brandt was being held, so I thought that, in the confusion in Berlin, it wouldn't be all that difficult just to go there and use my authority to get him out. And then too, my old friend Lüschen, head of Siemens, was still in Berlin; perhaps I could persuade him to leave with me.

"We left Sigrön early the next morning but were stopped dead about forty kilometers from Berlin by the thousands of vehicles of all kinds escaping from the city, which were taking up the full width of the road. Luckily we managed to get to an exit and, luckily again, the nearest town housed a divisional staff which had telephone communication with Berlin.

I rang the number I had been given for Brandt's place of detention, intend-ing to bully the officer in charge to let him go. But they told me Himmler had had him transferred north some days before; he was obviously protect-ing him, no doubt for his own purposes. Then I tried to reach Lüschen, but couldn't."

Speer said that this would have been the moment to turn around and go back to Hamburg. "Even now I don't have a rational explanation as to why I didn't," he said. "I was not tired of life—at least I *think* I wanted to survive, though at the time one didn't consciously ponder such things. Perhaps it was a need to see Hitler once more. Who knows? I certainly don't.

"Anyway, we made our way cross-country to Rechlin airport; I knew the commander there. And they prepared two *Storche* [single-engine reconnais-sance planes] and a two-seater training plane to fly us to Gatow, a few flying minutes from the center of Berlin. My Rechlin commander friend had given me an escort of twelve fighters who were going that way anyway to attack ground targets south of Potsdam. But anyway, it wasn't that dangerous—there was virtually no daylight Russian air presence, and even by land it was still possible to get out if one knew the back roads; the proof is that both Rib-bentrop and Schaub still got out that night by car."

Speer's descriptions in *Inside the Third Reich* of events at Rechlin and Gatow are different in some details from what he wrote at Spandau, and from what both he and Manfred von Poser told me, but in this instance I think it was simply his memory playing understandable tricks about basically irrelevant details.

In spite of his evident wish to see Hitler again, or "to be in at the end," he remained perfectly aware of Bormann's continuing intrigues and thus the possible risks to himself. But in Gatow, he said, he had briefly spoken to Luft-waffe General Christian, by then General Jodl's air adjutant. "He had just ar-rived from Hitler's bunker," Speer said, "and he would have known and warned me if it was dangerous for me to go there." As there was no such indication of danger, he had rung through to the Chancellery and told Schaub he was coming.

This was a story Speer had often told: twice in the Spandau version (nine months apart), once in *Inside the Third Reich,* each practically the same as—nine years after the book appeared—when he told it to me, sitting up on that sunny plateau in the Allgäu.

His central point in all these versions (except for one decisive exception which will appear later) remained constant. That trip to Berlin, though ap-pearing crucial to him at the time, was an "irrational act," brought about by feelings he understood neither in 1945 nor very much better later. In Spandau he wrote,

It would be wrong if I were to claim that I fully understood Hitler's iniquity at that time. I only learned to loathe and despise him from the bottom of my heart when I was confronted with the unimpeachable
documentation during the Nuremberg trial. It is of course true that there
was every reason for me to have come to this realization sooner.

But the fact of the matter is, I didn't. The truth is that for a reason I still
cannot explain to myself, perhaps like the thief who feels impelled to return to the scene of his crime, something deep inside myself drew me toward the Chancellery.

In Hamburg, on a bright, late-winter Sunday morning in 1986, only two
weeks after her days with us in London, Annemarie Kempf was describing
Speer's last trip to Berlin and her own feelings at that time. She had a room in
the Rudolf Steiner Home where she worked, and a summer cottage in Eutin,
the place where, by the side of the lake, she, Edith Maguira and the others
had lived for a few weeks in those trailers Cliever had found in April 1945.

Hamburg, one of the loveliest of Germany's large cities, makes good use of
the huge lake formed by damming the Alster, the Elbe tributary that tra-
versed the city in the Middle Ages. In warm weather it is dotted with sailboats, in the winter with ice hockey players and skating children. It was the
warmth of the sun and the sight of the whirling skaters that tempted us out-
doors onto the safe ice of the river, ending up, after an hour's part-walk,
part-slide, on the glassed-in terrace of a riverside restaurant for lunch.

"One was very torn about Hitler in those last months," Annemarie said.
"On the one hand, there was what we knew because of where we worked;
don't forget we had worked on the Führer conferences every day, so we always knew what was discussed. Not about any horrors—those would never
have been mentioned on the record, or in the presence of outsiders. But as
time went on what we learned was bad enough . . . how, always on his orders,
people died and our country was reduced to rubble. But then you see, overriding all this was what one had felt for so many years, a great all-encompass-
ing enthusiasm, loyalty; in some way, I suppose, a kind of love. For so many
of us, in that unique way, he had been the light of our lives; all that was very
strong, very important, and it did not easily die. . . ."

That day, April 21, when Speer and Manfred von Poser had arrived in
Hamburg, Annemarie said, Speer had seemed to her the most depressed she
had ever seen him. "He was never a suicidal character," she said. "But that
night and the next morning I did sense in him a deep fatigue. It was much
more than physical; it was an apathy, an indifference about what might happen to him, much more than the devil-may-care attitude which really was so
much part of his personality. I know now, but already sensed then, that it was
the real beginning of his sense of responsibility for the whole catastrophe—

Above: Hitler's birthday celebration at the Berghof in 1943, surrounded by the children of his intimates. The tall boy on his right is his godson, Martin Bormann; the girl holding his left hand is Hilde Speer. *Below:* Speer, accompanied by August Eigruber, Gauleiter of the Upper Danube District, talks with inmates of the Mauthausen concentration camp near Linz—his only recorded visit to a concentration camp.

Above: Speer, Admiral Karl
Dönitz and General Alfred Jodl
face Allied correspondents in
Flensburg, after their arrest on
May 24, 1945—the end of the
"Dönitz cabinet" formed after
Hitler's death. *Right:* Speer,
awaiting trial at Nuremberg,
writing in his cell.

The major war criminals in the courtroom of the Palace of Justice at Nuremberg, during the first session on November 20, 1945. Speer sits, arms folded, third from right in the second row.

Speer walking in the garden he created
during his imprisonment in Spandau

Margret and Albert Speer smile briefly for the press and TV cameras at midnight, September 30, 1966, when he was released.

At the family gathering the next day, Hilde and her husband Ulf with Speer

Margret and Albert Speer
outside their Heidelberg home
in 1978.

A.SPEER
Schloßwolfsbrunnenweg
50

The Speers' Heidelberg house
is prominently identified on
the gatepost, and the gates are
always open, not "barricaded . . .
guarded by dogs."

Top: Speer's desk is overlooked by a somber portrait of his mother. *Below:* The studio that Speer added to the farmhouse in the Bavarian Alps, which he purchased after the success of his books

Albert Speer, in 1978, with some of the twenty-five thousand letters he wrote in Spandau during his twenty-year imprisonment. They were written on any paper he could get—some on tobacco wrappers and toilet paper—and smuggled out.

Left: Robert Raphael Geis, the rabbi who became singularly important to Speer late in his life

Below: Georges Casalis, the French Calvinist chaplain in Spandau, who was the most important person in Speer's attempt "to become a different man"

Speer sits at a window in his Heidelberg
house, while talking to the author.

guilt, we now know, for suspected but, I'm still sure of it today, not fully known crimes."

Annemarie was both right and wrong; Speer had indeed become aware both of responsibility and guilt, but on separate levels—one that he (like the generals and many other Germans) could quite honorably acknowledge, but then another which for a number of reasons, among them the preservation of his own sanity, he suppressed and resisted. Up to a point, he readily admitted this that day on the Allgäu mountaintop.

"As we approached Berlin," he said then, "I had of course become aware of my responsibility: not for *crimes*—I'm not sure I thought that deeply or clearly then—but for these last years of the war which, let's face it, I had largely helped make possible. I didn't see myself as a 'war criminal'—a term by then quite familiar to us from British and American broadcasts—but I did think that I was at least co-responsible for the war going on so long, with none of us knowing how to stop it, how to stop Hitler."

The co-responsibility for the lost war was all he could face. Neither Hitler's crimes nor his own responsibility for the treatment of the slave laborers had yet been allowed to enter his mind.

"I did think I might be called to account for my part in prolonging the war," he continued, "though of course not to the degree I finally was. As we approached Berlin, I worried very much about my family, and I didn't really care one way or another how this last flight into Berlin would end. If it ended well and I got out, good. If it didn't, if it meant a confrontation with Hitler and a nasty end, well, that was all right too. Perhaps the Allies would count that on the credit side for my family.

"It was odd, though, because although I had announced my imminent arrival by phone, Hitler's adjutants, whom I found drinking upstairs in his Chancellery apartment, appeared quite startled to see me."

"We were amazed to see Speer," Traudl Junge told me subsequently. "There didn't seem to be any reason for his coming back, but we thought it was wonderful of him. And Eva Braun, with whom I had by that time become rather friendly, was really over the moon that he came, just as she had predicted. Everybody knew how much she liked him; he'd really been her only friend among the higher-ups for years. But more than that, she was so happy for Hitler."

"I must admit that I was apprehensive as to how I would be received," Speer continued, "until only moments later, Schaub having announced me to Hitler, I found Bormann waiting for me at the foot of the fifty steps at the deepest level of the Bunker we had built for Hitler. Bormann was unusually polite, the reason emerging very quickly when he suggested that, if the Führer asked for my opinion on what he should do, I would—wouldn't

I?—advise him to fly south. In fact, I had no intention whatever of doing that, but I didn't bother to disabuse him.

"Well, I had a comparatively long time with Hitler then. He looked very old, very tired, but you know, he was actually very calm, resigned it seemed to me, ready for the end. First he asked me some very searching questions about Dönitz. That indicated to me that he was going to name him his successor, which was fine with me: I considered Dönitz an honest man and a patriot. And what I wanted to avoid above all was that he would name me.

"After that, it wasn't a personal conversation we had—and yet in a way it was. Not personal in that he showed any interest in *me*, but personal in that he talked a little as he did that terrible night one long month before, on March 29—about the past, the hopes he had had, the disappointments he had suffered. And yet it was different from that other night. Because now, everything he said was imbued with that feeling of the end, his planned suicide. And he assured me that he felt no fear of it but was glad to die.

"Yes, he did also ask whether I thought he should stay in Berlin, or fly south, as Bormann and all the others were urging him to do. I told him that I felt that if Berlin went, everything was lost anyway and that to me it seemed better that he should end it all in Berlin, rather than at his weekend house in Bavaria. He said that had been his feeling too, but that he had wanted to hear what I thought. And then he went into all the details: that Eva Braun had decided to die with him, that he would shoot his dog Blondi before he died."

("Dr. Stumpfegger poisoned Blondi," Rochus Misch told me. "She died right away. And later they killed her puppies too.")

"And he was very precise about the orders he had issued about burning his body," Speer continued. "In retrospect it all sounds very dramatic, but you know, it wasn't. He sounded—how can I explain?—empty, depleted. And suddenly he stopped, as if there just wasn't anything else to say. And then to my surprise, I heard myself tell him that I had countermanded his orders over the past weeks wherever possible. He didn't say anything, there was no reaction. It was mad what I did, and yet I'm glad I went to see him, and I'm glad I did it. It was right. I still think now that it was right."

This "confession," which he first mentioned in *Inside the Third Reich* in 1970, then shortly afterwards in an interview with *Playboy*, and finally to me in 1977–78, is the "decisive exception" I mentioned earlier. In the book he associated it with an offer he says he made to stay with Hitler in Berlin. "For a moment," he wrote there, "his eyes filled with tears."

The same words appeared in *Playboy*, though here he assigned his offer to stay, or return once more to Berlin, to a later moment that night, when he made his final goodbyes to Hitler. This impulsive and touching last-minute confession to Hitler was mentioned by many reviewers and most historians writing since: it appeared to confirm the indifference to life and death he claimed to have felt, and to emphasize the ambivalence of his feelings toward Hitler.

Psychologically, it is possible that this is the way he remembered the occasion, because it was how he would have liked to behave, and the way he would have liked Hitler to react. But the fact is that none of it happened; our witness to this is Speer himself.

On September 3, 1952, the French weekly *Carrefour* published an extract of several pages from a forthcoming book, *L'Agonie de l'Allemagne,* by Georges Blond. The writer, drawing rather freely on previous publications, particularly Hugh Trevor-Roper's remarkable *The Last Days of Hitler,** used theatrical language and wholly invented dialogue to present thumbnail sketches of six of those closest to Hitler during those last days, including Speer.

In his essay entitled "L'Extravagant M. Speer," he compared the contemptuous treatment Hitler had meted out to the "loyal-to-the-grave" Göring with the indulgence he showed to Speer, who for months had systematically betrayed him. First giving a dramatic description of Speer's "perilous journey" to Berlin to join his Führer, flying through "a host of Russian fighter planes, with a 7-in-10 chance of being shot down," and "a 50 percent chance of death when attempting a landing near the Chancellery in Berlin," he soon gets to the meat of his embellished story:

> . . . Speer hastened to the Chancellery, went down to the bunker, and was immediately received by Hitler. "My Führer," he said, "I must speak to you." And then Speer confessed. He revealed to Hitler every aspect of his activities against him over the past weeks, without deleting anything. Hitler listened. Speer noticed that he was "profoundly moved by his frankness," but when he finished, nothing happened: no fury, no arrest, no relieving him of his functions. Hitler simply said that everything was now forgiven, forgotten, not to be spoken of again.

The Nuremberg prosecutors, wrote Blond, argued endlessly about Hitler's astonishing lenity. The psychiatrist Professor von Hasselbach, Blond said, had devoted several pages of his medical-psychiatric study of Hitler to it. "Hitler," the professor wrote (quite correctly), "could ferociously hate while at the same time be totally forgiving toward those he loved. . . ."

This copy of *Carrefour,* it appears, soon reached Speer via one of his

---

*In September 1945 Hugh Trevor-Roper was given the task of gathering for British Intelligence in Berlin all available evidence as to the precise fate of Hitler, to lay at rest persistent rumors that he had survived. The Russians, who knew he hadn't, did nothing to quiet the rumors and even started new ones. The results of Trevor-Roper's meticulous research, which had the full cooperation of both the British and the Americans, were published in March 1947 as *The Last Days of Hitler.* Eight more editions followed, as new information became available from various sources. It remains the classic source on the subject.

French guards. It is possible that the way his 1945 statement to Trevor-Roper had been misused contributed to his decision, a few weeks later on January 8, 1953, to begin his "Spandau draft" by writing about this trip to see Hitler, his feelings for Hitler and what really happened between them during those last meetings. Whatever he may have said later, what he said then in the "Spandau draft" has the unmistakable ring of truth.

Already by January 1945, he wrote (somewhat optimistically), he had definitely broken with Hitler, who, as had become abundantly clear, was acting against the interests of the people by continuing the war. He asked Wolters,

> What would you do if you discovered that your patron is guilty of high treason, say by serving the enemy as a spy, and thereby causing the death of thousands? You would try, wouldn't you, to persuade him of the error of his ways? I tried that, with my memorandums. But what if your efforts fail? Well, what remains then is the unavoidable obligation to denounce him and have him brought to justice, irrespective of his benevolence to you personally. Well, in my own way, that is precisely what I did in those last months wherever I could, though admittedly never without an inner feeling of regret. . . .
>
> Anyway, to put it briefly, to this day I cannot account for going on that last trip to Berlin, and I must therefore disabuse the French psychologist who wrote about "L'Extravagant Monsieur Speer" in *Carrefour*. It is essential for me to "de-heroize" this last trip of mine to Berlin. Neither Hitler nor I spoke one word of our personal relationship.
>
> *There can be no question of a touching scene or, even more than that, of a confession such as the Frenchman reported* [author's italics]. Even if either of us had wanted it, I doubt it could have happened: we were far more apart by then than anyone seeing it from outside could imagine.

And indeed why should there have been a "confession"? Hitler had already confronted him on March 29 with Bormann's information that Speer had been countermanding his orders. Speer continued to Wolters, that day in Spandau,

> Also . . . while he spoke of his suicide and all that, I had the feeling I was speaking with someone who was already dead. And the truth is that nothing he said provoked any feelings in me, positive or negative. . . . It was nothing. And that was the tragic end of it all. . . .

While certainly very nearly the end for Hitler and therefore, inevitably, an end to their relationship, it was of course anything but the "end of it all" for Speer who, on the contrary, would spend the remainder of his life searching for an answer to its mystery.

I showed the discrepancy between *Inside the Third Reich* and the "Spandau draft" to Speer's daughter Hilde and to Annemarie. Neither of the two people perhaps closest to Speer appeared shaken by it. "It looks as if he lied in the book," Hilde said. "If he lied, you have to say so."

Annemarie was no less definitive. "Yes, it is true," she said after carefully checking one against the other. "He says in the draft that there was no 'confession.' I had not seen the draft—I always accepted it had taken place. It was compatible with the circumstances, with Speer's feelings and with his character. . . ."

Maria von Below agreed but went further in analyzing what probably happened. "I'm not surprised about that lie," she said. "It fits in with everything one knows about his way of thinking. You see, he would have read this fantasy in *Carrefour,* laughed about it [or realized, with embarrassment, that it had started with something he had said during interrogation], and wrote in his draft, no doubt intending at the time to stick to this in an eventual publication, that of course he wouldn't have made such a confession—he wasn't crazy. But then, when he actually sat down fifteen years later to write his book, he would have mentally shrugged and said to himself, 'Oh, well, why not?' It did, after all, fit in well with the impression he then wanted to convey."

She didn't say this to "bad-mouth" Speer for in fact she liked him. She said it because that to her was the truth.

Back in Berlin, that night of April 24, Speer spent eight hours at the Bunker, first attending Hitler's brief situation conference and then another meeting after a radio message arrived from Göring asking whether, as Hitler intended to remain in Berlin, he should now assume leadership of the country. Pushed by Bormann to repudiate this loathed competitor once and for all, Hitler demanded that Göring resign all his offices and titles. Göring immediately complied, answering that a serious heart attack unfortunately forced him to renounce all his functions.

Shortly afterwards Speer's old friend Friedrich Lüschen arrived to see him but refused Speer's entreaties to leave Berlin. (He would be one of many to commit suicide a few days later.) Magda Goebbels, whom Speer then visited in her Bunker room, lay on her bed, suffering from angina attacks and looking deathly pale.

Both in his book and later to me, Speer expressed anger that Goebbels had not allowed them privacy for their goodbyes. "It was he, that monster," he said, "who, for the sake of appearing heroic to posterity, had forced this appalling decision [to kill their children] on her. And then he wouldn't even allow her a few minutes alone with me. Disgusting."

But she *was* Goebbels's wife, I said; they were about to kill their children and then themselves. Given the unique intimacy of the Greek tragedy these two people were about to enact together, why would Speer have thought that she had any desire, or that there was any place, for intimate goodbyes with anyone else?

"Well, we were friends," he said, sounding deflated.

Some time after midnight, when Hitler had retired for a brief rest, an orderly came to invite Speer to Eva Braun's room, which was entirely furnished with the pieces he had designed for her Chancellery apartment years before. "She told me that she had always loved my furniture," he told me, "and that she had wanted to have it around her now." He stayed with her, chatting, for more than two hours. "But that was the only sentimental or perhaps sad remark she made."

Saying she was sure he must be hungry, she ordered champagne and cakes and they talked about people they knew; the places they had visited together; her city, Munich; and her skiing trips with him and Margret (whom she still called "Frau Speer"). She told him how important it was that he had come, that Hitler had thought he too was against him. "And then she said, 'But you came. I told him you would. And that proved, didn't it, that you are with him.' I didn't know what to say, to her of all people, but I did tell her that I was not staying but leaving a bit later that night. She said, very calmly, that of course I must."

In all Speer's accounts of this last night at the Bunker, he expressed his deep admiration for this young woman, who, he said, was the only one to show dignity, and almost a kind of gay serenity. She told him that she had long thought that it was right for them to stay in Berlin, and the Führer had told her what Speer had said about it. "She said he had liked my telling him what I did and that I was quite right. And then she put her hand on my arm, just for a moment, and said she was really happy to be where she was and that she was not afraid. Oh, that girl . . ."

Around 3 a.m. the orderly came in to report that Hitler was up again, and Speer bid Eva Braun goodbye. "She wished me luck and sent greetings to my wife. It was extraordinary. Don't *you* think it was extraordinary? On the face of it, a simple Munich girl, a nobody . . . and yet she was a most remarkable woman. And Hitler had known this. He never said it; I don't think he often made her feel it; but he had sensed it. . . ."

His goodbye to Hitler a few minutes later took seconds, no more. " 'Oh, you are leaving? Good. Well, goodbye,' he said. His words were as cold as his hand," Speer said (and wrote in his book). "No good wishes, no thanks, no greetings to my family. . . ."

Did he not think, I asked him, that it was as extraordinary for him to expect a warm goodbye from Hitler as it was to have resented Goebbels's possessiveness of his wife a few hours earlier? He shook his head. "I see I disappoint you," he said.

DURING THE LAST six days of Hitler's life, confusion reigned both inside and outside the Bunker. In northern Germany, where the British were in almost complete possession, Dönitz, Keitel and Jodl desperately ignored Hitler's increasingly irrational orders to keep fighting.

The Americans, advancing both from the south and from the west, could easily have continued on to Berlin but stopped on a line preagreed with the Russians. By then, having long liberated all of the Eastern countries the Germans had conquered, and already occupying most of Silesia, Stalin had insisted on gaining this most valuable prize. This included the hundreds of thousands of Berliners who, hopeful that Hitler would stop the slaughter or too apathetic or tired to leave, now lived in cellars, the subways or in the simple air-raid shelters Speer had ordered to be built in 1940 when the air raids had started.

"We didn't really know what was happening," said Traudl Junge during one of our talks, "though God knows we were at the source. One's feelings were terribly split. On the one hand, we couldn't understand why it had to go on; on the other we heard Hitler giving new orders. By April 26 we were completely cut off except for a radio link to Field Marshal Keitel and the miraculously still-functioning telephone system inside Berlin over which Hitler kept calling this or that commander and giving them new instructions. Yes, we heard quite a bit of this; discipline or privacy hardly existed anymore. He phoned from anywhere; we sat around everywhere, everybody listened to everything.

"But it was very difficult to make sense of anything," she continued. "You see, even though we could see Hitler falling apart—he trembled, he cried, he was constantly mumbling—but even so, when we heard him issue directions to the generals, well, he *was* the Führer; he had always known, or seemed to know, what orders to give. How could we suddenly think that everything he now said was delusion? And then there was that other illusion, the beautiful Goebbels children, so natural, so well behaved, even there, even then. They laughed and made us laugh; they had tea with Uncle Adolf every afternoon, as they had often had, with little sandwiches and cakes laid out on a table with a stiffly ironed white tablecloth. They zoomed about as if the Bunker were a lovely adventure playground; they giggled and cuddled the puppies, and Hitler, yes, he laughed with them, chased the dogs with them under the table, and hugged little Heidi. How could we possibly reconcile that scene with what we knew was about to happen?"

What she described that last time we met sounded like scenes from a mad-house. At one point, she, Gerda Christian and Eva Braun, feeling claustro-phobic, had taken the dogs up the fifty steps and across the Chancellery garden into the much larger and wilder Foreign Ministry park. "It was so lovely," she said. "The sun was shining; there were snowdrops and crocuses in the new grass; we sat on some rocks and lit cigarettes and the dogs went wild in the freedom."

Eva Braun, who never smoked, lit a cigarette too. "Desperate situations call for desperate measures," she said. Afterwards she sucked a peppermint so that Hitler wouldn't smell the smoke on her breath.

"Down in the Bunker we hardly ever heard the guns," Traudl Junge said, "and there must have been a lull in the fighting when we came up because it was so quiet. But then suddenly the earth trembled with noises and we raced back, down the steps through the upper level, as deep as we could get. I was so frightened I felt sick."

On the twenty-seventh, there was a wedding. One of the kitchen maids married one of the drivers, and a party was held in Hitler's apartment up in the Chancellery, with a lot of champagne. "They danced to an accordion and a violin," she said. "I couldn't bear it—I went back downstairs."

(The day before they married, this young couple, who had apparently worked out a particularly ingenious escape plan, had offered to take the Goebbels children out with them the next day, but to no avail.)

On the twenty-eighth, she remembered, Hitler finally said it was all over. Eva Braun's brother in law, SS Gruppenführer Hermann Fegelein, who a year and a half before had replaced Karl Wolff as Himmler's liaison officer at Führer HQ, was summarily shot that night for having left the Bunker and being found in his Berlin apartment in civilian clothes. "Eva cried. Her sister was about to have their child," Traudl Junge continued. "Hitler said goodbye to a whole crowd of people who had been in neighboring bunkers and came over; they were lined up all along the corridors and up the stairs. He walked along the line, looked each of them in the face, as he had always done, and pressed each hand. Nobody said anything. A few people cried. I asked Eva if this was the end. She said no, not yet—we'd be told; he would want to say goodbye to us separately."

The previous day, Hitler had asked Nicolaus von Below what his plans were. "I told him that my family was safe," Below wrote in his memoirs, "and I would wait and see. . . . He gave me a cyanide pill."

When, four nights before, Speer and Manfred von Poser had left the Bun-ker and flown back to Rechlin, Speer decided on impulse to drop in on Himmler, who had established himself at his friend Dr. Gebhardt's hospital,

Hohenlychen. "Grotesquely," Speer said to me, "he received me in what had been my own sickroom, which he had turned into an office."

Speer remembered this meeting as something between Grimm's fairy tales and a painting by Hieronymus Bosch. Himmler told him that he was extremely busy setting up his future government. Europe, he said, would need him as Minister of Interior; Eisenhower would understand this as soon as they had spent an hour together. The fact of Hitler's dismissal of Göring was immaterial: for the people, he said, Göring was the successor, and he and Göring had a long-standing agreement that Himmler would be his Premier. He was in the process of organizing his cabinet; he had already been in touch with various people; Dönitz had been to see him, and Keitel was on his way. Wouldn't Speer, too, like to join his government, he said; that would surely be the best thing for his future.

"Not without malice," Speer said to me, "I made the countersuggestion that he might like to pay a farewell visit to Hitler, and offered him a lift in my *Storch,* which was standing on the hospital lawn." But Himmler said there was no point to it, and anyway he was too busy and his person was too important for Germany's future to risk such a flight. The arrival of Keitel ended the conversation. As he left, Speer said, he heard Keitel assure Himmler of his unconditional loyalty.

"What a sorry spectacle it all was," he said. "This more than anything perhaps symbolized for me the end of the Third Reich. This was the man who had made us tremble, who had coined the motto 'My Honor Is Named Loyalty,' for which tens of thousands died. Were we all painted with that same brush?"

Sometime during this bizarre encounter, Himmler had told Speer that for several days already he had been negotiating through Count Bernadotte the transfer of the concentration camps to the International Red Cross, and an end to the war. But it was to be three more days, in the afternoon of April 28, when the news of these negotiations had been leaked in Sweden, before Hitler, handed a Reuters report by his press chief, Heinz Lorenz, learned that even Himmler had betrayed him.

Below says this was the final and, he thought, decisive blow. Again, Misch had the most immediate impression of it: "He was sitting on that bench outside my switchboard room with a puppy in his lap when Lorenz, whom I had heard arrive at a run, handed him the paper on which he had jotted down the radio dispatch. Hitler's face went completely white, almost ashen. 'My God,' I thought, 'he is going to faint.' He slumped forward holding his head with his hands. The puppy plumped to the ground—silly how one remembers such trifles, but I can still hear that soft sound." But he had rallied very quickly, and disappeared into his study with Goebbels and Bormann.

Later that evening, Hitler tried to dissuade Goebbels from executing his plans. He wanted him and Bormann to survive, he said, and get to Dönitz. And he announced that he was going to marry Eva Braun. "Goebbels somehow located a registrar stationed nearby with the militia, and had him brought to the Bunker," wrote Below. "When he arrived, his face showed that he didn't know what hit him."

On the twenty-ninth, at 2 a.m., when Traudl Junge had at last fallen asleep for an hour, lying on her iron bedstead in a little box-room that had been her quarters for the past three months, she was awakened to be told the Führer wanted her.

"I quickly washed my face and went down to his study. A table in the corner had been laid as if for a party—glasses, small plates, cutlery—but I didn't know for what occasion. He was very quiet when I came in, but courteous as ever. He took my hand. Was I all right? he asked. Had I had a rest? I said I had, and he took me to the large conference room and told me to make myself comfortable, what he had to dictate would take some time, and would have to be transcribed as quickly as possible afterwards. Couriers would be waiting to take it out."

She had felt very strange as she took down Hitler's Political Testament. "You know, here we were," she said, "all of us doomed, I thought—the whole country doomed—and here, in what he was dictating to me there was not one word of compassion or regret, only awful, awful anger. I remember thinking, 'My God, he hasn't learned anything. It's all just the same.' " She hadn't known about the imminent ceremony. "It was only when he dictated his private will, in which he explained his last-minute decision to marry, that I found out.

"He stood like this," she said, remembering that night. She stood up, placed her hands on the table on which were the remainders of our tea and leaned forward. "Like this—almost all of the time."

She had taken down his dictation in shorthand and, when he had finished, settled down to typing the thirteen pages in three copies. She was to do it carefully, Hitler told her; there would not be time for any corrections.

While she typed, the marriage ceremony was taking place in the small conference, or map, room, with only the two witnesses, Bormann and Goebbels, present.

"It didn't take me long," she said. "There were ten pages of the Political Testament and just three for the private one. It would have gone even faster if Goebbels hadn't come in in the middle."

Goebbels, she said, had looked distraught. Hitler, he said, had just told him that after all he expected him to leave Berlin. "He said he couldn't; that, for the first time in his life, he would have to disobey the Führer—nothing would make him leave him or his city."

He then dictated a will of his own which eventually would be appended to one copy of Hitler's testament. All three of them, Hitler, Bormann and Goebbels, were in the room with her when she finished, and hurriedly took the copies to the map room.

"I joined the party in the study. [Magda Goebbels, SS General Burgdorf, Hewel, Axmann, Below, Gerda Christian, Hitler's valet Linge and, on and off, his aide Otto Günsche.] I sat down with them around the table and ate little sandwiches and drank champagne as they had apparently been doing for quite a while," Traudl Junge said. "Nobody said anything. We couldn't very well toast their future."

"They called me to the map room at 4 a.m.," Below wrote. "I was surprised when Hitler asked me to witness his private will, together with Goebbels and Bormann. But I also read the Political Testament and found his self-deception really depressing and his repeated anti-Semitic invectives embarrassing. . . ."

Hitler railed against the Jews five times in these ten pages. The war had not been of his making, he said, but brought about by international politicians of Jewish origin or acting on behalf of Jewish interests. Jewry, he said, was responsible for the death by starvation of millions of Aryan children in Europe, and he had decided on suicide in order not to provide "a show . . . stage-managed by the Jews."

In the second part of his Political Testament, he expelled Göring and Himmler from the party for having disloyally negotiated with the enemy; named Dönitz President of the Reich, Minister of War and Supreme Commander of the Armed Forces; Karl Hanke Reichsführer SS and head of the German Police; Paul Giesler (the architect's brother) Minister of the Interior; Goebbels Chancellor; Bormann head of the party; Seyss-Inquart Foreign Minister; Funk Minister of Economics; Schwerin-Krosigk Minister of Finance; Saur Minister for Armaments; Ley Head of the German Workers' Front; and Hupfauer Minister of Labor.

"Above all," he ended, "I hold the leadership to their strict commitment to the racial laws and to relentless resistance against the poisoner of all peoples—international Jewry."

It was said later by Speer's enemies that Hitler dropped him at the last minute to punish him after the "confession." But that confession never took place, and Eva Braun's words to Traudl Junge clearly confirm Hitler's lasting attachment to Speer. So one is tempted to wonder whether just as, by pointedly requesting Below, whom he liked very much, to sign his private but not his Political Testament, Hitler somehow managed to establish him as a private rather than political entity at his court, he might also have tried to protect Speer by leaving him out of that last damning document. While even suggesting the possibility of such farsighted compassion may be quixotic, the fact is that Speer's exclusion from this final government was considered a point in his favor by the Nuremberg prosecution, and was emphasized in his defense counsel's final address to the court.

Four men left later that day, April 29, each carrying a copy of the testaments. Major Willi Johannmeier, Hitler's last army adjutant, was to take only the Political Testament to Field Marshal Ferdinand Schörner, now the last Commander in Chief of the Army. Press Chief Lorenz, given the top copies of both Hitler's testaments and Goebbels's appendix, was told to make his way to Munich, and to see to it that the documents were safely deposited in order to preserve them for posterity.

SS Colonel Wilhelm Zander, one of Bormann's assistants, was to go to Dönitz, also taking a message from Bormann. Finally, Nicolaus von Below, who received Hitler's permission to leave at lunchtime but only left after the last situation report late that night, also went to Dönitz's headquarters with both testaments, plus an addendum addressed by Hitler to Keitel.

Just before lunch the next day, April 30, Eva Braun took Traudl Junge into her bedroom. "She took a beautiful silver fox cape out of her wardrobe," she said, "and handed it to me. 'Please take it,' she said, 'I want you to wear it and enjoy it.' After that we went into lunch with Hitler, and when it was over, he and Eva spent a little time on their own." She shook her head. "What do you think they could have said to each other?"

Hitler's aide, Otto Günsche, called them soon afterwards to say goodbye. "Hitler shook hands with each of us," Traudl Junge said, "holding our hands firmly as he always did, and looking into our eyes—that special look which people felt got right into them. But not that day," she said. "He looked at me, and murmured something, but I don't think he saw me, and I couldn't understand what he said."

Hitler and his wife then retired to their room. I have heard several descriptions of the minutes which followed, and also of the hours afterwards. The people who were there appear to carry the memory indelibly within them, but less as a sequential story than as something that cannot be real, something almost imagined, or seen in flashes.

How can one believe, for example, that while the suicide was being prepared or even taking place, and all movement had ceased in the Bunker, the sounds of music and revelry were suddenly clearly heard through the open doors from upstairs—a party with dancing and a great deal of schnapps was in progress in the by now windowless canteen of the almost ruined Chancellery.

"They had cleared the Führer level of the Bunker before it happened," said Rochus Misch. "The only people there were me at my switchboard, Günsche standing guard in front of Hitler's living room, and two orderlies, one with me, the other within sight of Günsche. That's the one he sent to tell me to phone them upstairs and tell them to be quiet. I rang and rang, but there was no answer; they probably couldn't even hear the phone. So I told the orderly to run up and tell them, but I'm sure he was too late."

Günsche had Hitler's precise orders about what was to be done. He and Eva Braun were to be given ten minutes before anyone came in, and then their bodies were to be carried upstairs into the "Honor Courtyard" and doused with petrol and burnt.

It was the longest ten minutes of his life, Günsche, who loved Hitler, was to say later. But as he stood there, suddenly there was the sound of running and Magda Goebbels, rushing down the corridor, banged against the door of the room. Not wishing to manhandle her, Günsche, at a loss as to how to act, instinctively knocked on Hitler's door as he had always done and opened it to ask him for directions. But the moment it was open, Magda Goebbels rushed past him into the room.

Within seconds she was out again, sobbing deeply. Hitler, Günsche told someone later, had sharply ordered her out. "Axmann came running too, then," Misch said, "but this time Günsche just said no and blocked the way. Then they both stood there. Quite soon afterwards—it was all very quick— Linge came and Kempka, and then Bormann and Goebbels and Burgdorf."

"When that door closed behind Hitler and Eva," Traudl Junge said, "all I wanted was to get out; I felt I was suffocating; I craved quiet and sleep. I wanted terribly not to be so frightened." She found herself rushing up the steps, without really knowing where she was aiming for, but then stopped halfway. "I suddenly remembered the children," she said. "I didn't think anybody had given them lunch." She turned out to be right. When she got back down as far as the kitchen, one small stairway up from the private apartments, she found that they had indeed been forgotten. They were sitting there around a table, she said, for once looking glum. "They said no, they hadn't had lunch. I told them the grownups were just terribly busy and got out some bread and ham and made them sandwiches. It was strange how quickly that cheered them up, how quickly they began to chatter. And then, suddenly, there was the sound of a shot and then dead silence. The children, startled I think, were motionless for a second, and then Helmuth shouted gaily, 'Bang on!' How right he was."

The children now had one night and one day to live. Again it was Rochus Misch who remembered it most vividly. That day had been very busy, he said. General Krebs, who had been military attaché in Moscow and spoke Russian, was sent—optimistically—with a white flag to find the Soviet commander. He was to offer the surrender of Berlin on the condition that those in the Bunker were allowed safe passage out. In the meantime General Mohnke organized escape plans if they became necessary.

The escape was to be attempted in four groups. The first, led by General Mohnke and including the four women, Günsche, Hewel, the navy liaison officer Admiral Voss, and the pilot Captain Baur, would lead the way. The others would follow along the tracks of the subway, eventually surfacing and somehow crossing the river Spree and the Russian lines. Almost none of it worked out as planned. Some people—such as Dr. Stumpfegger, who had helped Magda Goebbels kill her children—were hit by Russian shrapnel and died; some wisely slipped away from the groups and hid; some—such as Bormann—disappeared; some committed suicide. But most of them ended up like Misch, as prisoners of the Russians, spending the next years in prisons and gulags in the Soviet Union.

General Krebs was away negotiating with the Russians at least eight or nine hours, Misch said, when we talked in Berlin decades later. "He came back in the late morning. Of course the Soviets hadn't agreed. I never understood why those big generals imagined they might. Safe conduct, indeed," he said contemptuously, and his wife laughed outright. "I think they all lived in never-never land." But his voice changed when he got to the next part of the story.

"It was only just after 5 p.m.," he said, "when Frau Goebbels walked past me followed by the children. They were all wearing white nightgowns. She took them next door; an orderly arrived carrying a tray with six cups and a jug of chocolate. Later somebody said it was laced with sleeping pills. I saw her hug some, stroke others as they drank it. I don't think they knew about their Uncle Adolf's death; they laughed and chatted as always. A little later they passed me on their way upstairs, Heidi last, her mother holding her hand."

Misch left his switchboard for a moment and stood at the door; he and little Heidi had become particularly good pals. "Heidi turned around. I waved to her, she waved back with one hand, and then, suddenly, letting go of her mother's hand, she turned all the way around and, bursting into that happy clear laugh of hers, she scraped one forefinger along the other and chanted that little rhyme she always sang when she saw me: 'Misch, Misch, you are a fish.' [*Misch, Misch, Du bist ein Fisch.*] Her mother put her arm around her and pulled her gently up the steps, but she went on chanting it. I still hear it now." Misch and his wife were silent.

A little later Magda Goebbels had come back down and gone into her room, he said. "About an hour later I saw her again, going up the stairs with Dr. Stumpfegger." The place had once again become very quiet.*

"Not that long afterwards, not more than half an hour, she came back," Misch continued. "She was crying. She sat down at the long table in the conference room and played solitaire. Goebbels came and went but I didn't see them talk. A little later that evening they came past my door together. Goebbels stopped. He said, 'Good luck.' ["He stopped by me too," said Traudl Junge. "He shook my hand and said, 'All the best; you'll make it.' "] And then they killed themselves," said Misch, "upstairs, in the courtyard. The last thing Goebbels said, I think to Günsche, was 'That way you won't have to carry us.' "

Annemarie and I were on our way back along the frozen Alster when she told me about waiting for Speer, hoping against hope that he would return safely. "After Speer left for Berlin," she said, "Edith Maguira and I had just stayed on at the Atlantik, living from moment to moment. At that point I couldn't even think about what might be happening to him. But of course, in the end he was only away for two days, from the afternoon of the twenty-second to the evening of the twenty-fourth when, from the little entrance lobby of our suite, we suddenly heard that nonchalant voice: 'So, what's new here?' I honestly think I could have hit him."

"We had held on to the *Storch* to fly to Hamburg," Speer had told me. "Exceptionally, we could see some Russian fighters back of us on the horizon, so we flew low, using the woods on the Mecklenburg seaboard as a cover."

That low-level flight over precisely the waterways along which he and Margret had canoed twenty-two years before on their honeymoon, he said, suddenly waxing lyrical, was quite wonderful. Was it nostalgia he had felt, I asked. Regrets?

"No," he said. "Joy."

He was to have just one more moment of joy during the next days. "The morning after my return," he said, "we flew the *Storch* to Eutin and moved into our trailers. Cliever had done very well for us, parking them in the most beautiful lonely woods, within sight of the lake."

"There were finally quite a lot of us," Annemarie said. "Baumbach [Speer's pilot] had joined us and another flier; Cliever and us two women; and then General Holzheuer from Guderian's former staff arrived bringing

---

*James P. O'Donnell, quoting Misch in his book *The Berlin Bunker*, provides additional insight into his feelings: "I sat alone, paralyzed, not so much by fear as by frustrated compassion. . . . I began saying my rosary, praying for all six little souls. I prayed for the mother too. I guess I was praying she would relent."

some tank guards. Guderian had got a message through to him that Speer was to be kept safe. It was absolutely extraordinary. Here we were, in these quite primitive trailers—we called the one where we cooked and sat around at night our 'living room.' One, where Edith and I also slept, that served as our office, was our 'headquarters,' " she mocked, "and then one had four bunks for the five men. One had to sleep on the floor—they took turns. But guarding all this mess was this fully armed honor guard for Speer. I mean, it was extravagant, wasn't it?"

"Of course, we didn't *do* anything," Speer had told me. "I mean, there wasn't anything to do except every day or so to visit Dönitz at his naval base, or people from the Chief of Staff who like us had found their way into the area and, also like us, were doing nothing except waiting. We all waited."

("Speer at least knew what he was waiting for," Annemarie said, the disapproval she had felt so long ago still evident in her tone of voice, "Hitler's suicide. But we didn't know. God only knows why he didn't warn us, but he didn't.")

"The most significant event of that week for me," Speer had said, "was taking the *Storch* over to see my family on their isolated peninsula on the Baltic. This was the other moment of joy. I don't think I'll ever forget the faces of the children as long as I live, when that little plane landed, unannounced, on a field next to the house," he said. "They were so happy to see me, they were just delirious with excitement; I think the hours I spent there with them, my wife and those good friends who had taken them in, were the best we'd ever had."

"I think it was raining on May 1," Annemarie said. "Anyway, we were inside our living room trailer when the phone rang. It was Dönitz. One of us took the call—I don't even remember whether it was me or Edith; he didn't ask to speak to anyone in particular. As I remember, he just said, 'The Führer is no longer alive,' and then hung up. I remember I felt, well, taken aback, because of course, I hadn't known. Were we sad? Oh, I don't know. We were no longer in a state of mind where the word 'sad' could apply. Germany was in tatters. There was no future, and now *he* was dead too. Speer left a few minutes later, to join Dönitz, at Plön."

Although the local telephones still worked and radio connection with Berlin functioned until May 2, long-distance telephone communication had long ceased and no one at the "Northern Command" was aware of the drama still continuing in and outside the Bunker. History has recorded, of course, the names of the famous—or infamous—who died at their own hands, most of them with the help of those cyanide pills Himmler so generously distributed in April: Hitler and Goebbels; later Göring, just before he was to be hanged; Himmler himself when caught by the Allies; and the same for any number of his worst SS when they were captured. But it was to be months, in some cases years, before it became known how very many men, older and young, of high and low rank—many of whom had not been involved in any crimes—had committed suicide after Hitler's death.

In the Bunker itself, besides the principals already named, the two generals, Burgdorf and Krebs; the commander of the Leibstandarte, SS Captain Schedle; and one of his young officers, twenty-four-year-old SS Lieutenant Stehr—all shot themselves soon after the four groups of escapees had left. And in the neighboring bunker, which had been used as an emergency hospital for days, a number of seriously wounded soldiers, whose names we don't know, found means to kill themselves. The flying ace, Ritter von Greim, who with his friend Hanna Reitsch had made a daring flight in and out of Berlin at the last moment and was named Head of the Luftwaffe to replace Göring, killed himself a month later. So did Hanna Reitsch's whole family—her parents, brothers and sisters—immediately after Hitler's death. Ambassador Walter Hewel, who had managed to get out of Berlin, was only in his forties, recently married and certainly not guilty of any crime, killed himself. Many of the others became prisoners of the Russians within hours. Hitler's valet, Linge, tried to kill himself then; Rochus Misch stopped him. General Mohnke tried, too—Otto Günsche stopped *him*. They all survived Russian captivity.

Suicide in those early days was hardly an individual act—it was an epidemic, as if Hitler's hypnotic effect had endured beyond the grave.

Martin Bormann's "crown prince" son, Martin, was fifteen when his Nazi-elite school Feldafing (of which his father had been chairman) closed down on April 23, 1945. Each of the other boys was given RM 100 and told to find his way home, but Martin was given false identity documents (in the name of Martin Bergmann) and was driven to Salzburg, where some of his father's staff from Munich and the Berghof had taken over the *Gaststube* of an inn in a neighboring village.

"It was a small inn and a very small *Stube*," Martin said when we talked in 1991. "We sat on benches tightly packed together. It's impossible now to convey the atmosphere. The worst moment was when, at two o'clock in the morning of May 1, the news of Hitler's death came through on the radio. I remember it precisely, but I can't describe the stillness of that instant which lasted . . . for hours. Nobody said anything, but very soon afterwards people started to go outside, first one—then there was a shot. Then another, and yet another. Not a word inside, no other sound except those shots from outside, but one felt that that was all there was, that all of us would have to die."

And so finally Martin took the gun he had been given and stepped outside. "My world was shattered; I couldn't see any future at all. But then, out there, in the back of that inn, where bodies were already lying all over the small garden, there was another boy, older than I—he was eighteen. He was sitting on a log and told me to come and sit with him. The air smelled good, the birds sang, and we talked ourselves out of it. If we hadn't had each other at that moment, both of us would have gone—I know it."

Dönitz's headquarters that night was ruled by confusion, rather than despair. The radio signal which transmitted the part of Hitler's Political Testament which named Dönitz his successor and Goebbels and Bormann his principal ministers, was considered unacceptable. "Just imagine," Dönitz said to Speer, "what on earth do we do if Bormann really gets here. One can't work with that man." The decision was made—the first one taken by the new head of state—to destroy the signal, as if that could have destroyed Hitler's intention, Bormann's obedience to it had he really arrived, or the knowledge of what the testaments contained. The next day, Dönitz said, they would move to the larger naval base at Flensburg, and he would begin negotiations with Field Marshal Montgomery.

"That night," Speer told me, "I was assigned a small room in the navy barrack. When I unpacked my overnight bag, I saw that Annemarie Kempf had put in the red leather case with Hitler's portrait, which he had signed for me on my fortieth birthday six weeks before. I was quite all right, you know, until—I don't know why—I opened the case and stood the photograph up on the night table next to the bed. And then suddenly, standing there, I started to sob. I couldn't stop; it just went on and on until, still dressed, I fell asleep on the bed."

For a while, Speer felt that had been a kind of watershed that liberated him, but it wasn't. "That's when the dreams began," he said, "dreams of his knowing what I did, dreams of his saying that I wanted to kill him. They went on for years, and even now they sometimes come back. Sometimes he isn't even in the room in these dreams, but he is in the dreams, or he is the dream."

XXI

The One Interesting Person

Nuremberg, June 21, 1946

MR. JUSTICE JACKSON (cross-examining Speer): I will ask you about Exhibit 398-USA 894 . . . a statement by [former Krupp factory worker] Hofer, living in Essen: "From April 1943 I worked with Lowenkamp every day in Panzer Shop 4. Lowenkamp was brutal to the foreigners. He confiscated food which belonged to the POWs and took it home. Every day he maltreated Eastern workers, Russian POWs, French, Italian and other foreign civilians. He had a steel cabinet built which was so small that one could hardly stand in it." [Jackson presents photographs and describes the cabinets: "Their height was 1.52 meters, width and depth 40–50 centimeters (5 feet by 18 inches); there were a few sieve-like airholes at the top." He continues reading Hofer's statement:] "He locked up foreigners, women too, in the box, for forty-eight hours at a time, without giving them any food. They were not even released to relieve nature. It was forbidden for other people to give them any help. . . ."

We have upwards of a hundred different depositions; here is one more: "The undersigned Dahm [also a Krupp worker] personally saw how three Russian civilian workers were locked into the cupboard after they had first been beaten on New Year's Eve 1945. Two . . . had to stay locked in it the whole night and cold water was poured on them through the airholes. . . ."

There is a good deal more of this, but I will not bother to put it into the record. Is it your view that [these accounts] are exaggerated?

SPEER: I consider [them] a lie. I would say that among German people such things do not exist, and if such individual excesses occurred, they were punished. It is not possible to drag the German people in the dirt in such a way. . . . What is pictured here are quite normal lockers as used in every factory and not some special cabinets . . . and the air vents at the top . . . are ventilation holes. . . .

IT IS ABSURD to presume that Speer would have known about the precise nature of punishment and torture in concentration and labor camps, and his indignation at Mr. Justice Jackson's suggestion would have been entirely sincere.

Nonetheless, and leaving aside such special and specific knowledge, one of the great psychological mysteries about the Third Reich has always been Hitler's ability to convince a nation of culturally sophisticated men and women that wrong was right.

It is too simple to say, as many Germans do, that they "didn't know what was being done" or that they were all benighted and hypnotized. In truth it was, and is, more complicated. Whatever they did not know— and there was much of it—they all knew *something*. The real phenomenon was not that Hitler persuaded the Germans that wrong was right, but that they should accept the legitimacy of forbidden knowledge. As Carola von Poser said, they knew that there was danger in knowledge. Awareness of "these details"—as Hupfauer gratingly referred to the specifics of the SS crimes—of course lurked in the recesses of many minds, but it was determinedly and decisively suppressed until and even beyond the Nuremberg trials.

I discussed this phenomenon with Annemarie Kempf in Hamburg, still during the cold late winter in 1986, when in our talks we reached the period between Hitler's suicide and the wholesale arrest a few weeks later of virtually everybody who had been in his government, or with any semblance of importance in the party. She said the denial of knowledge applied to every single person she could think of, first in Flensburg, the seat of the Third Reich's post-Hitler government for a few weeks in May 1945, then in Dustbin, the V.I.P. camp to which the Americans sent most of the more important prisoners. It also applied to herself, she said ruefully, and of course, until well into the Nuremberg trial, to Speer.

"That second of May, the day after Hitler's death became known, was very busy," Annemarie said. "Dönitz appointed Speer Minister for Economics and Production and moved what was now the seat of government to Flensburg, a largish town near the Danish border and the naval base of Murvick. We moved there, too."

Speer had flown that day to Hamburg, where his friend Gauleiter Kaufmann was still battling against the party fanatics who wanted to destroy his city. A signed order Speer brought from Dönitz, now the head of state, finally enabled Kaufmann to hand Hamburg over to the British.

Back in Flensburg the same evening, Speer delivered to the German people a somewhat shortened version of the speech he had written and recorded three weeks before, over the local radio station, focusing it on reconstruction and dignity.

"For a few days we stayed on a large passenger ship, the *Patria*," said Annemarie. "But then [Speer's assistants] Cliever and Siebert got the Duke of Mecklenburg and Holstein to offer Speer hospitality at his beautiful waterside castle just a few miles away and the five of us—Speer, von Poser, Cliever, Maguira and I, and of course Speer's 'honor guard'—moved there, driving over to Flensburg every morning for the ten o'clock cabinet meeting."

"Can you believe this?" Speer had asked me. "*Cabinet* meeting? But it's true—there, in a former schoolroom still smelling of chalk, we solemnly met on the dot of ten every morning, sat down on brightly colored straight chairs around a brightly painted square table and discussed the nonexistent plans of a nonexistent country."

"After two days of this nonsense, Speer wrote an official letter to Dönitz," Annemarie said, "reminding him that they were living an illusion and that he thought the quicker they all faced reality, the better it would be for Germany."

Nonetheless, although finally agreeing on May 7 to unconditional surrender on the entire front, the Dönitz government remained *in situ* for another sixteen days. "I honestly think the British didn't immediately know what to do with us," Speer told me. "Hitler in his Bunker in Berlin would have been one thing, but an admiral in Flensburg was quite another. So they established their Control Commission in the same building where we had our offices, and left us politely to our silly meetings."

Reality arrived for Speer at his castle refuge a few days later in the persons of two young Americans, who early one afternoon knocked on his office door, onto which Annemarie had thumbtacked a large card with his name. "Excuse me," said the American lieutenant in perfect German, "can you tell me where I can find Speer?"

A week earlier, just after Hitler's suicide became known, Paul Nitze, Vice-

Chairman of the U.S. Strategic Bombing Survey* (USSBS), working out of London, had convoked two of his favorite juniors, Lieutenant Georg Sklarz and Technical Sergeant Harald Fassberg, to his office.

"You two get over there and find me Speer," he said. "I don't care what you have to do; just find him."

Paul Nitze, George Ball and John Kenneth Galbraith—all about Speer's age, with war jobs not unlike his—had had long careers in public service and academia when I visited them in April 1987, in Washington, D.C., Princeton, New Jersey, and Cambridge, Massachusetts, respectively. John Galbraith, during the war first Deputy Chief of the Office of Price Administration and then of Economic Security Policy, had been a member of Roosevelt's exclusive think tank. After the war, he served as Ambassador to India, taught at Harvard, wrote and lectured worldwide.

George Ball, a brilliant lawyer, was first General Counsel for Roosevelt's Lend-Lease Administration and then the Foreign Economy Administration. In 1944, he was named Director of the USSBS. After the war, Ball served as Undersecretary of State, U.S. Representative at the United Nations and eventually as counsel to private banks.

Paul Nitze, trained in banking, served during the war as Financial Director of the U.S. Office of Inter-American Affairs, of the U.S. Board of Economic Warfare, of the Foreign Procurement Department, and in 1944, was sent to London to head the USSBS. When I met him in his impressive office at the State Department, he had been one of America's top negotiators and advisor to Presidents for forty-five years.

"There had not been the least doubt in my mind, for months before the European war ended," said Nitze, "that Speer was the *one* man we had to find as quickly as possible. My two assistants, Sklarz and Fassberg, were very clever young people. Lieutenant Sklarz was, I think, of Czech origin; the young sergeant was Jewish; but what was important was that both of them had fluent German and lots of initiative." He laughed. "Sklarz was actually a musician, one of a two-man piano team; he played beautifully. And Fassberg didn't miss a trick—he could hear the grass grow. In addition, pretty important to me, both of them had a real good sense of humor.

"Of course, we didn't know where Speer might be; Berlin was the obvious place, and that would have been a tragedy because then the Russians had him, in which case he was a dead duck. But Sklarz and I had a hunch he was too clever to let himself be caught there. So then there was southern Ger-

*The U.S. Strategic Bombing Survey was to analyze the impact of the Allied bombing of Germany, both on production and on civilian morale, to learn anything which would assist the Americans in the continuing war against Japan.

many or, of course, the north, where Hitler's last government had established themselves; Sklarz made an educated guess that that's where he would have gone.

"So I gave them every authority at my disposal—and that was quite a bit: you know, planes, money, every laissez-passer on the books. And sure enough, it wasn't more than two days later that Sklarz called me up and said he'd found him.

"Later he told me that it had been quite eerie: there was this great big castle, and it looked deserted except for some little kids playing in the park. So my boys walked in and there was this huge hall with a curving staircase and lots of rooms downstairs but dead silence throughout. They went from door to door and within a few moments they found one with a card on it that said 'Reichsminister Speer.' They couldn't believe it. They knocked, and a voice said *'Herein,'* so they went in and there was this man they of course recognized at once from photographs we had. Do you know what he said? 'I know who you are,' he said. 'You are with the U.S. Strategic Bombing Survey.' And my sergeant asked where he could find a phone and Speer pointed at a phone on the desk and said, 'Help yourself; our phones work quite well.'

"So—can you believe this?—Sklarz called me, and I said, 'Hold on to him!' and he answered, 'He isn't going anywhere, sir; all he wants is to talk to you.'

"Well, I was in my DC-3 and over there before you could say 'knife,' and George Ball rushed over from Paris and Ken Galbraith flew in too after a few days. Altogether we had ten days with him during which he told us, I guess, all there was to tell about the effects of our and the Brits' strategic bombing. We needed to know for the war against Japan, but we knew—and believe me, *he* knew—that we also needed to know for the future, for whatever was going to happen with Russia. Any rational person was aware that something had to happen there sooner or later.

"Did I like Speer? Yes, I liked him. I like able men; he was a very, very talented person. Was he a moral man? That's a very different matter. I didn't say that. A 'good man'? I didn't say that either. We weren't looking for 'goodness' or 'morality' in him at that time. We were looking for absolutely vital information and knowledge and he was literally the only person in Germany who was in a position to provide it."

Nitze remembered ten days with Speer; Ball five or six; Galbraith, who came a little later, only about three. Annemarie remembered that the two young Americans came on May 12 and stayed until the end; Nitze and Ball arriving on the thirteenth, with "the third one coming a bit later." Throughout the talks, she told me, high-ranking officers came and went.

"It really was totally bizarre," she said. "Speer would attend Dönitz's 10 a.m. conference as usual and then come back. The Americans arrived at noon; Speer's guards would present arms—oh, yes, they were still armed—and then, before anything else, the four [later five] had 'breakfast' [actually lunch] prepared by the Duke's cook. They always had at least one interpreter sitting in, usually a rather nice man called Williams, an immigrant to America from Germany. They didn't have any secretarial help, so when they adjourned to a small salon next door, a beautiful room all in gold and red brocade, I would join them to transcribe the proceedings. Afterwards, Williams and Lieutenant Sklarz translated it into English."

"Speer was the one interesting person on the Nazi side," said George Ball. "His knowledge was absolutely astounding. And he was—or at least seemed—quite extraordinarily open. On our second day together, he said he thought it was a great shame the United States had not joined with Germany in the battle against the Russians. That was when we were just at the very beginning of the cold war, and he was touching a very raw nerve when he said that. He also said that one of Hitler's main problems—if not *the* main problem—was that he simply had no understanding whatsoever of foreign countries, and thus had no comprehension of the *power* of the U.S. and did not believe it when he was told.

"When Ken Galbraith arrived, he was very quickly very hard on Speer with questions about concentration camps; I hadn't asked, because I knew so little myself; Ken knew more. But Speer was very evasive about that—very, very evasive.

"But I was very impressed with the consistency of what he told us in Flensburg and what he later wrote in his book. Sometime during that week—during lunch one day, I think it was—I asked him whether he was sorry he hadn't been able to carry out his plans for Berlin and he answered, 'God, no; they were awful!' I thought that was remarkably honest.

"Did I like him? I don't know. For someone so distinguished, he was rather brash. I saw him again later, you know, during his long interrogations in 'Ashcan' [*sic*; he meant the VIP debriefing center Dustbin, near Frankfurt]. And there he said something really odd to me. 'There are going to be some war-crime trials,' he said. 'You are a young lawyer. How would you like to represent me? Many young lawyers have made their reputations defending notorious characters, and you could hardly find anyone more notorious than me.' I wasn't *that* young, just four years younger than he, in fact, but anyway, wasn't that a curious thing to say under the circumstances?"

"I suppose it might have seemed odd to Ball, who was there in his role as the victor," Annemarie told me. "But it wasn't odd for Speer—he probably thought it would be rather a joke if he arrived at a trial represented by an

American lawyer—that was his kind of humor. It wasn't that odd to me either. I mean, after all, he *was* Speer."

Of the Three Wise Men, as I would think of them later, Nitze seemed to me the most detached, and Galbraith the most bitter—he was the only one of the three who had already seen Dachau, Buchenwald and the awful photographs of Bergen-Belsen. "One was just beginning to hear rumors about Auschwitz," he said, "but the rest of it—Treblinka, Sobibor and the other horrific places—we knew nothing about.

"Do I think that Speer knew about all this? All he ever told us about was that story of one of his friends [Karl Hanke] who whispered to him sometime in 1944 never to visit a certain place in Silesia because something unspeakable was happening there, that's all."

("I asked him what he knew about the extermination of the Jews," said George Ball. "He said he couldn't comment because he hadn't known about it, but he added that it was his mistake not to have found out.")

"But, no, I don't believe he didn't know," continued Galbraith. "Certainly he knew all about the slave laborers. I remember his saying to us, 'You should hang Sauckel,' and then, a few weeks later, Sauckel said to us, 'You should hang Speer.' Nice people, weren't they?"

I asked if Galbraith considered it possible that Speer knew all these things but simply decided to eradicate them from his memory.

"It wouldn't have been a 'decision,' and it wouldn't have been simple at all," he said. "But, yes, I think it is entirely possible that by some unconscious process this is what happened in him.

"My first reaction to him? Well, of course he was physically very impressive. But that wasn't it—some of the others we met at Dustbin later looked all right too. It was quite simply, I think, that Speer was another caliber. He exuded personality, authority and—to me somewhat jarringly at times—humor. By any standards, he was quite exceptionally intelligent, with a phenomenal memory and breadth of technical knowledge. It is of course sad," he added, "that while Speer will be remembered as the genius of production he doubtlessly was, the men in Britain and America, such as Bevin, Beaverbrook, Leon Henderson or Robert Nathan, who were quite as brilliant organizers as he, are virtually forgotten."

(The Nobel Prize–winning economist Friedrich von Hayek, with whom I discussed this point in Freiburg in 1985, said the explanation was simple: "The great production geniuses in wartime Britain and America," he said, "were men experienced in finance, industry and economics who during the war worked *with* their governments and as part of them. Speer was a brilliant self-taught amateur who basically accomplished what he did *in spite of* his government; because whatever conventional bodies were set up—ministries of this and that—in the final analysis the sole ruler of Nazi Germany was Hitler, who was upheld by the primitive nonentities of the party. These were the people Speer had to deal with. He was the prime example of that phenomenon in Hitlerian Germany, though not the only one—a man born to honor, who chose to live in dishonor.")

"Above all," said Galbraith, "Speer, very early on, I believe—certainly by the time he was interrogated in Dustbin—had made a conscious plan for survival. While all of them, virtually without exception, said they knew nothing of any crimes, whether slave labor or concentration camps—a manifest lie— and they *all* declined to take any responsibility whatever, Speer from the word go admitted a universal kind of responsibility. At the same time, he adroitly avoided anything that touched even marginally upon these dangerous subjects. We tried to lead him toward them many, many times, but he very, very cleverly managed to divert us to other things, by flooding us with more and more details on air attacks and production statistics, which he knew were of immediate interest to us. I always had the distinct feeling he was holding such things in reserve, against the times he needed them for these—to him—so necessary diversions.

"Don't forget we had exceptional opportunities for comparison; we eventually saw all the key figures who were still alive: Göring; Funk; Ribbentrop; and the two generals, Keitel—a terribly narrow military mind—and Jodl, not so narrow but obviously distorted by his long exposure to Hitler. I am, you understand, only speaking of their minds, not their morals, although the more one saw the less one felt the two could be separated.

"Göring, of course, was still going through drug withdrawal when we met him, so one couldn't make an intellectual judgment. The American army method for this was quite ruthless, very different from now—they simply removed all drugs. In his case it meant that he couldn't even get codeine, with which he had been trying to get himself off morphine.* So no doubt he was going through a rough time. But even so, even in this state of physical distress and mental apathy, his fundamental arrogance showed through. And the others—all the others, including Seyss-Inquart and von Schirach—were, intellectually, terribly ordinary men.

"Speer was simply totally different, and his strategy from the beginning had been to highlight this difference whenever he could. He started this when he talked to us in Flensburg in May, and he maintained it through his many weeks of debriefing, first at Chesnay in Versailles near Eisenhower's headquarters, then when Ike moved to Frankfurt, at Dustbin, and finally

---

*According to G. M. Gilbert, after the severe withdrawal of all drugs at Mondorf, Göring *was* being given reduced doses of paracodeine at Nuremberg.

for nearly a year in Nuremberg. If he hadn't succeeded in these meticulously thought-out, self-promulgating tactics, he would have been hanged."

Paul Nitze, who by the time we met, had served under many Presidents,
from Roosevelt through Nixon to Reagan, though no more approving of
Speer, was perhaps just a degree more sympathetic.

"On our tenth day with him," he said, "I think it was the twenty-second of
May, Eisenhower's political advisor, Robert Murphy, joined us for dinner.
He told us that Speer was going to be arrested the next day and suggested we
should get everything we could out of him that night about Hitler in the
Bunker, and Hitler's will." ("I got a nice bottle of whiskey," Ball said, "and
we talked till 4 a.m.")

"Speer talked for hours then, about Hitler and all those around him, all
of whom he appeared to despise," Nitze went on. "Well, another of my favorites on our team was a very bright captain, Burt Klein. Was he Jewish? I
don't know; he may well have been. Anyway, he listened as we did for
hours, and then he suddenly said, 'Mr. Speer, I don't understand you. You
are telling us that you knew years ago that the war was lost for Germany.
For years, you say, you have been watching the horrible in-play among
these gangsters who surrounded Hitler—and surrounded you. Their personal ambitions were those of hyenas, their methods those of murderers,
their morals those of the gutter. You knew all this. And yet you stayed, not
only stayed but worked, planned with and supported them to the hilt. How
can you explain it? How can you justify it? How can you stand living with
yourself?'

"And Speer was silent for quite a while. And then he said, 'You cannot understand. You simply cannot understand what it is to live in a dictatorship;
you can't understand the game of danger, but above all you cannot understand the fear on which the whole thing is based. Nor, I suppose, have you
any concept of the charisma of a man such as Hitler.'

"Well," said Nitze, "Burt Klein just got up and left the room. I . . . Well, by
then I had served under two honest men—the most honest men I have
known: Roosevelt and Truman. And in a way, Speer was right; at that point, I
certainly didn't understand the effect that kind of environment could have.
Then I didn't understand . . . ," he added, and stopped.

Manfred von Poser, not surprisingly, had a different but, one might think,
not uninformed view of Speer's goals. "Speer had two very strong beliefs
which, now adopted worldwide, were then not only way ahead of their time
but dangerous to hold. On the one hand he believed in a maximum of individual initiative; he called it 'industrial self-responsibility,' but what it really
was, or what he envisaged it becoming in peacetime, was the separation of

industry—all industry, not only technical—from the state, i.e., a minimum
of state intervention and thus of state power.* And the second thing he believed in, and at considerable risk to himself had begun to put into practice as
far back as the early autumn of 1943 with the progressive French Minister of
Production, Bichelonne, was a European Community. It was in this sense he
wanted to talk to the Allies. He was certain that the only way toward a better
and peaceful future, not only for Germany but for all of Europe, was if Germany could eventually be part of an economic European entity. And he
thought that not only German but European interests could be served if the
Allies could be persuaded to leave the industrial organization of Germany as
he had so successfully set it up."

Annemarie Kempf hadn't attended that dinner with Murphy and the
USSBS, but she had taken down all the previous interrogations. "Every day,
after the Americans left," she told me, "he would sit there for a long time and
think. I would go next door to transcribe my shorthand notes, and when I
came back, quite often two or even more hours later, he would be sitting in
exactly the same position, still thinking. Years before, when I first came to
work for him, this capacity for intensive thinking had fascinated me. Since
then I have met and worked with many remarkable people from many walks
of life. But I have never again known anyone with a comparable capacity for
concentration.

"Of course, these conversations were very intense, very tiring, I think for
all the participants. And yet Speer was curiously relaxed even then. He had
not an ounce of servility in him, nor were they the kind of people who expected or, I suspect, would have respected it. He was very impressed by these
Americans, and so, frankly, was I. They were so totally different from anything I—or, I think, Speer—had imagined. I think neither of us would have
expected them to be such serious people, men of such substance."

"I felt a great sense of affinity with them," Speer told me. "My mind felt
closer to them than it would feel to anyone afterwards for years, and I felt a
terrible sense of regret, of loss, that in Germany I had known no one of this
quality—that there had not *been* anyone of this intellectual stature in the
world I inhabited all those years."

"In a way," Annemarie said, "this closeness he felt to those Americans
made the shock worse for him when it so dramatically ended, the morning
after that convivial evening with Murphy and the others."

Speer had managed to visit his family twice more during those last two

*Interestingly, one of the first clippings Speer sent me after we began corresponding in 1977 was a long
article from the *Frankfurter Allgemeine Zeitung* on the economic theories of Ludwig von Mises, one of
the founders of the Austrian—or Libertarian—School of Economics, who, as it happened, though Speer
didn't know this until much later, had been married to my mother from 1938 until he died in 1973.

weeks; it would be eight years before he would see any of the children again. But by the time Speer told me the story of his arrest, the morning after we had gone for our hike in the snow, he remembered it—or chose to remember it—more as farce.

"There was a little cloakroom off the downstairs hall in Glücksburg," he said, "and, in order not to occupy the bathroom several of us shared for too long in the mornings, I had got into the habit of getting up before everybody else, having my bath and then using the cloakroom to shave. ["He had always made quite a production of shaving," Margret told me later. "He uses his long bath to ponder, and while he shaves he sings, or hums."] It was probably because I was concentrating on my shave that I didn't hear the commotion outside."

It would appear that the British, very early that morning, had sent a unit of soldiers with antitank guns to surround Glücksburg and make the arrest. When they went to Speer's bedroom, he was not only not there but it looked to them as if he had rapidly departed, leaving wardrobe and drawers open and his pajamas on the floor. "I used to drop them on the floor when I wanted to remind myself to put them in the laundry," he explained. Orders were given to search the castle. "Everybody else was still in bed," he said, "and I'm afraid that included the luckless Mecklenburg-Holsteins, who had been kind hosts to me and were now very rudely awakened."

Speer thought it must have been a little while before sounds of heavy steps and orders in English did finally pierce the thick walls and paneled door of the little cloakroom. "My face was still covered with shaving cream," he said, "when I opened the door a little crack to see what was going on, and found myself confronted by about six astonished-looking men in British uniforms standing in a huddle four feet away. A sergeant—one of those extraordinary British sergeants, you know, who march up to you very loudly in parade step but then turn out to be extremely polite—said, 'Are you Albert Speer, sir?' and I said in my school English that, yes, I was Speer. Upon which, to my amazement, me with my bare torso and soapy face, he stood at attention and said, 'Sir, you are my prisoner.' After that, they became pretty casual, let me go up and pack an overnight case and talk to my people, who had of course rushed to my bedroom. Somebody—Annemarie or Maguira—even appeared with coffee, bread and Mecklenburg homemade jam. It was so silly; that's what I kept thinking about later—the coffee was too hot to drink, and I couldn't manage any of that good jam standing up."

In Flensburg, reunited with all the other members of the Dönitz government, they were subjected to what he referred to, very briefly, as a humiliating physical examination. "They were looking for poison capsules," he said, explaining it to me. He then made a few jocular remarks about the outrage of

his former ministerial colleagues at this "undignified treatment" but re-
frained from describing his own feelings. Except in the rarest instances, or
about illnesses, it was never possible to talk with Speer about physical matters; in that area, he was the most private of men.

As he told his story, I was intensely aware of where this arrest would lead
and what the next months in his life would uncover, and I began to wonder
how much, at this moment and in the weeks to come, he remembered, for
instance, about Dora (Jean Michel: ". . . no heat, no ventilation, not the smallest pail to wash in: death touched us with the cold, the sensation of choking,
the filth that impregnated us. . . . The latrines were barrels cut in half with
planks laid across . . . the SS guards' favorite joke . . . to watch the slaves sit on
the plank . . . and push them into the barrel. . . . They laughed and laughed
when we tried to get up and out of the shit. . . ." And then Speer had told me, "I
walked past these men and tried to meet their eyes. They wouldn't look at me.
. . . They stood at attention until we passed"). Sixty thousand were deported to
Dora, thirty thousand of whom died. Did he know that day in Flensburg that
this was what it would be all about for him? Did he realize that day or during
the next weeks that there *were* men and women who had somehow survived,
and that they would be heard against him?

Interestingly, in the "Spandau draft" he entirely ignored his arrest and the
details about his first interrogations; nor did he write about this period in his
subsequent thousands of letters to Wolters, his *Späne* (slivers, or wood shavings) or, of course, in his third series of correspondence, the Spanish-Illustrated, his hundreds of gently funny letters to the children.

Once again, I had not known about this omission at the time we talked,
and thus had no reason to question him about the reason for it. All I knew at
that time was what he had said in *Inside the Third Reich,* where he devoted six
rather self-consciously humorous pages to his four months of incarceration
before he learned that he would be one of the twenty-one principal defendants at the Nuremberg trial.

Annemarie Kempf and Theo Hupfauer to some extent shared these
months with Speer and reconstructed them for me. "I didn't see him for
about six weeks then," Annemarie said. "After Speer had been taken away,
some British soldiers came for Edith and me too. But then Speer's Americans
said they would need us, so the British released us. We went back to our trailers on Lake Eutin for a while; I borrowed a bicycle and went to see Frau
Speer, about seventy kilometers away, to tell her what had happened. She
took it calmly—I have rarely seen her be anything but cool. Cliever had
become ill and was in hospital, so almost as soon as I got back, I borrowed a
boat and rowed down the river Schlei to get to him. But I got a horrible sun-
stroke and was quite ill myself for a while. Finally—I think it was around the

last week of June—some Americans came and said that Speer needed us in Kransberg and could we also bring the clothes he'd left at Glücksburg."

Hupfauer meanwhile had avoided arrest for a while by the comparatively simple method of creating for himself and his friend Colonel Rommel—a nephew of the general—what he described as "ridiculously primitive false papers purporting to have been given to us by the U.S. occupation authorities." He and and young Rommel had slowly made their way south toward Sonthofen. "I was desperate to get closer to my family."

Hupfauer and his wife still sounded indignant when they told me what had happened there. "My wife had been thrown out of our house [the director's residence of the SS elite college]," Hupfauer said. "It was taken over by the French area commander, and my family had found refuge in a villa belonging to a general we knew."

"All we were allowed to take," said his wife, "was one suitcase each and a few broken-down things from the cellar. We had *nothing*."

"Well, when I had flown down from Berlin in mid-April," he corrected her, "I did bring you all the money we had in the bank."

"Yes—" she guffawed, "RM 25,000; what was that? And then, of course, we didn't know whether we wouldn't be taken by the Russians. Do you remember what I said, last thing, when you left?" He shook his head. "I said that if the Russians took us, I'd take poison and give the children poison too."

"Yes, yes," he said, looking long-suffering.

Hupfauer and his friend landed jobs as farmhands near Sonthofen. "We looked after the cows—well, actually I looked after the oxen."

Ironically, he was finally given away by his toddler son, Helmuth. While his mother was getting their bread ration in the local bakery, he happily announced in his baby language that *"Meins Vati ist da"* (My daddy is here). Twenty-four hours later, two Americans came to the farm. " 'You are Hupfauer,' they said, and that was that," he said.

Oddly enough, the Allies never quite realized his comparative importance, and although he would wander from one detention camp to another for months, finally ending up in Nuremberg, he was never held as a defendant, but only as a witness.

The most traumatic moment of his imprisonment, he said, was when, by mere chance in that first week, he briefly ended up in the prison of the very village where he had been in boarding school in 1917, when he was eleven. "Our school shared a wall with the local prison," he said, "and one day on our daily walk, we saw a knotted sheet hanging out of the window of a cell and heard with immense excitement that a prisoner had managed to escape that night. We had no idea what he was in prison for, but I remember how all of us hoped they wouldn't catch him. And then, would you believe it," he said, "they put me not only in that prison, but in that very cell.

"I reached my lowest point there. It brought back my whole life; my childhood, our delight at the man's escape . . . the capacity for joy and passion one had then . . . and now, here I was. And then, almost as soon as I sat down on the iron cot, a hand grenade exploded right outside my window. I suppose it was ridiculous, but I was sure it was meant for me: that they were trying to kill me. Actually it was a drunk American soldier playing silly games, nothing to do with me at all, but for me it was a kind of nadir, the only point in my life, I think, where I actually considered making an end of it."

Suicide?

"Yes, in a way; perhaps not in so many words, but yes, it was somewhere on the edge of my mind. Was this to be the end, or did I have the energy, the strength, the courage for a new beginning? Then I made myself think about my wife and the children. . . ."

Speer found those first weeks of imprisonment deeply depressing, even though he was neither alone nor badly treated. The "Dönitz government" group was first flown to Luxembourg, to the Palace Hotel in Mondorf, where they were reunited with the rest of the leadership of the Third Reich. Göring and Dönitz engaged in an extraordinary precedence battle, which was only resolved by avoiding having them arrive in a room at the same time, and by having them preside at different tables during meals. "I had a moment's pleasure when I found my friend Brandt there," Speer said. But Brandt, walking with him in the hotel park, told him that when the Americans found out what he had been involved with, "it'll all be over for me anyway."

"I don't think a death penalty was in anybody's mind then," Speer went on, "or, now that I remember Brandt's voice, *did* he perhaps think of it? I remember very clearly that although until quite late I had always had a weak spot for Göring, this changed in Mondorf. He was really quite revoltingly self-pitying and arrogant. One day at lunch, Brandt was talking about the mountains and about how sad he was to have lost their house there.

" 'Oh, come on,' said Göring. 'What possible reason can you have to complain when you had so little. But I, who had so much, think what it means to *me*.' I was sitting back to back with Dönitz, and I heard him murmur to his neighbor, 'Yes, and all stolen.' He was of course right—and that was the leadership of our Reich!"

After two weeks, Speer was told he was being transferred. "Somehow everybody thought I was being released, and this created an extraordinary atmosphere of optimism," he said. " 'There you are,' Göring said when he saw the limousine waiting for me in the driveway. 'I always knew they wouldn't be able to manage without us.' "

Speer's transfer to Versailles, where Eisenhower had established his head-quarters at the Trianon Palace Hotel (where Speer had stayed in 1937 when he was designing the German pavilion for the Paris World's Fair), was merely for further debriefing, though in marginally less luxurious circumstances. At the small palace of Chesnay, where he was given a minute back room on the third floor with an army cot, a chair and a narrow window covered with barbed wire, he found most of the technicians and scientists who had worked for him. "I was there for days rather than weeks," Speer said, "and nobody bothered me. Even so, it was somehow terribly claustrophobic. What saved my sanity there was when the British commandant took me out for a drive. It was strange, you know: twice, in those initial imprisonments, it was English-men who came to my help. This parachute major—I don't remember his name—drove me to Paris; we went through St. Germain and Bougival, where in years past I had often dined at the wonderful Coq Hardi with French artists—Vlaminck, Alfred Cortot [the pianist] and others—and then we walked along the *quais* in Paris and looked at the stalls. I was horribly sad, but I bought a print like any tourist and—so silly—it made me feel human."

A few days later, when Eisenhower moved his headquarters to Frankfurt, Speer and the technicians were moved too, this time in open trucks with wooden benches. After a night in Mannheim prison they reached Kransberg Castle—the very place Speer had reconditioned in 1939 as Göring's head-quarters. "I had added a two-story wing then for Göring's large staff of ser-vants," he said. All the technicians and scientists he had already seen in France, as well as other Germans who might have information on technical aspects of the war—rocket experts including Wernher von Braun, financiers such as Hjalmar Schacht, and designer-engineers such as Ernst Heinkel and Ferdinand Porsche—were brought here now, and lodged in that servants' wing.

"Porsche, that's who I shared a room with when I arrived," said Hupfauer. "Speer of course had a room on his own. But we were pretty free there and very well treated. We had the same food as the Americans; we could visit each other and go for walks in the park. Most of us—everybody really, except Speer—spent most of the days together. I started a sports group right away, gymnastics in the morning. Everybody came to that except Speer—and games in the afternoon. In the evening we had music. Speer isolated himself. All of us were allowed to have our secretaries there to get documentation to-gether; mine came too. But until Annemarie Kempf arrived, Speer saw no-body; after she came, he only saw her.

"I asked him once, 'Why? Why don't you join us?' And you know what he said? He said, 'I'm preparing myself for twenty years.' I remember saying, 'Go on—either they'll shoot us or let us go.' But he shook his head. I've thought about it often since. How did he guess? How just that figure twenty? Anyway, he remained aloof and alone. . . ."

Hupfauer didn't feel any beginning of remorse in Speer in Kransberg. "No, not really," he said. "We all knew that a trial was approaching, though the name Nuremberg had never been mentioned; and given that all the prisoners in Kransberg were technicians rather than politicians, I think we all thought in terms of being required as witnesses, not as defendants."

He hadn't thought of himself as a politician. "Why should I?" he said, sounding surprised at the idea. "I was a labor expert."

And Sonthofen? I asked. Was his appointment there as a labor expert?

"No," he said coldly, "as a figurehead."

"When Edith and I got to Kransberg," Annemarie recalled, "we really found ourselves almost entirely among friends. Everybody was there: Hettlage, Frank, Nagel, Hupfauer, Wernher von Braun; the directors of IG Farben, Thyssen, Krupp; the whole staff of the Berlin Geological Institute.* The women were lodged in double rooms in the tower. The men were in the annex, but we walked together in the little park, sat in the sun, ate together. Very good food and lots of it. We really were much better off than people outside."

But Speer, she said, had changed since Glücksburg. "He seemed very low when I arrived. I think one of the problems was that nothing much happened. They had brought an enormous amount of documentation, mostly from Berlin, but nobody did much or asked many questions. If you ask me what the difference was between him and all the others there, I can tell you two things. One, that all of the others basically felt it was unjust for them to be there; none of them—please believe me—*none* of them felt they had done anything wrong, or even that they had been *involved* in anything wrong. And thus, secondly, none of them felt any responsibility, or guilt.

"Speer didn't think he was there unjustly. And though Hupfauer is perhaps right when he says he didn't notice 'remorse' in him, this feeling of 'responsibility' I mentioned earlier became much stronger in him during these months at Kransberg. I am quite sure that by the time we learned he was to stand trial at Nuremberg, his mind was made up—not to plead guilty but formally to accept responsibility."

Annemarie didn't see that as a tactic or a strategy. "I know that's what his critics said later, but I don't think so. It was a moral imperative for him. It was from the start his lifeline, not to physical but to moral survival.

"Anyway, quite soon after I came, we began to work. He first dictated a long paper on the 'scorched earth'; then a very bright captain—I'm not sure

---

*Werner Heisenberg and the atom scientists were by then in England, segregated together—and carefully bugged—at Farm Hall.

whether he was American or British—asked him to write a paper on how he saw the future development of Germany within Europe. After that they asked him for an evaluation of all the personnel at the Ministry; that was actually in interrogations, but I took everything down and transcribed it. And then, of course finally, this British Intelligence officer came with whom he got on particularly well."

In 1978 Speer gave me copies of the two papers he was asked to write, and told me about his conversations with Captain Hoeffding, of British Army Intelligence. "He was a particularly intelligent and sensitive young man," Speer said. "He told me that 'they'—I presumed he meant the Dustbin authorities—had noticed how depressed I was and that, because they would need information from me for a long time, they were particularly interested in helping me keep up my morale. Captain Hoeffding said he thought my paper on Germany's future was interesting but rather discursive." He laughed. "He was quite right of course; you'll see when you read it. What was interesting to me, though, was that he understood the reason. He said they had asked me to write my thoughts about the future because they thought that would take my mind off the past. But what in fact happened in that paper was that I kept coming back to the past. And so he had decided that perhaps it would be better to use my own need to think or talk about the past to produce something useful. . . ."

(Speer did *not* tell me about the eight-page evaluation of his own ministry personnel that he did for his interrogators; I found that later in the U.S. National Archives. I asked Annemarie then how she thought the ministry people at Kransberg would have reacted, had they known that their former Minister was providing that kind of information for the victors.

"I think they would have been very upset," she said, "even though, as you will have noticed, he said virtually nothing negative, except of course about Saur and Dorsch." He evaluated Dorsch as a "reprehensible character, ruthless," and Saur as "too ambitious and not realist, but good in secondary or tertiary positions. Very diligent and extraordinary memory for figures.")

"When Captain Hoeffding suggested the profiles about Hitler's men," Speer continued, "he said that instead of asking me to do it on my own like the other paper, he would stay with me and help me along with questions. I worked on that from the beginning of July until almost the end of September. I found that extremely interesting to do, particularly because it required me to think about people's inner makeup rather than their more obvious external motives. It was a challenge for me. I enjoyed it and when I finished I felt better than I had felt in months."

A few days later he was told he would be charged with war crimes. Two weeks after that he was taken to Nuremberg.

XXII

A Common Responsibility

Nuremberg, November 21, 1945

LORD LAWRENCE (President of the court): I will now call upon the defendants to plead guilty or not guilty to the charges against them. They will proceed in turn to a point in the dock opposite the microphone. Hermann Wilhelm Göring.

GÖRING: Before I answer the question of the Tribunal whether or not I am guilty. . . .

LAWRENCE: I informed the court that the defendants were not entitled to make a statement. You must plead guilty or not guilty.

GÖRING: I declare myself in the sense of the indictment not guilty.

LAWRENCE: Rudolf Hess.

HESS: No.

LAWRENCE: That will be entered as a plea of not guilty. [Laughter.] If there is any disturbance in court, those who make it will have to leave the court. Joachim von Ribbentrop.

RIBBENTROP: I declare myself in the sense of the indictment not guilty. . . .

LAWRENCE: Albert Speer.

SPEER: Not guilty.

WHEN THE IDEA of an International War Crimes trial was first proposed to Churchill, he and his Foreign Secretary, Anthony Eden, vehemently opposed it; they favored summary execution for the principal Nazi leaders, and national tribunals to try those accused of violating lesser laws of war. That would have been a tragedy, and whatever our thoughts on the Nuremberg experiment, we must be thankful that it was decided on in preference to that other solution.

There are many excellent books and papers about the trial and every one of their authors has written at length about the more obvious drawbacks. So I will merely mention them in passing, and only in order to lend greater clarity to the proceedings as far as they concerned Speer.

There were two fundamental problems with the planning of Nuremberg. One, that in spite of the efforts to achieve judicial objectivity, it obviously *was* a trial of the vanquished by the victors. One alternative, a permanent War Crime Court as part of the International Court at The Hague, which rather than being set up for the sole purpose of trying the Nazi criminals would deal with *all* war crimes, whoever committed them, was barely considered. This was by no means only because one of the nations that would inevitably sit in judgment over the Germans was the Soviet Union, which had committed many of the same crimes, or because none of the nations involved, mindful of the future, dared to support such an unequivocal concept.

The main reason was that Hitler, perhaps more than any other politician or statesman in history, having deliberately and in full awareness offended against every conceivable rule of war and morality, had drawn upon himself the passionate loathing of most of the world.

The second problem was that in view of the huge scope of the undertaking—subjecting what was basically a whole political system to trial by law, the number of potential accused and witnesses, the extent of essential documentation, the security the trial would require and the costs it would incur and finally the fact that very few United Nations member states could be considered neutral—any solution but the one that was found must have seemed impracticable.

What had originally provoked the demand for a trial was the crimes against human beings the Nazis committed in their extermination, concentration and labor camps in Germany and occupied Europe. But although a number of declarations promised retribution (the St. James Declaration of 1942, the Moscow Declaration of 1943 and the Yalta Declaration of 1945), none of these were at all specific. Neither America nor Britain wanted to provoke Germany into reprisals against the many Allied POWs in German hands, and neither Britain nor America readily believed the tales of horror emerging from Eastern Europe, mainly from Jewish sources. The real preparation for the trial would only begin when the Allies were firmly re-established on European soil, but even then it took countless transatlantic conferences before a legal format was established. Already, deep rifts had become apparent among the four Allies in cultural and legal concepts which would bedevil the trial to the very end.

The eventual agreement, arrived at only reluctantly and with many hiccups, was to conduct the proceedings on the basis of four counts which far exceeded the original intention. (The first two were to remain for many people both logically and legally questionable.) The four counts were

COUNT ONE: "The common plan or conspiracy" to accomplish the planning . . . or waging a war of aggression, or a war in violation of international treaties, agreements or assurances.

COUNT TWO: "Crimes against peace"—the planning, preparing, initiating or waging of a war of aggression, or a war in violation of international treaties. . . .

COUNT THREE: "War crimes"—violations of the laws or customs of war, to include . . . murder, ill-treatment or deportation to slave labor or for any other purpose of civilian populations . . . prisoners of war . . . persons on the seas, killing of hostages, plunder . . . wanton destruction . . . or devastation not justified by military necessity.

COUNT FOUR: "Crimes against humanity"—namely murder, extermination, enslavement, deportation and other inhumane acts committed against any civilian population, before or during the war . . . or persecutions on political, racial or religious grounds . . . in connection with any crime within the jurisdiction of the Tribunal. . . .

Administratively and financially, the United States carried the major burden of the proceedings, and this, while inevitable, created immense psychological problems.

The principal problem, though unavoidable, was the participation of the Soviet Union. Brutally occupied by the Germans, with hundreds of thousands of its people horribly abused, the country had suffered more than any other participant in this war—twenty million Soviet men and women had died, an almost unimaginable figure. But the relationship between the Soviets and the United States was teetering on the edge of a volcano; the cold war that was soon to begin threw its shadow upon it from the start. (Churchill's "Iron Curtain" speech in Fulton, Missouri, was made in March 1946.)

France was in an ambivalent position because the government of Pétain and Laval had avidly collaborated with the Nazis, especially in the murder of the Jews. Nonetheless, France too had suffered a long and painful occupation, and tens of thousands of young Frenchmen had been deported for labor in Germany.

Britain, one might say, was Europe's beacon of integrity at the end of the war. She had carried the war alone for a year, had provided refuge to those who fled the German occupation, had supported for four years all those in Europe who fought the Nazis "underground" and, while under continuous and horribly effective bombardment herself, led the air attacks against Germany which were decisive in the eventual winning of the war. With her forces engaged in the liberation of Europe and the Far East, and host to hundreds of thousands of American soldiers, Britain had been the launching pad for the invasion.

By the end of it all she was nearly ruined; it cost her half a million dead or missing and led to the end of her empire. At Nuremberg, furthermore, Britain represented not only herself and her empire, but all those countries to whose governments in exile she gave hospitality during the war, all of which were martyred by the Nazis and none of whom had a direct say in the proceedings at Nuremberg.

By comparison to all these nations who had been so grievously hurt by the Nazis, America—both needed and resented by the others—was whole, healthy and rich. She was also, however, peculiarly deficient in any real knowledge about Europe. While the British assigned university graduates in history, law and economics to postwar research and examinations of Nazis in Germany, the Americans entrusted many of their investigations to eager but comparatively untrained German refugees, whose approach and methods tended to irritate the other Allies.

Speer was intensely aware of all these underlying currents, and by the end of the trial, although not at all sure that he would, could or even should stay alive, he would make use of all of them to help him survive.

Hans Flächsner, born in Berlin in the first year of the twentieth century, was forty-five years old when an American—"Like me, born in Berlin," he said—came to see him in August 1945. "He asked me whether I would be willing to serve as a defense lawyer in the Nuremberg trials which were being prepared. I think they tried first to pick only candidates who hadn't been in the [Nazi] party. I was an arch-liberal, very unsuitable for the Nazis, so it was all right in my case; but on the whole they had to give up on that one. Finally quite a few of the defense lawyers had been in the party."

Flächsner was an exceptionally modest and humorous man. I always saw him in his law office, in a large Berlin firm with impressive premises and many wealthy clients. Although well past retirement age, he still handled important cases. In 1945 he had had a one-man practice, and had not immediately agreed to accept the Nuremberg call.

Oddly enough, many years before, Flächsner had briefly been Göring's lawyer. "That was when I was about twenty-four," he said. "I think he picked me out of a hat." Göring had been wounded in the Munich Putsch on November 9, 1923. "He had thirteen bullet wounds," Flächsner said. "Comrades shot him full of morphine and smuggled him into Austria because in Germany he would have been arrested; that's what started his drug dependence. He went through three withdrawal cures after that. None of them worked. That's when I represented him, in three court suits for nonpayment of fees. True to form already then, he felt he shouldn't be asked to pay if the cures didn't work.

"Nuremberg wasn't something one could just decide to do without talking to one's family and one's friends," he said. "Professionally, of course, it was bound to be uniquely fascinating, but socially, well"—he smiled—"no single little lawyer could easily afford to be an island. The risk of alienating everybody one knew was very real. However, when the same man came again at the end of September, I did say yes. It was finally irresistible. But although I asked him, he didn't tell me which one I would represent.

"Then, on November 1, three Americans came—one colonel and two men from the U.S. Department of Justice—and they took me on a plane to Nuremberg and on arrival took me to breakfast at the Grand Hotel. That was fantastic," he said. During the hard first postwar months, Flächsner's weight had gone down to 109 pounds. "It was a lifesaver for me," he said. "I was hungry! After breakfast they took me to the court. I was very impressed. The Secretary of the Court, Colonel Williams [sic: Harold B. Willey], was a very warm man. I was to find that there were a lot of Americans like that—they were extraordinarily, well, nice, even lovable; it was an immensely pleasant discovery for me. They offered me the choice of Speer, Kaltenbrunner or Hess. I said, 'Only Speer.' "

When Flächsner arrived in Nuremberg, Speer had been in the prison there for a full month. "The first week was bad," he told me. "Later I read a good deal of prison literature and learned that all prisoners appear to feel this."

During that first week Speer was left strictly alone in a dark ground-floor cell whose only furniture was a straw pallet on the floor with three blankets—dirty ones, he said. It was across from Göring's cell. "When they opened the peepholes in our doors, which they did several times an hour, I could see him pace up and down," Speer told me. Otherwise he saw no one except the mess attendants, who brought a tray of food three times a day, and a German barber who, in total silence, shaved him after breakfast in the presence of a GI guard. He was allowed neither newspapers nor books. "Anyway, the one ceiling bulb would not have been strong enough to read by," he said; the light came on at 6 a.m. and was turned off at 8:30 a.m., "even though virtually no daylight came through the small barred window." It was turned on again at 6 p.m. and off for the night at 8 p.m.

(When I asked him, about ten days into our first three-week conversation, whether this regime had had the effect of reminding him of the slave laborers' suffering in the Krupp camps or in Dora, he looked nonplussed. "No," he said, slowly, he had never drawn such an analogy, and then he looked at me for quite a long time without saying anything. "You are quite dangerous," he said then.

I said that I wasn't trying to trick him. "No, I don't think you are," he said, "but you are asking me 'no win' questions, aren't you? Did you think that it *had* made me think of the slave laborers?"

I said, frankly, no, that I didn't think it would ever have occurred to him.

"Why not?" he asked.

"Because even in the worst circumstances," I replied, "you wouldn't have thought of yourself on the same or a similar plane."

He was again silent for a long time. "That is terrible," he finally said. "And more terrible still, it is true—or at least, it was true then. I can only hope it is no longer true.")

After that first week, he was moved into a cell on the fourth floor which had a clean cot, table and chair and, most important, a window, the small upper pane of which he could open. "The first day I was there," he said, "it was sunny outside; I took a blanket off the bed and spread it on the floor and lay in the sun. I was so happy, I can't tell you—so happy."

Over the next two weeks, he went through six interrogations by members of the Allied prosecution staff; he said he found the American Deputy Prosecutor Thomas Dodd the most aggressive. (Dodd's presentation of the case against Speer on December 11 would confirm the strong antipathy Speer had sensed in him.) He found the Soviets surprisingly polite, an impression he would have reason to modify when on June 21, 1946, he was sharply cross-examined by the Deputy Prosecutor for the USSR, M. Y. Raginsky.

By the time he and Flächsner met, he had known the charges against him for about two weeks. On October 19, Major Airey Neave had come to his cell, as well as those of all the other accused, to serve him with the indictment.

Neave, twenty-nine years old in 1945, had arrived on the British War

Crimes Executive via an Oxford degree in international law, a fluent knowledge of German and five years in British Intelligence. He was, as Rebecca
West would describe him, a very special man with "that special quality the
Romans call 'pietas.' " Thousands of people in Britain were devastated when,
in March 1979, then Member of Parliament for Abingdon, he was assas-
sinated by the IRA. It was less than a year after he published his famous book,
Nuremberg.

By the time Speer's cell was thrown open that October afternoon, Major
Neave, accompanied by Harold B. Willey, General Secretary of the Tribunal,
and Colonel Burton C. Andrus, governor of the prison, had already delivered
what Willey referred to lightly as "the bundle" to twelve of the defendants.
Neave, however, did not view lightly his assignment of serving these men
with what the American judges, Francis Biddle and his deputy judge, John
Parker, had described to him the day before as the "most important legal
document in the history of mankind." By the time he met the defendants, he
knew a lot about them and would study them and their reactions as though
he were a scientist looking through a microscope.

Neave was peculiarly well qualified for his assignment. He had had a very
special war, which included a number of painful encounters with the Gestapo when he was caught during an intelligence mission in Poland, a fairly
spectacular escape from the tough, elite POW camp Colditz and then three
years of training people of many nationalities for intelligence work in German-occupied Europe. Since the beginning of his posting to the British War
Crimes Executive, he had been in charge of gathering evidence against Gustav Krupp and his son Alfred who, at the Krupp factories and workshops in
Essen and Silesia, had employed about seventy thousand slave workers, many
of them women, under the most brutal conditions. Part of his research involved the evidence against the "architect of the Nazis' mass enslavement,
Albert Speer," as he put it in his book, which appeared to demonstrate that
under Speer's aegis 4,795,000 foreign workers had been torn from their
homes and forced to work for Hitler.

He introduced himself in each cell with the same words: "I am Major
Neave, the officer appointed by the International Military Tribunal to serve
upon you a copy of the indictment in which you are named as defendant."
The defendants were then handed a copy of the Charter in German and a list
of forty names of "approved" German lawyers. "I am also asked to explain to
you Article 16 of the Charter of the Tribunal. . . . You have the right to conduct your own defense before the tribunal or to have the assistance of counsel." He told each of them he would come back the next day, to hear his
decision.

It is fair to say that Neave had found every one of the twelve men on whom he served the indictments that afternoon, before he got to Speer, deeply distasteful. And although, as his book showed later, his reaction to Speer would be complex, he had no illusions about him either, especially after studying court proceedings such as the exchange that follows:

> Mr. Justice Jackson, cross-examining Speer on June 21, 1946: "I will read you Document 288 [an affidavit on conditions at Krupp's by Dr. Jäger, who also gave evidence in court]: 'The camp inmates were mostly Jewish women and girls from Hungary and Rumania . . . put to work at Krupp's at the beginning of 1944. The conditions they suffered were beneath all dignity: they were wakened at 5 a.m.; they could not wash, as there was no water; there was no drink or food served in the morning; they marched for three quarters of a hour, barely clothed or shod, in rain or snow to reach their factory. They worked ten to eleven hours from 6 a.m. . . .' I suppose you will say this is an exaggeration?"
>
> Speer answered carefully, ". . . I refuse to evade responsibility. But conditions were not . . . like this. . . . This seems to concern one of the small concentration camps near the factories, which were not open to inspection by the factories. . . . As far as I know . . . labor camps were not guarded by the SS. . . ."

The next document Mr. Justice Jackson turned to, D-313 (USA 901), was the testimony of a Polish camp doctor. "As I understand it," Jackson said, "this was a POW and labor camp for Polish, French and later also Russian POW workers, also serving Krupp at Essen. . . . I admit the distinction [between camps] is a little thin at times:

> "The camp was under the direction of the SS and Gestapo. Every day at least ten people were brought to me whose bodies were covered with bruises from the continual beatings with rubber tubes, steel switches or sticks. They writhed in agony and I had no medicines to help them. . . . The food consisted of a watery soup which was dirty and sandy, and sometimes foul cabbage which stank. The dishes out of which they ate were also used as toilets because they were too tired or too weak to go outside. People died daily of hunger or ill-treatment. . . . There, as well as in a nearby camp for Russian women, beating was the order of the day. The conditions lasted from the very beginning until the day the Americans arrived. . . ."

Speer protested: ". . . I should like to point out that . . . I do not believe that this description is correct, but I cannot speak about these things, since you will not expect me to be intimately acquainted with what happened in the camps of the firm of Krupp." If someone had asked the British Minister for Production, he said, about matters which were legitimately the business of the Minister for Labor, ". . . he would with justification have told you that he had something else to do at the time and no one would have raised a direct accusation against him on that account."

Like many others who would meet or listen to Speer in Nuremberg, Major Neave found himself fascinated by him. In his book he wrote about their first meeting:

> Speer was an impressive figure among the broken-down street politi-cians of the Nazi Party . . . a gifted and compelling man. His appearance was striking, even in his prison clothes. He was tall and dark with a strong, intelligent face and large thoughtful eyes. His manner was [that of] . . . an athletic university professor who had turned to public service. He was, I felt, a man of considerable distinction. . . . That afternoon [when he handed him the indictment], however, I felt repelled by his smoothness—he was, I felt, more beguiling and dangerous than Hitler who had died only six months before in the ruins of Berlin. . . .
>
> They could not have done without Speer. He was the exception . . . the only man in Hitler's entourage who sacrificed neither his will nor his rea-son . . . a man of great talent who did most to enable the Nazi dream to become a reality. . . .
>
> I read him the terms of the Charter of the Tribunal. He looked at me steadily. "There is a common responsibility for such horrible crimes," he said, "even in the authoritarian system."

"I was extremely depressed when I read the indictment," Speer said later. "It suddenly made it all horribly real. What so shook me was that they ap-peared to be charging me, not individually, but collectively it seemed to me, for everything that had been done."

In *Inside the Third Reich*, writing about his first meeting with Flächsner, he says he was immediately favorably impressed by his "friendly eyes, unassum-ing manner," and by his "sensible, unhistrionic attitude," and therefore signed the form accepting him as his counsel at once.

Flächsner remembers this somewhat differently. "He told me right away that he really wanted a former Prussian Minister called Schreiber. I tele-graphed this Schreiber immediately, and it was only when he didn't answer that Speer agreed to my representing him. But already in that first meeting, he told me that he wanted to admit guilt. I told him then and countless times afterwards that it was madness, that it could and probably would cost him his head. But he was adamant. He would shrug and say, 'So be it.' Are you sur-prised I came to admire such a man? He had this extraordinary sense of humor—I must admit, I found that quite exceptional under the depressing circumstances.

"Except for his determination to accept general responsibility, we had really no arguments. 'There is nothing you can say to change my mind,' he said time and again. 'I'm determined that there must never be a Hitler cult again, and whatever I can do to prevent it, I will do.' " He confirmed that Speer really hadn't expected to be charged. "It was an enormous shock to him. He had thought on the contrary that the Allies would use him, and they had happily left him in that belief for months while he gave them what was no doubt highly useful information, much of it against himself."

Flächsner said it was quite a while before he found out that all of Speer's official documents were in the hands of the prosecution, which made the task of defending him "not so easy." In the Kransberg "Exploitation Camp" (as the Allies named it), he said, Speer had taken a great liking to the British. "And so he just gave them his whole personal archive of ministerial records, and they ordered Annemarie Kempf to get them into shape—to organize them. In this sense Nuremberg really wasn't like an ordinary trial, in which anything the prosecution intends to present has to be disclosed to the defense. There were lots of things I never saw. If it hadn't been for Frau Kempf, I wouldn't even have known about the British having all this documentation. They certainly never let on about it."

"Yes, that's what happened in Kransberg," Annemarie confirmed. "Speer sort of fell in love with the British, and so he said they could have anything they wanted. Of course neither he nor we realized that it would all be used against him in the trial—after all, we didn't know he'd be tried, and they certainly didn't tell him. They just said in their offhand way he so admired, 'Oh, thanks very much.' After he was taken away they told Edith and me to get cracking and get it into some sort of order. Edith and I had nowhere to go, and also I knew perfectly well that if I wanted to help Speer, I needed to be within reach of the documents, and this was about as close as I could get. So we did that, and we also helped some other former ministry colleagues in their interrogations."

Officially, Annemarie Kempf and Edith Maguira stayed in Kransberg from June 1945 to December 1946. "We were correctly treated," she said, "and when I asked for travel permits to go and see my sick mother, they gave me a 'To Whom It May Concern' paper asking all Allied authorities to help me to return to Kransberg. That's how I went to Nuremberg."

"I was dumbfounded when she arrived," Flächsner said. "I mean, can you imagine? This beautiful young woman wandering around occupied Germany in order to come to Speer's help?"

"Well, they had DPs [displaced persons] on security duty where the lawyers had their offices in Nuremberg," Annemarie said. "They couldn't speak German or English, so I just showed them my impressive-looking Eisenhower HQ permit and said I was *Presse*—that's how I got in. Flächsner went to Speer right away and brought back a note saying I should help him. So Flächsner showed me a list of documents he would need, and he was in luck because some of them were already among those I had brought along just in case, some pinned to my underclothes, others held around my waist with elastic."

"It was unbelievable what she had brought," said Flächsner. " 'Do you want any of this?' she said. 'I've got lots more. I photocopied everything I gave to them, as a precaution.' God, what a woman! But above all, it brought home to me just *how* deficient we were in documentation. So she and I worked through the indictment and figured out what else we would probably need."

"The next day I went back to Kransberg and got it all together," Annemarie said. "We had found a room for me in Nuremberg with a nice woman, and that's where I stayed every time I went there after that." She laughed. "My poor mother had a *lot* of pretend illnesses over the next weeks; I went to and fro like a yo-yo."

"Of course, I had been told about some of the prosecution testimony," Flächsner said, "and Speer and I discussed these. You know, like those infamous punishment cupboards. Well, I was inclined to believe Speer that they were probably nothing but clothes lockers, but, on the other hand, it seemed obvious that these workers *had* been treated very roughly. But whatever was the truth about them, Speer cannot have known about that. One always thinks a Minister has to know everything, but it just isn't so, in any country."

He and Speer also discussed the statement by a German physician, Dr. Jäger, which was introduced by Jackson in his cross-examination of Speer. "When that was later written about by the media," he said, "they emphasized everything that was horrible, and they suppressed Dr. Jäger's other comments, such as when he said that in his opinion beatings of workers only happened rarely, and that it was not part of the system. He said that the German workers wouldn't have stood for it, and I think he was right. There was a strong tradition of workers' solidarity in Germany, and during the trial many instances were cited where German workers had intervened for foreigners and helped them with food and medicines."

Given the horrifying statistics of death in the labor camps and the sheer weight of the evidence on brutalities, his defense of Speer was very difficult. "I never thought we could get far—or anywhere—by questioning the integrity of the witnesses. Even when their testimony was perhaps overemotional, or somewhat exaggerated, I always felt that most of it was probably basically true and I didn't think it was in Speer's interest to express doubt. The atmosphere in the court did not encourage this. And the fact is that when Speer, under cross-examination by Jackson, tried to do this, he invariably failed to convince, as for example an exchange with Jackson about steel switches. Jackson, rather kindly, I thought, didn't enlarge on what I thought was an absurd reply, but it certainly didn't help Speer."

(On June 21, 1946, Jackson said to Speer during his cross-examination: "I will ask to have you shown Exhibit D-230: It is an inter-office record of the steel switches which have been found in the camp and they will be shown to you. Eighty of them were distributed [in this one Krupp labor camp alone] according to the reports."

SPEER: Shall I comment on this?
JACKSON: If you wish.
SPEER: Yes. Those are nothing but replacements for rubber truncheons. We had no rubber; and for that reason the guards probably had something like this. . . . But they did not immediately use these steel switches, any more than your police use their rubber truncheons. But they had to have something in their hands. It is the same thing all over the world.
JACKSON: Well, we won't argue the point.)

BEFORE THE BEGINNING of the trial, the defendants remained in solitary confinement, their only whispered contact during the half-hour walks around the prison courtyard, one behind the other at a distance of four feet, or during the Sunday church services which all of them (except Hess, Rosenberg and Streicher) attended. During this period of preparation, all the defendants were given a variety of psychological tests.

"I thought they were totally idiotic," Speer said. "Responding to them in the manner they expect presupposes either the subject's desire to cooperate or an obedient nature. Neither applied to me, so I decided to have fun with them and wrote total nonsense—especially the Rorschach test: inkspots indeed." (However, it seems that he was rather irked when he found out that, as a result, the psychologist Dr. Gilbert had rated him twelfth in intelligence among the twenty-one defendants, with an IQ of 128 against Schacht's 143. "Ridiculous!" Speer said, probably quite correctly.)

On October 24, four days after receiving the indictment, Robert Ley killed himself. He made a noose from the stripped edges of his army towel and fastened it to the toilet pipe. Dr. Gilbert and the prison psychiatrist had found him very agitated when they visited him the previous day. "Stand us against a wall and shoot us . . . well and good . . . you are victors," he had cried, his usual stammer intensified by his emotion. "But why should I be brought before a Tribunal like a c—c—c— [criminal]: I can't even get the word out."

Although Colonel Andrus had tried to withhold the manner of the suicide for several days, most of the prisoners, Speer thought, had somehow heard of it by the next day. Speer would say in *Inside the Third Reich* that he too considered suicide, but Flächsner didn't think so. When I asked Speer directly, he denied it. "Well," he added, "one fantasizes about such things, almost an intellectual exercise if you like—yes, I figured out how it *could* be done, but not with the intention of actually doing it."

During the weeks of interrogations, the prisoners had worn army fatigues dyed black. A week before the trial started, court orderlies came with their civilian clothes and took instructions as to what they wanted washed and cleaned. Throughout the trial, they would be issued clean underclothes, shirts, socks and handkerchiefs every day, and every night their suits were taken away for pressing.

On November 19, the day before the opening of the trial, the prisoners, without handcuffs, but with a GI guarding each, were taken to the empty courtroom to be assigned seats. Throughout the trial, MPs in dress uniform, with white helmets and belts, stood behind the defendants.

"I used the opportunity that afternoon to ask him once more to desist from his 'responsibility' plea," said Flächsner. "I said, 'Look where they have seated you. Don't think for a moment that any of this is haphazard; everything is planned, just like when they moved you to a south-facing cell on the fourth floor.* You have noticed, haven't you, that they didn't move Göring?' Speer was in the second row of the dock, number seventeen. 'The only ones on your other side are von Neurath and Fritzsche,' I said, 'both generally considered doubtful cases. Just keep a tight rein on that masochistic streak of yours,' I said, 'and we might be all right.' He just shook his head and patted my arm as if to console me. . . . The first day was nothing," he said. "They just read out the indictment, which all the defendants knew anyway."

"It was the first time we could talk freely to each other," Speer said. "Already it felt quite strange to be in one's own clothes; very strange how it makes one feel a man. But what gave one warmth was shaking hands with people, after all, one's own people. That first day the courtroom was cleared at lunchtime, but we stayed, and they brought us picnic trays."

As of the next day, they were divided up into groups to lunch in four small dining rooms in the Palace of Justice. The order of seating was made by the prison commander, Colonel Andrus, in consultation with the medical officers. For the first weeks Speer would eat alone with propaganda official Hans Fritzsche. "He was young, nice and sensitive," Speer said. "I couldn't think what he was doing there, and I was sure they'd have to acquit him." (They did.)

*Speer's stay on the fourth floor was brief. When the trial proper started, all twenty-one prisoners were moved into first-floor cells.

But two months later, on January 12, Speer warned Dr. Gilbert of the influence Göring was gaining over many of the defendants. "It is not a very good idea, you know, to let the defendants eat and walk together," he told the psychologist. "That is how Göring keeps whipping them into line."

It took over a month before Colonel Andrus finally asked Dr. Gilbert to draw up a new seating plan, separating the defendants into five groups, with Göring in a small room on his own.

Now Speer, Fritzsche, Schirach and Funk ate in what came to be called the Youth Lunchroom. Dr. Gilbert hoped that Speer and Fritzsche would wean the other two away from Göring's influence. The Elders' Lunchroom was for Papen, Neurath, Schacht and Dönitz, all old conservatives who, encouraged by Schacht, it was felt, might come to denounce Hitler.

In the third room, Frank, Seyss-Inquart, Keitel and Sauckel were put together, with the double purpose of removing Keitel from Göring and exposing him to impassioned denunciations of Hitler and confessions of guilt by Frank, who had rejoined the Catholic Church.

Room four was for the intractable Nazis: Raeder, Streicher, Hess and Ribbentrop, who, it was felt, would have neither positive or negative effect on each other. The fifth room was for Jodl, Frick, Kaltenbrunner and Rosenberg, who Dr. Gilbert appeared to think were almost prejudged men. "Raeder and Ribbentrop were disgusted to have been put with Streicher," Dr. Gilbert wrote in his *Nuremberg Diary*, ". . . and Göring was furious to have been isolated. . . ."

For Speer, Jackson's opening statement established the quality of the trial forever more. "It impressed me very deeply," he told me. "Much of what he said was what I had come to feel. It was extraordinary for me to hear my thoughts expressed by this American who, I knew perfectly well, would have a decisive influence on my fate." He was particularly glad that Jackson emphasized the difference between the accused and the German people:

> The privilege of opening the first trial in history for crimes against the peace of the world imposes a grave responsibility. The wrongs which we seek to condemn and punish have been so calculated, so malignant and so devastating, that civilization cannot tolerate their being ignored, because it cannot survive their being repeated. That four great nations, flushed with victory and stung with injury, stay the hand of vengeance and voluntarily submit their captive enemies to the judgment of the law is one of the most significant tributes that power has ever paid to reason. . . .
>
> We must never forget that the record on which we judge these defendants is the record on which history will judge us tomorrow. To pass these defendants a poisoned chalice is to put it to our lips as well. We must

summon such detachment and intellectual integrity to our task that this trial will commend itself to posterity as fulfilling humanity's aspirations to justice. . . .

The defendants are hard pressed, but they are not ill-used. . . . If these men are the first war leaders of a defeated nation to be prosecuted in the name of the law, they are also the first to be given a chance to plead for their lives in the name of the law. . . .

We would also make clear that we have no purpose to incriminate the whole German people. . . . If the German populace had willingly accepted the Nazi program, no storm troopers would have been needed . . . or concentration camps or the Gestapo. . . . The German no less than the non-German world has accounts to settle with these defendants. . . .

[If the law is to serve a useful purpose] it must condemn aggression by any other nations, including those which sit here now in judgment. . . . The real complaining party at your bar is Civilization. In all our countries it is still a struggling and imperfect thing. It does not plead that the United States or any other country has been blameless. . . . But it points to the dreadful sequence of aggressions and crimes I have recited, it points to the weariness of flesh, the exhaustion of resources, and the destruction of all that was beautiful or useful in this world. . . .

Civilization asks whether law is so laggard as to be utterly helpless to deal with crimes of this magnitude, by criminals of this order of importance. It does not expect that you, the Tribunal, can make war impossible. It does expect that your judicial action will put the forms of international law, its precepts, its prohibitions and most of all, its sanctions, on the side of peace, so that men and women of good will, in all countries, may have "leave to live by no man's leave, underneath the law."

Speer was right in feeling that Jackson's address was a moral delineation of the trial, but although almost universally admired and acclaimed, it could not affect the fundamental operational problems or avert their consequences.

The most basic of these was that the organization of the proceedings, and their formal framework, had been worked out largely by the Americans. While the American and British legal systems, if not identical, were certainly similar in their adversarial nature, the European judicial process, to which not only the French and Germans but also the Soviets at least formally subscribed, was—in theory at least—a joint search for truth.

For the Europeans therefore, the verbal battle between prosecution and defense, entirely normal and rather enjoyable to the Anglo-American judiciary, would remain problematic throughout. This applied most of all to the German defense lawyers, many of whom were quite as horrified as the rest of the court when they learned of the crimes which had been committed but who now, instead of being accepted by the prosecutors as colleagues in this search for truth, found themselves at times so closely identified with their clients that they frequently felt like co-accused.

The second considerable problem was that Jackson's idealistic assertion that the same law applied to all, in practice, of course, did no such thing. The Allies had no intention of allowing any documentary evidence whatever to emerge of their own misdeeds. Whenever a defense counsel plucked up his courage to ask for such documentation, it turned out to be "unfindable" or "irrelevant." And there in judgment sat the Soviets, who had invaded Poland and Finland and had maltreated populations in the Baltics, in Poland, in Germany and of course in their own country quite as brutally as the Nazis.*

But the British were also aware that they were treading a fine line when they supported the case against Admiral Raeder, who, under Counts One and Two of the indictment, was accused of having planned the invasion of Norway. The fact that Britain was all set to invade Norway but the Germans beat her to it did not help Raeder, who eventually, although the oldest of the defendants, would be sentenced to life in prison. (He was very ill in 1954, released in 1955 and died in 1960.)

It was quickly evident, Flächsner said, that the defendants were split into two groups, one supporting Göring, the other Speer. "These two men had very clearly assumed the leadership, and they had very different goals," he said.

"Göring wanted all of the accused to present a common front of pleading not guilty, and of denying the competence of the court to try them. His position was that during the Third Reich the laws of the Third Reich applied, and they could not be tried for obeying their own laws.

"Speer felt, and argued very strongly from the moment they were allowed to associate, that a dictatorship readily makes and unmakes its laws, which therefore are no longer moral but political instruments. Because of this, he said, universal law, representing civilized thought, superseded national law. Under the universal law of civilization—which he said richly included pre-Hitler German civilization—they had to consider themselves responsible, and they should stand together in this court as honorable men and say so, loud and clear.

"Frau Kempf was enormously helpful with the files she brought, but docu-

*The Soviets had succeeded in including the massacre of thousands of the Polish elite at Katyn in the indictment, as a *German* war crime, but presented only their own 1944 report as evidence. Several defense lawyers asked to present rebuttal witnesses, and it was agreed (after stormy exchanges) that three witnesses for the defense, and three by the Soviets, would be heard after all individual cases were finished. Circumstantially, it was clear that the Soviets had been responsible for the Katyn massacre, as documents recently released in Russia confirm. But not surprisingly, the Nuremberg court strenuously avoided reaching any decision.

mentation was still our worst problem," Flächsner continued. "We either didn't get prosecution material at all, or late, or they gave us official German documents not in the original text but retranslated from English, often very badly. There were many instances when I saw a document for the first time as the prosecution presented it. The fact that we defense lawyers then had to ask for a delay to allow us first to commission a correct translation, and then to study it, was considered by many of the Allied officials as bad will on our part—never a good thing for one's client."

Beautiful Luise Jodl, daughter and granddaughter of Prussian officers, who had been secretary to the General Staff for ten years and married General Alfred Jodl in March 1945, had managed in October to get herself officially appointed as secretary to her husband's Nuremberg defense team. "In many instances where the prosecution brought up points against Alfred, apparently on the basis of documents they had but we didn't have," she told me in 1985, when we talked in her small, book-filled flat in Munich, "we finally had to depend on Alfred's memory to challenge them.

"For instance, he was accused of having put himself at Hitler's disposal in 1933, when he was a Major General of the OKW [High Command of the Armed Forces], to assist him in his accession to power. In his position close to Hitler, the indictment said, he helped him to gain control over Germany. But this was quite untrue," she said. "He not only didn't know Hitler in 1933; he opposed him." They succeeded eventually in getting the British prosecution to drop this point.

"But there were worse difficulties than that," she continued. In one instance, it was only due to the kindness of a young American GI clerk that she became aware of a British document which showed that some British commandos who had been shot in Norway had worn civilian clothes under German uniforms. As this was prohibited under the international laws of war, it probably, in this particular instance, legitimized their execution. Usually, for this very reason, commandos would wear British uniforms under civilian clothes.

"The young American said I'd better copy the document," Luise Jodl said. "He didn't think I'd see it again otherwise—it was being 'filed.' You know, this young man was Jewish, and many of his relatives were murdered in the camps. Isn't it extraordinary that he, whose family was so desperately hurt by the regime on trial here, reached out to help the wife of an accused in this trial find the truth?"

Ordinarily, of course, the defendants' counsel could not hope for such assistance. Indeed, when Otto Stahmer, the counsel representing Göring, requested official German documents on Polish and Russian atrocities, the

British prosecutor successfully fought the application. "If you are trying to say that these documents would prove that if Germany offended against the laws of war, the others did the same, then in the opinion of the prosecution this is totally irrelevant," he said, and the court agreed.

Nothing that happened in Nuremberg was simple, Flächsner said. "For instance, quite a bit of Göring's attitude stemmed from his jealousy of Speer. I talked often with Göring; it wasn't that difficult. Once the guards were familiar with you, they were pretty accommodating."

Göring too, he said, had been devoted to Hitler. "I think he had been jealous of Speer for years; so many of them were. It really is quite extraordinary if one thinks how much these huge historical events were influenced by such emotions."

The other distinction which Flächsner saw as vitally affecting the proceedings was the differentiation in the court's conduct toward those of the accused who had something directly to do with the concentration camps and those who didn't. "Speer's position here was always ambiguous," he said. "Of course, he was accused of requesting and using forced labor, but I doubt that many people there held him directly responsible for the concentration camps. And there were things he said under cross-examination, or when I myself questioned him, which seemed to me—and I think to many others— very elegant." Thus, Speer very carefully avoided any mention of Milch [the head of the Luftwaffe] that could be construed to his friend's disadvantage; he repeatedly emphasized how much support he had had from Jodl about stopping the "scorched earth" measures. He brought up matters in defense of Hess, of Seyss-Inquart and of Dönitz. "And when it came to Sauckel, he said he was grateful for every worker Sauckel got for him."

"I did think that those were elegant gestures," said Flächsner. "There wasn't anybody else in that court who, so horrendously accused himself, took the risk of defending anyone else."

Luise Jodl was very aware of Speer's generosity in Nuremberg. "I really knew nothing about him until then," she told me. Ever since Nuremberg, her battle has been to dissociate Jodl's name in history from "the politicians and the brutes," people like Himmler, Kaltenbrunner, and Ley, who, she agrees, were criminals. She feels bitter about the fact that some of Jodl's own comrades, who had been good friends, referred negatively to him in their memoirs. "They did it to minimize the extent of their own involvement, their own guilt, of course," she said. "By comparison it was an act of great generosity when Speer, unasked, brought up my husband's help to him. . . ."

After Speer came out of prison, he invited her to come and see them in Heidelberg, and a little later they also met, by chance, in the Tyrol. "He had written me several very nice letters, and I was looking forward to meeting him, and her. But I finally found him very . . . impersonal, really unreachable in a way. Strange, as he could be so warm in letters."

But years later in *The Secret Diaries*, Speer had written that Jodl, under Hitler's influence, had finally betrayed the moral traditions of his calling. "I felt horribly bitter about that," she said. "How could he do that after what he himself said about Jodl in Nuremberg?"

She had had a special arrangement with her husband at Nuremberg: every day, at a precise time, she would stand for a while at a certain spot opposite the prison from where she could see the window of his cell. He was allowed to open up one small part of his high window, though they were forbidden to look out. But he could reach it sufficiently to wave from it with a handkerchief, and that's what he did, every day at that agreed time. And she too waved, rain, snow or sun, from below. She smiled. "Just a few times he disobeyed and somehow climbed up and looked." Jodl had told his lawyer that he couldn't really see her, but he saw the fluttering handkerchief and felt . . . warmed.

"I found out about the time of the executions," she told me, her fine face growing haggard. "I had gone to wave goodbye to him that day and I went back in the night, and just stood there until long after dawn. He knew I was there."

Flächsner said that Speer never talked about his family. "And I didn't bring them up; he didn't seem to want it. The only time I said anything was when he told me that his parents had made a joint will naming him as heir. I told him that this could create problems. His father was very rich; he owned stock in Dortmund Union and Heidelberg Cement. I suggested that the will should instead name Speer's children as his heirs." But he didn't know whether Speer communicated this advice to his father. "Perhaps to Wolters—he relied from the start entirely on Wolters.

"During the trial," Flächsner said, "when his case had started and I would come evenings to talk with him, he would often say, 'Oh, Flächsner, let's forget about the stupid trial—let's talk about other things. Were you ever in the Reich Chancellery?' I told him, yes, I had been there. He said, 'How did you like it?' It was difficult. I wanted to be honest. I said, well, there were very comfortable chairs [Speer had designed them], but that I was sort of surprised to find that only a quarter of the huge doors opened up—somehow it made the person coming in feel particularly small, confined. I said that surprised me, and it taught me that 'man is the measure of all things.' " (He was quoting Plato, who quoted Protagoras.)

"Well, he thought a while and then he said, 'Yes, you are right. Today I wouldn't do it that way.' "

Not for a moment had Flächsner felt that Speer's attitude of remorse was a sham—calculated tactics, as so many people claimed later. ("When he admitted guilt in Nuremberg," Leni Riefenstahl said to me once, "I thought that was very clever—clever as he was.")

"My God, if I think how often we went over this question," Flächsner said. "I wanted him to limit his responsibility to those matters over which he had control, and that did *not* include concentration camps. He had no influence there at all; the SS jealously guarded their rights."

Flächsner said that of course he had talked to Speer about the Jews. "I too, after all, knew in the 1930s that Jews were being badly treated, that they could no longer be judges or lawyers. And believe me, I often thanked God that I wasn't a Jew. I had Jewish friends and tried to help, and sometimes one could help. One knew it was miserable to be a Jew in Hitler's Germany, but one didn't know it was a catastrophe; one didn't know what happened to them. Until a day in 1943, when a client of mine who was a medic in Russia came back with photographs of executions of Jews, I knew absolutely nothing of this. I told him to burn or bury the photographs and to tell no one what he had seen. And I didn't tell anybody either, not even my wife. I know," he added quickly, "that wasn't right; but it was prudent. One wanted to survive—it was most unsafe to have seen such photographs.

"I don't think it was a secret that people were being executed; what we didn't know was that they were being systematically mass-murdered. I used to say to Speer that I couldn't understand why he wanted to take responsibility for things outside his competence. And that's when he said to me, 'If we had won the war, we would have shared in these men's triumphs, and this is why we must now share in the responsibility for the horrors.' That reminded me of myself when I saw those photographs, in 1943," he said. "And then I understood what he meant."

Flächsner was certain that the Ministry of Armaments and Munitions must have been informed about the Wannsee Conference on January 20, 1942, even if they didn't participate. It had never come up at Nuremberg, because Todt's death and Speer's appointment only happened afterwards. Strangely, he said, although the shadow of the extermination of the Jews hovered over the trial from beginning to end, it was not much discussed.

"Before Nuremberg," Flächsner said, "I had never heard the names of Treblinka, Sobibor, Belsec or Majdanek. I never even heard of Auschwitz. I did once vaguely hear of Mauthausen, but not in such a context."

Of course, Mauthausen was not that kind of camp, I said.

"No," he said, "not an extermination camp—it was a KZ." After sitting through a year of Nuremberg he certainly knew the difference between a concentration camp and an extermination camp, even if most Germans and for that matter the rest of the world didn't, or didn't want to admit it. "People on the whole cannot understand or confront that difference," he said. "Testimonies such as those given by that survivor from Treblinka [Samuel Rajzman] or [Rudolf] Höss, the commandant of Auschwitz, seemed so extreme, so intolerable, they confused rather than convinced. You see, they had all these witnesses—all very damaging to Speer—testifying to beatings and starvation in forced-labor and concentration camps. But somehow those horrors were, well, almost expected. One could be horrified and disgusted, but one could deal with them. I have always wondered whether, if they had brought more witnesses about the extermination camps, one could have dealt with gas-chamber murders of women and children. As it was, I don't think people did accept it—one somehow allowed it to pass one by. Did you notice that even Dr. Gilbert in his book barely mentions the gas chambers? As if even he could not bear to pronounce the word. Later, much later [in the 1960s], when the German N.S. [National Socialist] crime trials started, I think I understood."

Thirty-seven years after he had helped save Speer from the gallows, Flächsner was still unsure about what Speer had known about these things: "I asked him. I said, 'Herr Speer, you spent so much time at Führer HQ, so much time with army generals who had been in the East. Surely you don't expect me to believe that nobody there ever talked about these things?' And he answered, 'I know it sounds extraordinary. But you'll have to take it from me. Nobody there ever mentioned such a thing, ever.' "

After saying this, Flächsner leaned back in his chair, thinking quietly. "Even so," he finally said, "in this matter I don't think Speer was entirely open with me. Perhaps it was better that way; perhaps he shouldn't or couldn't have been. If he had told me he knew, what would I have done? Above all, how would I have felt? But I must admit I don't believe that it is possible that he knew nothing. I liked Speer. But I don't think that is possible."

IT WAS A CURIOUS aspect of the trial that while some if not all of the defendants, well supplied with news from the outside during that year, were very aware of the growing tension between the Americans and Soviets, all writers about the trial, many of whom (such as Airey Neave and Telford Taylor) participated in it, agree that within the trial situation relations between the Allies, if not invariably friendly, were certainly cordial. Both Bradley Smith and Taylor emphasize not only the competence but the apparent integrity of the Soviet lawyers. As Bradley Smith put it,

Although the Soviet representatives may have received closer direction than their Western counterparts, they were not radically different in their performance from the other judges. . . . All in all, it is reasonable to conclude that, although there were different degrees of independence granted to the Tribunal members, and although the individual judges made different use of their prerogatives, the defendants faced a court surprisingly free from outside control. . . .

Of all the defendants, though, Speer was the only one whose conduct toward the different prosecutors clearly showed his awareness of the changing political situation. Although this emerged most obviously in his arrogant and aggressive attitude when cross-examined by General Raginsky, the Assistant Prosecutor for the USSR, a more subtle demonstration was the process which on November 15 produced his much-discussed letter to the U.S. Prosecutor Robert Jackson. (Speer mistakenly dated it on the seventeenth, the date which has been used by historians ever since.)

The accusation, not so much against Speer but against Jackson, of "secret agreements" between them before the trial which allegedly "saved Speer's neck," emerged after years of rumors in the pages of a book on Nuremberg by one of Germany's more sensationalist writers on history, Werner Maser (*Nuremberg: A Nation on Trial*, Scribner's, 1979). In his chapter "Limits of Responsibility," Maser suggested that Jackson made his liking for Speer so obvious that observers at the trial suspected secret arrangements between them. Maser wrote,

> And indeed, as Jackson's private papers in his estate have shown and as Speer himself has meanwhile admitted, Jackson and Speer's secret correspondence resulted in an arrangement.

When I found that even Bradley Smith wondered about "that strange missive" (a letter Speer was alleged to have written to Jackson just before the trial opened) which has exercised the mind of every historian who has ever written about Speer or Nuremberg, I asked Speer himself about it.

He said that as soon as Maser's book had appeared, which implied that the author had had sight of Justice Jackson's papers, he had got in touch with Jackson's son. "He assured me that there was nothing in them that could possibly lend itself to the interpretation Maser gave," said Speer. "True, I didn't go to America to check them for myself, but then, as I understand it, nor did Maser."

He gave me the letter he had shown to the German media following Maser's accusation and on which Bradley Smith had already commented in his book. In this letter, Speer expressed his concern that the technical knowledge, which he had made freely available to the American-British intelligence teams who had questioned him prior to Nuremberg, might become available to "third parties," i.e., the USSR. "I gave this information [to the West] from conviction," he ended, "and I would feel despicable if I were forced, by third parties, to give this same information to them. . . ."

Smith saw this as a calculated move to gain Jackson's sympathy. ". . . Is it possible that Speer did not recognize that this approach was perfectly tuned to have such an effect, especially with the rising cold war mentality of a man like Robert Jackson?"

Perhaps—if Speer had on his own initiative addressed himself to Jackson. But this did not happen by Speer's choice. The U.S. National Archives has the records of two meetings between Speer and an American intelligence officer, Major John J. Monigan, which took place at least in part at Speer's request. In the first meeting, on November 2, 1945 (eighteen days before the trial would start, when Speer had not yet met his defense counsel), Monigan told Speer that they had been informed by Major Neave that Speer wished to discuss certain matters. His request, Monigan said, "has been considered by the British and . . . the Americans, and it is our wish that you prepare a statement concerning the matter which you wish to discuss, and we will work out the procedure to follow thereafter."

Speer told Monigan that he wished to discuss further the subjects he had worked through with the intelligence teams in Dustbin, and he particularly asked to speak with a British officer, Colonel Lawrence of the Office of Economic Warfare, who had led those discussions. He explained to Monigan that he had learned, toward the end of his stay at Dustbin, that there was a possibility that he would be handed over to the Russians. As he was in possession of a great deal of information regarding mistakes that had been made in the air war against Germany, which under certain circumstances could become useful in the future, "I think it would be wrong if I were [forced to] disclose . . . this information to anybody except the American authorities. . . ." There were matters he thought he could discuss in open court if asked, but he wished to point out that he had knowledge "which should remain on one side of the fence. I feel it is my duty to say that. I do not want to give the [technical] details here; I would like to state that to Colonel Lawrence. . . ."

"I see," said Major Monigan. "The purpose of talking to Colonel Lawrence would be to consider what information might be disclosed [and] which it might be undesirable to disclose." At the end of the interrogation, Monigan repeated his suggestion that Speer should prepare "a little statement . . . just a broad outline of the information that you have which should be considered by Colonel Lawrence or someone, on whether it should be disclosed."

"Yes," said Speer. "To whom shall I give this?"

"Well," replied Monigan, "if you prepare it and just address it to the Interrogation Office for transmittal, we will see that it gets to the right person." *Then the major added, "You might address it to Mr. Justice Jackson,* and I will see that it gets to the right person" (author's italics).

Two weeks later, on November 15, Monigan saw Speer again, mainly to inform him that he had not received the statement Speer had said he would prepare. Speer said he had written it immediately and handed it in "the very next day."

It was decided that Speer would be taken to his cell to get the copy he had made of the note he had written, and that he would then return to the major's office and recopy it. "I want to give the same statement," he said.

This record from the National Archives clearly demonstrates the falsity of the charges that Speer tried to influence Jackson by "secret agreements" or private correspondence.

The trial began five days later, but it would be seven months until Speer's case would be heard, between June 19 and June 30, 1946. He learned on the morning of June 20 that Jackson himself would cross-examine him. "I was glad," he told me. "I liked him; I thought he was a fair man."

By comparison with Göring, who, proving formidable in his lies and aggressive rejoinders, had infuriated Jackson and almost brought his crossexamination to a standstill, the quiet, civilized Speer with his ready admission of responsibility must have seemed a godsend to the Chief U.S. Prosecutor. It was no doubt the prospect of repairing his badly damaged prosecutorial reputation that prompted him to take on cross-examining Speer, the one defendant virtually everyone considered a controversial case, except the Russians, who were determined to hang him.

Two further points may be made about this alleged and now disproven "secret agreement." The first is that Robert Jackson was known as a "hard" justice, which indeed he showed by his "Opinion on Clemency," written for the War Department on September 26, 1946. This was to determine the outcome of all the appeals resulting from this first Nuremberg trial. "Clemency," he wrote, "is a matter of grace, not of right." Since none of the defendants had "rendered any service whatever to the prosecution," he said, there were no grounds for clemency. This hardly sounds like a man who would have entered into any secret agreements, with Speer or anyone else.

Furthermore, Jackson had always been a declared opponent of plea bargaining. Indeed, at the end of November 1945 he was instrumental in balking an attempt by the American Deputy Prosecutor (and head of the OSS), General William Donovan, to limit Göring's exposure to the court by a process which came very close to plea bargaining. Donovan's long stewardship of the OSS had convinced him of his talents for political mediation, under which the OSS entered into a number of inept if not immoral negotiations with various Nazis toward the end of the war, like those already mentioned with SS General Wolff. Donovan had evidently succeeded in building up something of a relationship with Göring. He proposed, first to Göring and then to Jackson, that Göring sign a questionnaire he had worked out which, while accepting the legitimacy of some of the charges and incriminating some of the other defendants, would essentially protect Göring from any but the most minimal confrontations in open court, where he would only be required to confirm the questionnaire.

After a number of bitter encounters with Donovan, Jackson vetoed the approach entirely, insisting that Göring, like everybody else, had to submit to cross-examination from all prosecutors. Donovan resigned a few days later and went home.

It was ironical that Göring, so grotesque for so many years, managed to make such a strong impression at Nuremberg. "The Americans made a great mistake there," Speer told me in 1978. "I know that judicially, and I suppose morally, they were obligated to get him off drugs, and I don't know what else they could have done. But psychologically, it produced for the world a lasting image of the Göring of twenty years earlier, and it made it impossible for the Tribunal to visualize the ineffectual, gross and corrupt personality this 'successor to Hitler,' this 'second man in the Reich,' had been. When you asked Germans during the war what they thought of Göring, whom they called *'der Fette'*—the fat one—they laughed. If you ask them now, after Nuremberg, you will hear them say, full of admiration, 'Ahhh, Göring!' Göring once said to me in Nuremberg, 'In fifty years, they'll build statues to me.' God preserve us, but he may turn out to be right."

The core of the case against Speer was his use of slave labor, but the real problem the Tribunal had to tackle was the question of mitigation. The fact that on the witness stand Speer was impressive with his clarity and intelligence, his devastating contempt for Hitler and his near admission of his use of slave labor did not essentially argue against his guilt. What did—or might have—was the indisputable fact that, since the Soviet Union had not signed the Geneva Convention, the Germans, though morally in the wrong, were technically within their rights to employ Soviet POWs in war industries.

The Tribunal's problem was firstly that, except for Speer's apparent indifference about the workers' treatment and his threat to have loafers *(Bumme-*

lanten) sent to concentration camps,* there was no evidence of any personal cruelty or misdeeds.

Secondly, there was a great deal of evidence, much of it supplied by Speer on the witness stand but supported by others, that he had informed Hitler early on that the war was lost, and that, at considerable risk to himself, he had sabotaged Hitler's "scorched earth" orders.

Thirdly, though never taken any more seriously than Speer's apparently reluctant presentation of it, there was his perhaps halfhearted but nonetheless real enough plan to kill Hitler, about which the court had the testimony of the man whose help he sought, industrialist Dieter Stahl.

For many historians and observers later, however, the most disturbing aspect of what many were sure was a manipulating Speer in Nuremberg was the Western Allies' reaction to his pleasant appearance, his reasonable tone, his apparently penitent demeanor and his openly contemptuous attitude toward the Soviets.

Flächsner was much more perceptive than some people—including Speer—gave him credit for. (Both Lord Lawrence and his deputy, the British judge Norman Birkett, mistook Flächsner's mildness for obtuseness and repeatedly treated him with open contempt.) He was well aware of Speer's manipulative gifts: "Perhaps one of the most extraordinary things about him during that year when, I assure you, he was fully aware of the dangers he was running," Flächsner said, "was that he remained exactly what he had always been: a game player. Of course this meant that he 'used' people, but, in a way, only intellectually or strategically. Because he was emotionally so distanced from others, he never played with them emotionally—if he liked you, he liked you and nothing would change it." He smiled. "Of course, for anyone who *loved* him this was difficult, for he didn't love. But game playing, which he most certainly, and brilliantly, did at Nuremberg, was almost an 'exercise' for him. Under those terrible circumstances, it served as a reassurance, in a way, that he was still what he had always been."

Flächsner often did not have an easy task when questioning his frequently verbose client. "Sometimes, when he quoted figures, which he reveled in," he said, "I just had to hope and pray that the court did not have sufficient knowledge at their fingertips to refute them." At one point, hoping to demonstrate that many prisoners preferred working in comparatively ordinary factories to starvation in the concentration camps—as was doubtless the case—he asked Speer,

---

*Fifteen years later, in a letter to Wolters from Spandau in which Speer reviewed the Nuremberg evidence with a view to possible negotiations for his early release, he advised Wolters that it would be best to leave the *"Bummelanten* matter" out of any discussions as "it is rather awkward."

Did you know, during your activities, that the workers from concentration camps had advantages if they worked in factories?

SPEER: Yes. My colleagues called my attention to this fact, and I also
heard it when I inspected the industries. Of course, a wrong impression
should not be created about the number of concentration camp inmates
who worked in German industry. In toto, 1 percent of the labor force
came from concentration camps.

Luckily for Speer, nobody seems to have analyzed that "in toto" figure: if,
as Speer had already said, his labor force in 1943 was 14 million, then 1 percent
would have been 140,000 (not, as he had told me, 45,000), and when, by late
1944, his labor force was doubled to 28 million, it would have meant an awesome 280,000 from concentration camps.

A little later that morning, Flächsner presented a letter to Speer from his
head of Armament Distribution, Walter Schieber, dated May 7, 1944:

> Because of the care which the manpower from camps receive from
> our factory managers in spite of all the difficulties, and the general decent
> and humane treatment which foreign and concentration camp laborers
> receive, both the Jewesses and concentration camp laborers work very
> efficiently and do everything in order not to be sent back to the concentra-
> tion camps.
>
> These facts really demand that we transfer still more concentration
> camp inmates into armament industries. . . . I have discussed this . . . in
> great detail with . . . [SS officers who] especially point out that the food
> situation of concentration camp inmates working in factories is con-
> stantly improved and that by granting additional protein foods, given
> under constant medical supervision, a marked increase in weight was ob-
> tained and thereby better work achieved.

"When you inspected establishments," continued Flächsner on this slippery slope, "did you ever see concentration camp inmates?"

"Of course," replied Speer. "When on inspection tours of industries, I occasionally saw inmates of concentration camps [recognizable, as they wore
striped uniforms], who, however, looked well fed."

It is doubtful that Flächsner would ever knowingly have led Speer into telling an outright lie, so we must suppose that even this devoted counsel sometimes simply made mistakes, as when he asked,

Herr Speer, what do you know about the working conditions in subterranean factories?

SPEER: The most modern equipment for the most modern weapons
had been housed in subterranean factories. This equipment required perfect conditions of work—air which was dry and free from dust, good

lighting facilities, and big fresh air installations so that the conditions which applied . . . would be about the same as those of a night shift in a regular industry.

I should like to add that, contrary to the impression which has been created here in court, these subterranean factories, almost without exception, were staffed with German workers. . . .

Flächsner did not know about the conditions for slave laborers at Dora and Landsberg, and Speer's visits to these dreadful places in 1943 and 1944. "I didn't know," he said, when I described them. "Thank God, the court didn't either."

As it turned out, though Jackson was certainly polite to Speer, he made it amply apparent when he thought Speer lied, and he did not give him an easy time over the most essential point: Speer's knowledge of the slave workers' suffering.

JACKSON: As Production Minister, you were vitally interested in reducing the sickness rate among workers, were you not?

SPEER: I was interested in a high output of work, that is obvious. . . .

JACKSON: Well . . . is it not a fact that the two greatest difficulties in manpower and production are sickness and rapid turnover? . . .

SPEER: These two factors were disturbing . . . but not as extensively as your words might suggest. Sickness made up a very small percentage. . . . However, propaganda pamphlets dropped from Allied aircraft were telling the workers to feign illness, and detailed instructions were given how to do it. And to prevent that, the authorities concerned introduced certain measures, which I considered proper.

JACKSON: What were those measures?

SPEER: I cannot tell you in detail because I myself did not institute these penalties . . . they were ordered by the Plenipotentiary for the Allocation of Labor [Sauckel] in collaboration with the police [Kaltenbrunner] or state authorities. . . .

JACKSON: Now, if you did not know what they were, how can you tell us that you approved of them? We always get to this blank wall that nobody knew what was being done. You knew that they were at least penalties of great severity, did you not?

SPEER: . . . What I knew is contained in the reports of the Central Planning Board; there you will get a picture of what I was told.

JACKSON: All right. Assume that these conditions had been called to your attention and that they existed. . . . Would you have taken it up with Krupp's? Or do you think they had no responsibility for these conditions?

SPEER: During visits to Krupp's, discussions certainly took place on the conditions which generally existed for workers after air attacks; this was of great concern for us . . . but I cannot remember ever being told that foreign workers or prisoners of war at Krupp's were in a particularly bad position. . . .

Speer, talking to me about Jackson's cross-examination, said that in trying to get him to admit that workers were ill-treated at Krupp's, he thought Jackson was after Krupp, rather than him, and read to me one of Justice Jackson's conciliatory remarks. "I am not claiming," said Jackson, "that you were personally responsible for these conditions, but only wish to point out to you what the regime did and to ask you in what way these measures affected your production efforts."

"He added," said Speer, "that what I would tell him about these conditions would not affect my position in the least. Which of course, made me realize that he wanted to use me against Krupp. And I was not going to be used."

Speer agreed, in response to my question, that the conditions and fate of the workers, except for their working capacity, were a matter of comparative indifference to him then. "I certainly can't claim to have been a humanist," he said, with bitter irony, and then added, "I have said it time and again. My objection to maltreatment was because it could not increase efficiency; it was not a moral issue for me. Now I can't even conceive of such conditions, or of feeling or reacting as I did then."

The only part of his own trial he enjoyed talking about was the way he dealt with the Russians. "They came at the end of my case," he said. "I knew I had done well with Jackson, and by that time, of course, one knew how the rest of the court felt about the Russians. By the time their prosecutor started on me, I was in a kind of euphoria, ridiculously cocky; I think I behaved badly. I'm rather sorry about this now. But one saw things differently then. . . ."

One of the first matters General Raginsky turned to was Speer's acknowledgement, in pretrial interrogation on November 14, 1945, that in *Mein Kampf* Hitler had bluntly stated his aggressive plans, in particular for the Soviet Union. Did Speer confirm this now?

SPEER: No. . . . I shall have to tell you that at the time I was ashamed to say that I had not read the whole of *Mein Kampf*. I thought that would sound rather absurd . . . [so] I cheated. . . .
RAGINSKY: You cheated at that time; maybe you are cheating now?
SPEER: No.

"It's difficult to explain now why I lied to the Russians about this during that earlier interrogation," he told me. "It was stupid: I was irritated by their investigator, who was very uninformed about me—someone from a lower echelon, I thought. I misjudged it. I didn't think anybody would believe me if I said I hadn't read the damned thing, but also I didn't think it was important or that anybody would call me on it. So I said I'd read it. It was the simplest thing to say. And then, when they did call me on it in open court, I admitted that I had lied, that I hadn't read it."

He ended that argument with Raginsky with typical bravado:

> I can only say that I was particularly relieved in 1939 when the nonaggression pact with Russia was signed. After all, your diplomats too must have read *Mein Kampf;* nonetheless, they signed the nonaggression pact. And they were certainly more intelligent than I am—I mean in political matters. . . .

Raginsky then came to Speer's ministerial appointment, quoting Speer's first ministerial speech to the Gauleiter:

You said, "I gave up all my activities, including my actual profession, architecture, to dedicate myself without reservation to the war task. The Führer expects that of us all." Do you still maintain that now?
SPEER: Yes. I believe that was the custom in your state too.
RAGINSKY: I am not asking you about our state. We are talking about your state. . . .
SPEER: . . . It appears that you cannot appreciate why in time of war one should accept the post of Armaments Minister. . . .
RAGINSKY: I understand you perfectly.
SPEER: Good.

Though all this sounds like the sparring of bad-tempered children, the Russians in fact brought up many points the other prosecutors had left out or avoided, all of which went toward supporting their eventual contention that Speer should receive a death sentence.

RAGINSKY: I will remind you briefly what you wrote about the principles of your ministry. "One thing, however, will be necessary, and that is energetic action, including the most severe punishment in cases when offenses are committed against the interests of the state. . . ."* Did you write this?
SPEER: Yes [but] may I ask you to read the whole paragraph. You left out a few sentences in the middle.
RAGINSKY: Yes, yes, I shall ask you some questions on that later; you can explain [then].

As he often did during the Russian's cross-examination, Lord Lawrence, the President of the Tribunal, came to Speer's aid: "No, no, General Ra-

---

*The speech is mentioned in Chapter XIII, page 316, but only the severe rules which were promulgated are quoted there.

ginsky," he said, "the Tribunal would prefer to have the comments now."
Minutes later, Raginsky questioned Speer on Russian forced laborers:

RAGINSKY: You knew, did you not, what kind of methods were used to
obtain [Russian] workers for your coal industry. Do you admit that?
SPEER: No, I do not admit it.
RAGINSKY: Do you acknowledge that, as a participant in a meeting at Hitler's headquarters (on January 4, 1944) and as a Reich Minister, you are
among those responsible for the forced deportation to Germany of several
million workers?
SPEER: But . . . this specific program was not carried through.
RAGINSKY: Defendant Speer, if you do not answer my questions, we shall
lose too much time.
LAWRENCE: But, General Raginsky, from the outset of this defendant's
evidence, if I understand it, he admitted that he knew that prisoners of
war and other workers were brought to Germany forcibly, against their
will. He has never denied it.
RAGINSKY: Yes, Mr. President, he admitted it. But the question now is
whether he admits that he himself is responsible. . . .
SPEER: . . . The Tribunal will decide the extent of my responsibility. I cannot. I explained [all this] yesterday, for about ten minutes. Either my explanation of yesterday is believed or not.
RAGINSKY: I do not want you to repeat what you said yesterday. If you do
not want to answer me, I prefer to pass on to the next question.
LAWRENCE: General Raginsky, if you asked him a question which was
asked yesterday, he must give the same answer if he wants to be consistent. . . . The witness says, "I did answer the question truthfully yesterday,
but if you want me to repeat it, I will, but it will take ten minutes." This is
what he said and it is a perfectly proper answer.

"Speer was very very depressed when his case was over," Flächsner said. "I
must admit, I didn't think we had a hope of acquittal—it would have been
grotesque. I thought he would get fifteen years, with revision after a few
years. But he was almost sure it would be a death sentence."

After finishing with the main defendants, the court battled for a month
with the knotty legal problem of the indicted Nazi organizations. The SS included the Waffen (armed) SS and the Reich Security Main Office (RSHA)
with its various departments such as the Security Service (SD), Security Police (SIPO) and the Gestapo, though this was separately charged because it
predated RSHA by several years. The Leadership Corps of the Nazi Party was
indicted as an organization, though many of its top men were also indicted as
individuals. The Reich Cabinet, like the Storm Troops (SA) after the 1934
Putsch, had largely lost any real power, and the General Staff and High Com-

mand was finally considered not to be a criminal organization. In the end only the SS, Gestapo and RSHA were declared criminal, with the proviso that no members even of these were to be punished without individual trials.

"But on July 27, Shawcross [the British prosecutor] delivered his final address, with that dreadful long quote about a killing of a group of Jews," Flächsner said. "I think that was Speer's zero point—he kept coming back to it in the days that followed. He was absolutely devastated: anybody who saw him then could never have doubted his feelings. But you see, most people never did believe that he could feel. After that [speech by Shawcross], all during August, he was not only certain that he would be sentenced to death, but he felt he should be, he had to be."

Over the first days of August, Speer wrote his final statement which he was to deliver on August 31, the last day of the trial. He wrote to Margret about it:

> I must be prepared for anything. . . . I cannot place my personal fate in the foreground; my concluding words will therefore not refer to my case at all. . . .

On August 10, after writing what Wolters felt was his last will, in which he appointed him not only his executor but his literary alter ego, he began on the first draft of his reminiscences on which he would work over the subsequent seven weeks. The stilted bureaucratic language of the introduction to what would become a 103-page manuscript clearly shows the tension Flächsner later described:

> I have now finished writing my closing statement for the court. It ends a career which, after early years of anonymity gave me huge responsibilities and fame and swept me to unimagined heights. It was a life which eventually turned an industrious responsible man into a traitor to the master he had faithfully served for ten years.
>
> After all the momentous events of those years, nothing can be more indicative of what life had become than that, at the end, the only real decision left was whether to serve the people, or the Führer, Adolf Hitler.
>
> I am not writing this in an effort to justify myself . . . but . . . I feel the need to provide my wife and my children for their later lives with a clear understanding of events and a summary of my many memories.
>
> The limited time at my disposal, and the external circumstances will not allow me, stylistically or otherwise, to produce the kind of account I would ordinarily hope to present, but the main thing is, I'm sincere in my purpose.
>
> Albert Speer, Nuremberg,
August 10, 1946
Prison, Cell 17.

[At the end he wrote:]
Original and 1 copy—Frau Speer, Heidelberg
1 copy—Rudi Wolters
1 copy—A.K. [Annemarie Kempf]

On August 31, the twenty-one defendants, in the order in which their cases had been heard, made their last statements. All of them, except Hess, who rambled, acknowledged the crimes of the regime. Göring said he "could not comprehend the ghastly mass murders the trial had revealed"; Keitel said he would "rather die than be entangled again in such horrors"; Rosenberg said that genocide was a crime which he had never envisaged; Frank warned of the consequences of turning away from God; Streicher condemned Hitler's mass killing of Jews; Funk spoke of feeling profound shame confronted by "these frightful crimes"; Schacht spoke of "the unspeakable misery [he] had tried so hard to prevent"; Raeder philosophized on the value of the Führer Principle; Schirach deplored how the youth of Germany had been deceived; Sauckel was "shocked in his innermost soul"; for Papen, "the power of evil had proved stronger than the power of God"; Seyss-Inquart deplored the "fearful excesses"; Neurath had "worked for the Fatherland"; and Fritzsche saw a "horrifying warning in the murder of five million people."

Not a single one of the defendants accepted personal blame for these crimes. Jodl and Hess were the only ones who defended them in any way, Speer the only one who tried to explain them. In all their cases, no one in court that day could have doubted their final fate.

"In a war such as this," said Jodl, "in which carpet bombing destroyed hundreds of thousands of women and children, and in which partisans used every single means to reach their goals, I cannot feel that hard measures, even when they seem doubtful under international law, are a crime before morality and conscience. Because I believe that duty toward one's people and one's Fatherland stands above all others, it was my highest obligation and an honor to fulfill this duty. I am proud of it. In a happier future, however, I hope that this duty will be replaced by a higher one: the responsibility for humanity."

"Hitler's dictatorship," said Speer, toward the end of his address, "was . . . one that employed to perfection the instruments of technology to dominate its own people. . . . Through technical devices such as radio and public address systems, used as they had never been used before, eighty million people were made subject, uncritically, to the will of one man. One of the results was a far-reaching supervision of the citizen of the state and the maintenance of a high degree of secrecy for criminal acts. . . . In five or ten years the technique of warfare will have progressed so far that it will be possible to fire rockets from continent to continent with uncanny precision . . . to use atomic power to destroy one million people in a matter of seconds in New York, without warning. . . . Science will be able to spread pestilence among humans and animals and destroy crops by insect warfare. . . . Chemistry will be capable of inflicting unspeakable suffering upon an increasingly helpless humanity. . . .

"This trial must contribute to laying down the ground rules for living in a humanistic society. What does my own fate signify, after all that has happened and in comparison with such a lofty goal? A nation which believes in its future," he ended, "will never perish. May God protect Germany and Western culture."

"The historians who criticized me for appearing to focus on the technical aspects of Hitler's regime," Speer said to me decades later, "thought that I was trying to present a picture of Nazi Germany as the prototype of a technological society, and myself as the prototype of technological man. And basically their argument was that the horrors Hitler produced—the extermination and concentration camps—had absolutely nothing to do with technology. Of course, if you consider Hitler's Germany from that point of view alone, then that is quite correct—the machinery of murder and the machinery of concentration camps were, if anything, primitive. But the whole point is that eighty million people were *not* persuaded to follow Hitler because they knew he was going to murder people in lime ditches and gas chambers; they did not follow him because he seemed evil, but because he seemed extraordinarily good. And what convinced them of this was Goebbels's brilliant propaganda, his unprecedented use of modern means of mass communication.

"Of course," he said, "when you are criticized, it is usually because you made mistakes, and I made mistakes even in that last statement. I was only interested in using it to re-establish some dignity for the German people who listened to it all on the radio, at the end of many months of listening—as many of them did—to the horrors which Nuremberg revealed. Now I know that I should have included what I felt so very strongly, that whatever was known or not known, it was our society that had produced these horrors or, better said, had given monsters a license for horrors, not as a result of technical perfection, but as a consequence of our moral disintegration. I didn't say it, and I was wrong."

On October 1, four weeks after the final statements, the court returned with the verdicts.

"The extraordinary thing," said Flächsner, "was that when they said twenty years, I honestly think it hit him harder than a death sentence would have. Somehow he had prepared himself for that—a kind of euphoria of guilt, of paying, of so many things. But the thought of twenty years—forty-one when he went in, sixty-one when he would come out—that was a tremendous shock. And somehow—it sounds grotesque and *he* never said it; *I* am saying it in retrospect—perhaps the fact that he didn't get the death sentence somehow diminished him in his own eyes."

It was nine months before all the inter-Allied problems were ironed out and the prisoners were transferred to Spandau prison in Berlin. Speer hated to talk about those months. "It was the blackest period of my life," he said. The blackest months of his life were the beginning of his life as a different man.

XXIII

Spandau: I

From the Spandau prison rules, as laid down by the Allied Control Commission:

On admission, the prisoners will undress completely and their bodies will be carefully searched. The search, which will be in the presence of the Directorate, will be carried out by four warders. All parts of the body, including the anus, will be searched for articles which might be smuggled into the institution. . . .

The discipline of the institution requires that prisoners should adopt a standing position whenever approached or in the presence of prison officers. They will salute by standing at attention or by passing by them in an upright posture at the same time removing their headgear. . . . The prisoners may approach an officer or warder only if ordered to do so or if they wish to make a request. . . .

Prisoners will be . . . addressed by their convict's number; in no circumstances by name.

Imprisonment will be in the form of solitary confinement. The cells will be isolated, but work, religious services and walks in the open air will be carried out together. When awakened, the prisoner will rise immediately and make his bed. He will then strip to the waist, wash, brush his teeth and rinse his mouth. Clothing, shoes and the cell, including furniture, will be cleaned in the time provided for this purpose and in the prescribed manner. . . . Approaching any window, including those in the cells, is strictly prohibited.

The prisoners may not talk or associate with one another nor with other persons except with special dispensation from the Directorate. They may not have in their possession any articles other than those authorized. . . . Work assigned by the Directorate will be carried out every day except Sundays and public holidays.

In Nuremberg on July 18, 1947, the day of the transfer to Spandau, the seven prisoners were awakened at 4 A.M. and, for the first time since the end of the trial, were handed their own clothes. For the first time in months, too, Speer told me, all seven of them—even Hess—all usually very selective in their choice of conversational partners, talked to one another as, tightly ringed by American soldiers, they stood together for hours in the prison office awaiting the command to leave.

"I still can't explain it to myself," Speer said, "but somehow the atmosphere was euphoric. I suppose it was the thought of getting away from Nuremberg with all it had come to mean." When the order came to move, each prisoner was handcuffed to an American soldier, and they were hurried into two military ambulances waiting in the courtyard. When the prison gates opened, the ambulances, three cars apart, were inserted into a waiting convoy of about ten personnel carriers. "It was very much a military operation, and I remember feeling ridiculously pleased that transporting us appeared to warrant all this security."

He got his greatest lift when, on their way to the military airport, they drove across a small new bridge over the river Pegnitz. "I could not remember when I had last felt so intensely excited," he said. "A new bridge; the people were working." His voice sounded somehow jubilant even after all those years. "The country was alive."

The euphoria endured throughout the short flight in a comfortable American DC-3 passenger plane. "It was the most beautiful day one can imagine," he said. "For the past months we had been allowed an hour's daily walk in the prison courtyard, but somehow at that airport in the countryside near Nuremberg the air smelled different: clean, flowery, alive." Again, that word "alive," and he would say it three more times in the next few minutes describing his reaction to what he saw from the low-flying plane: toiling peasants in the fields, chugging boats on a river, orderly and peaceful-looking hamlets and, "perhaps the most amazing," he said, the sight of walkers on country paths, with rucksacks on their backs. "For us it was all still going on, but here it was all over and people were on holiday—the kind of hiking holidays Margret and I had taken when we were young."

He had one more moment of comparative joy when, the plane circling over the city just before landing in Berlin, he saw spread beneath him his Olympic Stadium, the green lawns, which had been part of his design, well tended; his Chancellery, damaged but still massive, standing; and his East-West Axis, which he had handed over to Hitler on his fiftieth birthday. Speer had nonplussed his Führer that day with what had been announced as his first public speech, to which Hitler was scheduled to solemnly respond. *"Mein Führer,"* he had said, "I herewith report the completion of the East-West Axis. May the work speak for itself."

Stumping Hitler, who had expected a lengthy speech during which he could plan a suitable improvised response of similar duration, had been one of Speer's most gleeful memories when he told me about it. "It was a good joke," he said, "and what was nice was that Hitler accepted it as such. 'You got me there, you rascal, Speer,' he said. 'Two sentences indeed,' and then he had laughed. 'Still, I have to admit,' he had said, 'it was one of the best speeches I have ever heard.' "

Perhaps that, too, shot through his mind as he flew over that 125-meter-wide avenue. It had been planned as the approach to the largest building in the world, the "Kuppelhalle" (the Dome Hall). "For a moment I was totally happy. It had not all gone; I had left something," he said.

But this euphoria would disappear with shocking suddenness only minutes later when, again handcuffed to their guards, the prisoners were bundled into a bus—with windows painted black—which, preceded and followed by at least twenty Allied military vehicles, he thought some of them armored, drove at breakneck speed continuously sounding its horn until it sharply stopped when the prisoners, dazed by the trip, heard the closing clang of a heavy gate.

The draconian regime the Allied Control Commission had laid down for these prisoners was put into practice from the moment of their arrival at Spandau. Once again, Speer found himself incapable of recording in his books—or his letters from Spandau—these, the most humbling moments of the arrival formalities. "Everything happened very swiftly," he said, and added, with a note of irony in his voice, "they were very efficient. One had the feeling that every move had been carefully rehearsed."

Today nudity is nothing extraordinary. We not only undress readily enough in health and leisure centers or on beaches, but we are continually confronted by naked bodies in photographs, films and on TV, so much so that we hardly notice them anymore. But for men of Speer's and Schirach's generation—and even more that of Neurath, Raeder, Dönitz and Hess (of whom only the two naval officers, Raeder and Dönitz, had ever had any experience of communal living)—undressing in public and indeed in front of one another was profoundly embarrassing. "When I think of it now, it is so unimportant," Speer said, "and indeed, within a very short time the shared bathtime arrangements made us quite familiar with each other's looks [he couldn't quite bring himself to use the word "body"], but that day. . . ." He shook his head remembering it. "It was very much worse than that other occasion in Flensburg, perhaps because then there was almost an element of the ridiculous in the manner of our arrest, and we were held in a familiar place, with a window, with the sun shining in and noises of people from outside. In Spandau it was like entering a dungeon, bare, dark, musty"—for a second his nose moved as if he was smelling it in retrospect—"I couldn't think what the smell was, until they handed us the obviously disinfected, used prison clothes. The smell of disinfectant would always be with us, from then on."

It was clear that the presence of the four directors—American, British, French and Russian officers of rank—was the most humiliating part of it. "Each of us was given a pair of light blue trousers in thick cotton, a rough shirt, a battered-looking jacket, a pair of canvas shoes with wooden soles and a convict's cap, but we were told to remain undressed and wait, at attention, until each of us had passed a medical." That morning they were given socks but, incomprehensibly, no underclothes to replace their own, which were taken away. (Later that day these would be returned to them disinfected, and later still they were issued new uniforms, for which their measurements had been taken at Nuremberg, drill suits with U.S. Army battle jackets dyed black, and they would be allowed to ask in letters home for more underclothes and sweaters.)

"Hess said he felt faint, so the Russian director who appeared to be in charge said he could sit down on the floor," Speer told me. "As the rest of us stood there, the director added in a significant tone of voice that the clothes we had been given had been worn by convicts in Nazi concentration camps. This information was translated twice," he added drily.

How had all this made him feel? I asked.

"That I was now getting what I deserved," he answered, as drily. Had he really felt this, or was it just an afterthought now?

"My feelings then were very complex," he said, sounding irritated. "I'm putting them into simple terms for your benefit." I was surprised at this unusually aggressive reaction and, seeing it, he quickly changed his tone. "I assure you, nothing could have been better designed to make me feel very humble indeed."

Nothing except perhaps the next sequence in these events: the internal body search. There was perhaps a measure of consideration on the part of the four directors in deciding to disregard this particular part of the Control Commission's order, for it took place not *en groupe* and in a director's presence, but individually, in the comparative privacy of the medical office, and was carried out not by warders but by a male nurse.

"After that a quite friendly Russian doctor gave us a thorough physical examination," Speer said, "and then we were told to dress and were taken through another iron door that was locked behind us, into the cell block." The order in which they passed through this door determined the prison number they would carry to the end of their imprisonment and which that afternoon they would have to paint with indelible ink onto the fronts and backs of all their outer clothing. Speer was Number 5 and this—as the director had told them—was how he would be addressed from that moment on.

"That too," Speer said, "was somehow a logical next stage in our step-by-step diminution. I don't remember any sense of surprise or outrage, only a curious feeling of relief in submitting."

The instant when this sense of fatalistic submission to justified retribution was at its most intense came only moments later, when the heavy door of the bare cell that would be his home for nineteen years closed behind him. Three meters long, about two and a half meters wide and four meters high, the walls were painted what he described as "a sickly yellow," the ceiling white. A small barred window, high up, was covered with light brown plastic, though a section could be opened for ventilation. There was an eighty-one-by-forty-eight-centimeter wooden table fixed to a wall; a wooden chair; a water closet, with a wooden cover, in one corner; an open wardrobe, half of it shelves, half with hooks for clothes. Finally there was a black iron cot with a headrest, pillow, sheets and a covered American army mattress marked as having been produced in San Antonio, Texas. Folded symmetrically at the end of the bed were five grey woolen blankets, each of them stamped in large black letters "GBI." "That was the ultimate chastening for me," Speer said, "the ultimate irony too; I didn't think anything could happen that could demonstrate better the poetic justice of my presence in that dreadful place." The blankets had come from a labor camp run by Speer's Generalbauinspektorat.

THE SPANDAU COMPLEX had been built in 1876 on the orders of the Kaiser as a military prison with cells for six hundred men. Later it was used as military barracks and after World War I as a civil prison. Under Hitler, both military prisoners on remand and political detainees in transit to concentration camps were held there. When the decision was made in the winter of 1946 that four-powers-occupied Berlin was the logical place for the detention of any of the principals in the Nuremberg trials who would be given prison sentences, Spandau was the obvious choice.

The four occupying powers would share the responsibility for the prisoners. Spandau would be permanently staffed by military personnel from all four nations, but although all four directors would remain *in situ*, executive power would change in succession. In January, May and September it would be held by the British; in February, June and October by the French; in March, July and November by the Soviets; and in April, August and December by the Americans. The multinational staff was eventually to consist of seventy-eight people: thirty-two armed soldiers—eight from each nation—on permanent duty on the six watchtowers, and patrolling the electrified fence, eighteen warders, all military personnel from the four nations. (The British, Americans and French would be on duty around the clock; the Russians—doubtless to reduce the danger of closer relationships with the other three, always stronger at nighttime—would be withdrawn at 8 p.m. to return at 5 a.m.) There were also twenty-eight ancillaries, many of them citizens of other Allied countries.

Dutch male nurse Jan Boon, his wife and four-year-old son, Michael, moved into "Haus No. 22" inside the prison walls on January 1, 1947, when the whole place was still a construction site. In the absence of any knowledge of how many prisoners might eventually be sent to Spandau, either from the main trial or from others in preparation, thirty-two cells were prepared in the front tract of the main building, closing off the rest. The ceilings were lowered, new floors were laid, and the hygienic facilities were modernized. Boon and Toni Proost—the other medical orderly who had been recruited, also a Dutchman—assisted by a doctor and staff from the Berlin Health Council, set up an operating theater, sterilizing room and a ward with three beds provided by the nearby British Army Hospital.

Boon's experience of forced labor in the Third Reich was rather different from the one that has become familiar to us. Born in Holland into a Dutch Catholic family in 1912, he left school at seventeen to do his military service, during which he took army-sponsored courses in fire fighting and first aid. His dream was to study medicine, but realism would prevail and he went to work in a gin factory where his father was the manager. "It was a decent, quiet life," he said. "Work on weekdays, church on Sunday—it was good."

In 1940, after the German occupation of Holland, Boon, then twenty-eight, was in one of the first batches of Dutch forced laborers to be shipped to Berlin, where he was put to work in a machine factory of the Organization Todt. Nobody did him any harm in Germany, he said; the Dutch workers in that factory had been well treated, were allowed to live in private digs, received reasonable remuneration and the same rations as the German workers. "We were like anybody else," he said.

This claim is certainly borne out by the fact that when in 1942 he fell in love with a young woman who worked at the local post office where he posted his weekly letters home, his application for permission to marry her was immediately granted. And soon afterwards, when the new Frau Boon's doctor, a man named Schubert who had a large practice, was informed of Jan's dream to study medicine, he asked him to come and help out in his surgery weekends and evenings. The factory management readily adjusted his shifts to make it possible.

I first visited Boon in 1983 in the small house he had bought in 1956—his wife ran a small bar there for nineteen years—across the street from the prison. But shortly afterwards, they moved to northern Germany to live with their son and his family and I saw him again there later. Medium tall, medium blond, of medium build, he was—except for his enduring and rather romantic love for nursing and healing—a rather prosaic man. Had he been aware, I asked, that his was an unusually benign forced labor experience under the Nazis? He shook his head. He had only heard after the war about all the awful things which had happened. His own life, he repeated, had been "ordinary."

When the war ended, his mentor Dr. Schubert had opened a casualty hospital with thirty beds and teaching facilities and enabled Boon to take his formal nurse's training. At the end of 1946, a few weeks after qualifying, he received an enquiry from the local state employment office whether he would be interested in a nursing job at Spandau prison. "I was thunderstruck," he said. "One knew of course from the newspapers what was about to happen at Spandau. It was an experience not to be missed and a fantastic break in those hard times: good money, wonderful perks with free housing and utilities and above all, free food from the American and British commissaries. In a world of insecurity, we would be secure for an indefinite period." This period was to last thirty-three years, the rest of Jan's working life.

The other Dutch medic, Toni Proost, had also been a forced laborer during the war, and had worked in an armaments factory. When he fell ill, he was well treated in a hospital Speer had built before the war, and became an orderly there.

Boon and Proost were both on duty the day the prisoners arrived. "We were only told the day before, and had to sign an undertaking that we would keep secret everything we learned and heard at Spandau," Boon said. During the months before there had been regular seminars with Allied psychologists for those among the staff who would have close contact with the prisoners.

"They discussed each prisoner's personality, their history, the psychological tests they had undergone in Nuremberg and their prison conduct there." And they advised on the environment that was being readied—which color for the walls would be most soothing for the nerves; what would be best for the floors, tiles or linoleum (it ended up being concrete); and they counseled on discipline. Speer's impression was right: "We rehearsed every detail of their arrival for days," Jan said.

For the prisoners' medicals, Toni Proost weighed and measured them while Jan took their temperatures and did the body search. Was there any trouble about the internal examination? I asked. "Only with Hess, for whom it was in fact considered particularly important," he said. "It was always feared—already in Nuremberg—that he would kill himself. He refused, and had to be held, and that was unpleasant for everybody. They all had showers after their physical, and after they had dressed we cut their hair."

The prisoners arrived in the morning, so their first meal was lunch; it had been set out for them on individual trays on a table in the cell block, and each was directed to take one to his cell. "None of them had a lot of personal belongings, just toilet articles, as I remember, pajamas [they were issued straw slippers], photographs, and each of them brought a few books."

Jan said they had been told that no one was allowed to talk to the prisoners, except the warders on questions of prison routine or they themselves on medical matters. Later this changed, he said, but in the first months all orders were implicitly obeyed.

"One felt very isolated in the silence of that huge place," Speer said to me, describing Spandau, "but oddly enough, that wasn't so bad—after the tensions of Nuremberg, it gave one a kind of peace." What affected them more, he said, were the obligatory one-hour outings in the prison yard, walking ten paces apart clockwise around a large linden tree, hands clasped behind their backs, with six guards circling counterclockwise around them. "Like guard dogs," he said. "It was extraordinarily humiliating and—a sign how 'down' I was—I couldn't find any way to laugh it off. There seemed nothing to joke about and no one to joke with. The first two weeks I found myself becoming very lethargic, and during our walks I noticed that all the others also looked drawn and tired."

They had several immediate things to contend with. One was lack of exercise: "I didn't have the energy to exercise in my cell, as I certainly could have done and of course did later," he said. Food was insufficient as, not surprisingly, their meals were precisely in line with German civilian rations but—with the Russians in charge that July—without the supplements of fresh fruit or vegetables most Germans outside were able to find, and with which the Western Allies supplemented their diets later when they were in charge.

There was a total absence of any external stimulation—no one talked to them; they were not allowed newspapers, or for several weeks, music; and although books from the Spandau public library were made available almost at once, until much later that year the cells were insufficiently lit to allow more than sporadic reading. This was diametrically different from their imprisonment at Nuremberg during which not only did they live on American army rations, tastily prepared by an excellent German convict cook, but all of them were able to associate with many like-minded former associates and friends.

In addition, in Nuremberg Speer in particular had been interrogated almost daily by defense lawyers and prosecutors, and testified several times in the trials of former colleagues. Life then always held the prospect of a new next day. In those first hard weeks at Spandau, the prisoners had to face the realization that basically there was no new next day.

"There was an incredible greyness about it all," Speer recalled. "Now when I try to visualize it it is almost impossible, it was so—nothing."

Between his arrival on July 18 and mid-September, Speer wrote virtually no letters and few diary notes. The prisoners were permitted only one letter, out or in, every month; theoretically they were allowed a family visit every two months, but because it was only for fifteen minutes, few took advantage of it. "Margret couldn't afford it," Speer said.

The prison administrators obviously became aware of their charges' increasing depression, and dealt with it comparatively swiftly and wisely. Two weeks after the prisoners arrived—on August 2—they were told by the Americans, by then in charge, that they could work every day in the garden if they wished, for as long as they felt able.

Speer's letter to Margret on September 18 deals almost exclusively with the garden, about which, within his rather limited capacity for enthusiasm at the time, he sounds almost blissful:

> It is about 6,000 square meters of wilderness [about one and a half acres] full of nut trees and huge lilac bushes. Now we are all spending hours every day weeding; it is good for us. I already feel much better. I have big ideas for the garden, have designed a promenade I will lay, and plans for all kinds of flowers, a rock garden and, above all, fruit trees and vegetable plots for which I hope I will be allowed to have seeds sent me. I want to plant lettuce, tomatoes, cabbage, cauliflower, potatoes, beans and peas. It makes my mouth water even to write it. There is a lot to do, and I think the soil is healthy.
>
> Do not worry. Above all, do not let the children worry about me. Tell them their papa is becoming wonderfully domesticated: the first thing I do in the morning after washing and dressing is to wash my floor and

wipe all the furniture—i.e., the table, the chair and my WC. And then I make my bed into a sofa by spreading one of the blankets over it: it's quite nice then, and I use it for everything, to eat and write and read and rest. And if I want something from my table, I only have to reach out: marvelous. In future all bedrooms I design will be three by two and a half. Breakfast, which I consume comfortably on my trusty couch, is at 7:30, and afterwards I light my first pipe, bliss. I'm not unhappy.

This letter, only his second from Spandau, was certainly intended to allay his family's concern for him, above all the children's.

"When I was small," he told me, "I sometimes had terrible dreams, usually about my parents—my father dying, my mother being hurt in one way or another. Now of course, after my long acquaintance with [Erich] Fromm, I understand more about dreams and what they can reflect. But then I knew nothing except that children had vivid imaginations, and I wanted to forestall their imagining me living in a dungeon."

In a way this letter was the precursor of his Spanish- (for Spandau) Illustrated, from which he drew later for *The Secret Diaries.* He began this a few weeks later, and continued it until all the children had grown out of childhood, illustrating it with drawings—later even paintings—events from his daily life he thought might amuse them.

Within days of writing this letter, in which one could already sense a reviving life force, he would have the most important encounter of his years at Spandau, indeed of his postwar life.

In order to understand what happened to Speer over the subsequent three years, one has to understand the essence of a man such as Georges Casalis. The understanding of a mind and spirit such as his, and the use he put it to with Speer (and certainly many others), can give us hope, for it shows us what one human being can do for another. Casalis, the most unobtrusive and most unpretentious of men, was exceptional, but he would be the first to say that he was not unique. In fact I can imagine—can almost hear—his peal of laughter at the suggestion that he was anything but just a man, a teacher.

He always thought that it was purely an accident that he was assigned as pastor to the Spandau prisoners. "In a country under military occupation," he once said to me, "officers of the churches also become officials and as such, even though for the sake of courtesy my agreement was formally sought, it was in fact taken for granted."

And he thought they were right. However difficult it would be for a former *résistant* like himself, who had fought the Nazis throughout the occupation of France, to find in himself compassion and detachment for just these seven men, he was, he could see, the right and, at the time, the only choice. The prisoners were all Protestants, so a Protestant it had to be. The British and Americans, who had plenty of Protestant chaplains, happened to have none in 1947 who spoke German. For the French, he was the obvious choice as he was already pastor of the French community in Berlin. Furthermore, the fact that he had belonged to the French resistance—and doubtless more to its left wing than the right—made it easier for the Soviets to accept him.

Most of my many talks with Georges and his wife, Dorothée, took place in their small flat above what was then their working place, which was not a parish—by the early 1980s the French Protestant hierarchy considered him too much of a rebel to give him a conventional parish—but the Calvin Museum in Noyon.

For them it was the perfect job. From around March to September, they guided visitors around the museum, showed them films and talked to them about Calvin, and at night Georges wrote. In autumn and winter they worked in shantytowns and isolated mountain villages in South America, particularly Nicaragua. There, sharing the lives of the poorest of the poor, both of them found and gave others solace and strength.

On the face of it, informing people about Calvin seemed a curious assignment for the most liberal-thinking, the most compassionate and, one would have thought, least Calvinist of Protestants. "I do not believe in isms," Casalis explained, "whether Nazism, Communism, Judaism, Gaulleism, Catholicism or, for that matter, Lutheranism or Calvinism. I tell them about what, once the outer and perhaps more familiar skins were stripped away, Calvin was like as a man, perhaps not your kind of man or even my kind of man, but a man with moral principles."

The flat—two rooms, a tiny kitchen and even tinier bathroom, up a fairly rickety staircase from the museum—would have been excessively simple had it not been for Georges and Dorothée's wealth of books, her simple but wonderful food—an omelet, a salad, a runny Camembert—and the soft candlelight by which we ate and talked for hours, sustained with country wine and strong coffee, always deep into the night.

Georges recalled very vividly the first service he took in Spandau. "I was horribly nervous at the thought of meeting these seven men, who were at the very least co-responsible for the death of an untold number of my very special friends, the friends of my war. They had not only died, many of them had been betrayed, tortured, put to death in unspeakable pain. No, it wasn't easy. Well, I put on my soutane; I thought it might help for them to meet me a little formally, though that isn't my usual way at all. I had brought candles to the double cell I had been given as a chapel, and I lit them: Germans like candlelight and—as you see—I don't dislike it either.

"I remember as if it was yesterday, waiting for them at the door. I heard them come along that long corridor, not because they walked noisily, but because they were each dragging a chair—they didn't carry them, they dragged them. Perhaps it was a silent expression of . . . who can know what? Contempt? Resistance? Self-assertion? Anyway, after this, chairs were put permanently into the chapel.

"When they got there, I gave each my hand and said, 'Casalis,' and they each said their name. I replied, 'Good morning, Herr Dönitz, von Schirach, Speer, von Neurath, Raeder, Funk. Hess didn't come; he never came. And at the end of the service I again shook hands with each of them to say goodbye.'"

Throughout the years Casalis officiated at Spandau, the only prisoner who always asked to talk to him after the service was Speer. "Yes," he said, "I did feel I knew him very well indeed by the time I left"—he smiled sadly—"well enough that I should have realized that it was wrong of me to leave. Because of him, I should have stayed another three or four years."

Of the others, he said, Funk probably spoke with him most. "He was a highly intelligent man and liked to talk about the sermons in philosophical terms. The others? Well, all of them eventually talked to me about their families, which was already a sign of trust, and, yes, they also ended up talking about the Third Reich, von Neurath and Dönitz particularly, maintaining all along that they were guilty of nothing. In some ways, I suppose, they had a point; there were certainly numerous people in Germany immeasurably more guilty than they, who got away with it. Hess I can't talk about; he would never speak to me. Some of my colleagues later got to know him quite well, but I didn't; in those early years he absolutely refused to communicate, though after the first weeks, when I received permission to arrange weekly concerts for them—on records, of course—I was told he asked for his door to be opened so that he could hear the music.

"Schirach and Funk certainly did question their own morality, and at least with me they never denied either their involvement or their guilt. But of course, none of the self-doubts they expressed to me could compare in depth with those of Speer, who behind that wall of composure which, as you say, he had probably constructed around himself since childhood, was the most distraught man I had ever known. It was odd, you know. Basically he could get on with everybody—even, the only one among the seven, with the Russians—but, and it was both fascinating to observe and very sad for him, not with his co-prisoners, most of whom feared, despised and even hated him."

When Speer asked him after that first service whether he would help him become a different man, "I realized he meant helping him to learn to think and to study," Casalis said. "Not facts, but learn to expand his thinking into realms he had not yet entered. I told him that he must begin immediately to study Karl Barth, and I obtained Barth's books for him and permission from the prison to have them in his cell."

Barth's classic *Dogmatik,* which has influenced the thinking of countless Protestants, is nine thousand printed pages—thirty-seven volumes. Speer, tutored for the first three years by Casalis, read all of them over the years and studied them deeply. "He didn't only discuss them with me," Georges said, "but with all the pastors who followed me, though more with some than others, depending on their own interest and personalities.

"For me," he went on, "every Saturday of those three years became a special day. The whole Spandau experience was extraordinary, and in that context Speer was only a part of it. But as an individual, with a totally exceptional moral drive, he has remained in my mind for what is now forty years the most special part of this special experience."

Extraordinarily, except on two early occasions when Speer wrote to Hilde, he hardly mentioned Casalis in his letters from Spandau, and, as I ascertained as soon as he spoke of him to me, quite early in our talks, he does not figure in the Index of *The Secret Diaries.* I brought that up with Speer. If, as he told me, Casalis had been so important to him in Spandau, why hadn't he written about this in his book?

He shrugged. "I'm not sure; perhaps it was too important, or perhaps. . . ." He stopped. "Because I failed him."

Casalis's first weeks at Spandau were fairly uneventful except for his growing fascination with Speer. "I have no illusions about prisoners' interest in religion," he said. "I know them well. These particular, very conventional men, though probably conventionally 'religious' in their youth, had probably never really taken issue with faith—I'm sure they had all quite happily left their churches under Hitler to become what they called *gottgläubig,* believers in God. But I doubt that they ever gave a thought to God; National Socialism was the only religion they needed. Basically Hess, who refused to attend services—and of course Speer, who searched—were the only honest ones among them. But it's been my experience and that of other people who work in prisons that many prisoners who perhaps never in their lives darkened the door of a church will attend prison services, not because they suddenly 'get religion,' but because the service is a change from the awful monotony of prison life. And the pastor or priest or rabbi, if he is any good at all, should make himself a link for them, not with one secular interpretation of God but with all wider dimensions of life. In all prisons, I think, our function is to get across to prisoners that the power of morality is stronger than the morality of power. In the context of prison life this is by no means easy, for it necessarily confirms for most men the need—or the power—of power."

Casalis's first services at Spandau—the sermon always, as Karl Barth had advised him, the same for the prisoners on Saturday as he would deliver to Berlin's French Protestant congregation on Sunday—passed tranquilly enough. But on the sixth Saturday he very nearly came a cropper when he chose as his subject Jesus's healing of the leper. "They listened in dead silence," he recalled, "and except for Speer who smiled and shook hands as always—though even he didn't stay behind as he usually did—they filed out, stony-faced and refusing to shake hands. I was very taken aback, and I agonized over it all week. Had I perhaps been wrong? Should I be more careful in my choice of sermons from now on? Had this lost me the only just beginning trust of these men?

"The next week Raeder stood up at the end of the sermon, which I had again taken from Saint Mark, though choosing a particularly mild parable, and addressed me in the manner of the admiral dressing down the little navy chaplain. 'Last week, *Herr Pfarrer,*' he said, 'you deeply offended us. It is entirely impermissible to address us as lepers. We formally protest. We are here because we have been unjustly condemned; we are men who did nothing except their duty as soldiers who executed their orders. If our protest to you should prove ineffective, we shall be forced to take official actions.' And with that they stalked out.

"This time Speer stayed. 'I didn't stay last week,' he said, 'because I wanted to hear what they had to say right afterwards—the opportunity might not have come again.' And then he smiled that rather special smile of his. 'Well, you certainly threw the cat among the pigeons, didn't you?' But his tone was such that I immediately felt better—you see, another extraordinary gift of his was first of all the ability to put things into perspective and, secondly, to find humor in almost anything. 'All week,' he said, 'nothing was talked about except you.' [By this time they were allowed to talk during work and on walks—now in the garden, where Speer had already laid out a 270-meter-round path.] The whole group referred to themselves as 'the lepers,' he said. 'The lepers have to go in to dinner now; forward march, lepers, outside for the walk; lights out, for the lepers. Gallows humor, of course,' he said, 'but it got it out of their system. But for heaven's sake,' he said then, 'don't stop, don't spare our feelings; don't now start being careful or protective of us. You are exactly on course, exactly what is needed.' It was enormously encouraging for me.

"I was, after all, still pretty young and, pastorally speaking, not that experienced, you know. I had a very wise wife, but we were both thirty years old, with two small babies, living in an atmosphere both of us detested, that of an occupied country, and in a role we despised, that of the victors. I had been at war for all intents and purposes all my adult years, with no chance of any experience in ordinary living. Priests, I think, more than most people, need time and quiet to grow into their calling. I had never had either, and with all the horrors I had seen, both during and after the war, my mind, to my great confusion, had not yet been able to make the entire turn around from war to peace. And yet, if I was to contribute anything to these men who, whatever they admitted, were in great need, I could only do it from a position of peace and, in a deep sense, a position of equality."

By the following Saturday he decided to face them head-on and chose for his sermon Jesus's "Calling of Levi" (Luke 6:16) where Levi, a tax collector, held a great banquet for Jesus. The Pharisees and teachers of law complained that he should not eat and drink with tax collectors and sinners, but Jesus answered them, "It is not the healthy who need a doctor, but the sick. I have not come to call the righteous, but sinners to repentance."

And here, in the middle of the sermon, Georges stopped. "I'm a little reluctant now to preach as I do normally," he said to them. "Am I going to cause offense with the words from the Bible? And if I do, how can I be of help to you? How can you accept the help of the Bible? How can I help you understand that if I speak of the sinner and the sick—and the lepers—it is not the words, or simply the words you must hear, but parables, which you can each hear or interpret as you wish, as you need. But first and foremost, please remember always that in my own interpretation of the parables, to me the first sinner and first sick person is always myself. We are together in this experiment here, in this attempt at finding common ground between you and your inner selves, between you and me, and between the things Jesus said and what we can accept or find in them. I am in that no different from you. I search."

From that moment on, except for Hess, the group accepted him. "On one occasion," he said, "the only one while I was there, even Hess came toward me." On December 19, 1948, the Casalises' small son, Etienne, died of diphtheria. "It was surprising to me how these men at Spandau behaved when I saw them the following Saturday; they showed me quite extraordinary tenderness and compassion. I will never forget that. That was not only Speer—it was all of them, some showing it more than others. Speer was very near tears; it wouldn't have taken much for us to cry together, which I could neither have permitted nor borne."

Certainly, the ever-strengthening relationship between Casalis and Speer, and Speer's resultant concentration on what he would call his "study-program," explains the comparative paucity of letters to his family or friends during that time. This is in spite of the fact that as of October 14, 1947, when Toni Proost quite unexpectedly offered to smuggle letters out for him, he could have written anything he wanted, to anyone of his choice. Still, for the next three years, he took amazingly little advantage of this opportunity. Although the thought of writing "a Hitler biography" was somewhere in the back of his mind, and he did now and then jot down this or that anecdote he remembered, and sent it off to Annemarie Kempf, these were rare occasions.

"I never knew about Speer's writing in Spandau until after he came out," Casalis said. "Of course, he didn't write to any great extent while I was there, but even so, it is quite extraordinary and has never ceased to astonish me that he must already have known then that he would want to write, and didn't tell me.

"It didn't hurt me when I found out, because I know that a prisoner—all prisoners—are always an ambivalent entity; one lives with them in a perpetual state of half-truths or half-reality. And this certainly applied to Speer too. In a way it is the defense of their id: they can't give it up, even to someone they come to trust; if they did, it would destroy whatever 'self' they have retained. So you see, it isn't deliberate or even unconscious dishonesty. It is an instinctive self-protective process. So everything they show is always only partly really open, really true.

"While I was there, I'm quite sure Speer was concentrating on creating and then developing a rhythm of working, thinking and indeed living which would make it possible for him to grow into that 'different man.' That was his intention, of that I am certain. Afterwards, when I left—perhaps *because* I left?—he used that rhythm, that discipline he had learned, for the alternate purpose which, I now know, had always been marginally in his mind, though he abandoned it for the brief time we worked together.

"In those first years I knew Speer," he said, "he was resigned to his punishment—that much was absolutely true in him. He talked to me about a great many things: private, emotional and intellectual things. The content of our conversations changed somewhat, became, let us say, less desperate as he began to read, understand and was able to discuss his reading of Barth and of course of other works. But during those years, his reading, his studies, his thoughts originated in and were dominated by his very profound sense of guilt which was entirely centered on the murder of the Jews—to such a degree, indeed, that he seemed oblivious to Hitler's many other crimes."

The Gauleiter conference in Posen, Casalis agreed, had been the decisive moment, even though he believed that Speer knew about the Jews before, if not the gruesome details. But after the war, he had to make a decision about Posen. If he admitted to having been there, then he had to admit to knowledge; if he couldn't admit to knowledge, then he had, at all cost, to maintain his claim that he had neither been present when Himmler made his awful disclosures nor been told about them subsequently. Casalis—like Hilde—didn't see how he could have admitted *that* knowledge and still remain alive.

"All this weighed incredibly heavily on his mind," Casalis said, "and certainly whatever the risk, I saw it as part of my task, as you later saw yours, to help him confront the truth, deal with it, and having done so, remain alive."

What one could never forget, however, when considering Speer's battle, he said, was that he waged it alone, and in an extremely hostile environment. "A microcosm of Germany's confusion and defensiveness," he said, "actively directed toward him all hours of every day, whether in words or in silence."

Casalis was as struck as I was by the extent of hostility toward Speer from so many other people in other countries. "Of course cynics before, during and long after this time," he said, "condemned him over and over for whatever he did and tried and said; many of my colleagues in the faith joined this deplorable chorus. It was a curiously pathological reaction. Because the crimes under Hitler had been so dreadful and because—yes, let us confront this—most of the so-called free world had stood by, not only idly but some, even worse, in the depth of their black souls approvingly, they now could not admit that one of the 'sinners'—oh, yes, he was very much one of the sinners—wanted to repent. You see, an admission of guilt, if it is real and true, in our Christian and even some Judaic cultures is tantamount to seeking and finding forgiveness.

"And here is the point about Speer and some of his critics. They could not forgive themselves, so most certainly they could not forgive him. [Casalis's judgments were necessarily strongly influenced by his total condemnation of *French* collaborators and *French* Nazis, whom he considered if anything more guilty than the Germans. His wide experience in the resistance, of French traitors and Western Allied political prejudices toward the left factions in the resistance, which frequently had fatal results, made him very cynical toward many postwar reactions.] I tell you," he said, "the postwar attitudes, the disgusting retroactive moralizing of intellectuals, both in Europe and America, was one of the many reasons why I thought that for this deep and brilliant man—who to my mind had very little chance of finding people any more receptive to him as 'a different man' than they were to the Speer they thought they knew—the best and most rewarding life would be a contemplative one, and it was toward this solution I tried to work with him."

Speer had talked to Casalis very soon and quite extensively, he said, about his relationship with, and his feelings for, Hitler. "How could he not have?" Georges said. "The memory of this man and of those years was for a long time foremost in his mind. And for a long time he saw his breaking with Hitler as an emotional rather than a moral act. I must say that it did often make me wonder about him. I never had any reason to believe—and I know you don't either—that Speer was a homosexual or even had homosexual feelings in the now familiar and largely accepted sense. But his descriptions of his relationship with Hitler showed very clearly a *kind* of erotic attachment. There was no doubt whatever in my mind that this man had loved, and even perhaps still did love, that man.

"Of course, when we talked, there were untold questions I wanted to ask him, but I couldn't; contrary to historians or psychiatrists, a pastor's task is not to probe or to interrogate men, but to help them live. A pastor cannot request self-revelation; he can only, if it occurs by the other's initiative, accept and respond to it."

Of course Speer lied to him, Casalis said, but the lies were expressions of his need. "At the moment of being told lies," Georges said, "I didn't realize he was lying. You see, he lied to me only about facts, not about his inner life. He constructed for me a path on which he thought I could walk with him a while." Speer had, for example, told him that Hitler, in moments of hysterical anger, had "gnawed carpets" (which Speer explicitly denied to me). "He told me that," Casalis said, "because representing Hitler as a madman was perhaps a help to him in those first years of prison; it briefly allowed him the consolation, the illusion, that he had been seduced by a madman. Later, talking about his illness in 1944, he told me he had been in a coma for forty days; he told you his experience of having died. It is a mystery how he chose whom to tell what, and which of these things were more true than others, but in both of these particular ones, there was an important element of truth. When he told me about the 'coma,' he needed to think of himself as having been in such a 'coma' during a period of enormous changes inside him. When he told you, whom he trusted somewhat the same way as he did me, about having had a death vision, he perhaps needed to have you share his imagination or possibly a very private experience. It was a present he gave you.

"If he didn't tell Annemarie Kempf—or his wife—about either of these, despite the fact that they were closer to him than either you or I, it was because they were physically *there* at the time, and he couldn't share with them a metamorphosis he felt was happening in him, of which these experiences, imagined or real, were an integral part.

"The [near] death experience," Georges continued, "as he described it to you, is fairly familiar now, has been written about many times almost exactly as he described it to you. He may of course have had this experience. On the other hand, could he have read about it and adapted it to himself? Could he have wanted to have felt it, or perhaps want to have been—or to be—dead? All this is highly possible. Equally, of course, during this very significant period for him, January to May 1944, when we can assume he went through this metamorphosis, he might well have wanted to have been asleep—he might have wished it didn't really happen, that his illusions didn't really die, that his love for Hitler didn't end. All this is possible, all of it part of the human experience. I remember many times driving away from Spandau after these talks and saying to myself, '*Merde,* what an oddball.'

"Don't forget, for years I had been and still was very seriously involved in politics. To me, in a world like ours, to be religious is tantamount to having a social conscience, and a social conscience means politics. Thus, religion essentially never has and doesn't exist without politics. And I said to myself, how did a man like that, a man with such feelings of love, ever fit into serious politics? And the answer is, of course, he didn't—he fell into it, unknowing. Indulging his emotions, he played at it, never realizing or never facing that it was a most dangerous game. It was not that he didn't come to realize that it could cost him his head—he knew terribly well how to play the game to protect his life. But he didn't know, and until Nuremberg and Spandau didn't admit to himself, that it could cost him his soul."

AFTER SPEER was sentenced, Annemarie went back to the trailer camp at Eutin, which was now her only home. Her troubled family joined her, she said—her mother, who had cancer; her sister, suffering from multiple sclerosis; and her brother, who had come out of the army with emphysema. She and her brother got work on a farm, at thirty pfennigs an hour, and soon afterwards the Eutin community, adopting—as had been the case all over Germany—the self-help building movement Speer had suggested in his last radio speech, gave them a plot of land to build two cottages for themselves. "One for my mother and me, and one for my brother and his family," she told me. "We cleaned umpteen thousands of bricks, and a year or so later, with some help of course from architect friends, we had two little houses."

In Kransberg she had formed a close friendship with the former director general of BMW, Wilhelm Schärf, a known opponent of the Nazis, who was there as a consultant rather than a prisoner.

"Thanks to his advice," said Annemarie, "the Americans got a lot of the BMW technicians out before the plant was transferred to the Russians. He was a wonderful man and enormously helpful to me. I was very desperate about life then, not because the war had been lost, but because of the terrible unhappiness it had caused—Hitler had caused. Schärf had for years been very interested in anthropology, and he got me involved in it. It filled a void in me and gave me hope. All during the house building in Eutin, I was planning my future, which from the start I knew would somehow have to involve helping children."

But then, toward the end of 1949, one of Speer's former industrialist friends who had become a member of parliament offered her a job in Bonn.

"I think it is fair to say," she said, "that although I had other plans by then, I deliberately went there because I thought that it might be of use to Speer." She stayed there for five years with the sole purpose of being near politicians who might be willing to help obtain an early release for him.

"After a few years, you see," Annemarie said, "his resolution to 'pay his dues,' to serve out every minute of his sentence, gave way to determination—really more in tune with what I call his 'pre-Casalis' personality—to fight the system and get himself an early release. In the course of time all of us were mobilized toward that effort—Rudi Wolters, Hilde, me and anyone we could interest in his fate.

"I don't know how much use my presence in Bonn was," she said. "There were of course small things I could achieve, like getting the decision that they couldn't have newspapers modified and that sort of thing, but most things one tried didn't work out. What one could do, was to try to convey a different image of Speer's personality, and this usually worked. But I think finally it was more of a comfort to me, than of practical use to him."

After Toni Proost's extraordinary offer in October 1947, Annemarie Kempf told me during our first series of talks in Hamburg in 1982, Speer did begin to send her occasional dated notes. "And he quite soon started that Spanish-Illustrated, his to me rather heartbreaking attempt to make it all sound funny for the children," she said. "He addressed these to me, but there was very little of it for the first three years. The first *Cassiber* [secret consignment from a prison] of any size didn't arrive until 1950."

Two years later he began writing to Wolters, she said, and of course in January 1953 he started his "Spandau draft" for his memoirs, which became *Inside the Third Reich*. Once Speer really started to write in Spandau, he very carefully organized to whom he sent what. As of 1952–53 it was Wolters who received the bulk of everything: first the "Spandau draft"—written in up to forty-page letters entirely from memory—and when Speer was through with that, for years appendixes for it, afterthoughts to much he had written there.

"To me," said Annemarie, "he sent everything to do with Bonn—suggestions for easing of the Spandau rules; drafts for letters to and from well-known personalities, to government officials and foreign heads of state suggesting his early release; suggestions—in later years mostly for Hilde, who became very effective in this kind of public relations for her father—for contacts with foreign dignitaries by high-ranking Germans, sympathetic American and British legal personalities, and top journalists. Most of his many communications to me were of that kind.

"His *Späne*,* the Spanish-Illustrated—his collective letters to the chil-

*German proverb: "*Wo gehobelt, da fallen Späne*" ("Where there is planing, there are shavings").

dren—and the ones he wrote to individual children, went via either Rudi or me, or in later years Hilde. His main need was to organize everything himself, to keep everything under his control. He insisted that all *Cassibers* in and out were sent according to 'astrological dates' he instructed us on; he said it was the only way he could systematize his work. I think it was actually more for his morale than any 'system,' but although I sympathized with his need for it, about eight years later when I became very busy and had to travel a lot, I couldn't keep up with the 'astrologicals' "—she smiled—"and had to deal with it on my own more mundane schedule. Albert understood, but Rudi was furious, and for a while my relationship with him collapsed. A couple of years later, on Albert's plea, because he needed us to work for him together, we patched it up."

The frequent dates which go through *The Secret Diaries* seem to indicate that he had made and kept notes from the beginning, and throughout his time in prison, but Annemarie said that wasn't the case.

"For many years this was precisely the problem. Officially they were quite free to write anything they liked on the few pages of paper they were given; but at suppertime every evening they were required to hand in what they had written and, except for their monthly official letter home, which was censored and posted, anything written was shredded. [In later years, they would be given a notebook which they could keep until it was full—then *it* was shredded.] Later, when he really started to write, both on any bits of paper he had— tobacco, cigarette or chocolate wrappings, and even toilet paper, for years his most important source of supply, and later on writing paper which we managed to smuggle in—he simply flouted that rule and took the most appalling risks, usually hiding his writings in his shoes and, when he got going, sometimes forty or fifty pages in the top of his socks under his trouser legs.

"As he explained in his Preface to *The Secret Diaries*, and this applied equally to his first book, the thousands of original letters and transcribed pages Rudi Wolters and his family handed over to him after his release from Spandau, all depended on that phenomenal memory of his which, ever since he was a boy, as he told you, had allowed him to store up experiences and impressions as if his mind were an archive.

"In earlier years, we knew that he had only to look at a document, a letter or a newspaper article to be able to recite it verbatim when needed. I often saw him astonish Hitler, industrialists or the military at conferences with these feats of memory. Throughout the years at Spandau, he worked methodically to keep this facility in training, by learning books by heart. When he came out, he could recite much of the Bible, the New Testament as well as the Old, and all kinds of books—reference works, novels and poetry, now often in English, French and Latin."

He wrote in his Preface to *The Secret Diaries* that everything in it was authentic, and this was perfectly true, she said. "But he first reorganized his Spandau letters—to Wolters, to me and to his children—to fit the concept of each of the books, and then, as had to be done, he supplemented his original writings with other things he remembered, plus the necessary dates and documentation from the historical archives, his own and the Federal Archives."

When I talked to her, I had of course read *The Secret Diaries, Inside the Third Reich* and *Infiltrations* but had not yet seen the Wolters archive. It was only as I studied these letters and compared them with the printed text, that I realized one surprising element of his "reorganization." The specific letters to Wolters, which came to constitute the "Spandau draft," were carefully dated by Speer at the start of each letter and again within the text when one letter was written over several days. Marion Riesser, in her transcripts, meticulously included all these dates. This typescript, as already noted, shows him beginning his task on January 8, 1953, and completing it on January 9, 1954. However, in *The Secret Diaries,* he reported instead that he had taken *two* years to finish it, and gave various progress reports throughout the two years. Thus, his first mention of writing his memoirs in *The Secret Diaries* is dated March 8, 1953, when "after hesitations and false starts":

> I began writing as if it was the most natural thing in the world. . . . I have made it easy for myself. I did not begin with Hitler, but with my childhood.

In reality, he had begun the memoirs in a letter dated January 8, 1953—"In April [1945], I heard of the order to prepare all the Berlin bridges for destruction"—and writes for five pages how he persuaded the general in charge not to destroy them. Then, in the same letter, he writes nine pages about his final visit to Hitler. He never did write about his childhood in the "Spandau draft"; that information was later drawn from his letters to the children. *The Secret Diaries* continues,

> May 2: My friend's secretary is typing up the closely written pages. . . . My friend . . . complains because I have called Hitler a criminal, but there is no dodging that. Certainly I shall be losing a good many friends. . . .
>
> November 28: I have been informed from Coburg [his code for Coesfeld, to "protect" Wolters] that there are already 350 typewritten pages filled. . . . For many events I lack data and material from memorandums. . . . There will have to be another version . . . after my release. . . . I have not proceeded chronologically. From my youth, I jumped to my period as a government Minister. I plan to take up the decade as Hitler's architect last of all. Today I began the section on July 20, 1944.

In reality, between July 3 and July 12, 1953, he wrote twenty-one pages on the July 20 plot, and then started a new letter: "My dear friend, I now continue with the description of the tragedy of the Twentieth of July. As you will have gathered, in retrospect my sympathy is with the men who tried to do something about the approaching catastrophe. It is very difficult for me now to say what my attitude toward this event was then." The next mention of his memoirs in *The Secret Diaries* was dated January 4, 1954: "I have by this time reached the Ardennes offensive, which the Americans call the Battle of the Bulge. . . ."

But in fact he had written about the Ardennes five months earlier, July 26, 1953: "In November 1944 Hitler told me in complete confidence that he planned a major offensive in the West. . . . The Western Allies were weak and incapable of hard fighting, and that it must therefore be possible to break through in the center . . . advancing to Antwerp . . . thus forming a huge pocket which would force large parts of the U.S. and British armies to capitulate. . . ."

His description in *The Secret Diaries* of coming to the end of his memoirs was very like that in his draft, except that it was dated one year later. In the draft he wrote, on December 26, 1953, "I have only a final paragraph to write, and an epilogue. This will make a thousand pages—I'm glad I didn't know how much work it would be when I started one year ago." His book said,

> December 29 [1954]: My estimate was pretty close. I wanted to conclude the memoirs on January 1, and today I brought the book to a conclusion as best I could. . . . From Heidelberg, I hear that it mounts up to some 1,100 pages. . . . This is the end of a laborious, sometimes upsetting task that has taken me two years.

It is obvious in studying the "Spandau draft," from which he created *Inside the Third Reich*, that he had to transform the original material, which jumped from subject to subject with additions thrown in helter-skelter as they entered his mind, into a logical orderly account. His decision to claim that the original took from March 1953 to December 1954 was taken then, and he gives those dates in his Afterword. Then he reinforced it in *The Secret Diaries* with repeated references to how the work was progressing, associating various subjects to specific dates—all of them wrong.

I have consulted the few people familiar with the draft, in Koblenz, in Munich and in Berlin. Everyone agrees that while there is no reason whatsoever to suspect his motivations here, equally there is no rational explanation for this curious divergence from the facts.

But sometimes explanations are simpler than one thinks or seeks. The consensus of those who knew Speer well is that when he worked through the reams of letters in 1967, it may have occurred to him that no one could believe he wrote them all in one year. For want of a better explanation, I conclude that in his often airy but always pragmatic way, he simply decided to turn that one incredibly creative year into two.

CASALIS LEFT BERLIN in June 1950; Speer records in *The Secret Diaries* that he saw him last on June 1. "I was very sad seeing him go," he told me, "but at that point I really thought the strength he had given me, in life as much as in God, you understand, would carry me through." But after only a few weeks he realized he couldn't manage on his own. "I had to face the fact that I am very dependent on external influences," he wrote two and a half years later to the then sixteen-year-old Hilde. "If I have a Casalis I can manage. But without such a catalyst I fall apart: all my good intentions evaporate."

After a period of intense apathy and depression, he reverted almost entirely, away from his difficult spiritual search, to his concentration on himself, not as a different Speer of the future, but as an adapted version of the persona of his extraordinary past. Nonetheless, he retained the three most essential things of his three years' tutelage with Casalis: a conviction that life had a wider meaning than that provided by intelligence and logic, the saving grace of disciplined reading and, however desperately "blocking" the worst part of it, a real inner awareness of guilt.

It took him almost two years to come to terms with Casalis's departure, a period during which, spending as much time as possible working in the garden, he slowly created a "program of living" for himself. The first step was the work in the garden, esthetically the most creative thing he was to do in those twenty years.

"When he arrived, it was a comparatively small wilderness," said Eugene Bird, who had been an American guard officer at the beginning and became the U.S. Spandau director toward the end. "When he left it was like a wonderfully laid-out park, with a profusion of flowers of every description, a vegetable plot—lettuce, tomatoes and berries to supplement their, and sometimes our own, diets—and an orchard with dozens of apple and plum trees." (Speer wrote to his children on June 16, 1953: "I was myself surprised today when I inspected my garden. When I counted, I found that I'm the 'owner' of 800 strawberry bushes, 100 lilac trees now 2 meters high, 100 chestnut and 50 hazelnut trees.")

His reading was equally or even more important in his new life. On July 3, 1955, writing to Wolters, he described his reading program, but he had by then already sent him three lists of books he had read—by the beginning of 1956 it would be about 1,500. "I don't know whether I ever told you my reading method," he wrote. "I'm allowed three books in my cell at any one time, plus the Bible. One of them is usually on architecture, one on something more demanding—philosophy, theology or science—and the third, for recreation, a novel or a travel book. I start my reading about 5:30 p.m. with the 'heavy'; after 10–20 pages, depending on how difficult it is (pedantic as ever, I decide on its 'grade' as soon as I get it, and determine the number of pages I can read every day), I change to architecture and, always interrupted at least four times by the newspapers which the guards pass from cell to cell—what a chore they are, and yet one feels obligated to peruse them—I end up for the last half-hour before the lights go out with my light reading, which I also indulge in for a bit in the morning before getting up."

It took him about five years to create some sort of modus vivendi with his co-prisoners. He never had any problems with onetime Foreign Minister Neurath. "I never knew him to be anything but a gentleman," he wrote to Wolters at Christmas 1954, a month after Neurath, old and sick, had been granted an early release. Speer and Funk eventually forged a kind of tie almost entirely based on their shared passion for humor and for music. Speer wrote to the children, in the same cheerful letter (June 16) which described his garden,

> Let me show you the kind of grave problems we have: Saturday, before the service, is our bath time, two of us at a time, as there are two tubs in the bathroom. As there are seven of us, the last has to bathe alone and that is usually me. Well, last week Funk asked me whether I minded if he went last—there is a Russian guard he can't stand who goes on duty at 11 a.m. and always makes a point of immediately looking in on the bathers, who at that time are usually Funk and Hess. I said fine, I'd bathe with Hess. As it happened, I got to the bathroom just before Hess and got into "my" tub; over the course of time we have come to feel proprietary about all kinds of things, among them the tubs. Hess comes in and asks, "What are you doing in my tub?" As you know, I am a peaceful man. "Oh, is this your tub?" I say and, with water pouring off me, get out of it and take the other. Hess bathes very quickly and is out while I'm still splashing about—you might send me a duck to play with next! Funk comes in, ready for his bath, and makes a serious face. "What are you doing in my tub?" says he. "That has been mine for six years." I know he is half joking so I burst out laughing. "To punish you," he says, "I'm going to play nothing but Wagner at the service." As you know, he plays the organ—beautifully. And indeed, that was what he did. . . . Terrible, terrible Wagner, from *Lohengrin* to *Götterdämmerung* for forty-five minutes. Well, there you are—a look-in on our daily life.

Speer's most difficult relations would always be with his former *"Du"* friend Dönitz, who could never believe Speer's assurance that it had not been he who had persuaded Hitler to appoint him his successor. And the man he least trusted, from the beginning to the day they were both released, was Schirach.

("Schirach was the one I talked to most," said Jan Boon. "He was the second youngest there, but he was somehow a terribly idle man. He did crossword puzzles every day, and of course he read, but, contrary to all the others, particularly Hess and Speer, he seemed to have no resources. All he ever seemed to want was to talk—to somebody, about nothing.")

The one person with whom Speer succeeded surprisingly well was Hess. "Speer was the only one who showed Hess any kindness," Boon said rather grudgingly, for he never liked Speer. "He was arrogant," he said. "He would tell us what to do, for instance, about Hess; he would instruct me how to deal with him. Well, I didn't need Speer for that. We were always afraid Hess would kill himself—he tried twice. But on the whole, one knew what to do: I quite often gave him placebo injections when he screamed with some—we were sure imaginary—pain. And our ruse invariably worked."

Speer, he said, was condescending, and there was never anything impulsive from him. "Except," he added, "when any of the prisoners were sick. I have to admit, just like with Hess, whom he basically helped every day, that when any of the others needed help—their cells cleaned, their food brought, books changed—Speer was there to do it."

"I had of course known Hess for years," Speer said, "but always *'mit Distanz.'*" He smiled. "He was, if anything, even more reserved than I." For much of the twenty years at Spandau, Speer and Hess had adjacent cells. "It was only there I came to understand the degree of his sensitivity and vulnerability, but also of his very real strength," Speer said. "I grew to like him very much. He was emotional about his family, even sentimental, and, yes, he was an eccentric in many ways; but he had more integrity than perhaps any of us there. He was very kind to me," he added, "which, given the position I had taken at Nuremberg and maintained throughout my time at Spandau, was all the more remarkable in that his own loyalty to Hitler was unquestionable, and unquestioning. But as an essentially religious man and a philosopher, he had both compassion and patience. He could disagree entirely with your opinions, but"—again he smiled—"very democratic really, he accorded you the right to hold them.

"There was a curious fellowship between him and me," he said. "We were both loners; we were both insatiable readers, and we were both disliked by our fellow prisoners. But there was something more important. We had both been close to Hitler, had both reveled in this closeness and then—we discussed this repeatedly in Spandau—had both had to acknowledge to our-selves its limitations. Hitler had no friend, could not feel friendship, perhaps did not know what it was. So, in a way, we had an important emotional defeat in common. Hess told me that even in prison in Landsberg, when Hitler was dictating *Mein Kampf* to him—and they lived in closer proximity than he and I did in Spandau—Hitler, despite the superficial conviviality and even joviality he often displayed, was aloof and alone."

But there was something else between himself and Hess, he said. Both of them had adopted a moral position that divided them from the others. "Hess's attitude, really until the end of his life," Speer said, "was that National Socialism was alive, not dead; that it and Hitler, as 'the greatest man Germany had produced,' as he called him in his final words at Nuremberg, could never die. To him Hitler remained the *Führer,* and he remained the *Führer Deputy.* For many years he insisted on being addressed by this title (Führer Stellvertreter) by all of us—and the Nazi principles remained the principles of his life.

"I, on the other hand, had publicly rejected both Hitler and the principles, and continued to do this throughout my time at Spandau. Strangely enough, we could acknowledge these diametric differences between us but still respect and to a degree support each other. He, of course," Speer said, "was humanly more perceptive than I. One day, in the early 1960s, I think, when it really did look as if the Allies would release us all, I said to him that when we were out, I would come up to the Allgäu to see him; we would sit over a good bottle of wine and perhaps find it in us to laugh about some of our memories of Spandau. And he said, 'If ever we are all out, none of us will ever see each other again; most certainly, we shall never laugh about Spandau.' He was right, on both counts."

BY MAY 1952 Margret had visited Speer four times. His mother had a stroke in May 1952 and died a month later. His father's death five years earlier, while Speer was still in Nuremberg prison, and his realization that there was nothing he could do to help his mother over her bereavement, had been "unbelievably painful," as he would recall for me. From what he said, however, it was clear that the "unbelievable pain" was less for his father's death, which he had then been expecting for some time, than for his inability to "be with my mother at that time." And his mother's death, though again expected, was nothing short of traumatic for him.

"Nothing that had happened in my private life, not even my father's death," he said, "was as excruciating. Now I had no more hope."

This conversation, once again, took place late at night in his studio in the

Allgäu. It was in that room, late at night, with a glass of good wine next to him and after some quiet time listening to music, that he was most apt to reveal his deeper feelings. His sentence about having "no more hope" was said slowly, sadly, but I thought quite spontaneously; he had not pondered how to phrase it or put it into specific context. I asked him what he meant by "no more hope." He looked surprised and shook his head. "I don't know what I meant," he said.

Annemarie Kempf, to whom I quoted this years later, thought she did know. "Her death came at what I think was just about the zero point of those two years after Casalis left. Except for his very first letters after Toni Proost offered to smuggle mail out, when he was euphoric in this newfound freedom to communicate, virtually every one of the few letters or notes I had during that time reflected his depression, each one basically more so than the preceding one. But shortly after her death," she said, "he wrote the most desperate letter I was ever to receive from him. I had known his mother, and I'm afraid disliked her. She was arrogant and pretentious. I had seen her quite a few times, in Berlin and in Berchtesgaden, where she often took charge of the house when Speer and his wife were away on holidays. His father, a very distinguished and upright man, never came there, but when she did, Hitler, who was thoughtful that way, knowing that she was there, sometimes had her invited to supper at the Berghof. Afterwards she would talk unendingly about having been seated next to Hitler and hinted at confidences he made to her which, by then knowing quite a bit about Hitler's social habits, we were quite sure never took place."

But Annemarie's dislike for Speer's mother dated principally to the time when Speer's brother Ernst died at Stalingrad. "Not surprisingly, she totally lost her composure and pursued Speer with telephone calls, some of which I had to take in his absence," Annemarie recalled. "She sent him the most dreadful messages, her voice sounding almost vicious. During the subsequent week I inadvertently heard him on the telephone with her several times. Twice afterwards—I have always remained surprised about this—he handed me, without comment, letters she wrote to him. They were terrible letters, and he was devastated by them, more by his mother, I thought, than by the fact that his father too, at the time, appeared, quite irrationally, to hold him responsible for his brother's death. Although he never explicitly talked to me about his childhood feelings about her, I must admit that, knowing her, I guessed some of them, though perhaps not their true extent. So I was extremely worried about him when she died, but not altogether surprised at the strength of his reaction. His love for his mother was unrequited. When he became so wildly successful, she was no doubt proud of him, but more of herself as the mother of the Führer's favorite. But I never thought she loved him. Now that I understand even more, I believe that he tried all his life to get her to love him, and I think, until she died, he must have hoped there would still be an opportunity for it to happen. And that hope, of course, had to die with her."

In February 1952, Speer heard that Hilde, still only fifteen, had won an American Field Service competition to spend a year as a high school student in America. "I had very mixed feelings about it," he told me. "I became terribly worried about what they would tell her about me. Somehow, the thought of her being exposed to . . . criticism of me suddenly made me terribly aware for the first time of what my children could feel."

Three months later, in early June 1952, after the State Department had refused Hilde a visa, he wrote Margret a stern letter:

> I'm sorry for her but it may be for the best: perhaps she is rather young for this, and too open to influences and "Americanization" of a kind she may not understand. I thought it was a great mistake that she wrote me about this trip in an "official" letter—there are people here who don't wish us well and who carefully read what is said to me. And perhaps you don't realize this: all "official" letters are copied and sent to the four powers for information. You should never forget that. It is in fact necessary that you censor the children's letters: Hilde also once mentioned visiting Breker [the sculptor]—who most certainly would not want anybody's attention drawn to him—and that I knew Cortot [the pianist] well in Paris: not good for Cortot, either. *And* she mentioned Coesfeld, which could be fatal to R. [Rudi Wolters]. You must all avoid mentioning names. Also, *you* must not say anything positive: in your next "official" say that Flächsner needs to act for me again but that you aren't sure we can afford it; write how difficult everything is, Omi's [his mother's] illness, so expensive, last money soon gone and that you don't know what to do then. Also that you don't know how you will be able to visit me in the autumn since up to now Omi always gave you money for the trips, etc., etc. Important though: when you write something that is untrue, insert the word "nevertheless" to let me know.
>
> I'm wondering whether it might be a good thing for you to write and thank the people who organize these student exchanges—after all, they had the best intentions. There were always two groups among the Americans I met: one who wanted nothing more than to put me in charge of reconstruction, already in 1946, and the other . . . well, you can imagine. . . .

From what he says here it is very clear that, whatever his feelings of guilt, it had not yet occurred to him that there could be a third group in America and elsewhere, by no means necessarily Jews, who deplored him on principle, simply on moral grounds.

A few days later, the U.S. Army paper *Stars and Stripes* announced that after intervention by the former High Commissioner John McCloy, the State Department had reversed themselves about Hilde Speer, and that a distinguished Jewish family had offered her hospitality.

In *The Secret Diaries* Speer wrote that he had been very moved about this offer. "I would have found it almost unbelievable," he told me, "if it hadn't been for the fact that all along there had been American Jews, both in Nuremberg and by then in Spandau, who had shown me the most incredible kindness. So, yes, I was moved, and I was shamed. But I was also worried. . . ."

On June 23, less than four weeks before Hilde would leave, he wrote her a long letter of advice. The change of tone in his letters at this time suggests that this was a real turning point for him, the end of the two-year psychological bridge from the time when Casalis left him as a man in the beginning stages of transformation toward a different future to the time when, his mind almost exclusively on himself, he decided to take the easier way out—for the most part returning to the past. He wrote,

> I want to congratulate you but also add my bit of "wise" advice! First of all, do all you can to avoid confrontations. . . . You won't be able to evade journalists and indeed, unless your hosts suggest it, you shouldn't. If they ask you political questions, just point out your age. . . . You should not mention that you knew Hitler, nor that you lived on the Obersalzberg. They will not understand why you haven't visited me in prison . . . [so] tell them it is your parents' decision; that we decided it would only make you sad. Schirach's children . . . usually leave in tears. I couldn't stand it and would perhaps lose my self-control. If they ask, it wouldn't do any harm if you tell them that I never complain in my letters and that I try to cheer you up. . . . You should absolutely read three books: Trevor-Roper's *The Last Days of Hitler;* Gilbert's *Nuremberg Diary;* and a book by Musmano whose title I don't know, but it was published in the U.S.A. If you read those, you'll be able to answer any attacks on me.
>
> I read in the paper that you may be staying for part of the year with a nice Jewish family. If so, you should be very happy about it: I am certain they will do everything to make you feel at ease. Our doctors in Nuremberg were Jews and despite the hate-filled atmosphere there, they couldn't have been more decent or kinder. I never had any problems with them, and they always acknowledged that I never said anything in speeches or otherwise that anyone could object to. . . . Please write . . . and I will answer. Let the Americans teach you what I have always admired in them and in the British: their self-control. Don't be too critical—people are different and there is great value in these differences. It is a very important

event in your life. . . . I am so proud of you. I know you will do well (and thereby do well for me, too).

P.S.: Copy on a piece of paper which of my bits of advice you accept and send it to Frau Kempf; I'd like to know. And I rely on your discretion.

P.P.S.: Secret language: If something is wrong, but you don't want to, or can't, say so, then put the word "nevertheless" before the sentence. Thus if you say, "Nevertheless, I'm fine," it means you are not fine at all. I'd rather know. You can find the three books I mentioned in any U.S. library.

The letter shows that he had no concept of who or what his daughter really was. From this moment on his letters become more frequent; he began to write several times a week to Wolters and, via him, to Margret and Anne-marie Kempf. He also wrote, in August 1952, to Dr. Werner Schütz, a distinguished lawyer (soon to be named Minister of Culture), who had offered to represent him in any official steps with the Allies, and in matters of inheritance as well:

I'm infinitely grateful for your offer. I'm not convinced anything positive can happen for me, but by all means, let us quietly prepare, just in case. Since we are lucky enough to have this chance to communicate, perhaps you would like to take me through the Nuremberg verdict paragraph by paragraph; I'm only too happy to answer any question. My guilt, as I voluntarily stated even before the trial, is, in my opinion, limited to the fact that I demanded that workers be brought to Germany who came against their will, and that I did not stop my demands even when I knew that they were brought by force. And given the huge numbers involved, this is without doubt a serious point against me. . . . What is very important to me now is to protect my wife and the children from any further exposure. . . .

He wrote the same day to Annemarie Kempf:

Don't get too impatient if you are not successful with your attempts. It makes me really happy to hear how energetically and loyally you represent my interests. It seems immodest that I accept your help as if it was my due, and yet I have a feeling you prefer that to any of the many thank-yous I could express. But be patient. . . . I am.

Hilde's American hosts, it turned out, were a distinguished Quaker family. Richard Day was an eminent pediatrician, his wife, Ida, an untiring worker for others. They had two passions: for music (all the family played instruments) and for inviting young people in trouble to live with them in their comfortable, rambling house in Hastings-on-Hudson, New York. Their

three daughters—Kate, ten (in 1952); Betty, fifteen; and Sally, seventeen—
would later remember about eighty young foreigners who had lived with
them between the late 1930s and the mid-1960s: European refugees from the
Nazis, South Americans fleeing juntas or communists, and Hilde, who was to
remain unique in their experience.

The whole family met Hilde on her arrival in Boston. "It happened at the
beginning of our holiday," Ida told me, "which we always spent on our
boat—a small ketch on which we lived on top of each other during the
month of August. We had been told that she was brilliant but shy, and we
thought that would be the best way to get acquainted with her."

When I visited them in 1986, Ida was seventy-nine and Richard was eighty-
one years old. (Richard would die three years later; Ida followed him in 1993.)
They had given up the big house in Hastings when Dick, as I was immediately asked to call him, was offered a professorship first in Brooklyn and then
in Pittsburgh. Later they had retired to a smallish clapboard house with a
wonderfully untidy garden in Westbrook, a small town in Connecticut.
Photos showed that there was astonishingly little difference between their
looks the day we met there and thirty-four years earlier when Hilde met them
first, when they were forty-five and forty-seven. They had remained straight-
backed, their tanned faces full of life, with blue eyes in which one could see
both steel and a twinkle. They, as well as their home and garden, might have
stepped straight out of a painting titled *American Pioneers*. What extraordinary luck it was that Hilde should have ended up with them.

"We had read in *Time* magazine in February about her winning the American Field Service competition," Ida Day said, "and not long afterwards the
principal of Hastings High School called and asked whether we would have
her to stay with us. We were absolutely disgusted three months later when
the State Department refused her the visa. She had won the competition fair
and square. Going in for this prize, which she had done with her mother's
support but over her father's objections, had already been an act of considerable courage; there was no reason in the world why our government should
now penalize her for her father's past." The Days were in the process of
mounting a lobbying campaign against the State Department decision when
they were informed that the objection had been withdrawn.

"I have a curiously precise memory of my first sight of her," Dick said; he
had no doubt looked at Hilde with the eyes of an experienced children's doctor. "With her small thin face and those grave, grave eyes, she looked like a
woman of twenty-five in the body of a particularly underdeveloped teenager.
'What have we here?' I thought."

"What I remember best about that first day," Ida said, "was her diving off the side of our boat and swimming faster than I had ever seen anyone move in the water; she was more like a fine little fish than any human child."

"It was quite strange that Hilde should have ended up with us," said Kate, a cellist who lives in London, where we talked after I met her family. "Our parents had been passionately anti-Nazi, and quite a few of our guests had been victims of the Nazis." This applied particularly, she said, to three young Dutch girls named Wiener—one of them had been a great friend of Anne Frank's—who came to live with the Days in 1945, almost straight out of Belsen (where their mother had died), and who, for the Day family, came to personify all of the Nazi horror. "My mother became very attached to them," Kate said.

"They were very traumatized, very needy, and like all institutionalized children, very receptive to love," Ida said of the Wiener girls. "Seeing them change, almost day by day, was wonderfully rewarding."

"Hilde became equally rewarding for us," Dick said, "but it took time. When she arrived, she was the most self-contained, closed-up and disciplined young person I had ever seen. I could see no happiness in her, no joy in being alive. To us, who lived sort of helter-skelter, she was, I suppose, quite a shock. She was so terribly controlled, so . . . correct."

"She was unfailingly polite, punctual and incredibly tidy about her things and her person," said Ida. "On the other hand, she seemed entirely incapable of spontaneous acts, either in expressing affection, sympathy, or in helping others—in the house, other children, or me—for any reason other than obligation."

"Of all the young people who came here, virtually all of whom had had a hard time in life," Dick said, "I think, oddly enough, that Hilde, whose childhood had been one of exceptional privilege, was the one in deepest confusion. With most of the others, we somehow succeeded quickly in reducing the effect of their various traumas. With Hilde it was slow, and I attributed this entirely to her very deep conflicts about her father. Oddly enough, though she was the politest child we ever had here, for the first months she was not easy to live with. One could never, well, forget her; one was always aware of her, with concern." He smiled, looking at Ida. "I advised patience but I could sense a brewing storm."

"It happened about six or seven weeks into her stay with us," Betty, their middle daughter, remembered. She had come to visit her family and to talk with me about Hilde. "Mother just burst out. Usually, when she didn't like something we did, she told us and that was that; I think with Hilde, she had suppressed her irritation so hard for weeks that when she let go, it was entirely out of proportion and awesome to behold. She just let her have it. She told her everything about her that she objected to. I actually felt pretty bad about Hilde being yelled at like that. While Mother took her to task, she just stood there, straight as a die and took it. Later, upstairs, I listened whether she cried; I would have gone to her if she had, but I didn't hear anything."

Kate, remembering that time, smiled: "It wouldn't have been good manners to be heard, but she cried all right; I can remember seeing tears in her eyes for three days when she thought nobody was looking. I was too young to know much, but later I did wonder whether the very strong feelings my mother had had for the three Wiener girls had something to do with the anger she showed that day to Hilde."

"I was terribly upset with Mother for doing that," said Betty, "but the fact is that somehow it must have been the right thing to do. For from that day on, Hilde was a different girl—it was almost as if it had given her a badly needed release."

"America was immensely important for me," Hilde had told me in Berlin, the year before I met the Days. "I loved it. The Days were unimaginably kind and warm—and discreet too; immense care had been taken to shield me. The whole family were part of this care for me."

That care had not been without cost. "Three of our best friends, who were Jewish, wouldn't enter our house during the year Hilde was there," Dick said.

That Christmas, the Days gave Hilde a flute, and the girls' trio—Sally played the harp, Betsy the violin and Kate the cello—soon turned into a quartet. Hilde would write to them at Christmas 1986 that she was still playing on that flute.

Kate showed me photographs of a laughing Hilde. "Those were taken in the spring," she said, "when she had changed." And Betty remembered her elder sister coming home from boarding school that Christmas and saying, "Hilde doesn't have cold eyes anymore."

"We liked her when she came," Ida said, "and we grew to love her; I love her to this day. And also, she taught us a great deal." Dick took her hand. "She taught Ida and me to stop hating Nazis—I still hated their ideas, but no longer the people. And that was very important to me, and very good for me."

Betty remembered that in late spring of 1953 Hilde began talking quite a lot about her father. "She asked my parents whether she should still love him in spite of what he had done, and Mother said, 'He is still your father—you must love him, and, more than that, you must very clearly show him your love.'"

By this time, of course, Speer had written her many letters. She had become immensely important to him. "Important because I had begun to realize how extraordinary she was," he told me. "I could see from her letters how she was growing, how deep—much deeper than mine—her mind was, and I was so proud of her. You know, I found myself living in and through her; I think I told her this later. I hope I did. But I don't want to lie to you—part of her importance to me was that she was in America; that she met many people who might help me; and indeed that she lived in close proximity to John McCloy, who had become my main hope."*

Hilde was well aware of her father's hopes for some benefit from her efforts. She had written to McCloy at the very beginning of her American stay; the McCloys invited her over for tea. The Nuremberg sentence on her father, he told her, was disproportionate. He would do all he could to help get him an early release. Speer replied on October 10, 1952:

> It is the most encouraging news you could have given me. McCloy has great influence, as has Eisenhower [elected President soon after this], and I think they are close. If both of them are positively inclined toward me—and I was told in 1946 that Eisenhower was—I really begin to feel hope.

Without doubt Speer's most creative year was 1953. In the twelve months from January 8, 1953, to January 9, 1954, he wrote, as already discussed, the entire "Spandau draft" of his memoirs, which became *Inside the Third Reich*. But in this year he also wrote dozens of other letters, to Wolters, Annemarie Kempf, his lawyers, other members of his family, individual children and many of the collective Spanish-Illustrated letters. And aside from this, he entertained a fairly copious correspondence with Hilde. "It was as if his brain and his energy became almost manic," Annemarie said later. "I never did understand how he managed it all. I finally just marveled."

It was during this year that he wrote time and again to Hilde about faith. For example, on January 9, 1953:

> My parents didn't go to church . . . and in school the chaplain was in the unintelligent habit of imposing the learning of Psalms by heart as a punishment! You can imagine how that called forth my spirit of contradiction. Your mother and I did marry in church, but I can't claim to have felt anything then: we just did it to please her parents. And so, even though when you were born we were still formally members of the church, we didn't have you baptized. . . . It really wasn't that Hitler forced anything on us—on the contrary, he forbade his closest circle, Hess,

---

*John J. McCloy had a distinguished legal career before he became Assistant Secretary of War from 1941 to 1945. In 1947 he headed the new World Bank and in 1949 succeeded the U.S. military governor, General Lucius Clay, to become the first civilian High Commissioner for Germany, as well as chairman of the Allied High Commission, until 1952, the period in which sovereignty was being returned to the West German Republic. He returned to the United States in 1953 as chairman of the Chase National Bank. His career of public service continued for the rest of his life, and included working under Kennedy, Johnson and Nixon on arms control and disarmament.

Goebbels, Göring, etc., to leave their churches, and he himself, as you may know, never formally renounced the Catholic Church. You may say that was just political expediency, but I'm not sure I would agree: I suspect that in the way of many Catholics, he somehow couldn't give it up. I think they always believe that renouncing the church would bring God's wrath upon them. When your mother and I did leave the [Protestant] church, it was in reaction to the political opposition of the churches to Hitler—I suppose it was a sort of statement of loyalty. Silly. But we did decide together to make Albert attend Sunday school in Berchtesgaden—perhaps the only sensible thing we did. [His own attitude changed, he wrote, in the summer of 1944, after his illness.]

And then, of course, there was Nuremberg, with two exceedingly kind American chaplains at a time when kindness was in low supply, and . . . then of course, in Spandau, there was Casalis, the most unique man I have known. . . . You write that in your discussions about God, rational consideration argues against rather than for His existence. Well, I am against applying reason to God, for the miracles of nature show that reason has nothing to do with it, or Him. How do you explain that the peas I deliberately planted in the spring in a deep hole unfailingly pierced fifteen centimeters of earth to shoot straight up out of the ground? And what about the fern I planted by mistake upside down? It turned itself around, to grow straight up, bypassing its own root. I know, you can find reasons: the nature of growth; Schopenhauer's "Will for Life" [*sic*] or whatever. Of course one can always say no, but if you are honest you have to admit that these are miracles, which become more mysterious the more you ponder them. . . . I have read and thought so much by now, and I suppose the *knowledge* I gain will remain with me later. I only hope though that I won't lose the *feeling* for faith once I'm back in ordinary life. . . . As you see, it is ethics which particularly interest me. . . . I read again and again what Jaspers said: "Evil will rule unless I confront it at all times in myself and in others. . . ."

This preoccupation with evil—more specifically, with Hitler's evil—is reflected in almost all of the "Spandau draft" and in at least some of his many other letters to Wolters. But Wolters's extreme sensitivity to Speer's fate at Spandau and his consideration for his feelings meant that Wolters only rarely allowed himself any criticism; in all the correspondence I have seen, I have only found three specific instances, and even these were very restrained— "Much more restrained than Wolters felt, I assure you," Marion Riesser said.

The first and most explicit one was in a letter Wolters wrote to Speer in early April 1953. Speer replied on April 20:

I can see you would like me to be more positive about Hitler. But if I'm to write honestly, I cannot do that. That would really be a falsification of subjective [*sic*] truth. This kind of retrospective embellishment happens to most writers of memoirs when, probably unconsciously, they repress the negative aspects of their lives or the events they describe. . . . Perhaps this is what is happening already now in our country and to our people. It is, in the final analysis too painful to face that one has sacrificed children or parents for ideals one can now only condemn. I fear that, just as happened after Napoleon's fall, when for a long time only negative opinions were voiced, this restraint may repeat itself here and—just as happened then—result in a historical rebound, with German historians fifteen or twenty years from now presenting a Hitler repainted in positive colors.

Again Speer shows historical perspicacity here, for this is exactly what happened, if rather later than he predicted, in the famous *Historikerstreit,* the historians' quarrel over the nature of the Nazi past which raged in the late 1980s. Some sought to exculpate the Germans for the murder of the Jews by arguing that genocide was not planned or intended by anyone but grew out of century-old circumstances in European life, particularly as a response to Russian communism—seen as linked to world Jewry—and its brutal methods. The German army, they claimed (against passionate arguments from many other German historians), was fighting on the Eastern front to save European civilization.

The *Historikerstreit* was in fact a kind of apex of German postwar reactions, a perhaps not unnatural result of almost forty years of mea culpas and national (as opposed to nationalist) restraint. Ever since 1945 Germans had been told to be ashamed, and ashamed basically of one thing only—millions of words had been written in books and the media about Hitler's Third Reich, and spoken in theaters, films, radio, educational institutions and in parliament, all of them focusing on that one crime, the murder of the Jews. This—in many ways certainly justified—singularism is reflected in Speer's own feelings of guilt being entirely concentrated on this supreme outrage, to the exclusion of all the others.

Speer continued in his letter to Wolters,

> You criticize me for calling Hitler a criminal and you are of course right that, as this is a value judgment which the reader should make for himself, it is inappropriate in a book of memoirs. But if I say it, not once but many times, then I do so deliberately, in a way to remind myself. Of what? Of what I learned so graphically in Nuremberg: that upon his orders families—yes, imagine it, *families*—a man with his wife and small children—had to die [*mussten in den Tod gehen*] just because they were Jews. Being myself the father of young children, I have sufficient imagination to picture myself in their place. . . .
>
> Of course, nobody who was close to Hitler, or committed to him, wants

to hear this. I understand that and expect furious attacks. As I am by nature weak, I prefer to put them off until after I'm dead. But I need for you to believe, firstly that I am aware what I risk if I continue in this vein, but secondly, that I hope to God that I will have the strength to go on doing so. I beg of you to take very seriously what I'm saying here, for putting it into words is very, very difficult for me, and I probably can't do it again. . . .

On May 13, 1953, when Hilde was beginning to plan her return to Germany two months hence, he replied to two letters she had written—the most important one on her birthday, April 17, and the other, about her future, on April 24.

She should not forget to write thank-you letters both to McCloy and the U.S. Secretary of State Dean Acheson, both of whom had shown her kindness during her stay. And no doubt hoping that she would bring back yet more encouragement for him from these two important men, he added, "I suggest you write those in good time so that they still have time to reply to Hastings before you leave." About her question to him as to what he thought she might do in the future, he suggested she sit down before reading his reply as it might shock her. "I get the impression," he said, "that what interests you most is . . . politics!! . . . in the sense of being able to do something to help people [the term he used was "the masses"] with the problems of living in a different, better society."

This, given Hilde's later switch from academic to an active political life, seems again remarkably perceptive. Did she think, I asked her at one point, when she was staying with my husband and me in London, that her father's words had influenced her in her later decisions to join the Alternative Party and become its representative on the Berlin Council? "Not at all," she said somewhat airily. "His advice went in one ear and out the other." Even in the 1980s, Hilde found talking about her father so difficult that she sometimes put on a casual attitude which she was certainly far from feeling.

Not about everything though. Although she admitted it only with reluctance (like everything else that invaded her privacy and touched her deeper feelings), she was certainly affected by the next letter Speer wrote to her, on the following day, May 14, in reply to her long-pondered request, penned finally on her birthday, asking him to explain to her how he could have remained part of a system that was so evil. It was the only time, until years after his release from Spandau, that the subject would arise between them.

He wrote at length, not because there was all that much to say, but because, to start out with, he prevaricated (as he would always do when confronted with this precise question). Even so, his method with her, whom he loved and whose approval he desperately wanted, was less discursive than it would be with others in the future. Nonetheless, here too, he tried, rather desperately, to avoid her fundamental question even while appearing, cleverly, to expand on it. Hilde was unable—or perhaps unwilling—to recall the words of her letter to him when talking to me, and of course none of the smuggled letters he received (contrary to those he sent) survived; he tore them into small pieces and flushed them down the toilet. But what she did tell me indicated that, in order to moderate its impact, she had phrased her long-pondered-over question of conscience in general rather than only personal terms. It was perhaps all the more hurtful for this remarkable young girl when in the first part of his letter, with its curiously condescending tone, he seemed to slur over her decision to be gentle and her willingness to understand. Nonetheless, almost as if he had reached a decision halfway through, in the second part of the letter he made a rare effort to confront himself, beginning with the paragraph already cited in the Prologue:

> You ask . . . about the Nazis . . . how could an intelligent person go along with such a thing. I want to show you by specifically using myself as an example how this might happen. Let me say the hardest bit first: unless one wants, cowardly, to avoid confronting the truth, one has to say that there can be no excuse; there is no justification. . . . [And] in that sense I am convinced of my own guilt. There are things, you see, for which one has to carry the blame, even if purely factually one might find excuses: the immensity of the crime precludes any attempt at self-justification.

> I should tell you that I don't discuss this with anyone here: I loathe peddling my feelings—they belong to one's inner self. Of course, writing to you about it is something different. Otherwise I have only discussed it with my friend, Pastor Casalis. . . . In Nuremberg too [where he pointedly accepted "co-responsibility" but never "guilt"] I avoided a direct confrontation with the term "guilt," and I succeeded in this by never justifying myself.

> To reassure you, however: of the dreadful things, I knew nothing. The Americans told me later that they never thought I did. Even so, I'm not entirely content to leave it at that, for I ask myself what, given my lofty position, I could have found out, had I wanted to. Even then, perhaps not everything, but certainly a great deal. . . . I see my fate, if you like, as God's judgment: not for having infringed any laws—for my transgressions in that sense were comparatively minimal—but for the deeper guilt of having so readily and unthinkingly gone along. . . .

> In Sophocles's *Oedipus,* he is horribly punished by Providence for having killed his mother and father, although it was not his fault and any court today would have acquitted him. But according to the moral precepts of ancient Greece, he is nonetheless called to account for it. I cannot explain even to myself why I think that is right, but I do. . . .

He had flattered Hilde that he could discuss these personal things with her but not with anyone else, except in the past "with my friend, Pastor Casalis, who is now gone." But then his tone changed and—as would happen so often when he spoke to me—one can sense honesty and pain in what followed. He continued,

> I have often asked myself what I would have done if I had come to feel a share in the responsibility for the things Hitler did in areas other than those in which I was directly involved. And unfortunately, if I'm honest, my reply has to be negative—the tasks Hitler had confided to me, first in architecture, then in government, his "friendship," the passionate conviction he radiated, the power his favor conferred on me, all this was quite simply overwhelming and had become so indispensable to me that to hang on to it I would probably have swallowed anything.
>
> True, as you will have read, much later I did oppose him in many ways. But, in the context of your question, that cannot serve as a justification of my previous passivity. . . . The truth is that I only woke up to what he was doing—what he *was*—when I had to acknowledge to myself that he intended to pull the German people down into perdition with him. And really, all I did then was only in an effort to prevent that.
>
> So you see, mine was not a moral opposition. I didn't try to act against him because he persecuted the Jews or started the war. Even then I was able to tell myself that *that* was outside my competence, was not my business.
>
> And the undeniable fact that we had all been conditioned to this attitude is no justification either, I know it. The truth is that my active opposition only began when, by ordering the industries of France, Belgium, Holland—and finally Germany proper—to be eradicated, he extended his evil intentions to *my* area of responsibility.
>
> I hope you will feel that I have said *something* in reply to your question. I have learned to understand that unfettered ambition can destroy one's innate awareness of ethical principles. Can one transmit such understanding, gained through catastrophe, to others? To anyone young one feels close to? [He cannot bring himself to say "loves."] I don't know: I can only wish for you to feel supported not by any ideology, but by faith in the miracle that is the creation.

Very, very affectionately,
your Papa

In a postscript, ambivalent as ever, he recommends once more that upon her return to Germany she should read Dr. Gilbert's *Nuremberg Diary* (which was very favorable to him): "It will broaden your knowledge."

XXIV

Spandau: II

HILDE, and a few years later her husband, Ulf, a brilliant young sociologist, were the only members of Speer's family to whom he ever wrote about his thoughts. Besides Hilde, his third child, Fritz, interested both him and Wolters most. Wolters wrote to Speer on August 22, 1953: "I want to congratulate you on Fritz. This child is a genius in mathematics. Intellectually he stands miles above the others. He is, on the other hand, very 'closed,' very much like his father!!"

"The children, especially the boys," said Speer, "needed a father. Rudi did this for some of them—he was especially good with Fritz, though Margret always said that Arnold, who is three years younger, was always trailing after Rudi even more than Fritz. But it was about Fritz that Rudi most often wrote to me. He always said Fritz was the most intelligent of my children." He shook his head. "They all seem terribly intelligent to me. They've all done awfully well, you know." He paused and then added, "Much better, I think, than if I had been there." It wasn't said sadly—just as a fact.

Speer felt enormous empathy with Fritz and wrote him often, the letters even more personal than those he wrote to Hilde and almost entirely focused, not on himself, but on this complicated and—he sensed—unhappy boy. "Sadly," he told me once, "it never worked between us after I came out. I never understood why. He fought me more and sees me even less than any of the others. Yes, perhaps because we are the most alike."

Except for a few letters he would write later, to two of the children at a time after they had been allowed to visit him together, and several congratulations he sent to his eldest son, Albert, after he won architectural competitions, all his family letters were either on practical matters or about his Spandau life—to the younger children, always reported in humorous terms—or they were brief comments about their successes or problems at school and later at university.

Wolters was always the exception. In 1953, even while sending him the long letters which made up the "Spandau draft," Speer also wrote him separately then and later—about his financial concerns for Margret, his irritations with his difficult brother Hermann, his continuous problems with his co-prisoners, but also about more pleasant moments such as finishing an architectural design of a house for one of the American guards. "It makes me really happy to design a house for people to live in," he wrote. "It strengthens my determination to return to architecture when I come out. I am so happy about Pie's and Ap's suggestions." (Two of his former associates, the builder Karl Piepenburg and the architect Otto Apel, both of whom had made huge postwar careers, had sent him messages asking him to join them as a consultant upon regaining his freedom. He put all his hopes in these invitations, but they were dashed when both these loyal friends died in 1966, only a few months before he was released.) His letter continued, "Yesterday an American prosecutor came to get my testimony for————'s trial. He addressed me as Herr Speer—except for Casalis, the first time I heard these words in eight years; I felt almost giddy with pleasure. One does forget here that one is anything but a number."

He was getting to be on good terms with a new British director: "A man who knows how to behave—how helpful," and he writes about the courtesy of the old Neurath on March 19, Speer's birthday. "He came to my cell after lunch. 'What can I wish you?' he said sadly, and then just quietly held my hand—a present of humanity; I could have cried." And late that night Funk showed him unexpected kindness in slipping him a drink of cognac in a metal mug. "Where could he have got that wonderful old brandy?"

Jan Boon told me that Funk regularly received cognac and caviar. "At one point the guards smuggled in the cognac in urine bottles—they said that was the safest. They had quite a commerce going," he said, "things like champagne, caviar, pressed duck. All of the prisoners got things from outside. I also helped them, but only by smuggling letters out and by occasionally slipping them some brandy, white wine or good coffee in the guise of medicine. Why not?"

Until Dönitz was released in September 1956, he remained the bane of Speer's existence. Speer wrote to Wolters on April 14, 1953:

> Yesterday he got at me all day. "If it was up to the Americans," he said, "you'd get out ahead of me. The American Jews would make sure of it. But now it's German public opinion that counts." What gets me . . . is that he makes me out a sycophant. Yes, it's true, I'm civil to Jews who are civil to me—I always have been and always will be. I would say that after what has happened, they have more reason to think ill of me than I of them. Hess, with whom I discuss it all, is as cross with himself as I am with myself. "I don't understand it either," he said. "When Raeder has a go at me, I simply can't think of anything to say. In the evening in my cell, I am furious for not having given as good as I got. Is it the same for you?"
> . . . I can tell you that I'm often at the end of my tether. The smallest

things become absolutely enormous. The other day—my wife was to come the next afternoon—I decided to sew on some missing buttons. After finally having managed to thread the needle, it disappeared. I couldn't find it. I first looked all over the bed, including, ridiculously enough, under the pillow, then took the whole bed apart, took off my jacket and then my trousers thinking it might have got stuck in them and, still not finding it, found myself bathed in nervous sweat.

When finally, exhausted, I collapsed on the bed, I saw needle and thread, clear as day, lying on the floor at my feet. You won't believe it, but my heart beat so hard, I had trouble breathing. And then the next day, my wife's visit: always the saddest half-hour one can imagine, for her, I fear, quite as much as for me. Sometimes I feel I should spare us both these visits, and yet . . . and yet. . . .

I try—I really try—never to show my occasional despair. What is most difficult for me is not having anybody to talk to here. I fear I am rather more sensitive than the others. Well, I suppose I can't very well ask for a second architect to be locked up here for my sake, can I? . . . It *is* a relief to be able to tell you what troubles me. Nonetheless don't worry, I'll stick it out. . . .

Georges and Dorothée Casalis got to know Margret Speer quite well over the years of Speer's imprisonment. "During the time I officiated in Spandau," Georges said during one of his visits to us in Munich, "the wives, including Margret Speer, would quite regularly see me in my Berlin office whenever they visited their husbands, or even outside 'visiting months.' If they needed to tell each other privately something of importance which they didn't want to subject to the censors' eyes, it was quite legitimate for me as their pastor to pass messages to and fro. But I never visited any of the wives until after I left Spandau.

"Over the years after that, I probably saw Margret Speer about six times, whenever I was anywhere near Heidelberg. She was very impressive, a woman of total integrity and dignity who probably shed some tears but never showed it, never asked for any favors. It was remarkable how she had managed to create a harmonious atmosphere and a joyous home for those six children. There was a lot of laughter in that house. I admired her very much."

Dorothée Casalis, a theologian in her own right and an exceptionally intelligent and humorous woman of great charm and perception, saw Margret somewhat differently. "It was difficult to find anything we had in common," she said. "Georges and I were such activists, and she of course was the antithesis to political. I'm sure she was in many ways very moral, and yet somehow one couldn't associate the concept of morality, in our sense, with her. Actually, I felt much closer to Hilde's personality—even as a young girl, she was quite amazing." Dorothée remembered the small and dainty Margret as "rather Wagnerian. She never spoke directly about her former life, but I knew from the other wives that she really was very closely bound to the Berghof, to Hitler, and she seemed to me to reflect his most familiar ideals. She was very 'Gretchen,' you know, even in her way of dressing. It wasn't a matter of money, it was her personality, and why not? It's true, she never complained, but true too that I felt in her the opposite of the almost obsessive awareness of guilt that Georges found in Speer. German society at that time, you see, did not feel guilty; or if ordinary Germans did—unlike many writers, artists and priests we knew—they repressed or hid it and only demonstrated their feeling of having been betrayed and vanquished. And I certainly sensed those feelings in Margret.

"For people like Georges and me, who had fought them, this was difficult. It was difficult to offer Margret warmth. Georges tried very hard with her, and I think she finally came to look for it in him and accept it from him. But not from me." What had been very obvious, however, Dorothée said, was the strength of Margret's relationship with Speer, and with her children. "She certainly loved Speer," she said. "It was by no means only marital obligation—it was love too. But, sadly for her, it was not in her nature—or in his—to give or receive love in the complete sense we know. They were two people with considerable sexual problems—I could see that when I met her during Speer's Spandau time and understood it even better years later when I met him. I honestly didn't think that either of them knew the meaning of sexuality. She was above all a mother; perhaps her attitude even to Speer was that of a mother—or a sister?"

("My mother—" said Hilde, while her mother was still alive, "and you can believe me that I know—never looked at another man in all those years. Beautiful, and still young as she was, there was nobody in her life, ever. It simply would not have done. Her sense of what was proper, what she owed to the family and how she had to preserve my father's self-respect, was like a rock. Nothing in the world could have budged it, I think. She was and is always loyal to her own.")

Margret's letters to Wolters, if not to Speer, for she too tended to protect him, clearly demonstrate that underlying stubborn strength. They also show her frequent annoyance with her husband's ever-increasing self-absorption and his determination to remain in control. In addition, every one of her letters as of the end of 1953 (contrary to Speer's) shows her deep embarrassment at accepting financial help from a fund Wolters had managed to set up—the so-called School Fund—with monthly contributions from most of Speer's former architects and some of the industrialists who had worked with him during the war. She wrote to Wolters at the end of 1953:

I had an annoying letter from Albert today. I was furious and didn't react kindly. He wants us to manage without touching any of the capital, but I think this is ridiculous. Now that our funds have been released [by the Allies, who after his arrest in 1945 had blocked Speer's fortune and put a lien on any future inheritance], we cannot allow you to look after us as you have been doing. I think we should manage with half of that amount and make it up from capital. After all, we are not paupers. Albert seems to think we are extravagant because we live in the villa [the Speer family house they had recently moved back to, when it was released by the Allies]. He doesn't seem to understand—not only that there are seven of us, but also that it is only thanks to the additional room that I can take in paying guests, which is hard work. Nor does he seem to understand how much gratitude we owe you for all your help. But there are limits. I know it is partly that he can't know what life costs now, but with our background I am ashamed to accept what you are providing for us and I beg of you to explain this to him. You are the only one he listens to. It is probably the winter and Christmastime—always very hard for him—that make him so pessimistic. But after all, I live outside and can't sleep for worrying how to manage, and on top if it all, have this continuous trouble with his idiot of a brother. I won't let either of them tyrannize and torment me, even though he *is* in prison. You tell him that. . . .

And a year later she writes to Wolters, complaining about the now fourteen-year-old Arnold:

Now he has to be tutored in Latin at DM 50 per month, which I could well use to buy the new trousers he also wants. Other boys his age *give* lessons; nobody ever succeeds by laziness. Albert keeps going on about Fritz and his "drinking." Good God, he's only been drunk once. Is that so surprising, at seventeen? He is very aware of his faults, so please feel free to discuss them with him. You help him more that way than by restraint and silence. I'm asking a lot of you, but as long as he has no father and there is no man in the family, you are all we have. . . . As always, I liked your letter to Albert a lot; if he didn't have you. . . . But I'm pretty depressed.

Speer, meanwhile, writing around the same time, is euphoric. Seven months earlier, as already mentioned, Albert and Hilde had visited him together, and this had been such a great success that at the end of it he had offered them a celebratory lunch at his favorite Berlin restaurant, the super-chic Horcher's, which Wolters was instructed to pay for out of the School Fund. A year later, Hilde would repeat this combined visit (the second one since the authorities slightly changed the visiting rules), this time with her sister, Margret. He wrote to Wolters,

> It was wonderful; they did it really enchantingly. Margret bears an almost scary resemblance to my mother—you can imagine how that shook me. I think they were determined to . . . make this half-hour we had into a time of fun, and it worked. I think it is nine years since I have so unreservedly escaped the prison world. Those two could wind me around their little fingers without any trouble whatsoever. . . .

It is possible to consider Speer's years at Spandau in the context of milestones. If the first was, without doubt, Casalis; the second his creation of a garden; and the third the almost incredible achievement of the "Spandau draft"; then the fourth was his decision to "Walk around the World." When I asked him what had made him think of that, he said readily, "The danger of giving up keeping fit, just because it is so boring." That morning we had discussed the two elements which had always ruled his life, self-discipline and obsessions.

"I had worked it out—if I did thirty circuits of the path I had laid out in the garden, that would be seven kilometers a day. I asked Hess, who sat and watched me, if he would mark down each time I passed him, so that I wouldn't lose count. He had a marvelous idea. He gave me thirty peas and said, 'Put these in one pocket and move one to the other pocket each round. That will do it.' "

In September 1954, he decided to think of his exercise rounds as a walk from Berlin to his home in Heidelberg. "It was a more imaginative goal than just completing the circuit thirty times, as I had been doing. That was successful, so I kept on going, across the mountains to Italy, and finally decided to see just how far I could get. After preparing for the walks by studying maps, travelogues and art history books, I focused imaginatively on the differences in the landscapes, the rivers, flowers, plants, trees and rocks. In the cities I came through, I thought of churches, museums, great buildings and works of art." He smiled at me. "It would break into what you rightly call my 'obsessive' concentration on the past, of which I was perfectly aware."

He had concluded from studying a world atlas that, taking the shortest route throughout, he would achieve his goal at just under forty thousand kilometers. "In a manner of speaking, Rudi Wolters accompanied me on these walks," he said. "He advised me on distances, warned me of natural barriers: raging rivers, glaciers, unclimbable mountains, and sent me descriptions of the wonders of the world I would encounter."

Thus when Speer approached Siberia in his walk, Wolters wrote, "I am well acquainted with the Altai. It is the huge mountain chain near Novosibirsk where I spent a year. A famous mountain excursion is the Bjelucha, the goal of all Siberian climbers, as is the Elbrus in the Caucasus. Will you have time to climb them? . . . Oddly enough, we spoke of this before, when at the beginning of the Russian campaign I gave you a detailed map of the huge coal-mining part of that region. I remember your passing it on (!) [to Hitler]."

On other occasions Wolters gave Speer precise directions on how to walk and instructions on what to see. "Opposite the Hermitage [in Leningrad] you might like to see the Fortress of Peter and Paul; just a few minutes will be enough." Or yet again proving his tremendous empathy with Speer's effort: "For the trek through the huge uninhabited wastes of Siberia, I would strongly advise you to be kind to yourself and take a train. Saves time too, as you can do it at night! But don't sleep too much. It would be a crime to miss seeing these unending snowy mountain chains and prairies and the sea of stars above. If you open the top slat in your compartment window, you can smell the purity of the air even in your sleeper. Only, careful—if you expose your face too long, your mouth and nose will freeze. But you remember that feeling from Dnepropetrovsk, I know. However, the Ukraine is the tropics by comparison to the Siberia you are now meeting."

Speer replied in March 1957,

I suspect you of giving me reduced kilometer figures for distances to make it easier for me. I note from one of my travel books that Delhi–Calcutta is 1,820 kilometers, not 1,400 as you told me. Ahhh? What do you say, you kind rascal? [On November 29, 1957, he reported that he had reached Calcutta.]

On September 29, 1966, the day of his last walk, he would have covered 31,936 kilometers. "I suppose it too became an obsession," he said. "But what's wrong with that, if it makes one happy?"

ON NOVEMBER 6, 1954, Speer's only supporter among the prisoners, Konstantin von Neurath, old and sick, had been granted early release, an event the lobbying of Speer's many friends had presumably helped to bring about. "I was glad but devastated at the thought of being without him," Speer told me. Four days later, "to calm himself" he walked twenty-four kilometers, more than three times his daily stint, and two days later he was in bed with his "Achilles' heel"—his troublesome leg was swollen to twice its size. Was it just the physical strain or was it mental stress, as it had been after Posen and Dora? Just as in 1944, within two weeks the initial symptom developed into bronchitis which, as ten years before, turned into pulmonary infarction.

"They chose to call it pneumonia, probably to avoid transferring him to hospital, where he certainly belonged," said Jan Boon. "But he had an embolism. He was in an oxygen tent for three weeks. I nursed him days; they sent in American male nurses for the nights. Later they said I saved his life." Had Jan found Speer nicer when he was ill and dependent? "No, not really. His thank-yous were from his *Kinderstube* [nursery manners], not his heart."

The years 1955 and 1956 appear to have been dreary: he walked, he read, he tried to rule his home roost and distribute bounty from prison irrespective of the fact that Wolters could only meet his demands by tapping the School Fund. At Easter 1955 he informed Wolters that he had worked out an exam competition for the children, to supplement their modest pocket money:

> Their marks will be divided into two groups: Group A, Math, Languages, History, Sciences. Group B, Religion, Music, Art, etc. For every top mark in Group A you will give them DM 80, for (2) DM 25, (3) DM 8 and (4) DM 4. In Group B: a (1) gets DM 15 etc. For any (5) or (6) [failing marks] you deduct DM 40, 20, 15 and 8.

He calculated that this scheme, plus birthday and Christmas presents, would cost the School Fund some DM 1,200.

> To this please add, like every year, the cost of a holiday trip for our "friend" [his secret courier, the medic Toni Proost]. Of course, next year is Margret's fiftieth birthday and I am pondering what to do about that. And we should do something for AK [Annemarie]—a trip? Perhaps a fortnight skiing in the Tyrol? DM 4–500. Well, these are my long-distance methods of keeping in touch. It is amazing, though, that in spite of these ten years now, and although they had virtually nothing of me during my three years as Minister, the children still seem gratifyingly attached.

In view of the financial pressures he attempted to impose on Margret, his airy instructions to Wolters for outlays of several thousand deutschmarks seem almost contemptuous.

Annemarie Kempf laughed when I read this to her. "Yes, I know," she said. "He always did look upon that fund as quite legitimately his own. He was after all incarcerated behind walls, while the contributors, all men who had climbed up on his coattails, he felt were sitting pretty. But as the years went on, he certainly carried it too far. I think he knew it, but the more Rudi reported mutiny in the ranks, the more stubborn he became. Although some of the contributions continued until he came out, in the final years it was

Religion, faith, + prayers

hardly relevant anymore. Margret had sold some land, and there was some money, and anyway by that time most of the children were grown up and didn't need help anymore.

"Yes, I remember Rudi Wolters did send me skiing money once, and I was livid, not so much at Albert as at him. I sent it back by return mail and told him that although one could just about find excuses for Albert turning megalomaniac in his isolation, there was none for him. I used the opportunity to tell him everything I thought was wrong with the way the two of them were handling things—it was the beginning of our estrangement."

Speer told me later that this estrangement between Annemarie and Rudi, which less than a year later resulted in Annemarie's announcement that they were to consider her "out of it all," was mainly due to Annemarie's desire, not to be in charge, but to be given more to do for him. "The whole problem," Speer wrote to Wolters at the time, "is that she is somehow in competition with you, and because of everything you are doing and are able to do, she must necessarily lose this 'competition.' Could you not force yourself to consult her, even if you don't need her advice? It would help me."

"Whatever it was," he told me, "it was a real blow, because in fact she had always done an incredible amount for me. Up to a point, she did go on after this, but not hand in hand with Rudi; it made things very awkward." It was to be more than five years before Speer's pleas finally healed the breach. "Only superficially," Annemarie said. (She thought it only had been two years.) "You see, I knew how Rudi really felt [about Speer]; Albert didn't."

✳   In these depressing years he turned more and more to poetry, prison literature and prayers. "I have already seen," he wrote to Hilde, "that when I feel depressed, not knowing how to go on here, then my 'faith' takes over from my 'will.' But when I feel well, it immediately works the other way. I only hope I won't lose the *feeling* for faith. Will I continue going to church when I come back to you? I wonder. . . . I read as many books on theology as I can, and one of them, a thick one on all religions, has convinced me that the Jewish religion is morally superior to all others—Christianity after all grew out of it. . . . I think one can compare faith to a mountain which can be climbed on one side easily, gently, almost like walking over green fields—that is the faith of a child. From the other side, however, the path is almost insurmountably steep and full of rocks, driving the climber back over and over, to try again. . . .

"I think that only prisoners can understand that in the worst moments, one can find some relief in a primitive prayer," he continued a little later, citing a prayer Dietrich Bonhoeffer wrote in April 1945 for his co-prisoners in the concentration camp of Flossenburg before all of them were hanged.

In the dawn of the day I call to Thee
Help me pray
Direct my thoughts to Thee
I cannot manage on my own
It is dark within me, but there is light in Thee
I am lonely, but Thou will not leave me
I am faint of heart, but know Thou will help me
I am troubled, but know that in Thee is peace
I am bitter, but in Thee is endurance
I do not understand Thy ways
But Thou understandeth them for me.

"I think that, somewhat as for monks," he concluded this entry, "this time here is not as pointless as I sometimes feel. What I fear however, is that, once I'm back at liberty, the unhappy memories will overshadow the good and valuable ones. . . . I can only hope that, at least in my unconscious, something good will remain."

Meanwhile 1955 and the first half of 1956 continued unhappily. "The young British officers used to be very friendly," he wrote that summer, "but now a new lot has arrived. They were shown a film on the Nuremberg trials before their tour of duty began. Result: icy conduct toward us."

In June 1956 Hilde went on a second trip to America, which she had grown to love. And even before her return, Margret received a letter from John McCloy.

Dear Mrs. Speer:
    Hilde has sent me your letter of April 22 and the folder which explained your husband's situation very fully. I don't know what I can do to be effective, but I promise you that I will do something. I may make a few inquiries at the State Department to see what the best method of approach would be. I have a firm conviction that your husband should be released and I would be happy if I could do anything that would expedite such a development. I shall try to keep you informed as to what steps I am taking and any other information I may be able to gather.
    It is very nice to have Hilde in this country again. She always makes a very good impression wherever she goes.
                                                        Sincerely,
                                                        John J. McCloy

This was exactly the encouragement Speer needed. On June 8, 1956, he wrote how glad he was to hear of the wealth of experiences and impressions Hilde was gathering on her travels. "The most important to me," he said, honest with her as ever, "was that McCloy immediately reacted to the letter you brought him. I was quite overcome by the tone of his letter to Mama and his evident willingness to help. This unreserved generosity is to me typical of Americans. Can you imagine a highly placed German official offering to extend himself like this for a foreigner in my position?" (It was of course precisely what numerous highly placed Germans were to do in the years to come for foreigners in trouble: in China, in South Africa and in Russia.)

Hilde had written about the lively political discussions she was having with the Days. Speer wrote back,

> I only wish I could join in. I entirely agree with Mrs. Day—as I expressed very clearly in my final words at Nuremberg, which I know you have never read—that in our time of perilous technical developments, no problem whatever can be solved by force of arms. . . . In West Germany, our basic problem is that we are in the immoral position of benefiting from something which is not good but bad—the tension between East and West—to which essentially we owe our out-of-all-proportion high living standard and our equally out-of-proportion standing in Europe, to neither of which we have as yet a moral right. I of course don't know how many Germans pray for the continuation of this tension, but I fear only too many, for it is certain that the reunification of Germany, with the accompanying rebalancing of all of the East-West situation, would at least temporarily have to vastly reduce our expectations and realign our position in the European scheme. . . .

This was one of the best and longest letters he would write to Hilde, forty-seven handwritten pages about the resemblance between the conflicts created by the Reformation in the sixteenth century, which seemed insurmountable at the time, and the current conflicts between East and West. Then, he wrote, the result had been the totally useless and devastating Thirty Years' War:

> Today unless a détente can be achieved by means of human intelligence, mediation and arbitration, the eventual catastrophes will be worse. As your grandfather's hero, the pioneering Pan-European Coudenhove-Kalergi, preached so many years ago—the restriction of human beings within strictly defined national borders is the antithesis of freedom.
>
> Forgive this long epistle, but it is good to talk to a young mind like yours rather than the fossilized ones in my present immediate circle. I do hope you young people will have the generosity and the vision to see the world not nationally, but as a whole. . . .

From that moment on he seemed imbued with new energy, submerging both Wolters and Hilde for months in a veritable flood of advice and directions on the management of his affairs. With McCloy clearly willing to open new doors toward his release, now was the moment to approach others: Robert Murphy, Allen Dulles and of course Eisenhower (now President—a few years later it would be Kennedy whose support they sought). And the men leading the new, strong West German government: Konrad Adenauer, Ludwig Erhard, Franz Josef Strauss, Willy Brandt ("But be *careful* with him; I know he is a splendid chap, but something of a prima donna"). Perhaps de Gaulle, and in the end even some of the Russians, should be approached. Even Margret was infected by the profusion of activity. "She is suddenly writing to everybody she knows," he told Wolters. "I had forgotten she knows so many people. And now she says that perhaps she herself should go to Russia. A wife's pleas? Rudi—I don't think so. . . ."

When by the end of 1957 nothing happened as a result of all these undertakings, he fell back into black depression. Raeder, Dönitz and Funk had been released, and he, Schirach and Hess were entirely dependent on each other for company. Toni Proost had been in a panic for months because the Russians briefly but pointedly detained him (during a day trip to the Eastern sector to visit his mother-in-law) and suggested, with a clear implication of blackmail, that he should become their informer at Spandau. He finally announced his decision to retire. "I can hardly bear the idea," wrote Speer.

Added to this, Annemarie, who for more that twenty years had found solutions for his practical problems, had not returned to the fold. "Is it the saintly life she leads? Who could have predicted that?" he asked Wolters. "I am shaken by the anger in her letters. *That* isn't all that holy, is it?" It was a curious view of Annemarie's dedication to her children, but, as she would frequently remind me later, mockery with a touch of maliciousness had often been his reaction to opposition. His letter continued,

> But in case this is really the end of our letters [because of Proost's departure] and I don't get another chance, let me say thank you for everything you have done for me and my family over the years; your support has been the most important element in my holding out. The knowledge of your friendship will continue to sustain me even if there are no more letters. Please be nice to AK, even if it's hard: I need her for afterwards.

And a few days later, in the same letter, he added words which somehow don't quite ring true:

> Even if we find a way to continue, I wouldn't blame you at all if you decided to apply your energies to better purposes. If it weren't for the children and my wife, I'd be of a good mind to stop torturing you with my affairs.

But only a few paragraphs on, the old Speer re-emerges:

> Perhaps rather than only addressing yourselves to heads of state and Ministers, you should use those who have been close to us and who are

almost all now in influential positions: administrators who have entered government and architects who are building cities on the one hand, industrialists who are the backbone of the economic miracle on the other. Krupp, Siemens, Osram, all of them know *somebody* who could help. And don't forget the artists like my friend Wilhelm Kempff.

And he suggests Christmas presents: *The Brothers Karamazov* for Annemarie, six antique glasses for Margret together with a bottle of her favorite scent, Houbigant, an earthenware vase, a tin of the special ham she liked and some Dortmund beer. Books for all the children; for Toni Proost and his wife, wine, champagne for New Year's Eve and an envelope with DM 100 for their daughter, Christine. "Please send my glass collection to be auctioned. Whatever remains of the money, pass it on to Margret." His Christmas wish for himself is a new pipe—he had worn out the two he had: Dunhill or Petersen, he specifies, and sends a design of the desired shape. "Also, if possible, could you send me excerpts from Churchill's memoirs relevant to Germany, and [Alan] Bullock's new book?"

In 1958, with Toni Proost now living in a small house in Eutin he obtained with Annemarie's help, a new team took over Speer's correspondence: an American guard he would never name who agreed to take in and bring out everything, receiving and posting it via a young woman doctor in Berlin. "An American officer has also volunteered," he wrote Wolters. "We'll have to be careful or I'll be writing letters day and night to satisfy their generosity."

By 1959, Speer's optimism—or fatalism, as he had begun to call it—and his sense of humor were fully re-established. "My fears these last few months," he wrote to Wolters on January 2, 1959, "caused me to think deeply on the value and importance of our friendship. I reproach myself for accepting it so lightly, and for my often stupid, childishly bad manners. It would be different if you'd give *me* a piece of *your* mind sometimes. You are too considerate, but I expect you to make up for this thoroughly later. . . ."

For Speer's birthday that year Wolters had outdone himself. "Here is the menu of the Gala Dinner," Speer wrote: "Beluga caviar with new potatoes; French goose liver with truffles on oriental white bread; Siberian roast [probably venison]; Westphalian ham, black bread and country butter, and with it your exceptional Winkler Massenpflug 1957. Afterwards oriental coffee with cream, mocha chocolate, pralines, fruit." He marveled the next day,

The wine was exceptional, and the caviar quite fantastic, even though for us experts Beluga comes second to that other outrageously expensive one we tasted together at the Kuban bridgehead, remember? [But] I reveled in it all, thank you, thank you, thank you.

Hilde went to Britain in early 1960 and was jubilant about her reception at the Foreign Office, where she was very seriously advised on tactics. "They told her *not* to do what Hess's and von Schirach's families are doing," Wolters wrote. "They said it was not sensible to try to force the issue through the media." He, of course, entirely agreed, he said, for the German media were outrageous with their continuous harping on the Holocaust. "The whole world, believe me, is appalled at the extent to which we Germans keep throwing dirt on ourselves and our reputation." But Speer had now served two-thirds of his sentence and something *must* happen, Wolters said, and proposed that Speer should "allow" Hilde, who was most concerned about her studies, to interrupt them for one or two terms in order to devote all her time to his interests. "She is simply the most effective ambassador you have; there is no getting around it. And if you agree to this, I think the other children should help her financially so that she doesn't suffer through it. No news from Annemarie," he added. "I tried, by means of a silk scarf, but no reaction."

("My father 'allow' me to interrupt my studies?" Hilde said to me later. "Wolters must have been crazy. How dare he? Of course I didn't.")

Nonetheless, two months later she traveled to Paris, where Khrushchev was meeting with de Gaulle, and again, even though the press got wind of—and sniped at—her efforts, returned feeling optimistic. "I don't share her admiration for the 'nice French government men,' " Wolters wrote. "I was a nice German government man too and happily promised anything to people who tried to get requests to you through me, and then threw them straight into the wastepaper basket. No doubt the same applies to those surrounding France's most powerful man."

Shortly after this, Speer advised Hilde to give up the idea of going to Moscow. "I really do think they not only have other worries, but are so meticulous about protocol that the only way they will even consider a change in the status of Spandau is if the request comes both from the three Western powers and, very strongly, from the German government. Wait until after the new summit Khrushchev has requested; try him in April or May—he may be ripe for it by then."

A little later, information reached them that de Gaulle had suggested in a top-level meeting that Speer should be released. "I have to put brakes on my optimism," he wrote Hilde when he heard that. "But whatever comes or does not come of it, what a triumph for you."

Hilde continued to encourage him with positive little tidbits throughout 1961, even though, beginning on her Ph.D., she was now not only busy with her studies but preparing for her wedding in July. "You will be getting some money via AK," Speer wrote her shortly before the day. "Please buy a large bunch of pink roses for your mother and give it to her from me, the morning of your wedding. . . . I'm not pleased with my wedding letter to you and Ulf—I couldn't say what I wanted and the letters kept getting blurred; my dotage no doubt. In the afternoon, while it is happening, I'll be listening to *Figaro*. Thank God it's on."

(Nine months later, in April 1962, he would repeat almost the same pattern when Margret, his second daughter, was married, also to an academic, in oriental studies. This time he heard Mozart's *Coronation Mass* and, offered a celebratory glass of rum by a friendly British guard, drank to Margret's health.)

For the next five years Ulf, patient and sensitive with an exceptional intellect, was to become the recipient of very special letters from Speer, different from all the others.

Jan Boon, though by no means an observant man, had not been so wrong about Speer. Even though capable of surprising moments of humility, Speer *was* arrogant. This innate arrogance of the German upper-class male led to his being incapable of considering Margret anything but a "wife," in the sense of a necessarily loyal appendage—thereby confirming her own low estimation of herself. He always saw Wolters as his appreciated but inevitably inferior number two, and Annemarie, who was without a doubt the most loyal friend he had to the day he died, was never anything in his mind but his "wonderful indispensable secretary"—which was how he described her to me.

Hilde, although he certainly loved her and was proud of her as his favorite child, was in the final analysis a *girl*, which qualitatively simply wasn't the same as a man. He immediately and unreservedly liked and accepted Ulf because he trusted Hilde's instinct, but it was for the young and highly educated *man* that he very quickly developed an intense intellectual need.

With him, more than anyone since Casalis, he wanted to communicate and converse, in his case neither particularly focusing on nor, for that matter, avoiding the past. Here was a man with whom he shared no guilt and no regrets, no common experiences and no secrets. In addition, contrary perhaps to Casalis, Ulf made no demands on him. He was neither generationally nor emotionally involved with Speer or his history. Ulf's own letters (as quoted by Speer in his replies) convey a considerable degree of neutrality—he was a courteous man and friendly by nature, but his was a limited interest and he was thus an intellectual but not a moral or emotional challenge for Speer. Speer's several hundred letters to Ulf show clearly how comfortable he felt with this comparative detachment and how galvanized he was by the novel stimulation of this exchange.

His letters to Hilde, Wolters and Annemarie became even more exclusively dedicated to practicalities. Ideas—on anything from artistic creation to linguistics, to social and divine justice, the nature of good and evil and the genesis of man—were now entirely reserved for Ulf.

Hilde did not mind. "Of course not," she said, smiling, "I was grateful. We were all pretty worn out with these letters. Ulf came to them fresh, without prejudice and, above all, without the encumbrance of a common past. He was affected by my father's circumstances, but not weighed down; he talked to him as he talked to anybody intelligent, and as such it was interesting for him rather than a chore."

"Ah, how different the germination of ideas of an intellectual or an artist," Speer wrote, when Ulf mentioned his difficulties in getting a new concept on paper. "In former times I often thought how much easier it was to be a Minister than an architect. But the wonderful torture of that empty piece of drawing paper—I long for it." And a few months later:

> Is human character and personality determined at birth? How much can circumstances of family, background and education, and their own individual efforts affect that nature? *Is* there an element of fate as the Christian church appears to teach? But then, can one really hold men responsible for their actions? A frightening thought for those of us who are trying to solve that very problem, for does it not either indict Christian teaching or even creation? God?
>
> [He was deep in Dostoevsky, he wrote.] It is finally *Karamazov* I prefer. Except for Shakespeare's plays, I cannot think of another work of literature that goes so deeply into the problems of guilt, predisposition and human brutality.
>
> [Five months later he returned to the same subject.] On your level—of the intellectual—ethical requirements are established with this level of human beings in mind. It seems right to me that an elite demands of itself elite ethics. But it is right only as long as you are aware that you are being perhaps intolerably elitist, virtually excluding 99 percent of the human race. Does this not mean that you are in a manner of speaking relegating yourselves into a vacuum? I threw the scary thought of non-responsibility into the ring of our discussion, but my own belief is that, whatever the individual's predisposition, human freedom—on which the human being's dignity depends—consists of creating something out of or in addition to predisposition and chance. . . .
>
> By the way, I looked up your biblical quotation "Love thy neighbor as thyself." I always thought there was something wrong with this expression of self-love, and I now see that the real translation from Greek is "Love thy neighbor as you are yourself loved." How do you suppose that went wrong, in all translations?

· · · ·

By now Speer and Ulf had met. Two months after her marriage in July 1961 Hilde had received permission to bring Ulf to the prison. "It was difficult, wasn't it? I hope you were not disappointed," Speer wrote Ulf two days later. "We had said so much on paper, that we were mute when sitting face to face. . . . Let me explain the state of 'subtemperature' [*Unterkühlung*] which I imposed upon myself a long time ago to make life possible. If I had ever lived fully here, I think I would have had to die. But an uninterrupted state of 'subtemperature' is also insupportable, for—as you see in Hess—it leads to both apathy and fantasizing.

"I have usually succeeded in replacing or avoiding apathy by physical means—my 'Walk around the World,' during which I live in a world of imagination. My life otherwise, of course, is one of solitude and silence; on average I talk no more than five minutes a day. I use letters and writing—as Hess uses fantasizing—to produce 'feeling.' But what is not possible, is to transmute one into the other. It means that I, who am by nature reserved, can abandon this restraint and come to life in letters—sometimes I fear even sounding exalted, which is also against my nature, as you may already know—but what I can't do is apply this 'letter' dimension of being above my self-enforced subtemperature, to normal intercourse. This is what you saw, and no doubt found yourself surprised by when we met in person. But it is not really alarming. It will only become difficult when I have to return to living in 'normal temperature' one day."

By 1962 and 1963 nobody really had any hope of Speer's early release. "We just went through the motions," Hilde said. Even so, this included new visits to Brandt, Lübke and Erhard, as well as again to George Ball, finding them all, as usual, well intentioned. Toward the end of 1963, Pastor Martin Niemöller sent Speer his "warm greetings" and Fabian von Schlabrendorff, one of the few anti-Hitler activists to escape the hangman after the July 20 bomb plot, let him know that he was taking up his case.

"He says he is going to see Kennedy about me," Speer wrote to Ulf on November 2, 1963. "I'll believe it when it happens. In the meantime however, the Russians here have become quite amiable—it's a little scary. Yesterday I was lying on my bed munching chocolate when the Russian director, usually an ogre, came in. I prepared to jump up, but he gave me a gentle wave. 'No, please, don't bother; stay where you are, be comfortable. Everything all right? Everything happy?'

"I nearly swallowed a whole nut and just managed to nod ardently, keeping lips pressed together. I thought if I smiled he would see my teeth covered with chocolate, not very dignified."

Three weeks later, Kennedy was dead. "This dreadful, dreadful event," he wrote. "The guards called it in to us, half an hour after it happened, but I couldn't take it in, could not believe it. And I mourn more from day to day. To me, Kennedy was more a Roman than a Berliner. . . . Is there any sense in this tragedy? Could it be to remind us all that we are building on sand? All personal troubles vanish in the face of such a tragedy."

A real surprise came in April 1964 when Schlabrendorff obtained, first from the Soviet Ambassador in Washington and then in Moscow, the virtual promise of Speer's release on three conditions: that he would never again engage in political activities ("I could agree to that in a hurry," he wrote to Wolters, who had been instrumental in bringing about this demarche), that he had independent means to survive without such activities ("Here they joke; they *must* know!") and that a deal with Krupp would be arranged that they would trade with the USSR. "There we are. That's what it's really all about. How naive to have ever thought it could be anything else. Well, that ensures that I'm here to the end. And honestly, I don't mind anymore. I find I don't care. My hopes throughout these years were really only on one level— somewhere inside I was always resigned to continue my Trappist existence to the last moment. The ambivalence between my hopes against hope, and this very real and not unhappy resignation is, I suppose, part of my prison psychosis."

"The last two years," Speer told me, "we had no trouble whatever with the Allied guards—they seemed to feel, and said quite openly, that our being there was grotesque."

Toward the end of that year, Eugene Bird took over as American director. "My predecessor, Colonel Drake, introduced the three remaining prisoners to me several months before, in April," he told me. "Speer was working in the garden with his jacket tied around his waist. He stood up and said a nice hello in perfect English. Colonel Drake pointed around the garden and said, 'We call this Speer's Garden of Eden; he planted all these wonderful trees and experimented by crossing a lot of flowers. It's a paradise now.' And it was too; I'd never seen such a garden. . . .

"When I assumed my duties, it was easy enough to manage Schirach—I never trusted him, but he was agreeable enough; his English was better than mine. Hess was really difficult to talk to: 'How are you?' 'Bad.' 'The weather?' 'Bad.' 'Food all right?' 'Bad.' I finally sometimes skipped seeing him because he was so difficult, and went on to Speer. On one occasion Speer remarked that he had noticed that I often didn't talk to the old man. 'If you are short of time,' he said, 'I wish you'd skip me and see him longer. He hasn't said anything to me, but I think it's important. One of these days, you see, he'll be on his own with you, and he will need by then to have got to know you well.'

"I thought that was really nice of him. I was told that Speer always stood up for all the others, especially Hess. When he was sick, it was always Speer who cleaned his room. Schirach didn't like Speer, said he was a traitor . . . but when he had his eye trouble, it was Speer who read to him for hours. Still, he wasn't a yes-man, he wasn't really easy to get along with. He'd insist on his rights as a prisoner but—the only one of the three—he never complained about *being* a prisoner. And he was always doing something. He read over five thousand books; I looked up the lists. . . ."

The other directors had told him, he said, that Speer felt he carried the guilt of all of Germany. "He got on awfully well with the last Russian director, who came just before I left, Colonel Lazaroff. He thought Speer was the most remarkable man."

Bird was planning to build a house in Berlin. "Speer designed it for me, and he gave me an estimate which came closer to what it cost than the architect who finally built it," said Bird. "One day he said, 'Where is my fee? A former Hitler architect comes expensive.' He asked for a piece of paper and wrote, 'Payment for architect: DM 20, signed Speer,' and said, 'Go and buy some flowers for your wife with the twenty you owe me.' Within three weeks of his being released, he came to see the house."

Bird said he attended visits by Hess's family—"One had to: we were concerned about him until the end"—but never Speer's. "I knew how difficult it was. Those terrible long pauses—nothing to say—and then the goodbyes, the children so heartbreakingly relieved it was over. I couldn't stand seeing it. In the end only Lazaroff went, and he deliberately turned away to give them privacy."

("When the children were younger," the Speers' housekeeper, Clara Samuels, told me, "for weeks before those visits they would say, 'Oh, God, it's coming up again. What can we *say?*' ")

"We suspected he was writing, but we never knew for sure," Bird said. "Just once, a rubber band he had around his trouser leg broke and some papers fell out. I pretended not to see; what was the point? Then, when he came to see me after he was out, he told me he had written thousands of pages. I really could hardly believe it. I still don't know how he did it."

By 1965, several publishers had let the Speers know of their interest in Speer's memoirs: first, in 1948, Blanche Knopf; in 1950, the German publisher Heliopolis; and finally, in 1963, Wolf Jobst Siedler at Propyläen.

Speer wrote to Wolters in October 1964,

I'm quite aware that to plan publishing may be one of my worst idiocies, perhaps indeed a fatal one. But as it so happens, I am one of the few who may be able to report objectively, not from any French or British or even German point of view, but from a position beyond and above national interest.

In agreement with H. [another publisher who had written] I vaguely
see the project in five parts: 1) Trial and "Spain" [Spandau], 4–500 pages;
2) What you call the "scientific bit," but I call simply all production
and armaments—horribly boring I fear; 3) Building plans; 4) What do
you think of a combination of the *Chronik* (with my solemn undertaking to suppress the author's name!) and the Führer protocols as well as
the various Memorandums with, retrospectively, my comments? and
5) I might want to discuss the books and writings of various of my
contemporaries....

His parenthetical remark following the fourth point is particularly important, for it strongly suggests that Wolters had already asked Speer not to use
his name in connection with the *Chronik,* no doubt because of the danger a
resurrection of his wartime history could pose for a busy architect with a
large public practice. As was the custom between these two, Wolters would
have couched this serious request in humorous terms, and he could hardly
have expected Speer as a result to suppress so totally Wolters's role during
the twenty years in Spandau.

Speer, however, writing his acknowledgements years later, may well have
seen potential hazards for himself in publicizing the identity of this too
knowledgeable friend. This request may have provided a welcome justification for leaving Wolters out altogether. After all, he could tell himself, Wolters had quite pointedly himself suggested discretion.

Even though these serious publishers' offers were on the table by 1962,
Speer's letters to Ulf show that he was still of two minds about publishing his
memoirs in his lifetime. Although ambivalence was part of his nature, the
possibility remains that if the two friends who had made definite offers to
him to join their firms upon his release had survived, he might after all have
returned in some manner or other to architecture, keeping the publication of
his memoirs on ice until his retirement or, as he indicated to Ulf in 1962,
until after his death.

"I'm flirting with the idea," he wrote then, "that sometime in the twenty-
first century someone will dig up all the nonsense I've been penning and
publish it as historical documentation. It'll make about fifteen hundred
printed pages, as I have now been writing (with some interruptions) for
about ten years."

By November 1965, however (although both Piepenburg and Apel were
then still alive), he seemed to have gone a long way toward making up his
mind. "There is a chap named Siedler," he wrote to Ulf:

Could you keep an ear out as to what people say about him? I'm interested whether he is reactionary or petit-bourgeois.... Though I doubt

it—he sounds more Prussian than anything else. That too could be a problem, or maybe not; maybe it would be a counterweight to me, who am more of a Rhinelander—or Winelander! If I do decide to write, for later publication of course, I shall need a modern young publisher who has his finger on the pulse of the new generation. I need to know how they feel. . . .

Nineteen sixty-five was the year in which he came to terms with the approach of his freedom the following year. In April Wolters wrote Speer a bitter-funny letter:

> When *it* happens, it will have been twenty years since I saw you last. What will there be between us old codgers, aside of course from happy memories of skiing tours in the long distant past; the taste in both our mouths of that "best of all caviars" eaten in the Russian snow, and in yours of Beluga found by me in our Economic Miracle's department store delicatessen and wrapped and posted by your admirer Marion? Will you come to me mainly to take receipt of the promised gift I have held for you in our cellar—that long-cured Westphalian ham, and those patiently waiting bottles of your favorite nectar: Johannisberger 1937? Could these things of the senses end up being all that is between us? I am so happy that the moment approaches, but my heart is heavy. . . .

And Annemarie wrote to Speer, around Christmas:

> I wonder how it will be when—Phase 3 of our lives—we finally confront each other again. Do you understand what I am doing with my children? Can I really envision what you have been through? Have you known how much my mind was with you, all these years? Will we be able to live up to ourselves? I think we may still have some surprises in store.

Sometime not long before, Speer had asked Wolters about Marion's history, and Wolters, tongue in cheek as he often was, relished writing him that the young beauty who had found refuge in "your great offices, O Führer-Architect and Minister," had not been what Nazi Germany considered "a pure Aryan."

"I thought it was funny," Marion told me. "Wolters really thought that Speer didn't know that his organizations were providing a safety net for a number of people in jeopardy. Maybe he had forgotten. For though often not knowing the people concerned, Speer of course knew *about* them. Perhaps Wolters *wanted* to forget it."

She did not think, as Annemarie did, that Wolters wished Speer ill. "But he was frightened for him; I think he was frightened of the reality of Speer."

By the last months of 1965, de Gaulle had openly suggested that Spandau be closed, and Couve de Murville was ordered to so inform Soviet Foreign Minister Andrei Gromyko; Averell Harriman had specifically requested the four-power council in Berlin to release Speer; Henry Kissinger had told Schlabrendorff it was a matter of weeks; Nuremberg prosecutor Lord Shawcross was quoted in *Stern* as saying that both he and John McCloy had repeatedly tried to get Speer released; and a French general, looking at Speer's family photographs in his Spandau cell, had said, *"Bientôt, vous les verrez"* ("Soon you'll be seeing them").

"I actually found myself joking with him," Speer wrote to Ulf. "In the French army, I said, what is *'bientôt'*? Nonetheless, you will laugh, I know, but minutes after he left I found myself telling one of my favorite guards what to do with my Sony radio, just in case. But really, I don't believe it, and I don't care."

Over the next months he would write again and again—to Hilde, Ulf, Annemarie, Wolters, Fritz, Albert and even to twenty-year-old Ernst (who during the last visit found himself hardly able to utter anything except "yes" and "no")—with detailed plans for The Day; what he would wear; what he needed; who should come when and where; whom he would see and whom he would not see; where they would go upon leaving Spandau, by what mode of transport and where after the first stop; how long they would stay in one place or another; what they would do, eat, say. . . .

The question of how to handle the media would preoccupy him for months. Try to evade them? Plant "friendly" press people on his route? Confront all of them head-on? *Stern* offered in excess of DM 300,000 for a first interview. He said no. Siedler offered a country house in Switzerland as soon as he wanted to start writing. He said perhaps. He wrote Wolters that Coesfeld would be his first port of call after he had spent a week or two with the family—in a hunting lodge in the north, it was finally decided. Marion wrote a quivering letter. "I can't wait," she bubbled. "We are wondering what the uncle ["Uncle Alex" had been one of his silly pseudonyms] from Spain [Spandau] will bring us as presents from his trip."

It was the silly season, "but it *was* infectious," Hilde said. "We let him dream his dreams, and meanwhile got on with it, but it was quite exciting. I think my brothers and sisters were pretty anxious; my mother too, but I less. I felt I knew him pretty well, and I liked him."

"I want to give Mama a present of a beautiful golden watch," he wrote Hilde. "Rudi has saved up some money for me—about DM 1,500 to 2,000. I'm looking through the ads and I thought you might buy it for me (a Longines, I think) and then secretly slip it to me so that I can give it to her. Don't write and say it's a waste: it isn't, it isn't. Firstly, it's the end of a twenty-year separation, and secondly, oh, a gesture of thank you for bringing you up as she has."

"I'm wondering," he wrote to Ulf, "whether you could find out whether there is a sleeping pill that puts one out for five hours. I might want it for Day X which, as you know, is going to last until midnight! I'm considering putting myself to sleep around 6 p.m. in order to wake up fresh at 11 p.m. I am quite ridiculously happy. And, heaven knows why, I'm just remembering a silly occasion on the Obersalzberg where the 'Sultan's' [Hitler's] hat hung in the cloakroom. Disrespectful as we young ones were, one adjutant after the other tried on this *Reichshut,* and one after the other found it sinking down over his ears to the level of their noses. That showed the size of *his* brain, they called out in amazement. But then, when I put it on, it fit me to a tee—well, almost; it was a little small. Can't tell you what that did to my self-confidence, and probably my reputation. Goodness, what idiots we were."

Margret came—the last Spandau visit. "It should have been one long bout of joy," he wrote to Wolters, "but both of us found ourselves being quiet and thoughtful. I looked at her, and I know she looked at me the same way. . . . We have both become old." He wrote Ulf in January,

I've decided I must return myself to discipline. I am stepping up my walking—I am in Mexico and proceeding west. I'm having difficulty keeping my mind on what I'm reading so have started to translate a two-hundred-page book from French to German. When it's finished, I'll translate it back into French. At twenty-two pages each month that'll take care of the time that's left. . . . I love the family cassette you sent me . . . all the happiness in your voices. In Hilde's I felt real laughter. If I may put it this way, she has a truly enchanting voice. Of course, when she visited here, none of this could ever show up. . . .

[To Hilde in February 1966:] I wouldn't mind writing an article for *Der Spiegel*—they've offered DM 50,000; it's less than all the others, but I would prefer to go with them. Also, if I write for them, it might neutralize their potential criticism. They could send me questions now, and I could prepare a draft. How about that?

[And in March:] Everything I have written so far will have to be rewritten. So don't think of it in the Illustrated style—this was only a means to an end which served its purpose then, but could quite wrongly make me seem a cynic. You remind me of what I said twenty years ago about the "dirty money writing would earn." Of course I haven't forgotten. But even so, I don't want to *give* my work away—we can't afford it. I have to think what I have lost in earning power. The potential really is, as Schirach has said, in the millions—there will be enough left to give away. [Which shows that he thought of charity from the start.] As alas, I am an object of contemporary history, I shouldn't try to shirk it. . . . If I could build, I wouldn't even think of writing. But—with Pie and Apel dead? And of course I want to earn. The idea of dragging us through the coming years, just getting by, is a nightmare. . . . It would be an advantage to tie up with a good publisher quickly—it would legitimize some restraint. Please tell Siedler I'd like to meet with him as soon as possible after I come out. We can discuss my book later as much as you like—you know that I have always wanted you to be the first to read it, but the whole family must advise me if they can and wish to. Enough of this for now. More important: the suit you and Fritz are getting for me. A thinnish tweed seems nicest. Above all, please, discreet: in case of doubt, whatever is simplest and least conspicuous.

[To Ulf, on April 30:] Pity you can't hold an open-air seminar on one of my lovely lawns here—you'd enjoy that. The orchard blooms like the one at the Heidelberg house, and the flowers are literally shooting out of the ground. A strange thought that I will never witness this again here: not exactly a regret, but a shadow. . . . There are times when the future frightens me and I think that perhaps the best thing for me to do when I come out would be somehow to re-create my Spandau life—a small isolated room somewhere, a kind of cell, a garden, silence and music, communication with others only by letters—perhaps that way I would be a better man. . . . I know it's nothing but a dream for I'm weak. Once I'm out, I'll let it all happen. . . .

[On September 7:] Each of the family has a commission, yours is Project Briefcase. Buy a dark brown leather briefcase, about thirty-five by twenty-five, -six centimeters deep; you'll have to get it to me before we leave Berlin.

Into the briefcase: a dark brown portfolio, with DM 200–300 from Rudi; a notebook with lined, removable pages. Also with telephone numbers of: Nein [his former pilot] in Erlangen; the hunting lodge (and its address); the airport where I arrive with Pan Am (with Nein to be there), Hermann, Wolf, Sybille [Hermann Speer's children], Flächsner, Wolters, Albert in Frankfurt, unless he is meeting us; yours in Berlin ditto; Arnold's in Kiel ditto; Hofer [a friend in public relations they had engaged to help with the media] and any others you think useful.

Pills: Miltau, Bellergal, Sympathol, Multibionta, Helfergin, sleeping pills and Depuraflax. A simple pair of sunglasses, cheap and of glass. A photocopy of my official letter of September 17. A book about copyright; writing paper; electric shaver, also a Gillette razor with blades, soap, shaving lotion; Mama's watch beautifully wrapped (Hilde), toothpicks, car and hiking maps . . . and combs for everybody for delousing—that's a secret: I want to place one at each table setting at our first meal together ... a precaution!!! (joke).

On September 19 he sent Hilde a precise list of menus and drinks. ("It was beginning to drive us bonkers," she said.)

> The pastor will come to Heidelberg on September 29 with a bouquet I shall pick that day in my garden for Mama. Ask her to invite him and his wife to come visit us later; I've already mentioned it to him, but he will need to hear it from her, lest he thinks it is only my last-week-of-prison euphoria. I would have invited him anyway but I have arranged with him that he will keep a special eye on Hess for me from now on, so he is doubly important to me as a link to that poor man. It is the one thing I cannot bear to think about, Hess here alone. . . .

> [September 25:] This I expect is the last letter; the last in reply to all the extraordinary energy and love you expended in the effort to shorten my time in Spandau. You wrote once that you were disappointed that your mission failed. But I can see no failure. Thanks to you, I wandered from hope to hope and that was vital, for without hope one cannot live. . . . But what was most important to me was the love you manifested by taking on this ungrateful task. This love from you to me was the greatest gift, never to be lost or forgotten—it will remain within me, always. That is what I wanted to tell you, at the end of all these many thousands of words. No "thank you" can be enough.

Here he pronounced the word "love," as far as we know, for the first time in twenty years of writing, and perhaps all of his adult life. Fifteen years later, in a different, but for him an equally unprecedented way, he would receive and acknowledge love once more.

But that golden September of 1966, all that lay ahead of him. Twelve years before, he had started on his 40,000-kilometer walk around the world, and he had covered 31,936 kilometers. On September 30 the friendly American guard who had been smuggling things in and out for eight years had a last task. He sent a telegram for him to Wolters, to reach him precisely at midnight: "Please pick me up thirty-five kilometers south of Guadalajara, Mexico."

XXV

A Twilight of Knowing

THE NIGHT from September 30 to October 1, 1966, was warm, with millions of stars in a clear sky. Only Flächsner had accompanied Margret to the prison that night. "There were huge TV spotlights all over the place, lighting it up as if it were noon," he told me. "The streets leading up to the prison were black with people."

This was the third time Flächsner and I met in his comfortable Berlin office, where we talked, always for several hours, sitting in deep armchairs grouped around a glass table.

Of all of the people who had worked with or for Speer, he was probably the most underrated, both by the judges in Nuremberg, where especially the British had little patience with the usually more long-winded style of German advocacy, and, unfairly I feel, by Speer himself. Though probably not brilliant, Flächsner was an intelligent man of integrity, courage and compassion. He was not a dominant personality and, like so many Germans, had a wide streak of romanticism and a propensity for hero worship, some of which he came to expend on Speer. Nonetheless, he saw him clearly enough. "He always seemed to want me to tell him what I really thought," he said. A few minutes after midnight that October 1, 1966, Flächsner did tell him.

"We had come in a black Mercedes, lent to the family by the industrialist Ernst Wolf Mommsen," he said. "When the prison doors opened, precisely one minute after midnight, and Speer and Schirach, almost encircled by British soldiers, came out together, his wife ran up the steps to meet him.

"I was right behind her, and I'm trying to remember exactly what happened. They didn't embrace: I really think they shook hands. There was something so reticent, so reserved about them. I'm not that demonstrative myself, but I remember the thought shooting through my mind, 'What *will* they be like with each other on their own?' She had been very quiet while we waited—I felt concerned about them.

"What *was* funny was that he automatically made as if to get into the seat next to the driver. ["I always had," Speer told me. "It was a habit."] Imagine how that would have looked, me in the back with his wife, he in front with the driver! I pushed him into the back.

"They just sat there; he waved once to someone in the crowd—he said later he thought he had seen one of his favorite British guards—but then they didn't budge, didn't talk, didn't seem to look at each other. It was eerie. I do remember very clearly that a cold shiver went down my back: *What* was going on there? What didn't I know?

"Perhaps in reaction to this coolness between them, on the drive to the Hotel Gerlus in the Grunewald, where they were going to spend the night, I found myself talking to him as I hadn't in all those years. I said, 'Herr Speer, it isn't only that you were away from your family for twenty-one years, but you were hardly with them before that either. In those years—a lifetime really—your wife has brought up six children on her own, helping them to become people capable of counting for something in life. You need to keep remembering that,' I told him—to my own amazement, I might add—and then stopped, feeling I had gone too far.

"Well, he didn't take it amiss; he listened; he always had a great talent for listening to opinions and even advice. And when we got to the hotel, a small, very exclusive place where the owner, who had known him well in bygone days, was waiting to welcome him, he asked me to stay. They had a suite— perfectly beautiful, very luxurious and full of flowers. We drank a wonderful bottle of wine, made small talk, he rang Wolters and some others, and a bit later he went down and gave a press conference. I admired that, and I admired the way he did it."

Flächsner's hero worship showed more clearly here than at any other time. "The hotel hall was bursting with journalists and photographers. He was extraordinary. He said—I remember it word for word—'Ladies and gentlemen, you will understand that I can only be brief tonight, for this evening belongs to my wife, this evening is hers. So please ask me only concrete questions, and I'll answer them.' Some idiot called out, 'It isn't your business to say *anything,*' and he ignored him. They asked him this and that about Spandau, and then at the end—not more than six, seven minutes—they asked how he saw his future, and he said, 'I'm an architect, and I hope to find people who will let me practice my profession.' "

All the children, with wives and husbands, were at the borrowed lodge in Schleswig-Holstein the next day when Margret and Speer arrived. "It was a desperate atmosphere, almost at once," Hilde said. "It was very sad because everybody tried so hard."

Annemarie went to see them there after a few days. As only the family had been allowed to visit him in Spandau—each of the children once a year—she hadn't laid eyes on him in twenty-one years. "At first sight, it was astonishing how unchanged he was," she said. "Older, of course, but not that old; he didn't look in the least worn, or flabby. I thought there was a depth to his eyes I hadn't remembered. But on the whole," she shrugged, "he was the Speer I knew.

"The family had planted a lot of false trails to mislead the press," she said. "They were quite right: *Spiegel* promptly described one of the wrong places, and the media descended on it in droves. The place we'd found for them, though a little small as it turned out, was comfortable but simple—very much the kind of thing Speer had always liked. But I sensed that it had all gone wrong the moment I got there. Everybody was at such awful pains to be terribly, terribly at ease."

"I knew almost at once that they wanted something from me I didn't know how to give," Speer told me. "It was in the air from the moment we were there together, *en famille*. What I mostly felt was this terrible embarrassment, this total strangeness, an estrangement infinitely worse even than I had felt during those terrible prison visits. What happened in me was, well, really outrageous, and I knew it was—an awful regret at being there; an awful longing almost at once for Spandau, my rhythm there—the pattern of twenty years, my solitude, my imaginary walks, my thinking. I knew within days that it would not, could not change."

"I should have known," Margret said on one occasion in the Allgäu while we were cooking. "It had been too long. You see, at first he talked about Spandau, about the people there, what was said, what he did. And even though he had written unendingly about all this, the children *were* interested. But after a while they wanted him to ask them about themselves, what was important to *them*, their ideas, their plans. They wanted him to want to get to know them. In his letters to them, it had sounded as if that was what he wanted too. And they tried, almost each one of them tried. But they soon saw he didn't listen. I suppose it was asking too much. . . ."

Annemarie, who had been so closely involved with organizing this family reunion, worried about it afterwards for years. "But I don't know what we could have planned that would have been better, less of a strain, and that would have avoided this fiasco," she said. "It certainly had an immense—a disproportionate—effect on the family's future relations with him. They never got over it."

Given the circumstances it could hardly have been different, I suggested. "That's what I mean," she said. "Perhaps it shouldn't have been a family get-together like this. There were too many people, all trying to say and feel things of import. But it was what he—and they—wanted at the time. Of course he wanted to see them all, and they him, and the children were longing to have him meet their husbands and wives.

"I made an attempt to break up what seemed to me to be becoming an emotional disaster area by organizing an excursion to a nearby floating restaurant I knew he had liked in the past, the Finauer Fähre, but it didn't help much." She smiled. "It was there I noticed a silly but real change. When cheese was handed around he picked it up with his fingers to put it on his plate. A stupid thing to notice, but I remember saying to myself, 'Well, old boy, you are going to have to relearn table manners,' and later Margret told me that this thought had occurred to her on several occasions during those first days." Annemarie had left after one day. "I first went to see Rudi, and then to Heidelberg to deal with the mail, the phone and prepare the house."

During that stay in the hunting lodge, I once asked Margret, had he ever talked to them about his moral doubts, about his spiritual search? After all, he *had* written about it at least to some of the children, and to Ulf. They were all grown-up people. Surely they would have been capable of understanding?

She shook her head. "No, he never talked about those things, then or later." She paused. "You are right, perhaps he would have if I had encouraged him, and, yes, now that you are putting it this way, the children probably *would* have been interested in that. It was probably my fault. I thought—then and for years afterwards—that we should forget about it all. I—" She hesitated before going on and then laughed a special, somehow embarrassed laugh. "I remember being terribly afraid . . . of words. I kept cutting him off in mid-sentence. I just wanted him to talk about ordinary things, be an ordinary man."

But of course he wasn't an ordinary man.

"I know, but I couldn't accept it. I never did this again later, but somehow, I didn't want the children . . . I didn't myself want to be . . ." She wanted to say "part of that past," but again she stopped and then said, conclusively, "I just wanted him to live in the 'now,' not in the past."

Later I understood that it was precisely the "moral doubts" she hadn't wanted to hear about. Not because she didn't suspect that he had them, but because she had never been able to face her own.

"What they wanted and needed," Speer said when I raised this subject with him, "I could not provide. I could do it in my imagination, I could extend it to letters; but I couldn't do it face to face. I just wasn't that sort of man, and I didn't know how to pretend to be. It was hopeless."

"Seen in retrospect, it was really quite dreadful," Hilde said. "One by one my sister and brothers gave up. There was no communication, and feelings about it became worse, not just every day but every hour; so they left."

"It took me a long time to realize that I must have been deluded," Margret said with that brief laugh that wasn't laughter. "I really thought he'd come back as my husband, the father of his children, ready to live in Heidelberg, open a small architect's office and live a small life. *Small*," she repeated, bitterly.

"I knew he wanted to write," Hilde said, "but I had no idea it would lead to the sort of conspicuousness which he immediately—I soon realized—sought and of course received."

"You know, the way it all went," Speer said, "the things that happened, and the way I made or let them happen . . . I had really foreseen it all. Even before leaving Spandau I had realized that rather than a prison, it had become a refuge for me, the place where I had come to live my fullest life—my *real* life, or what my life perhaps should have been. I remember, I wrote something like this—I think to Ulf—some ridiculous idea of retreating to a mountain or a monastery or something.*

"Well, perhaps it wasn't as ridiculous as all that, because there were only two alternatives. One which I might—just *might*—have done if the opportunity had ever come along, and that was to try to return to architecture. Perhaps then I would have lived more with and for the family, the children. But it never did come along, and of course I know now that it never could have—I mean, even if my two friends who made me offers while I was still in prison had survived. How could any firm have afforded to be identified with me? For most people, even now, I'm a kind of a freak; only the simplest people—the peasants on the mountain—can speak to me like a normal human being. In private life now, few of the people I used to know well want to know me. Oh, they are polite, but. . . ."

"So really," he laughed, mocking himself, "short of making my little dream come true, entering a monastery perhaps, all I could do was what half of me really wanted to do anyway—live in the past, and through that be whatever I could become." And then, as often happened when what he said had been revealing, his tone changed abruptly, becoming almost flippant. "In a way, for the children everything that happened was probably the best. The reason for their successes now is probably that I wasn't around when they grew up." He smiled. "*That* would have weighed on them too."

"There has never been any doubt in my mind that, whatever his writing ambitions were, Speer's primary intention had been to return to architecture," Annemarie said. "He really was a very realistic man, you know. He knew a mark had a hundred pfennigs, and he was perfectly aware that he would have to earn money. He felt a profound obligation both to himself and to his family to make a new 'go' of it—yes, to succeed. And as everybody else he knew had had twenty years to do it in, he had to do it very quickly if he was going to do it at all. But it was architecture he wanted to do it with. However, as he told you, he realized very soon that this wasn't going to be possible. Too many people still considered him a social leper. That's when he fully

---

*See letter to Ulf, April 30, 1966 (Chapter XXIV, page 660).

turned toward writing, and also drew back from attempting to see former friends. It happened very quickly, and I think it was a very painful time for him."

It had begun less than two weeks after he left Spandau, when he went to see Rudi Wolters in Coesfeld. "Part of all the plans he made at Spandau was that sad illusion that everybody would receive him with open arms," Annemarie said. "One of the first people he wanted to see was Mommsen, the friend who had loaned a car to the family. Speer phoned him, among others, the night of his release and told Wolters that he had invited him to join them at Wolters's house in Coesfeld, two weeks later.

"Well, as you can imagine, neither of the two men thought that was a very good idea. Under the moral pressure of that immediate phone call Mommsen agreed, but unhappily, and Wolters, not surprisingly, was furious to have Speer immediately impose on him, order him about."

("More than furious," Fritz Wolters told me. "I think my father was really hurt by Speer wanting Mommsen there on the first day he would spend in Coesfeld. He arranged it, but it rankled to the end.")

"It's interesting that in his diary notes," Annemarie said, "Rudi didn't mention my visit to him that first week on my way back from Schleswig-Holstein. You see, I had known for years how he really felt about Albert, and having seen what was happening at the family meeting, I was desperate to pre-empt a similar debacle during the Coesfeld visit, to which I knew Albert was intensely looking forward."

She thought that Wolters avoided mentioning her visit in his diary because they had had a bitter confrontation. "He was totally intransigent, rather frightening really," she said. ("My father could become absolutely wild if he was opposed, with tantrums that shook the walls," said Fritz. "As a child, it scared me witless.") "He screamed and yelled, stamped his foot, thumped the table," Annemarie continued. "I begged him to allow this first visit to pass in peace, to keep faith with Albert just one more time, however much he disagreed with his opinions, and I finally said that he owed him that much. But he replied that no, he now owed him *nothing*. He had done what he could those twenty years to make his life easier and to help the family, but now it was over. 'We are too far apart,' he said, and he was right. They were."

And yet, on the face of it, that first *Wiedersehen* of the two friends went off merrily enough. Wolters wrote in his *Segments,*

We hadn't seen each other in almost twenty-two years, but our *Wiedersehen* in Coesfeld was just as casual as our goodbye had been in 1945. 'How goes it, long time no see,' he said, as if it was nothing, just shaking my hand. Even so, that night I brought up the promised Prince Metternich Johannisberger 1937, solemnly handed over my *Chronik,* the photographs of his buildings and plans for Berlin, his Spandau letters in original and transcripts and his other writings, twenty years of press cuttings, and my final account of the School Fund, from which I was able to present him with the not unrespectable balance—DM 25,000—which would enable him to buy a dashing automobile ten days later. . . .

And finally, I was also able at last to get rid of the Westphalian ham I had promised him in a fit of enthusiasm on the day Stalin died. "I promise you the best ham ever from our Westphalian pig, born on this memorable March 5, 1953," I had written him that day. At that point we were sure he would be released in 1956 after serving [half] his sentence, and I had planned to have that pig slaughtered accordingly; who would have thought that it would have another ten years to live?

[Nonetheless] I knew that day of that still merry first reunion that the Spandau friendship was over. As he stood there, in person, I saw him suddenly quite differently than I had previously, in my mind. It was something like his first sight of Hitler after his long illness, when he no longer saw the remarkable eyes to which he had so long succumbed, but only a "broad nose." . . .

Wolters's son, Fritz, had long admired Speer, "for his stand at Nuremberg, in Spandau and afterwards," he said. "He at least had the courage to change his mind, while my father and his old cronies . . ." He left the sentence unfinished. "When he came to Coesfeld that first time," he went on, "Mommsen came with his wife and a big chauffeur-driven Jaguar. The chauffeur had gone off for a beer, leaving the car blocking our narrow driveway. Mommsen didn't drive, so he asked his wife to move the car, but she said she really didn't dare. 'Just give me the keys, I'll drive it out,' said Speer, who hadn't touched a car in twenty years and certainly never a Jag. And lo and behold, nobody dared to say boo. Good as gold, quiet as little lambs, they handed over the keys to this million-mark or whatever car, and with total self-assurance he drove it faultlessly around the narrow curve, and returned the keys with a flourish." ("Just the kind of thing he'd relish," said Annemarie. "Real tongue-in-cheek, little-boy nonsense.")

"When Herr Speer arrived home," said former housekeeper Clara Samuels, "it was really strange. Yes, he had changed—he was very reticent; we had to get used to each other slowly. He was immediately very busy, lots of people came to see him—I don't know who they were, but I think they were all strangers. Frau Speer went out a lot—one could see she didn't want to take part in all that. She went to see friends, to take saunas, to walk. During meals [Clara sat at table with them for family meals] we talked about everyday things. I had known them for so long, I could see that he was very concerned about his wife," she said, "but they were people who just couldn't show this to each other—they couldn't talk either. It was heartbreaking. . . ."

Three weeks after his release from Spandau, Speer wrote to Wolf Jobst Siedler, suggesting they should meet and offering to come to Berlin to see him. Siedler wrote back and made a counterproposal to come to Heidelberg.

Siedler, at the age of forty publisher and editor-in-chief of Propyläen, the trade books part of the giant Ullstein publishing empire—a success in his field not too unlike that of the young Speer under Hitler—was particularly well equipped to take on this controversial author. Highly intelligent and attractive, he grew up in an exemplary intellectual family, with a liberal, decently anti-Nazi father who had a large circle of like-minded friends, including throughout the Hitler period a considerable number of Jews— some of whom he and his friend, the physicist Otto Hahn, hid and fed. Siedler himself was imprisoned at seventeen for subversion, then released after ten months to serve at the Eastern front.

By the time Siedler and I sat down in his office in Berlin in 1985 to talk about Speer (through whom we had originally met in 1978), he had long since left Ullstein and was running his own Siedler Verlag with immense success.

Siedler had first written to Margret Speer in 1963 and told her he thought that Speer should write a book. He didn't see such a project as a "quickie," he said. Perhaps once Speer was released, he and she would like to go to live in Switzerland—he was prepared to finance the rental of a chalet there, he wrote, and a long period for "writing slowly."

He had later managed to get a letter directly to Speer in Spandau, he said. "I told him that I had no idea what his ideas were now and that I myself had no sympathy for the Nazis, but that, whatever his present politics were, I felt he was the only one of the Hitler circle who was intellectually equipped to bear witness. I told him that I had already written to his wife that Ullstein would finance him for six months after he left Spandau, to sit and write in some Swiss village. I had heard that he loved mountains, and I did think it might be useful for him to start the work away from everyone and outside Germany. Of course, when I wrote to his wife, and then to him, I had absolutely no idea that he had already written a first draft, that so much material was already available.

"When, in 1966, I said I'd come and see him in Heidelberg," Siedler said, "he rang me up. He said he knew about the world of books; authors went to see publishers, not the other way round. I tried to persuade him that this had changed, but he insisted and I finally realized he wanted desperately to come to Berlin."

They met a few days later for lunch at Schlicher's, a restaurant Speer knew

well from the past. There was ample reason why the passionately liberal Siedler should have been suspicious of Speer, whose past represented everything
he detested. But intellectually and even physically curiously similar, it took
only minutes for them to grow to like each other. "He looked honest,"
Speer—always terse in descriptions—told me.

"He was amazingly trusting," Siedler said. "We talked for the briefest
time. By that time he had been offered hundreds of thousands of D-Marks
[Deutschmarks] and dollars by magazines in Germany, France and America,
and had said no to all of them. But there, at lunch in Berlin with me, he insisted that we should fix the contract then and there. It was lying on my desk
at the office—I had thought we might go there after lunch. I finally sent my
driver to pick it up. It was an extraordinary way to put a writer under contract, but that's what he wanted, so that's what I did. When it came, I asked
him to read it—I said I'd leave him alone for a bit so he could read without
me watching him. But he said no, it wasn't necessary. 'Either there is trust
between us or there isn't,' he said. I said he should be careful about trust, it
had got him into hot water before. But he just smiled and signed it."

Had you read the contract? I had once asked Speer. "No, whatever for?" he
replied. "I liked him."

Although Speer, from that moment on and for the next two years, concentrated almost entirely on the book, he did give one major interview he had
already planned, to two journalists from *Der Spiegel.*

"I wanted to do this," he told me, "not because of the fee but because I
wanted to talk to young people." But he had a whole family of young people,
I said, why didn't he talk to them?

"Because I needed people who had nothing to do with me, who felt no
need to protect me and who would not, I thought, hesitate to attack or contradict me. And indeed, I was amazed and fascinated by the questions the
journalists asked. And I realized that if this was what young people wanted to
know, then there were still things I hadn't sufficiently considered, and thus
many answers missing in my 'Spandau draft.' It was after this interview that I
asked Siedler whether he could think of someone young who could ask me
questions from time to time while I worked. And that's when he came up
with [Joachim] Fest."

Seen from today's perspective when newspaper journalists, in competition
with TV, have become more combative, the *Spiegel* interview seems fairly
restrained.

Wolters, as he had written to Speer years before, was highly critical of all
the German media, but probably most of all of the left-liberal *Spiegel.* And he
was appalled by, and fought from the start, Speer's intention to use them as
his "platform" upon leaving prison. In a critical letter (November 30, 1966),

which he said he had "pondered for a long time" (after reading the article), he told Speer he was convinced that the *Spiegel* journalists' "opinionated questions" were carefully aimed toward achieving essentially predetermined replies:

> And indeed, the opinions you duly expressed, so precisely in line with what has been taught in our schools and universities for the past twenty years, provided exactly what the press wants to hear. . . . However difficult it is, in your memoirs you should perhaps concentrate entirely on what really happened, leaving aside what the world thinks of it now.
>
> As Hitler was one of the prime political movers of the first half of this century, anything said about him by those who were close to him is essential for the establishment of historical truth. . . . In this sense . . . improvised statements to the press are not only irresponsible and misleading, but also possibly harmful to your future credibility.
>
> Your reply to *Spiegel*'s question, "Would you unequivocally blame Germany for the war?" "No, not Germany: Hitler," is precisely the kind of dangerous oversimplification made entirely from today's perspective that I mean. You will surely remember that in 1939 we were all of the opinion that Hitler *was* Germany. Although we were certainly depressed rather than enthusiastic about the war in Poland, we surely considered that the responsibility for it was to be found in the provocative conduct by the Poles, and that it was the British who made of it a world war. Is that not how all of us saw it then?
>
> Of course, after the drumming the masses have received from the media since 1945, hardly anyone doubts Hitler's sole responsibility, which after all forms the basis of our foreign policy—Hitler the devil, his collaborators the devil's generals, the devil's doctors, the devil's architects and so on. If anyone entertained the hope, however, that this demonization would free the German *people* of blame, they have been richly disillusioned. For the victors—i.e., most of the world—the devil and his subdevils were and remain the *Germans, all* Germans. . . .
>
> Don't you think that [in your future writing], rather than repeating these clichés, it would be worth arousing the interest and understanding [of our new generations] with a truer and wider picture of the past, which necessarily must include not only Germans, but all Europeans and even all of Western civilization?
>
> In old friendship, your
> R.

"I know my father expected to help Speer with his book," Fritz Wolters told me. "I heard him say this repeatedly, and it also emerges very clearly from the first letters he wrote to him, after his release."

Marion Riesser thought differently. "This was perhaps so much earlier, when Speer began the 'Spandau draft,' and at that time officially appointed Wolters his literary executor and, incidentally, also said that he would dedicate the book to him," she said. "But when a few years later he changed his mind and made Hilde his executor, Wolters ceased to think that he would have—or wanted to have—any part in the eventual work."

Speer talked with me many times about his books and described his original plans for them during our first few days together. He said he had communicated very little with Wolters once he started to work. "I went to stay in Portugal for a while, with the Brüggemanns, friends of Rudi's who had a house there," he said, rather curtly. "It was he who organized that, and that's where I started to work. But talk about it, no. From the moment I signed up with Siedler, he was the only one I talked with."

His original plan had been for one book of reminiscences, but when Siedler saw the enormous amount of material, he decided it had to be two books. "But it was my decision what would go into which book," Speer said. "The letters I wrote in Spandau had always been radically different from each other, and in order to emphasize this, I gave them specific headings. Thus all those which basically were my draft for my memoirs—which became *Inside the Third Reich*—I called 'Arias.' All those which were additions, corrections or afterthoughts to the 'Arias' were the *Späne* [shavings]. The third category was on the one hand the letters to the children, the Spanish-Illustrated, on the other hand many letters to Wolters, about events, people, books I read, dreams I dreamed, and then about more mundane things like money and all that. In this category there were also many letters to individual children. It was largely from this third category that, five years later, I selected the material for *The Secret Diaries*.

"And then there was a fourth small category of letters to Wolters, on which I put a special mark and which were to be put away, untouched, until I returned." These, he said, were the most difficult, his private thoughts and searches "about my own morality, faith . . . or lack of both."

Would Wolters have read those? I asked.

"I don't think so," Speer replied. "He is a very honorable man; my special mark was on the envelopes, and they were returned to me in the envelopes."

He was confronted with about ten thousand typed (transcribed) pages when he had to make his choice as to what to use for each of the two books.

"It was not too difficult to decide what would go into the Reminiscences,"* he said. "It had to be my twelve years with Hitler. Basically, what you find in the book—though organized differently, and with some post-Spandau additions of documents and so on—is largely taken almost verba-

*In German, he referred to *Inside the Third Reich* as his *Erinnerungen* (Reminiscences).

tim from the 'Arias' I wrote in Spandau. *The Secret Diaries* represented a very different problem, requiring far more selection and organization," he said.

(It was after he said this, as we sat in a bright little conservatory next to his study in Heidelberg, that he took stacks of the original letters and transcripts out of his archive there. I spent hours on successive nights reading parts of them—my first sight of the documents I have been studying since his death.)

"When my father started to work on the Reminiscences," Hilde said, "he sent my sister Margret and me chapters as he completed them. I went along with it for a while—a little longer than Margret—but then I also stopped. I didn't want the role he wished to assign to me. But I liked the book well enough when it was finished."

She did not feel the same way about *The Secret Diaries*. "He again sent me chapters, but there I gave up much quicker. For that book to be true in an absolute sense, it would have had to be a psychological self-portrait. I didn't think it was that, so I wanted nothing to do with it. He had selected so carefully from the letters that finally it was a 'laundered' book. Not in the sense of politics or his guilt, but really, at a much deeper level, he had removed or withheld almost all his private feelings. And finally I am glad about that. If that book had been 'right,' in the sense I mean, then it would have been too much: he would have had to bare his soul, and those of others too—as indeed he did in his letters, those thousands and thousands of pages he did *not* include in the books. I really think he quite deliberately drew the line at exposing his private person, his private life, his deepest thoughts, and I think he was right."

"It is true that Hilde felt that ideally I should have written the *Diaries* differently," Speer said. "I disagreed. Not because it would have been less successful, but because writing it as I did came closest to showing what Spandau had been for me. I couldn't do more, but I also couldn't do less—more would have been intolerable, less would have been dishonest. It is true, though, that what was finally published has some added material. I don't feel I have to apologize for that. I started work on that book in 1972, six years after I was released from Spandau, three years after the Reminiscences were published in Germany. By that time I had had the most concentrated period you can imagine of catching up with twenty-one years of thinking in Germany. And I had also by then met a number of very special people. *Grosse Köpfe, grosse Geister*—great minds, great spirits. I couldn't simply close myself off from developing my reflections, all the more since most of what I added had probably been in my unconscious all along anyway.

"But whether it was or not, to fulfill the purpose of that book, which was not only to record what happened from day to day—which I did as far as I possibly could both from my notes and from my memory—but how the human personality can and must adapt and change, the thoughts I added quite simply belonged in it."

Both books, he said, contain things other than those he wrote in prison. "But why not? What do people want? In prison, my horizon was very limited. When I came out, it was inevitable that I would experience things, learn things, learn to understand and see things differently in relation to the prison-freedom context—of *course* I had to apply that to what I wrote. Thoughts cannot be timed like calendars or clocks; they span timeless worlds inside one. Writing is the link. At least, that is how I saw it, and still see it now."

He was surprisingly philosophical about the many accusations against him. "They accuse me of altering the original notes, of adding to them, of changing my mind about the format and, finally, of writing the books for money. Will you tell me of one autobiography where each of these points would not apply? Furthermore, they accuse me of hiding or lying about my political convictions and the extent of my relationship with Hitler, of compromising my architecture, of sinister motivations for my stand at Nuremberg and for writing my books, and of lying about my knowledge of the murder of the Jews. Well, you will be in a position to judge for yourself."

When he enumerated these accusations, he put the principal one at the end, almost as if to try me out. He did not mention another accusation by many of his most bitter critics, which he was really sensitive about—that he had not really written the books, that Joachim Fest had been his ghostwriter.

"This was total nonsense," Siedler later confirmed. "Naturally I talked to him quite frequently during his years of writing; sometimes he rang to discuss something or—as many writers need—to get some encouragement, and sometimes I called him to talk about specific chapters he sent me. As you know, for the Reminiscences he had asked me to find a 'young historian,' and Fest's contract for this project—he had nothing to do with *The Secret Diaries*—was as a historical consultant. I don't think he ever saw him without me, and oddly enough, given the length of the writing process and the complexity of the subject, our actual meetings were comparatively rare. As I remember, we actually met just seven or eight times. Once we spent five or six days together in Bozen [Bolzano, in South Tyrol]; we went to Heidelberg, I think, six times, staying about three days on each occasion. And once we spent a wonderful summer weekend in Sylt [on the North Sea]. Our wives were always along. Fest and I would spend the days with Speer working through things, talking and walking, while our wives would go their way and we'd meet up for meals."

Fest's advice, including on research in which he was very experienced, had been invaluable, Siedler said. "But he had no part in the second stage of the work—the actual editing of five thousand typed pages down to what would become six hundred pages in print. He had nothing to do with writing." But both Fest and Siedler himself, he said, had asked Speer many questions, the answers to which were essential to the book. Among these of course, were questions about the Kristallnacht and the Jews.

"I knew, of course," Speer told me, "that this issue was uppermost in everybody's mind; it had been uppermost in mine for more than twenty years. When I left Spandau I soon saw that my feelings were paralleled by many of the best people in Germany and by many of the young. When Siedler and I first discussed the book, I said that I felt I should state my position about concentration camps and the murder of the Jews right at the start. I was almost thinking in terms of a special foreword. But Siedler felt it wasn't necessary; he thought the reader would find it as he read the book. Rationally, he was right: I was writing my Reminiscences, and if this was to be what I myself *remembered*, then, literally speaking, the extermination of the Jews could not be part of it. Still, I thought he was wrong and I felt very unhappy about it."

A number of critics—Lucy Dawidowicz, Geoffrey Barraclough, Rebecca West, Matthias Schmidt, Elias Canetti, Heinz Höhne and others—would point out how feeble and impersonal his comments on this central issue were, and how little there was of them except where, "for the sake of the American market" some of them said, he had "inserted extra bits" in the English-language edition. But the fact is that although his mention of the Kristallnacht was entirely the result of Siedler and Fest's intervention, Siedler confirmed that the decision about how the question of the Jews and Speer's feelings of guilt were to be handled in the German edition was made not by Speer, but by him.

"In his first draft after Spandau," Siedler told me in 1985, "the question of the Jews and his feelings of guilt came up in every third paragraph. I felt that a German readership simply could not cope with all these mea culpas. We argued for days about it. He fought me like a tiger, and when I won, it was really only because he tired of the battle. 'Do what you like,' he finally said.

"Some time later, Gerry Gross, the editor at Macmillan in New York who was reading the English-language translation, rang me and said that for American readers there simply wasn't enough about the murder of the Jews and Speer's own feelings of culpability. I said, 'If that's all you are worried about, I've got in my drawer pages and pages I took out, and you are welcome to them. They put some of them back in their edition, and that's how it happened."

Years later when I asked Siedler whether he could help me any further on those extra pages he had mentioned to me seven years earlier, he said that although he could not remember the details, he certainly recalled discussing the problem occasionally with Gerry Gross. Gerry, he said, was always asking that Speer should deal with the moral aspect of his personal responsibility. He himself, he said, had found Speer's "eternal proclamations" of his guilt rather embarrassing. He remembered advising him to leave the decision about his guilt to others. "However," he said, "when all is said and done, he probably *did* feel this guilt. If he didn't, why would he have consigned such a large part of his royalties to the victims?"

Gross, now vice president of Boston University, had a clear if slightly different memory of his conversation with Siedler when we talked over lunch at the Century Club in New York City in December 1992. (By that time, however, all the editions, in German and other languages, of *Inside the Third Reich* had incorporated the same additions, and in the two subsequent books, *The Secret Diaries* and *Infiltrations*, Speer focused increasingly on the terrible issue of the murder of the Jews.

The Century is a renowned New York club, which primarily serves the literary world. The walls of the dining rooms are lined with shelves to the ceiling holding tens of thousands of books from our own and earlier times. Service is unobtrusive, voices are low, and a club rule prohibits business transactions during meals—no notebooks or papers are permitted on the dining tables. It makes for a quiet atmosphere.

"Something certainly happened about extra material," Gerry Gross said. "It was actually our then publisher, Peter Rittner, who felt very strongly that the American edition had to have more about Speer's *feelings*. I'm sure I discussed it first with Wolf, though I don't recall his offering pages he had taken out. My impression, probably mistaken in view of how Siedler remembers it, is that previous to our request, there hadn't been any additional pages. What I do remember very vividly is talking with Speer himself about it. He was exceptionally receptive to criticism and suggestions. I told him that we, Rittner and I, felt the American edition needed something additional from him about his own feelings on what happened to the Jews.

"Speer merely said something on the order of 'Oh, yes? All right,' and then he sent us two pages right away. They were pretty much exactly what we had hoped for, and it was enough. After this one time, even though I saw him whenever I was in Germany, we never talked about anything like this again."

With Siedler, I interjected, he had "fought like a tiger" on this issue. Gross smiled. "It was, I think, a very different relationship; I saw a good deal of him, but except for this matter and a few other small points in the manuscript which we went over after the translation had been completed, we didn't really discuss the substance of the book. What I mean is that while Siedler, and I suppose Fest with him, had to tackle him on what I'm sure were many sensitive issues during the writing, by the time I came on the scene, the book was *there*. So our relationship was, well, much more detached, more relaxed, I suppose."

Gross did not become a friend of Speer's, as Siedler had. "Friends? No, I wouldn't say that. I was fascinated by him; what he wrote was extraordinary, for me *The Secret Diaries* even more than *Inside the Third Reich*. He was a most extraordinary man."

But he did not feel comfortable with him, I suggested, and he looked at me thoughtfully. "Comfortable? No. Excited, stimulated, yes. As I remember it now," he said after a while, "it's true, our conversations were always very much on the surface. My son was just becoming an architect, and we talked about architecture, and about art and travel, and of course we talked about publishing matters—publicity, money and all that. Now that I come to think of it, it's true, we never talked about anything to do with his past, or about Hitler. But . . ." Again he reflected quietly for a time. "I don't know," he finally said. "Something drew me to him."

Curiosity? Hope that perhaps one day they *could* communicate on things which were important to *him*? "Perhaps," he said. "On one occasion I bumped into him, unplanned, at the Frankfurt Book Fair. He asked me to have dinner with him, and I declined, saying my wife was with me. Usually, because she really disliked Germany, she spent whatever time I had to be there with our daughter, who was then living in Geneva.

"He immediately invited her too. When I telephoned her at the hotel, she said absolutely not—nothing in the world could make her sit down at table with 'that man.' He called her himself then, and she agreed, but by the time I came to pick her up she was almost ill with panic. I think I really wanted her to meet him. She did it for me. It was very brave of her, and I have given her credit for it ever since. Nothing happened, you know. We just had dinner in a nice place, and he and I chitchatted as usual. She said very little. But when we got back to our room, she burst into tears and cried, it seemed to me, for hours.

"I've never been sure whether Speer knew nothing about the murder of the Jews until after the war," he said. "Logically, it seems impossible that he didn't know. Eugene Davidson [who wrote the Introduction to the American edition of *Inside the Third Reich*] got to know him well, and believed him. But I don't think my wife ever did."

I asked Gross to what extent he thought Speer had been motivated by money in writing his books.

"Very little," he said, and showed me a note Speer had scribbled during dinner with him on September 24, 1972, about his revenues (in dollars) from 1967 to 1972.

His total income from Ullstein, to whom Speer had given world rights (and who by then, as Wolf Jobst Siedler told me, had sold 500,000 hardbacks of *Inside the Third Reich* in Germany and, as the book had by then gone into both hardback and paperback editions in foreign languages, millions of copies elsewhere), had been $577,000. Of this he had contributed $102,000 to charities in Europe and the United States; $263,000 went for income tax; $96,000 for secretarial help, transport and support of relatives; and $93,000 on family expenses. His casual arithmetic indicated that he had lost money; but he had, in fact, a tiny surplus of $23,000 over four years.

By the time I met Speer, two and a half years after *The Secret Diaries* was published in 1975, he had probably earned most of the large sums he would earn. Just as he had scribbled down the above figures for Gerry Gross in 1972, he showed me his account books in 1978. As one can imagine, everything was carefully entered in them.

After taxes, family obligations, gifts to people who had helped him—Toni Proost and his family, and others from the Spandau days—and the usual running expenses, Speer was left with DM 850,000, at that time approximately half a million dollars. "The total," he said, "is enough to keep Margret and me going gently—I mean to the end—if I don't earn any further sums of consequence with my future books."

("Both my parents were quite old-fashioned about money," Hilde said later. "Before the books, there was also money, but it was 'capital,' and for people of their generation, capital can't be touched. Certainly they couldn't have lived on the income of that, which was comparatively modest." She laughed. "Well, not *that* modest, but then it really wasn't his way, was it, to live even *that* modestly." What he liked, she said with a smile, was living modestly in luxury.)

"I suppose I shouldn't have liked Speer," Gerry Gross said. "Many people would say I couldn't have. But, yes, I think I did. I liked him and don't quite know why. Perhaps it was because, even though we never talked about it, I did feel he was looking for truth, inside himself."

Gross remembered that when he and Speer had first discussed the American contract, he had suggested that Speer might wish to contribute to some American Jewish aid organizations once the royalties began to come in, and he immediately agreed. But until I told him, Gross had never known that (without anyone's knowledge except Annemarie Kempf, Siedler, former U.S. prosecutor Robert Kempner and later Wolters) Speer had been anonymously contributing to several Jewish organizations in Europe from the time he began to earn money, and continued to do so until he died.

"He came to see me very soon after his first book came out," Kempner told me. "He told me he had given Annemarie Kempf money for the children's home she was working for, and he asked where else he might help without anyone knowing. I told him about a place in Frankfurt where Jewish camp survivors were being cared for. He started there, and then added the convent in Maastricht where Edith Stein had lived, until she was sent to Auschwitz, where she died. Some of the nuns who had helped her were still alive then—they never knew where the large sum he sent them came from, nor did the place in Frankfurt, or other Jewish organizations he later helped." Speer, said Kempner, had always carried a medallion of Edith Stein in his pocket.*

"Both my books—the Reminiscences and then *The Secret Diaries,*" Speer told me, "did of course go through a long process of structuring and corrections. In Spandau, as you know, I had no documentation at my disposal since we were not allowed to read anything on the Third Reich. So I spent months afterwards working with documentation from the Federal Archives in Koblenz and other archives, checking facts and dates in the records of my own ministry and in books published since the war."

"Speer was given considerable help here," I was told by Hedwig Singer, who always assisted Speer at the Federal Archives, and after his death organized the Speer Archive when it was transferred to Koblenz. "All the material Speer needed for his Reminiscences went to him by mail. He would tell us in writing what he needed, and we would make photocopies—most of them from his ministry records, the Führer conferences and official publications—and send them to him. His main problem was dates, and he checked all of these with us very carefully, in writing and of course also by phone, talking either to the Chief Archivist [Alfred] Wagner or myself. I must say, though, that for the Reminiscences I don't recall his asking for anything to do with foreign workers or Jews. He did tell us once that his two secretaries had smuggled out a lot for his defense at Nuremberg—Annemarie Kempf presumably looked after those records afterwards.

"We never met Speer until July 1969, when he came to the archives with a stack of papers including a copy of the *Chronik*. Of course we did not know then that it was a cut version, though he told us it was a copy. [See Chapter IX.] Six months later, in January 1970, he wrote that a part of it had been found in the Imperial War Museum and that he had seen with dismay that the copy he had given us had been cut. And he said that if there was an original, only Rudolf Wolters had it. He certainly gave us the impression that he wished to clear up this matter. Wolters was the only one of his former people

---

*Edith Stein was born in 1891 to prosperous Jewish parents in Breslau. She converted to Catholicism in the 1920s and entered the Carmelite order in 1933. She wrote to Pius XI urging him to condemn Hitler for his anti-Semitic acts. In 1938 she was sent to a convent in Holland to escape the Nazis. She was taken by the SS from the convent in 1942 and sent to Auschwitz, where she died two days later. Under Pope John Paul II she was beatified in 1987, a halfway stage to sainthood.

he ever gave us an address for. He was extremely discreet about all his former friends."

In later years, said Frau Singer, when Speer worked for long periods in the archives, in order to make it unnecessary for him to sit in the general reading room, he either worked in her room or was lent offices of people who were on holiday.

"He was here a great deal, first in 1972–73 when the Goldhagen-Posen scandal broke [see Chapter XV]," she said, "and then later in 1979, when he worked on his third book, *Der Sklavenstaat* [U.S. title, *Infiltrations*]. Shortly before he died he was also beginning to research a fourth book which he finally never wrote, on production and armaments." But in all the time he was at the Federal Archives, until quite shortly before his death in 1981, Singer said, the archive directors would never see him: "He was and remained a 'hot iron' " (*"heisses Eisen,"* the German equivalent of "hot potato").

Although admiring Speer's intelligence and diligence, Hedwig Singer had evidently never succumbed to his charm. But having been so closely connected with his research, she had mixed feelings about his books.

"I liked his Reminiscences. I feel that it is a unique record of the Hitler period," she said. "The quintessence of *The Secret Diaries* seemed to me to be his continuing involvement with Hitler, psychologically highly interesting, of course, but I dislike all this soul striptease. *Sklavenstaat,* I thought, started well but it completely fell apart—it was sad, because he did so much research for that, and finally it didn't show at all."

He had told her that settling his accounts with Himmler was more important to him than anything else. "But finally, rather than attacking or explaining Himmler, he ended up mostly defending himself. Of course, in the final analysis, that's what all his books were," she said, "a defense of himself. It really wasn't so much that he tried to 'justify' himself. He was entirely consistent for all these years of writing in maintaining his position of penitence—and I didn't think it was a pose—but of course, inevitably, this led him to defending himself. It is only human."

When Siedler started Speer on this book, he had not expected a huge success. "I didn't think I'd lose money," he said, "but of course I had no idea what kind of a man he had become, and whether he could write. We were very careful. The only risk I proposed taking, to start out with, was to back him for a limited time of writing, and then we intended to start with a small printing. He accepted a small advance on royalties in 1968, but by that time we had interest from publishers everywhere. Even so," he said, "nobody in the world could have dreamed that it would become *the* postwar best-seller. There were, of course, many critical reviews, but it really seemed as if the reading public didn't care *what* reviews said; they bought the book anyway.

Of course, when *Die Welt* paid DM 600,000 for serialization, I knew we had it made."

Wolters wrote in his *Segments of a Life:*

> The publicity buildup by Ullstein of Speer was brilliant. It reminded me of the pre-publication ballyhoo in the twenties about Erich Maria Remarque's *Im Westen Nichts Neues* [*All Quiet on the Western Front*].

Not unexpectedly, Wolters was critical about *Inside the Third Reich.* He had nothing but admiration for the structure of the book, he told Speer in a letter. Everything seemed to him like a carefully constructed piece of architecture, climax after climax culminating in "your extraordinary description of your goodbye to your East-West Axis, your Reich Chancellery, and to your patron in the inferno that was the Bunker in those last days of our Greater Reich." But then he took him to task for yet again confessing to his own and thus, "without intending it," to Germany's guilt. "When one gets to the end of your book, one is led to believe that the author would now walk through life wearing a hairshirt, distributing his fortune to the victims of National Socialism, and, renouncing all vanities and enjoyments of life, live on locusts and wild honey."

"When Speer appeared in Coesfeld shortly after receiving my letter," Wolters wrote later, "the huge sales of the book had eclipsed all criticism. 'Where are the locusts?' he laughed, sitting down to lunch. . . ."

The almost tumultuous reception given to Speer's book—rare for a book of nonfiction and certainly unprecedented for any memoirs of the Hitler period—was expressed in print and the spoken word with a mixture of admiration and anger, servility and aggression. Speer, as Annemarie would put it, was more than anything else "childishly delighted." The publishers, understandably enough, well aware that "success breeds success," were quick to exploit the phenomenon by ever-increasing publicity, not too difficult as the media apparently couldn't get enough of Speer. (Six years later, this whole process was to be equalled by the success of *The Secret Diaries.*)

The fervor—both favorable and critical—of this reception has to be viewed in the context of the time. In September 1969, when the Reminiscences were published in Germany, it coincided, one might say, with the beginning of the end of one cycle of development—twenty-five years during which every West German politician or public personality of stature, every writer of standing, every newspaper of honor, every filmmaker with any pretension of depth and millions of people with a new sense of morality, above all a whole generation of young people, had gone through the first struggles with the dreadful inheritance of the Hitler years.

This, although opposed by many older Germans, was perhaps most steadily kept in their minds by the N.S. (National Socialist) crimes trials being pursued since 1958 in West German courts. Between 1958 and 1968, 150 major Nazi-crimes trials took place in the eleven *Länder* (states) of West Germany, and they have continued ever since. A huge special judicial machinery was set up, with hundreds of investigating prosecutors over the years traveling the world in search of evidence and witnesses.

Some of these trials were huge proceedings lasting many months or even several years and were meticulously reported almost daily in the press. In 1962 the Bergen-Belsen trial was held in Hanover; the Treblinka trial in Düsseldorf and the Auschwitz trial in Frankfurt took place in 1964. These dealt with large numbers of accused and resulted in long prison sentences, many for life. In 1968 the Einsatz Kommando 1005 trial, in Hamburg, brought to justice some of the murderers who shot hundreds of thousands of Jews, Russians and Poles behind the Eastern front. And in 1970 Franz Stangl, commandant of Sobibor and Treblinka—extradited from Brazil after twenty years there—was sentenced in Düsseldorf to life imprisonment.

Paralleling these efforts of the German lawmakers were the hundreds of films and documentaries which filled the screens and, via television, entered millions of homes. Contrary to what was claimed, particularly in the English-speaking world, this was not a country that closed its eyes to its recent past, however much the older generations might have wished it.

Speer's first book, appearing at the apex of this period, seemed made to order for both camps of Germans: the young seeking authentic information from the one man apparently capable of supplying it; the older people seeking reflections of their own happy memories and moments of glory, and reassurance that the horrors with which, tragically enough, they saw themselves identified weren't their fault.

The book's enormous success in Germany was doubtlessly due to Speer's considerable ability to satisfy the needs of the younger readers—those of the generation who had been children during the war and were now young parents. Among his own generation of readers, however, above all his former friends, many were bitterly disappointed. Even if there was little emphasis on Hitler's atrocities, they were never denied. And furthermore, wherever they were referred to, even if between the lines, the ultimate responsibility for them was clearly assigned to Hitler.

"People didn't blame Speer for coming out against Hitler—they themselves held it against Hitler that he lost the war," said Theo Hupfauer, who was to remain one of Speer's most loyal supporters. "What many so bitterly resented was that Speer, who had been the 'favorite of the czar,' annihilated him in the book. This had a far greater effect because it came from *him.*

"They had just about come to terms with Nuremberg and what they believed to have been lying evidence" ("those 'faked horror' films they forced them to watch in court," as Wolters had written). Hupfauer said, "But Speer's confirmation in his first book and even more in his subsequent ones, that all this was not lies but the truth, basically lost him the goodwill of most of his peer group."

"When I first read Speer's manuscript of his Reminiscences," Annemarie said, "I also felt, 'My God, does he have to do this, *must* it be?' Speer always said it did have to be, that people who had not lived through the Third Reich had not understood what it was, and thus what we felt while it lasted and afterwards."

But she came to feel that he was right, she said. "I think he tried to be fair. He tried to bring to life the enthusiasm, the hope that we felt—we who were so totally immersed in it—and our devastation later. But, because he couldn't or didn't wish to think in terms of emotions, he didn't quite succeed with this. All he could do was call Hitler a 'criminal,' and you know the consequences this had for him among so many of his associates, even the closest. I myself think that it isn't—as Wolters said—that the word 'criminal' is too much, but rather that it is too little. I think Speer was shocked when he realized how many people of our generation expected his memoirs to defend rather than explain our position under Hitler. While he was enormously relieved to find that the younger generations were almost entirely on the side of those who had resisted, or at the very least had afterwards forsworn Hitler, it was an enormous shock for him to discover that the majority of people of his own generation—above all most of his former friends—considered both those who had resisted and those like himself, who later admitted to a share in the responsibility for the crimes, as traitors. The fact is that Speer was almost entirely 'out of sync' with almost everyone he knew when he started on his book. It was immensely painful for him."

"I am astonished about A. Sp.," his old friend, the sculptor Arno Breker wrote to Wolters in September 1971. "I have to radically change my view of him. . . ."

For almost five years, from October 1966 to the spring of 1971, the Wolters-Speer relationship had somehow limped along. They had spoken on the phone a few times, usually on Speer's initiative, and Speer had occasionally dropped in at Coesfeld. "But it was very much on the basis of their pre-Spandau semijocular relationship," Annemarie said. "A meeting of minds had become impossible, so they didn't 'talk,' and I knew that eventually it would come to an explosion."

This "explosion" was preceded by considerable correspondence between Wolters and members of Speer's—or Hitler's—former circle who were outraged after reading *Inside the Third Reich*, but it finally erupted after the republication in *Quick* magazine of the long interview which Speer had given early in 1971 to Eric Norden of the American *Playboy*.

Speer told me that he felt Norden's editing of the long discussions—he did not speak German, and Speer had specifically authorized him to "tidy up" his English—had resulted in a number of dramatized interpretations. Nonetheless, Norden had very carefully read *Inside the Third Reich* and all of Speer's published statements and asked perceptive questions. Certainly in these twenty-seven pages, he got Speer to explain more about himself than he had in the book, or would in *The Secret Diaries* or in any of his many other interviews until his conversations with me, seven years later.

Wolters, however, was livid and on May 24, 1971, wrote him what was intended to be a final letter:

What on earth is the matter with you, that even after the unending admissions of guilt in your Reminiscences you cannot stop representing yourself ever more radically as a criminal for whom twenty years in prison was "too little"?

If you are really convinced that "there can't be any atonement in this lifetime for sins of such huge dimensions," then there appears to be a vast and incomprehensible discrepancy between your humble confessions and your present way of life. For the former would lead one to expect a Speer in sackcloth and ashes; I, however, know you as a merry fellow who undertakes one lovely journey after another and who happily regales his old chums with tales of his literary and financial successes. Of course, I have nothing against the merry Speer, but contrary to this I have to say that both your public mea culpas and your accusations [not only against the active perpetrators but] against your former colleagues (Göring, Goebbels, Bormann, etc.) who, being dead, cannot defend themselves, are agony to me.

What are your friends to say when you describe yourself "morally fatally contaminated"? And always only *you* and always only in the restricted context of Germany, while you never, never take issue with the present wars and acts of horror being committed in the Near and Far East.

Your defense of the victors' court at Nuremberg must seem extravagant even to the former prosecutors of that show trial. But I can well understand. If you rejected Nuremberg, your crime thesis would collapse, and then what?

In this letter, my dear Albert, I am saying everything I think. . . . I hope and think that the day will come when you will no longer find it necessary to confess your sins to all and sundry in order to persuade yourself of your virtue.

But I propose that we put off seeing each other again until the end of this phase, i.e., when your exclusive interest in your rehabilitation has ceased.

Speer replied coolly, on June 5, 1971:

> Your unusual letter requires an unusual and to me distasteful reply. In general it is customary in civilized countries and more than that, among friends, that a delinquent is given a chance to speak before being sentenced. I could say a great deal about the *Playboy* interview, but for the moment it is enough that I tell you that it was restructured, with words and formulations entirely foreign to me. Whole passages were clearly taken from the book and rewritten in the manner of bad ghostwriting. . . . But on the whole the interview as printed corresponds with my opinions and I imagine that this is what is decisive for you. What I wrote in the book on the question of my guilt already angered you during the Spandau time. But it remains valid. Whether or not there are people who merely see this as opportunism is irrelevant to me. *Your* reaction, it is true, dismays me but I realize that, given your position in this matter from the start, it was perhaps inevitable.
>
> To claim that my moral attitude is incompatible with my way of life is denying the fact that one can quite legitimately lead a good life despite or indeed because of such an attitude.
>
> Besides . . . I arranged more than a year ago a modification to my contract with Propyläen providing that much of my worldwide earnings be consigned to charity. It leaves me, after taxes, with about 12 percent of my earnings. . . .
>
> I should be very glad if you decide one day to pull down the barrier you have now put up between us. I'm sure you will understand that this move can not now come from me. Be well.
>
> Your old,
> Albert

"Rudi wasn't the only one who was shocked by the *Playboy* interview," Speer told me. "I was unhappy about it myself, but when he wrote so sharply I couldn't admit that. It was sad. I had given that interview on tape in my—as you know—not that wonderful English. This reporter was a nice man, so I told him just to go ahead and correct my English. I don't think he deliberately changed anything; it's just that some of the words that finally appeared were rather stronger—different from the way I talk, or for that matter feel. He quoted me as saying that 'blood is on my hands; I have not tried to wash it off,' or that I had devoted fifteen years of my life 'to building a graveyard,' or that, in my ignorance about the fate of the Jews, I was like 'a man following a trail of bloodstained footprints through the snow without realizing someone had been injured.' Can you imagine me expressing myself that way? It was all horribly journalese, and when translated back into German quite dreadful.

"So it was not too surprising that Wolters said this was the end, that after this he could have nothing to do with me. Well, the door is not *quite* closed—his wife Erika doesn't agree with him and our wives are close friends. He sends us a Westphalian ham at Christmas and we send them a pot of honey from our hives. But that's all. You see, he—and his like-minded friends—call what I do 'soiling one's own nest.' " He shrugged. "I can see their point. I don't blame them. It's just—because I've never had *many* friends—with one or two of them, but of course Rudi most of all, it does hurt."

After hearing this, I remarked how extraordinary Wolters's devotion seemed to me: the twenty years of unceasing efforts for him; the setting up and administration of the School Fund and the constant urging of some quite reluctant former friends to contribute—by the end, a total of DM 158,000; Wolters's care for Speer's children, particularly Fritz; his imaginative input in the "Walk around the World"; his long letters, unfailingly at least one a month. ("You have no idea how difficult that was," another one of Wolters's former secretaries told me. "Every day we made notes of anything that happened that might possibly interest him—in the papers, on TV, in the office, in films or plays that we saw. And even so, when the day came, Wolters always groaned, 'What *can* I tell him?' There was always such a danger of hurting him, of being tactless, but above all, by some wrong word, some thoughtless story, emphasizing and making worse his isolation.")

Finally and most of all, there was the work Marion Riesser did—for Wolters surely as much as for Speer—in transcribing the twenty-five thousand letters. Was it not an excess of friendship?

He was silent for a long time, and I finally asked him why.

"What you say gives me to think," he said and added, as if it had never occurred to him before, "Perhaps it *was* extraordinary." In the final analysis, given the many years so many people had depended on him, he evidently had accepted as his due what they did for him later. "But," he added then, after a moment's thought, "it is difficult to recognize that treason can be honorable and loyalty wrong. There is so much one has to admit to in oneself before one can accept that radical moral turnabout."

NOT LONG AFTER the publication of the Reminiscences, Speer's interview with *Playboy* and Rudi Wolters's letter, Theo Hupfauer, hearing from Annemarie how isolated Speer felt, decided to try to build bridges for him with some of his former friends. He would invite people to a weekend get-together in some pleasant spot in Munich, and they would go on from there.

"It was entirely Hupfauer's initiative," Annemarie said. "Of course he asked Speer, but he just shrugged and said, 'All right, if you like.' Since Spandau he was always terribly compliant."

Speer looked resigned rather than compliant when he told me about this initiative eight years later. "I had little hope that many would come," he said. "After all, by that time I had been out for five years, and hardly any of them had raised a finger in my direction."

Maybe not, I said, but most of them had contributed to Wolters's School Fund for nearly twenty years, hadn't they?

He shrugged. "What is money—if there *is* money?"

Of about forty people Hupfauer invited, about twenty came. Annemarie was the only woman. "The meetings—two or three more were held later—were on Friday evenings, in a private house belonging to one of the Munich industrialists, but everybody stayed at the Hotel Marienbad," she said.

"We tried to make it very informal," Hupfauer told me. "There was a buffet, but we sat in groups rather than at one table. Speer was meant to go from group to group. All the people who came were very successful men; the street was full of huge chauffeur-driven Mercedeses. The problem was that none of them were interested in talking about the past; they were all very involved in the present—politics, economics, world affairs. The last thing any of them wanted to think about was Hitler, and that was all Speer *could* think about."

Annemarie said that it had been immensely difficult: "Time and again I would find Speer sitting on his own, staring at the ceiling. He said it was useless and that we shouldn't have bothered."

"Whenever I noticed it," Hupfauer said, "I'd take some people over to him; he would make an effort, and by the end of the evening there would be something like conversation."

"We tried it a few more times, over the years," Annemarie said, "but fewer people came every time. It became embarrassing. Hupfauer tried very hard but it could never work. They lived in the present; he lived in the past, and none of them could understand that or in a way forgive him for it. He was a living reminder of what they wanted to forget."

Speer did become overexposed fairly quickly. He did not complain about this; on the contrary, from the moment the first book was completed, virtually to the moment of his death, he made himself available to anybody who asked to see him.

In Heidelberg, at the beginning of our conversations in 1978, the mail brought dozens of letters every day, and the telephone, answered by Frau Speer in a clear but halting voice that sounded oddly girlish, rang continuously—journalists, researchers, historians and just people wanting to talk about the past. Every letter was answered, by hand; every caller given a time when Speer would speak to them. An American, a former Eighth Air Force pilot, wanted to come by for an autograph; a Heidelberg pensioner, also a stranger, who requested "just a few minutes to ask a few questions," was invited up for tea.

"He seems to make himself available to everybody," I remarked to Margret Speer. "Yes," she said, "he feels he must. All the more now, because most of the others are dead, or dying."

"For a long time after I came out of Spandau," Speer told me later, "Margret didn't want to hear about the past. She didn't ask to read the manuscript. In fact she didn't read the first book until very recently. One day, perhaps two years ago, she had shown somebody in who had come to talk or interview me, I don't remember which, and she sort of stood around in the doorway, looking—I don't know how to describe it—curious, I suppose. So I said, 'Why don't you come in? Wouldn't you like to sit with us?' And she did, and since then she almost always stays and listens, and by now she has read both books."

"What else could I do?" she asked, when we discussed it a week later. "The children are gone; we shall be more and more alone. The past is his life; it always will be. It had to be done, otherwise," she paused, and then ended, "one is so alone."

"Why *do* you see everybody who phones, anybody who rings the doorbell?" I asked him once after, with his customary courtesy, he had seen out a particularly dense and gushing visitor from abroad who had wanted his autograph and ended up wasting nearly an hour of his time.

"Well," he said, sounding helpless as he often did, "how could I know what he'd be like? He *could* have turned out interesting."

But was he really interested in all these people? I asked. Was he being sincere with all that charm, or was he accepting yet another penance with this indiscriminate acceptance of all comers? "Could it be that?" he asked with interest. "I don't *think* I'm being insincere; I don't mean to be."

Quite often, as I once pointed out to him after yet another few hours with visitors—this time two students of theology, one American, one German—he *played* at modesty. Did he perhaps see himself as fundamentally modest? I asked him.

He smiled, that unfailingly captivating smile—there were times when he could be very warm. "No, I'm not that modest," he conceded and then shrugged. "Any man who has once been in the center of public life misses it, needs the recognition. It becomes very much part of one's lifeblood. It's pointless to deny that. But it is true, too," he repeated, "that one is always on the lookout for interesting people."

Interesting people to him, he said, were those who worked seriously on "his" subject: Erich Fromm *(The Anatomy of Human Self-destruction)*, Carl Zuckmayer *(The Devil's General)*, Eugene Davidson *(The Trial of the Germans)*.

"Fromm came, and the very first time we talked for six hours; we've spoken and written often since; a fascinating man. Zuckmayr—we used to go for long walks; he was wonderfully warm, I don't know why he liked me. Davidson too has been very nice to me; I see him whenever he comes to Europe, and we correspond. And I am always glad when young people come to see me, they refresh me."

But in fact, as would become increasingly apparent over the subsequent months and years, it was in print that he managed to contribute something to those who sought to understand. In live interviews for radio or television, he was increasingly hampered by the sharpness of his young questioners, and by the growing inability of his mind to go beyond almost rote replies.

"I am so aware of this," he told me. "In these discussions my mind appears enclosed, locked into one channel from which I can't escape. I can't find the words to get me out of it, or beyond it."

He tried two ways of breaking the pattern. One was to return to the spiritual search which had so effectively sustained him in the first years in Spandau. The second was to plan future books, beginning with *The Secret Diaries* as soon as the main editions—German and English—of his reminiscences—*Inside the Third Reich*—had been dealt with. ("I asked him once," said Hupfauer, "how many more books he wanted to write. He laughed and said that if he wrote everything he *could* write, he'd have to live to be a hundred.")

Late in the afternoon the day we discussed this—it was the sixth day we spent together—he suddenly seemed irritable and nervous and with the change a little less smooth, or even handsome. He seemed tired, I said. Should we stop?

"No," he replied, "I'm just asking myself, as you did this morning, why I do it. I have so much of my own work to do." (At that point in 1978, he was already researching *Der Sklavenstaat* *(Infiltrations)* and planned two further books. Propyläen would publish a book on his architecture that year, and during our time together we added the one on the profiles we intended to do together.) "Why *do* I subject myself to these interviews, again and again, always knowing . . ." He caught himself. "I don't mean anything against *you*. But even now, I know that you too are only holding back on the essential question. It will come; it always comes; always the same one; everything always leads up to it."

And this was certainly true, for every single interview he gave began or ended with the one question everyone wanted the answer to: what had he known about the Jews? For the media—if not for his millions of readers—everything he wrote, everything he knew, everything he thought paled in importance beside this, was at best only of marginal interest, and at worst unacceptable.

To this question his answer had always remained the same—he should have known, he could have known, but he hadn't known. "Why don't *you* ask it at last?" he said with weary irritation. "Why not get it over with? You are going to ask it in the end."

There was a psychological structure to our conversations, I said. Both for his and my sake, we would have to comply with it if we didn't want it to break down. "We will talk about this when we know each other better," I said. "When the right moment comes."

He looked at me for a moment, the bushy black eyebrows raised, the fatigue gone. "You are going to keep me waiting, are you?" he said, and suddenly smiled. "Interesting."

But later that day he spoke of it, unasked. "It is on my mind all the time," he said, his face drawn. "I awake with it, spend my day with it, go to sleep with it and dream it. But my reply—I know it—has long become routine. I can no longer answer it with emotion, and people resent this."

At the very beginning, in Heidelberg, I had explained to Speer how I wanted to conduct these conversations, and told Margret that at some point or other I would hope to talk a little with her too, about the past. Although she greeted this announcement with barely concealed dismay, she eventually agreed. "But later," she said, putting off the evil moment, "when we are quiet, up in the mountains."

(THE NIGHT BEFORE this carefully scheduled conversation two weeks later, Speer came up to my room after we had already said goodnight. "I just wanted to say," he started, "you know, Margret is very, very nervous about talking with you about these things. She needs a little reassurance if she is going to get any sleep."

I knew the reassurance she needed, and I also knew by then the limitations of what she would—or could—say. And I told him to tell her that I would not bring up the subject of the Jews.

He nodded, and briefly—so briefly I hardly felt it—touched my arm. "Thank you," he said. "She will sleep now."

Almost four years later, shortly after Speer's death, Hilde and I were talking about her mother. "I wish she would talk to you again now," Hilde said.

"There is so much in her, so many guilt feelings of her own which need to come out, to give her peace."

Margret very nearly did. She would have if some of her children, who, understandably enough, wanted to be rid of the Speer legend, had not prevented her. "I wish, I wish I could see you," she said when she phoned me sometime in the 1980s, I can't remember when, from the house on the mountain where she had fled to be alone. I could come, I said, any time she liked. "Perhaps one day," she said in that hesitant small voice of hers. "Perhaps it will again become possible, up here. I want . . ." She stopped.

You want what, Margret? I asked.

"One day," she said.

That day was not to be: she died, of cancer, quite soon afterwards.)

"THE ATTITUDE toward Speer was very ambiguous," psychoanalyst Margarete Mitscherlich told me. She and her husband, Alexander, wrote together the now classic *The Inability to Mourn*. When *The Secret Diaries* appeared in 1975, Alexander wrote an analysis of the Speer-Hitler relationship, which Speer himself later described to me as probably the most perspicacious.

"I remember being on a television program with Speer, Wolf Jobst Siedler and Joachim Fest," Margarete said. "The condescension with which both these younger men treated Speer was extraordinary. It was sad and embarrassing, as indeed was Speer's humility."

She was quite right, but very few people were able to detect the real humility that did exist in Speer. Of all his intimates and friends, I found only four people who understood it: Annemarie; Casalis, who had discovered it very soon in Spandau; the Benedictine monk Father Athanasius, who observed it during ten years of retreats in the monastery at Maria Laach, which will be described a little later; and Robert Raphael Geis, who sensed it even before he met Speer in 1970. Anyone else I mentioned it to merely looked perplexed.

On November 24, 1969, two months after his Reminiscences had been published, Speer received a letter from Geis. It was to begin a relationship that was to cause "Aba" Geis, as he was called by the many people who loved him, a great deal of trouble from the Jewish hierarchy. By this time Geis—still the hothead he had been when he fought the Jewish elders in Hitler's Germany in the 1930s, and now once again anathema to the heads of the minute Jewish community in West Germany—had abandoned his vain efforts to retain a rabbinical appointment, and was writing, lecturing and working as a member of the boards of UNESCO (United Nations Educational, Scientific, and Cultural Organization), the West German Rundfunk and, above all, the German Evangelical Church's Working Group of Christians and Jews, which he and Dietrich Goldschmidt had set up.

"Meeting Geis was a huge experience for me," Speer told me. This fateful encounter, as many others at that time, occurred after Geis had seen Speer on television. He wrote from Düsseldorf,

> *Sehr geehrter* [Most Honored—a very formal greeting] Herr Speer,
> In 1963, I read G. M. Gilbert's *Nuremberg Diary*, and after that I thought of you time and again. You were different from the other accused at the Nuremberg trial and I found the sentence you were given too severe. . . .
> Not long ago I saw parts of two of your TV interviews and was again impressed by you. You will have to go on bearing your lot, as I and the survivors must bear ours. But I did want to tell you that even where I don't understand you, I respect you. But even more than that, as a devout Jew I feel that there has to be forgiveness, and I am profoundly convinced that you are under the star of this forgiveness, for you are today an honest man. I haven't read your book yet, but I will one day soon. But I didn't want to delay until then sending you these few words.
> With warm greetings, your
>
> > Raphael Geis

"I think," Speer told me, "that the day I received that letter was one of the most important days of my life." The next day, on November 25, he replied, addressing Geis with equal formality:

> *Sehr geehrter* Herr Geis,
> I have read the last lines of your letter to several of my children over the telephone, and every time I did it made me cry. I know you won't consider this—and my telling you of it—excessive sentimentality. I have had many letters as a result of the book or TV interviews, both from former friends and enemies, and among them a few kind ones from Jews. But about yours there is something very special. It touches the core of all my despair and my doubts, and allows me hope for redemption.
> I don't wish to seem immodest, but you would make me very happy if you would allow me to send you my book. May I?
> The wishes you, a devout Jew, send me for inner peace are, believe me, the most wonderful present I have ever received. I think perhaps that no one could help me as much as you to make it come true.
> With warm greetings, your grateful
>
> > Albert Speer

If Speer, as he told me, lived and dreamed in Nuremberg, Spandau and afterwards the murder of the Jews, Geis lived and dreamed "an indestructible longing for his German homeland," until he finally managed to return to Germany in 1952. It is an incredible, almost unbelievable parallel between these two men of different faith but very similar upbringing.

After having tried vainly for six years to accommodate himself to life in Israel, Geis and his new wife, Susanne—seventeen years younger than he; they had been married for a year—returned to Europe in 1946. They first stayed for ten difficult months in Britain, where his parents, Moritz and Sittah, had found refuge but where he found no employment. They survived on Susanne's earnings from working in a center for children rescued from concentration camps. After a temporary teaching job in Zurich, he was named in August 1949 rabbi to an immigrant community in Amsterdam where, now parents of a girl, Jael, and a boy, Gabriel, they stayed until at long last he was called back to Germany as provincial rabbi of the state of Baden.

His great wish, to serve as rabbi to a community of camp survivors, was to remain unfulfilled; there was no stable community of Jewish camp survivors, nor did those who briefly stayed in one or another UNRRA (United Nations Relief and Rehabilitation Administration) facility wish for the presence of a rabbi. They were restless, angry, deeply suspicious and not infrequently violent people, many of them ravenous for revenge and, as a security of sorts, for possessions, however obtained. Their principal need was to get out of Germany as fast as possible, and most of them were rapidly "processed" by Israeli and U.S. Jewish organizations for immigration to Israel or overseas. Spiritual matters were very low on their list of priorities in those first post-Hitler years.

But by the time Geis finally got back to Germany, his writings and lectures had made him very well known, both as a profoundly spiritual Jew, a born teacher, and as a man determined to work toward Christian-Jewish reconciliation. "He was full of love," Susanne Geis told me, shaking her head. "I could never get anywhere near this 'perfection.'"

Geis had replied to Speer's letter by return mail. No, he said, he saw him as far too masculine to risk being sentimental:

> If you find yourself in tears, be grateful for them. When I was a young rabbi in Munich, at the beginning of the Third Reich, I couldn't allow myself tears, because I had to be strong for the confused and frightened Jews in my care. That is how I survived Buchenwald, and I remained as stiffly still when [three years later] I learned of the end of my sister and her family in Auschwitz. Why do I write you this? Certainly not in order to open up a mercifully drawn curtain, but to tell you that my own fate in the Third Reich until 1939 taught me that one cannot categorize human beings. I knew, for instance, high-ranking Nazis whose helpfulness was exemplary, and I knew of Jews who denounced me to the Gestapo. I always

understood about the quality of the world's so-called compassion or conscience. Without the cowardly silence of the great powers, Hitler could
never have become the awful reaper of death he became. And in the subsequent years? Vietnam, Greece, Spain, South America, South Africa, the
American blacks—the awful dying, torturing and starving that is still continuing? If one does not wish to despair and if one recognizes that the battle is on many fronts, then one knows that the first victory is to say time
and again "Yes" to individual human beings. So you see, while there are
those whose hand I wouldn't shake, I can look upon you as a comrade,
because I sense you to be true. I should be happy to have your book. And
perhaps we can find a way to meet one day—it would be good.

                                            your Raphael Geis

There were to be many more, increasingly warm letters between them,
until four months later, in March 1970, they finally met in the Black Forest
where Aba and Susanne Geis were on holiday and invited the Speers to join
them for a day and a night.

I met Susanne Geis in the early spring of 1986 in Baden-Baden, a lovely spa
on the edge of the Black Forest, where she and her husband had lived for
years. Susanne is beautiful, quiet, with a wonderful gaiety and warmth. Her
husband had died in 1972. She continued to live in the charming apartment
in Baden-Baden they had found together and where she and I were to talk
many times. "I was very apprehensive," Susanne said. "To help me, Aba also
invited our doctor and his wife, the Sprengers, who were close friends from
Karlsruhe. They arrived in the morning, the Speers in the afternoon. I didn't
at all share my husband's enthusiasm. I was, and remained, very suspicious
of Speer. He never quite succeeded in persuading me of his good faith."

The inn in the Black Forest was relatively simple, and they spent the first
hours driving to another village for afternoon coffee. "Then we had dinner,
and afterwards stayed talking around the table in the *Gaststube.*" The conversation, she said, was largely about Speer and his time in Spandau. "I was
pretty appalled by Mrs. Sprenger, who immediately asked Speer the most direct questions. It made me squirm.

"My husband was a very good pastor. He certainly must have known or
guessed what Margret Speer had been through, and he got her to talk. She
said her husband had hardly been home throughout the war, or much before
then either. He had never been much of a husband or father in the usual
sense of the term, so [the Spandau time] wasn't *that* different for her and the
children. She said all this in that light girlish voice of hers, sounding almost as
if she felt nothing as she said it. Aside from that, I rarely heard her say anything during the ten times or so we all met over the next two years. But, then,

I too was fairly silent when my husband was around—that is how women were conditioned then, you know."

Susanne's feelings about Speer had not changed over the years. "In a way I found him scary, and it never changed. I don't mean I disliked him; it enervated me—irritated me, if you like—that he only had the past on his mind. My husband was sad about that too; he wrote him in one of his letters to stop exposing himself eternally to questions about it.

"Aba could put up with all his holding forth, his 'instructing' everybody, and his stories about all the people with 'names' he met. But I felt it was all partly masochism, and partly just enjoying his fame. I remember one of the stories he told us, about going to a reception at a castle in Bavaria full of past and present dignitaries, including Strauss*—whom we deeply distrusted. I didn't like it at all that he attended functions like that, and my husband didn't like it much either."

Perhaps he did some of these things unthinkingly, out of a curious kind of naiveté, I suggested. "Funny that you say that," she replied. "Aba also thought that for such a sophisticated man he had an extraordinarily naive side. Actually, if I liked anything about him, I liked that."

Both Geis children, like much of the Jewish community, deeply disapproved of their father's relationship with Speer, but never told him. "They only talked to me about it after Aba had died," Susanne said.

"But there *were* nice things about him," she said. "I liked the way he talked about Hilde, of whom he was so proud, and also her husband, whom he admired. He was fascinated by their radically different way of life in a cooperative, living very closely to their baby. And he talked about his architect son, Albert, and his wife, Ruth, who was on television and whom he respected a lot.

"He also spoke of his grandchildren, the children of his youngest son, Ernst, and his wife, Irmgard, with whom they increasingly shared the Heidelberg house. He loved that the grandchildren were entirely unself-conscious about him—he was just their grandfather, and that was very special for him. I thought all that was nice. And then, he loved giving presents, and he really thought about them. One day he arrived bringing two ancient theological volumes Aba had longed to have. They must have cost him untold thousands," she said, "but that made no difference to him; money in that sense was entirely immaterial to him."

She pointed to one of the earliest letters in the Geis-Speer correspondence, where Speer, with apologies, asked whether Geis knew of anyone he could

*Franz Josef Strauss, a right-wing Bavarian politician who had been Federal Minister of Defense and then of Finance, and was later Prime Minister of Bavaria.

help financially and of course anonymously, via him. "Aba saw nothing wrong with it," Susanne said, "but in a much later letter returned some money to him. 'Five thousand is much too much,' he wrote sternly. 'You must not be so excessive: nobody expects it, anonymously or not!' "

About the time he met Aba and Susanne Geis, in the spring of 1970, Speer further expanded his spiritual research. He began to go regularly on retreats in the beautiful Benedictine monastery of Maria Laach, under the guidance of the then thirty-nine-year-old Father Athanasius, a tall, imposing man and an exceptionally talented priest. Born in Bremen and having grown up in Berlin with a banker father, he was a man of the age and background Speer responded to best.

"He came here regularly once or twice a year," Father Athanasius told me, "and contrary to the other guests who stay two days in a guest wing, he always stayed with us in the *Klausur* [seclusion] for five days. No one urged him, but he insisted on sharing our lives completely: the five daily masses, beginning with the morning Latin mass at 5:30, and our silent meals. During the meals, one of the brothers reads aloud, by no means always holy books. In fact, two of the books we read, though obviously not while he was there, were Speer's *Reminiscences* and later *The Secret Diaries.*" His eyes twinkled. "Our reading taste is very catholic—in the English sense of the term."

They found Speer to be an easy guest. "He was very quiet, very attentive to what was going on around him. During our Latin mass—he knew Latin —he would sit without a book to help him, just listening silently, living the experience."

Father Athanasius remembered that he once asked Speer whether he didn't find the retreat strenuous. "Most people find it a strain," he said. "But Speer had said no, not for him. He said, 'It's a return to a life I knew very well indeed—my life at Spandau was not that different. And I grew to cherish it.'

"When he came first," the priest said, "he told me he wanted to talk to me as he might have talked to his son if he had been able to—which he wasn't. But after all that, he didn't really talk that much: it was almost as if what he really wanted was to be silent with me. I don't think I have ever known a man as aware, as Speer was, of his deficiencies."

From reading the history of the period, including Speer's own book, Father Athanasius said, he hadn't expected this at all. "I asked him once, after his architecture book came out, full of all these monumental buldings, all that splendor, you know, what he liked most about his architecture. 'You won't find it here,' he said. 'It was a chair I designed; a beautiful—I thought—ultraplain chair. I was proud of that. I loved it.' "

Father Athanasius had found that very touching. "I always felt that he was singularly deficient in imagination, that he was an executant [of art] rather than a creator," he said. "But then, there was that chair which he said he loved." He shook his head. "It was the only time in the ten years I knew him that he pronounced the word 'love.' "

Did Father Athanasius not feel that Speer's reaction to the retreat—and to Spandau, particularly his "Walk around the World"—was proof of imagination? I asked.

"No," he replied, "it was proof of discipline: everything about Speer was discipline. I often wondered what happened to him as a child to make him into what he was, a brilliant man incapable of abstract thinking and, I think, incapable of sensual love and thus, finally, an incomplete man." Strange, compassionate and perhaps prophetic words from a priest.

That spring of 1970 brought Speer two more important encounters. Invited by a Protestant theologian of Jewish descent, Lili Simon, to join a spiritual think tank which had been meeting regularly for several years in the evangelical Youth Academy in Radevormwald, south of Wuppertal, he came face to face for the first time in nineteen years with Georges Casalis.

"I hadn't heard from him at all since his release from Spandau," Georges told me. "And, yes, if I'm truthful I suppose I was a little surprised—put off about it. I mean, there he apparently was, telling everybody how close I was to him; well, very nice, but when, I asked myself, was he going to budge in our direction? But I thought it wasn't up to me to take the initiative—I still think I was right. Our relationship had been too private, too special. It was *he* who had to come to *me*.

"But he didn't, and so we didn't meet until Lili Simon invited us both to this conference. [As Aba Geis was also a very discreet pastor, Casalis didn't know that it was at Speer's request and Geis's suggestion that Lili Simon invited them together.] I didn't say anything about it when he came up to me," said Georges. "He was a bit embarrassed. Also, at this conference, he was very quiet, didn't say a word, and he was right—there was nothing for him *to* say in that company. He listened and that was good, and we talked little on that occasion.

"You know, it is very difficult, very complicated for people who have received help from someone at a moment of great need to return to such a person, to turn back to such a person. It is not that it is difficult to acknowledge what has been done for them. The real difficulty is to go on knowing someone who, at a time of crisis, has got to know you so deeply. I knew this, of course, and that is why, although I often thought about Speer after his release, I couldn't—as I told you—make the first move.

"I saw him three more times after Radevormwald; once in Heidelberg, once in Paris, and then—the longest time we spent together—when I drove him once to Lille, in my little Citroen 2CV car. We continued our Spandau conversations, but obviously from a different position. In Spandau he was the prisoner, living what he called then his 'sixteenth-century life': a continuity of reflection, of studying, of opening his mind and spirit to suffering. His talks with me then were very central to all of this, and, yes, I could see that they started something in and for him, and created in him a new dimension, a new space. But in the very public existence of his post-publication life, someone like me was necessarily marginal."

Glad as he was that Speer had regained his freedom, Georges felt, from a spiritual point of view, that Speer's leaving Spandau had been a regression. "But," he added, "and this was surprising and really very moving, he did talk to me again about existential matters, about the things he had discovered in Spandau. And so, really, I was very glad."

Speer wrote to Geis a few days after Radevormwald,

> My encounter with Casalis was all I hoped. Exactly like more than twenty years ago, there he was, my conscience, that *conscience* which I continually manage to diminish and repress by superficial overuse. . . .

Speer's other significant meeting that spring weekend in Radevormwald was with the son and daughter-in-law of the writer and thinker who had been his spiritual companion through his twenty years at Spandau, Karl Barth. Rosemarie and Markus Barth, both theologians, arrived late from their home just outside Basel, and although Markus was to be one of the speakers, neither knew Speer was going to be there.

"I saw this tall man with those striking eyebrows sitting across the room," Rosemarie Barth told me, "and I wondered who this extraordinary-looking man was. He looked like a monk, like someone totally isolated but with a curiously open face. I really was very interested in this stranger."

I met the Barths in their house in the Basel suburbs. It is on the edge of the city but, with the living room and bedroom windows overlooking woods and fields as far as the eye can see, one might be somewhere deep in the countryside. The house had a wonderful feel, of children having grown up, of years having been lived, of hundreds of books having been read, and many written. Markus Barth is a tall, slim, slightly stooped man, grey-haired, twinkle-eyed, the classical professor, one thinks, rather than the pastor he was for a long time. Rosemarie is small and attractive. He has more humor, but she is more intuitive.

"She *is* my intuition," he says. He had read Speer's first book, "perhaps not before that unexpected first meeting, but certainly before they came to see us soon afterwards. Meeting him, I was convinced that he had sincerely repented."

Markus said that one had to see Speer very much in the context of his background and the time in which he grew up. "The educated *grande bourgeoisie* in Germany were particularly anti-Semitic," he said. "Don't you ever let them tell you they weren't. So whatever his father was—as you tell me, Pan-European or whatever—Speer grew up in such an atmosphere. The potential for National Socialism was particularly strong in that part of German society."

The Speers visited them twice. "And I went to see them in Heidelberg three times," Markus said. "Twice more we met at the conferences Lili Simon organized in Radevormwald, and once or twice afterwards in Maria Laach, with Father Athanasius."

What he had never understood, he said, was how for even a minute Speer could claim ignorance of the Nazi horrors against the Jews. He himself as a young man, sponsored by his father, had become a member of the Swiss Aktion Nationaler Widerstand (Swiss Action Group of National Resistance). "We met regularly," he said, "and we knew about the mass exterminations of Jews by the autumn of 1942. So you see, for me it really is and always has been impossible to credit that our little Swiss resistance group—mostly young people of no 'importance' whatsoever—meeting in deep secret to prepare for a possible German occupation of Switzerland, should have known about these horrors in considerable detail, and that the German Reichsminister for Armaments should have been in ignorance of them."

But he had not put this to Speer. "When I met him I felt it was up to God to forgive. It was not my role to delve into Speer, to ask him whether he had really admitted everything. Of course," Markus said, "he had studied my father's *Dogmatik* so intensely, he may have come to the conclusion that nothing he could *do*—that only thinking—could help him, could lead him to salvation. Perhaps he was right."

"His solution," Rosemarie said, "was not to speak of repentance but of responsibility, and I think that was probably right; he could 'carry'—manage—that."

Geis, she said, with his gift for empathy, would have felt how Speer suffered from his guilt. "And of course, Geis hadn't met many men who *suffered* from having had something to do with the extermination of the Jews, so this must have been a huge experience for him. And to meet a Jew like Geis, this most exceptional spirit," she said, "must have been a truly fantastic thing for Speer. That's the impression he conveyed at that first conference. He seemed so very expectant, so full of hope and trust. It was very, very impressive and touching. Everyone who was there felt it and reacted to it. As I said when we began to talk, he did seem then like a man of innocence, a very honest man, searching."

"Yes," said Markus, "but he changed—we could see him change over the years. Something gave; something broke. There was a despair or a defeat; otherwise he would not have done a book on his architecture, which he had so denigrated before. And he would never have written that dreadful SS book."

Although the breakup with Wolters in 1971 was a shock, the increasing depth of Geis's friendship, the renewed connection with Casalis, the new acquaintance with the Barths and the beginning relationship with Father Athanasius were powerful compensations for Speer. All through 1971, while very busy with the promotion for the American and British publication of *Inside the Third Reich,* Speer's correspondence shows intense preoccupation with his renewed spiritual search and the well-being of the men who were helping him.

He was then—and would be for the subsequent fourteen months—extremely worried about Geis's frail health. "His concern was quite overwhelming," Susanne Geis told me. "It made me feel better about him—it warmed me." After she telephoned him to put off a planned visit, as Geis was again ill, Speer wrote her on January 6, 1971:

> Dear Mrs. Geis,
>   I think of your husband time and time again every day. The longer I know him to be unwell, the more I am aware of what he means to me. Without wishing to compare your anxiety about him with mine, I did want to tell you that I have rarely been so distressed by anything since my release as by your phone call.
>
>   May God be with him. . . .

Following his recovery from yet another bout of angina pectoris, rheumatism in his right arm limited Geis's correspondence to the most urgent problems, which always included the battle to bring Christians and Jews together. For the last months of his life, it also involved his mediating between Markus Barth and Georges Casalis, who, probably largely owing to Georges's entirely humanistic and politically left interpretation of Christianity, had had a serious falling out since May 1970. Nonetheless, the Geises and the Speers met three times in 1971 and twice more in 1972. Geis's last letter to Speer, exactly two years after the first, is dated November 23, 1971. After deploring and advising against a libel suit which Speer was considering, he ended with a plea for more calm in his life:

> If only you could start leading a normal life, consisting of a bit of calm in the present and a quieter and more contemplative future. This constant dragging yourself into the past cannot be good for anyone. If I had been you I would long since have refused to see any reporters!

But, be well anyway. Warmest greetings to you and your dear wife from us both,

your
R. Geis

Although Speer didn't know about it, Geis was having very serious troubles with the press in Israel about his friendship with Speer. One Israeli writer (of German origin), Ben Chorin, had gone so far as to suggest (wrongly) that Geis was trying to get Speer into a big job in Bonn. Just two days earlier Geis had written to his old friend Moshe Tavor, correspondent in Israel for the prestigious *Frankfurter Allgemeine Zeitung,* to ask for advice and help. Could his journalist friend do anything to pour oil on these troubled waters?

Indirectly, Speer was in Geis's mind almost to the end. Five days before he died (on May 18, 1972), Geis wrote to Georges Casalis, who had become one of his most cherished friends, and whose concern for Speer he shared:

Beloved Friend,

How wonderful that you exist. . . . My dear friend, we stand very isolated in life. Precisely because we take seriously the Message of Love, of which the others speak without really wishing for it, we are alone in this battle, alone because we are vulnerable. It does hurt badly at times but we must persevere.

Our happiness, yours and mine, are our wives, are they not? Susanne and I embrace you both, so warmly,

your
Aba

"I had only known him for three years," Casalis said, "but I loved that man more than many people I have known all my life." We were sitting in that small sitting room in Noyon, late at night. "He became *the* friend of my maturing years," Georges said. "I loved his friendship with Speer; it was— oh, God—it was so *right.* And you know, even though it makes one cry to think of it, even the fact that he was driven to *fight* for it against the philistines was right."

Wasn't it sad that Speer hadn't known this? I commented. Georges grinned, in that unique way which turned his so wonderfully alive face into one big warm laugh. "He will," he said, pointing upwards jokingly. "Just give him time."

XXVI

The Great Lie

THE RELATIONSHIPS between Speer and the three spiritual mentors of his life after Hitler, the protestant Georges Casalis, the Catholic Father Athanasius and the Jewish Aba Geis, were exceptionally warm and of exceptional importance to each of them.

But when the catastrophe of Erich Goldhagen's *Midstream* article hit Speer at the very end of 1971, he found himself unable to speak to any of them about it. Over the next few months, while he was already despairingly searching for proof in Koblenz which would somehow clear him, he met each of them several times—Geis twice more before he died in May 1972—but mentioned to none of them what he would describe to me six years later as "the worst thing that had happened to me since Nuremberg."

His silence about this traumatic crisis to these three men whose affection and respect had become a lifeline for him was deliberate. He could no more have told them—Geis least of all—a lie about Posen than he could have told them, or the world, the truth.

When I mentioned this to Annemarie, her reply, for the first time in my experience, was evasive. She said that Speer had been absolutely devastated when Geis died. "But I have to say that, already for several months before then, he was so involved in trying to clear himself of the Goldhagen slur, he saw no one and went nowhere except to Koblenz."

Most unusual for Annemarie—she was not only mistaken about that but, unconsciously I thought, was avoiding my question. The point I had made to her was that the only thing that could have prevented Speer from telling Geis about this terrible trouble was the fact that Goldhagen's accusation, however unfortunately phrased, was essentially justified. This was simply impossible for Annemarie to accept.

She had certainly known nothing in 1943 about Himmler's speech in Posen, but, having read it after the war, it was inconceivable to her that Speer could have heard it or even known of it. Her mind, so open to all human problems or pain, was curiously closed to this possibility; she was unable to deal with it. It was during one of our many discussions about what finally became Speer's four-year-long attempt to prove that he *could not* have been at Posen that she suddenly said, quite resignedly, "It will never end, will it, this business about the Jews? It will go on and on, won't it?"

She was in agreement with my belief that Speer's feelings of guilt about that one aspect of Hitler's reign ruled all of his postwar life. Did she, I asked her (who, as an unconscious act of contrition, I was convinced, was giving her life to caring for children, some of whom under Hitler's eugenic rules would have been killed), think it was wrong that "the business about the Jews" had permeated not just Speer's conscience—and Germany's—but the world's?

Annemarie, who, with that unlined face and those clear, dark blue eyes, always looked so young, suddenly turned old before my eyes—her next words, more than anything else she had said over the years, showed me how deep her feelings had been, and her distraught face proved how deep they had remained.

"Of course," she said, "if Hitler had this solution of the 'Jewish question' in mind from the start, if *that* solution could even *enter* his mind, then everything he was and did was an abuse of our confidence, our loyalty, our faith. Because then there was *never* any national integrity, any nobility in the movement, in the sense in which we believed we were living it. My God," she said,"if this was in his mind"—she stopped and then went on—"then there was *never* anything pure about it. It means that we were betrayed to the very depth of our beings."

My research into all the circumstances concerning Speer and the events and consequences of Posen in October 1943 was greatly complicated by the fact that no one still alive who had attended Himmler's speech was willing to admit to their presence there that day. In their refusal to confront that memory, they were, of course, not unlike Speer. The difference between him and almost all of them, however, was that they denied not only hearing this dreadful speech and all personal knowledge of these murders, but any suggestion that Hitler had committed any wrong—except the one of losing the war. Speer, on the other hand, who did more than any other man to help him win that war, ended up shattered by its futility, convinced of Hitler's crimes and determined to share the overall responsibility for them.

By the time Professor Goldhagen, citing Himmler addressing Speer directly in Posen, appeared to prove that Speer had been present during that awful speech, Speer had maintained for twenty-six years that he had been in ignorance of the extermination of the Jews until Nuremberg.

Although, alone among the twenty-one accused, he had been prepared and indeed determined from the beginning of the trial to accept a share in the responsibility for all Nazi crimes, this had been a gesture he felt honor-bound to make as a member of Hitler's government. But—so he wrote in

Spandau—it had only been during the trial, listening to the specific testimonies about the murder of the Jews, that this formal acceptance of responsibility became an emotional awareness of personal guilt.

This, I believe, was the beginning of what Alexander Mitscherlich would later refer to as his *Lebenslüge,* the Great Lie of his life.

For while he may indeed not have known about the gas chambers until Nuremberg, and until then, as he told me, may not have been able imaginatively to visualize whole families being killed, I believe that after Posen— whether he actually attended Himmler's speech or not—he knew about the long-planned and almost completed genocide of the Jews, including the women and children. And however far removed he himself was from these systematic murders, once he knew of them and yet continued to work for Hitler, he became an active participant in the crime.

Speer's tragedy, a paradox of Greek dimensions, manifested itself clearly during his illness in 1944. After Posen and then Dora, recognizing both the crimes and, intolerably, his own involvement and thus his guilt, he essentially needed and longed to die. But in the final analysis, his will to live was stronger than his need to atone. His strength was his weakness.

But even that was not all. For even though in that hospital room in Hohenlychen, morality had reawakened in him, and he confronted, one might say in extremis, his personal culpability, there was also still this link, this need, this tie to Hitler, the deepest—perhaps the only real—emotion he had ever felt.

"Who is this man?" he asked himself when he saw Hitler again. "How could I never have seen how ugly he is, his sallow skin, his broad nose?" Thus, for a moment, he tried to reduce the profoundly disturbing moral condemnation he had arrived at, not only of Hitler but of himself, into a question of esthetic perception rather than of shared guilt.

The moment passed. It is almost grotesque to think that with untold thousands dying, emotion continued to rule Speer's actions. His love for Hitler took a long time to wane, and granting himself that time, indulging those emotions, was probably his gravest compromise. For it allowed his final act of self-deception—that he could not give up, could not leave, could not take that all-important moral stand because, so he told himself, all he could do was to work ever harder to try to save the country, the people, from destruction, from dishonor; for Hitler, from Hitler—he no longer knew which.

It was a grinding conflict which did not remain unperceived. Those closest to him—Annemarie, Poser, Below, even Hupfauer—were always aware of it. And the Twentieth of July conspirators evidently sensed it too; hence his name on their list for the future government, with a question mark.

His fight against Hitler's "scorched earth" plan was waged not in anger, but in sadness and despair. Neither this nor even Hitler's death freed him from his terrible attachment. It was only years later, after the trauma of Nuremberg, in the monastic peace of Spandau and with Casalis's—his next catalyst's—help, that morality and repentance became the ruling factors of his life.

And even though there would be many fluctuations in the years to come, essentially these two elements remained the focus of his life. As Markus and Rosemarie Barth would put it, the very special thing about Speer was not his formal acceptance of responsibility in Nuremberg, but his inner awareness of personal guilt and his suffering for it ever afterwards.

Although in the course of time the intensity of these feelings became more internalized, they were kept alive by being for twenty years the principal expression of his opposition to his fellow prisoners in Spandau, and, after his release, to most of his onetime friends. He was a very stubborn man and, as Siedler quite rightly felt, he could revel in being different, whatever the cost. But equally, his radical opposition to Hitler took on new life after Spandau when he found himself at one on this issue with almost all the young in Germany—perhaps one of the greatest joys of his post-Spandau life.

By 1971, when the Posen-Goldhagen controversy had arisen, just as he was about to begin work on his second book, he had re-established his name. The majority of his huge new public were these new generations whom he loved with that very special German romantic admiration he had always had for "youth." ("Every statesman over fifty," he once remarked to me, "should have a deputy under thirty-five. Not to replace them if they die, but to influence them while they live.") Certainly there had been critical reviews of his first book in Germany as well as abroad, but they were by far in the minority.

"The reviews I have read," said Geoffrey Barraclough in January 1971, in the bitter attack on Speer in the *New York Review of Books*, "with a couple of honorable exceptions take Speer at his own evaluation. . . ."

Although in conversation or argument Speer—always almost too prepared to suggest or admit his own mistakes or faults—readily quoted his critics, he let himself be carried along by the public approval evidenced by the huge sale of his books. But this was the surface. His real comfort, the greatest he was offered since Spandau, was, without any doubt, the stand taken by Aba Geis.

Until the advent of Geis, Siedler had been his literary and, to a degree, his political mentor. But after Geis entered his life, Speer threw off the dependence on his publisher's tutelage. With his second book, *The Secret Diaries*, he intended to address not his own generation but the young. And doing so, he would write more freely and accept no more advice, either on his opinions on Hitler or, more to the point, on his interpretations of his own involvement and his condemnation of the Nazi crimes.

Goldhagen's accusation at this stage of his life had an almost cataclysmic effect on him. Here he was, two years after the sensational success of *Inside the Third Reich*, at the beginning of producing his second book, suddenly confronted with an event which could put it all at risk—his credibility, his role as the one apparently sane and repentant voice from the Third Reich, his third great career, his whole new honorable life and his friendship with Geis.

It was, as he told me later, "devastating." It was the moment when the entire structure of his Great Lie threatened to collapse, burying him beneath the wreckage. This brought the whole issue newly and destructively to the fore. Now, instead of searching inside himself for the strength to confront the truth, as Casalis had encouraged him to do at the start, or to learn to live quietly with the blocking of it, as Geis had so generously advised, he had to find proof of the lie, thereby, of course, in terrifying detail and degree, extending and expanding it beyond anything he had done before.

Up to a point, perhaps because the great public no longer cared, he succeeded, but at great cost to himself. Robert Jay Lifton has written very convincingly that human beings who cannot face a terrible truth "block" it or "double their conscience." I thought for a long time that this applied to Speer. But after his account to me of the Goldhagen episode—with the physical manifestations of his pain, impossible to simulate—and my subsequent long investigation into Posen, I reached the conclusion that, much harder than "blocking" the truth, which in its most extreme form can mean no longer being consciously aware of lying, Speer was living a lie, saw no way of ending it and—I think his one great merit—suffered atrociously under it. It is this pain which flourished in the isolation of Spandau, created the remarkable "Spandau draft," opened the door to Geis and eventually made a fine work of *The Secret Diaries*.

In a review Speer once brought out to show me, Lucy Dawidowicz had written, "What his *Diaries* do not mention, are any sleepless nights . . . or dreams about Auschwitz."

"But that is exactly what *does* give me sleepless nights," he said, sounding very weary. This was the last day of our original three weeks together.

"I think I know what you knew about the Jews," I said. "But could you yourself not go a little further?"

He had known that this question would come up that day. "I can say," he said slowly, "that I sensed [*dass ich ahnte*] . . . that dreadful things were happening with the Jews. . . ." This was no longer the man I had found glib, smooth and almost theatrically charming when we first met. Deadly serious, deeply tired, there was not a shred of glibness left.

But if you "sensed," I said, "then you knew. You cannot sense or suspect into a void. You knew."

He was silent for a long moment, then got up, went to his study and came back with a piece of paper. "Read this. Do as you wish with it; and then let us speak of it no more."

In April 1977, Speer received a letter from D. Diamond, director of the South African (Jewish) Board of Deputies, asking him to assist the Board in their legal action against the publishers and distributors of the pamphlet *Did Six Million Die? The Hoax of the Twentieth Century* to prevent its distribution in South Africa.

The request to Speer was that he should affirm on oath that: a) contrary to what the pamphlet claimed, there had indeed been a plan to exterminate the Jews of Europe; b) that he had heard of this plan and could testify that it existed; c) that it was implemented and how he knew that it was implemented.

Speer's affidavit in reply, which I translated from his original German, consisted of three pages in which, point after point, he described the background to the exterminations and the devastating admissions of those directly implicated accused at the Nuremberg trial. After paying, as often before, a tribute to Nuremberg as an attempt to create a better world, he ended with the most revealing words he had ever written:

I still recognize today that the grounds upon which I was convicted by the International Military Tribunal were correct. More than this, I still consider it essential today to take upon myself the responsibility, and thus the blame in general, for all crimes which were committed after I became a member of Hitler's government on February 8, 1942. It is not individual acts or omissions, however grave, which weigh upon me, but my conduct as part of the leadership. This is why I accepted an overall responsibility in the Nuremberg trial and reaffirm this now.

However, to this day I still consider my main guilt to be my tacit acceptance [Billigung] *of the persecution and the murder of millions of Jews* [author's italics].

With those words, especially the hard-to-translate *Billigung*, Speer associated himself for the first time directly with the murder of the Jews. Three months later, when *Die Zeit Magazin*, the color supplement of Germany's influential weekly, obtained the German rights to my profile of Speer, the contract provided that the retranslation into German would be rechecked with Speer, and most specifically this last paragraph.

Just as he had not registered any objection when I had given him the English draft to read, here again he accepted the profile as written, except that in a handwritten note to *Die Zeit* he asked for a footnote to be added in which he explained the term *"Billigung,"* which I translated as "tacit consent," to mean "looking away, not by knowledge of an order or its execution. The first," he wrote, "is as grave as the second."

"Why did you say this so directly now, after denying it for so long?" I asked him. He shrugged. "For this purpose, and with these people," he said, "I didn't wish to—I couldn't—hedge." (*wollte ich nicht—komte ich nicht—handeln.*)

If Speer had said as much in Nuremberg, he would have been hanged.

Postscript

ON NOVEMBER 30, 1980, more than two years after my profile of Speer had been published, first in the *Sunday Times Magazine* and then in *Die Zeit* magazine, I received a long letter from him telling me how unhappy he had been about the conclusions I had drawn from our weeks of talks.

Between those talks and the arrival of this letter, Speer had telephoned me in London probably thirty or forty times—on average every two weeks or so—and we had exchanged letters about our projected book collaboration. He had been working for a year and a half on *Der Sklavenstaat*, which was to be published in Germany in early 1981 by his new publisher, DVA, and in America as *Infiltrations* that autumn. DVA was also planning a new edition of his book on his architecture for 1981, with a revised foreword by him. A letter from DVA, which he sent on to me, therefore advised him to put off our planned profiles of Hitler's men until 1982. All this had been agreed and many other things had been discussed. Above all, we had been concerned over a new flareup of his circulation troubles, which in June 1980 brought on another embolism. However, he had recovered, as he and Margret announced to my husband and me in a cheerful postcard from the French Basque coast in September. The letter less than three months later amazed me.

He said in it that he had been terribly hurt by my article. After the dedication I had written for him in my book *Into That Darkness,* he had expected me to have an attitude different from all "those others" who had been trying for so long to "catch him out and pass judgment" on him. The question of his "knowledge" was absolutely central to his life, he said, and it was a great disappointment to find that after all the time we spent together, I had tried to accuse him of "knowledge" without mentioning any of his counterarguments.

If I mentioned his meeting with Selzner, the political commissar in Dnepropetrovsk, he said, I could only do it because he had volunteered the information. When he did so, he had immediately added that it would have been impossible for Selzner to tell him anything about the actions of the Einsatzgruppen in his area, because if he, Speer, had then confronted Hitler with

this, Selzner would have risked censure or worse for giving away secret information. "Various other examples like this which I gave you were then used in
the article to prove the contrary," he wrote. "I found it quite natural to show
you my correspondence with the South African Jewish organization. But the
sentence you took from it wasn't meant as you interpreted it, and also was
more sharply emphasized than I would have done."

His position, he continued, was that he had been convicted by a "high
court" and had served his sentence, day by day. "Following this I am today a
free man who has paid his debt to society."

He said he had used much sharper words in his book than I had, and accepted blame even though he had been "cleared" of blame. "Who else, aside
from me, has written in this sense after having served his sentence? Funk,
Raeder, Dönitz, Schirach? None of them."

He had not bothered to tell me of his reservations when I came to show
him the draft and we sat together over the corrections; he hadn't felt like
it, he said. "Also, I didn't know then that the article would appear in Germany. . . . But don't take all this too tragically. You have a difficult profession,
I know, which forces you to enter and disclose the private lives of others.

"Anyway, it is all long past, long settled in my mind; I enjoy being with
you and like you very much; the fact that we can write this way to each other
is proof of this. . . . And I look forward to our work together next year on the
new book.

"With warmest greetings, also from Margret, to dear Don, your Albert."

WHY THIS LETTER two years later? I asked him on the phone
that very night.

"Ah," he said, "there is a reason . . . but let us not talk of this now; forget
the letter. . . ." When I said that I couldn't do that, and if this is how he felt
I could not possibly work with him on a book, he answered, "Nonsense,
nonsense, we will see each other soon and of course we will do the book
together. . . ."

He telephoned two or three more times during the first months of 1981,
and on March 30 he sent me an advance copy of *Der Sklavenstaat*. "Hope you
don't grumble!!" was written in English on one side of the title page; on the
other he had written a dedication, in German: "Dear Gitta, this is meant to
be an attempt to show young people who long for 'law and order' where *not*
to look for an example. With warmest wishes, yours. . . ."

The book was very bad, a mélange of bitter accusations against himself and
a furious attack on Himmler and his methods of creating a slave state by in-

filtrating every state organization, "doubling," or duplicating, the officials with his own people.

How had I liked it? Speer asked me in his next phone call, about three days after the book had arrived. I was not crazy about it, I said. "Well, I'm not either," he said. "I think I've done myself a lot of harm with it."

After this, our communication lapsed for several months. I was working in Italy, he—I presumed—was resting after promoting the new book.

It was very late on the evening of Friday, August 7, when he rang next. He had evidently had a few glasses of wine—which usually didn't affect him aside from relaxing him—and sounded totally unlike himself. As usual, he first asked to speak to my husband, Don, who looked amused as he listened. "He is sozzled," he said when he handed back the receiver.

"What I wanted to tell you," Speer said happily, "was that after all I think I haven't done so badly. After all, I *was* Hitler's architect; I *was* his Minister of Armaments and Production; I *did* serve twenty years in Spandau and, coming out, *did* make another good career. Not bad after all, was it?"

Who was I talking to? I asked; "Not the Albert *I* know? What's happened?" I asked.

"Ah, well," he said, his voice inexpressibly joyful, "I have after all had another *Erlebnis* [experience, adventure]. . . ."

"Experience?" I asked, "What sort of experience?"

"Ah . . . one day soon, we will sit down together over a glass of wine," he promised, "and I'll tell you. Goo-o-od-bye."

IT WAS TO BE several weeks before I would learn what Speer's *Erlebnis* had been, and thus at last understand the metamorphosis that had induced him to write in November 1980—two years late—that baffling unhappy letter and, ten months later, to inform me, most uncharacteristically, that he thought after all he had done pretty well in his life.

Sometime in 1979 or early 1980, it appears, he had received a letter from a young woman. She had an English surname, a German first name and wrote in German. She had just read *The Secret Diaries,* she wrote, and had to tell him that it was the most wonderful book she had ever read. It was apparently a quiet and modest letter: she was married, she said, to an Englishman; they had two children, and her husband's job had taken them overseas, to Germany and now back to England.

Being a young German woman in an English environment, she said, was not always easy, and she had often felt unhappy about the things she heard people say; she had felt bad for her children, too, because they had a German-born mother. But all this was changed for her since she had read his book; it had made her cry and it had made her happy and that's what she had wanted to tell him. She hoped he wouldn't mind.

Speer was apparently very touched by the simplicity of this letter. Writing back, he invited her to come and see him next time she was in Germany.

"I saw Speer last in 1980," Wolf Jobst Siedler told me in 1984, in Berlin. "He had sent me the manuscript of his SS book, and we talked about it, I think over lunch. I told him I couldn't help him with it; it would have taken me six months to get it into what I considered publishable shape. He took my 'no' very well—he always took criticism very well."

Afterwards, they had a long talk, Siedler said. Speer told him again what he had said many times over the years, that he was the only man he could confide in. "And he said that sometimes a man needed another man to talk to," he said. And then, to his astonishment, Speer told him about his friendship with someone he described as a young Englishwoman—he showed Siedler a photograph he took out of his wallet.

"It was of them together on a terrace," Siedler said. "It was a house he had rented in the south of France, Speer told me. The very good-looking lady—under forty I would think—slim, tall, long blond hair, was in a white negligee, and Speer next to her in slacks and a thin white turtleneck sweater, silk I think. They were laughing. It was obviously a self-photo taken in the sun. In the context of the Speer I had known for fourteen years, it was about as unlikely a situation as one could imagine."

"It is extraordinary," Siedler quoted Speer as saying, "I had to be in my seventies to have a first real erotic experience with a woman." They had, it seems, fallen in love at first sight when he was still writing his SS book.

It is, of course, tempting to be wise after the events, but I had wondered, when he sent me the advance copy of the SS book, how he, who was so meticulous, so careful, and above all, so intelligent, could have handed in such an unfinished and—because of it I thought—confusing book, in which he condemned the appalling actions of others while admitting (it almost seemed only in order to deny) his own part in specific crimes.

He himself, as emerged from his telephone call after he had sent the book to me, was clearly aware of its deficiencies. Now all was explained. He had fallen in love. At seventy-five he was for the first time sexually in love, with a beautiful young woman for whom this experience must certainly also have been a milestone in her life.

He was, as he had always been, physically a very attractive man, a fact I perhaps did less than justice to in my descriptions. Even so, I doubt that this or, for that matter, the great personal charm he was capable of was his main attraction for her.

It must have been exactly as she had told him in that first letter. That wonderful book, *The Secret Diaries,* had shown her not only a man other than any she had ever known, but a different German of the generation—her own parents' generation—she had for so long been required to despise and condemn. It changed her feeling about the past, about history and essentially, too, I suspect, about herself.

I would learn later that she had come to England first in the late 1950s, early 1960s, as an au pair. I remember that time well, and the young au pairs who came to us during those years to help look after our children. I remember their bewilderment. It was difficult for a child of that generation of Germans or Austrians to be confronted daily, in British newspapers and on TV, with the subject of the Nazi horrors. They had seen this in Germany as well, but it was a culture shock to find themselves identified abroad with Hitler's crimes, blamed for being their parents' children, blamed for being German. Though, paradoxically, many of them left loving England, every one of these young girls I knew had somehow been marked, some of them seared by the experience.

In the case of Speer's last friend—for that is what she became—it would appear that she "drew the consequences" of her experiences in England as a young girl. Not much later, back in Germany, she met a young Englishman, loved him, married him, had children with him and "became" English (she would be described as "an Englishwoman" to Margret, Hilde, Annemarie and Margret's closest friend, Erika Wolters—the only ones who were to be told, until Siedler—and none of them knew at first that she was actually German).

Her mother, Hilde told me later, had been devastated by this late invasion of her life. "I was heartbroken for her," she said. "After everything she had gone through, everything she had done for us, for him. 'This too, now,' she said to me. 'Did this really have to be?' "

How had Margret found out about it? I asked. She shrugged.

"Found out?" she repeated, her tone of voice unusually bitter. "He used to 'report absent' [*er meldete sich ab*] when he went to meet her."

For Speer, meeting this lovely creature, who unconditionally admired him and unquestioningly believed in him, in the middle of trying to write a book he should probably never have undertaken, must have been overwhelming. He had always been a devotee of youth and physical beauty, in women as well as men. Margret had been beautiful, but until this moment, his esthetic need for these qualities had never been transmuted into the natural sequence of shared physical joy.

Speer always was a mental-and-romantic rather than physical-and-sexual force. His love for Margret—and he did love her—grew out of his romantic need for simplicity, a genuineness and moderation he found in her and her family, which they embraced in their early marriage. Margret succeeded in communicating this to their children, and, after Speer returned, he and she maintained it in their private lives to the end.

Although he experienced sexual love for the first time at this late point, this emotion had a second and unprecedented dimension. It was linked with an infinitely valuable gift this young woman was able to bestow upon him— unlimited and uncritical acceptance of him as the man she found in *The Secret Diaries*: the best man he had ever been.

She didn't know—how could she?—that her no doubt passionate approval, delivered in terms he had never experienced, would free him from the questioning self he had been for so long. How could she, innocent and unknowing, realize that this, in the long run, would have destroyed that very "best" in him she had come to love?

Nonetheless, how liberated he must have felt when it happened, and how clearly it explained his letter to me, and that subsequent phone call full of joy.

As Hilde said much later, with that quiet generosity that is so particularly hers, "What an extraordinary thing to happen to him—I can't help feeling glad for him."

WHAT SPEER hadn't told me in that euphoric telephone call on August 7, 1981, was that three weeks later he would be in London for twenty-four hours to take part in a BBC documentary. His visit was during a long bank holiday weekend in Britain which, not knowing he was coming, we spent in the country.

When we came home in the evening on Tuesday, September 1, our answering machine was blinking.

"Here Albert," said the familiar voice in his Germanic English. "I'm here just for a day, talking with the BBC, but you it seems are not at home. How sad. I wanted to surprise you. Well, come to see us in Germany soon. How is my friend Don? Goodbye."

That was the first message on the tape, without date or time. The next one was from ITV. Could they talk to me about Albert Speer? "That's funny," I said to my husband. "ITV wants him and the BBC have got him." And then came Canadian Broadcasting from Toronto—which had called only minutes before we got back. Could I ring back collect, any time up to 2:30 a.m. my time, for a radio interview about Albert Speer's death?

It was impossible—it had to be a mistake. I rang Margret in the Allgäu. Alone up on the mountain—she had expected him back that night—she must have been sitting by the phone (which I knew was on the desk in his study), for she picked it up at the first ring. Her voice sounded light and shy, as it always had, but oddly fluttery and somehow disembodied. It was true, she said with that matter-of-factness that sometimes comes with shock; he had just died.

She said they thought it was a stroke; it had happened at his London hotel, the Park Court, just as he was about to leave for the airport and home. He had died at ten o'clock, German time, at St. Mary's Hospital, Paddington. "Hadn't I seen him?" she asked.

WALLY DUNNAGE was a retired police officer who was chief security officer at Speer's London hotel. "It was about 4:30 in the afternoon when the phone rang in my office," he said, telling me about the day Speer died. "The duty manager said a guest had collapsed in his room and that an ambulance had been called.

"When I got to Room 516, the door was opened by a lady—she was about thirty-five to forty, with long fair hair, about five feet eight inches tall, of medium build. She wore a thin cardigan over a dress, or perhaps a skirt and blouse. She looked very pale, very distressed.

"An elderly man was lying on his back on the bed; he didn't appear to be breathing, and his skin was clammy cold. The lady said she thought he might have had a stroke. I pressed the center of his chest. There was a sound and he seemed to start breathing. I turned him sideways into the recovery position and worked on him until, only minutes later, the paramedics arrived. I went outside then, as one does, and the lady did, too.

" 'Do you know who this is?' she said to me. I said, 'No.'

" 'This is Albert Speer,' she said."

Angelita de la Torre was the young floor maid on duty that afternoon and was there when Dunnage came out of the room. "Wally had given him the kiss of life, I think," she said, in her lilting Spanish accent. "He must have worked very hard on him—his face was grey, he was absolutely drained. 'Imagine,' he said to me, '*me* looking after *him.*'

"I didn't know what he meant, but very soon afterwards," she said, "we heard a news bulletin on the radio; that's when we understood who he was."

"He was a guest of the BBC," said the hotel's manager. "They rang and said to take care of the gentleman's things: his son would come to pick them up. Our housekeeper—she was German, you know—she said she'd like to see Albert Speer's son."

"We couldn't believe it," said BBC producer Jane Ellison, an attractive young woman who had been production assistant on the documentary on

Hitler and art, for which Speer had been invited to London to be interviewed by historian Norman Stone.

"It was only Speer's second visit to England since the war," she said. "On his first, in 1970, also at the invitation of the BBC, he had been put under guard as a former war criminal, and it took hours of negotiation with the Home Office before he was permitted to land. There wasn't anything like that this time. It had all been carefully cleared ahead of time. He'd arrived the previous afternoon and had a long working dinner with Norman."

"He was in excellent form," said Stone, Professor of Modern History at Oxford, and a renowned raconteur. "I picked him up at his hotel on Sunday at six; he said he'd left his house in the Allgäu at seven in the morning, but he didn't seem a bit tired. In fact I'd say he was pleased as Punch to be in London. We planned the interview—and then went on talking about the past until quite late, two in the morning I think, but he was fine, remarkably sharp. Of course, he loved talking about it all, didn't he?"

"We got him from the hotel very early the next morning and shot the interview for several hours," said Jane. "He seemed perfectly all right, not even tired after that late night. We thought he was amazing—we were all fascinated by him. We knew he was due to fly home that afternoon, so Norman suggested lunch, but he said—very chirpily as I remember—that he was lunching with a lady. ["I was sure it was you," Norman told me.] So we dropped him off at his hotel—I think it was about one o'clock," Jane continued.

"When—at about four, I think—I was told he had been taken to St. Mary's with a probable stroke, I rushed there. The registrar told me he had been brought in in a coma, and that a relative or friend who had come in the ambulance with him was sitting in front of the emergency room.

"She was tall and blond, looking distraught. She said that no, she wasn't a relative. She murmured something about helping him with work—publishers, letters in English. She spoke with a very slight German accent and later—we sat together for hours—she told me all about herself. And she said that she had notified Speer's family of what had happened."

"She telephoned my mother late that afternoon," said Hilde. "She had known about the relationship all along, but to learn from *her* that he was dying—it really was too much, you know, almost grotesque."

"After a while," Jane Ellison went on, "I sensed that they must have had much more than a casual working relationship. She really was quite desperate; it was very obvious that she loved him deeply.

"The door to the emergency room was open; it wasn't very private. We watched them work on him, but after two hours or so they said they were taking him up into a side ward and then we went to sit there.

"She knew a lot about his family, his children. She talked about his books, about him too, as a person, but I can't remember just what she said because, well, it wasn't very rational. She was horribly upset, crying much of the time.

"The hospital had had no idea who he was. We had registered him at the hotel under our producer's name, Dave Wallace, because we didn't want him bothered by the media—and so they probably sent him in the ambulance as Dave Wallace too. I don't know how it got out, but suddenly the hospital switchboard was jammed with media calls. It was a shambles."

Dr. Edwin Keal, a leading chest consultant, had been called in as soon as the hospital realized they had a VIP on their hands. "Oh, yes," he said, "I knew exactly who he was—it was my war, you know; I'm of that generation. It was quite extraordinary to have that man spending his last hours in an anonymous ward, in London—which he had perhaps been more instrumental than anyone else in trying to destroy. Of course, one didn't think of all that until much later." He smiled. "We did wonder, though, about the attractive young person who had brought him in."

"And then of course he died," said Jane, "and there were all the arrangements to be made. My office at the BBC was in an uproar, with the calls from all over the world I had fielded for hours now coming to them. By that time they knew that Speer's daughter-in-law, who was a doctor, would fly over early next morning to take care of the formalities, and fly the body back to Germany.

"We stayed at the hospital until very late, I think it was ten or so," Jane said. "I was exhausted and the friend looked worn to a frazzle. She told me where she lived—a suburb. Perhaps I should have driven her out there but, I didn't; I dropped her off at Waterloo. She looked forlorn but was a bit more composed by then, and said she'd be all right. I took her name and address and said I'd get in touch, but I never did. What could one say to her?"

Dr. Keal had never had any hope, he said. "It was a very dense trauma with massive damage. I don't suppose he would have wanted to survive like that, not that man."

He was right. "Margret and I have discussed our attitude toward artificial prolongation of life," Speer had told me about a little over a year before he died, when, in June 1980—not long after the beginning of his love affair and his conversation with Siedler, I realized later—he had another of the embolisms which always seemed to hit him at moments of emotional stress. "We both feel that if anything happened to either of us, we would not wish our lives to be artificially extended. If such a thing as an incapacitating stroke happened to me, I would want her to tell them to let me go, and I think she would want me to do the same for her."

•   •   •

As I began writing the end of this book, I stopped to look once more at Speer on the videotape the BBC had sent me, of the documentary he had taken part in on the last day of his life. It was screened three and a half months after he had died, on December 14, 1981.

He looked extraordinarily young in it, and slimmer than I had ever seen him. But what struck me perhaps more than anything else was that here, on that screen, on that final day of his life, the two dimensions he had always had were so apparent.

On the one hand, there was the pragmatic Speer, in a documentary he had doubtless been eager to do, in which the questions put to him were above all about Hitler's architectural plans for his native city of Linz. Speer's answers are, of course, very knowledgeable; after all, he was entirely familiar, no one more than he, with Hitler's mania for architecture and his manner of dealing with its practitioners. But it was interesting how, with perfect aplomb, although he was largely ad-libbing, he managed to generalize his replies to specific questions on Linz in such a way that it never became apparent that (although he had designed the city's new art gallery) it was not he Hitler had appointed chief architect for his beloved Linz, where he planned to spend his old age and die, but Speer's old rival Hermann Giesler.

By the same token, when the documentary showed old German newsreel film of Hitler's dawn tour, in June 1940, of the splendors of architecture in the conquered Paris—the Invalides, the Eiffel Tower, the Opéra, the Arc de Triomphe, Sacré-Coeur on top of Montmartre—although Hitler, in the lead car of the motorcade, sat between Giesler and Speer, Giesler does not figure in Speer's description of that extraordinary occasion.

It reminded me of Annemarie's saying with a smile, "Success—that's what he wanted." It made me smile too, though more with resignation than indulgence. It was true, but far from the whole truth.

He was ecstatic upon entering Hitler's service; unfaithful on demand to the pure concept of architecture he had so wholeheartedly espoused from his first mentor, Tessenow; blinkered from the very beginning to his Führer's monstrous obsessions; oblivious to (rather than ignorant of) the suffering they would so immediately cause—concentration camps for Christians and communists, civic obliteration for Jews, death for the handicapped, the genetically sick, the senile. He enthusiastically embraced Hitler's war when it began, was jubilant about his conquests, and when he—the artist—was appointed to high government office, he readily did all and more than was required. He manipulated, cajoled, intrigued against and threatened those who interfered with his power and his aims, demanded rather than merely participated in the brutal subjugation of foreign workers for slave labor and unconsciously or consciously blinded himself to licensed murder.

Speer himself killed no one and felt no enmity, hatred or even dislike for the millions in Eastern Europe, Christians and Jews, who were systematically slaughtered: he felt nothing.

There was a dimension missing in him, a capacity to feel which his childhood had blotted out, allowing him to experience not love but only romanticized substitutes for love.

Pity, compassion, sympathy and empathy were not part of his emotional vocabulary. He could feel deeply but only indirectly—through music, through landscapes, through art, eventually through visual hyperbole, often in settings of his own creation: his Cathedral of Light, the flags, the thousands of men at attention motionless like pillars, the blond children, rows upon rows of them with shining eyes and arms stiffly raised. This became beauty to him and, another substitute for love, allowed him to *feel*.

But then, via Posen and Dora, at long last he acknowledged Hitler's madness; through the revelations of Nuremberg and the confrontation with the reactions of the civilized world came his realization and horror at what had been done, his feelings of personal guilt, his wish, almost, for death and yet fear of execution, the shame of being spared, the prospect of twenty years' incarceration until, a young forty-one when he went in, he would come out old, at sixty-one. Out of all this, through his illumination with Casalis, his discovery of humility, the gift to him of his young daughter's excellence, the joy he found in solitude, but most of all, his continuing and tormenting awareness of guilt—out of all this, there came to be another Speer.

In this Speer, obsessed with a history he understood perhaps like no other man, I found a great deal to like over the four years I knew him. This, I feel, had become the real Speer; the one I am convinced that—after the euphoria of his late-life passion had passed—he would have become again, had he lived on. This was a very serious man who knew more about that bane of our century, Hitler, than anyone else. This was an erudite and solitary man who, recognizing his deficiencies in human relations, had read five thousand books in prison to try to understand the universe and human beings, an effort he succeeded in with his mind but failed in with his heart. Empathy is finally a gift, and cannot be learned, so, essentially, returning into the world after twenty years, he remained alone.

Unforgiven by so many for having served Hitler, he elected to spend the rest of his life in confrontation with this past, unforgiving of himself for having so nearly loved a monster.

I came to understand and value Speer's battle with himself and saw in it the re-emergence of the intrinsic morality he manifested as a boy and youth. It seemed to me it was some kind of victory that this man—just this man—weighed down by intolerable and unmanageable guilt, with the help of a Protestant chaplain, a Catholic monk and a Jewish rabbi, tried to become a different man.

REFERENCES
NOTES
INDEX

References

As the following sources are frequently used, they will be abbreviated as shown. Some, such as the Goebbels diaries and letters in my possession, are identified in the text by date, and not separately referenced. Other sources follow this short list. Where several editions of a book are listed, page references will be to the first mentioned, unless otherwise noted.

BELOW — Below, Nicolaus von. *Als Hitlers Adjutant 1937–45*. Mainz: Hase und Koehler, 1980.

CHRONIK — The office journal, or *Chronik*, kept by Wolters during Speer's work as GBI and later as Minister of Armaments and War Production. Fully discussed in Chapter V and in Chapter IX.

DIARIES — Speer, *Spandau: The Secret Diaries*. New York: Pocket Books, 1977.

FINAL — Reitlinger, Gerald. *The Final Solution: The Attempt to Exterminate the Jews of Europe, 1939–1945*. Second Revised Edition. London: Valentine, Mitchell, 1968.

GEIS — *Leiden an der Unerlöstheit, Robert Raphael Geis, 1906–1972, Briefe, Reden, Aufsätze*. Herausgegeben von Dietrich Goldschmidt in Zusammenarbeit mit Ingrid Ueberschär. Munich: Chr. Kaiser, 1985.

IMT — Proceedings of the International Military Tribunal are from the edition in English published in Nuremberg in 1948 by the Secretariat of the Tribunal as *Trial of the Major War Criminals* in twenty-three volumes. References are usually listed by volume and page, but my chapter headings are identified in the text by date and persons speaking, so are not otherwise referenced.

ITD — Sereny, Gitta. *Into That Darkness*. New York: Vintage Books, 1983; London: Andre Deutsch, 1991; Pimlico, 1995.

ITTR — Speer, Albert. *Inside the Third Reich*. New York: Collier Books/Macmillan, 1981; London: Weidenfeld and Nicolson, 1970; Phoenix, 1995. In the text this is sometimes referred to as his *Erinnerungen* (Reminiscences), but to readers in English *Inside the Third Reich* is more familiar.

NRMBG — The Nuremberg draft was 103 pages of memoir written by Speer before and during the trial, in anticipation of his possible execution. Speer in Spandau refers to this as the *Urfassung* (original version).

SEGMENTS — Wolters, Rudolf. *Lebensabrisse* (Segments of a Life). Privately published, now in the Wolters Archive in the Federal Archive, Koblenz.

SLAVE — Speer, *Der Sklaven Staat*. Stuttgart: Deutsche Verlags-Anstalt, 1981. Translated passages by author. English edition, *The Slave State*. London: Weidenfeld and Nicolson, 1981. American edition, *Infiltrations: Heinrich Himmler's Master Plan for SS Supremacy*. New York: Macmillan, 1981.

SPANDAU — The "Spandau draft" refers to the 1,200 pages (when transcribed) Speer wrote to

Wolters from prison between January 8, 1953, and January 1954. Within the Wolters Archive *(Nachlass)*, held at the Federal Archive in Koblenz, they form NL 7 to NL 11, and are referenced by volume, date and sometimes the page.

Archive sources for documents will be abbreviated as follows:

NA RG   National Archives (War Crimes), Washington, D.C.
BA   Bundesarchiv (Federal Archive), Koblenz
IFZ   Institut für Zeitgeschichte (Institute for Contemporary History, Munich)
PRO   Public Records Office, Kew

Other Sources

Bismarck, Klaus von. *Aufbruch aus Pommern, Erinnerungen und Perspektiven.* Munich: Piper, 1992.

Blond, Georges. *L'Agonie de l'Allemagne.* Paris: Librairie Artheme Fayard, 1952.

Breitman, Richard. *The Architect of Genocide: Himmler and the Final Solution.* New York: Alfred A. Knopf, 1991; London: The Bodley Head, 1991; Paladin, 1992.

Breitman, Richard, and Laqueur, Walter. *Breaking the Silence.* New York: Simon and Schuster, 1986.

Browning, Christopher R. *Ordinary Men.* New York: HarperCollins, 1992.

Bullock, Alan. *Hitler and Stalin: Parallel Lives.* London: HarperCollins, 1991; New York: Alfred A. Knopf, 1992.

Burckhardt, Carl J. *Meine Danziger Mission: 1937–1939.* Zurich/Munich: 1960.

Butz, Arthur R. *Did Six Million Die? The Hoax of the Twentieth Century.* Ladbroke Southam: Historical Review Press, 1976.

Carrefour. French newspaper that reprinted on September 3, 1953, a passage about Speer from *L'Agonie de l'Allemagne,* by George Blond.

Churchill, Winston. *The Second World War: Their Finest Hour,* 1949, and *Triumph and Tragedy,* 1953, Boston: Houghton Mifflin; *The Grand Alliance,* Vol. III, London: Cassell, 1950; London: Penguin, 1976.

Fest, Joachim C. *Hitler.* Frankfurt: Propyläen, 1973; New York: Harcourt Brace Jovanovich, 1974; London: Weidenfeld and Nicolson, 1974.

Friedlander, Saul. *Kurt Gerstein, or the Ambiguity of Good.* London: Weidenfeld and Nicolson, 1967.

Fromm, Erich. *Anatomy of Human Destructiveness.* New York: Holt, Rinehart and Winston, 1973.

Galante, Pierre, and Silianoff, Eugene. *Last Witnesses in the Bunker.* London: Sidgwick and Jackson, 1989.

Giesler, Hermann. *Ein anderer Hitler.* Leoni am Starnberger See: Druffel, 1982.

Gilbert, G. M. *Nuremberg Diary.* New York: Signet, 1961.

Goebbels, Joseph. *Die Tagebücher von Joseph Goebbels, Sämtliche Fragmente.* Herausgegeben von Elke Fröhlich im Auftrag des Instituts für Zeitgeschichte. Munich: K. G. Saur, first volume, 1987 (nine volumes to date).

Gruchmann, Lothar. *Euthanasie und Justiz im Dritten Reich,* in *Vierteljahres Hefte für Zeitgeschichte,* Heft 3/72. Munich: R. Oldenburgh Verlag.

Hagen, Walter. *Die Geheime Front.* Linz-Wien: Nibelungen-Verlag, 1950.

Hitler, Adolf. *Mein Kampf.* Munich: F. Eher, 1935.

Hitler's Tabletalk, 1941–44. Introduction by Hugh Trevor-Roper. London: Weidenfeld and Nicolson, 1953. For a full discussion of various versions of the *Tabletalk,* see Note for Chapter IX.

Hossbach, Friedrich. *Zwischen Wehrmacht und Hitler 1934–1938.* Göttingen: Vandenhoeck und Ruprecht, 1949.

Jäckel, Eberhard. *Sämtliche Aufzeichnungen, 1904–1924.* Stuttgart: Deutsche Verlags-Anstalt, 1980.

Janssen, Gregor. *Das Ministerium Speer.* Frankfurt am Main: Ullstein, 1968.

Kehrl, Hans. *Krisenmanager im Dritten Reich.* Düsseldorf: Droste Verlag, 1973.

Kempner, Robert M. W. *Eichmann und Komplizen.* Zurich: Europa Verlag, 1961.

Klee, Ernst. *Euthanasie im NS Staat.* Frankfurt am Main: Fischer, 1983.

Klee, Ernst, and Dressen, Willi, editors. *Gott Mit Uns.* Frankfurt am Main: Fischer 1992.

Klee, Ernst, Dressen, Willi, and Riess, Volker, editors. *Schöne Zeiten.* Frankfurt am Main: Fischer, 1988. English edition, *Those Were the Days,* London: Hamish Hamilton, 1991.

Levi, Primo. *If This Is a Man.* London: Orion, 1959.

Lifton, Robert Jay. *The Broken Connection.* New York: Simon and Schuster, 1979.

———. *The Nazi Doctors.* New York: Basic Books, 1986; London: Macmillan, 1986.

Maser, Werner. *Nuremberg: A Nation on Trial.* New York: Scribners, 1979; London: Alan Lane, 1979; Penguin, 1980.

Michel, Jean. *Dora.* Paris: Editions Lattès, 1975; London: Weidenfeld and Nicolson, 1979.

Mitscherlich, Alexander and Margarete. *The Inability to Mourn.* New York: Grove Press, 1975.

Morse, Arthur. *While Six Million Died.* London: Secker and Warburg, 1968.

Neave, Airey. *Nuremberg.* London: Hodder and Stoughton, 1978. Page references are to the Coronet edition, 1980.

O'Donnell, James P. *The Berlin Bunker.* London: Arrow, 1979.

Oven, Wilfred von. *Verrat und Widerstand im Dritten Reich.* Coburg: 1978.

Playboy. Speer interview by Eric Norden, June 1971.

Powers, Thomas. *Heisenberg's War.* New York: Alfred A. Knopf, 1993; London: Jonathan Cape, 1993; Penguin, 1994.

Reif, Adelbert, editor. *Albert Speer, Kontroversen um ein Deutsches Phänomen.* Munich: Bernard und Graefe, 1978.

Riefenstahl, Leni. *Memoiren.* Munich: Albrecht Knaus, 1987.

Rohland, Walter. *Bewegte Zeiten: Erinnerungen eines Eisenhütten Mannes.* Stuttgart: Seewald Verlag, 1978.

Schirach, Henrietta von. *Der Preis der Herrlichkeit.* Munich: F. A. Herbig, 1975.

Schmidt, Matthias. *Albert Speer: End of a Myth.* New York: St Martin's Press, 1984.

Schmidt, Paul. *Statist auf Diplomatischer Bühne, 1923–45.* Bonn: Athenäum, 1961.

Schröder, Christa, with Joachimsthaler, Anton. *Er war mein Chef.* Munich: Langen-Müller, 1985.

Schröder, Christa, with Zoller, Albert. *Hitler privat, Erlebnisbericht seiner Geheimsekretarin.* Dusseldorf: Droste Verlag, 1949.

Smith, Bradley. *Reaching Judgment at Nuremberg.* London: Andre Deutsch, 1977.

Smith, Bradley, with Peterson, Agnes F., editors. *Heinrich Himmler, Geheimreden 1933–1945.* Frankfurt am Main: Propyläen, 1974.

Stahlberg, Alexander. *Bounden Duty: Memoirs of a German Officer 1932–1945.* London: Brassey's, 1990, p. 316. German edition, *Die verdammte Pflicht.* Berlin: Ullstein, 1987.

Taylor, Telford. *The Anatomy of the Nuremberg Trials.* New York: Knopf, 1992; London: Bloomsbury, 1992.

Todorov, Tzvetan. *Face a l'Extreme.* Paris: Editions du Seuil, 1991.

Toland, John. *Adolf Hitler.* New York: Doubleday, 1976; London: Ballantine, 1978.

Trevor-Roper, Hugh. *The Last Days of Hitler.* London: Macmillan. I have used the Papermac edition, 1987, reprinted 1991. A fourth edition reprinted 1995.

Vassiltchikov, Maria (Missie). *Berlin Diaries: 1940–1945.* London: Chatto and Windus, 1986.

Notes

Schirach, *Der Preis der Herrlichkeit,* p.
51; BELOW, p. 340.
115 Troost dies: ITTR, p. 49.
Röhm Putsch: Ibid., pp. 51–53.

Chapter V

128 Maifeld design: ITTR, p. 26.
130 request re Klinke: Führer conference,
April 14, 1943: collection of documents
for Speer, Wolters Archive, Koblenz.
Klinke eulogy: *CHRONIK,* May 1943,
p. 58.
133 memoirs: Leni Riefenstahl, *Memoires.*
Munich: Albrecht Knaus, 1987.
137 BBC interview: *Panorama:* Roll 3, p. 18;
Rolls 4/1, 4/2.
140 Berlin project: SPANDAU, NL 11,
10.12.53 pp. 25, 114 ff.
141 "my old university friend": Ibid., p, 31.

Chapter VI

144 "Make a good job of it": SPANDAU,
NL 11, 5.11.53, p. 49.
145 Wolters to GBI: SEGMENTS, pp.
17–18.
150 four meetings: Ibid., p. 187.
158 Speer's father: ITTR, p. 133.

Chapter VII

164 Kristallnacht: ITTR, pp. 111–13.
173 murderous laws: FINAL, p. 7.
175 Elbogen-Geis letter: GEIS, pp. 55 ff.

Chapter VIII

179 "If Hilter had died": Toland, *Adolf
Hitler,* p. 409.
"*Heil Hitler*": Ibid., p. 398.
185 the great hall: ITTR, pp. 151–60.
186 "most secret" meeting: Friedrich
Hossbach, *Zwischen Wehrmacht und
Hitler 1934–1938.* Göttingen:
Vandenhoeck und Ruprecht, 1949, pp.
119, 165–7.

187 Comment on "most secret" meeting:
BELOW, pp. 48–50.
189 Anschluss: ITTR, pp. 107–9, and
SPANDAU, NL 11, 17.12.53, p. 41.
196 Bouhler and Brandt: FINAL, p. 134.
198 medical research: Public Records
Office, Kew, FO 371, No. 66582.

Chapter IX

205 Schmundt notes: BELOW, pp. 164–65.
207 Hitler-Stalin link: ITTR, p. 161.
208 "Everything I undertake is directed
against the Russians": Burckhardt,
Meine Danziger Mission: 1937–1939, as
quoted in Bullock, *Hitler and Stalin:
Parallel Lives,* p. 639.
212 Poland the social laboratory: Bullock,
Hitler and Stalin: Parallel Lives, p. 652.
213 "parts and fragments": Himmler
memo, discussed in Breitman, *The
Architect of Genocide: Himmler and the
Final Solution,* p. 118 and note. NA RG
242. His reference: T-175/R 94/2615221.
"Special Train": Himmler note, IMT,
Doc. No. NO-1881, Office of Chief of
Counsel for War Crimes.
214 *Tabletalk:* Notes on Hitler's
monologues were mostly made by
Heinrich Heim, a young Bormann aide,
between July 5, 1941, and March 20,
1942. During his absence on two trips
buying art for Hitler, another aide,
Henry Picker, briefly replaced him from
March 21 to July 31, 1942. Occasional
notes were also made until November
29, 1944, some by Heim and some by
two others. The notes were given to
Bormann each morning, who edited the
staff-prepared transcripts and kept two
copies. One, in the Brown House in
Munich, was burnt at the end of the
war. The other, at the Berghof in
Berchtesgaden, survived as the
Bormann *Vermerke* and came into the
possession of François Genoud, a Swiss
who purchased publication rights for
many Nazi documents from various
heirs.
    Dr. Picker published his own notes

(plus some of Heim's which he had copied at the Brown House) in 1951 as *Hitler's Tischgespräche im Führerhauptquartier 1941–42* (Bonn: Athenäum Verlag). This version was arranged by themes, not chronologically. In 1963 he published a new version chronologically arranged and edited by Professor Percy E. Schramm, with commentary by Dr. Andreas Hillgruber (Stuttgart: Seewald Verlag).

Genoud, with the much more complete text, published a French version in 1952, *Libres Propos sur la Guerre et la Paix, recueillis sur l'ordre de Martin Bormann,* and an English version in 1953, *Hitler's Table Talk 1941–44,* with an introduction by Hugh Trevor-Roper (London: Weidenfeld and Nicolson). A second edition was published in 1973, with a new preface explaining the origins of the two versions.

A German edition based on the whole of Heim's Bormann *Vermerke,* edited by Werner Jochmann, was published in 1980, *Adolf Hitler, Monologe im Führerhauptquartier 1941–44* (Hamburg: Albrecht Knaus), and has the advantage of naming most of those present at each meal. Earlier versions omitted all but special guests, so that regulars like Speer were sometimes not named.

This passage is from the 1973 English version; others are translated from the 1980 German edition.

218 **"Our armies at home":** Churchill, *The Second World War: Their Finest Hour,* p. 256.

220 **Berlin Jews:** Minutes of meeting at Propaganda Ministry in Berlin, March 21, 1941, NA RG 242, T-81/R 676/15485604-5.

221 **"to escape the evacuation":** IMT, Vol. XVI, p. 519.
"When I think about": Speer, *Infiltrations,* p. 355 (see SLAVE).

223 **"Jewish real estate":** *CHRONIK,* Wolters Archive, Koblenz, R3 1662.

228 **Speer's iniquity:** Matthias Schmidt, *Albert Speer: End of a Myth.* New York: St. Martin's Press, 1984, pp. 183–89.

229 **two notes: housing:** Federal Archive, Koblenz, R-3 1662, pp. 48, 51, 60.

Chapter X

232 **In the little Speer does say:** ITTR, pp. 176–77.

235 **Todt to Speer:** Ibid., p. 193.

236 **Bormann's role:** Giesler, *Ein Anderer Hitler,* pp. 342–44.

237 **"Adolf Hitler loved Albert Speer":** Mitscherlich, Alexander, *Frankfurter Allgemeine Zeitung,* November 1, 1975.

238 **Barbarossa:** Bullock, *Hitler and Stalin: Parallel Lives,* p. 692.

240 **Hess flight:** ITTR, p. 174, and BELOW, p. 273.

244 **Hess in England:** Churchill, *The Second World War: The Grand Alliance,* p. 45.

245 **Commissar Order:** IMT, Vol. XXI, pp. 32, 40.
"Our task in Russia": Fest, *Hitler,* p. 885, quoted from Halder's diary, *Kriegstagebuch: Tägliche Aufzeichnungen des Chefs des Generalstats des Heers, 1939–42.* Stuttgart, 1962–64 (no publisher given by Fest).

247 **"Hitler's concept":** BELOW, p. 279.

253 **"close at hand":** FINAL, p. 84.
Einsatzgruppe: SS Obersturm-bannführer Ehlers is quoted in Klee, Dressen, and Riess, editors, *Those Were the Days,* p. 82.

254 **first pogrom:** Ibid., p. 27.
"increasingly nervous": BELOW, pp. 278–9.
"Hitler told me": SPANDALL, NL 11, 26.12.53, p. 34.

256 **killing in Kovno:** Klee, Dressen, and Riess, editors, *Schöne Zeiten,* p. 35. (Name was withheld.)
Fort VII: Ibid., p. 42.

257 **final report:** Ibid., pp. 52–62.
sterilization: Brack quoted in Breitman, *The Architect of Genocide: Himmler and the Final Solution,* p.

152–3. His reference: NA RG 238, NO 203, National Archives RG (War Crimes), NO series.

258 **Erwin Schulz:** Klee, Dressen, and Riess, editors, *Schöne Zeiten*, p. 85.

259 **report to Himmler:** Ibid., p. 167.

260 **Slutsk: a bad effect:** Browning, *Ordinary Men*, pp. 16–23, and note 28, p. 196; Klee, Dressen, and Riess, editors, *Schöne Zeiten*, pp. 164–67.
"the most humane manner": Wilhelm Kube to Heinrich Lohse, in Klee, Dressen, and Riess, editors, *Those Were the Days*, p. 180 ff. (For background, see *Lithuanian Jewry*, vol. IV, Tel Aviv: 1984; Karl Jäger's "Conclusive List," December 1941, in *Those Were the Days*; Reitlinger, *The Final Solution* [Tel Aviv: 1960]; *Jews from the Third Reich*, by Dina Porat; *The Einsatzgruppen Reports*, edited by Yarad Shmul Krakowski and Shmul Spector [New York: 1989].).
"the scourge of humanity": Fest, *Hitler*, p. 887.

261 **"Final Solution":** FINAL, p. 85.
Goebbels at HQ: BELOW, pp. 290–91.

263 **Kommissar Befehl:** Bismarck, *Aufbruch aus Pommern*, pp. 135–37, 170–72.

270 **Majer Neumann:** FINAL, p. 250.

272 **Babi Yar:** ITD, p. 97.

Chapter XI

275 **flight to HQ:** NRMBG, pp. 5–6.
Todt is depressed: ITTR, p. 191.
talk about Russia: Speer Archive, 1.3.1953, p. 422.

276 **"I was content":** ITTR, p. 192.
given new job: Ibid., p. 197.

277 **mysterious crash:** Ibid., p. 196; Speer papers given to author.

279 **"The plane Todt had":** BELOW, pp. 305–6.
Todt mystery: Wolters's letter, NL 7, 16.3.53, pp. 1–2.

280 **premonition:** ITTR, p. 197.
Frau Todt: Wolters Archive, Koblenz. NL 47, letters.

283 **"Prison camp in Minsk":** Klee and Dressen, editors, *Gott Mitt Uns*, p. 138.

284 **letter about POWs:** Ibid., p. 142.

287 **Hitler's men:** Profiles of Hitler's men by Speer, which he gave to the author. **"hypnotic quality":** NRMBG, p. 4.

288 **"one extraordinary deficiency":** ITTR, p. 126.

Chapter XII

291 **Speer starts new job:** CHRONIK and SEGMENTS, p. 24.

295 **organization of Ministry:** SPANDAU, Wolters to Speer, NL 7, 16.3.53, p. 3; Speer to Wolters, NL 7, 14.3.53, pp. 1–22.

300 **Saur:** SPANDAU, NL 7, 14.3.53, pp. 19, 22.

302 **concert with Speer:** Wolters's diary, March 1942, p. 245. Wolters Archive, Koblenz.

Chapter XIII

304 **"Over the objections":** ITTR, p. 212.

305 **"like the sword of Damocles":** Janssen, *Das Ministerium Speer*, pp. 65–66.

307 **Hitler's humor:** ITTR, p. 180.

311 **female servants:** Ibid., p. 221.
"Whether [Eastern] nations live": Himmler to Hitler Youth.

312 **"I must share":** ITTR, p. 219.
"gloomy section": SPANDAU, NL 7, 21–23.3.53, pp. 15 ff.

314 **cheap labor:** *Tabletalk*, May 4, 1942.
"mistakes were fatal": SPANDAU, NL 7, 21–23.3.53, p. 19.

315 **"ruthless methods":** Ibid., p. 20.
"mass deportation": Dodd, IMT, Vol. III, p. 404.
"The aim of this": Sauckel letter, ibid., p. 405.

316 **farm workers:** Baden Directives, IMT, December 12, 1945, Doc. EC-68, Exhibit No. USA-205.
domestic workers: Sauckel directions, IMT, Vol. III, p. 406.
report to Hitler: IMT, Vol. III, p. 484.

317 **atom scientists:** SPANDAU, NL 8, 2.4.53, pp. 14–17; NL 9, 3.7.53, pp. 15–16; ITTR, pp. 226–29.

318 **"insane hate":** SPANDAU, NL 8, 2.4.53, p. 15.

319 **Heisenberg:** Ibid.; Powers, *Heisenberg's War*, pp. 121–28.

320 **bomb dates:** ITTR, p. 227; SPANDAU, NL 9, 3.7.53; DIARIES, p. 426.

329 **offered SS rank:** ITTR, p. 227; SPANDAU, NL 7, 21.3.53, pp. 24–25. **SS admission:** IMT, Doc. 3568-PS, Exhibit No. USA-575.

331 **concentration camps:** Ibid., Vol. XVI, p. 516.

333 **Rohland on workers:** Rohland, *Bewegte Zeiten, Erinnerungen eines Eisenbutten Mannes*, p. 148.

334 **"countless prisoners of war":** Bräutigam memorandum, October 25, 1942, IMT, Vol. III, pp. 422–23.

335 **"I in no way deny":** Rosenberg, December 21, 1942, IMT, December 12, 1945, Doc. D18-PS, Exhbit No. USA-186.

337 **"We leave Lemberg":** Wolters's diary, pp. 252–53.

Chapter XIV

340 **films of camps:** Gilbert, *Nuremberg Diary*, p. 48.

341 **acres of corpses:** Ibid., p. 152. **"our children now?":** Ibid., p. 162.

342 **hair shaved off:** Rajzman, IMT, Vol. XVI, pp. 326–29.

344 **more than a million:** ITD, pp. 141–42.

345 **Korherr report:** Korherr Report, IFZ, Munich.

349 **Wannsee:** Kempner, *Eichmann und Komplizen*, pp. 155 ff.

351 **Wolff letters:** FINAL, pp. 273–74. Reference: Trials of War Criminals 1951, Vol. V, p. 277.

353 **Turner letter:** Turner letter, IFZ, Munich.

354 **"he had to report it":** BELOW, p. 320. **Von dem Bussche:** Documentary film, *The Restless Conscience: Resistance to Hitler Within Germany, 1933–1945*, by Hava Kohav Beller, shown on WNET, New York, December 30, 1992.

355 **Gerstein:** Play, *The Representative*, by Rolf Hochhuth; *A Spy for God*, by Pierre Joffroy; *Kurt Gerstein, or the Ambiguity of Good*, by Saul Friedlander.

364 **Stalingrad:** SPANDAU, NL 8, 10.4.53, p. 26.

365 **his brother ill:** NRMBG, p. 12. **"In mid-January":** ITTR, p. 250.

366 **"It was very clear":** BELOW, p. 306.

367 **"The army can":** Himmler directive, November 2, 1942.

368 **"if . . . 'asocial' ":** Sauckel directive, November 26, 1942.

Chapter XV

370 **"At Führer HQ":** SPANDAU, NL 8, 20.4.53.

373 **"He viewed the situation":** NRMBG, p. 22.

375 **"Göring showed his":** SPANDAU, NL 8, 20.4.53, p. 21.

377 **Speer as successor:** Kehrl, *Krisenmanager im Dritten Reich*, pp. 334–35.

378 **Speer to Himmler:** Speer letter, February 1, 1943, IFZ, Munich.

379 **"Special Instructions":** Attached to *Ostbahn* timetable, Krakau, August 26, 1942. Federal Archives, Koblenz.

380 **"Utilization of Textiles":** Pohl to Funk, Federal Archive, Koblenz, B/Ch 186.

381 **Gypsies:** Pohl to Brandt, IFZ, Munich, 8378.

382 **"150 skeletons":** Letter (signature illegible), November 2, 1942, IFZ, Munich, 5706. **Natzweiler:** Berger to Eichmann. IFZ, Munich, MA 466/5094.

383 **"a new planning program":** Speer to Himmler, April 5, 1943, IFZ, Vol. I, 815/43. **"luxury construction":** Pohl to Himmler, IFZ, Munich. **"they discovered":** SLAVE, p. 71.

385 **"For months we had":** ITTR, p. 269.

388 **"On his return":** CHRONIK, October 4–5, 1943.

389 **special train:** Sleeper List, October 5, 1943, MA 697/861–866, IFZ, Munich.

390 **"please take note":** ITTR, p. 312. **Himmler:** Posen speech, October 6, 1943; Smith and Peterson, editors, *Heinrich Himmler: Geheimreden 1933 bis*

1945. Frankfurt am Main: Propyläen, 1974.

393 **bitter attack:** Goldhagen article, *Midstream,* October 1971; Speer's answer in Reif, editor, *Albert Speer, Kontroversen um ein deutsches Phänomen,* p. 395.

402 **Hitler reprimand:** ITTR, p. 316.
telephone calls ceased: Ibid., p. 317.

403 **"Opposition to Speer":** SEGMENTS, p. 341.
creation of Dora: Führerprotokoll, August 19–22, point 21, Federal Archive, Koblenz.

404 **visit to Dora:** ITTR, p. 370.
Dora from inside: Michel, *Dora,* various pages.

406 **Christmas:** SPANDAU, NL 9, 26.6.53, p. 7; ITTR, pp. 319–21.

Chapter XVI

410 **a retrospective study:** Gebhardt notes given to author by Speer.

413 **"I'm informed":** Letters to Sauckel, in Janssen, *Das Ministerium Speer,* p. 158.
to Hitler: Ibid., January 29, 1944.

414 **"He and I both feel":** Ibid.

415 **Funk story:** ITTR, pp. 331–32.

418 **"An astonishing recovery":** Dr. Koch notes, given to author by Speer.

419 **"beat them to death":** FINAL, p. 450, quoting Paul Schmidt, *Statist und Diplomatische Bühne, 1923–1945.*

420 **"In Poland":** Ibid.

422 **many visitors:** CHRONIK, dates as listed.
ugly Hitler: ITTR, p. 334.

423 **Gebhardt in Meran:** Ibid., p. 335.

424 **"intends to leave":** Gebhardt to Himmler, Wolters Archive, Koblenz.

425 **"your great skill":** Speer to Gebhardt, ibid.
"special time for me": SPANDAU, NL 9, 24.6.53, p. 18.

426 **warning to Hitler:** ITTR, p. 337.

427 **Brugmann's plane:** SEGMENTS, p. 281.

429 **Hitler's feelings:** BELOW, p. 368.

431 **"We suggested":** Ibid., p. 363.

433 **"We are planning":** Churchill, *The Second World War: Triumph and Tragedy,* p. 8.

434 **"40,000–50,000 youths":** IMT, Vol. III, pp. 406–8.

Chapter XVII

443 **"safeguarding of Rumanian oil":** ITTR, p. 382.

444 **Lunch invitation:** Ibid., p. 380.

445 **Major Remer:** Ibid., p. 387.

446 **"new excitement":** SPANDAU, NL 9, 3.7.53, p. 31.

447 **Fromm:** Speer letters: to Frau Fromm (September 6, 1944), to Zeitzler (August 21, 1944, and February 20, 1945), given to author by Speer; see also Janssen, *Das Ministerium Speer,* p. 270.
Stauffenberg: ITTR, p. 378; SPANDAU, NL 9, 3.7.53, p. 22.
against the coup: NRMBG, Part II, p. 31.

448 **between the lines:** ITTR, pp. 391–92.
"his hearty laughter": Oven, *Verrat und Widerstand im Dritten Reich,* p. 43.

449 **"What clearly emerged":** SPANDAU, NL 9, 12.7.53.P.2.
Kaltenbrunner: ITTR, pp. 391–92.

453 **Adam von Trott:** Maria Vassiltchikov, *Berlin Diaries: 1940–1945,* p. 230.

455 **"Hitler loved the film":** SPANDAU, NL 9, 12.7.53, p. 7; Toland, *Adolf Hitler,* p. 818; BELOW, p. 404.

Chapter XVIII

461 **"I was appalled":** BELOW, p. 385.

462 **"He was now clinging":** Ibid., pp. 385–86.

463 **Karl Hanke:** ITTR, pp. 375–76; BELOW, p. 178.

469 **800,000 Jews:** FINAL, p. 500.

470 **"It was a great worry":** SPANDAU, NL 9, 23.7.53, pp. 26–28.

471 **poison gases:** IMT, Vol. XVI, p. 526.
Robert Ley: NRMBG III, p. 18.

474 **"in a state of despair":** BELOW, p. 398.

476 *Mein Kampf* **quoted:** ITTR, p. 429.
Reference: Adolf Hitler, *Mein Kampf,* 1935 edition, pp. 104, 693.

477 "The tension of the raid": SPANDAU,
    NL 10, 9.8.53, pp. 4–5.
483 Guderian: Ibid., NL 10, 9.8.53, pp.
    13–15.
484 "Speer asks me": BELOW, p. 404.

Chapter XIX

489 "scorched earth": Janssen, *Das
    Ministerium Speer*, pp. 313–17.
493 "When I returned": SPANDAU, NL
    10, 5.9.53, p. 4.
494 Last letter: ITTR, pp. 453–54.
497 "When I got down": SPANDAU, NL
    10, 5.9.53, pp. 4–6.
500 Seyss-Inquart: Neave, *Nuremberg*, pp.
    179–81.
    "This was one": SPANDAU, NL 10,
    5.9.53, p. 4.
501 "These offers were": Ibid., p. 7.
502 "If I can do anything": Ibid., p. 20.
    "His plan was to": SEGMENTS, pp.
    345–46.
503 "When I asked who": Letter to Marion
    Riesser given to author.
504 "I booked for us": SPANDAU, NL 10,
    5.9.53, pp. 26–27.
505 "She adapted herself": BELOW, p.
    409.
    "We were appalled": SPANDAU, NL
    10, 5.9.53, p. 27.
507 "It was unforgettable": BELOW, p.
    409.
509 last letter to Hanke: Wolters Archive,
    BA, R3/1625. Letters, Wolters Archive,
    Koblenz.
510 "A few months later": ITTR, p. 423.
512 "The younger ones": Schröder, *Er war
    mein Chef*, pp. 200–201.

Chapter XX

523 Traudl Junge: Galante and Silianoff,
    Last Witnesses in the Bunker, pp. 142–44.
524 Last trip to Berlin: ITTR, pp. 476 ff.;
    SPANDAU, NL 7, 8.1.53, pp. 8–15.
528 "confession": ITTR, p. 480; *Playboy*,
    June 1971; Blond, *L'Agonie de
    l'Allemagne*, in *Carrefour*.
530 "What would you do": SPANDAU,

NL 7, 8.1.53, pp. 7–13, and NL 10, 17.9.53,
pp. 9–16.

Chapter XXI

552 Göring's drugs: Gilbert, *Nuremberg
    Diary*, p. 17.
556 Speer's arrest: ITTR, p. 500.

Chapter XXII

564 declarations: Taylor, *The Anatomy of
    the Nuremberg Trials*, pp. 21 ff., Chapter
    2, "The Nuremberg Ideas."
    four counts: Ibid., Appendix A, p. 648,
    Appendix B, p. 654.
568 the indictment: Neave, *Nuremberg*, pp.
    62 ff.
569 the Jäger affidavit: IMT, Vol. XVI, pp.
    537, 546.
    Polish doctor: Ibid., p. 558.
570 "an impressive figure": Neave,
    Nuremberg, p. 149.
573 "steel switches": IMT, Vol. XVI, p.
    546.
    Ley's suicide: Gilbert, *Nuremberg
    Diary*, p. 13.
575 warning about Göring: Ibid., p. 115.
    Jackson opens: IMT, Vol. II, pp. 98 ff.
583 "Although the Soviet": Smith,
    Reaching Judgment at Nuremberg, p. 8.
    Maser wrote: Maser, *Nuremberg: A
    Nation on Trial*, p. 181–219.
    letter to Jackson: Smith, *Reaching
    Judgment at Nuremberg*, p. 221.
584 Monigan: National Archives,
    Washington.
585 "Opinion on Clemency": Taylor, *The
    Anatomy of the Nuremberg Trials*, p.
    603.
    plea bargaining: Ibid., p. 181.
586 loafers: IMT, Vol XVI, p. 516.
588 "Did you know": Ibid., p. 442.
    Schieber: Ibid., p. 443.
    "working conditions": Ibid., pp.
    443–44.
589 "As Production Minister": Ibid., p.
    561.
590 Raginsky: Ibid., p. 565.
591 "I can only say": Ibid., p. 566.

591 "You said, 'I gave up' ": Ibid., p. 570.
    "I will remind you": Ibid., p. 571.
592 "You knew, did you not": Ibid., p. 580.
593 "I have now finished": NRMBG, p. 1.
594 **Jodl:** IMT, Vol. XXII, p. 400.
    Speer's address: Ibid., pp. 405 ff.

Chapter XXIII

617 **Preface:** DIARIES, p. xiii.
626 **offer to Hilde:** Ibid., June 17–18, 1952, p.
    219.

Chapter XXIV

646 **"In the dawn":** Dietrich Bonhoeffer,
    quoted in letter to Hilde, May
    1953.
661 **end of "Walk":** DIARIES, p. 497.

Chapter XXV

667 **"We hadn't seen":** SEGMENTS, p.
    499.
681 **"The publicity":** Ibid., p. 506.

Chapter XXVI

706 **cannot face:** Lifton, *The Nazi Doctors,*
    pp. 418 ff.
707 **hoax:** Butz, *Did Six Million Die?,* pp.
    6–8.

Postscript

718 **TV film:** BBC film, *The Great Art
    Dictator,* Program No. E3000, shown
    December 14, 1981.

Photographic Credits